T0141208

Internet of Things

This book addresses the fundamental technologies, architectures, application domains, and future research directions of the Internet of Things (IoT). It also discusses how to create your own IoT system according to applications requirements, and it presents a broader view of recent trends in the IoT domain and open research issues. This book encompasses various research areas such as wireless networking, advanced signal processing, IoT, and ubiquitous computing. *Internet of Things: Theory to Practice* discusses the basics and fundamentals of IoT and real-time applications, as well as the associated challenges and open research issues. The book includes several case studies about the use of IoT in day-to-day life. The authors review various advanced computing technologies—such as cloud computing, fog computing, edge computing, and Big Data analytics—that will play crucial roles in future IoT-based services. The book provides a detailed role of blockchain technology, Narrowband IoT (NB-IoT), wireless body area network (WBAN), LoRa (a long-range low power platform), and Industrial IoT (IIoT) in the 5G world. This book is intended for university/college students, as well as amateur electronic hobbyists and industry professionals who are looking to stay current in the IoT domain.

Pramod R. Gunjal works as an IoT application technical consultant in India. His research interests are Internet of Things, embedded systems, wireless sensor networks, robotics and automation, and embedded system design.

Satish R. Jondhale is currently working as an assistant professor in the Electronics and Telecommunication Department at Amrutvahini College of Engineering, Sangamner, Maharashtra, India. His research interests are signal processing, target localization and tracking, wireless sensor networks, artificial neural networks and applications, image processing, and embedded system design.

Jaime Lloret is currently full professor in the Polytechnic University of Valencia, Spain. Previously, he worked as a network designer and administrator in several enterprises. He is also the Chair of the Integrated Management Coastal Research Institute (IGIC). Since 2016 till today he is the Spanish researcher with highest h-index in the TELECOMMUNICATIONS list according to Clarivate Analytics Ranking. Moreover, he is included in the world's top 2% scientists according to the Stanford University List since 2020.

Karishma Agrawal received her Master of Engineering degree in 2023 from Thammasat University, specializing in the field of electrical and computer engineering. Her academic pursuits have been focused on signal analysis, control systems, Internet of Things (IoT), and computational mathematics.

Internet of Things

Theory to Practice

Pramod R. Gunjal, Satish R. Jondhale,
Jaime Lloret and Karishma Agrawal

CRC Press is an imprint of the
Taylor & Francis Group, an informa business

Designed cover image: © Shutterstock

First published 2024
by CRC Press
2385 NW Executive Center Drive, Suite 320, Boca Raton FL 33431

and by CRC Press
4 Park Square, Milton Park, Abingdon, Oxon, OX14 4RN

CRC Press is an imprint of Taylor & Francis Group, LLC

ISBN: 978-1-032-25168-4 (hbk)
ISBN: 978-1-032-25393-0 (pbk)
ISBN: 978-1-003-28294-5 (ebk)

DOI: 10.1201/9781003282945

Typeset in Times LT Std
by Apex CoVantage, LLC

Contents

Preface

The Internet of Things (IoT) is all about connecting the unconnected. Most of the objects in our day-to-day lives are not connected to a computer network, but this paradigm is changing rapidly. The "things" in the IoT can be anything from household appliances, machines, goods, buildings, and vehicles to people, animals, and plants. With the IoT, all physical objects are interconnected and capable of exchanging data with each other without human intervention. They can be accessed and controlled remotely, and this is the prime objective behind IoT. The IoT is the evolutionary step of the internet that creates a worldwide infrastructure by connecting various kinds of things around us, and thereby has the ability to make our lives happier and simpler. For instance, we have all had the "*where are my keys?*" experience before. Well, in the era of IoT, we probably will not need our keys anymore. Our phones will be the keys, and we could open the doors using phones, or using our biometric information such as palm prints, fingerprints, or scans of iris, retina, palm veins, face, and voice. Thus, basically, the IoT consists of allowing things to connect to the (existing) internet, allowing the interaction of the virtual world with the physical world. The IoT promises to unlock the real world the way that the internet unlocked millions of computers just a few decades ago. The IoT is supposed to have a potential to connect about 60 billion items by 2030. It is believed that IoT will improve healthcare infrastructure, energy efficiency, remote monitoring, transportation aids, national security, and control of physical assets and productivity through applications as diverse as home security to condition monitoring on the factory floor. IoT will provide the infrastructure over which the new emerging artificial intelligence (AI) revolution will be based. A short summary of this book follows.

Chapter 1 focuses on "Fundamentals of the Internet of Things." It gives and outline of challenges and open research issues in IoT.

Chapter 2 explores the concept of "Things in the Internet of Things." It covers basics of sensors, actuators, wireless sensor networks, and the Internet of Hybrid Energy Harvesting Things in IoT.

Chapter 3 covers "Wireless Protocols and Technologies for the Internet of Things." Specifically, it discusses WPAN technologies and IP-based networking protocols for IoT.

Chapter 4 includes detailed discussion of "Data Handling and Analytics" technologies. It also covers the Relationship between Big Data and the Internet of Things, and challenges in IoT with Big Data analytics.

Chapter 5 elaborates on "Roles of Cloud Computing, Fog Computing, and Edge Computing," along with cloud analytics for IoT Application, further discussion on data analysis options—edge, cloud, or combination—which can be better for the future of IoT.

Chapter 6 focuses briefly on "The Internet of Things in the Era of 5G." This technology will increase cellular bandwidth by huge amounts, making it much easier for IoT to network large numbers of devices together.

This chapter also covers the trends of Narrowband IoT (NB-IoT) and the Industrial Internet of Things.

Chapter 7 deals with "The Role of Blockchain Technology in the Internet of Things." It briefly addresses how to secure the IoT with blockchain, the concept of thingbots, and the future of botnets in the IoT.

Chapter 8 focuses on "A Practical Approach to Development of the Internet of Things" in the view of various essential aspects like Python programming language and embedded suites for IoT. It also includes open service platforms for IoT cloud computing like ThingSpeak, with a case study on how to use ThingSpeak for IoT.

Chapter 9 discusses briefly "The Internet of Things for Healthcare" about IoT as a key in the digital healthcare system, how IoT helps in healthcare and makes broader use of technologies in the medical field. It also incorporates challenges, security issues and risks of IoT in healthcare. Wireless Body Area Network (WBAN) and its architecture are explained so as to understand the role of IoT enabling wearable devices in the medical field as Internet of Medical Things.

This book addresses fundamental IoT technologies, architectures, application domains, and future research directions. It does not only attempt to cover the theoretical fundamentals of IoT, but it also discusses how to create your own IoT system according to applications requirements, as well as presenting a broader view of recent trends in the IoT domain and open research issues. The intended audience of the book is university/college students, and academic and industrial professionals working in the IoT domain. To ease reading, we have tried to provide illustrations as much as possible. The contents of the book flow from a basic overview of IoT, with details on "classical" protocols, to more research trends possible in the near future. It assumes readers have a basic concept of how computers work and can competently use a computer, i.e., can switch the computer on, log in, run some programs, and copy files to and from a universal serial bus (USB) memory stick. This book can be used as a core textbook, as well as a background-reading textbook as a syllabus context, and reinforcement of concepts can be achieved for those who are already working on this concept and desire to work for research in the IoT domain. We believe that this book can be easily adopted by students, colleges, and most of the universities at the national and international levels as a part of their syllabi for the most streams of study and application.

About Our Authors

Mr. Pramod R. Gunjal received his B.E. in electronics engineering in 2013 and completed his Masters of Engineering in electronics engineering with digital systems as a specialization in 2015 from Savitribai Phule Pune University, Pune, India. He has been working as an IoT applications technical consultant in India. Previously, he was an assistant professor in the Electronics and Telecommunication Engineering Department at Amrutvahini College of Engineering, Sangamner, Maharashtra, India for more than six years. His research interests are IoT, embedded systems, wireless sensor networks, robotics and automation, and embedded system design.

Dr. Satish R. Jondhale received his B.E. in electronics and telecommunication in 2006, his M.E. in electronics and telecommunication in 2012, and his Ph.D. in electronics and telecommunication in 2019 from Savitribai Phule Pune University, Pune, India. He has been working as an assistant professor in the Electronics and Telecommunication Department at Amrutvahini College of Engineering, Sangamner, Maharashtra, India for more than a decade. His research interests are signal processing, target localization and tracking, wireless sensor networks, artificial neural networks and applications, image processing and embedded system design.

Prof. Jaime Lloret received his B.Sc. and M.Sc. degrees in physics in 1997, his B.Sc. and M.Sc. degrees in electronic engineering in 2003, and his Ph.D. in telecommunication engineering (Doktoringenieur) in 2006. He is a Cisco-certified network professional instructor and he has seven Cisco Networking Academy certifications. He also has the Hewlett-Packard information technology (IT) architect certification. He worked as a network designer and administrator in several enterprises. He is currently an associate professor in the Polytechnic University of Valencia. He is also the Chair of the Integrated Management Coastal Research Institute (IGIC).

Karishma Agrawal is an accomplished researcher who achieved her Master of Engineering (2023) from Thammasat University, specializing in the field of electrical and computer engineering. Her academic pursuits have been focused on signal analysis, control systems, IoT, and computational mathematics. With a passion for advancing knowledge, Karishma has contributed significantly to the field, evidenced by her numerous research papers featured in esteemed journals and conference proceedings, including those available on IEEE Xplore. A deeper understanding of her research journey, her publications, h-index, and research caliber can be explored via ResearchGate at {www.researchgate.net/profile/Karishma-Agrawal} and Google Scholar at {https://scholar.google.com/citations?user=3TvAOEoAAAAJ&hl=en}.

1 Fundamentals of the Internet of Things

1.1 INTRODUCTION AND BACKGROUND OF THE INTERNET OF THINGS

Internet of Things (IoT) is a system made of physical devices (things) connected by the internet and capable of accumulating and sharing data across a network. The IoT is a vast, interconnected network of physical devices, also known as "things," which are equipped with unique identifiers in the form of Internet Protocol (IP) addresses. These devices have embedded technologies or are equipped with sensors that allow them to collect and transmit data to other devices or systems, enabling them to interact with their environment and process valuable information [1, 2]. The IoT is a rapidly growing technology that is revolutionizing the way we live, work, and interact with the world around us. At its core, IoT refers to the interconnectivity of physical objects and devices through the use of sensors, software, and network connectivity, enabling them to collect and exchange data. This data can then be analyzed and used to optimize processes, improve efficiency, and enhance user experiences. IoT has the potential to transform numerous industries and areas of our lives, from smart homes and cities to healthcare and transportation. With the proliferation of connected devices and the increasing availability of data, IoT is paving the way for new applications and innovations that were once only dreamed of. IoT technology has its roots in the early 1980s when computer scientist John Romkey created the first internet-connected appliance, a toaster that could be turned on and off over the internet [3]. However, it was not until the early 2000s that the concept of IoT gained significant attention with the development of RFID (radio frequency identification) technology and the increasing availability of internet connectivity [4, 5]. In 2008, the number of devices connected to the internet surpassed the number of people on Earth, and the potential for IoT to revolutionize industries from healthcare to manufacturing became increasingly clear. Today, the IoT ecosystem is vast and varied, encompassing everything from smart homes and wearable technology to autonomous vehicles and industrial automation systems. As the technology continues to evolve and become more sophisticated, it has the potential to fundamentally transform the way we live and work. In summary, IoT can be defined as a system of interconnected physical objects, devices, and appliances that are embedded with sensors, software, and network connectivity which enable them to collect, exchange, and analyze data to optimize processes, improve efficiency, and enhance user experiences. There are

DOI: 10.1201/9781003282945-1

several definitions of IoT in the literature from different sources [1, 6, 7], including the following.

> The Internet of Things (IoT) refers to the interconnectivity of uniquely identifiable embedded computing devices within the existing Internet infrastructure.
>
> International Data Corporation (IDC)

> IoT is a system of interrelated physical devices, vehicles, home appliances, and other items embedded with sensors, software, and network connectivity that enable these objects to collect and exchange data.
>
> Gartner

> IoT is the extension of Internet connectivity into physical devices and everyday objects, enabling them to send and receive data.
>
> Cisco

> The Internet of Things (IoT) is the network of physical objects—devices, vehicles, buildings, and other items—embedded with sensors, software, and network connectivity that enables these objects to collect and exchange data.
>
> McKinsey & Company

> The Internet of Things (IoT) is the network of devices, vehicles, and home appliances that contain electronics, software, sensors, actuators, and connectivity, which allows these things to connect, interact and exchange data.
>
> IBM

With the help of IoT, the world has become more interconnected than ever, allowing for seamless communication and data exchange across a range of devices and platforms. Things in terms of IoT are objects of the physical world (physical things) or of the information world (virtual world) which are capable of being identified and integrated into communication networks. Simply, things are associated with information, which can be static and/or dynamic. Physical things exist in the physical world and are capable of being sensed, actuated, and connected. Examples of physical things include the surrounding environment, industrial robots, goods, and electrical equipment [8]. Virtual things exist in the information world and are capable of being stored, processed, and accessed. Examples of virtual things include multimedia content and application software. An IoT system consists of sensors/devices which "talk" to the cloud through some kind of connectivity [9]. Once the data gets to the cloud, software processes it and then might decide (the execution of instructions in software) to perform an action—such as sending an alert or automatically adjusting the sensors/devices without the need for the user. As IoT continues to grow and evolve, there are challenges to overcome, such as security and privacy concerns, interoperability issues, and the need for standardization [10, 11]. However, the benefits of IoT are too great to ignore, and the technology is expected to become even more prevalent in the coming years. In this book, we will explore the basics of IoT,

FIGURE 1.1 Speciality of an IoT.

its underlying technologies, its current and potential applications, and the challenges and opportunities that come with it. We will also delve into the ethical and societal implications of IoT and discuss how we can ensure that this technology is used to benefit society as a whole. Figure 1.1 illustrates the gravity of the world of IoT in the form of its characteristics.

1.1.1 Need for IoT

The IoT is a rapidly growing technology that connects physical devices, vehicles, buildings, and other items with the internet, enabling them to collect and exchange data. The need for IoT arises from the desire to make our daily lives more convenient, efficient, and secure. There are several reasons why one might need IoT. IoT can streamline processes and improve efficiency in several ways. For example, in a smart home, IoT-enabled devices can be connected to a central hub, allowing users to control all of their devices from a single interface [12]. This can save time and reduce the need for manual intervention. In a manufacturing plant, IoT sensors can be used to track equipment performance, identify maintenance needs, and optimize production processes. IoT can help businesses save money by reducing waste and optimizing processes. For example, in a logistics company, IoT sensors can be used to track shipments and optimize delivery routes, reducing fuel costs and improving delivery times. In a smart building, IoT sensors can be used to monitor energy usage and automatically adjust heating and cooling settings to conserve energy [13]. IoT can improve safety and security in several ways. For example, in a smart city, IoT sensors can be used to monitor traffic patterns and alert authorities to accidents or traffic congestion. In a smart home, IoT-enabled security cameras and sensors can be used to detect intruders and alert homeowners to potential threats. IoT can enhance customer experiences by providing personalized and timely services. For example, in a retail store, IoT sensors can be used to track customers' movements and suggest products or promotions based on their behavior. In a smart home, IoT-enabled devices can be used to create custom lighting and temperature settings based on individual preferences. IoT can provide businesses with valuable data insights that can be used to make better-informed decisions. For example, in a healthcare facility, IoT sensors can be used to monitor patient health and identify potential issues before they become serious [10, 14]. In a manufacturing plant, IoT sensors can be used to collect data on equipment performance and identify areas for improvement. Overall, IoT has the potential to transform the way we live and work, improving efficiency, safety, and convenience, while also providing valuable data insights for better decision-making. Some of the key benefits and needs of IoT include the following [11, 12, 15, 16].

1. **Automation and Control:** IoT devices can be programmed to automatically perform certain actions based on real-time data, allowing for improved efficiency and control.
2. **Increased Efficiency:** IoT devices can collect and transmit data that can be used to optimize processes and reduce waste.
3. **Improved Safety and Security:** IoT devices can be used to monitor and secure homes, businesses, and public spaces, providing early warning systems for potential threats.
4. **Better Decision-Making:** IoT devices can collect and analyze vast amounts of data, providing valuable insights that can be used to inform decision-making in various industries.
5. **Cost Savings:** IoT devices can reduce costs by optimizing processes, reducing the need for manual labor.

Overall, the need for IoT arises from the desire to make our world a smarter, more connected, and more efficient place.

1.1.2 Is IoT the Future?

IoT devices are becoming a part of the mainstream electronics culture and people are adopting smart devices into their homes faster than ever [12]. The more data that IoT devices collect, the smarter they will become. The future seems ripe with a host of endless possibilities which only go to show that the evolution of IoT and the growth of IoT technologies have gone past the point of no return. Technology today not only pushes past barricades we once thought insurmountable but also moves us toward a world where equal access to the internet and its resulting technological marvels will be available to everyone. IoT will continue to evolve in many ways which will amaze and astound us, ultimately creating a truly limitless potential for everyone. IoT is considered one of the most promising and rapidly evolving technologies of the future. The number of IoT devices is expected to grow exponentially in the coming years, with an estimated 41.6 billion devices projected to be in use by 2025, according to a report by IDC [17]. This growth is being driven by the increasing demand for automation, optimization, and data insights across a range of industries and use cases. IoT has the potential to transform industries such as healthcare, transportation, manufacturing, and agriculture, among others. It can help businesses and organizations to collect valuable data insights, optimize processes, and reduce costs, leading to increased productivity and efficiency. Moreover, IoT technology is evolving at a rapid pace, with advancements being made in areas such as edge computing, AI, and 5G (fifth-generation technology cellular) networks, among others [18–20]. These advancements are expected to further expand the capabilities and applications of IoT technology, making it even more essential in the future.

The future of the IoT is expected to be a major disruptive force in the years to come, transforming the way we live, work, and interact with technology. IoT refers to the interconnected network of physical devices, vehicles, home appliances, and other items embedded with electronics, software, sensors, and connectivity, allowing these objects to collect and exchange data. The number of IoT devices is projected to continue to grow rapidly in the future. As more devices are connected, there will be an even greater amount of data generated, which can be used to optimize processes and make better decisions [8, 21]. As IoT continues to grow, there will be an increasing focus on integrating AI and machine learning into IoT systems, allowing for even more powerful insights and decision-making. 5G networks promise to deliver higher speeds, lower latency, and greater capacity than previous wireless networks [22]. This will be particularly important for IoT applications, which require reliable and fast connections. The adoption of 5G networks is expected to accelerate the growth of IoT devices and applications. As the number of IoT devices grows, there will be an increasing focus on security and privacy. IoT devices can collect sensitive data, and any security breaches could have serious consequences. Therefore, there will be a greater focus on securing IoT devices and ensuring that user data is protected. In summary, the future of IoT is likely to be characterized by the growth of devices, the integration of AI and machine learning, the development of edge computing, the adoption of 5G networks, and a greater focus on security and privacy [23, 24]. Some of the key trends and advancements expected in the future of IoT include the following [17, 25–27].

1. **Increased Connectivity:** The number of connected devices is expected to continue to grow, resulting in a more connected and integrated world.
2. **Edge Computing:** Edge computing will become increasingly important as more devices are added to the IoT network, allowing for faster data processing and reducing the need for data to be sent to centralized servers.
3. **5G Technology:** The rollout of 5G networks will enable faster and more reliable connectivity, leading to new and improved IoT applications.
4. **Artificial Intelligence:** The integration of AI into IoT devices will enable more advanced capabilities such as predictive maintenance, enhanced security, and more efficient energy use.
5. **Cyber-Security:** As the number of connected devices grows, the importance of securing IoT networks will become even more critical, and new technologies and protocols will emerge to address these challenges.

6. **Smart Homes and Cities:** IoT will play a key role in creating smart homes and cities, with connected devices improving energy efficiency, reducing waste, and making our living spaces more convenient and comfortable.
7. **Wearables:** The rise of wearable technology will lead to an increased demand for connected devices, such as fitness trackers, smartwatches, and medical devices.

Overall, the future of IoT is expected to bring about many exciting advancements and opportunities, changing the way we live and work, and leading to a more connected and efficient world.

1.1.3 What Is IoT, and How Does It Work?

The IoT is a system of interrelated computing devices, mechanical and digital machines, objects, animals, and/or people that are provided with unique identifiers (UIDs) and the ability to transfer data over a network without requiring human-to-human or human-to-computer interaction [28, 29]. A *thing* in the IoT can be a person with a heart monitor implant, a farm animal with a biochip transponder, an automobile that has built-in sensors to alert the driver when tire pressure is low, or any other natural or man-made object that can be assigned an IP address and is able to transfer data over a network. Increasingly, organizations in a variety of industries are using IoT to operate more efficiently, better understand customers to deliver enhanced customer service, improve decision-making, and increase the value of the business.

An IoT ecosystem consists of web-enabled smart devices that use embedded systems—such as processors, sensors, and communication hardware—to collect, send, and act on data they acquire from their environments [14, 27]. IoT devices share the sensor data they collect by connecting to an IoT gateway or other edge device where data is either sent to the cloud to be analyzed or analyzed locally. Sometimes, these devices communicate with other related devices and act on the information they get from one another. The devices do most of the work without human intervention, although people can interact with the devices—for instance, to set them up, give them instructions, or access the data. The connectivity, networking, and communication protocols used with these web-enabled devices largely depend on the specific IoT applications deployed. IoT can also make use of artificial intelligence (AI) and machine learning to aid in making data collecting processes easier and more dynamic. An IoT-based system typically involves the following components [1, 2, 7].

1. **Devices:** IoT devices are physical objects that are connected to the internet and equipped with sensors, processors, and communication hardware. These devices can range from simple sensors to complex machines, such as smart cars or home automation systems.
2. **Sensors:** IoT devices are typically equipped with various sensors that can collect data such as temperature, humidity, light, motion, and sound. These sensors can also collect more complex data such as GPS location, images, and video.

3. **Connectivity:** IoT devices are connected to the internet through various wireless or wired technologies such as Wi-Fi, Bluetooth, cellular, or Ethernet. This connectivity enables them to communicate with other devices, applications, and services.
4. **Data Processing:** The collected data is processed either locally (on the device) or in the cloud. Local processing is useful when low latency is required, and cloud processing is useful when large amounts of data need to be processed and analyzed.
5. **Applications:** IoT applications can be built to make use of the data collected by IoT devices. These applications can range from simple mobile apps to complex business applications that integrate with other systems.
6. **Security:** IoT systems need to be secure to protect against unauthorized access and data breaches. Security measures include authentication, encryption, and access control.

An IoT-based system is shown in Figure 1.2, illustrating how one typically works [11, 27].

1. The IoT devices collect data from their sensors and transmit it to a gateway device.
2. The gateway device aggregates the data from multiple devices and sends it to the cloud for processing and analysis.
3. The cloud-based system processes the data, applies analytics algorithms, and generates insights and alerts.
4. The IoT applications access the processed data and present it to users in a meaningful way, such as through a dashboard, notification, or report.
5. The system may also send commands or instructions back to the IoT devices based on the processed data or user input.
6. The system continuously monitors and manages the devices, connectivity, and security to ensure reliable and secure operation.

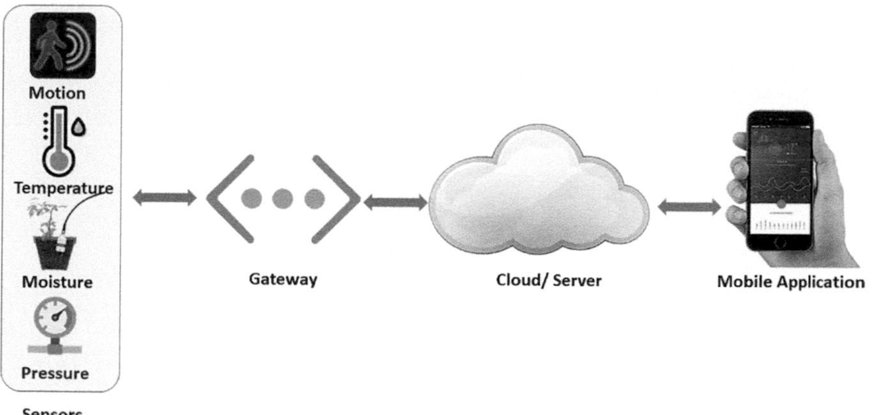

FIGURE 1.2 Working of an IoT.

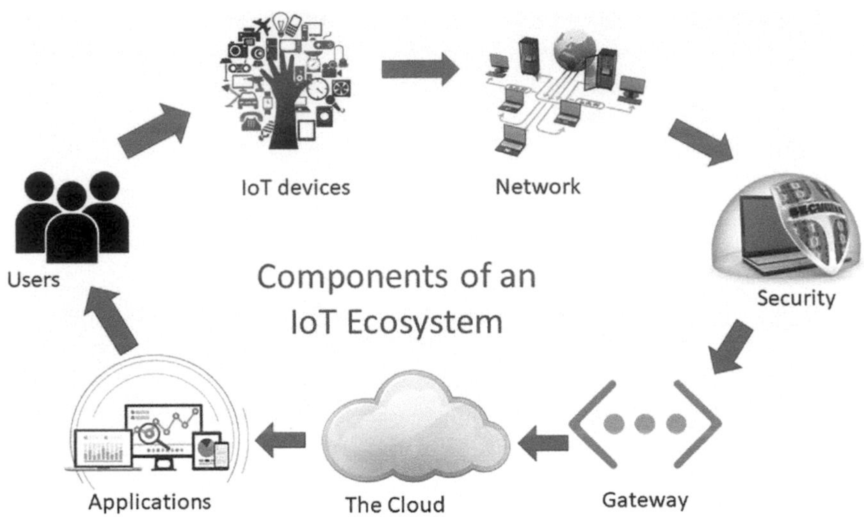

FIGURE 1.3 Seven components of an IoT ecosystem.

IoT-based systems and IoT ecosystems are different concepts, although they are related to each other. An IoT-based system is a specific implementation of IoT technology that involves a network of physical devices connected to the internet which can collect, process, and exchange data [7]. Figure 1.3 shows seven components of an IoT ecosystem. An IoT-based system typically includes devices, sensors, connectivity, data processing, applications, and security measures. On the other hand, an IoT ecosystem is a broader concept that encompasses all the elements involved in the development, deployment, and use of IoT technology [30, 31]. An IoT ecosystem includes hardware and software vendors, IoT service providers, connectivity providers, system integrators, application developers, and end-users. The IoT ecosystem involves the interactions and interdependencies between these different players, as well as the regulatory and policy frameworks that govern IoT technology. In other words, an IoT-based system is a specific use case of IoT technology, while an IoT ecosystem is the larger context within which IoT technology operates.

A successful IoT-based system is typically dependent on the larger IoT ecosystem within which it operates, including the availability of compatible devices, connectivity, and software, as well as the support of various stakeholders involved in the ecosystem. In the following list is how the IoT ecosystem works [29–31].

1. **Devices:** The first component of the IoT ecosystem are the devices themselves. These can range from smart home devices like thermostats to industrial sensors on manufacturing equipment. Each device is equipped with sensors, processors, and communication interfaces that enable it to collect and transmit data.
2. **Connectivity:** IoT devices require a communication infrastructure to exchange data. This can be achieved through wired or wireless networks, such as Wi-Fi, Bluetooth, or cellular.

3. **Data Management:** Once the data is collected from the devices, it needs to be stored, processed, and analyzed. This is done through data management systems that can process and store large amounts of data, such as cloud platforms or on-premises data centers.
4. **Application Layer:** The application layer is where the data collected from the devices is transformed into meaningful insights and actions. Applications can range from simple dashboards that display real-time data to complex algorithms that use machine learning to make predictions based on the data.
5. **Security:** IoT devices and systems are vulnerable to cyber-attacks, and security is thus a crucial component of the IoT ecosystem. Security measures such as encryption, firewalls, and access control help to protect sensitive data and ensure the privacy and safety of users.
6. **Interoperability:** For the IoT ecosystem to work effectively, devices from different manufacturers must be able to communicate and exchange data with each other. Interoperability standards, such as those developed by the Open Connectivity Foundation (OCF) and the AllSeen Alliance, help to ensure compatibility between devices [32, 33].

In summary, the IoT ecosystem is a complex network of interconnected devices, communication networks, data management systems, and applications that work together to provide valuable insights and control over a wide range of physical objects.

1.1.4 History of IoT

The IoT is a term used to describe the interconnected network of physical devices, vehicles, home appliances, and other items embedded with electronics, software, sensors, and connectivity which enables these objects to connect and exchange data with each other. The concept of the IoT can be traced back to the late 1990s and early 2000s, when researchers and technology experts first started exploring the idea of connecting everyday devices to the internet [1, 2]. One of the earliest examples of IoT technology was a Coca-Cola machine at Carnegie Mellon University, which was connected to the internet in 1982 and allowed users to check the availability of drinks remotely [34]. Over the next few years, the development of wireless networks, advancements in miniaturization, and the growth of the internet paved the way for the development of the IoT. In 1999, Kevin Ashton, a British technology pioneer, coined the term "IoT" to describe the interconnected network of devices and objects [35]. In the early 2000s, the IoT began to gain momentum, with the introduction of smartphones and the growth of home automation systems. In 2006, Amazon introduced the Amazon Echo, a smart speaker that uses voice commands to control smart home devices and access information from the internet [36]. Since then, the IoT has continued to grow and evolve, with an increasing number of devices being connected to the internet. Today, the IoT is being used in a wide range of applications, from smart homes and cities to industrial systems and healthcare. Figure 1.4 gives insight into the history of the IoT, showing how the term IoT has evolved in the technological world over the period of last three decades.

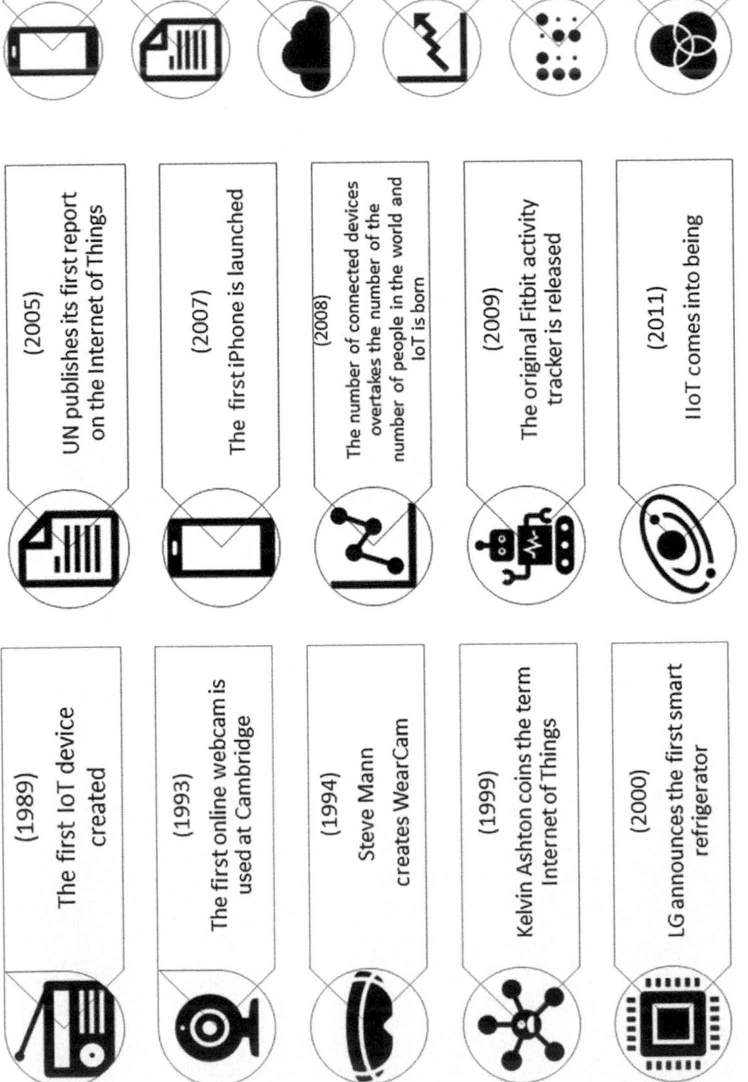

FIGURE 1.4 The history of the Internet of Things.

LG announced the first smart refrigerator in 2000, the first iPhone was launched in 2007, and by 2008, the number of connected devices exceeded the number of people on the planet [2, 31]. In 2009, Google started testing driverless cars, and in 2011, Google's Nest smart thermostat hit the market, allowing remote control of central heating and cooling. The concept of IoT started to gain some popularity in the summer of 2010. Information leaked that Google's StreetView service had not only made 360-degree pictures but had also stored tons of data of people's Wi-Fi networks [37]. People were debating whether this was the start of a new Google strategy to not only index the internet but also index the physical world. The same year, the Chinese government announced it would make the IoT a strategic priority in its updated Five-Year Plan. In 2011, Gartner—the market research company that invented the famous "hype-cycle for emerging technologies"—included a new emerging phenomenon on its list: "The Internet of Things" [6]. The next year, the theme of Europe's biggest internet conference LeWeb was the "Internet of Things." At the same time, popular tech-focused magazines like *Forbes*, *Fast Company*, and *Wired* starting using IoT as their vocabulary to describe the phenomenon. In October of 2013, IDC published a report stating that the IoT would be a $8.9 trillion market in 2020 [17]. The term IoT reached mass market awareness when in January 2014, Google announced the purchase of Nest for US$3.2 billion. At the same time, the Consumer Electronics Show (CES) in Las Vegas was held under the theme of IoT. Despite its tremendous growth, the IoT is still in its early stages and is expected to continue to evolve and grow in the coming years, with the development of new technologies and increasing demand for connected devices.

1.1.5 About Things in IoT

Things in IoT refer to physical objects or devices that are connected to the internet and have the ability to collect, process, and exchange data. These devices can range from simple sensors to complex machines such as smartphones, smart homes, wearables, medical devices, vehicles, and industrial equipment. The key characteristics of things in IoT include the following [2, 3].

1. **Connected:** Things in IoT are connected to the internet through various wired or wireless technologies such as Wi-Fi, Bluetooth, Zigbee, near field communication (NFC), or cellular networks. This connectivity enables them to communicate with other devices, services, and applications.
2. **Intelligent:** Things in IoT are equipped with sensors, processors, and software that enable them to collect and process data, and to make decisions or take actions based on that data. This intelligence can range from simple data logging to complex machine learning algorithms.
3. **Sensors:** Things in IoT are equipped with sensors that can collect various types of data such as temperature, humidity, motion, location, or light. These sensors can be integrated into the device or attached externally.
4. **Processors:** Things in IoT have processors or microcontrollers that can process and store data, run software, and make decisions or take actions based on that data.

5. **Software:** Things in IoT can run various types of software such as firmware, operating systems, and applications. This software can be programmed to perform certain tasks or respond to certain events.
6. **Communication Protocols:** Things in IoT use various communication protocols such as MQTT (Message Queuing Telemetry Transport), CoAP (Constrained Application Protocol), or HTTP (Hypertext Transfer Protocol) to exchange data with other devices or services. These protocols enable secure and efficient communication between devices.
7. **Power Source:** Things in IoT can be powered by various sources such as batteries, solar panels, or electrical outlets. The choice of power source depends on the device's usage, location, and lifespan.
8. **Autonomous:** Things in IoT can operate without human intervention or control. They can be programmed to perform certain tasks or respond to certain events automatically, based on predefined rules or algorithms.
9. **Interoperable:** Things in IoT can work with other devices or services that use different technologies or standards. This interoperability enables them to share data and services with other devices or applications.
10. **Secure:** Things in IoT need to be secure to protect against unauthorized access or data breaches. This security can be achieved through various measures such as encryption, authentication, access control, and device management.

In summary, things in IoT are physical objects or devices that are connected to the internet and have the ability to collect, process, and exchange data, enabling various industries and applications to become more efficient, intelligent, and secure. Examples of things in IoT include the following [1–3].

1. **Smart Thermostats:** These are devices that can control the temperature of a home or building based on user preferences and usage patterns.
2. **Wearables:** These are devices that can be worn on the body and can monitor various health parameters such as heart rate, blood pressure, or sleep patterns.
3. **Smart Appliances:** These are devices such as refrigerators, washing machines, or ovens that can be connected to the internet and can be controlled remotely.
4. **Industrial Sensors:** These are devices that can monitor various parameters such as temperature, pressure, or vibration in industrial processes and can optimize efficiency and productivity.

1.1.6 About the Internet in IoT

The internet in IoT is the global network of interconnected devices and systems that enables communication and data exchange between them. The internet serves as the backbone of IoT, connecting billions of devices and enabling them to share information and services. The internet in IoT is characterized by the following aspects.

1. **Connectivity:** The internet in IoT provides connectivity between devices through various communication protocols [38]. Wi-Fi is a commonly used protocol for home and office networks, while cellular networks are used for

devices that require mobility, such as vehicles or wearables. Bluetooth is often used for short-range communication between devices, while Zigbee is used for low-power, low–data-rate communication. NFC is used for contactless payments, and RFID is used for tracking and identification.

2. **Data Exchange:** The internet in IoT facilitates the exchange of data between devices, services, and applications [12, 27]. This data can be used for various purposes, such as monitoring and controlling devices, analyzing usage patterns, or providing insights for decision-making. For example, a smart thermostat can collect temperature and humidity data from sensors in a room and adjust the temperature based on the user's preferences and usage patterns. A fleet management system can collect location and performance data from vehicles and optimize routes and maintenance schedules.
3. **Cloud-Based Services:** The internet in IoT enables devices to connect to cloud-based services that can provide additional functionality and intelligence. These services can include data storage, analytics, machine learning, and AI [9]. For example, a smart security system can use machine learning algorithms to detect and prevent intrusions, while a smart home system can use voice recognition to control devices and services.
4. **Security:** The internet in IoT requires robust security measures to protect against data breaches and cyber-attacks. These measures can include encryption, authentication, access control, and device management [39, 40]. Devices and services must be designed with security in mind, and users must be educated on best practices for securing their devices and networks. For example, a smart lock system must be designed to prevent unauthorized access and ensure data privacy.
5. **Standards:** The internet in IoT requires common standards and protocols to ensure interoperability between devices and services [39]. These standards can be established by industry groups or regulatory bodies. Standards ensure that devices can communicate and work together seamlessly, regardless of their manufacturer or technology. For example, the Open Connectivity Foundation (OCF) has developed standards for IoT devices to ensure interoperability and security.
6. **Scalability:** The internet in IoT must be scalable to accommodate the increasing number of devices and data that are being generated. This scalability can be achieved through technologies such as edge computing and distributed systems [20, 26]. Edge computing enables data processing and analysis to be performed closer to the source of data, reducing latency and bandwidth requirements. Distributed systems enable data to be stored and processed across multiple devices and locations, providing redundancy and fault tolerance.

1.2 CHARACTERISTICS OF IOT

The IoT is a network of physical objects that are remotely monitored and controlled using internet technologies. The characteristics of the IoT are often described together with how we define IoT. The IoT is a term that is often used to describe a collection of interconnected devices, objects, vehicles, and buildings. It refers to the idea that

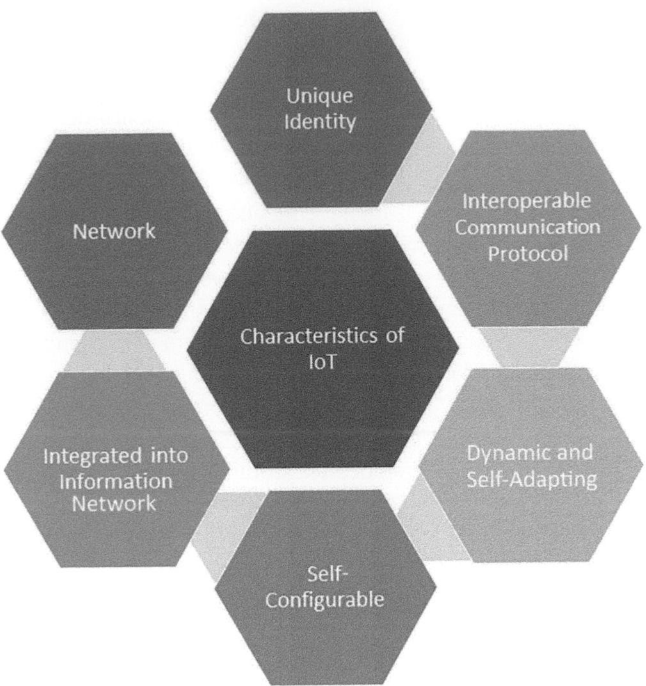

FIGURE 1.5 Characteristics of IoT.

all these different items will be able to talk to each other and share information. This allows the IoT to create new experiences for its users. As more and more objects are connected, the IoT will allow for more personalized experiences. Figure 1.5 shows the major characteristics of the IoT. Each of these characteristics are explained in detail in what follows.

1. **Unique Identity:** For effective coordination between the "things" in IoT applications, all the "things" are assigned (deployed) with a unique identity [28, 29]. So, a "thing" can be monitored, updated, and controlled remotely due to its unique identity. Identity is the unique characteristic of a person, group, place, or thing. Every identity has a name and an identification number. The combination of the name and number makes up the identity. This is what helps identify people and things on the internet. Identity is a concept that is found in many aspects of IoT. Device identity is the one thing that makes an IoT device unique and identifiable. Identity can be used to distinguish between different devices, give them a name, and allow them to be controlled. For Example, An IP address of a device is a unique identifier that represents a device in a network.
2. **Interoperable Communication Protocol:** In IoT applications, all the "things" are deployed in the network of communication. Various protocols are available for device to device and device to communication network.

IoT interoperability is the capacity for multiple components within an IoT deployment to effectively communicate, share data, and perform together to achieve a shared outcome [30, 41]. Organizations must be able to transmit and understand data throughout all the connections from devices to the cloud. Since the emergence of IoT, different communities developed different proprietary protocols which may not be interoperable across different devices. These protocols are being standardized so that they can be used across different devices. Some of the interoperable or standardized protocols are Transmission Control Protocol (TCP), User Datagram Protocol (UDP), IEEE 802.15.4, 6LoWPAN, etc.

3. **Dynamic and Self-Adapting:** IoT-based applications and devices are made aware of the environment in such a way that changes in parameters of their surroundings change the context and the IoT applications can accommodate such changes based on user's context. Such intelligent systems can be designed and are called self-adapting IoT applications. In the context of the IoT, self-adaptation is a salient property of smart objects. It allows them to be self-configured and adapted to extreme conditions while ensuring the target system objectives such as comfort, automation, security and safety goals [30, 42]. In IoT, the sensors or devices respond to dynamic events and have the ability to adapt to the change in the environment. Consider a surveillance system whereby cameras are installed for monitoring a location. Whenever there are no objects in front of the camera, the camera will be in a low power mode. Whenever an object is detected, the camera resumes its activity of monitoring that object. This is the dynamic behavior. The cameras also respond to changes in the environment. If it is night time, the cameras might shift to infrared mode and vice versa during day time. Also, the cameras can adjust their picture clarity based on the environment. Thus, IoT devices can self-adapt to changes in the environment.
4. **Self-Configurable:** Self-configuration (sometimes referred to as reconfiguration) and adaptive coordination (sometimes referred to as adaptation) refer to the spectrum of changes that a system makes to itself in response to occurrences in its environment and internally. Most of the small IoT devices such as sensors, actuators, etc., once deployed have much less direct user interaction. Due to this, many such devices are capable of fetching the latest software updates and setting up basic networking and status checks themselves or with very little user intervention. The IoT sensors or devices have the capability to obtain the instructions from a remote location for installing, updating, or other management-related tasks [27, 43]. These nodes from time to time receive updates or instructions from a remote management server to update the firmware, or remote startup and shutdown. In a weather monitoring system, several sensor nodes or devices will be placed at different locations in a vast area.
5. **Integrated into an Information Network:** IoT devices are typically configured in such a way that they can communicate between other devices in the IoT-based environment to create an information network [27, 43]. IoT devices can describe themselves using the unique identity to other devices

or to a network, and are dynamically discovered in the network by other devices and/or network. All the sensors or different devices in IoT are connected to the internet or other communication pathway. The data from sensors is aggregated and pre-processed at the local site or in the cloud. Information can be extracted from the data and appropriate decision can be made. As an example, consider a fire monitoring system in which different sensors are spread across the trees in a forest. These sensors send the data to a local sink node which is connected to the internet. This data is analyzed and alerts are generated which are taken care of by the appropriate personnel.

1.3 IOT ARCHITECTURES

IoT architectures are the frameworks and structures that define how IoT devices, networks, and applications communicate and interact with each other. There are several IoT architecture models, but they generally fall into the following three categories [26, 44, 45].

1. **Device-Centric Architecture:** In this architecture model, IoT devices are the primary focus and the data generated by these devices is transmitted to a central server or cloud-based platform for processing and analysis. This architecture is characterized by low complexity, low latency, and low bandwidth requirements.
2. **Gateway-Centric Architecture:** In this architecture model, a gateway device is used to aggregate and pre-process data from multiple IoT devices before transmitting it to the central server or cloud-based platform [46]. The gateway device acts as an intermediary between the devices and the server, and it can perform functions such as data filtering, compression, and encryption. This architecture is characterized by higher complexity, higher latency, and higher bandwidth requirements.
3. **Cloud-Centric Architecture:** In this architecture model, the central server or cloud-based platform plays a central role in the IoT system. All IoT devices transmit their data directly to the cloud platform, where it is stored, processed, and analyzed [9, 47]. This architecture is characterized by high complexity, high latency, and high bandwidth requirements.

IoT architectures can vary depending on the specific application and use case. Factors such as scalability, reliability, security, and cost must be considered when designing an IoT architecture [44, 45]. It is important to choose an architecture that can support the desired functionality and performance of the IoT system, while also meeting the constraints of the environment and network infrastructure. There are also several subcategories of IoT architectures that combine elements of the previously discussed models, including the following.

1. **Edge Computing Architecture:** In this architecture model, data processing and analysis are performed at the edge of the network, closer to the source

of data [48]. This approach can reduce latency and bandwidth requirements by minimizing the amount of data that needs to be transmitted to the central server or cloud-based platform.

2. **Distributed Architecture:** In this architecture model, data processing and analysis are performed across multiple devices and locations, providing redundancy and fault tolerance. This approach can improve scalability and reliability by distributing the workload and data storage across the network.
3. **Hybrid Architecture:** In this architecture model, a combination of device-centric, gateway-centric, and cloud-centric approaches are used to balance the requirements of the IoT system [44, 45]. For example, some data may be processed at the edge of the network, while other data may be transmitted directly to the cloud-based platform.

1.3.1 Functional Building Blocks of IoT

The functional building blocks of IoT are the essential components that make up an IoT system. These building blocks are the core elements required to create and operate an IoT solution. IoT systems include several functional blocks such as devices, communication, security, services, and application. The functional blocks provide sensing, identification, actuation, management, and communication capability [1, 2]. These functional blocks consist of devices that handle the communication between the server and the host, enable monitoring control functions, manage the data transfer, secure the IoT system using authentication and different functions, and provide an interface for controlling and monitoring various terms. These functional building blocks can be combined in various ways to create IoT solutions that meet specific requirements and use cases [44]. Understanding the role and function of each building block is essential for designing and deploying effective IoT systems. Figure 1.6 shows a General overview of IoT's functional blocks.

1.3.2 Physical Design of IoT

The physical design of an IoT system refers to the hardware and physical components that are used to create the system, which includes the sensors, actuators, connectivity, and other physical components that are required to collect, process, and transmit data [1, 2]. Physical design is more than creating products. The physical design of IoT is all about forming an overall intelligent system, as shown in Figure 1.7. The design must be oriented toward the end-user's needs. In logical design, one understands the logical relationship of the objects. However, in physical design, one understands the most effective method of storing and accessing those objects. Physical design of an IoT system refers to the individual node devices and their protocols that are utilized to create a functional IoT ecosystem. Each node device can perform tasks such as remote sensing, actuating, monitoring, etc., by relying on physically connected devices. It may also be capable of transmitting information through different types of wireless or wired connections.

The things/devices in the IoT system are used for building connections, data processing, providing storage, providing interfaces, and providing graphical

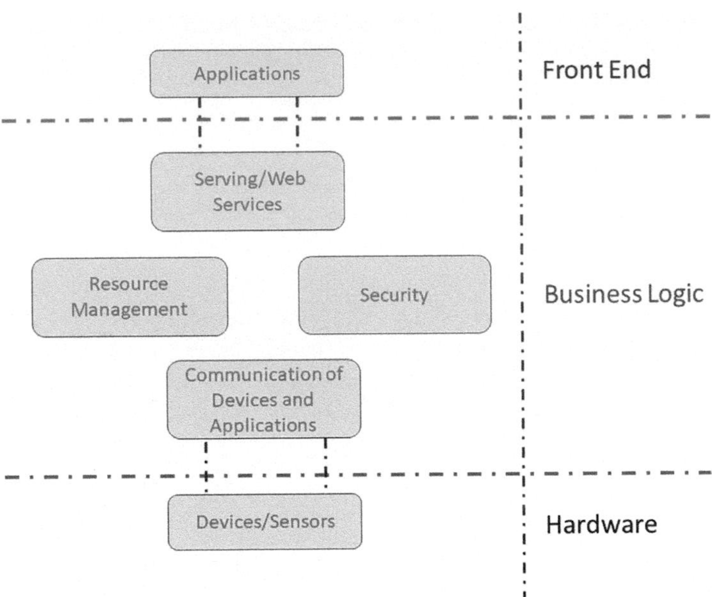

FIGURE 1.6 General overview of IoT: functional blocks.

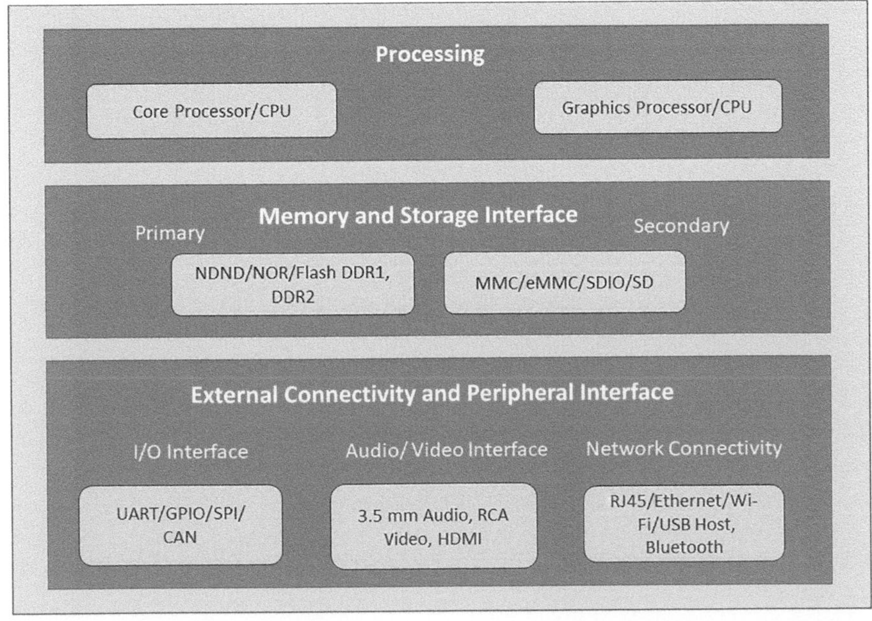

FIGURE 1.7 Physical design of IoT.

interfaces [2]. The devices generate data, and the data is used to perform analysis and do operations for improving the system. For instance, a moisture sensor is used to obtain the moisture data from a location, and the system analyzes it to give an output. Thus, the physical design of an IoT system is a critical aspect of the overall design and implementation of the system. Careful consideration must be given to the selection of hardware components, communication technologies, power supply, and other factors to ensure that the system meets the performance, reliability, and scalability requirements of the application [38, 45].

1.3.3 Logical Design of IoT

The logical design of IoT is an abstract representation of processes and entities without going into the lower-level details of the implementation [29, 45]. Logical design is less detailed than physical design and is more conceptual. It is the basic outline of how you want all those devices to talk and exchange information, but it does not specify a particular technology or product. A logical design for an IoT system is the actual design of how its components (computers, sensors, and actuators) should be arranged to complete a particular function. It does not go into the depth of describing how each component will be built with low-level programming specifics. Figure 1.8 shows the protocol layers in IoT. The logical design of an IoT system refers to an abstract representation of entities and processes without going into the low-level specifies of implementation. it uses functional blocks, communication models, and communication APIs (application programming interfaces) to implement a system.

In short, the logical design of an IoT system refers to the software and logical components that are used to create the system. This includes the software architecture, data flow, and communication protocols used to manage and analyze the data collected by the physical components of the system [29, 31]. The logical design of an IoT system is critical to its overall functionality and usability. The software architecture, data flow, communication protocols, data storage and management, analytics, and user interfaces

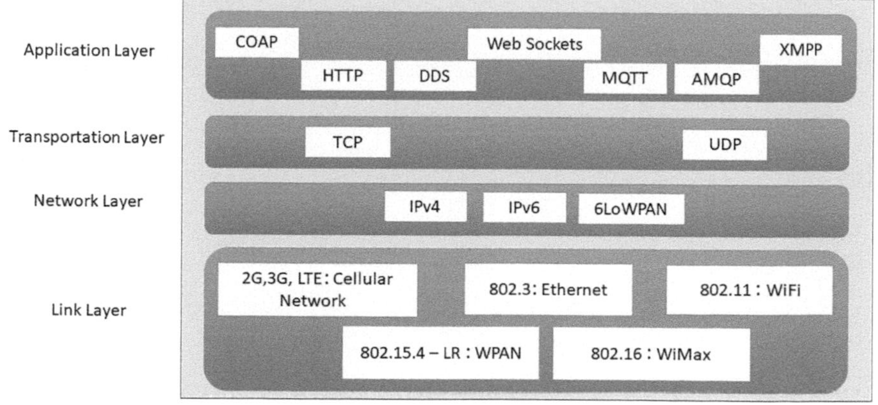

FIGURE 1.8 Protocol layers in IoT.

must all be carefully designed and implemented to ensure that the system meets the requirements of the application and provides a seamless user experience.

There are several different types of models available in an IoT system that is used to communicate between the system and server like the Request-Response Model, Publish-Subscribe Model, Push-Pull Model, Exclusive Pair Model, etc. [49].

- Logical design of IoT refers to its functional blocks, which helps to explain how IoT-based applications are implemented and the communication model which will elaborate how the data is sent and receive in case of IoT-based communication.
- Communication in IoT-based application can be carried out in various ways.

1.4 COMMUNICATION MODELS AND APIs

The IoT communication models and APIs are essential components of an IoT system. Communication models define the way in which IoT devices and sensors communicate with each other and with the cloud-based platform, while APIs provide a standard interface for developers to interact with the IoT system [49–51]. Following are some of the key IoT communication models.

1.4.1 Request-Response Communication Model

This model is a communication model in which a client sends the request for data to the server and the server responds according to the request. when a server receives a request, it fetches the data, retrieves the resources and prepares the response, and then sends the data back to the client. Figure 1.9 shows the Request-Response Communication model.

In simple terms, we can say that in the request-response model server send the response of equivalent to the request of the client. in this model, HTTP works as a request-response protocol between a client and server.

1.4.1.1 Example

When we search a query on a browser, the browser submits an HTTP request to the server and then the server returns a response to the browser (client). Figure 1.10 shows the Simplified Request-Response Communication model.

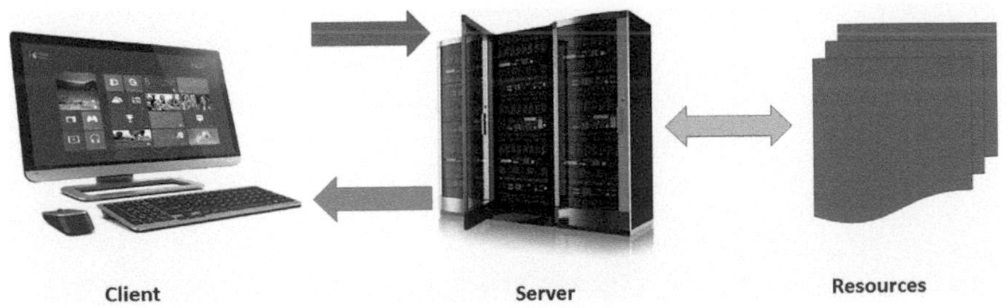

FIGURE 1.9 Request-Response Communication Model.

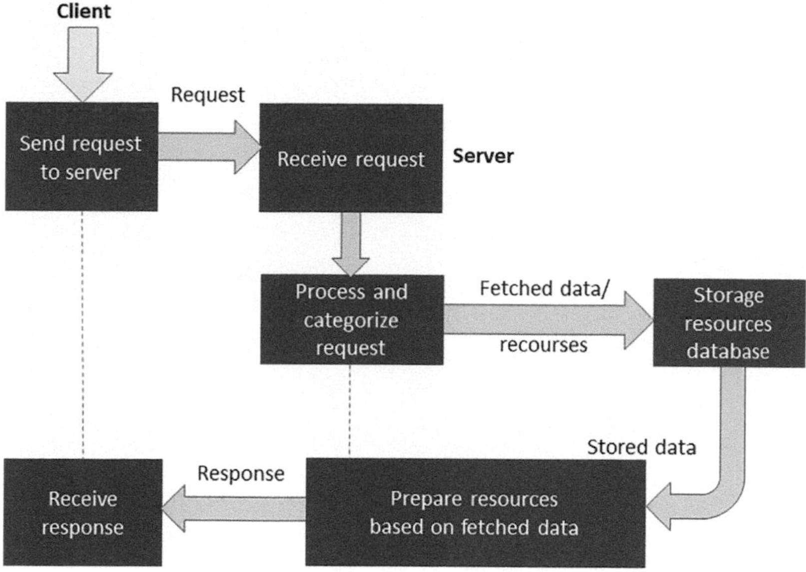

FIGURE 1.10 Simplified Request-Response Communication Model.

1.4.2 Publish-Subscribe Communication Model

In this communication model, we have a broker between publisher and consumer. Here, publishers are the source of data, but they are not aware of consumers. They send the data managed by the brokers, and when a consumer subscribes to a topic that is managed by the broker and when the broker receives data from the publisher, it sends the data to all the subscribed consumers [50]. Figure 1.11 shows the Publish-Subscribe Communication Model.

1.4.2.1 Example

Many times, we subscribe to a website's newsletters using our email address. These email addresses are managed by some third-party services and when a new article is published on the website, it is directly sent to the broker and then the broker sends these new data or posts to all the subscribers.

1.4.3 Push-Pull Communication Model

This is a communication model in which the data push by the producers in a queue and the consumers pull the data from the queues. Here also, producers are not aware of the consumers [51]. Figure 1.12 illustrates the Push-Pull Communication Model in detail.

1.4.3.1 Example

When we visit a website, we see a number of posts that are published in a queue, and according to our requirements, we click on a post and start reading it.

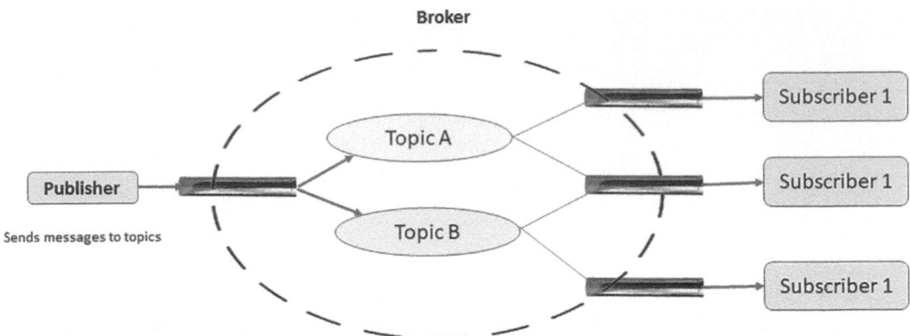

FIGURE 1.11 Publish-Subscribe Communication Model.

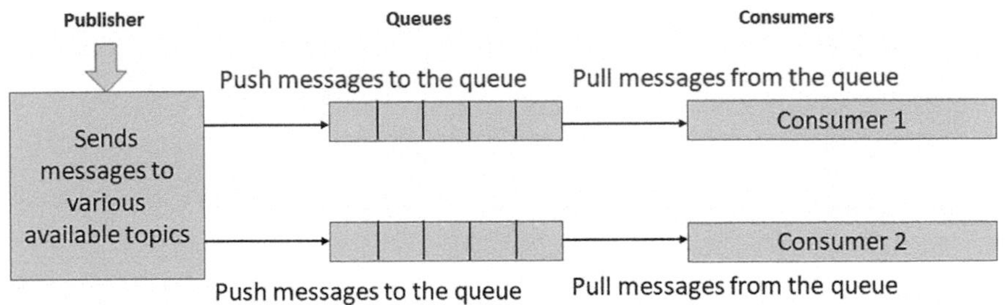

FIGURE 1.12 Push-Pull Communication Model.

1.4.4 Exclusive Pair Communication Model

This is a bidirectional fully duplex communication model that uses a persistent connection between the client and server [49]. Here, we first set up a connection between the client and the server which remains open until the client sends a close connection request to the server. Figure 1.13 explains how the Exclusive Pair Communication model works.

The IoT APIs are a set of protocols, routines, and tools that allow developers to access and interact with IoT devices, sensors, and platforms. APIs provide a standard interface for developers to integrate IoT functionality into their applications, enabling them to collect and analyze data, automate processes, and control devices. IoT APIs are typically used to perform the following tasks [44, 49, 51].

1. **Data Collection:** IoT APIs enable developers to collect data from sensors, devices, and other sources in the IoT system. This data can be used to analyze trends, detect anomalies, and make decisions in real time.
2. **Device Management:** IoT APIs enable developers to monitor and control devices in the IoT system. This includes tasks such as configuring settings, updating firmware, and performing diagnostics.
3. **Integration:** IoT APIs enable developers to integrate IoT functionality into their applications, such as home automation, industrial control, and smart

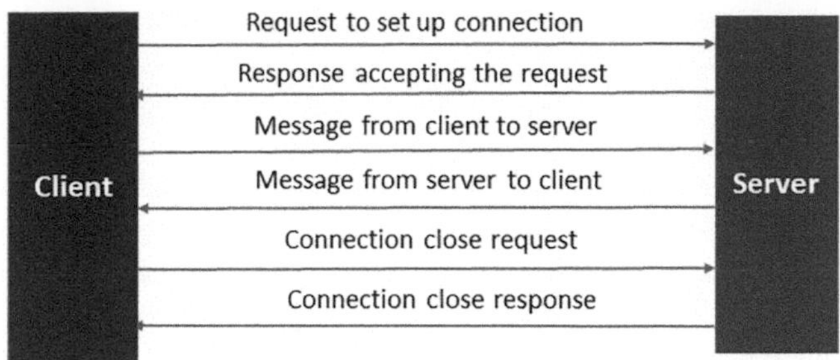

FIGURE 1.13 Exclusive Pair Communication Model.

cities. APIs provide a standard interface for developers to access and interact with IoT systems, making it easier to create customized solutions.

4. **Analytics:** IoT APIs enable developers to perform advanced analytics on the data collected from the IoT system. This includes tasks such as machine learning, predictive analytics, and data visualization.
5. **Security:** IoT APIs provide security features such as authentication, authorization, and encryption to protect sensitive data and ensure that only authorized users have access to the IoT system.

There are several types of IoT APIs, including the following.

1. **RESTful APIs:** REST (Representational State Transfer) APIs are a type of web service that use the HTTP protocol to access and interact with resources; it is an architectural style used for developing web-based applications that use HTTP as the primary communication protocol. RESTful APIs are a type of web service that adheres to the principles of the REST architecture. RESTful APIs are typically used to retrieve, create, update, and delete resources over HTTP [52]. RESTful APIs provide a standard set of commands, such as GET, POST, PUT, and DELETE, that can be used to read, create, update, or delete data from the IoT system. RESTful APIs are widely used in IoT systems because they are lightweight, flexible, and scalable. They provide a standard interface for developers to access and interact with IoT systems, making it easier to create customized solutions. However, designing a good RESTful API can be complex, and it is important to follow best practices to ensure that the API is efficient, secure, and maintainable. They are widely used in many different IoT applications, from smart homes and cities to industrial automation and agriculture.
2. **MQTT API:** MQTT is a lightweight messaging protocol that is often used in IoT systems. MQTT provides a publish-subscribe model and is optimized for low-bandwidth, high-latency networks [53, 54]. The MQTT API provides a standard interface for developers to interact with MQTT-based IoT systems.
3. **CoAP API:** CoAP (Constrained Application Protocol) is a lightweight protocol that is designed for use in IoT systems with limited resources, such

as low-power devices or networks with low bandwidth [51, 54]. CoAP provides a request-response model and is designed to be efficient and scalable. The CoAP API provides a standard interface for developers to interact with CoAP-based IoT systems.

4. **WebSocket API:** WebSocket is a communication protocol that enables bidirectional communication between devices and the cloud-based platform [47]. WebSocket is designed to provide low-latency, real-time communication and is often used in IoT systems to enable real-time data streaming and device control. The WebSocket API provides a standard interface for developers to interact with WebSocket-based IoT systems.

In summary, IoT APIs provide a standardized way for developers to access and interact with IoT systems. This enables developers to build custom applications that leverage the power of IoT data and devices, leading to improved efficiency, productivity, and customer experiences.

1.5 ENABLING TECHNOLOGIES IN IOT

Enabling technologies of IoT refers to the underlying technologies and infrastructure that enable the deployment and functioning of IoT systems. These technologies include hardware components, software platforms, and communication protocols that allow IoT devices to connect to the internet, communicate with each other, and perform tasks. Enabling technologies of IoT include wireless sensor networks (WSNs), embedded systems, cloud computing, Big Data analytics, machine learning, RFID, and Bluetooth Low Energy (BLE) [55, 56]. Each of these technologies plays a critical role in enabling the functionality of IoT systems. WSNs, for example, are essential for collecting data from a large number of devices over a wide area, while embedded systems provide the necessary computing power and connectivity to perform tasks like data collection, processing, and communication [57, 58]. Cloud computing is used for storage, processing, and analysis of the large amounts of data generated by IoT devices. Big Data analytics is used to extract insights from the data, while machine learning algorithms enable devices to analyze data in real time and make decisions based on that analysis [8]. RFID is used for identification and tracking of objects, while BLE is a low-power, low-cost way for devices to communicate with each other over short distances. Together, these enabling technologies provide the infrastructure, computing power, and communication capabilities required for IoT systems to function effectively. We will next discuss in detail the enabling technologies in IoT.

1. **Wireless Sensor Networks (WSNs):** These networks are a critical enabling technology in the context of IoT. A WSN is a network of spatially distributed sensors connected wirelessly to a central server, which can be used to monitor physical or environmental conditions such as temperature, humidity, pressure, and motion. These networks are composed of a large number of low-cost and low-power wireless sensor nodes, which are distributed throughout the environment and are capable of sensing, processing,

and communicating data wirelessly. In IoT, WSNs are used to collect and transmit data from a large number of sensors distributed over a wide area [59]. These sensors are typically embedded in physical objects, such as machines, vehicles, or environmental systems, and can be used to monitor their performance, detect faults or anomalies, and optimize their operation. The data collected by WSNs is sent to a central server or cloud platform, where it can be analyzed and processed in real time, allowing for more efficient and effective decision-making. WSNs are an essential technology for IoT because they enable the collection of data from a large number of devices over a wide area. WSNs consist of small, low-power devices called sensors that are deployed in large numbers to monitor physical and environmental conditions such as temperature, humidity, and pressure. The sensors use wireless communication protocols like Zigbee, Wi-Fi, or Bluetooth to send data to a central hub, which then processes and analyzes the data.

The primary advantages of WSNs in IoT are their low cost, low power consumption, and wireless connectivity, which make them ideal for use in large-scale and distributed IoT applications. WSNs can be used in a variety of IoT applications, such as smart homes, industrial automation, agriculture, healthcare, and environmental monitoring. For example, in smart homes, WSNs can be used to monitor temperature, humidity, and light levels, and control appliances such as lighting, heating, and air conditioning. In industrial automation, WSNs can be used to monitor and control the performance of machines and equipment, reducing downtime and maintenance costs. In agriculture, WSNs can be used to monitor soil moisture, temperature, and other environmental factors, helping farmers to optimize crop yields and reduce water usage. However, there are also challenges associated with the use of WSNs in IoT, such as energy efficiency, security, and scalability. To overcome these challenges, researchers are developing new technologies and protocols—such as low-power wireless communication protocols, energy harvesting techniques, and secure data transfer mechanisms—to make WSNs more efficient, secure, and scalable [60, 61].

2. **Embedded Systems:** Embedded systems are specialized computer systems that are designed to perform a specific task. They are used in IoT devices to provide the necessary computing power and connectivity to perform tasks like data collection, processing, and communication. These systems are optimized for low power consumption and are typically based on microcontrollers or single-board computers like Raspberry Pi or Arduino. In IoT, embedded systems are used to control and monitor physical devices—such as sensors, actuators, and other devices—and enable communication between these devices and the internet. These systems typically include microcontrollers, which are small, low-power processors designed for use in embedded systems, and are often used in conjunction with sensors, actuators, and other hardware components. One of the primary advantages of embedded systems in IoT is their ability to provide real-time monitoring and control of physical devices [26, 62]. This enables devices to respond quickly to changing environmental conditions and perform complex tasks,

such as monitoring and controlling multiple sensors or actuators simultaneously. For example, embedded systems can be used in smart homes to control lighting and heating systems, monitor security systems, and interact with other connected devices.

Another advantage of embedded systems in IoT is their low power consumption and small form factor. This makes them ideal for use in battery-powered devices, such as sensors and wearables, where power efficiency is critical. Additionally, embedded systems can be designed to operate in harsh environments, such as extreme temperatures or high humidity, making them well suited for use in industrial automation and environmental monitoring applications [63, 64]. However, there are also challenges associated with the use of embedded systems in IoT. These include the need for specialized expertise in hardware and software design, the need to optimize power consumption and performance, and the need to ensure the security of embedded systems in the face of potential cyber-threats. To overcome these challenges, researchers are developing new tools and techniques for designing and testing embedded systems, as well as new security protocols and standards for ensuring the safety and reliability of IoT devices.

3. **Cloud Computing:** Cloud computing provides on-demand access to computing resources over the internet. It is an essential technology for IoT because it provides the necessary storage, processing, and analytics capabilities required to manage the large amounts of data generated by IoT devices. Cloud computing enables IoT devices to store, process, and analyze data in real time, making it possible to derive insights and take action based on the data generated by IoT devices [9, 34]. Cloud providers like Amazon Web Services, Microsoft Azure, and Google Cloud offer IoT-specific services like IoT data storage, IoT data processing, and IoT analytics. In the context of IoT, cloud computing refers to the use of cloud services and infrastructure to support the deployment, management, and scaling of IoT applications and services. This involves the use of cloud-based platforms, such as Amazon Web Services (AWS), Microsoft Azure, and Google Cloud Platform, to store and process IoT data, and to provide the computing resources necessary to run IoT applications and services.

   One of the primary benefits of cloud computing in IoT is the ability to store and process massive amounts of data generated by connected devices. Cloud-based platforms provide the scalability and flexibility required to handle the huge volumes of data generated by IoT devices, enabling organizations to gain valuable insights into consumer behavior, environmental conditions, and other key factors. Cloud computing also enables real-time processing and analysis of IoT data, making it possible to respond quickly to changing conditions and take action based on the data generated by connected devices. This is particularly important in applications—such as industrial automation and smart cities—whereby real-time monitoring and control are critical. Another advantage of cloud computing in IoT is the ability to reduce the cost and complexity of IoT deployments. By leveraging cloud-based platforms and services, organizations can avoid the need to invest in expensive infrastructure and hardware, and can instead focus on developing and deploying IoT applications and services [47, 65, 66]. However, there are also challenges associated with the use of cloud computing in IoT. These include concerns about data privacy and security, as well as the need to ensure interoperability and standardization across different cloud platforms and IoT devices. To address these challenges, researchers and industry experts are developing new standards and protocols for ensuring the safety and reliability of IoT systems, and are working to develop more secure and interoperable cloud-based platforms and services.

Due to the rapid growth of technology, the problem of storing, processing, and accessing large amounts of data has arisen. Great innovation relates to the mutual use of IoT and cloud technologies [34, 47]. In combination, it will be possible to use powerful processing of sensory data streams and new monitoring services. As an example, sensor data can be uploaded and saved using cloud computing for later use as intelligent monitoring and activation using other devices. The goal is to transform data into insights and thus drive cost-effective and productive action. There are many benefits of combining these services, including the following.

a) IoT cloud computing provides many connectivity options, implying large network access. People use a wide range of devices to gain access to cloud computing resources: mobile devices, tablets, laptops. This is convenient for users but creates the problem of a need for network access points.
b) Developers can use IoT cloud computing on demand. In other words, it is a web service accessed without special permission or any help. The only requirement is internet access.
c) Based on the request, users can scale the service according to their needs. Fast and flexible means you can expand storage space, edit software settings, and work with the number of users. Due to this characteristic, it is possible to provide deep computing power and storage.
d) Cloud computing implies the pooling of resources. It influences increased collaboration and builds close connections between users.
e) As the number of IoT devices and automation in use grows, security concerns emerge. Cloud solutions provide companies with reliable authentication and encryption protocols.
f) Finally, IoT cloud computing is convenient because you get exactly as much from the service as you pay. This means that costs vary depending on use: the provider measures your usage statistics. A growing network of objects with IP addresses is needed to connect to the internet and exchange data between the components of the network.

It is important to note that cloud architecture must be well designed since reliability, security, economy, and performance optimization depends upon it. Using well-designed continuous integration and continuous deployment (CI/CD) pipelines, structured services, and sandboxed environments results in a secure environment and agile development.

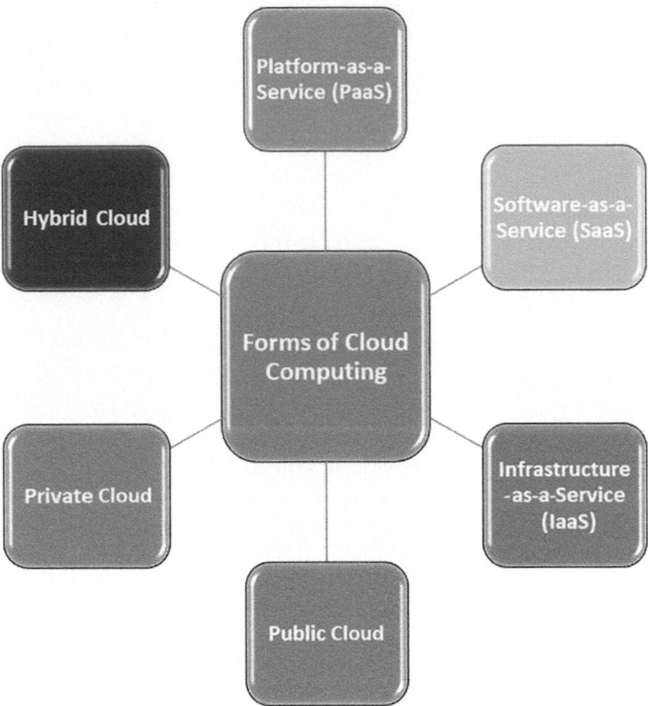

FIGURE 1.14 Forms of cloud computing.

Cloud computing encompasses the delivery of data to data centers over the internet. IBM divides cloud computing into five different categories, as shown in Figure 1.14 [67].

a) **Platform-as-a-Service (PaaS):** The cloud contains everything you need to build and deliver cloud applications, so there is no need to buy and maintain equipment, software, etc.
b) **Software-as-a-Service (SaaS):** In this case, applications run in the cloud and other companies operate devices that connect to users' computers through a web browser.
c) **Infrastructure-as-a-Service (IaaS):** IaaS is an option providing companies with storage, servers, networks, and hubs processing data for each use.
d) **Public Cloud:** Companies manage spaces and provide users with quick access through the public network.
e) **Private Cloud:** The same as a public cloud, but only one person has access here, which can be an organization, an individual company, or a user.

4. **Big Data Analytics:** Big Data analytics is the process of extracting insights from large, complex datasets. It is an essential technology for IoT because it enables organizations to derive insights and make informed decisions based on the data generated by IoT devices [8]. IoT data can be analyzed using

machine learning algorithms, statistical techniques, and data visualization tools to uncover patterns and trends that would be difficult to identify using traditional data analysis methods. Big Data analytics enables organizations to make sense of the massive amounts of data generated by connected devices. IoT devices generate a vast array of data, including sensor readings, video feeds, and other data streams, which can be used to gain insights into consumer behavior, operational performance, and other key factors. In the context of IoT, Big Data analytics refers to the use of advanced analytical techniques to analyze and process the data generated by connected devices. This involves the use of sophisticated algorithms and machine learning models to identify patterns, trends, and insights in the data, and to use this information to inform decision-making and drive business value.

One of the primary benefits of Big Data analytics in IoT is the ability to identify new opportunities and areas for improvement. By analyzing data from connected devices, organizations can gain a deeper understanding of customer behavior, identify operational inefficiencies, and uncover new business opportunities. Big Data analytics also enables real-time decision-making in IoT applications, enabling organizations to respond quickly to changing conditions and make more informed decisions based on real-time data [8, 21]. This is particularly important in applications such as smart cities, whereby real-time data analysis is critical for managing traffic flows, optimizing energy usage, and improving public safety. Another advantage of Big Data analytics in IoT is the ability to automate processes and reduce manual intervention. By using machine learning and AI techniques, organizations can automate the analysis of data from connected devices, reducing the need for manual intervention and increasing the efficiency of IoT deployments [8, 68]. However, there are also challenges associated with the use of Big Data analytics in IoT. These include concerns around data privacy and security, as well as the need to ensure interoperability and standardization across different IoT devices and platforms. To address these challenges, researchers and industry experts are developing new standards and protocols for ensuring the safety and reliability of IoT systems, and they are working to develop more secure and interoperable IoT platforms and services.

5. **Machine Learning:** Machine learning is a type of AI that enables machines to learn from data and improve their performance over time. It is an essential technology for IoT because it enables devices to analyze data in real time and make decisions based on that analysis. Machine learning algorithms can be used to detect anomalies, predict equipment failure, and optimize processes in IoT systems. It has become an essential component of IoT systems due to the increasing amount of data generated by IoT devices. In the context of IoT, machine learning algorithms can be used to analyze the data generated by sensors and other devices to derive insights, make predictions, and automate decision-making processes [8, 68]. Following are some of the key reasons why machine learning is important for IoT.

a) **Handling Large Data Volumes:** IoT devices generate large volumes of data, which can be difficult to process and analyze using traditional methods. Machine learning algorithms can help to handle this data by identifying patterns and trends that are not visible to the human eye, and can be used to make predictions and identify potential problems before they occur [69].

b) **Automating Decision-Making:** Machine learning algorithms can be trained to make decisions based on the data generated by IoT devices. This can help to automate decision-making processes, such as identifying anomalies, detecting faults, and optimizing performance [70].

c) **Predictive Maintenance:** IoT devices can generate data on the health and performance of equipment, such as machinery and vehicles. Machine learning algorithms can be used to analyze this data to predict when maintenance is required, allowing for proactive maintenance to be carried out before a failure occurs [69, 70].

d) **Personalization:** IoT devices can generate data on the preferences and behavior of users. Machine learning algorithms can be used to analyze this data to personalize services and products, such as recommending products and services based on past behavior and preferences [71].

e) **Optimization:** Machine learning algorithms can be used to optimize the performance of IoT systems by analyzing data on usage patterns and environmental factors, such as temperature and humidity. This can help to reduce energy consumption and improve the efficiency of IoT systems [70, 71].

In summary, machine learning is important in the context of IoT because it can help to handle large data volumes, automate decision-making, enable predictive maintenance, personalize services and products, and optimize the performance of IoT systems. Machine learning algorithms can help to derive insights from the data generated by IoT devices and enable more intelligent decision-making processes.

6. **RFID:** Radio frequency identification (RFID) is a technology that uses radio waves to identify and track objects. It is an essential technology for IoT because it enables devices to communicate with each other and exchange data without human intervention. RFID tags are attached to objects and can be scanned by RFID readers to retrieve information about the object's location, status, or history. In the context of IoT, RFID plays a critical role in enabling devices to communicate with each other and exchange data [4, 72]. Following are some of the key reasons why RFID is important for IoT.

a) **Tracking and Monitoring:** RFID technology can be used to track and monitor the location and movement of objects in real time. This can be useful in a wide range of industries, such as logistics, healthcare, and retail.

b) **Asset Management:** RFID tags can be used to manage assets, such as inventory, equipment, and vehicles. This can help to reduce the cost of lost or stolen assets, improve inventory accuracy, and streamline supply chain operations.

c) **Automation:** RFID technology can be used to automate processes and reduce the need for human intervention. For example, RFID-enabled machines can automatically reorder parts when inventory levels get low, or trigger alerts when equipment requires maintenance.

d) **Security:** RFID tags can be used to secure assets and prevent theft. For example, RFID tags can be used to track the movement of high-value items, such as electronics or jewelry, and trigger an alarm if they are removed from the premises without authorization.

e) **Analytics:** RFID data can be used to derive insights and make data-driven decisions. For example, RFID data can be used to identify trends in customer behavior, optimize inventory levels, and improve supply chain efficiency.

In summary, RFID technology plays a critical role in the context of IoT by enabling devices to communicate with each other and exchange data. RFID technology can be used to track and monitor objects in real time, manage assets, automate processes, improve security, and derive insights from data [44, 72]. By leveraging RFID technology, IoT systems can become more intelligent, efficient, and secure.

7. **Bluetooth Low Energy (BLE):** BLE is a wireless communication protocol that is used for short-range communication between devices. It is an essential technology for IoT because it provides a low-power, low-cost way for devices to communicate with each other [73]. BLE is commonly used in IoT applications such as smart homes, healthcare, and asset tracking. Following are some of the key reasons why BLE is important for IoT [73, 74].

a) **Low Power Consumption:** BLE is designed to be energy efficient, which makes it an ideal communication protocol for devices with limited power supplies, such as sensors and wearables. BLE can operate on a single coin cell battery for several years, which makes it ideal for IoT devices that are deployed in remote locations.

b) **Short-Range Communication:** BLE is designed for short-range communication, which makes it ideal for use cases when devices need to communicate within a limited area, such as a room or a building. BLE has a range of up to 100 meters, which makes it ideal for indoor IoT applications.

c) **Interoperability:** BLE is a widely adopted standard, which means that devices from different manufacturers can communicate with each other. This makes it easier to build IoT systems that incorporate devices from multiple vendors.

d) **Security:** BLE provides built-in security features, such as encryption and authentication, which makes it a secure communication protocol for IoT devices. This is particularly important for applications where sensitive data is being transmitted, such as healthcare and financial services.

e) **Cost Effectiveness:** BLE is a low-cost communication protocol, which makes it ideal for IoT devices that need to be produced in large quantities. This also makes it easier for businesses to adopt IoT technology, as they can leverage off-the-shelf BLE components and modules.

In summary, BLE is an important communication protocol in the context of IoT due to its low power consumption, short-range communication capabilities, interoperability, security features, and cost effectiveness. By leveraging BLE technology, IoT systems can become more efficient, secure, and cost effective, which can help to accelerate the adoption of IoT technology across a wide range of industries. Overall, all of the enabling technologies discussed in this chapter provide the necessary infrastructure, computing power, and communication capabilities required to connect devices, collect and analyze data, and derive insights that drive business value in IoT systems.

1.5.1 The Identifiers in IoT

In any system of interacting components, identification of these components is needed in order to ensure the correct composition and operation of the system. This applies to all lifecycle phases of a system from development to assembly, commissioning, operations, maintenance, and even end of life. Especially in case of flexible and dynamic interactions between system components, identification plays an important role. Identifiers are used to provide identification. In general, an identifier is a pattern to uniquely identify a single entity (instance identifier) or a class of entities (i.e. type identifier) within a specific context. In the context of IoT, an identifier is a unique name or code that is used to identify a specific device, sensor, or object connected to the internet [56, 75]. These identifiers play a crucial role in enabling the IoT devices to communicate and interact with each other and with the cloud-based IoT applications. In conclusion, identifiers play a critical role in IoT networks, as they are used to identify, authenticate, and communicate with devices, objects, and sensors. Following are some commonly used identifiers in IoT.

1. **MAC Address:** A MAC (media access control) address is a unique identifier assigned to a network interface controller (NIC) for use as a network address in communications within a network segment [76]. MAC addresses are used at the data link layer (Layer 2) of the open systems interconnection (OSI) model and are usually assigned by the manufacturer of the network interface card. MAC addresses are used to identify devices on a local network, such as Wi-Fi or Ethernet networks. MAC addresses are typically assigned by the manufacturer of a device, and they are used to ensure that data packets are correctly delivered to the intended recipient. For example, you may have a smart thermostat in your home that is connected to your home Wi-Fi network. The MAC address of the thermostat is used to uniquely identify the device on the network, allowing it to communicate with other devices on the same network, such as your smartphone or a cloud-based IoT application.
2. **IP Address:** An Internet Protocol (IP) address is a numerical label assigned to each device connected to a computer network that uses IP for communication. IP addresses are used to route data packets between devices and to identify the location of devices on the internet [75, 76]. For example, when you access a cloud-based IoT application on your smartphone to control your smart thermostat, the application uses the IP address of the thermostat to send commands to the device over the internet.

3. **UUID:** A UUID (Universally Unique Identifier) is a 128-bit value used to identify a device or object in the IoT network [77]. It is a random number that is generated by the device or server, and it is guaranteed to be unique. For example, if you have a fleet of trucks that are connected to the IoT network, each truck will have a unique UUID assigned to it that identifies it on the network.
4. **QR Code:** A quick response (QR) code is a two-dimensional barcode that is used to identify a device or object in the IoT network [75, 76]. It is a machine-readable code that can be scanned by a smartphone or other device to retrieve information about the device or object. For example, if you have a smart appliance in your home, it may have a QR code on the back that you can scan to retrieve information about the device, such as its model number, serial number, and other details.

The Alliance for Internet of Things Innovation (AIOTI) is a European Commission-initiated body that aims to promote innovation in the field of IoT. When it comes to classification of identifiers in IoT, AIOTI proposes the following categorization [78, 79].

1. **Device Identifier:** A unique identifier assigned to a physical device in the IoT ecosystem. This identifier is used to distinguish one device from another and can be used for device authentication and access control.
2. **Service Identifier:** A unique identifier assigned to a specific service within the IoT ecosystem. This identifier is used to distinguish one service from another and can be used for service discovery and routing.
3. **Application Identifier:** A unique identifier assigned to a specific application within the IoT ecosystem. This identifier is used to distinguish one application from another and can be used for application discovery and routing.
4. **User Identifier:** A unique identifier assigned to a user within the IoT ecosystem. This identifier is used to distinguish one user from another and can be used for user authentication and access control.

Overall, these identifiers play a critical role in enabling communication and interaction between various components within the IoT ecosystem, and their proper management is essential to ensure secure and efficient operation of IoT systems.

1.5.2 IoT Frameworks and Its Design Ethics

The IoT frameworks are a set of software tools and protocols that enable the deployment and management of IoT devices and applications. These frameworks provide a comprehensive set of functionalities that are required to build, deploy, and manage IoT applications [41, 80]. Some of the important features of IoT frameworks include device management, data management, communication protocols, security, and analytics.

As IoT applications become more prevalent, it is important to consider the ethical implications of IoT framework design. Following are some of the key ethical considerations that should be taken into account during the design of IoT frameworks [79, 81].

1. **Privacy and Data Protection:** One of the primary concerns with IoT devices and applications is the potential for privacy breaches. IoT frameworks should be designed with strong privacy and data protection mechanisms to ensure that user data is kept secure.
2. **Transparency and User Control:** IoT frameworks should be transparent about what data is being collected and how it is being used. Users should have control over their data and be able to decide whether to share it or not.
3. **Inclusivity and Accessibility:** IoT frameworks should be designed with inclusivity and accessibility in mind. This means that the needs of all users, including those with disabilities, should be taken into account.
4. **Sustainability and Environmental Impact:** IoT frameworks should be designed with sustainability and environmental impact in mind. This includes considering the energy efficiency of devices and applications, as well as the disposal of electronic waste.
5. **Ethical Use:** IoT frameworks should be designed with ethical use in mind. This means that the potential social, economic, and environmental impact of IoT applications should be considered, and the potential for harm should be minimized.

1.6 TOWARD THE INTERNET OF THINGS APPLICATIONS

The IoT is a network of connected devices, objects, and systems that can communicate and exchange data with each other over the internet. The applications of IoT are vast and diverse, ranging from smart homes and industrial automation to healthcare, transportation, and agriculture. By using IoT-enabled devices and systems, individuals, businesses, and governments can optimize processes, reduce costs, and improve safety and sustainability. However, the widespread adoption of IoT also poses significant challenges, including data security and privacy concerns, interoperability between devices and systems, and the need for standards and regulations [15, 82, 83]. Despite these challenges, the IoT has enormous potential to transform the way we live, work, and interact with the world around us, making it an exciting area of technological innovation and development.

1.6.1 Strategic Research and Innovation Directions

The IoT is a rapidly evolving field with numerous research and innovation directions. Some of the strategic research and innovation directions for IoT include the following.

1. **Data Analytics and Machine Learning:** One of the major challenges in IoT data analytics and machine learning is the ability to handle and process

large amounts of data generated by IoT devices. This requires the development of new algorithms and models that can efficiently process and analyze data in real time. Another challenge is the need for data privacy and security, as sensitive data generated by IoT devices can be vulnerable to cyber-attacks. Suitable examples of this research direction include the development of advanced machine learning algorithms for real-time analytics of sensor data in industrial automation, and the use of predictive analytics to improve healthcare outcomes by analyzing data from wearable health devices [11, 24, 83].

2. **Security and Privacy:** The security and privacy of IoT devices and systems are major concerns, particularly given the potential for data breaches and cyber-attacks. IoT devices are often deployed in remote or unsecured locations, making them vulnerable to attacks. Research in this area is focused on developing new security and encryption techniques to ensure the confidentiality, integrity, and availability of data generated by IoT devices [40, 84]. Suitable examples of this research direction include the use of blockchain technology to enhance security and privacy in IoT systems, and the development of secure hardware platforms for IoT devices.
3. **Edge Computing:** Edge computing involves processing and analyzing data on IoT devices themselves, rather than sending the data to a centralized cloud server [26, 65]. This enables faster response times and reduces the need for large amounts of data transfer, making it ideal for real-time IoT applications. However, edge computing also presents challenges such as limited computational resources, network connectivity issues, and data security concerns. Suitable examples of this research direction include the development of lightweight machine learning models for edge devices, and the use of edge computing for autonomous vehicle applications.
4. **Interoperability and Standardization:** Interoperability and standardization are critical for the seamless integration of different IoT devices and systems [41]. This requires the development of new communication protocols and standards that enable different devices and systems to communicate with each other. One of the major challenges in this area is the lack of standardization in IoT, as there are many different platforms and protocols that do not necessarily interoperate. Suitable examples of this research direction include the development of standard communication protocols such as MQTT and CoAP, and the use of semantic technologies to enable interoperability between different IoT platforms.
5. **Energy Efficiency:** IoT devices often have limited power and operate in remote or hard-to-reach locations, making energy efficiency a critical concern. Research in this area is focused on developing new energy-efficient hardware and software solutions, as well as on optimizing the power consumption of IoT devices and systems. One of the major challenges in this area is the need to balance energy efficiency with performance and functionality. Suitable examples of this research direction include the use of low-power wireless communication protocols such as LoRaWAN and Sigfox, and the development of energy harvesting techniques for IoT devices [85].

Overall, these strategic research and innovation directions for IoT are critical for addressing the challenges and opportunities of this rapidly evolving field, and for unlocking the full potential of the IoT in various domains.

1.6.2 IoT Smart X Applications

IoT Smart X applications refer to the use of IoT technologies and systems to create intelligent and interconnected solutions that improve various aspects of life [86]. The "Smart X" label represents different fields or domains that can benefit from IoT technologies. These applications aim to increase efficiency, reduce costs, and enhance the quality of life for individuals and communities. The IoT ecosystem consists of various devices, sensors, and systems that can communicate with each other and collect data in real time. This data can be analyzed using advanced analytics and machine learning algorithms to provide insights that can help improve decision-making, productivity, and efficiency.

Examples of IoT Smart X applications include smart homes, smart cities, smart transportation, smart agriculture, and smart healthcare [87]. Smart homes, for instance, use IoT devices and systems to automate and optimize various home appliances and devices. Smart city applications use IoT technologies to optimize urban infrastructure, services, and systems, making them more efficient, sustainable, and accessible. Smart transportation applications aim to improve transportation systems and reduce traffic congestion, emissions, and accidents through the use of IoT technologies. Smart agriculture applications use IoT technologies to optimize farming practices and increase crop yields. Smart healthcare applications use IoT technologies to improve patient outcomes and reduce healthcare costs. Following is a discussion of key IoT Smart X applications in detail.

1. **Smart Homes:** Smart homes are one of the most popular IoT Smart X applications, which use IoT devices and systems to automate and optimize various home appliances and devices. Smart home systems can include smart lighting, smart thermostats, smart locks and security systems, among others [12]. These devices can be controlled and monitored remotely through a smartphone or tablet, making it convenient and easy for homeowners to manage their homes. The IoT allows homeowners to automate and remotely manage a wide range of home systems and appliances, such as lighting, heating and cooling, security systems, entertainment systems, and more. Smart homes typically involve the installation of smart devices, which are equipped with sensors and connected to the internet, allowing them to collect and share data with other devices and systems. This data can then be analyzed and used to automate various processes and improve the efficiency and convenience of daily life. Figure 1.15 visualizes a typical Smart homes scenario.

   One of the key benefits of smart homes is the ability to control and manage different devices and systems from a central hub, such as a smartphone or a voice-controlled device like Amazon Alexa or Google Home [88]. This allows homeowners to easily adjust their home environment to their

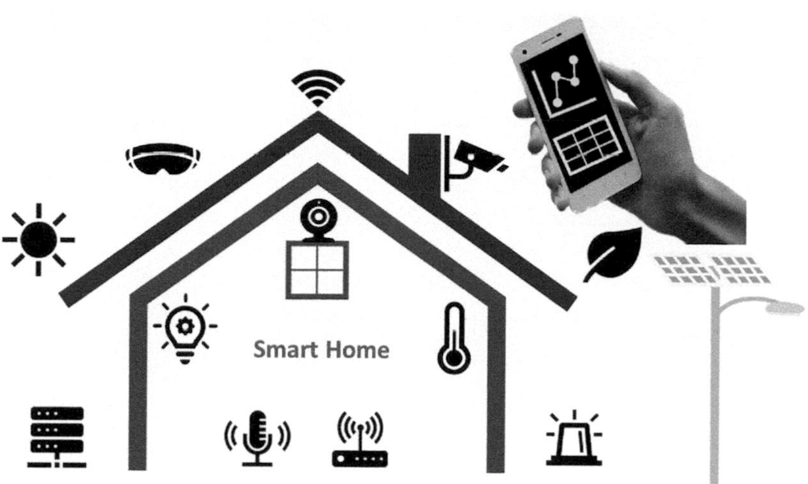

FIGURE 1.15 Typical smart home scenario.

preferences and needs, even when they are not physically present in the home. Other benefits of smart homes include improved energy efficiency, increased security, and greater convenience. For example, homeowners can set their heating and cooling systems to turn off when they leave the house, or schedule their lights to turn on and off at certain times of the day, which can save energy and reduce costs. Smart security systems can also alert homeowners when there is suspicious activity, and can even trigger alarms or contact emergency services if necessary. Overall, smart homes represent an exciting and rapidly growing field within the IoT industry, with many new devices and applications being developed all the time to make homes more connected, efficient, and secure.

Thus, the IoT Smart X applications have enormous potential to transform various aspects of life, from homes and cities to transportation and healthcare, among others. These applications can improve efficiency, reduce costs, and enhance the quality of life for individuals and communities. However, they also pose significant challenges, including data privacy and security concerns, interoperability between devices and systems, and the need for standards and regulations. To fully realize the benefits of IoT Smart X applications, it is essential to address these challenges and develop robust and secure systems that can support these applications.

2. **Smart Cities:** Smart cities are one of the most exciting and rapidly growing IoT Smart X applications that have been gaining popularity in recent years. Smart cities leverage advanced technologies such as IoT sensors, cloud computing, data analytics, and machine learning to enhance urban infrastructure and services, making them more efficient, sustainable, and livable [87, 89]. The main goal of smart cities is to improve the quality of life of citizens by providing better services, reducing costs, and optimizing

resources. Figure 1.16 shows the typical overview of a smart city. Following are some examples of how IoT is transforming the urban landscape.

a) **Traffic Management:** IoT sensors can monitor traffic flow in real time, providing real-time data to traffic management systems to optimize routes, reduce congestion, and improve safety. Smart traffic lights can adjust the signal timing based on traffic volumes, and smart parking systems can guide drivers to available parking spots, reducing traffic congestion.
b) **Waste Management:** IoT sensors can monitor waste bins' fill levels, optimizing the collection process and reducing the cost of waste collection. This can lead to significant cost savings and reduce the environmental impact of waste collection.
c) **Energy Management:** IoT sensors can monitor energy usage in buildings and other urban infrastructure, providing real-time data to optimize energy consumption, reduce costs, and lower carbon emissions. For example, smart street lighting can automatically adjust brightness and turn off when not in use, reducing energy waste.
d) **Public Safety:** IoT sensors can monitor public spaces, detecting potential safety hazards such as fire, flooding, and crime. Real-time data can be used to alert authorities, allowing them to respond quickly and prevent damage or injury.
e) **Environmental Monitoring:** IoT sensors can monitor environmental factors such as air quality, water quality, and noise levels, providing real-time data to city authorities and citizens. This data can be used to identify areas of concern and develop targeted solutions to improve environmental conditions.

Overall, smart cities represent a significant opportunity to create more sustainable, efficient, and livable urban environments. As IoT technologies continue to advance, we can expect to see more innovative solutions that

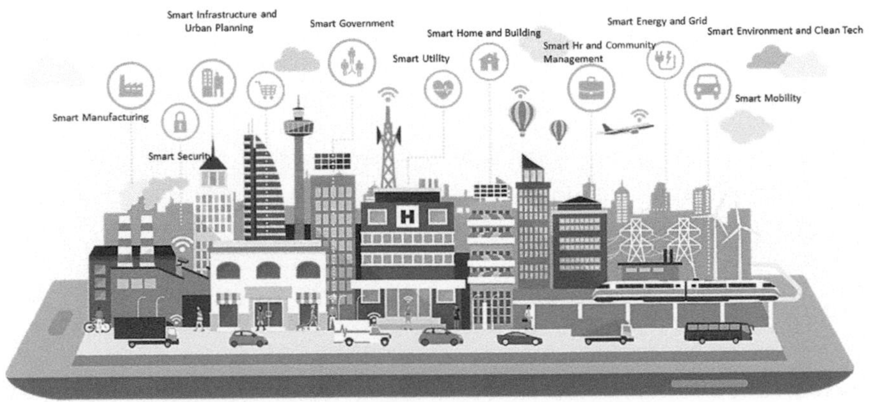

FIGURE 1.16 Typical overview of a smart city.

improve the quality of life for citizens and create more vibrant and connected urban communities.

3. **Smart Healthcare:** Smart healthcare is a rapidly growing IoT Smart X application that has the potential to revolutionize healthcare delivery and improve patient outcomes. Smart healthcare leverages advanced technologies such as IoT sensors, wearables, mobile apps, cloud computing, and data analytics to create intelligent and connected healthcare systems that can enhance patient care, reduce costs, and improve efficiency [15, 40]. Figure 1.17 illustrates the smart wearables in smart healthcare, and Figure 1.18 shows patient engagement. Following are some examples of how IoT is transforming healthcare.
   a) **Remote Monitoring:** IoT sensors and wearables can monitor patients' vital signs, activity levels, and medication adherence remotely, providing real-time data to healthcare providers. This can enable early detection of health issues, improve medication management, and reduce hospital readmissions.
   b) **Predictive Analytics:** IoT data can be used to develop predictive models that can identify patients at risk of developing health issues, such as chronic diseases. This can enable healthcare providers to develop targeted interventions to prevent or manage these conditions more effectively.
   c) **Telemedicine:** IoT technologies can enable virtual consultations between patients and healthcare providers, reducing the need for in-person visits and improving access to care, particularly for patients in remote or underserved areas.
   d) **Patient Engagement:** IoT technologies can improve patient engagement by providing patients with personalized health information, enabling

FIGURE 1.17 Smart healthcare: smart wearables.

FIGURE 1.18 Smart healthcare: patient engagement.

them to manage their health more effectively. For example, mobile apps can remind patients to take their medications, track their activity levels, and provide educational materials on their condition.

e) **Health System Optimization:** IoT data can be used to optimize healthcare delivery systems, reducing costs and improving efficiency. For example, IoT data can be used to optimize hospital bed allocation, reduce wait times, and improve patient flow through hospitals.

Overall, smart healthcare has the potential to transform the healthcare industry, improving patient outcomes, reducing costs, and enhancing the patient experience. As IoT technologies continue to advance, we can expect to see more innovative solutions that enhance healthcare delivery and improve patient care.

4. **Smart Agriculture:** IoT sensors can help farmers monitor soil moisture levels, temperature, and other environmental factors to optimize crop yields and reduce water usage. For instance, smart irrigation systems can automatically adjust watering schedules based on weather conditions, while drones equipped with sensors can capture data about health and growth of crops. Sensors, devices, and other technologies can be used to collect data on various aspects of agriculture, such as soil moisture, temperature, rainfall, and crop growth. This data is then analyzed to provide insights and optimize agricultural processes. In the context of IoT Smart X applications, smart agriculture can be enhanced by integrating with other smart applications such as smart irrigation, smart pest control, smart fertilization, and smart harvesting [90, 91]. These applications utilize IoT sensors and devices to gather data on crop growth and environmental conditions, and then use this data to automatically adjust farming processes in real time. Figure 1.19 shown shows IoT-based smart agriculture with IoT applications.

   Smart irrigation systems, for example, use IoT sensors to monitor soil moisture levels and weather conditions to determine the optimal amount of

FIGURE 1.19 IoT-based smart agriculture.

water needed for crops. This data is then used to automatically adjust irrigation schedules and water delivery, reducing water waste and maximizing crop yield. Similarly, smart pest control systems use IoT sensors to monitor pest populations and identify areas of infestation. This information is then used to automatically deploy targeted pest control measures, reducing the need for harmful pesticides and improving crop health. Smart fertilization systems use IoT sensors to monitor soil nutrient levels and crop growth, providing precise fertilizer recommendations to optimize crop yields and reduce waste. Finally, smart harvesting systems use IoT sensors to monitor crop maturity and readiness for harvest, providing real-time data on when to harvest crops and reducing waste from overripe or underripe produce. Overall, smart agriculture in the context of IoT Smart X application offers a powerful tool for farmers and agricultural managers to optimize farming processes, reduce waste, and increase crop yields [90, 91]. By leveraging IoT sensors and devices, farmers can gain valuable insights into their crops and the environment, allowing them to make data-driven decisions and improve their bottom line.

5. **Automotive Applications:** Automotive applications of IoT Smart X refer to the integration of IoT technology into vehicles to make them more connected, efficient, and safe. In the automotive sector, IoT has enabled greater transportation efficiency and management capabilities and is leading us to a future of intelligent, autonomous vehicles. Overall, the integration of IoT technology into automotive applications can create a safer, more efficient, and more connected driving experience [60, 73]. Figure 1.20 illustrates how IoT can be utilized in automotive applications.

FIGURE 1.20 Application of IoT in the automotive sector.

Following are some examples.

a) **Connected Cars:** IoT technology can enable vehicles to connect to the internet, allowing for real-time updates on traffic, weather, and road conditions [92]. Connected cars can also communicate with other vehicles on the road, creating a safer and more efficient driving experience.
b) **Predictive Maintenance:** IoT sensors can be installed in vehicles to monitor and predict maintenance needs, such as tire wear, brake pad wear, and compromised engine performance [93]. Predictive maintenance can reduce the likelihood of breakdowns and help drivers avoid costly repairs.
c) **Fleet Management:** IoT technology can be used to track the location and performance of vehicles in a fleet, enabling managers to optimize routes, monitor fuel consumption, and schedule maintenance more efficiently [94].
d) **Driver Assistance:** IoT technology can enable vehicles to assist drivers in various ways, such as automatically adjusting speed based on traffic conditions, alerting drivers to potential collisions, and assisting with parking.
e) **Smart Traffic Management:** IoT technology can be used to create smarter traffic management systems, enabling traffic lights to communicate with each other and optimize traffic flow based on real-time conditions [94, 95].

6. **Military Applications:** IoT Smart X applications can also be used in the military to create smarter and more efficient military operations [57, 96]. Figure 1.21 shows the IoT military applications.

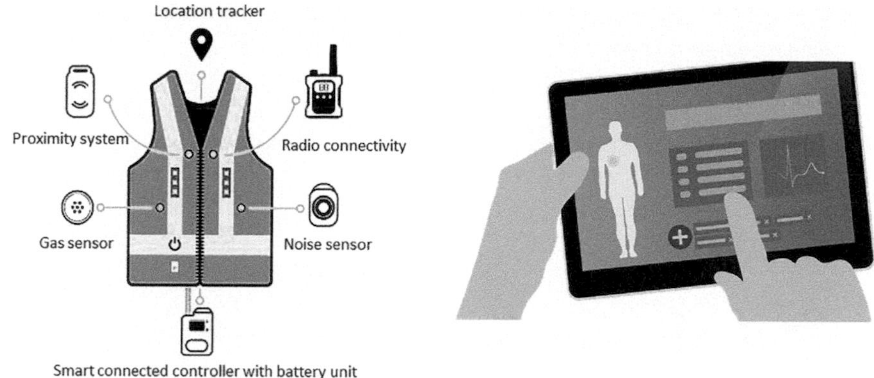

FIGURE 1.21 IoT in military applications.

Following are some examples.

a) **Smart Logistics:** IoT technology can be used to track and monitor military equipment, supplies, and personnel. This can help military logistics teams to optimize supply chains, ensure the right equipment and supplies are available at the right time, and reduce waste.
b) **Smart Maintenance:** IoT technology can be used to monitor and predict maintenance needs for military vehicles, aircraft, and other equipment. This can help prevent breakdowns and ensure equipment is always in top condition.
c) **Smart Energy Management:** IoT technology can be used to monitor and manage energy usage at military bases, enabling more efficient use of resources and reducing energy costs.
d) **Smart Battlefield Management:** IoT technology can be used to create smarter battlefield management systems, enabling military leaders to make faster and more informed decisions based on real-time data from sensors, cameras, and other sources.
e) **Smart Training:** IoT technology can be used to create more realistic and effective military training programs. This can include the use of virtual reality and other immersive technologies to simulate real-world scenarios and enhance training outcomes.

Overall, the integration of IoT technology into military applications can create more efficient, effective, and safer military operations, enabling military forces to better accomplish their missions. However, it is important to consider the potential security risks associated with IoT technology, especially in military applications, and take appropriate measures to ensure the security of sensitive data and systems

7. **Energy Management:** IoT Smart X applications can be used in energy management to create smarter and more efficient energy systems. IoT energy management is a process that includes planning and management of energy consumption patterns in different industries. These solutions can be utilized to manage and optimize energy consumption patterns by taking complete control of energy data at the most fundamental and granular level [97, 98]. IoT can be employed for improving energy efficiency, increasing the share of renewable energy, and reducing environmental impacts of the energy use. Figure 1.22 shows the IoT as energy management. Following are some examples.
   a) **Smart Grids:** IoT technology can be used to monitor and control energy distribution on the grid, enabling more efficient energy use, reducing waste, and preventing blackouts.
   b) **Smart Metering:** IoT technology can be used to track energy usage in homes and businesses, providing real-time data to both consumers and energy providers. This can help consumers to better understand and manage their energy usage, while enabling energy providers to optimize energy supply and demand.
   c) **Smart Energy Storage:** IoT technology can be used to monitor and manage energy storage systems, including batteries and other energy storage devices. This can help optimize energy storage and usage, reduce waste, and increase the efficiency of renewable energy source.
   d) **Smart Demand Response:** IoT technology can be used to create smarter demand response systems, enabling energy providers to quickly and efficiently respond to changes in energy demand. This can help reduce energy costs, prevent blackouts, and improve overall energy system reliability.

Overall, the integration of IoT technology into energy management applications can create more efficient and sustainable energy systems, reduce waste, and lower energy costs for consumers and businesses.

1.7 CHALLENGES AND OPEN RESEARCH ISSUES IN IOT

Taking into account the challenges of IoT is necessary to ensure that IoT systems are secure, interoperable, scalable, energy-efficient, well-managed, user-friendly, and socially responsible. Addressing these challenges can also help to unlock the full potential of IoT and drive innovation and growth in various sectors. As IoT continues to grow and evolve, it brings with it several challenges and open research issues, including security and privacy, scalability and interoperability, energy efficiency, data management, standards and regulations, human–computer interaction, and ethical and social issues [10, 42, 56, 89, 99].

1.7.1 Security and Privacy Issues in IoT

IoT is the emerging technology which will change the way we interact with devices. In the future, almost every electronic device will be a smart device which can compute

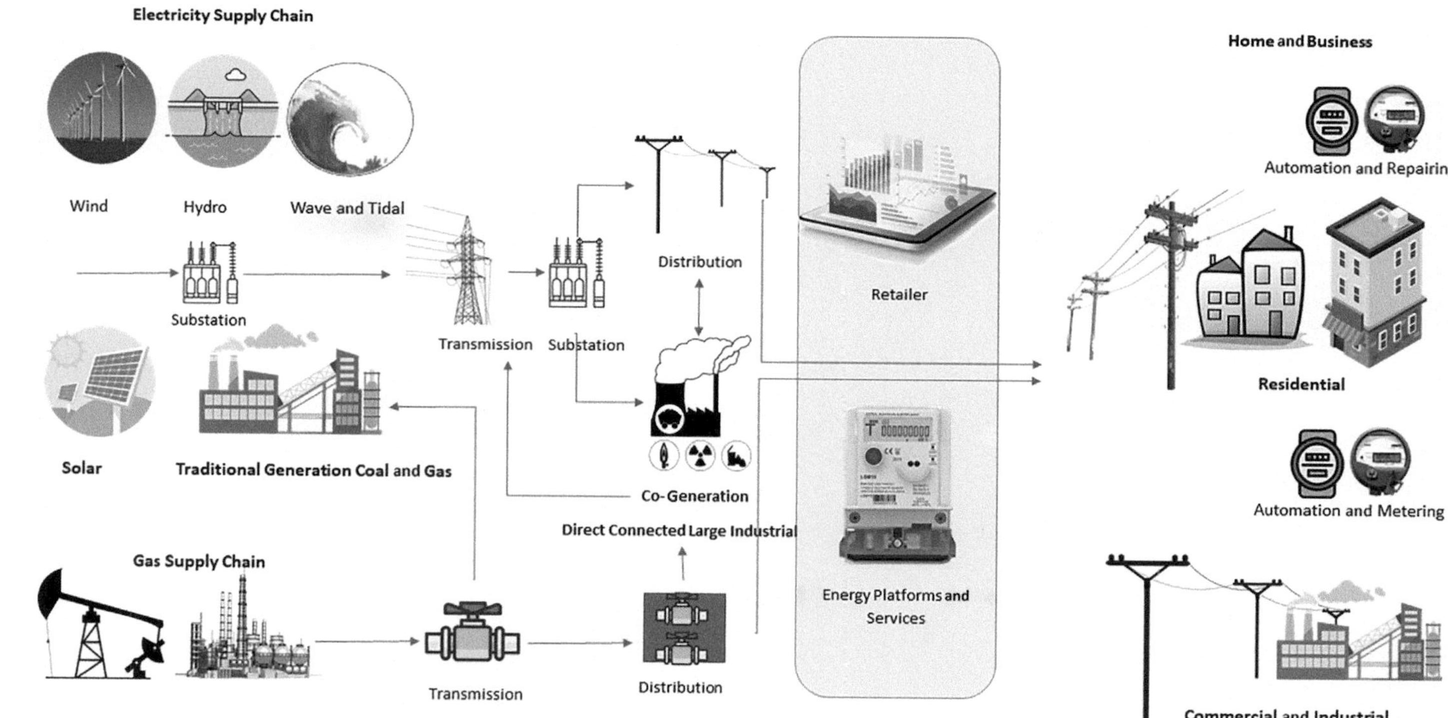

FIGURE 1.22 IoT as energy management.

and communicate with handheld and other infrastructure devices. As most of the devices may be battery-operated, due to less need for processing power, the security and privacy is a major issue in IoT. Authentication, identification and device heterogeneity are the major security and privacy concerns in IoT. With a growing number of connected devices, security and privacy are major concerns in IoT. Attackers can exploit vulnerabilities in IoT devices to gain access to sensitive information or to launch cyber-attacks. Researchers are exploring ways to enhance IoT security, including secure communication protocols, access control mechanisms, and data encryption techniques [19, 40, 82]. Failure to address security and privacy concerns can lead to serious consequences such as loss of sensitive information or unauthorized access to devices and systems. This can have a significant impact on individuals and organizations, and may result in legal, financial, and reputational damage.

Security and privacy are critical issues in IoT, and addressing them is essential for the successful development and deployment of IoT systems. Following are some ways to deal with security and privacy issues in IoT [45, 74, 82, 100].

1. **Use Secure Communication Protocols:** IoT devices should use secure communication protocols, such as Transport Layer Security (TLS) or Datagram Transport Layer Security (DTLS), to encrypt communication and ensure data integrity.
2. **Implement Access Control Mechanisms:** IoT devices should implement access control mechanisms to restrict access to sensitive data and functions. This includes user authentication, authorization, and role-based access control.
3. **Encrypt Data:** IoT devices should encrypt sensitive data to prevent unauthorized access and ensure confidentiality. This includes data at rest, in transit, and in use.
4. **Conduct Regular Security Audits:** Regular security audits can help identify vulnerabilities and ensure that IoT devices and systems are secure. This includes testing for common vulnerabilities, such as buffer overflows, SQL (Structured Query Language) injection, and cross-site scripting (XSS).
5. **Use Intrusion Detection and Prevention Systems:** Intrusion detection and prevention systems can help detect and prevent attacks on IoT devices and systems. This includes detecting unusual network traffic, unauthorized access attempts, and malware infections.
6. **Implement Privacy-Preserving Techniques:** Privacy-preserving techniques, such as differential privacy and homomorphic encryption, can help protect sensitive data while still allowing data analysis and processing.
7. **Establish Best Practices and Standards:** Establishing best practices and standards for IoT security and privacy can help ensure that IoT devices and systems are designed and implemented in a secure and privacy-preserving manner. This includes establishing security and privacy guidelines, certification programs, and industry standards.

Overall, dealing with security and privacy issues in IoT requires a comprehensive approach that includes secure communication protocols, access control mechanisms, encryption, security audits, intrusion detection and prevention systems, privacy-preserving techniques, and best practices and standards. By addressing these issues, IoT devices and systems can be made more secure and privacy-preserving, which is essential for the successful development and deployment of IoT.

1.7.2 Tackling Jamming Attacks in IoT

Jamming attacks in IoT are a type of cyber-attack whereby an attacker floods the wireless communication channel with high-power radio signals, causing the IoT devices to lose connectivity with the network. The jamming signals interfere with the communication channel, making it difficult for legitimate devices to transmit or receive data. This type of attack is also known as a denial of service (DoS) attack, as it denies access to the network to legitimate users [74, 101, 102]. IoT devices are particularly vulnerable to jamming attacks because they often rely on wireless communication channels and are designed to consume low power. Jamming attacks can be carried out using relatively low-cost equipment, and the attacker does not need to have detailed knowledge of the IoT device or network to launch an attack.

The impact of a jamming attack on an IoT system can vary depending on the type of application. For example, in a smart home system, a jamming attack may result in the loss of connectivity of smart home devices such as security cameras, sensors, and smart locks, while in an industrial automation system, a jamming attack may cause a shutdown of the entire system, leading to production losses and safety hazards [70, 103]. To mitigate the impact of jamming attacks, IoT systems need to be designed with security in mind, and appropriate countermeasures need to be put in place to prevent or mitigate the effects of a jamming attack. Tackling jamming attacks in IoT involves several strategies, including:

1. **Physical Layer Security:** Physical layer security is a technique used to secure the wireless communication channel between IoT devices and the network. This technique involves the use of signal modulation schemes and spread spectrum techniques to make it difficult for an attacker to interfere with the communication channel [70, 103]. For example, using frequency hopping spread spectrum (FHSS) or direct sequence spread spectrum (DSSS) can make it difficult for an attacker to jam the communication channel.
2. **Signal Processing Techniques:** Signal processing techniques can be used to detect and mitigate the effects of jamming attacks [104]. For example, energy detection can be used to detect the presence of jamming signals in the communication channel, and interference cancellation can be used to remove the effects of the jamming signals from the received signal.
3. **Dynamic Channel Allocation:** Dynamic channel allocation is a technique used to dynamically allocate channels for communication based on the channel conditions. This technique can be used to avoid using channels that are jammed or have a high level of interference [105].
4. **Diversity Techniques:** Diversity techniques involve using multiple communication channels or antennas to transmit and receive data. This technique

can improve the reliability of communication and make it more difficult for an attacker to jam all the communication channels or antennas [105, 106].

5. **Jamming-Resistant Protocols:** Jamming-resistant protocols are protocols designed specifically to mitigate the effects of jamming attacks. These protocols use techniques such as frequency hopping, spread spectrum, and adaptive modulation to make it difficult for an attacker to jam the communication channel [104, 105].

In conclusion, tackling jamming attacks in IoT requires a combination of techniques and strategies. These include physical layer security, signal processing techniques, dynamic channel allocation, diversity techniques, and jamming-resistant protocols. By implementing these strategies, IoT devices can be made more resilient to jamming attacks, thereby improving the security and reliability of the IoT network.

1.7.3 Encryption

Encryption is a technique used to secure data transmitted over IoT networks. IoT devices generate a vast amount of data that can be sensitive and needs to be protected from unauthorized access. Encryption ensures that data is secure by transforming it into an unreadable format that can only be decrypted using a secret key. Encryption is a process of transforming data into an unreadable format that can only be decrypted using a secret key or password. Encryption is an essential technique used to secure data transmitted over IoT networks, as it ensures that data is protected from unauthorized access and can only be accessed by authorized users. In IoT, encryption can be applied at various levels of the network stack, including the application layer, transport layer, and network layer [94, 107]. At the application layer, encryption can be used to secure data transmitted between IoT devices and the application server. For example, in a smart home system, encryption can be used to secure data transmitted between a smart lock and the application server, such as user credentials or lock access logs. At the transport layer, encryption can be used to secure data transmitted between IoT devices and the network. Transport Layer Security (TLS) is a commonly used encryption protocol that can be used to secure data transmitted over TCP/IP connections [108]. TLS uses a combination of symmetric and asymmetric encryption techniques to ensure the confidentiality and integrity of data transmitted over the network. At the network layer, encryption can be used to secure data transmitted over the internet. Internet Protocol Security (IPsec) is a commonly used encryption protocol that can be used to secure data transmitted over IP networks. IPsec provides authentication, encryption, and integrity services to ensure that data transmitted over the network is secure.

Encryption in IoT typically uses two main types of encryption algorithms: symmetric key encryption and asymmetric key encryption [107, 108]. Symmetric key encryption uses the same key to encrypt and decrypt data, while asymmetric key encryption uses a pair of keys: a public key for encryption and a private key for decryption. Asymmetric key encryption is typically used for secure communication between IoT devices and the server, while symmetric key encryption is used for securing data transmitted between IoT devices. IoT systems also need to implement secure key management practices to ensure the secure distribution and management of encryption keys. Key management includes the generation, distribution, storage, and revocation of keys. It is essential to ensure that keys are not compromised or lost, as this can result in the compromise of sensitive data transmitted over the IoT network.

In summary, encryption is a crucial technique for securing IoT networks and protecting sensitive data transmitted over these networks. It ensures that data is secure by transforming it into an unreadable format that can only be decrypted using a secret key, and it can be applied at different levels of the network stack [63, 69]. To implement encryption successfully, IoT systems need to implement secure key management practices to ensure the secure distribution and management of encryption keys.

1.7.4 Privacy Challenges and Their Solutions in IoT

Privacy is a critical concern in IoT, as the vast amount of data generated by IoT devices can contain sensitive information about individuals, their behavior, and their environment. Privacy challenges in IoT can arise at various stages of data processing, including data collection, storage, transmission, and analysis [40, 75]. We will next discuss some of the privacy challenges in IoT and their solutions.

1. **Data Collection:** IoT devices can collect a vast amount of data about individuals, including their location, health status, and behavior patterns. This data can be used for various purposes, such as improving product design, enhancing user experiences, and enabling personalized services. However, privacy concerns can arise if this data is collected without the user's knowledge or consent. To address this challenge, IoT devices should implement transparent data collection practices that inform users about what data is collected, how it is used, and who has access to it [42, 75]. Devices should also collect only the data necessary for their intended purposes and provide users with the option to opt out of data collection.
2. **Data Storage:** IoT devices generate a vast amount of data that needs to be stored securely. Privacy concerns can arise if this data is stored without appropriate security measures, such as encryption, access controls, and auditing. To address this challenge, IoT devices should implement secure data storage practices that ensure that data is protected from unauthorized access, modification, and deletion [4]. Data should be encrypted both in transit and at rest, and access to data should be restricted to authorized personnel only.
3. **Data Transmission:** IoT devices often transmit data over wireless networks, which can be intercepted by attackers. Privacy concerns can arise if this data is transmitted without appropriate security measures, such as encryption and authentication. To address this challenge, IoT devices should implement secure data transmission practices that ensure that data is protected from interception and unauthorized access [19, 40]. Data should be encrypted in transit, and communication should be authenticated to ensure that only authorized devices can access the data.

4. **Data Analysis:** IoT devices can generate insights and predictions based on the data they collect. Privacy concerns can arise if these insights contain sensitive information about individuals, such as their health status, financial status, or location. To address this challenge, IoT devices should implement privacy-preserving data analysis techniques that ensure that sensitive information is not disclosed [109]. For example, data can be anonymized or aggregated to protect user privacy.
5. **Consent and Control:** Users need to have control over the data collected by IoT devices and how it is used. Privacy concerns can arise if users do not have the ability to control the data collected about them or if they are not given the opportunity to provide their consent. To address this challenge, IoT devices should implement user-centric privacy practices that give users control over their data. This can include privacy settings that allow users to manage their data sharing preferences, data deletion options that allow users to delete their data from the device, and data portability options that allow users to transfer their data to another device or service.

In summary, privacy is a critical concern in IoT, and there are several privacy challenges that need to be addressed. The solutions to these challenges involve implementing transparent data collection practices, secure data storage and transmission practices, privacy-preserving data analysis techniques, and user-centric privacy practices that give users control over their data. By implementing these solutions, IoT systems can ensure that the privacy of users is protected.

1.7.5 Design and Development Challenges

IoT is a rapidly growing field that involves connecting various devices and sensors to the internet to enable them to communicate with each other and with users. While IoT offers many benefits, such as increased efficiency and automation, it also presents several design and development challenges. Following are some of the most common challenges in IoT, with a specific case study to deal with it.

1. **Security:** Security is one of the most significant challenges in IoT design and development. Connected devices are vulnerable to cyber-attacks, and data breaches can result in serious consequences. IoT devices may have limited resources for implementing security measures, such as encryption, authentication, and access control. Developers must take into account the specific security requirements of each device and network, and design robust security protocols that can withstand potential attacks. In 2016, a massive distributed denial of service (DDoS) attack was launched on Dyn, a domain name system (DNS) provider, which caused major websites like Twitter and Netflix to go offline for several hours [101, 102, 110]. The attack was orchestrated using hundreds of thousands of unsecured IoT devices, including cameras and routers. This incident highlighted the importance of IoT security, and since then, many manufacturers have implemented

security features like encryption and two-factor authentication to prevent unauthorized access and attacks.

2. **Interoperability:** IoT involves connecting various devices and sensors from different manufacturers, which can make interoperability a significant challenge. Devices may use different communication protocols, data formats, and operating systems, making it difficult for them to communicate with each other seamlessly. Developers need to create open standards and protocols that enable different devices to work together, while also ensuring that security is not compromised. The Open Connectivity Foundation (OCF) is an industry group that aims to create open standards for IoT interoperability. The OCF has developed a universal communication protocol called IoTivity, which enables different devices to communicate with each other regardless of manufacturer, operating system, or communication protocol [32, 33, 111]. IoTivity is supported by many major technology companies, including Samsung and Intel.
3. **Power Consumption:** Many IoT devices are designed to operate on battery power, which can be a challenge in terms of power consumption. IoT devices that require frequent data transmission and processing may consume a lot of power, reducing battery life and requiring frequent battery replacement. Developers must find ways to optimize power consumption, such as reducing data transmission frequency or using low-power modes, to extend battery life and reduce maintenance costs [60, 112]. Nest, a smart home device manufacturer, uses a machine learning algorithm to optimize the power consumption of its smart thermostats. The algorithm learns the user's behavior patterns and adjusts the temperature settings accordingly, reducing energy consumption and extending battery life.
4. **Scalability:** As the number of connected devices increases, scalability becomes a significant challenge. IoT systems must be able to handle large amounts of data from numerous devices and sensors, without compromising performance. Developers must design systems that can scale up or down easily, without requiring significant modifications. Amazon Web Services (AWS) IoT platform provides a scalable solution for IoT data management and processing [88, 113]. AWS IoT enables developers to securely connect and manage millions of devices and analyze the data they generate in real time.
5. **Data Management:** IoT generates vast amounts of data that must be managed effectively to extract useful insights. Developers must design systems that can handle large volumes of data and process it quickly, while also ensuring data privacy and security [75]. They must also determine how to store and analyze data, and how to present it in a meaningful way to users. The city of Barcelona, Spain, implemented an IoT system to manage waste collection [114]. Sensors were placed in garbage bins to monitor their fill levels, and the data was transmitted to a central system for analysis. This data was used to optimize waste collection routes and schedules, reducing collection costs and improving the efficiency of waste management.

6. **Reliability:** IoT systems must be reliable and available 24/7. Device failures, network outages, and software bugs can all disrupt IoT systems, causing significant problems. Developers must design systems that can detect and recover from failures quickly, without causing significant disruptions to users. Rolls-Royce, a manufacturer of aircraft engines, uses IoT sensors to monitor engine performance in real time [75]. The sensors transmit data to a central system, which analyzes the data and provides predictive maintenance alerts. This enables Rolls-Royce to detect potential engine failures before they occur, minimizing downtime and ensuring reliable performance.

In conclusion, IoT offers many benefits, but designing and developing IoT systems is not without its challenges. Developers must address issues such as security, interoperability, power consumption, scalability, data management, and reliability to create effective and efficient IoT systems. As the IoT landscape continues to evolve, developers must stay abreast of new challenges and solutions to create robust, scalable, and secure IoT systems.

1.7.6 Securing IoT Using Blockchain Technology

IoT has revolutionized the way we interact with technology, making it possible to connect and control physical objects remotely. However, this increased connectivity also introduces new security risks, as IoT devices are vulnerable to cyber-attacks and data breaches. There are several key techniques that can be used to secure the IoT ecosystem, including blockchain technology, device identity management, secure communication protocols, secure software updates, physical security, privacy protection, and DDoS protection [10, 23, 40, 62, 109].

Blockchain technology is a type of distributed ledger technology (DLT) that allows for the secure and transparent storage and transfer of digital information. A blockchain is essentially a database or ledger that is distributed across a network of computers or nodes. Each node has a copy of the blockchain and can validate transactions and add new blocks to the chain. In the context of IoT, blockchain technology can provide a secure and decentralized system for managing IoT devices and data. IoT devices generate vast amounts of data, much of which is sensitive and needs to be protected from cyber-attacks and data breaches. Blockchain technology can help to address these security concerns by providing the following benefits [99, 109, 115, 116].

1. **Immutable Record-Keeping:** Blockchain technology provides an immutable and transparent record of all transactions and data exchanges, which can help to prevent fraud, tampering, and unauthorized access to IoT devices and data.
2. **Decentralized Control:** Blockchain technology allows for decentralized control and management of IoT devices, reducing the risk of a single point of failure or attack. This can make it harder for cybercriminals to compromise the entire IoT network.
3. **Secure Data Sharing:** Blockchain technology can enable secure data sharing between IoT devices and users without compromising the privacy and

security of the data. This can help to build trust among users and increase the adoption of IoT technology.
4. **Smart Contracts:** Smart contracts, which are self-executing contracts with the terms of the agreement directly written into code, can be used to automate and secure transactions between IoT devices and users. This can help to reduce the risk of fraud and errors.
5. **Faster and More Efficient Transactions:** Blockchain technology can enable faster and more efficient transactions between IoT devices and users, as it eliminates the need for intermediaries and reduces transaction costs.

One example of the use of blockchain technology in the IoT is the IBM Watson IoT Platform, which uses blockchain to secure and manage IoT devices and data [117, 118]. The platform is designed to enable businesses to securely share data and collaborate with their partners, customers, and suppliers. The IBM Watson IoT Platform uses a private blockchain to provide a secure and transparent record of all transactions and data exchanges between IoT devices and users. The blockchain provides a tamper-proof record of all transactions, which helps to prevent fraud, tampering, and unauthorized access to IoT devices and data. One example of how the IBM Watson IoT Platform can be used is in the supply chain management industry. A company can use the platform to track and monitor the movement of goods from the manufacturer to the end-user. IoT devices can be attached to the goods, providing real-time data on their location, temperature, and other important metrics. The data collected by the IoT devices can be securely stored on the blockchain, providing a transparent and tamper-proof record of the goods' journey. This can help to prevent fraud, theft, and counterfeiting, while also improving supply chain efficiency and reducing cost. In summary, the IBM Watson IoT Platform is an example of how blockchain technology can be used to secure and manage IoT devices and data. By using blockchain, businesses can create a secure, transparent, and tamper-proof system for managing IoT devices and data, helping to prevent cyber-attacks and data breaches, while also improving business efficiency and reducing costs.

Overall, blockchain technology can play an important role in securing the IoT ecosystem, providing a secure, decentralized, and transparent system for managing IoT devices and data. By using blockchain technology, organizations can help to prevent cyber-attacks and data breaches, protect sensitive user data, and build trust among users. Developing a blockchain-based IoT network comes with its own set of challenges, which must be addressed to ensure the successful implementation of such a network. Some of the key challenges include the following [83, 119–121].

1. **Scalability:** Blockchain technology is known for its scalability challenges, especially when it comes to processing large volumes of transactions. This can be a significant challenge when implementing a blockchain-based IoT network, which can involve millions or even billions of devices generating large volumes of data.
2. **Interoperability:** IoT devices come in different shapes, sizes, and functionalities, making it challenging to develop a blockchain network that is

compatible with all devices. Ensuring interoperability across different devices is a critical challenge that must be addressed when developing a blockchain-based IoT network.

3. **Security:** While blockchain technology is considered to be highly secure, it is not immune to cyber-attacks. IoT devices can also be vulnerable to cyber-attacks, making it critical to develop a secure and tamper-proof network that can protect against potential security threats.
4. **Integration with Existing Systems:** Developing a blockchain-based IoT network requires integration with existing systems and platforms, which can be a challenge due to differences in architecture and protocols.
5. **Cost:** Developing a blockchain-based IoT network can be expensive, requiring significant investments in infrastructure, hardware, and software.

In summary, developing a blockchain-based IoT network comes with its own set of challenges, which must be addressed to ensure the successful implementation of such a network. These challenges include scalability, interoperability, security, integration with existing systems, and cost. Addressing these challenges requires a comprehensive approach that involves collaboration among different stakeholders, and the use of innovative technologies and solutions.

REFERENCES

[1] J. Khan and M. Yuce, *Internet of Things (IoT) Systems and Applications*, New York, Jenny Stanford Publishing, 2021.

[2] A. Kolah, "Internet of Things, for Things and by Things," *EDPACS*, Philadelphia, United States, vol. 59, no. 1, 2019, doi: 10.1080/07366981.2019.1565338.

[3] OFIS, "Kenali Apa Itu Internet of Things, Cara Kerja & Manfaatnya," *Ofis*, Indonesia, 2020.

[4] G. Jezic, *Agents and Multi-Agent Systems: Technologies and Applications,* Springer, Singapore, 2020, June 2020, doi: https://doi.org/10.1007/978-981-13-8679-4.

[5] M. Nitti, V. Pilloni, G. Colistra, and L. Atzori, "The Virtual Object as a Major Element of the Internet of Things: A Survey," *IEEE Commun. Surv. Tutor.*, vol. 18, no. 2, 2016, doi: 10.1109/COMST.2015.2498304.

[6] Gartner Inc., "Definition of E-Learning—Gartner Information Technology Glossary," *Information Technology Glossary*, 2020.

[7] K. Sorri, N. Mustafee, and M. Seppänen, "Revisiting IoT Definitions: A Framework Towards Comprehensive Use," *Technol. Forecast. Soc. Change*, vol. 179, 2022, doi: 10.1016/j.techfore.2022.121623.

[8] H. Yoo, R. C. Park, and K. Chung, "IoT-Based Health Big-Data Process Technologies: A Survey," *KSII Trans. Internet Inf. Syst.*, vol. 15, no. 3, 2021, doi: 10.3837/tiis.2021.03.009.

[9] P. P. Ray, "A Survey of IoT Cloud Platforms," *Futur. Comput. Inform. J.*, vol. 1, no. 1–2, 2016, doi: 10.1016/j.fcij.2017.02.001.

[10] M. Frustaci, P. Pace, G. Aloi, and G. Fortino, "Evaluating Critical Security Issues of the IoT World: Present and Future Challenges," *IEEE Internet Things J.*, vol. 5, no. 4, 2018, doi: 10.1109/JIOT.2017.2767291.

[11] W. Iqbal, H. Abbas, M. Daneshmand, B. Rauf, and Y. A. Bangash, "An in-Depth Analysis of IoT Security Requirements, Challenges, and Their Countermeasures via Software-Defined Security," *IEEE Internet Things J.*, vol. 7, no. 10, 2020, doi: 10.1109/JIOT.2020.2997651.

[12] N. Bansal, "Designing Internet of Things Solutions with Microsoft Azure: A Survey of Secure and Smart Industrial Applications," Springer International Publishing (Apress Berkeley, CA), New York, United States, 2020, doi: 10.1007/978-1-4842-6041-8.

[13] K. Priya Dharshini, D. Gopalakrishnan, C. K. Shankar, and R. Ramya, "A Survey on IoT Applications in Smart Cities," *EAI/Springer Innovations in Communication and Computing*, Springer Cham, Germany, 2022, doi: 10.1007/978-3-030-66607-1_9.

[14] J. Ding, M. Nemati, C. Ranaweera, and J. Choi, "IoT Connectivity Technologies and Applications: A Survey," *IEEE Access*, vol. 8, 2020, doi: 10.1109/ACCESS.2020.2985932.

[15] S. Selvaraj and S. Sundaravaradhan, "Challenges and Opportunities in IoT Healthcare Systems: A Systematic Review," *SN Appl. Sci.*, vol. 2, no. 1, 2020, doi: 10.1007/s42452-019-1925-y.

[16] P. Bajpai, A. K. Sood, and R. J. Enbody, "The Art of Mapping IoT Devices in Networks," *Netw. Secur.*, vol. 2018, no. 4, 2018, doi: 10.1016/S1353-4858(18)30033-3.

[17] IDC Study, "AIoT: How IoT Leaders Are Breaking Away," *SAS Inst. Inc*, 2019.

[18] J. M. C. Brito, "Technological Trends for 5G Networks Influence of E-Health and IoT Applications," *Int. J. E-Health Med. Commun.*, vol. 9, no. 1, 2018, doi: 10.4018/IJEHMC.2018010101.

[19] B. D. Deebak and F. AL-Turjman, "How to Exploit 5G Networks for IoT e-Health Security and Privacy Challenges," *IEEE Internet Things Mag.*, vol. 4, no. 3, 2021, doi: 10.1109/iotm.0101.2000048.

[20] A. H. Sharmila and N. Jaisankar, "Edge Intelligent Agent Assisted Hybrid Hierarchical Blockchain for Continuous Healthcare Monitoring & Recommendation System in 5G WBAN-IoT," *Comput. Netw.*, vol. 200, 2021, doi: 10.1016/j.comnet.2021.108508.

[21] T. Saheb and L. Izadi, "Paradigm of IoT Big Data Analytics in the Healthcare Industry: A Review of Scientific Literature and Mapping of Research Trends," *Telemat. Inform.*, vol. 41, 2019, doi: 10.1016/j.tele.2019.03.005.

[22] A. Ahad, M. Tahir, M. A. Sheikh, K. I. Ahmed, A. Mughees, and A. Numani, "Technologies Trend Towards 5g Network for Smart Health-Care Using IoT: A Review," *Sensors (Switzerland)*, vol. 20, no. 14, 2020, doi: 10.3390/s20144047.

[23] M. Roopak, G. Yun Tian, and J. Chambers, "Deep Learning Models for Cyber Security in IoT Networks," in *2019 IEEE 9th Annual Computing and Communication Workshop and Conference, CCWC 2019*, 2019, doi: 10.1109/CCWC.2019.8666588.

[24] J. S. Park and J. H. Park, "Future Trends of IoT, 5G Mobile Networks, and AI: Challenges, Opportunities, and Solutions," *J. Inf. Process. Syst.*, vol. 16, no. 4, 2020, doi: 10.3745/JIPS.03.0146.

[25] B.-S. P. Lin, "Toward an AI-Enabled SDN-Based 5G & IoT Network," *Netw. Commun. Technol.*, vol. 5, no. 2, 2020, doi: 10.5539/nct.v5n2p7.

[26] M. Chiang and T. Zhang, "Fog and IoT: An Overview of Research Opportunities," *IEEE Internet Things J.*, vol. 3, no. 6, 2016, doi: 10.1109/JIOT.2016.2584538.

[27] V. D. Gowda, S. B. Sridhara, K. B. Naveen, M. Ramesha, and G. N. Pai, "Internet of Things: Internet Revolution, Impact, Technology Road Map and Features," *Adv. Math. Sci. J.*, vol. 9, no. 7, 2020, doi: 10.37418/amsj.9.7.11.

[28] Y. Xing, A. Hu, J. Zhang, J. Yu, G. Li, and T. Wang, "Design of a Robust Radio-Frequency Fingerprint Identification Scheme for Multimode LFM Radar," *IEEE Internet Things J.*, vol. 7, no. 10, 2020, doi: 10.1109/JIOT.2020.3003692.

[29] J. Horalek and F. Holik, "Design and Realization of the Intelligent System for Identification of the IoT Devices," *J. Telecommun. Electron. Comput. Eng.*, vol. 10, no. 1–8, 2018.

[30] S. Schmid *et al.*, "An Architecture for Interoperable IoT Ecosystems," in *Lecture Notes in Computer Science (including subseries Lecture Notes in Artificial Intelligence and Lecture Notes in Bioinformatics)*, 2017, doi: 10.1007/978-3-319-56877-5_3.

[31] I. Lee, "The Internet of Things for Enterprises: An Ecosystem, Architecture, and IoT Service Business Model," *Internet Things (Netherlands)*, vol. 7, 2019, doi: 10.1016/j.iot.2019.100078.

[32] A. Rayes and S. Salam, "Industry Organizations and Standards Landscape," in *Internet of Things From Hype to Reality*, Springer Cham, Switzerland AG, 2019, doi: 10.1007/978-3-319-99516-8_11.

[33] H. S. Oh, S. B. Seo, G. T. Lee, W. S. Jeon, and M. G. Lee, "OCF-to-ZigBee (O2Z) Bridging Technique and IoTivity-Based Implementation," *IEEE Internet Things J.*, vol. 8, no. 22, 2021, doi: 10.1109/JIOT.2020.3024206.

[34] A. Groves and P. Schulte, "The Journey into IoT and the Cloud with Coca-Cola," in *The Race for 5G Supremacy*, WORLD SCIENTIFIC, Singapore, 2020, doi: 10.1142/9789811218712_0005.

[35] W. E. Zhang *et al.*, "The 10 Research Topics in the Internet of Things," in *Proceedings—2020 IEEE 6th International Conference on Collaboration and Internet Computing, CIC 2020*, 2020, doi: 10.1109/CIC50333.2020.00015.

[36] S. Li, K. K. R. Choo, Q. Sun, W. J. Buchanan, and J. Cao, "IoT Forensics: Amazon Echo as a Use Case," *IEEE Internet Things J.*, vol. 6, no. 4, 2019, doi: 10.1109/JIOT.2019.2906946.

[37] A. Sponselee and A. Dooremalen, "Virtual Garden for People with Dementia," *Technol. Disabil.*, vol. 31, 2019.

[38] V. Kumar, "Selecting IoT Connectivity Protocols for Rural Development Applications," *J. Mob. Multimed.*, vol. 17, no. 1–3, 2021, doi: 10.13052/jmm1550-4646.171323.

[39] M. N. Bhuiyan, M. M. Rahman, M. M. Billah, and D. Saha, "Internet of Things (IoT): A Review of Its Enabling Technologies in Healthcare Applications, Standards Protocols, Security, and Market Opportunities," *IEEE Internet Things J.*, vol. 8, no. 13, 2021, doi: 10.1109/JIOT.2021.3062630.

[40] A. Chacko and T. Hayajneh, "Security and Privacy Issues with IoT in Healthcare," *EAI Endorsed Trans. Pervasive Heal. Technol.*, vol. 4, no. 14, 2018, doi: 10.4108/eai.13-7-2018.155079.

[41] K. Ndlovu, M. Mars, and R. E. Scott, "Interoperability Frameworks Linking mHealth Applications to Electronic Record Systems," *BMC Health Serv. Res.*, vol. 21, no. 1, 2021, doi: 10.1186/s12913-021-06473-6.

[42] B. Farahani, F. Firouzi, V. Chang, M. Badaroglu, N. Constant, and K. Mankodiya, "Towards Fog-Driven IoT eHealth: Promises and Challenges of IoT in Medicine and Healthcare," *Futur. Gener. Comput. Syst.*, vol. 78, 2018, doi: 10.1016/j.future.2017.04.036.

[43] A. M. Koya and P. P. Deepthi, "Plug and Play Self-Configurable IoT Gateway Node for Telemonitoring of ECG," *Comput. Biol. Med.*, vol. 112, 2019, doi: 10.1016/j.compbiomed.2019.103359.

[44] S. Dhanasekar, E. Ilankhatir, S. Divakar, and D. Vennila, "A Survey on IoT Architecture," *Int. J. Adv. Sci. Res. Dev.*, vol. 6, no. 4, 2019, doi: 10.26836/ijasrd/2019/v6/i4/60402.

[45] P. Datta and B. Sharma, "A Survey on IoT Architectures, Protocols, Security and Smart City Based Applications," in *8th International Conference on Computing, Communications and Networking Technologies, ICCCNT 2017*, 2017, doi: 10.1109/ICCCNT.2017.8203943.

[46] S. K. Datta, C. Bonnet, and N. Nikaein, "An IoT gateway Centric Architecture to Provide Novel M2M Services," in *2014 IEEE World Forum on Internet of Things, WF-IoT 2014*, 2014, doi: 10.1109/WF-IoT.2014.6803221.

[47] P. Verma and S. K. Sood, "Cloud-Centric IoT Based Disease Diagnosis Healthcare Framework," *J. Parallel Distrib. Comput.*, vol. 116, 2018, doi: 10.1016/j.jpdc.2017.11.018.

[48] D. C. Klonoff, "Fog Computing and Edge Computing Architectures for Processing Data from Diabetes Devices Connected to the Medical Internet of Things," *J. Diabetes Sci. Technol.*, vol. 11, no. 4, 2017, doi: 10.1177/1932296817717007.

[49] V. Thoutam, "A Comprehensive Review on Communication Enablers and Communication Models of IoT," *J. Community Pharm. Pract.*, vol. 1, no. 2, 2021, doi: 10.55529/jcpp.12.1.8.

[50] A. Pozo, Á. Alonso, and J. Salvachúa, "Evaluation of an IoT Application-Scoped Access Control Model Over a Publish/Subscribe Architecture Based on Fiware," *Sensors (Switzerland)*, vol. 20, no. 15, 2020, doi: 10.3390/s20154341.

[51] R. C. Sofia and P. M. Mendes, "An Overview on Push-Based Communication Models for Information-Centric Networking," *Future Internet*, vol. 11, no. 3, 2019, doi: 10.3390/fi11030074.

[52] R. Maurya, "Application of Restful APIs in IOT: A Review," *Int. J. Res. Appl. Sci. Eng. Technol.*, vol. 9, no. 2, 2021, doi: 10.22214/ijraset.2021.33013.

[53] M. Dave, J. Doshi, and H. Arolkar, "MQTT-CoAP Interconnector: IoT Interoperability Solution for Application Layer Protocols," in *Proceedings of the 4th International Conference on IoT in Social, Mobile, Analytics and Cloud, ISMAC 2020*, 2020, doi: 10.1109/I-SMAC49090.2020.9243377.

[54] R. Banno, J. Sun, S. Takeuchi, and K. Shudo, "Interworking Layer of Distributed MQTT Brokers*," *IEICE Trans. Inf. Syst.*, vol. E102D, no. 12, 2019, doi: 10.1587/transinf.2019PAK0001.

[55] S. K. Goudos, P. I. Dallas, S. Chatziefthymiou, and S. Kyriazakos, "A Survey of IoT Key Enabling and Future Technologies: 5G, Mobile IoT, Sematic Web and Applications," *Wirel. Pers. Commun.*, vol. 97, no. 2, 2017, doi: 10.1007/s11277-017-4647-8.

[56] A. Čolaković and M. Hadžialić, "Internet of Things (IoT): A Review of Enabling Technologies, Challenges, and Open Research Issues," *Comput. Netw.*, vol. 144, 2018, doi: 10.1016/j.comnet.2018.07.017.

[57] S. R. Jondhale, R. Maheswar, and J. Lloret, "Fundamentals of Wireless Sensor Networks," in *EAI/Springer Innovations in Communication and Computing*, Springer, Cham, Switzerland AG, 2022, doi: 10.1007/978-3-030-74061-0_1.

[58] S. R. Jondhale, V. Mohan, B. B. Sharma, J. Lloret, and S. V. Athawale, "Support Vector Regression for Mobile Target Localization in Indoor Environments," *Sensors*, vol. 22, no. 1, 2022, doi: 10.3390/s22010358.

[59] S. R. Jondhale, A. S. Jondhale, P. S. Deshpande, and J. Lloret, "Improved Trilateration for Indoor Localization: Neural Network and Centroid-Based Approach," *Int. J. Distrib. Sens. Netw.*, vol. 17, no. 11, 2021, doi: 10.1177/15501477211053997.

[60] M. Saravanan, J. Ajayan, S. R. Jondhale, and P. Mohankumar, "An Overview of Energy Harvesting Techniques for Future Internet of Things Applications," in *EAI/Springer Innovations in Communication and Computing*, Springer Cham, Switzerland AG, 2020, doi: 10.1007/978-3-030-34328-6_7.

[61] S. R. Jondhale, M. A. Wakchaure, B. S. Agarkar, and S. B. Tambe, "Improved Generalized Regression Neural Network for Target Localization," *Wirel. Pers. Commun.*, vol. 125, no. 2, 2022, doi: 10.1007/s11277-022-09627-9.

[62] S. J. Hsiao and W. T. Sung, "Employing Blockchain Technology to Strengthen Security of Wireless Sensor Networks," *IEEE Access*, vol. 9, 2021, doi: 10.1109/ACCESS.2021.3079708.

[63] S. Khan, W. K. Lee, and S. O. Hwang, "AEchain: A Lightweight Blockchain for IoT Applications," *IEEE Consum. Electron. Mag.*, vol. 11, no. 2, 2022, doi: 10.1109/MCE.2021.3060373.

[64] D. Lu *et al.*, "XTSeH: A Trusted Platform Module Sharing Scheme Towards Smart IoT-eHealth Devices," *IEEE J. Sel. Areas Commun.*, vol. 39, no. 2, 2021, doi: 10.1109/JSAC.2020.3020658.

[65] Z. Yang, B. Liang, and W. Ji, "An Intelligent End-Edge-Cloud Architecture for Visual IoT-Assisted Healthcare Systems," *IEEE Internet Things J.*, vol. 8, no. 23, 2021, doi: 10.1109/JIOT.2021.3052778.

[66] M. Zhang *et al.*, "Tripod: Towards a Scalable, Efficient and Resilient Cloud Gateway," *IEEE J. Sel. Areas Commun.*, vol. 37, no. 3, 2019, doi: 10.1109/JSAC.2019.2894189.

[67] IBM, "Defining IaaS, PaaS and SaaS," *IaaS, PaaS and SaaS—IBM Cloud Service Models*, 2019.

[68] V. Jagadeeswari, V. Subramaniyaswamy, R. Logesh, and V. Vijayakumar, "A Study on Medical Internet of Things and Big Data in Personalized Healthcare System," *Heal. Inf. Sci. Syst.*, vol. 6, no. 1, 2018, doi: 10.1007/s13755-018-0049-x.

[69] M. A. Al-Garadi, A. Mohamed, A. K. Al-Ali, X. Du, I. Ali, and M. Guizani, "A Survey of Machine and Deep Learning Methods for Internet of Things (IoT) Security," *IEEE Commun. Surv. Tutor.*, vol. 22, no. 3, 2020, doi: 10.1109/COMST.2020.2988293.

[70] F. Hussain, R. Hussain, S. A. Hassan, and E. Hossain, "Machine Learning in IoT Security: Current Solutions and Future Challenges," *IEEE Commun. Surv. Tutor.*, vol. 22, no. 3, 2020, doi: 10.1109/COMST.2020.2986444.

[71] F. Al-Turjman and I. Baali, "Machine Learning for Wearable IoT-Based Applications: A Survey," *Trans. Emerg. Telecommun. Technol.*, vol. 33, no. 8, 2022, doi: 10.1002/ett.3635.

[72] A. V. Baidiuk, "The Use of Radio Frequency Identification Technologies for Preventing the Spread of Coronavirus," *Electron. Acoust. Eng.*, vol. 4, no. 3, 2021, doi: 10.20535/2617-0965.eae.228210.

[73] J. Yang, C. Poellabauer, P. Mitra, and C. Neubecker, "Beyond Beaconing: Emerging Applications and Challenges of BLE," *Ad Hoc Netw.*, vol. 97, 2020, doi: 10.1016/j.adhoc.2019.102015.

[74] A. Barua, M. A. Al Alamin, M. S. Hossain, and E. Hossain, "Security and Privacy Threats for Bluetooth Low Energy in IoT and Wearable Devices: A Comprehensive Survey," *IEEE Open J. Commun. Soc.*, vol. 3, 2022, doi: 10.1109/OJCOMS.2022.3149732.

[75] M. Akil, L. Islami, S. Fischer-Hübner, L. A. Martucci, and A. Zuccato, "Privacy-Preserving Identifiers for IoT: A Systematic Literature Review," *IEEE Access*, vol. 8, 2020, doi: 10.1109/ACCESS.2020.3023659.

[76] H. Aftab, K. Gilani, J. E. Lee, L. Nkenyereye, S. M. Jeong, and J. S. Song, "Analysis of Identifiers in IoT Platforms," *Digit. Commun. Netw.*, vol. 6, no. 3, 2020, doi: 10.1016/j.dcan.2019.05.003.

[77] M. Dvorak and P. Dolezel, "An IoT Approach to Positioning of a Robotic Vehicle," in *Advances in Intelligent Systems and Computing*, Springer Verlag, Vol. 763, pp. 99–108, 2019, doi: 10.1007/978-3-319-91186-1_12.

[78] AIOTI, "AIOTI—The Alliance for the Internet of Things Innovation," *Website*, 2018.

[79] A. Felkner *et al.*, "Industry and Standardization Aspects," in *Studies in Big Data*, Springer Science and Business Media Deutschland GmbH, Berlin, Germany, Vol. 75, pp. 99–124, 2021, doi: 10.1007/978-3-030-62312-8_4.

[80] M. Alshamrani, "IoT and Artificial Intelligence Implementations for Remote Healthcare Monitoring Systems: A Survey," *J. King Saud Univ.—Comput. Inf. Sci.*, vol. 34, no. 8, 2022, doi: 10.1016/j.jksuci.2021.06.005.

[81] M. Vermanen, M. M. Rantanen, and V. Harkke, "Ethical Framework for IoT Deployment in SMEs: Individual Perspective," *Internet Res.*, vol. 32, no. 7, 2021, doi: 10.1108/INTR-08-2019-0361.

[82] D. Pishva, "IoT: Their Conveniences, Security Challenges and Possible Solutions," *Adv. Sci. Technol. Eng. Syst.*, vol. 2, no. 3, 2017, doi: 10.25046/aj0203153.

[83] B. K. Mohanta, D. Jena, U. Satapathy, and S. Patnaik, "Survey on IoT Security: Challenges and Solution Using Machine Learning, Artificial Intelligence and Blockchain Technology," *Internet Things (Netherlands)*, vol. 11, 2020, doi: 10.1016/j.iot.2020.100227.

[84] T. Matsumoto, M. Ikeda, M. Nagata, and Y. Uemura, "Secure Cryptographic Unit as Root-of-Trust for IoT Era," *IEICE Trans. Electron.*, no. 7, 2021, doi: 10.1587/transele.2020CDI0001.

[85] A. Ikpehai *et al.*, "Low-Power Wide Area Network Technologies for Internet-of-Things: A Comparative Review," *IEEE Internet Things J.*, vol. 6, no. 2, 2019, doi: 10.1109/JIOT.2018.2883728.

[86] N. Saeed, M.-S. Alouini, and T. Y. Al-Naffouri, "Towards the Internet of x-Things: New Possibilities for Underwater, Underground, and Outer Space Exploration," 2019, arXiv.

[87] K. C. Chu, E. Turatsinze, K. C. Chang, Y. W. Zhou, F. H. Chang, and M. T. Wang, "A Survey of Common IOT Communication Protocols and IOT Smart-X Applications of 5G Cellular," in *Smart Innovation, Systems and Technologies*, Springer Science and Business Media Deutschland GmbH, Berlin, Germany, Vol. 211, pp. 114–122, 2021, doi: 10.1007/978-981-33-6420-2_15.

[88] S. D. Arya and S. Patel, "Implementation of Google Assistant & Amazon Alexa on Raspberry Pi," arXiv, pp. 18–21, 2020.

[89] S. Hakak, W. Z. Khan, G. A. Gilkar, M. Imran, and N. Guizani, "Securing Smart Cities Through Blockchain Technology: Architecture, Requirements, and Challenges," *IEEE Netw.*, vol. 34, no. 1, 2020, doi: 10.1109/MNET.001.1900178.

[90] W. Tao, L. Zhao, G. Wang, and R. Liang, "Review of the Internet of Things Communication Technologies in Smart Agriculture and Challenges," *Comput. Electron. Agric.*, vol. 189, 2021, doi: 10.1016/j.compag.2021.106352.

[91] J. Yang, A. Sharma, and R. Kumar, "IoT-Based Framework for Smart Agriculture," *Int. J. Agric. Environ. Inf. Syst.*, vol. 12, no. 2, 2021, doi: 10.4018/IJAEIS.20210401.oa1.

[92] E. J. C. Nacpil, Z. Wang, and K. Nakano, "Application of Physiological Sensors for Personalization in Semi-Autonomous Driving: A Review," *IEEE Sens. J.*, vol. 21, no. 18, 2021, doi: 10.1109/JSEN.2021.3100038.

[93] K. S. Yi and J. Y. Lee, "Vehicle Dynamics Control Applications to Automobiles: Survey and Some New Trends," *J. Inst. Control. Robot. Syst.*, vol. 20, no. 3, 2014, doi: 10.5302/J.ICROS.2014.14.9017.

[94] J. Zhang, Y. Wang, S. Li, and S. Shi, "An Architecture for IoT-Enabled Smart Transportation Security System: A Geospatial Approach," *IEEE Internet Things J.*, vol. 8, no. 8, 2021, doi: 10.1109/JIOT.2020.3041386.

[95] F. Zantalis, G. Koulouras, S. Karabetsos, and D. Kandris, "A Review of Machine Learning and IoT in Smart Transportation," *Future Internet*, vol. 11, no. 4, 2019, doi: 10.3390/FI11040094.

[96] E. E. Egbogah and A. O. Fapojuwo, "Achieving Energy Efficient Transmission in Wireless Body Area Networks for the Physiological Monitoring of Military Soldiers," in *Proceedings—IEEE Military Communications Conference MILCOM*, 2013, doi: 10.1109/MILCOM.2013.233.

[97] S. Benhamaid, A. Bouabdallah, and H. Lakhlef, "Recent Advances in Energy Management for Green-IoT: An Up-to-Date and Comprehensive Survey," *J. Netw. Comput. Appl.*, vol. 198, 2022, doi: 10.1016/j.jnca.2021.103257.

[98] Y. Liu, C. Yang, L. Jiang, S. Xie, and Y. Zhang, "Intelligent Edge Computing for IoT-Based Energy Management in Smart Cities," *IEEE Netw.*, vol. 33, no. 2, 2019, doi: 10.1109/MNET.2019.1800254.

[99] J. Xie *et al.*, "A Survey of Blockchain Technology Applied to Smart Cities: Research Issues and Challenges," *IEEE Commun. Surv. Tutor.*, vol. 21, no. 3, 2019, doi: 10.1109/COMST.2019.2899617.

[100] J. Sengupta, S. Ruj, and S. Das Bit, "A Comprehensive Survey on Attacks, Security Issues and Blockchain Solutions for IoT and IIoT," *J. Netw. Comput. Appl.*, vol. 149, 2020, doi: 10.1016/j.jnca.2019.102481.

[101] D. K. Bhattacharyya and J. K. Kalita, *DDoS Attacks: Evolution, Detection, Prevention, Reaction, and Tolerance*, CRC Press, New York, pp. 1–283, 2016.

[102] N. Hoque, D. K. Bhattacharyya, and J. K. Kalita, "Botnet in DDoS Attacks: Trends and Challenges," *IEEE Commun. Surv. Tutor.*, vol. 17, no. 4, 2015, doi: 10.1109/COMST.2015.2457491.

[103] M. Fuller, M. Jenkins, and K. Tjølsen, "Security Analysis of the August Smart Lock," *Minor*, pp. 1–16, 2017.

[104] A. A. Fadele, M. Othman, I. A. T. Hashem, I. Yaqoob, M. Imran, and M. Shoaib, "A Novel Countermeasure Technique for Reactive Jamming Attack in Internet of Things," *Multimed. Tools Appl.*, vol. 78, no. 21, 2019, doi: 10.1007/s11042-018-6684-z.

[105] A. Gouissem, K. Abualsaud, E. Yaacoub, T. Khattab, and M. Guizani, "Game Theory for Anti-Jamming Strategy in Multichannel Slow Fading IoT Networks," *IEEE Internet Things J.*, vol. 8, no. 23, 2021, doi: 10.1109/JIOT.2021.3066384.

[106] M. López, A. Peinado, and A. Ortiz, "An Extensive Validation of a SIR Epidemic Model to Study the Propagation of Jamming Attacks Against IoT Wireless Networks," *Comput. Netw.*, vol. 165, 2019, doi: 10.1016/j.comnet.2019.106945.

[107] H. Xiong, T. Yao, H. Wang, J. Feng, and S. Yu, "A Survey of Public-Key Encryption with Search Functionality for Cloud-Assisted IoT," *IEEE Internet Things J.*, vol. 9, no. 1, 2022, doi: 10.1109/JIOT.2021.3109440.

[108] P. Li, J. Su, and X. Wang, "ITLS: Lightweight Transport-Layer Security Protocol for IoT with Minimal Latency and Perfect Forward Secrecy," *IEEE Internet Things J.*, vol. 7, no. 8, 2020, doi: 10.1109/JIOT.2020.2988126.

[109] K. Curran and J. Curran, "Blockchain Security and Potential Future Use Cases," in *Blockchain for Cybersecurity and Privacy*, CRC Press, pp. 75–83, 2020, doi: 10.1201/9780429324932-5.

[110] Q. Shafi and A. Basit, "DDoS Botnet Prevention Using Blockchain in Software Defined Internet of Things," in *Proceedings of 2019 16th International Bhurban Conference on Applied Sciences and Technology, IBCAST 2019*, 2019, doi: 10.1109/IBCAST.2019.8667147.

[111] W. Jin, Y. G. Hong, and D. H. Kim, "Design and Implementation of a Wireless IoT Healthcare System Based on OCF IoTivity," *Int. J. Grid Distrib. Comput.*, vol. 11, no. 4, 2018, doi: 10.14257/ijgdc.2018.11.4.08.

[112] S. K. Singh, Y. Pan, and J. H. Park, "Blockchain-enabled Secure Framework for Energy-Efficient Smart Parking in Sustainable City Environment," *Sustain. Cities Soc.*, vol. 76, 2022, doi: 10.1016/j.scs.2021.103364.

[113] I. Al_Barazanchi *et al.*, "Blockchain Technology—Based Solutions for IOT Security," *Iraqi J. Comput. Sci. Math.*, vol. 3, no. 1, pp. 53–63, 2022, doi: 10.52866/ijcsm.2022.01.01.006.

[114] G. Bel and M. Sebő, "Watch Your Neighbor: Strategic Competition in Waste Collection and Service Quality," *Waste Manag.*, vol. 127, 2021, doi: 10.1016/j.wasman.2021.04.032.

[115] F. Gîrbacia, D. Voinea, R. Boboc, M. Duguleană, and C. C. Postelnicu, "Toward Blockchain Adoption for the Automotive Industry," *IOP Conf. Ser. Mater. Sci. Eng.*, vol. 1220, no. 1, 2022, doi: 10.1088/1757-899x/1220/1/012026.

[116] A. Ekramifard, H. Amintoosi, and A. H. Seno, "A Systematic Literature Review on Blockchain-Based Solutions for IoT Security," in *Lecture Notes on Data Engineering and Communications Technologies*, Springer Science and Business Media Deutschland GmbH, Berlin, Germany, 2020, doi: 10.1007/978-3-030-37309-2_25.

[117] M. I. Ahmed and G. Kannan, "Secure End to End Communications and Data Analytics in IoT Integrated Application Using IBM Watson IoT Platform," *Wirel. Pers. Commun.*, vol. 120, no. 1, 2021, doi: 10.1007/s11277-021-08439-7.

[118] IBM, "IBM Watson IoT Platform," *Console.Bluemix.Net*, 2020.

[119] B. Singhal, G. Dhameja, and P. S. Panda, "How Blockchain Works," in *Beginning Blockchain*, Apress, New York, United States, pp. 31–148, 2018, doi: 10.1007/978-1-4842-3444-0_2.

[120] P. K. Sharma, N. Kumar, and J. H. Park, "Blockchain Technology Toward Green IoT: Opportunities and Challenges," *IEEE Netw.*, vol. 34, no. 4, 2020, doi: 10.1109/MNET.001.1900526.

[121] M. S. Ali, M. Vecchio, M. Pincheira, K. Dolui, F. Antonelli, and M. H. Rehmani, "Applications of Blockchains in the Internet of Things: A Comprehensive Survey," *IEEE Commun. Surv. Tutor.*, vol. 21, no. 2, 2019, doi: 10.1109/COMST.2018.2886932.

2 Things in the Internet of Things

2.1 SENSORS AND ACTUATORS IN IOT

Sensors and actuators are essential components of the IoT ecosystem. Sensors are devices that detect physical or environmental conditions—such as temperature, humidity, pressure, light, and sound—and convert them into electrical signals. Basically, sensors are devices that detect and respond to changes in the physical environment, such as temperature, humidity, pressure, light, sound, and motion. They convert physical signals into electrical signals, which can be processed by IoT devices and transmitted to the cloud for further analysis [1, 2]. In IoT applications, sensors are used to collect data from the environment, monitor equipment and processes, and provide feedback for control and decision-making purposes. These signals can then be processed by other IoT devices or transmitted to a central server for further analysis. Actuators, on the other hand, are devices that receive signals from the IoT system and take physical actions based on those signals. They convert electrical signals into physical actions, such as movement, rotation, or vibration. In IoT applications, actuators are used to control and automate physical processes, such as turning equipment on and off, adjusting temperature and humidity, and activating alarms and notifications [1, 3]. For example, an actuator could be used to turn on a light or adjust the temperature of a room based on data received from a sensor. In the context of IoT, sensors and actuators work together to collect and transmit data from the physical world to the digital world, and vice versa. This enables IoT systems to make automated decisions and take actions based on real-time data from the physical environment. The sensors and actuators are critical components of IoT systems, enabling the collection and processing of data from the physical world and the automation of actions based on that data. Together, sensors and actuators enable IoT devices to sense the physical environment, collect and process real-time data, and interact with the physical world [4–6]. Figure 2.1 shows a simplified IoT architecture. Sensors and actuators are essential for building smart and connected systems in various fields, including healthcare, manufacturing, transportation, agriculture, and home automation.

In a basic IoT system, sensors are connected to a microcontroller or other computing device, which collects data from the sensors and processes it. The processed data is then transmitted to a cloud server or other data center, where it can be analyzed and used to make decisions. Actuators are connected to the same microcontroller or computing device and receive signals from the cloud server based on the data collected by the sensors. The actuators then take physical actions based on those signals, such as turning on a motor, opening a valve, or adjusting a temperature. The flow of data in this system is typically bidirectional, with sensors transmitting data

DOI: 10.1201/9781003282945-2

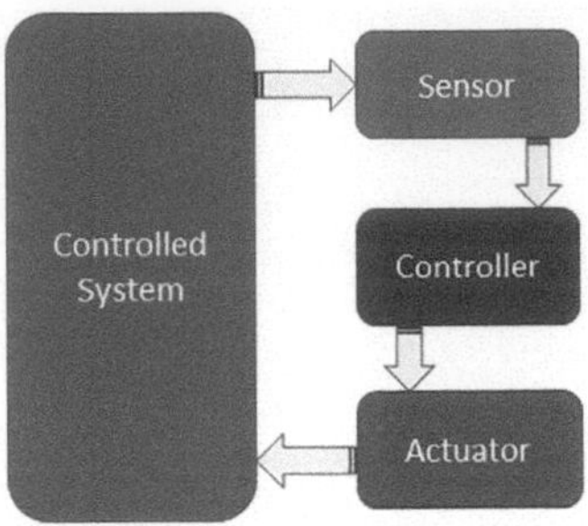

FIGURE 2.1 A simplified IoT architecture.

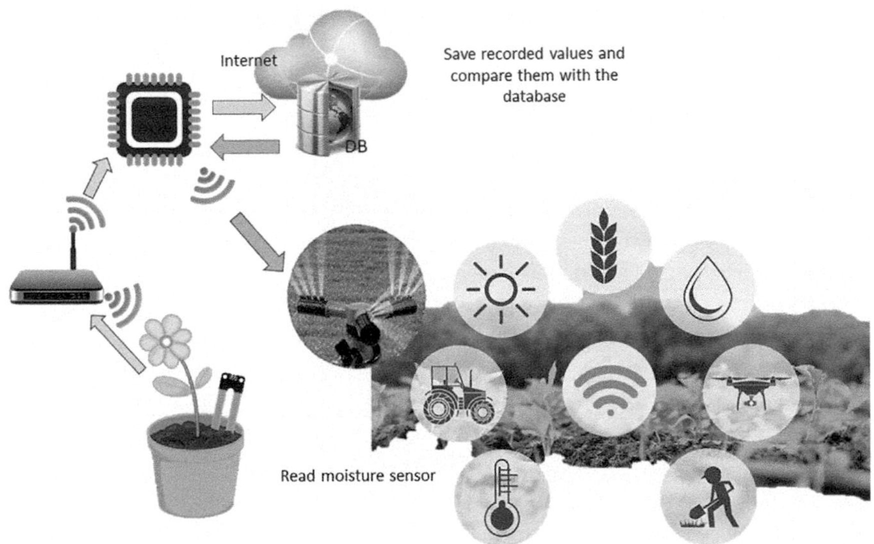

FIGURE 2.2 An IoT-based agriculture unit.

to the cloud server and actuators receiving signals from the cloud server [7, 8]. This allows for real-time monitoring and control of physical systems, enabling greater efficiency, safety, and automation. Figure 2.2 illustrates IoT-based agriculture unit as an example.

There are a wide variety of sensors and actuators used in IoT applications, each with its own unique capabilities and use cases. Following are some common types of sensors used in IoT.

1. **Temperature Sensors:** These sensors can detect changes in temperature and are commonly used in HVAC (heating, ventilation, and air conditioning) systems, refrigeration systems, and weather monitoring [9]. Temperature sensors are used to measure the temperature of the environment. They can be used in a wide range of applications such as smart homes, healthcare,

agriculture, and manufacturing. There are several types of temperature sensors that are commonly used in IoT-based applications. The choice of temperature sensor will depend on the specific application and the accuracy, range, and cost requirements. We will next discuss important types of temperature sensors used in IoT-based applications.

a) **Thermocouples:** Thermocouples are temperature sensors that use the Seebeck effect to measure temperature. They consist of two dissimilar metals that are joined at one end, and as the temperature changes, a voltage is generated that can be measured to determine the temperature [10].
b) **Resistance Temperature Detectors (RTDs):** RTDs are temperature sensors that measure the resistance of a metal wire as the temperature changes. As the temperature increases, the resistance of the wire also increases, and this change in resistance can be measured to determine the temperature [11].
c) **Thermistors:** Thermistors are temperature sensors that use the change in resistance of a semiconductor material as the temperature changes. They are highly sensitive and can provide accurate temperature readings, but they require calibration to ensure accuracy [9].
f) **Infrared Sensors:** Infrared sensors use infrared radiation to measure the temperature of an object. They work by detecting the amount of infrared radiation emitted by an object, which is directly proportional to the object's temperature [9].
g) **Digital Temperature Sensors:** Digital temperature sensors are integrated circuits that provide temperature measurements in a digital format. They are often used in IoT-based applications, as they are easy to integrate into digital systems [9].

2. **Humidity Sensors:** These sensors can measure the amount of moisture in the air and are commonly used in HVAC systems, agriculture, and building management [11]. They are used to measure the relative humidity of the environment. They are commonly used in HVAC systems, smart homes, and agriculture. The choice of humidity sensors for an IoT-based application will depend on various factors, including accuracy, sensitivity, response time, cost, and environmental conditions. There are several types of humidity sensors commonly used in IoT-based applications. Some of the most popular types include the following.
   a) **Capacitive Humidity Sensors:** These sensors measure the changes in capacitance of a material when it absorbs or releases moisture. Capacitive sensors are commonly used in HVAC systems, weather monitoring stations, and other applications for which accurate humidity measurement is required [11, 12].
   b) **Resistive Humidity Sensors:** These sensors work by measuring the resistance of a material when it absorbs moisture. Resistive sensors are commonly used in consumer electronics such as smartphones, tablets, and smartwatches [1, 13].
   c) **Thermal Conductivity Humidity Sensors:** These sensors measure the changes in the thermal conductivity of a material when it absorbs or

releases moisture. They are commonly used in industrial applications for which humidity measurement is critical for process control [1].

d) **Optical Humidity Sensors:** These sensors work by measuring changes in the refractive index of a material when it absorbs or releases moisture. Optical sensors are commonly used in medical and laboratory applications for which high accuracy is required [6].

e) **SAW (Surface Acoustic Wave) Humidity Sensors:** These sensors measure the changes in the propagation of acoustic waves through a material when it absorbs or releases moisture. SAW sensors are commonly used in automotive and aerospace applications for which reliability is critical [6].

3. **Light Sensors:** These sensors can detect changes in light levels and are used in lighting control systems, security systems, and agriculture. Light sensors are used to measure the amount of light in an environment. They are commonly used in smart homes, automotive applications, and street lighting. The choice of light sensor for an IoT-based application will depend on various factors, including sensitivity, response time, cost, and environmental conditions [14, 15]. There are several types of light sensors commonly used in IoT-based applications. Some of the most popular types include the following.

a) **Photovoltaic Sensors:** These sensors convert light energy into electrical energy. They are commonly used in solar panels and other applications for which light intensity measurement is important [16].

b) **Photoconductive Sensors:** These sensors work by changing their electrical resistance when exposed to light. They are commonly used in consumer electronics such as cameras and automatic light switches [14].

c) **Photodiode Sensors:** These sensors work by generating a current when exposed to light. They are commonly used in optical communication systems, barcode scanners, and other applications for which rapid response time is required [16].

d) **Phototransistor Sensors:** These sensors work by amplifying the current generated by a photodiode. They are commonly used in security systems, motion detectors, and other applications for which low light levels need to be detected [15].

e) **Light-Dependent Resistor (LDR) Sensors:** These sensors work by changing their resistance when exposed to light. They are commonly used in streetlights, outdoor lighting, and other applications for which automatic control of lighting is required [17].

f) **RGB Color Sensors:** These sensors can detect different colors of light and are commonly used in applications such as color sorting, color matching, and display calibration [18].

4. **Motion Sensors:** These sensors can detect movement and are commonly used in security systems and occupancy detection. They are used to detect motion in an environment. They are commonly used in security systems, smart homes, and automotive applications. Some of the most common types of motion sensors include passive infrared (PIR), ultrasonic, and microwave

sensors. The choice of motion sensor for an IoT-based application will depend on various factors, including accuracy, sensitivity, response time, cost, and environmental conditions. For example, a PIR sensor may be a suitable choice for a security system that needs to detect human movement, while an accelerometer may be a better choice for a fitness tracker that needs to detect movement of the user's wrist [14]. In what follows, we will discuss these types one by one.

a) **Passive Infrared (PIR) Sensors:** These sensors detect changes in infrared radiation, such as body heat. They are commonly used in home security systems and automatic lighting systems. They are highly sensitive and have a low false alarm rate, while ultrasonic sensors are highly accurate and can detect small movements [14].
b) **Ultrasonic Sensors:** These sensors emit high-frequency sound waves and detect their reflection off nearby objects [19]. They are commonly used in parking sensors, intrusion detection systems, and automatic doors.
c) **Microwave Sensors:** These sensors emit microwave radiation and detect changes in their reflection off nearby objects [20]. Microwave sensors have a long range and can detect motion through walls. They are commonly used in automatic doors, speed detection systems, and intrusion detection systems.
d) **Accelerometers:** These sensors detect changes in acceleration, tilt, and vibration [19, 20]. They are commonly used in fitness trackers, smartwatches, and other wearable devices.
e) **Gyroscopes:** These sensors detect changes in orientation and angular velocity. They are commonly used in navigation systems, drones, and robotics [21].
f) **Magnetometers:** These sensors detect changes in magnetic fields. They are commonly used in navigation systems, metal detectors, and compasses.
g) **Pressure Sensors:** These sensors detect changes in pressure and can be used to detect motion. They are commonly used in smartphones and gaming controllers.

5. **Proximity Sensors:** These sensors can detect the presence of an object in close proximity and are used in automated manufacturing and robotics. Proximity sensors are a type of sensor which is commonly used in IoT-based systems to detect the presence or absence of an object or a person within a specific distance range. Proximity sensors work by emitting a signal (such as electromagnetic radiation, sound waves, or infrared light) and then measuring the time it takes for the signal to bounce back after being reflected by an object [22]. This measurement is then used to determine the proximity of the object. Proximity sensors have many advantages over other types of sensors, such as high reliability, fast response time, and the ability to operate in harsh environments. They are also easy to integrate with other electronic systems and can be used in a wide range of applications, from automotive and aerospace to consumer electronics and home automation. However, they

also have some limitations, such as limited detection range, susceptibility to interference from other electronic devices, and the need for a direct line of sight to the object being detected. There are several types of proximity sensors available, including the following [23, 24].

a) **Inductive Proximity Sensors:** These sensors detect the presence of metallic objects using electromagnetic fields. They are commonly used in manufacturing and automation applications.
b) **Capacitive Proximity Sensors:** These sensors detect the presence of objects based on their electrical properties. They are commonly used in touchscreens and level detection applications.
c) **Ultrasonic Proximity Sensors:** These sensors use sound waves to detect the presence of objects. They are commonly used in robotics, automotive, and security applications.
d) **Infrared Proximity Sensors:** These sensors use infrared light to detect the presence of objects. They are commonly used in consumer electronics and home automation systems.
e) **Magnetic Proximity Sensors:** These sensors detect the presence of magnetic fields, which are emitted by certain types of objects. They are commonly used in automotive and industrial applications.

6. **Pressure Sensors:** These sensors can detect changes in pressure and are commonly used in industrial processes, automotive systems, and medical devices [25]. Pressure sensors are used to measure the pressure of gases or liquids. They are commonly used in HVAC systems, automotive applications, and manufacturing. Pressure sensors are used to monitor and control pressure levels in hydraulic and pneumatic systems. Pressure sensors are used in tire pressure monitoring systems, engine oil pressure monitoring systems, and airbag systems. Pressure sensors are used in blood pressure monitors, ventilators, and dialysis machines. They can also be used in weather stations and other environmental monitoring systems to measure barometric pressure and altitude. Some of the most common types of pressure sensors include piezoelectric, capacitive, and strain gauge sensors. Piezoelectric sensors are highly sensitive and have a fast response time, while capacitive sensors are highly accurate and have a low noise level. Strain gauge sensors are highly accurate and can measure both pressure and temperature. The choice of pressure sensor for an IoT-based application will depend on various factors, including accuracy, sensitivity, response time, cost, and environmental conditions [26, 27]. In what follows, we discuss these types in detail with their possible application areas.

a) **Piezoresistive Pressure Sensors:** These sensors use the change in resistance of a material when subjected to pressure. They are commonly used in automotive, aerospace, and industrial applications.
b) **Capacitive Pressure Sensors:** These sensors use the change in capacitance of a material when subjected to pressure. They are commonly used in medical devices, consumer electronics, and automotive applications.
c) **Piezoelectric Pressure Sensors:** These sensors use the piezoelectric effect to generate an electrical charge when subjected to pressure. They

are commonly used in vibration monitoring, acoustic emission testing, and structural health monitoring.

d) **Optical Pressure Sensors:** These sensors use optical fibers to measure pressure changes by detecting changes in light intensity. They are commonly used in aerospace and medical applications.
e) **Strain Gauge Pressure Sensors:** These sensors use a strain gauge to measure the deformation of a material when subjected to pressure. They are commonly used in industrial applications, such as hydraulic and pneumatic systems.

7. **Gas Sensors:** These sensors can detect the presence of gases in the air and are used in environmental monitoring, industrial safety, and indoor air quality monitoring. Gas sensors are a type of sensor that are commonly used in IoT-based systems to detect the presence of various gases in the environment. They are used in a wide range of applications, including industrial safety, environmental monitoring, and indoor air quality monitoring. Gas sensors work by measuring the concentration of a particular gas in the air. They can detect a wide variety of gases, including carbon monoxide, methane, ammonia, nitrogen oxides, and volatile organic compounds (VOCs) [28, 29]. There are several types of gas sensors available, including electrochemical sensors, semiconductor sensors, and infrared sensors. Electrochemical sensors are the most commonly used gas sensors in IoT-based systems. They operate by measuring the current generated by a chemical reaction between the gas and an electrode. They are highly sensitive and accurate, and they have long lifespans. Semiconductor gas sensors operate by measuring the change in resistance of a semiconductor material in the presence of a gas. They are low-cost and have a fast response time, but they are less accurate than electrochemical sensors. Infrared gas sensors use an infrared beam to detect the presence of a gas. They are highly accurate and can detect a wide range of gases, but they are also more expensive and require more power than other types of gas sensors. Gas sensors in IoT-based systems are typically connected to a wireless network, such as Wi-Fi or Bluetooth, to transmit data to a central server or cloud-based platform [30]. The data can then be analyzed and used to monitor air quality, detect leaks, or alert users to potential safety hazards. In some applications, such as industrial safety, gas sensors may also be connected to an alarm or shut-off system to automatically trigger an emergency response. Overall, gas sensors are an important component of many IoT-based systems, and their use is becoming increasingly widespread as the demand for real-time environmental monitoring and safety systems continues to grow.
8. **Sound Sensors:** These sensors can detect changes in sound levels and are commonly used in noise pollution monitoring, acoustic sensing, and speech recognition. Sound sensors, also known as acoustic sensors or microphones, are a type of sensor commonly used in IoT-based systems to detect and measure sound levels in the environment [6]. They are used in a variety of applications, including noise monitoring, smart homes, and industrial automation. Sound sensors work by converting sound waves into electrical

signals that can be processed and analyzed by electronic systems. They can detect a wide range of frequencies, from very low frequencies (infrasound) to very high frequencies (ultrasound). Sound sensors can also be used to detect specific sounds, such as alarms, sirens, or human voices. There are several types of sound sensors available, including condenser microphones, dynamic microphones, and piezoelectric sensors [31, 32]. Condenser microphones are the most commonly used sound sensor in IoT-based systems. They are highly sensitive and can detect even low levels of sound, but they also require a power source and are more expensive than other types of microphones. Dynamic microphones are less sensitive but are more durable and require less power. Piezoelectric sensors use a crystal that generates an electrical charge in response to pressure or vibration, making them suitable for detecting sounds in harsh environments. Sound sensors in IoT-based systems are typically connected to a wireless network, such as Wi-Fi or Bluetooth, to transmit data to a central server or cloud-based platform. The data can then be analyzed and used to monitor noise levels, detect unusual sounds, or trigger automated responses, such as turning devices on or off, or sending notifications to users.

Actuators play a vital role in IoT systems, allowing them to control and manipulate physical devices such as appliances, lights, and HVAC systems [3]. The choice of the type of electric actuator depends on the specific requirements of the application, such as power consumption, speed, torque, and precision. Following are some of the most common types of actuators used in IoT-based applications.

1. **Electric Actuators:** These are actuators that use electric motors to produce linear or rotary motion. Electric actuators are widely used in home automation and industrial applications such as conveyor belts, pumps, and valves. Examples of electric actuators include stepper motors, servo motors, and linear actuators. There are several types of electric actuators used in various applications, including the following [33, 34].
   a) **DC Motors:** DC motors are the simplest type of electric actuators and are used in a wide range of applications. They are typically small and inexpensive, making them suitable for low-power applications. DC motors are commonly used in toys, robotics, and home automation.
   b) **Stepper Motors:** Stepper motors are a type of electric actuator that moves in small steps, making them ideal for precise positioning applications. They are widely used in 3D printers, computer numerical control (CNC) machines, and robotics.
   c) **Servo Motors:** Servo motors are a type of electric actuator that provides accurate control of speed, position, and torque. They are widely used in industrial automation, robotics, and aerospace applications.
   d) **Linear Actuators:** Linear actuators are electric actuators that produce linear motion. They are commonly used in applications such as medical equipment, industrial automation, and automotive systems. Linear actuators can be driven by DC motors, stepper motors, or servo motors.

e) **Gear Motors:** Gear motors are electric actuators that combine an electric motor with a gearbox. They provide high torque and are commonly used in industrial automation, robotics, and automotive systems.
f) **Brushless DC Motors:** Brushless direct current (DC) motors are a type of electric actuator that provides high efficiency and low noise. They are widely used in applications such as drones, electric vehicles, and medical equipment.

2. **Hydraulic Actuators:** These actuators use hydraulic fluid to produce linear or rotary motion. Hydraulic actuators are commonly used in heavy-duty applications such as construction equipment and industrial machinery. Examples of hydraulic actuators include hydraulic cylinders, hydraulic motors, and hydraulic pumps. The choice of the type of hydraulic actuator depends on the specific requirements of the application, such as force, speed, and precision. Hydraulic actuators are generally more powerful than electric actuators and are often used in heavy-duty applications for which high force and precision are required [35, 36].
   a) **Hydraulic Cylinders:** Hydraulic cylinders are the most common type of hydraulic actuator. They convert the pressure of the hydraulic fluid into linear motion. Hydraulic cylinders are widely used in industrial machinery, construction equipment, and aerospace applications.
   b) **Hydraulic Motors:** Hydraulic motors convert the pressure of the hydraulic fluid into rotary motion. They are commonly used in heavy-duty applications such as construction equipment, agricultural machinery, and mining equipment.
   c) **Hydraulic Pumps:** Hydraulic pumps are devices that convert mechanical energy into hydraulic energy. They are used to pressurize the hydraulic fluid, which is then used to power other hydraulic components such as cylinders and motors. Hydraulic pumps are commonly used in industrial machinery, construction equipment, and transportation systems.
   d) **Hydraulic Valves:** Hydraulic valves are devices that control the flow and direction of hydraulic fluid. They are used to regulate the speed and force of hydraulic actuators. Hydraulic valves are commonly used in industrial machinery, construction equipment, and transportation systems.
   e) **Hydraulic Accumulators:** Hydraulic accumulators are devices that store hydraulic energy in the form of pressurized fluid. They are used to supplement the output of hydraulic pumps, reduce pressure spikes, and improve the performance of hydraulic systems. Hydraulic accumulators are commonly used in industrial machinery, transportation systems, and energy storage systems.
3. **Pneumatic Actuators:** These actuators use compressed air to produce linear or rotary motion. Pneumatic actuators are commonly used in industrial applications such as assembly lines and packaging machinery. The choice of the type of pneumatic actuator depends on the specific requirements of the application, such as force, speed, and precision. Pneumatic actuators are generally less powerful than hydraulic actuators but are often more economical and easier to maintain. They are commonly used in applications that

require fast and repetitive motion, such as packaging machinery and assembly lines. Examples of pneumatic actuators include pneumatic cylinders, pneumatic motors, and pneumatic valves [37, 38].

a) **Pneumatic Cylinders:** Pneumatic cylinders are the most common type of pneumatic actuator. They convert the pressure of the compressed air into linear motion. Pneumatic cylinders are widely used in industrial automation, packaging machinery, and material handling systems.
b) **Pneumatic Motors:** Pneumatic motors convert the pressure of the compressed air into rotary motion. They are commonly used in applications such as assembly lines, robotics, and transportation systems.
c) **Pneumatic Valves:** Pneumatic valves are devices that control the flow and direction of compressed air. They are used to regulate the speed and force of pneumatic actuators. Pneumatic valves are commonly used in industrial automation, packaging machinery, and material handling systems.
d) **Pneumatic Grippers:** Pneumatic grippers are devices that use compressed air to grip and hold objects. They are commonly used in robotic arms, assembly lines, and material handling systems.
e) **Pneumatic Pumps:** Pneumatic pumps are devices that use compressed air to move fluid or gas. They are commonly used in industrial applications such as chemical processing, food and beverage processing, and wastewater treatment.

4. **Piezoelectric Actuators:** These are actuators that use the piezoelectric effect to produce motion. When an electric field is applied to certain materials, such as quartz or ceramics, they undergo a small deformation or shape change, which can be used to produce motion [39]. Piezoelectric actuators are commonly used in precision positioning applications such as in semiconductor manufacturing and medical devices. Piezoelectric actuators are not as commonly used in IoT applications as other types of actuators, but they can still be found in some applications. The choice of the type of piezoelectric actuator used in IoT applications depends on the specific requirements of the application, such as size, power consumption, and accuracy. Piezoelectric actuators are commonly used in IoT applications for which small size, low power consumption, and high precision are required. Some of the piezoelectric actuators used in IoT include the following [39, 40].

a) **Piezoelectric Valves:** Piezoelectric valves use a piezoelectric element to control the flow of fluid or gas in a system. They are commonly used in medical devices, such as infusion pumps, for which precise control of fluid flow is required.
b) **Piezoelectric Sensors:** Piezoelectric sensors use the piezoelectric effect to detect changes in pressure, force, or acceleration. They are commonly used in IoT applications, such as structural health monitoring, vibration monitoring, and condition monitoring of machinery.
c) **Piezoelectric Micro-Actuators:** Piezoelectric micro-actuators are tiny actuators that can produce very small displacements. They are commonly used in IoT applications, such as microfluidics and biomedical devices.

d) **Piezoelectric Energy Harvesters:** Piezoelectric energy harvesters use the piezoelectric effect to convert mechanical energy into electrical energy. They are commonly used in IoT applications, such as wireless sensors and wearables, for which the harvested energy can be used to power the devices.

Overall, the specific type of sensor or actuator used in an IoT system will depend on the specific application and the data that needs to be collected or acted upon.

2.1.1 Case Studies: RFID Principles, Components, and Applications

RFID (radio frequency identification) is a wireless technology used to identify and track objects using radio waves [41, 42]. RFID systems consist of three main components: tags, readers, and antennas. RFID tags are small, wireless devices that can be attached to or embedded in objects, while RFID readers use radio waves to communicate with the tags and gather data. Antennas are used to transmit and receive radio signals between the tags and readers. We will next discuss each of the RFID components in detail.

- **RFID Tag:** An RFID tag is a small wireless device that can be attached to or embedded in objects for identification and tracking purposes using radio waves. RFID tags typically consist of an antenna and a microchip, which contains unique identifying information that can be read by RFID readers. There are two main types of RFID tags: passive and active. Passive RFID tags do not have their own power source and rely on the energy from an RFID reader to power the microchip and transmit data. Active RFID tags, on the other hand, have their own power source and can transmit data over longer distances than can passive tags. RFID tags can be used in a variety of applications, such as inventory management, supply chain management (SCM), and asset tracking. In inventory management, RFID tags can be attached to products and used to track inventory levels in real time. In SCM, RFID tags can be used to track the movement of goods throughout the supply chain, providing real-time information about the location and status of each item. In asset tracking, RFID tags can be attached to equipment or other assets to track their location and maintenance history. RFID tags have a number of advantages over other identification and tracking technologies. They can be read from a distance without the need for line of sight, and can be read quickly and efficiently, making them ideal for high-volume applications [41, 42]. RFID tags are also durable and can be used in harsh environments such as in manufacturing or outdoor settings. Overall, RFID tags are a versatile and powerful tool for identification and tracking in a wide range of applications.
- **RFID Reader:** An RFID reader is a device that uses radio waves to communicate with RFID tags and collect data. RFID readers typically consist of an antenna, a radio frequency (RF) module, and a processor. The antenna is used to transmit and receive radio signals, while the RF module converts

the signals to digital data that can be processed by the reader's processor. There are two main types of RFID readers: fixed and handheld. Fixed RFID readers are typically installed in a fixed location, such as a warehouse or distribution center, and are used to collect data from RFID tags as they pass by the reader. Handheld RFID readers, on the other hand, are portable devices that can be used to collect data from RFID tags in the field. RFID readers can be used in a variety of applications, such as inventory management, SCM, and asset tracking [42, 43]. In inventory management, RFID readers can be used to track inventory levels in real time, providing accurate and up-to-date information on the location and quantity of products. In SCM, RFID readers can be used to track the movement of goods throughout the supply chain, providing real-time visibility into the location and status of each item. In asset tracking, RFID readers can be used to track the location and maintenance history of equipment or other assets. RFID readers have a number of advantages over other data collection technologies. They can read multiple tags simultaneously, without the need for line of sight, and can read tags from a distance, allowing for high-volume data collection. RFID readers are also durable and can be used in harsh environments, such as in manufacturing or outdoor settings. Overall, RFID readers are a powerful tool for collecting and managing data in a wide range of applications. By providing real-time visibility into the movement of objects, RFID readers can help organizations optimize their operations, reduce costs, and increase efficiency.

- **RFID Middleware:** RFID middleware is software that sits between RFID readers and enterprise applications, providing a bridge between the physical world of RFID tags and the digital world of enterprise systems. RFID middleware is designed to manage the flow of data between RFID readers and enterprise applications, providing a centralized platform for collecting, filtering, and analyzing RFID data [44]. RFID middleware typically includes a range of features and functionalities, such as data filtering, event management, and integration with enterprise systems. Data filtering allows the middleware to capture and process only relevant data, reducing the amount of data that needs to be transmitted to enterprise systems. Event management allows the middleware to trigger actions based on specific RFID events, such as when a tag is read or when a threshold is exceeded. Integration with enterprise systems allows the middleware to transmit RFID data to other enterprise systems, such as enterprise resource planning (ERP) systems, warehouse management systems (WMS), or manufacturing execution systems (MES). RFID middleware can be deployed in a variety of ways, such as on-premises, cloud-based, or hybrid architectures. On-premises deployments allow organizations to maintain complete control of the middleware infrastructure, while cloud-based deployments offer scalability and flexibility. Hybrid deployments offer a combination of the two, allowing organizations to leverage both on-premises and cloud-based capabilities. Overall, RFID middleware plays a critical role in managing and analyzing RFID data, providing a centralized platform for collecting, filtering, and integrating

RFID data with enterprise systems [44, 45]. By providing real-time visibility into the movement of objects, RFID middleware can help organizations optimize their operations, reduce costs, and increase efficiency.

One example of an RFID application is inventory management, whereby RFID tags can be used to track and manage inventory levels in real time. For example, a clothing retailer could attach RFID tags to each piece of clothing in their inventory. RFID readers could then be placed throughout the store, allowing the retailer to track the movement of each item in real time. This could help the retailer optimize their inventory levels, reduce theft, and improve the overall customer experience. Another example of an RFID application is in SCM, whereby RFID tags can be used to track the movement of goods throughout the supply chain. RFID tags can be placed on products or packaging, and readers can be used to scan the tags at various points in the supply chain. This allows companies to monitor the movement of products and identify any potential issues or delays. For example, Walmart has implemented RFID technology in its supply chain to improve inventory management and reduce costs [46]. By using RFID tags on products, Walmart can track inventory levels in real time, improve the accuracy of its inventory data, and reduce the need for manual inventory counts. For example, an automotive manufacturer could attach RFID tags to each component of a car as it moves through the production process. RFID readers could then be used to track the movement of each component as it moves from one stage of production to the next, providing real-time visibility into the production process and helping to optimize efficiency. RFID technology is also used in healthcare to track medical equipment, supplies, and patient records. RFID tags can be attached to patient wristbands, medical equipment, and medication packaging, and readers can be used to scan the tags to identify patients, equipment, and medication. This improves patient safety and reduces the risk of medication errors. For example, hospitals can use RFID tags to track patient movements and ensure that they receive the right medications at the right time.

RFID technology can be used to track and manage assets such as equipment, tools, and vehicles. RFID tags can be attached to these assets, and readers can be used to scan the tags to identify their location and status. This helps companies keep track of their assets, monitor maintenance schedules, and prevent theft. For example, hospitals use RFID to track medical equipment and ensure that it is readily available when needed. This improves patient care and saves time for medical staff who no longer have to search for missing equipment. RFID technology can be used to track and manage livestock, such as cows and sheep. RFID tags can be attached to the animals, and readers can be used to scan the tags to identify each animal and its status. This helps farmers keep track of their animals, monitor their health, and improve overall efficiency. For example, farmers can use RFID to track the movement of cows and monitor their milk production. This helps farmers identify any potential issues with their cows and improve overall efficiency. RFID technology can be used to manage library collections, automate check-in and check-out processes, and prevent theft. RFID tags can be attached to library materials, and readers can be used to scan the tags to identify the materials and their status. This makes it easier for library staff to manage their collections and improve the overall user experience for patrons. For example, libraries can use RFID to automate the check-in and check-out process,

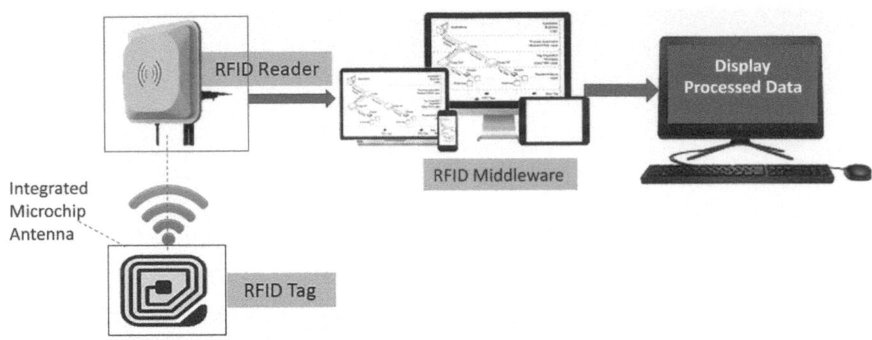

FIGURE 2.3 RFID-based communication system.

allowing patrons to quickly and easily borrow and return materials. RFID technology can be used for access control in buildings and other secure areas. RFID tags can be given to employees, visitors, and other authorized individuals, and readers can be used to scan the tags to grant access to specific areas. This allows for more efficient and secure access control, as RFID tags can be programmed to allow or deny access to specific areas based on an individual's authorization level. For example, companies can use RFID to restrict access to certain areas of their building based on an employee's job function or security clearance level. Overall, RFID technology offers a range of benefits for a variety of applications, including inventory management, supply chain management, and healthcare [1, 46, 47]. By providing real-time visibility into the movement of objects, RFID systems can help improve efficiency, reduce costs, and increase safety and security.

We will next discuss a typical scenario of a RFID-based communication system using a case study, as shown in Figure 2.3.

Background: A large warehouse handles the storage and distribution of various products. The warehouse management team faced challenges in accurately tracking inventory, locating items, and ensuring efficient communication between staff members.

Solution: To address these challenges, the warehouse implemented an RFID-based communication system. The system utilized RFID technology to enable seamless communication and efficient inventory management as shown in Figure 2.3.

Implementation

a) **RFID Tags:** Each product in the warehouse was affixed with an RFID tag containing a unique identifier. The RFID tags were either attached directly to the product or incorporated into product packaging.
b) **RFID Readers:** RFID readers were strategically placed throughout the warehouse. These readers emitted radio waves and captured information from the RFID tags within their range.

c) **Communication Infrastructure:** The RFID readers were connected to a centralized communication infrastructure, which included servers and a database. The infrastructure facilitated the collection, processing, and storage of data obtained from RFID tags.
d) **Real-Time Inventory Tracking:** As products moved within the warehouse, the RFID tags attached to them were automatically detected by the RFID readers. This allowed for real-time tracking of inventory movement and accurate inventory counts. The system could quickly identify the location of specific products within the warehouse.
e) **Communication Devices:** Warehouse staff members were equipped with handheld RFID scanners or RFID-enabled mobile devices. These devices could read the RFID tags and communicate with the central system.
f) **Seamless Communication:** With the RFID-enabled devices, staff members could easily communicate with each other and the central system. They could scan RFID tags to retrieve information about products, check inventory levels, and update the status of items.
g) **Alerts and Notifications:** The RFID-based communication system sent real-time alerts and notifications to the appropriate staff members. For example, if an item was placed in the wrong location or required immediate attention, the system would generate an alert to inform the responsible person.

Benefits

a) **Improved Inventory Accuracy:** The RFID-based communication system significantly enhanced inventory accuracy by providing real-time visibility into the location and movement of products. This reduced inventory discrepancies, minimized stockouts, and improved order fulfillment.
b) **Efficient Item Localization:** With RFID technology, staff members could quickly locate specific items within the warehouse. This saved time and effort previously spent searching for products.
c) **Enhanced Communication:** The RFID-enabled devices enabled seamless communication between staff members and the central system. This improved coordination, response times, and overall operational efficiency.
d) **Increased Productivity:** The automated tracking and communication capabilities of the RFID system streamlined warehouse operations, resulting in increased productivity. Staff members could perform tasks more efficiently and make informed decisions based on real-time data.
e) **Reduced Errors and Losses:** The accurate tracking and real-time alerts of the RFID system helped minimize errors, prevent misplaced items, and reduce losses due to inventory discrepancies or theft.

Conclusion

The implementation of an RFID-based communication system in the warehouse improved inventory management, streamlined operations, and facilitated efficient communication between staff members. The system's

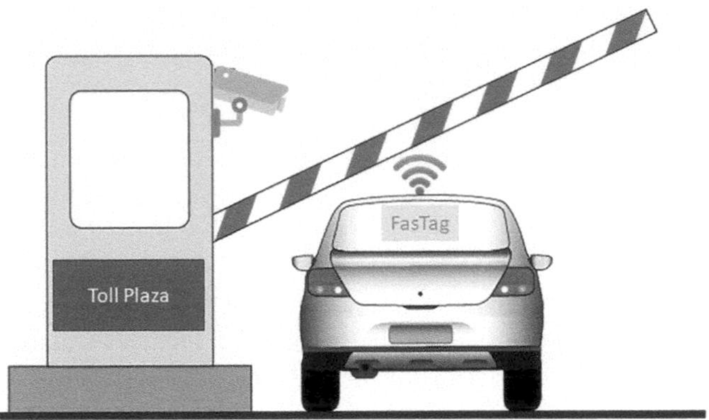

FIGURE 2.4 Use of RFID on toll plaza.

real-time tracking, seamless communication, and accurate inventory information significantly enhanced productivity and reduced errors, leading to improved overall warehouse performance.

We will next discuss a typical scenario using of RFID at a toll plaza using a case study, as shown in Figure 2.4.

Background: A busy toll plaza on a major highway faced challenges in effectively managing toll collection, reducing congestion, and improving overall operational efficiency. To address these issues, the toll plaza implemented an RFID-based IoT communication system.

Solution: The RFID-based IoT communication system integrated RFID technology with IoT capabilities to enable seamless communication, efficient toll collection, and enhanced traffic management. Figure 2.4 shows the use of RFID technology at a toll plaza.

Implementation

a) **RFID Tags:** Each vehicle was equipped with an RFID tag containing a unique identifier. The RFID tags were either affixed to the windshields or integrated into the vehicle registration documents.
b) **RFID Readers:** RFID readers were installed at the entry and exit points of the toll plaza. These readers emitted radio waves and captured information from the RFID tags within their range.
c) **IoT Gateway:** The RFID readers were connected to an IoT gateway, which served as a central communication hub. The IoT gateway collected data from the RFID readers and communicated with the toll plaza's central server.
d) **Real-Time Vehicle Identification:** As a vehicle approached the toll plaza, the RFID reader at the entry point detected the RFID tag and transmitted the vehicle's identification information to the central server. This allowed for real-time vehicle identification and verification.

e) **Toll Collection:** Once the vehicle was identified and verified, the toll plaza's system automatically calculated the toll amount based on the vehicle type, distance traveled, and other relevant factors. The driver could then make the payment using cash, a card, or an electronic payment system.
f) **Traffic Monitoring and Management:** The RFID-based IoT communication system also provided real-time traffic data. The RFID readers continuously collected vehicle information, including entry and exit timestamps. This data was analyzed to monitor traffic flow, identify congestion points, and make informed decisions regarding traffic management.
g) **Integration with Other Systems:** The RFID-based IoT system was integrated with other toll plaza systems, such as surveillance cameras, automated barriers, and electronic signage. This integration allowed for seamless coordination and improved operational efficiency.

Benefits

a) **Faster Toll Collection:** The RFID-based system enabled quick and automated vehicle identification, reducing the time taken for toll collection. This resulted in shorter waiting times for drivers and decreased congestion at the toll plaza.
b) **Improved Accuracy:** The automated vehicle identification and toll calculation reduced errors associated with manual collection methods. This improved the accuracy of toll collection and minimized revenue leakage.
c) **Enhanced Traffic Management:** The real-time traffic data collected by the RFID system allowed toll plaza authorities to monitor traffic patterns, identify congestion points, and take proactive measures to manage traffic flow. This helped to reduce congestion and improve overall traffic management.
d) **Convenient and Secure Payments:** The RFID-based IoT system facilitated various payment options, including cash, cards, and electronic payment systems. This provided drivers with convenience while ensuring secure transactions.
e) **Operational Efficiency:** The automated toll collection and real-time data analysis provided by the RFID-based system improved overall operational efficiency at the toll plaza. It reduced the need for manual intervention, minimized errors, and streamlined toll collection processes.

Conclusion

The implementation of an RFID-based IoT communication system at the toll plaza resulted in faster and more efficient toll collection, improved traffic management, and enhanced operational efficiency. The system's real-time vehicle identification, automated toll calculation, and integration with other systems provided convenience to drivers and enabled toll plaza authorities to make informed decisions based on real-time traffic data. The RFID-based IoT system played a vital role in reducing congestion, enhancing revenue collection, and improving the overall toll plaza experience.

2.2 PILLARS OF EMBEDDED IOT AND PHYSICAL DEVICES

Embedded IoT (EIoT) refers to the integration of IoT technology into physical devices, enabling them to collect and share data. The pillars of EIoT and physical devices are the key components that make up a robust and reliable system for IoT devices to function effectively [48]. These pillars include the following.

1. **Hardware:** Hardware refers to the physical components that make up an IoT device. These components include sensors, processors, memory, power sources, and other electronic components that are necessary for the device to function properly [49]. The hardware plays a critical role in collecting and processing data from the environment and transmitting it to other devices or the cloud. For example, a temperature sensor collects data on the surrounding temperature and sends it to the device's processor for processing and analysis. The hardware must be designed and manufactured to be durable, reliable, and energy-efficient, as many IoT devices are deployed in harsh or remote environments.
2. **Software:** Software refers to the code that controls the hardware and enables it to perform specific tasks. It includes the operating system, firmware, and application software. The software plays a critical role in managing the hardware, processing and analyzing data, and communicating with other devices or the cloud. For example, the firmware on a smart thermostat controls the temperature sensor, reads the data, and adjusts the thermostat accordingly [9, 10]. The application software allows users to interact with the device and control its settings. The software must be designed and written to be reliable, efficient, and secure, as many IoT devices are deployed in environments in which downtime or failure could have serious consequences.
3. **Connectivity:** Connectivity refers to the ability of IoT devices to communicate with each other or with the cloud. This can be achieved through various communication protocols such as Wi-Fi, Bluetooth, Zigbee, and cellular networks [50, 51]. The connectivity pillar enables IoT devices to transmit data to other devices or the cloud, receive commands or updates, and interact with other IoT devices in the network. For example, a smart home security system may use Zigbee to communicate between devices and Wi-Fi to connect to the internet and cloud services. The connectivity must be reliable, secure, and efficient, as many IoT devices operate in environments with limited bandwidth, intermittent connectivity, or interference.
4. **Security:** Security is an essential aspect of EIoT, as it ensures the protection of data and devices from unauthorized access or malicious attacks. It includes encryption, authentication, and access control mechanisms. The security pillar is critical in protecting sensitive data, preventing unauthorized access to the device, and ensuring that IoT devices are not used as a vector for attacks on other devices or networks [52, 53]. For example, a smart home security system must be secured against unauthorized access or hacking attempts to prevent intruders from gaining access to the home network. The security must be designed and implemented to be robust, scalable, and updatable, as new security threats are constantly emerging.

Together, these pillars provide the foundational elements for the integration of physical devices and embedded systems with the IoT. By leveraging these pillars, organizations can develop innovative solutions that enable the creation of intelligent systems, improve efficiency, and enhance the quality of life for individuals and communities. The hardware, software, connectivity, and security must be designed and implemented to work together seamlessly and efficiently, ensuring that IoT devices are reliable and secure, and that they perform optimally.

2.2.1 Machine-to-Machine

Machine-to-machine (M2M) communication is a critical pillar of EIoT that enables devices and systems to communicate with each other and exchange data without human intervention [1, 33]. M2M communication refers to the direct communication between two or more devices without human intervention. This means that devices can share data and coordinate their actions with other devices in real time, without the need for human input. M2M communication is a critical component of IoT, as it enables devices to interact with each other and perform automated tasks without the need for human intervention. M2M communication enables devices to interact with each other in real time, allowing for the creation of complex systems that can automatically respond to changes in the environment. M2M communication is enabled by a range of technologies including wireless networks, sensors, actuators, and embedded systems. These technologies enable devices to collect and transmit data to other devices and systems, allowing for the creation of intelligent systems that can automate complex tasks and improve efficiency. Speaking more clearly, it can be enabled through various communication protocols such as MQTT, CoAP, and DDS [26, 54]. These protocols allow devices to communicate with each other in a secure and efficient manner, and enable data to be transmitted in real time. M2M communication is used in various IoT applications such as smart homes, smart cities, and industrial IoT.

M2M communication enables devices to communicate with each other and exchange data in a seamless and automated manner, making it a fundamental aspect of the IoT and the Fourth Industrial Revolution, which is also known as "Industry 4.0" [55]. M2M communication requires at least two devices that can communicate with each other. These devices can be anything from sensors and actuators to computers and smartphones. The devices must be able to communicate with each other using a communication protocol. This can be wired or wireless, and can use various technologies such as Bluetooth, Wi-Fi, cellular networks, or satellite communication. M2M communication involves the transmission of data between devices. This can include data such as sensor readings, commands, or status updates. Once the data is transmitted, it must be processed by the receiving device. This can involve analyzing the data, making decisions, and sending commands back to the sending device. M2M communication can involve sensitive information, so it is important to ensure that the communication is secure. This can include encryption, authentication, and access control. M2M communication is often used in large-scale systems in which there may be thousands or even millions of devices communicating with each other.

As such, the system must be scalable to accommodate this level of communication. To ensure interoperability between different devices and systems, there are various standards that have been developed for M2M communication. Examples include the Message Queuing Telemetry Transport (MQTT) protocol and the Constrained Application Protocol (CoAP) [55].

M2M communication has a wide range of applications in various industries, such as healthcare, transportation, manufacturing, and agriculture. In healthcare, M2M communication can be used to monitor patient vital signs and transmit data to healthcare providers in real time, allowing for faster and more accurate diagnosis and treatment. In transportation, M2M communication can be used to monitor vehicle performance and optimize routes, reducing fuel consumption and improving safety. In manufacturing, M2M communication can be used to monitor machine performance and predict maintenance needs, reducing downtime and improving efficiency. In a smart home, the temperature sensor can communicate with the thermostat and adjust the temperature automatically, without the need for manual input. Similarly, in a smart city, traffic sensors can communicate with traffic lights and adjust the traffic flow depending on the traffic conditions. Overall, M2M communication is a critical pillar of EIoT that enables devices and systems to communicate and exchange data in real time [48, 56]. By leveraging M2M communication, organizations can develop innovative solutions that improve efficiency, reduce costs, and enhance the quality of life for individuals and communities.

2.2.2 IoT and M2M

M2M communication refers to the exchange of information between two or more machines without human intervention. This technology has been in use for decades in various industrial applications such as monitoring and controlling production lines, tracking inventory, and managing supply chain logistics. Some people also consider M2M as a subset of IoT that specifically refers to the direct communication between machines and devices without human intervention. M2M communication enables devices to interact and exchange data in real time, allowing for the creation of complex systems that can automatically respond to changes in the environment [57, 58]. On the other hand, IoT is a network of physical devices, vehicles, home appliances, and other items embedded with sensors, software, and connectivity, enabling them to exchange data and interact with each other. IoT can provide a wealth of data that can be used for various purposes, including monitoring and control. IoT refers to the network of physical devices, vehicles, buildings, and other objects that are embedded with sensors, software, and network connectivity that enable them to collect and exchange data. IoT enables devices to connect and interact with each other, allowing for the creation of intelligent systems that can automate tasks, monitor environments, and optimize processes. IoT and M2M are two critical pillars of EIoT that enable the integration of physical devices and systems embedded with the internet and each other. The combination of IoT and M2M can provide significant benefits in various industries, enabling better monitoring, control, and automation of processes and devices, leading to increased efficiency, cost savings, and improved user experiences. Together, IoT and M2M enable the creation of intelligent systems that can improve efficiency, reduce costs, and enhance the quality of life for individuals and communities [56, 59]. By leveraging IoT and M2M, organizations can develop innovative solutions that enable the integration of physical devices and embedded systems with the internet and each other, unlocking new opportunities for automation, data collection, and analysis.

When these two technologies are combined, they can provide a wide range of benefits. For example, IoT can provide real-time data on the status of machines, which can be used for predictive maintenance. M2M communication can be used to automatically trigger maintenance tasks, such as ordering replacement parts or scheduling repairs, based on the data received from IoT sensors [57]. Another example of how IoT and M2M can work together is in the area of smart homes. IoT devices such as smart thermostats, lighting systems, and security cameras can communicate with each other through M2M communication, enabling homeowners to control various aspects of their home remotely or through voice commands. Following are a few typical case studies of how IoT and M2M have been used in real-world applications [55, 60–62].

1. **Smart Agriculture:** One example of IoT and M2M combination is the use of smart sensors in agriculture. These sensors can monitor soil moisture, temperature, humidity, and other environmental factors that affect plant growth. The data collected is transmitted to a central server via M2M communication, where it is analyzed to optimize irrigation and fertilization, reducing waste and increasing crop yields.
2. **Smart Cities:** Another example is the use of IoT and M2M in smart cities. By embedding sensors in streetlights, waste management systems, and public transportation, city planners can optimize traffic flow, reduce energy consumption, and improve safety. Data collected from these sensors can be transmitted via M2M communication to a central server, where it is analyzed to provide insights into city operations and enable more efficient resource allocation.
3. **Industrial Automation:** In the manufacturing industry, IoT and M2M can be used to automate processes and increase efficiency. For example, sensors can be used to monitor machine health and predict failures, allowing maintenance to be scheduled before breakdowns occur. M2M communication can also be used to automatically trigger orders for replacement parts, reducing downtime and improving productivity.
4. **Healthcare:** In the healthcare industry, IoT and M2M can be used to monitor patient health remotely. Wearable devices can collect data on vital signs such as heart rate, blood pressure, and oxygen levels, and transmit it to healthcare providers via M2M communication. This allows for early detection of potential health issues, and can enable providers to deliver more personalized care.
5. **Energy Management:** IoT and M2M can also be used to optimize energy management in buildings. By installing sensors to monitor energy usage, building operators can identify areas where energy is being wasted and take action to reduce consumption. M2M communication can be used to

automatically adjust heating and cooling systems, lighting, and other building systems based on occupancy and usage patterns, further reducing energy waste.

2.2.3 Software-Defined Networking

Software-defined networking (SDN) is a critical pillar of IoT that enables the creation of intelligent, dynamic networks that can adapt to changing conditions and requirements [63, 64]. The SDN is a network architecture approach that separates the control plane from the data plane in networking devices. This separation enables network administrators to centrally manage and control network traffic flow and access, making it easier to configure, optimize, and secure the network. In IoT, SDN enables the creation of intelligent networks that can automatically adapt to changing traffic patterns, device requirements, and security threats. SDN enables network administrators to define policies and rules that govern network traffic and access, allowing them to dynamically allocate network resources to devices and applications based on their requirements. SDN enables network administrators to configure network devices, policies, and traffic flow dynamically, depending on the needs of the network and applications. SDN is important for IoT applications, as it enables network administrators to manage large-scale IoT networks more efficiently and reduce network latency [65]. For example, in a smart factory, SDN can be used to optimize the flow of data between IoT devices and cloud services, ensuring that data is transmitted quickly and efficiently. SDN also enables network virtualization, allowing multiple virtual networks to coexist on a single physical network infrastructure. This enables organizations to create secure, isolated networks for specific applications or user groups, reducing the risk of unauthorized access and data breaches. Overall, SDN is a critical pillar of IoT that enables the creation of intelligent, dynamic networks that can adapt to changing conditions and requirements. By leveraging SDN, organizations can develop innovative solutions that enable the integration of physical devices and embedded systems with the internet, improving efficiency, security, and reliability.

SDN is important for IoT applications, as it enables network administrators to manage large-scale IoT networks more efficiently and reduce network latency. SDN allows network administrators to configure network devices and policies based on the requirements of the IoT applications, enabling them to optimize the flow of data between IoT devices and cloud services [66, 67]. SDN is used in various IoT applications such as smart cities, industrial IoT, and healthcare IoT. For example, in a smart factory, SDN can be used to optimize the flow of data between IoT devices and cloud services, ensuring that data is transmitted quickly and efficiently. SDN can also be used to manage the security of IoT networks, enabling network administrators to monitor network traffic and detect security threats in real time. In conclusion, M2M communication and SDN are important pillars of EIoT, as they enable and manage IoT devices and networks more efficiently. M2M communication enables devices to communicate with each other and perform automated tasks, while SDN enables network administrators to manage IoT networks more efficiently and reduce network latency. Both M2M communication and SDN are critical components of IoT, enabling the development of scalable, reliable, and secure IoT applications.

2.2.4 Wireless Sensor Networks

Wireless Sensor Networks (WSNs) are a critical pillar of IoT that enable the collection and transmission of data from physical devices and embedded systems in real time, without the need for wired connections [68, 69]. WSNs consist of small, battery-powered sensors that are embedded in physical devices and environments, such as buildings, vehicles, and factories. These sensors are equipped with wireless communication capabilities, enabling them to communicate with each other and with centralized network controllers. WSNs enable the collection of data from remote and hard-to-reach environments, enabling organizations to monitor and control physical systems and processes in real time. WSNs can be used to monitor environmental conditions such as temperature, humidity, and air quality, as well as to monitor machine performance and detect faults and anomalies.

WSNs can also be used to control physical systems, such as lighting, heating, and ventilation, enabling organizations to optimize energy consumption and reduce costs [59, 70]. In addition, WSNs can be used for asset tracking, enabling organizations to track the location and movement of goods and equipment in real time. Overall, WSNs are a critical pillar of IoT that enable the collection and transmission of data from physical devices and embedded systems in real time. By leveraging WSNs, organizations can develop innovative solutions that enable the integration of physical systems and processes with the internet, improving efficiency, reducing costs, and enhancing the quality of life for individuals and communities.

2.2.5 SCADA

Supervisory control and data acquisition (SCADA) is a critical pillar of IoT that enables the remote monitoring and control of industrial processes and equipment in real time. SCADA systems consist of a network of sensors, controllers, and software applications that work together to monitor and control industrial processes and equipment. These systems enable operators to remotely monitor and control industrial processes from a centralized location, improving efficiency, reducing costs, and enhancing safety. In IoT, SCADA systems can be used to monitor and control a wide range of industrial processes and equipment, including manufacturing plants, power generation facilities, and oil and gas pipelines. These systems can collect and analyze real-time data from sensors and devices, enabling operators to detect anomalies and respond to them before they escalate into critical issues.

SCADA systems also enable the integration of physical systems and processes with the internet, enabling operators to remotely monitor and control industrial processes and equipment from anywhere in the world. This enables organizations to optimize their operations, reduce downtime, and improve overall productivity. Overall, SCADA is a critical pillar of IoT that enables the remote monitoring and control of industrial processes and equipment in real time. By leveraging SCADA, organizations can develop innovative solutions that enable the integration of physical systems and processes with the internet, improving efficiency, reducing costs, and enhancing safety.

2.3 WIRELESS SENSOR NETWORKS

WSN is a type of wireless network that consists of a large number of small, low-cost, and battery-powered sensor nodes that communicate with each other wirelessly to collect data from a specific area. In other words, the WSN is a collection of autonomous, wireless devices called nodes or sensors that can sense, process, and communicate data wirelessly with other nodes in the network to perform monitoring, control, or decision-making tasks [68, 71]. WSN is mainly used for monitoring and collecting data from a specific environment, such as temperature, humidity, and pressure in a building, or soil moisture and temperature in agriculture. According to the Institute of Electrical and Electronics Engineers (IEEE), a wireless sensor network (WSN) is a self-configuring network of small, low-power, and lightweight devices called sensor nodes that can sense and collect data from their environment and communicate the data to a base station or other nodes in the network. There are several extended versions of WSN which are designed to address specific requirements or limitations of traditional WSNs. For instance, in mobile sensor networks, sensor nodes are mobile, and they can move around and self-organize to collect data from a larger area [72]. Mobile sensor networks are suitable for applications such as wildlife monitoring, battlefield surveillance, and disaster response. Multimedia sensor networks (MSNs) are WSNs that can handle multimedia data, such as audio and video. MSNs are useful in applications that require real-time video surveillance, multimedia streaming, and content-based retrieval. Underground sensor networks are WSNs that are deployed underground, such as in mining or oil and gas exploration. They use special sensors and communication protocols that can operate in harsh and dynamic underground environments. Body sensor networks (BSN) are WSNs that are integrated into wearable devices such as smartwatches or health monitors to collect and analyze physiological data from the human body [73]. BSNs are useful in healthcare applications such as remote patient monitoring and disease management. Flying sensor networks (FSN) are WSNs that use unmanned aerial vehicles (UAVs) or drones to collect data from the air. FSNs are useful in applications such as environmental monitoring, disaster response, and surveillance.

Ubiquitous sensor networks (USNs) and wireless sensor and actuator networks (WSANs) can also be considered as advanced forms or specialized versions of WSNs [69]. USNs focus on providing seamless and pervasive sensing and monitoring capabilities throughout an entire environment, such as a city or a building. USNs use a large number of sensors that are distributed throughout the environment to collect data on various parameters such as temperature, humidity, light, and sound. The data collected by these sensors is then analyzed to provide a comprehensive view of the environment. Unlike traditional WSNs that are often designed for specific applications, USNs are intended to be ubiquitous and support a variety of applications and services. USNs typically consist of a large number of heterogeneous sensor nodes that can sense and collect data from their surroundings. These nodes are equipped with various types of sensors such as temperature, humidity, light, sound, and motion sensors, and can communicate with each other using wireless communication technologies such as Wi-Fi, Bluetooth, Zigbee, or cellular networks. The data collected by the sensor nodes can be processed locally or transmitted to a central server for further processing and analysis. The processed data can then be used to provide various services such as environmental monitoring, traffic control, health monitoring, and smart home automation. USNs have several advantages in IoT, including their ability to operate in diverse environments and their scalability. They can also provide real-time data and support a variety of applications and services. However, USNs also face several challenges such as energy consumption, security, and data management. As such, developing efficient algorithms and protocols for data collection, processing, and management in USNs is an active area of research in the IoT field. WSANs are a type of wireless network that integrates sensing and actuation capabilities, allowing for automated control of physical systems in real time. WSANs are designed to provide a scalable, reliable, and efficient communication platform between sensors, actuators, and other devices in the network. WSANs consist of several sensor nodes that collect data from the environment and transmit it to a central coordinator or gateway. Actuator nodes receive control signals from the central coordinator and perform actions in the physical world. The communication between the sensor and actuator nodes is typically wireless and may use various communication protocols such as Zigbee, Bluetooth, or Wi-Fi. WSANs have several advantages in IoT applications, including their ability to automate physical systems, reduce manual intervention, and improve system performance and efficiency [74, 75]. For example, in a smart building application, WSANs can be used to monitor and control temperature, lighting, and air conditioning systems based on occupancy and usage patterns.

Designing WSNs is a challenging task that requires a deep understanding of the network architecture, the application requirements, and the environment in which the network will be deployed. Since most of the sensor nodes in a WSN are battery powered and have limited energy resources, energy efficiency is one of the major design challenges. Researchers are constantly looking for ways to reduce the energy consumption of WSNs, including developing energy-efficient protocols, data aggregation techniques, and routing algorithms [76]. WSNs may consist of thousands of sensor nodes, and it is challenging to design a scalable network architecture that can handle a large number of nodes. The network should be able to handle node additions, deletions, and reconfigurations without affecting the overall network performance. WSNs may be deployed in critical applications such as military, healthcare, and industrial systems, and the data collected by these networks may be sensitive. Therefore, security is a major concern in WSN design, including authentication, encryption, and secure routing [77]. WSNs collect a massive amount of data, and it is challenging to transmit all this data to the sink node. Therefore, data aggregation and fusion techniques are required to reduce the amount of data that needs to be transmitted, thereby reducing energy consumption and improving network scalability. Some WSN applications, such as healthcare and industrial systems, require a high level of reliability, low latency, and high data throughput. Therefore, designing WSNs with high quality of service (QoS) is a significant challenge. WSNs are often deployed in harsh and inaccessible environments, making it challenging to deploy and manage the network. The nodes may be exposed to harsh weather conditions, and the network may be deployed in hazardous areas. Therefore, designing WSNs that are easy to deploy and manage is a major challenge.

2.3.1 History and Context

The history of WSNs for IoT can be traced back to the early 1990s when researchers started exploring the concept of wireless sensor networks as a means of collecting data from remote and hard-to-reach environments [78, 79]. In the late 1990s, the US Defense Advanced Research Projects Agency (DARPA) launched the Sensor Information Technology (SensIT) program, which aimed to develop WSNs for military applications. The program led to the development of several key technologies, including low-power radio transceivers, energy-efficient protocols, and data processing algorithms. In the early 2000s, researchers began exploring the use of WSNs for civilian applications, such as environmental monitoring and smart agriculture. These applications required low-cost and energy-efficient sensors that could collect and transmit data in real time, leading to the development of new sensor technologies and communication protocols.

Publication of the IEEE 802.15.4 standard in 2003 provided a standardized communication protocol for WSNs. This standard enabled the development of low-cost and energy-efficient sensor nodes that could communicate with each other and with centralized network controllers. In the mid-2000s, the emergence of the IoT concept led to a renewed interest in WSNs, as researchers and developers recognized the potential of WSNs as a critical component of IoT [59, 80]. This led to the development of new WSN technologies and applications, including wireless mesh networks, body area networks, and smart homes and buildings. Today, WSNs are a critical component of IoT, enabling the collection and transmission of data from physical devices and embedded systems in real time, without the need for wired connections. WSNs are used in a wide range of applications, including environmental monitoring, smart cities, and industrial automation.

2.3.2 Connecting Nodes

In a WSN, nodes are connected wirelessly to enable communication and data transfer. The nodes in a WSN typically consist of sensors, actuators, and a central control unit that coordinates communication and data transfer between nodes. WSNs play a critical role in IoT by enabling the collection and transmission of data from physical devices and embedded systems. WSNs are used to monitor and control a wide range of systems and processes, including environmental monitoring, industrial automation, smart cities, and healthcare. To connect nodes in a WSN, various wireless communication technologies are used, including Bluetooth, Zigbee, and Wi-Fi [78, 79]. These technologies provide reliable and low-power communication, enabling nodes to communicate with each other over long distances without the need for wired connections.

In IoT, WSNs enable the collection of data from physical devices and embedded systems, which is then transmitted to cloud-based platforms for storage and analysis. This data can be used to gain insights into system performance, optimize operations, and improve efficiency. WSNs also enable the remote monitoring and control of systems and processes, enabling operators to detect and respond to issues in real time. This helps to reduce downtime and improve overall system reliability and safety. Overall, the role of WSNs in IoT is critical, enabling the collection and transmission of data from physical devices and embedded systems, and facilitating the integration of physical systems and processes with the internet [68, 81]. The development of new WSN technologies and applications is expected to continue, as researchers and developers explore new ways of leveraging WSNs to improve efficiency, reduce costs, and enhance the quality of life for individuals and communities.

2.3.3 Networking Nodes

WSN senses and gathers together data using sensors distributed spatially in a geographic region and collects it to a centralized location with the help of wired, wireless, or sometimes hybrid networks for processing. WSN is used to detect physical and environmental changes like temperature, pressure, motion, heat, etc. WSN focuses on sensing and gathering data and routing it for further processing. WSN has multiple nodes ranging from a few hundred to thousands in number scattered throughout a vast geographical region [78, 79]. Each of these nodes at least has a sensor attached to it obviously for the sensing purpose. Sometimes a single mode has multiple sensors attached to it (temperature, pressure, etc.). A node has an electronic circuit interface for the sensor inside, a microcontroller, and a radio transceiver with an antenna and battery as an energy source. These nodes sense data and have routing capability; this data is processed and provided to the end-user in the upper layers as shown in Figure 2.5, while Figure 2.6 shows the levels of networking nodes.

The WSNs are composed of a large number of tiny sensor nodes that communicate wirelessly with each other. These nodes are deployed in a variety of topologies depending on the application requirements. The choice of topology for a WSN depends on the application requirements, network size, power consumption, and scalability [78, 82, 83]. Each topology has its own advantages and disadvantages, and it is essential to choose the proper topology to ensure the successful deployment and operation of the WSN. Following are some of the most common topologies of WSNs.

1. **Star Topology:** In a star topology, all the sensor nodes are connected to a central node, which acts as a base station [83]. The base station collects data from the sensor nodes and forwards it to the sink node or the central server. This topology is easy to set up, and the base station can easily communicate

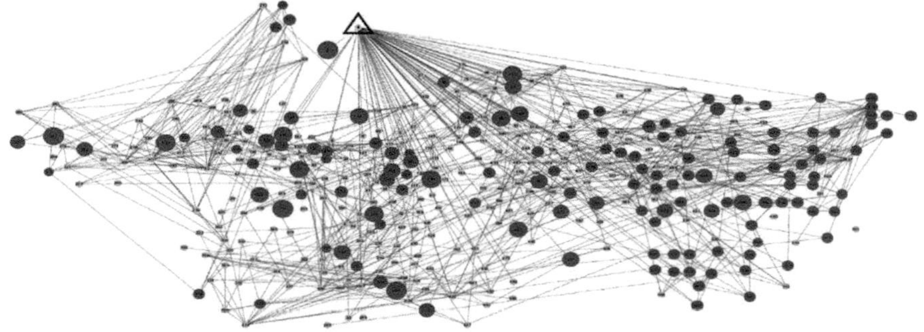

FIGURE 2.5: Networking nodes.

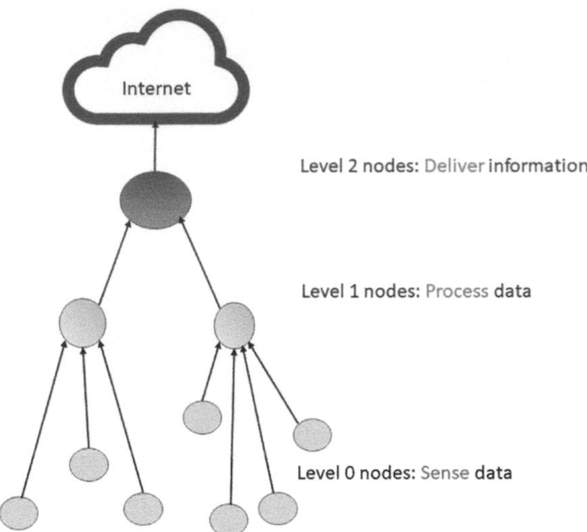

FIGURE 2.6 Levels of networking nodes.

with each node. However, it is not suitable for large networks, as the distance between the nodes and the base station can be a limitation.

2. **Mesh Topology:** In a mesh topology, the sensor nodes communicate with each other directly or through intermediate nodes, forming a mesh network. In this topology, the nodes act as both sensors and routers, which means that they can forward data from other nodes to the base station [82]. The mesh topology is scalable and robust, as it can continue to work even if some nodes fail. However, it requires more power and is more complex to set up than a star topology.
3. **Tree Topology:** In a tree topology, the sensor nodes are arranged in a hierarchical tree-like structure with the base station at the root of the tree [82]. The nodes are connected to their parent nodes, and the data flows upwards towards the base station. This topology is efficient for collecting data from a large area, and it requires less power than a mesh topology. However, it is not very scalable, and the network can become congested as data moves up the tree.
4. **Hybrid Topology:** Hybrid topology is a combination of two or more topologies. For example, a WSN can have a star topology in the center, with mesh topology nodes on the periphery. This topology is useful for applications that require a combination of features such as high reliability, scalability, and low power consumption [82, 83]. The hybrid topology can be designed to suit specific application requirements, but it requires more complex setup and management.
5. **Cluster Topology:** In a cluster topology, the nodes are grouped into clusters, and each cluster has a cluster head that acts as a coordinator for the nodes in the cluster. The cluster heads are responsible for collecting data

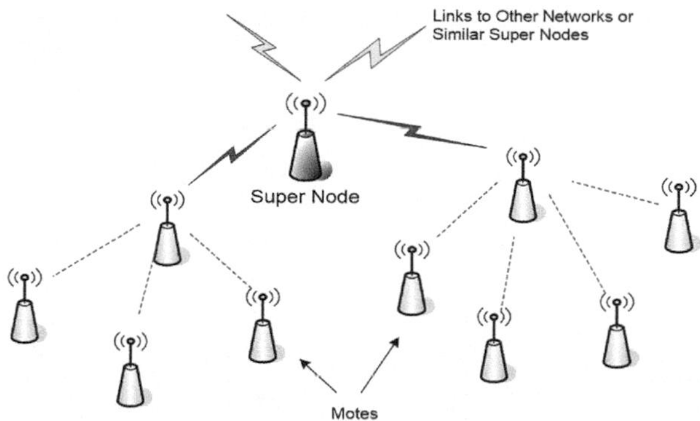

FIGURE 2.7 Routing in wireless sensor networks (WSNs).

from the nodes in their cluster and forwarding it to the base station. This topology is scalable and energy-efficient as the cluster heads can manage the nodes in their cluster and reduce the energy consumption of individual nodes [82, 83]. However, it requires more complex management, and the cluster heads can become a bottleneck in the network.

Figure 2.7 shows the routing of packets is executed in a typical WSN network. Routing protocols play a crucial role in the operation of WSNs. They are responsible for ensuring that data packets are delivered from the source node to the destination node efficiently and reliably.

Following are some of the important routing protocols used in WSNs.

1. **LEACH (Low Energy Adaptive Clustering Hierarchy):** LEACH is a clustering-based protocol that organizes the sensor nodes into clusters and elects a cluster head in each cluster [78, 81]. The cluster heads collect data from their cluster members and forward it to the base station. LEACH is energy-efficient, as it reduces the energy consumption of individual nodes and prolongs the network lifetime.
2. **AODV (Ad Hoc On-Demand Distance Vector):** AODV is a reactive protocol that establishes a route between the source node and the destination node only when there is data to be transmitted [84]. AODV uses a route discovery process to find the shortest path to the destination node. It is efficient in terms of bandwidth usage and adapts to network changes quickly, and it is a reactive routing protocol, meaning that it only establishes routes when they are needed. This helps to conserve energy and bandwidth, as nodes do not need to always maintain routing tables for all possible destinations. In AODV, nodes broadcast route request (RREQ) packets to discover routes to a destination node. When a node receives an RREQ packet, it checks its routing table to see if it has a route to the destination. If it does not have a route, it broadcasts the RREQ packet to its neighbors. This process continues until the destination node is reached, or a node with a route to

the destination is found. Once a route is established, data packets can be sent along the route. AODV has several advantages in IoT and WSNs. It is scalable, energy-efficient, and well suited for networks with dynamic topology changes, and also provides a low-latency route discovery mechanism, enabling real-time data transmission. However, AODV also has some limitations. It may not be suitable for networks with high traffic loads, as frequent route discoveries and updates can cause network congestion [85]. It may also be vulnerable to security attacks, as malicious nodes can manipulate the routing information and disrupt network operations.

3. **DSR (Dynamic Source Routing):** DSR is another reactive protocol that discovers the route between the source node and the destination node on demand. DSR maintains a cache of all the routes it has discovered, which makes it faster than AODV in some situations [85, 86]. DSR is also robust to network changes and can adapt to topology changes quickly. DSR is a reactive routing protocol used in WSNs and IoT. Like AODV, DSR only establishes routes when needed, which helps to conserve energy and bandwidth. In DSR, when a source node wants to send data to a destination node, it first broadcasts a route request (RREQ) packet to its neighbors. Each intermediate node receiving the RREQ packet stores the source node's address and broadcasts the packet to its neighbors if it has not already seen it. The destination node, upon receiving the RREQ packet, sends a route reply (RREP) packet back to the source node, containing the list of nodes that the data should be forwarded through. Once the source node receives the RREP packet, it can send the data to the destination node by using the route information contained in the RREP packet. The intermediate nodes on the route cache the route information so that subsequent packets from the same source can be sent more efficiently.

   DSR has several advantages in IoT and WSNs. It is simple, scalable, and well suited for networks with low to moderate traffic loads. It is also resilient to node failures and able to adapt to changes in network topology. However, DSR also has some limitations. It may not be suitable for networks with high traffic loads or high mobility, as frequent route discoveries and updates can cause network congestion. It also has higher latency compared to some other routing protocols, as it requires multiple message exchanges to establish a route. Finally, DSR may be vulnerable to security attacks, as malicious nodes can manipulate the routing information and disrupt network operations.
4. **SPIN (Sensor Protocols for Information via Negotiation):** SPIN is a data-centric routing protocol that transmits data based on the data content rather than the node address [86]. SPIN uses data aggregation techniques to reduce the number of transmissions and conserve energy. SPIN is efficient in terms of bandwidth usage and is suitable for applications that require data aggregation.
5. **TEEN (Threshold-Sensitive Energy Efficient Sensor Network Protocol):** TEEN is an event-driven protocol that transmits data only

when certain events occur. TEEN uses a threshold-based mechanism to detect events and reduce energy consumption. TEEN is efficient in terms of energy consumption and is suitable for applications that require event detection [81, 86].

2.3.4 WSN and IoT

WSNs and the IoT are closely related technologies that are commonly used in the field of wireless communication and data transfer. WSNs are networks of wireless sensors that can be used to collect data from the environment, such as temperature, humidity, and light levels. These sensors communicate with each other through wireless communication protocols and transmit the collected data to a central node or base station for processing and analysis [78, 81]. IoT, on the other hand, refers to the connection of various devices to the internet, allowing the devices to communicate with each other and exchange data [6, 87]. This can include everything from smartphones and laptops to smart home devices and industrial equipment. In many ways, WSNs can be seen as a subset of IoT, as they are essentially networks of sensors that are designed to collect and transmit data. However, IoT also includes a wider range of devices and technologies that are not necessarily focused solely on data collection. Furthermore, IoT often involves the use of cloud computing and Big Data analytics to process and analyze the vast amounts of data generated by connected devices. In this sense, WSNs and IoT technologies are complementary, as WSNs can provide valuable data to IoT systems, which can then be used to gain insights and make decisions in real time.

There is a relation between the WSN and IoT technologies. First, both WSNs and IoT are wireless communication technologies that rely on the use of sensors and other devices to collect data from the environment [88]. WSNs are typically used in applications whereby a large number of sensors need to be deployed in a specific area, such as environmental monitoring or industrial control systems. IoT, on the other hand, can include a wide range of devices and technologies, from wearables and smart home devices to connected vehicles and industrial equipment. Second, both WSNs and IoT rely on wireless communication protocols to transmit data between devices [88, 89]. WSNs often use protocols such as Zigbee or Bluetooth Low Energy (BLE), while IoT devices can use a variety of protocols, including Wi-Fi, cellular, and low-power wide-area (LPWA) technologies like LoRaWAN or NB-IoT. Third, both WSNs and IoT generate large amounts of data that need to be processed and analyzed. In the case of WSNs, the data is typically transmitted to a central node or base station, where it can be aggregated and processed. IoT devices, on the other hand, may transmit data directly to the cloud, where it can be processed using Big Data analytics tools. Finally, WSNs and IoT can be used together to create more powerful and effective systems. For example, WSNs can be used to collect data from the environment and transmit it to an IoT system, where it can be combined with other data sources to gain deeper insights and make more informed decisions. Alternatively, IoT devices can be used to control and manage WSNs, allowing users to monitor and manage sensor networks from a centralized platform [88]. In summary, the relationship between WSNs and IoT is one of interdependence and mutual benefit. Both technologies rely on wireless communication and sensor data to operate, and both generate large amounts of data that can be processed and analyzed to gain valuable insights. By working together, WSNs and IoT can create more powerful and effective systems that can be used in a wide range of applications, from environmental monitoring to industrial automation and beyond.

The preference between WSN and IoT technologies really depends on the specific application and use case. Both technologies have their own advantages and disadvantages, and the choice between them will depend on factors such as the size and scope of the deployment, the type of data that needs to be collected and analyzed, and the desired level of control and customization [30, 79, 88]. In general, WSNs are often preferred for applications whereby a large number of sensors need to be deployed in a specific area, such as environmental monitoring or precision agriculture. WSNs can be highly customized and optimized for specific applications, and they can be designed to operate in harsh or remote environments where other communication technologies may not be suitable. On the other hand, IoT technologies are often preferred for applications where a wider range of devices and data sources need to be integrated and managed. IoT systems can incorporate a variety of devices, from wearables and smartphones to smart home appliances and industrial equipment, and they can be used to collect and analyze data from a wide range of sources. Ultimately, the choice between WSN and IoT will depend on the specific needs and requirements of the application. Both technologies have their own strengths and weaknesses, and the most appropriate solution will depend on a variety of factors, including the size and scope of the deployment, the type of data that needs to be collected and analyzed, and the desired level of control and customization.

There are many applications in which WSN and IoT technologies are used together to create more powerful and effective systems. One example of such an application is in precision agriculture [90, 91], a farming technique that uses data and technology to optimize crop yields and reduce waste. WSNs can be used to monitor environmental conditions such as soil moisture, temperature, and humidity, while IoT devices such as drones and smart tractors can be used to collect and transmit data on crop health and growth. For example, a farmer might deploy a network of WSNs in fields to monitor soil moisture levels and temperature. The data collected by the sensors can be transmitted to a central hub or cloud platform, where it can be analyzed and combined with other data sources such as weather forecasts and crop yield data. IoT devices such as drones and smart tractors can also be used to collect data on crop health and growth. Drones equipped with cameras and sensors can be used to capture high-resolution images of crops, which can be analyzed using machine learning algorithms to identify areas of stress or disease. Smart tractors equipped with GPS and precision sensors can be used to plant seeds and apply fertilizers and pesticides with greater accuracy and efficiency, reducing waste and improving yields. By combining WSN and IoT technologies in this way, farmers can gain a deeper understanding of their crops and make more informed decisions about how to manage them. This can lead to significant improvements in crop yields, reduced costs, and more sustainable farming practices.

2.4 TWO PILLARS OF THE WEB: WEB OF THINGS AND CLOUD OF THINGS

The Web of Things (WoT) and the Cloud of Things (CoT) are two terms used in the context of the IoT to describe different approaches for connecting devices and enabling IoT applications [92]. The WoT and the CoT are two key pillars of the IoT landscape, enabling the creation and management of connected devices and systems. Both WoT and CoT are important concepts in the IoT ecosystem, as they enable different types of IoT applications and use cases. WoT provides a standardized way for devices to communicate and interact with each other, while CoT provides a centralized platform for managing and analyzing IoT data. The main difference between WoT and CoT is their approach to connecting IoT devices. WoT focuses on connecting devices directly to the web, while CoT focuses on connecting devices to the cloud for centralized management and analysis.

The WoT is a framework for connecting physical devices to the web, allowing them to be accessed and controlled remotely via web-based applications [93, 94]. The WoT is an approach that aims to create a universal, standardized way for IoT devices to communicate and interact with each other over the web. The WoT architecture is built around the concept of "things" that are identified by uniform resource identifiers (URIs) and can be accessed and manipulated using standard web protocols such as Hypertext Transfer Protocol (HTTP) and Representational State Transfer (REST). In this model, devices are connected directly to the web, and users can interact with them using web browsers or other web-based applications. The WoT is built on standard web technologies such as HTTP, hypertext markup language (HTML), and JavaScript, enabling developers to create web interfaces for IoT devices and integrate them with other web services. The WoT provides a standardized way to connect devices to the web, enabling interoperability between devices from different manufacturers and reducing the complexity of IoT development. By creating a common language for IoT devices, WoT makes it easier to build and manage IoT systems and enables new use cases such as smart homes, industrial automation, and smart cities [94, 95]. For instance, a smart home is a home that is equipped with internet-connected devices that can be controlled remotely using a mobile device or computer. WoT enables these devices to communicate with each other and with other services over the web. For example, a smart thermostat can use WoT to communicate with a smart speaker to turn on/off lights, adjust the temperature, or even order groceries. WoT can be used to optimize crop yields and reduce water usage by enabling sensors to monitor soil moisture levels and temperature. Farmers can use this data to make informed decisions about when to water their crops and when to harvest them. For example, WoT can be used to create an irrigation system that can automatically water plants when the soil moisture level falls below a certain threshold. WoT can be used to monitor patients remotely, allowing healthcare providers to monitor a patient's vital signs and health status in real time. For example, patients can use WoT-enabled devices to monitor their blood sugar levels, heart rate, and blood pressure, and this data can be shared with their healthcare provider for analysis and intervention.

On the other hand, the CoT is a model that focuses on connecting IoT devices to the cloud, where data is processed and analyzed using cloud computing resources

[96, 97]. In this approach, devices are connected to a cloud platform, which provides the necessary infrastructure for managing and analyzing the data generated by the devices. The cloud platform can provide services such as data storage, data processing, and data visualization, and can also integrate with other cloud-based services and applications. It is a platform for hosting and managing IoT data and applications in the cloud. The CoT provides a scalable and flexible infrastructure for collecting, storing, processing, and analyzing IoT data, enabling real-time insights and decision-making. The CoT enables organizations to leverage the power of cloud computing to manage their IoT systems more efficiently and to develop new applications and services that leverage the vast amounts of data generated by IoT devices. By providing a centralized platform for IoT management, the CoT also enhances security and privacy by enabling fine-grained access control and data management policies. The CoT has the potential to transform industries and services by enabling the centralized management and analysis of data generated by IoT devices, allowing for real-time decision-making and optimization [92, 96]. For instance, the CoT can be used to optimize the manufacturing process by collecting data from sensors on machines and analyzing this data in the cloud. This allows manufacturers to identify inefficiencies and improve the overall manufacturing process. For example, CoT can be used to monitor the performance of equipment and predict maintenance needs, reducing downtime and improving productivity. CoT can be used to optimize energy usage by monitoring energy consumption and using this data to make informed decisions about energy usage. For example, CoT can be used to monitor energy usage in a building and adjust temperature settings automatically to optimize energy usage.

2.4.1 Web of Things versus Internet of Things

The terms WoT and IoT are often used interchangeably, but they refer to two distinct concepts. The IoT focuses on the physical layer of connectivity and the collection of data, while the WoT adds an additional layer of web-based functionality and user interfaces, allowing users to interact with IoT devices in more natural and intuitive ways [93, 98]. The IoT refers to the network of physical devices, vehicles, buildings, and other objects that are embedded with sensors, software, and network connectivity, allowing them to collect and exchange data. The IoT enables the creation of new applications and services that can improve efficiency, reduce costs, and enhance the quality of life. The WoT, on the other hand, is a framework for connecting IoT devices to the web, allowing them to be accessed and controlled remotely via web-based applications. The WoT is an approach that extends the capabilities of the IoT by enabling IoT devices to communicate and interact with each other using standard web technologies and protocols. This enables devices to be connected to the internet and to each other in a standardized and secure way, which can facilitate data sharing and integration across different devices and services. The WoT is built on standard web technologies such as HTTP, HTML, and JavaScript, enabling developers to create web interfaces for IoT devices and integrate them with other web services. The WoT approach is based on the principles of the World Wide Web, which is an open, decentralized, and scalable system for sharing and accessing information over the internet. The WoT extends these principles to the realm of IoT devices, allowing devices to be accessed and controlled using standard web technologies such as HTTP, REST, and JavaScript Object Notation (JSON). Following are some of the key features and benefits of the WoT [93–95, 98].

1. **Standardization:** The WoT provides a standardized way for devices to communicate and interact with each other over the web. This enables interoperability between different devices and services, allowing data to be shared and integrated across different platforms and applications.
2. **Scalability:** The WoT is a scalable approach that can accommodate a wide range of devices and services. It can handle large volumes of data and can be extended to support new devices and services as they become available.
3. **Security:** The WoT provides a secure framework for connecting IoT devices to the web. It uses standard web security protocols such as HTTPS (Hypertext Transfer Protocol Secure) and OAuth (Open Authorization, an open standard for access delegation) to ensure that data is transmitted and stored securely.
4. **Accessibility:** The WoT enables devices to be accessed and controlled from anywhere, using any device with a web browser. This allows for remote monitoring and control of devices, which can be particularly useful in applications such as home automation and healthcare.

IoT and WoT are transforming the healthcare industry, enabling remote monitoring of patients and real-time data analytics [99, 100]. Wearable devices such as smartwatches and fitness trackers are used to monitor vital signs, while smart pill dispensers remind patients to take their medication on time. These devices can send alerts to healthcare providers in case of any abnormalities, enabling prompt medical attention. IoT and WoT are being used in industrial automation to improve productivity, efficiency, and safety. Smart sensors are used to monitor various parameters such as temperature, pressure, and humidity, which can be analyzed in real time to identify any anomalies or potential problems. This data can be used to optimize production processes and reduce downtime. IoT and WoT are being used in the transportation industry to improve safety, efficiency, and sustainability. Smart traffic management systems are used to monitor traffic flow and adjust traffic signals accordingly. GPS-enabled devices are used to track vehicles in real time, enabling logistics companies to optimize their delivery routes and reduce fuel consumption. In summary, the IoT is the underlying network of connected devices, while the WoT is a framework for connecting those devices to the web and enabling web-based interactions and functionality.

2.4.2 Architecture Standardization for WoT

The architecture for the WoT is a set of design principles and technical specifications that define how WoT devices and services can be integrated and interact with each other. Figure 2.8 shows the three-tiered architecture for WoT. The WoT architecture

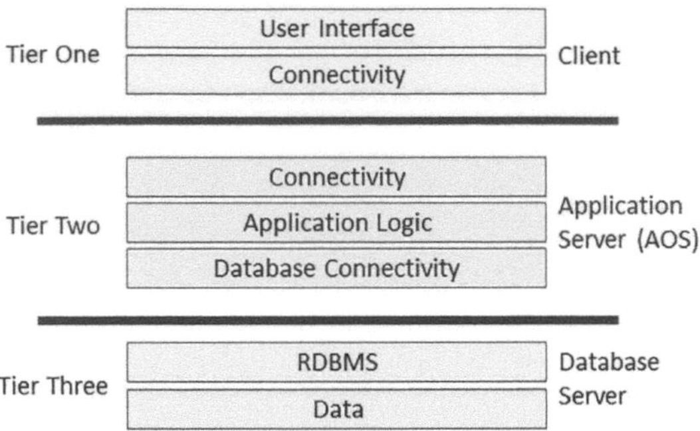

FIGURE 2.8 Three-tiered architecture for WoT.

is designed to enable seamless communication and interoperability between WoT devices and services over the web [96, 101, 102]. It provides a set of standardized interfaces, protocols, and data formats that allow developers to create and integrate WoT things into the larger web ecosystem. The WoT architecture is based on the key components such as WoT thing, WoT interface, WoT binding, WoT gateway, and WoT ecosystem [99, 100]. The WoT thing is a physical or virtual entity that represents a device or service in the WoT ecosystem. It exposes its functionality and data as a set of properties, actions, and events through a standardized interface called the Thing Description (TD). The TD is a JSON-LD (JSON for Linked Data) document that describes the WoT thing's capabilities, interactions, and metadata. The WoT interface is a set of abstract concepts and specifications that define how WoT Things can interact with each other over the web. It includes a set of protocols, data formats, and security mechanisms that enable seamless communication and interoperability between WoT devices and services. The WoT Interface is designed to be flexible, scalable, and modular, allowing for easy integration with existing web technologies. The WoT binding is a software component that bridges the gap between the WoT thing and the WoT interface. It translates the WoT thing's TD into a set of protocols and data formats that can be understood and processed by the WoT interface. The WoT binding also provides a set of APIs that allow developers to interact with the WoT thing and perform various operations, such as reading and writing properties, invoking actions, and subscribing to events. The WoT gateway is a software component that acts as an intermediary between the WoT things and the external world. It provides a unified interface that enables users to discover, monitor, and control WoT things from any device or platform. The WoT gateway also provides various value-added services, such as device management, data analytics, and security. The WoT ecosystem is a network of WoT things, WoT interfaces, WoT bindings, and WoT gateways that work together to create a seamless and interoperable web of devices and services. The WoT ecosystem is designed to be open, collaborative, and standards-based, allowing for easy integration with third-party systems and services.

The WoT is an emerging field and there are several standardization efforts underway to establish a common architecture for WoT systems. Following are some of the key standardization efforts.

1. **W3C WoT Architecture:** The World Wide Web Consortium (W3C) has launched a WoT Interest Group to develop a common architecture for WoT systems [103]. The WoT architecture includes three layers: the application layer, the protocol binding layer, and the TD layer. The TD layer provides a standardized way of describing the characteristics and capabilities of WoT devices, while the protocol binding layer defines how devices communicate with each other. Figure 2.9 shows the W3C WoT architecture.
2. **OASIS Open Connectivity Foundation (OCF):** OCF is a standards organization that is developing open standards for IoT and WoT systems [104]. OCF has developed a common data model that allows devices to communicate with each other, and a set of protocols that enable secure communication between devices.
3. **Industrial Internet Consortium (IIC):** The IIC is a global organization that is developing standards for industrial IoT and WoT systems. The IIC has developed a reference architecture that provides guidelines for designing and deploying IoT and WoT systems in industrial settings [105].
4. **OneM2M:** OneM2M is a global standards organization that is developing a common platform for IoT and WoT systems. OneM2M provides a standardized set of APIs and protocols for IoT devices to communicate with each other, and a set of security and privacy guidelines to protect sensitive data [106].

By establishing common standards and architectures for WoT systems, these standardization efforts aim to promote interoperability between different devices and systems, reduce development costs and complexity, and facilitate the deployment of large-scale IoT and WoT systems.

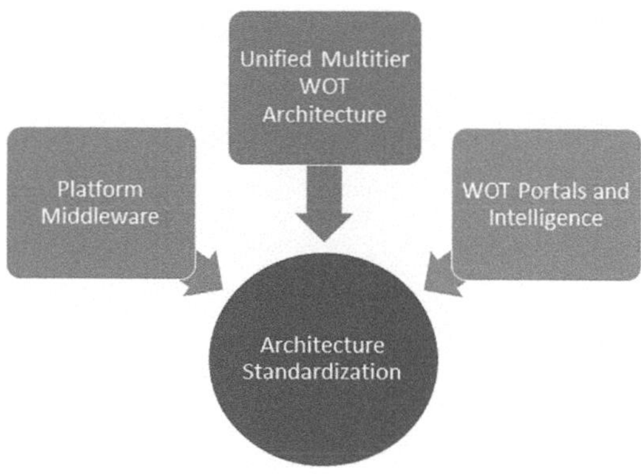

FIGURE 2.9 W3C WoT architecture.

2.4.3 Platform Middleware for WoT

Platform middleware for the WoT is a software layer that provides services and tools for managing and integrating WoT devices and applications. It serves as a bridge between the physical devices and the software applications that use them, enabling developers to build complex WoT systems more easily. Following are some of the key functions that platform middleware for WoT typically provides [93–95, 102].

1. **Device Management:** Platform middleware for WoT provides tools for managing and configuring WoT devices, such as registering and deregistering devices, updating firmware, and managing access control.
2. **Data Management:** Platform middleware for WoT provides services for collecting, storing, and analyzing WoT data, such as time series data, sensor readings, and other types of data generated by WoT devices.
3. **Protocol Translation:** Platform middleware for WoT provides services for translating data between different protocols and formats, enabling devices and applications to communicate with each other more easily.
4. **Security:** Platform middleware for WoT provides tools and services for securing WoT devices and applications, such as authentication, authorization, and encryption.
5. **Integration with Cloud Platforms:** Platform middleware for WoT provides services for integrating WoT devices and data with cloud platforms, such as Amazon Web Services, Microsoft Azure, and Google Cloud Platform.
6. **Analytics and Machine Learning:** Platform middleware for WoT provides tools and services for analyzing and processing WoT data using machine learning algorithms, enabling developers to build intelligent WoT applications and services.

Some examples of platform middleware for WoT include Eclipse IoT, Node-RED, and FIWARE. These platforms provide a range of tools and services for building and managing WoT systems and are designed to be flexible and adaptable to different use cases and deployment scenarios. Examples of platform middleware for WoT is shown in Figure 2.10.

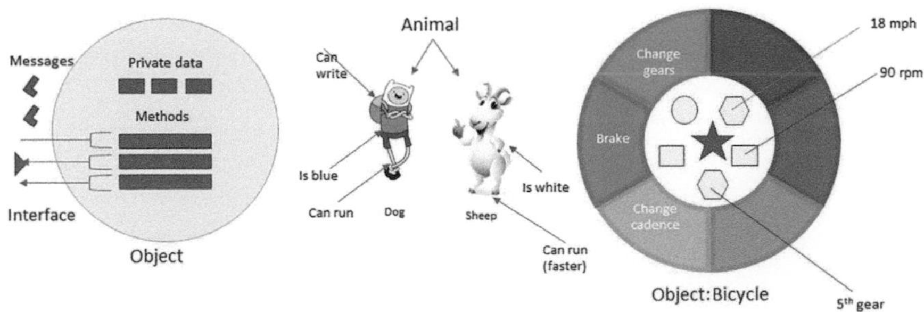

FIGURE 2.10 Examples of platform middleware for WoT.

2.4.4 Unified Multitier WoT Architecture

Unified Multitier WoT Architecture is a proposed framework for implementing WoT systems that aims to provide a comprehensive and standardized approach to WoT architecture. The architecture is designed to address the complexities and challenges of large-scale WoT deployments, including interoperability, security, and scalability [94, 107]. The architecture consists of four main tiers, each of which performs specific functions:

1. **Perception Tier:** The Perception Tier is responsible for collecting data from physical devices and sensors. It includes devices such as sensors, actuators, gateways, and edge computing nodes that collect and process data from the physical world.
2. **Network Tier:** The Network Tier is responsible for communicating and managing data between the Perception Tier and the Application Tier. It includes network protocols, gateways, and routers that ensure reliable communication between devices.
3. **Service Tier:** The Service Tier provides a set of services and APIs that enable access to WoT data and functionality. It includes servers, cloud platforms, and middleware that provide services such as data management, analytics, and security.
4. **Application Tier:** The Application Tier is responsible for providing end-user applications and interfaces for interacting with WoT data and functionality. It includes web and mobile applications, dashboards, and other user interfaces.

The Unified Multitier WoT Architecture is designed to be flexible and adaptable to different use cases and deployment scenarios. Figure 2.11 shows the Unified

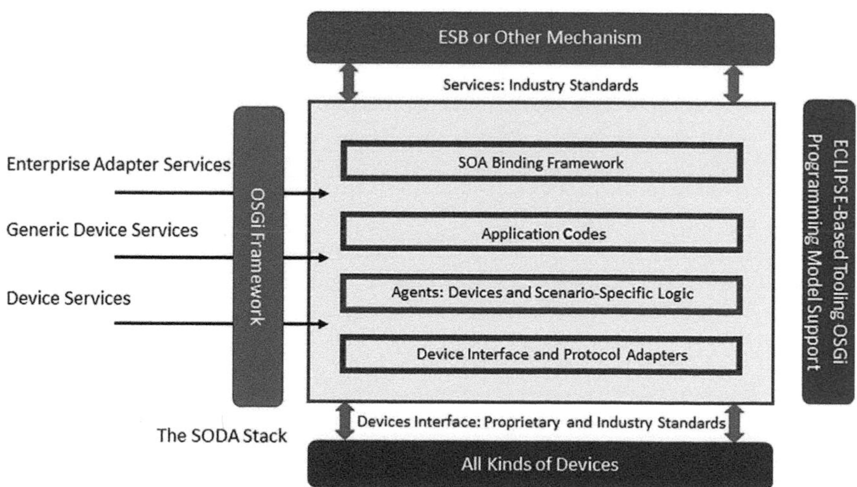

FIGURE 2.11 Unified Multitier WoT Architecture.

Multitier WoT Architecture. It is intended to provide a standardized approach to WoT architecture that promotes interoperability between different devices and systems, reduces development costs and complexity, and facilitates the deployment of large-scale WoT systems.

2.4.5 WoT Portals and Business Intelligence

WoT portals are web-based interfaces that allow users to interact with and control IoT devices and services. These portals can provide a centralized dashboard that aggregates data from various devices and presents it in an easy-to-understand format, allowing users to monitor and control their IoT systems in real time [94, 108]. Business intelligence (BI) refers to the tools, techniques, and processes used to analyze and extract insights from data. In the context of IoT, BI can be used to gain insights into the performance of IoT systems, identify patterns and trends, and make data-driven decisions to optimize operations and improve efficiencies. WoT portals can be integrated with BI tools to provide advanced analytics and data visualization capabilities. This allows users to analyze and visualize data from their IoT systems, identify key performance indicators (KPIs), and gain insights into how their systems are performing. By monitoring KPIs, users can identify areas for improvement, optimize processes, and reduce costs.

For example, a WoT portal for a smart building could be integrated with a BI tool to analyze data from various sensors and devices to identify patterns and trends in energy usage. This information could be used to optimize HVAC systems, reduce energy consumption, and improve building efficiency. Similarly, a WoT portal for a manufacturing plant could be integrated with a BI tool to monitor production metrics such as cycle times, throughput, and defect rates. This information could be used to identify bottlenecks, optimize production processes, and improve overall efficiency. Overall, WoT portals and BI tools can provide valuable insights and analytics for businesses and organizations looking to optimize their IoT systems and improve operational efficiencies [101, 108].

2.5 MULTIMEDIA INTERNET OF THINGS

Multimedia Internet of Things (MIoT) is a term used to describe the integration of multimedia content with IoT devices and applications. MIoT is based on the idea of adding multimedia capabilities, such as audio and video, to traditional IoT devices like sensors and actuators [109]. The main goal of MIoT is to enable new and innovative applications that can leverage multimedia content, such as video surveillance, augmented reality, and smart homes. By adding multimedia capabilities to IoT devices, MIoT can enable more immersive and interactive experiences for users and provide richer and more contextual data for applications. Figure 2.12 illustrates the MIoT in better view.

MIoT faces several technical challenges, including the need for high-bandwidth and low-latency networks to support multimedia content, as well as the need for new protocols and standards to support multimedia data formats and communication [109, 110]. Additionally, MIoT applications require more complex processing and

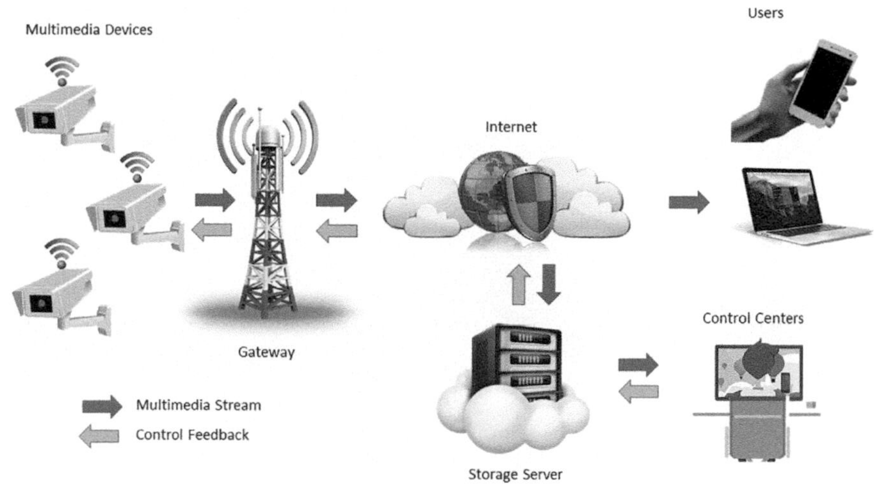

FIGURE 2.12 Multimedia Internet of Things.

storage capabilities, which may require more powerful and specialized hardware. To address these challenges, researchers and developers are exploring new technologies such as 5G networks, edge computing, and AI-powered multimedia processing. These technologies can enable MIoT applications to be more efficient, secure, and scalable. Overall, MIoT represents an exciting new frontier in the evolution of IoT and has the potential to transform many industries and applications, including entertainment, healthcare, transportation, and more.

2.6 INTERNET OF MOBILE THINGS

The Internet of Mobile Things (IoMT) is a term used to describe the integration of mobile devices into the IoT ecosystem [111]. IoMT refers to the connection and communication between mobile devices, such as smartphones and tablets, and IoT devices such as sensors, smart appliances, and other connected devices. Figure 2.13 portrays an overview of the IoMT.

IoMT allows for mobile devices to be used as remote controls for IoT devices, as well as for collecting and analyzing data from sensors and other IoT devices. This integration of mobile devices with IoT can enable new use cases and applications, such as smart homes, smart cities, and industrial IoT. Some of the benefits of IoMT include the following [111, 112].

1. **Greater Control:** With IoMT, mobile devices can act as a remote control for IoT devices, allowing users to manage and control IoT devices from anywhere.
2. **Improved Efficiency:** IoMT can help improve the efficiency of IoT devices and systems by enabling faster and more accurate data collection and analysis.

FIGURE 2.13 Overview of the Internet of Mobile Things (IoMT).

3. **Enhanced User Experience:** IoMT can provide a more seamless and intuitive user experience, as mobile devices are often more familiar and easier to use than traditional IoT interfaces.
4. **Increased Accessibility:** IoMT can make IoT devices more accessible and inclusive, as mobile devices are ubiquitous and often more affordable than dedicated IoT interfaces.

However, IoMT also poses some challenges, such as security and privacy concerns, as well as the need for new protocols and standards to support the integration of mobile devices with IoT devices [112]. Overall, IoMT represents an exciting new frontier in the evolution of IoT and has the potential to transform many industries and applications, including healthcare, transportation, and more.

2.7 INTERNET OF SHIPS

The Internet of Ships (IoS) is a term used to describe the integration of maritime vessels and shipping logistics with the IoT ecosystem [113]. IoS refers to the connection and communication between ships, ports, and other shipping infrastructure, as well as the data collected and analyzed from various IoT devices on board ships. Figure 2.14 illustrates an overview of the IoS, which can enable new use cases and applications in the shipping industry, such as predictive maintenance, real-time tracking of cargo and ships, and optimized route planning. It can also improve safety and security, as IoT devices can monitor and detect potential hazards and threats.

Some of the benefits of IoS include the following [113, 114].

1. **Improved Efficiency:** IoS can help improve the efficiency of shipping operations by providing real-time data on weather, traffic, and other factors that can affect shipping schedules and routes.

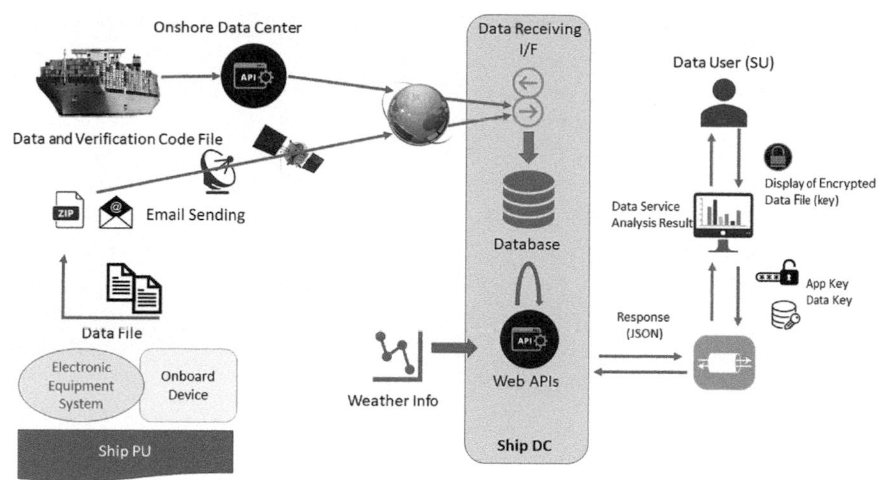

FIGURE 2.14 Overview of the Internet of Ships (IoS).

2. **Enhanced Safety:** IoS can help improve the safety of ships and crews by providing real-time monitoring and detection of potential hazards such as collisions, piracy, and environmental hazards.
3. **Better Decision-Making:** IoS can provide real-time data and analytics to shipping companies, enabling them to make more informed decisions about operations, routes, and logistics.
4. **Cost Savings:** IoS can help reduce costs by optimizing routes, reducing fuel consumption, and improving maintenance schedules.

However, IoS also poses some challenges, such as the need for standardized protocols and data formats, as well as the need for secure and reliable communication networks. Overall, IoS represents an exciting new frontier in the evolution of IoT and has the potential to transform the shipping industry and the way we move goods around the world.

2.8 INTERNET OF HYBRID ENERGY HARVESTING THINGS

The need for energy harvesting techniques for IoT arises from the fact that many IoT devices are designed to be deployed in remote or hard-to-reach locations where it is difficult or costly to replace batteries or provide wired power [6]. In addition, IoT devices are often required to operate for long periods of time without maintenance, which means that they need to have a reliable and self-sustaining power source. Energy harvesting techniques provide a way to capture and store energy from the environment to power IoT devices, so as to eliminate the need for regular battery replacements or wired power, which can be expensive and time-consuming [115, 116]. They also provide a more sustainable and environmentally friendly way to power IoT devices, as they can use renewable sources of energy such as solar or thermal energy. In addition to the cost and sustainability benefits, energy harvesting techniques also provide a greater degree of flexibility and autonomy for IoT devices. Devices can be deployed in more locations and with greater ease, and they can operate for longer periods of time without maintenance or intervention. This makes energy harvesting techniques an essential component of many IoT applications, particularly those that require remote sensing, monitoring, or control.

Internet of Hybrid Energy Harvesting Things (IoHEHT) is a term used to describe a system that combines energy harvesting techniques with traditional power sources to provide a reliable and sustainable power supply for IoT devices [117]. IoHEHT has the potential to enable a wide range of new IoT applications and use cases, particularly in remote or hard-to-reach locations where traditional power sources may not be available. It also has the potential to improve the sustainability and environmental impact of IoT systems by reducing reliance on disposable batteries or non-renewable power sources.

2.8.1 Concepts

The IoHEHT is a concept that combines two important trends in the IoT space: energy harvesting and hybridization (See Figure 2.15). IoHEHT refers to the idea of creating smart, connected devices that are powered by multiple energy sources, including technologies which harvest ambient energy, such as solar, kinetic, and thermal energy [116, 117]. IoHEHT is designed to address the limitations of both energy harvesting and traditional power sources. Energy harvesting techniques are often limited in their ability to provide consistent and reliable power, while traditional power sources such as batteries or wired connections may not be practical for certain IoT applications. By combining the two, IoHEHT provides a more robust and flexible power supply for IoT devices. For example, a device may use solar panels or thermoelectric generators to harvest energy from the environment during the day then

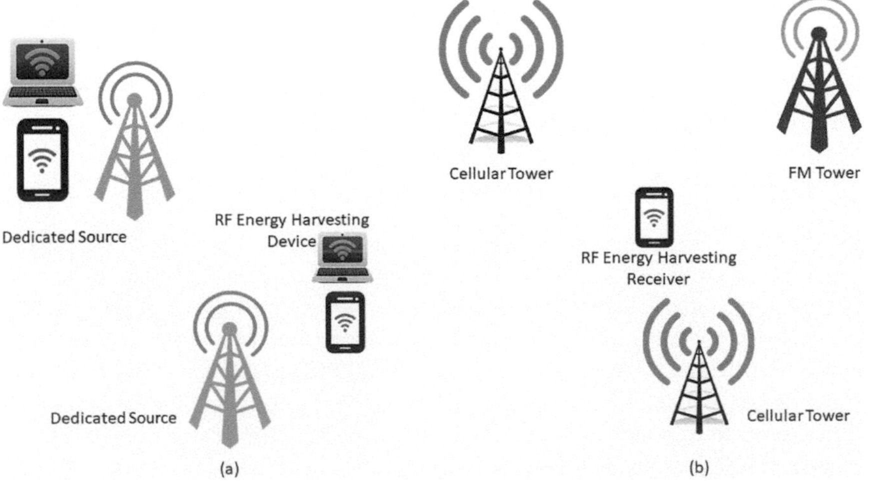

FIGURE 2.15 Overview of Internet of Hybrid Energy Harvesting Things (IoHEHT).

switch to battery power at night. Alternatively, a device may use energy harvesting to supplement the power provided by a wired connection, allowing it to operate for longer periods of time without interruption.

The goal of IoHEHT is to create self-sustaining, energy-efficient devices that can operate for extended periods of time without requiring a traditional power source. This is particularly important in remote or hard-to-reach locations where battery replacement or recharging is difficult or impossible. The IoHEHT ecosystem includes a variety of devices, sensors, and actuators that are designed to work together and communicate with each other through wireless networks such as Bluetooth, Zigbee, or Wi-Fi. These devices can be used in a wide range of applications, including environmental monitoring, smart agriculture, building automation, and healthcare. Some of the key benefits of IoHEHT include the following [115, 117, 118].

1. **Reduced Environmental Impact:** IoHEHT can help reduce the environmental impact of IoT devices by reducing the need for traditional power sources and batteries.
2. **Increased Reliability:** IoHEHT devices can operate for extended periods of time without requiring maintenance or battery replacement, increasing their reliability and reducing the risk of downtime.
3. **Cost Savings:** IoHEHT devices can help reduce costs by eliminating the need for frequent battery replacement and reducing the amount of energy consumed by traditional power sources.
4. **Improved Efficiency:** IoHEHT devices can be designed to operate more efficiently than traditional IoT devices by using multiple energy sources and optimizing their power usage.

Overall, IoHEHT represents an exciting new area of research and development in the IoT space, with the potential to transform the way we think about smart, connected devices and their power requirements.

2.8.2 Comparison of Existing Energy Harvesting Techniques

A comparison of some of the most common energy harvesting techniques used in IoT devices follows [115, 116, 119].

1. **Solar Energy Harvesting:** This technique is widely used in IoT devices because it is a reliable and efficient source of power. It is especially useful in applications that require continuous power, such as environmental sensors or surveillance cameras. However, it may not be as effective in areas with limited sunlight or during cloudy weather.
2. **Kinetic Energy Harvesting:** This technique involves capturing energy from motion or vibrations. It can be used in IoT devices such as wearable sensors or smart shoes. The energy generated from kinetic energy harvesting is typically small, so it may not be suitable for high-power devices.
3. **Thermal Energy Harvesting:** This technique involves capturing energy from temperature differences. It can be used in IoT devices that are located

in areas with significant temperature differences, such as industrial or manufacturing plants. However, thermal energy harvesting may not be as efficient in environments where the temperature differences are small.

4. **RF Energy Harvesting:** This technique involves capturing energy from radio frequency signals. It can be used in IoT devices that communicate wirelessly using protocols such as Wi-Fi or Bluetooth. RF energy harvesting can be effective in both indoor and outdoor environments, but the amount of energy that can be harvested is relatively small.
5. **Piezoelectric Energy Harvesting:** This technique involves capturing energy from mechanical stress or strain. It can be used in IoT devices that are subject to pressure or vibration, such as sensors placed on bridges or highways. However, the amount of energy that can be harvested is relatively small.

Overall, the choice of energy harvesting technique for an IoT device will depend on a variety of factors, including the power requirements of the device, the environmental conditions where the device will be used, and the availability of different types of energy sources.

2.8.3 Existing Energy Harvesting Techniques

There are several existing energy harvesting techniques that can be used for IoT systems. Following are some of the most commonly used ones [115, 120, 121].

1. **Solar Energy Harvesting:** This technique involves using solar panels to convert sunlight into electrical energy. The harvested energy can be used to power IoT devices or stored in batteries or supercapacitors. Solar energy harvesting is commonly used in outdoor IoT applications such as environmental monitoring, precision agriculture, and smart cities. For example, a smart irrigation system can use solar energy harvesting to power its sensors and controllers, which can help farmers to optimize water usage and increase crop yields.
2. **Thermal Energy Harvesting:** This technique involves using temperature differences to generate electrical energy. Thermoelectric generators are used to convert the temperature differences into electrical energy, which can then be used to power IoT devices. Thermal energy harvesting can be used in environments with temperature differences, such as industrial settings or building automation systems. For example, a smart building automation system can use thermal energy harvesting to power its sensors and controllers, which can help to optimize energy usage and reduce costs.
3. **Vibration Energy Harvesting:** This technique uses piezoelectric materials to convert mechanical vibrations into electrical energy. It can be used in environments where there is constant vibration, such as in machines or vehicles. For example, a wireless sensor network in a factory can use vibration energy harvesting to power its sensors and transmitters, which can help to monitor machine health and predict maintenance needs.

4. **RF Energy Harvesting:** This technique involves harvesting energy from radio waves that are present in the environment. The energy can be captured using antennas and rectifiers and then stored in capacitors or batteries. RF energy harvesting can be used in wireless IoT applications such as asset tracking or smart home systems. For example, a smart home system can use RF energy harvesting to power its wireless sensors and switches, which can help to automate lighting and climate control.
5. **Human Motion Energy Harvesting:** This technique uses piezoelectric materials to convert the mechanical energy from human motion into electrical energy. It can be used to power wearable IoT devices such as fitness trackers or smartwatches. For example, a smartwatch can use human motion energy harvesting to power its sensors and displays, which can help to track fitness metrics and provide notifications.
6. **Wind Energy Harvesting:** This technique involves using small wind turbines to generate electricity from wind energy. It can be used in locations where wind energy is abundant, such as in outdoor environments. For example, a remote monitoring system for environmental conditions can use wind energy harvesting to power its sensors and transmitters, which can help to collect and transmit data from remote locations.

These are just a few examples of how each energy harvesting technique can be used for IoT systems. The choice of technique depends on the specific application and environmental conditions. While energy harvesting techniques provide a promising solution to powering IoT devices, there are several challenges associated with them. For instance, energy harvesting techniques produce a limited amount of power, which may not be enough to power some IoT devices [121]. This is especially true for devices that require high power consumption or operate in low-light or low-temperature conditions. The energy output of energy harvesting devices can be unpredictable due to changing environmental conditions, which can make it difficult to plan and manage power usage. For example, solar panels may not produce energy on cloudy days, and vibration energy harvesting may not work if the machine or vehicle is not in use. Energy harvesting devices may need to be integrated with existing infrastructure, which can be challenging due to compatibility issues or space limitations. This is especially true for retrofitting energy harvesting technology into existing buildings or machines. The cost of energy harvesting devices and their installation can be high, which can make it difficult for some IoT applications to adopt this technology [115, 116]. The cost effectiveness of energy harvesting depends on the specific application and the expected lifespan of the IoT device. Energy harvesting devices may require periodic maintenance and calibration, which can add to the overall cost of the system. For example, solar panels may need to be cleaned to maintain their efficiency, and vibration energy harvesting systems may need to be recalibrated periodically to optimize their performance. Some energy harvesting techniques may have an impact on the environment. For example, wind turbines may have an impact on bird populations, and solar panels may require the use of toxic materials during manufacturing.

2.8.4 Hybrid Energy Harvesting

Hybrid energy harvesting refers to the use of multiple energy harvesting techniques in combination to increase the overall energy output and reliability of an IoT system. Hybrid energy harvesting is becoming increasingly popular in IoT applications, as it can provide a more robust and sustainable power source compared to using a single energy harvesting technique [122, 123]. In simpler words, it involves combining two or more energy harvesting techniques to power IoT devices. This approach allows for a more reliable and consistent power supply, as it takes advantage of multiple energy sources that may be available in the environment. For example, a hybrid energy harvesting system for an IoT device could combine solar energy harvesting with kinetic energy harvesting. During the day, the device could use solar energy to power its operations, while at night or during periods of low sunlight, the device could switch to using energy harvested from motion or vibrations. The use of hybrid energy harvesting can also help to address some of the challenges associated with individual energy harvesting techniques, such as the unpredictability of energy supply or limited power output. By combining multiple energy harvesting techniques, hybrid energy harvesting can provide a more robust and sustainable power source for IoT systems.

Another example could be a hybrid energy harvesting system that combines thermal and RF energy harvesting [124]. In this case, the device could use thermal energy harvested from temperature differences during the day, while at night or during periods of low temperature differences, it could switch to using energy harvested from radio frequency signals. The advantage of hybrid energy harvesting is that it allows for a more reliable and consistent power supply for IoT devices, as it takes advantage of multiple energy sources that may be available in the environment. Additionally, by combining multiple energy harvesting techniques, it may be possible to generate more power than using any single technique alone, thereby increasing the overall energy efficiency of the system [117, 121]. However, designing and implementing a hybrid energy harvesting system for IoT devices can be challenging, as it requires careful consideration of the power requirements of the device, the environmental conditions where the device will be used, and the availability and compatibility of different energy sources. Another example of hybrid energy harvesting is the combination of vibration and thermal energy harvesting techniques. In an industrial setting, a machine may generate both mechanical vibration and heat. A hybrid energy harvesting system can use vibration and thermal energy harvesting techniques to generate energy from both sources, which can help to power sensors and transmitters used for machine monitoring and maintenance.

REFERENCES

[1] S. Dhanasekar, E. Ilankhatir, S. Divakar, and D. Vennila, "A Survey on IoT Architecture," *Int. J. Adv. Sci. Res. Dev.*, vol. 6, no. 4, 2019, doi: 10.26836/ijasrd/2019/v6/i4/60402.

[2] M. Chiang and T. Zhang, "Fog and IoT: An Overview of Research Opportunities," *IEEE Internet Things J.*, vol. 3, no. 6, 2016, doi: 10.1109/JIOT.2016.2584538.

[3] A. Markus, M. Biro, G. Kecskemeti, and A. Kertesz, "Actuator Behaviour Modelling in IoT-Fog-Cloud Simulation," *PeerJ Comput. Sci.*, vol. 7, 2021, doi: 10.7717/PEERJ-CS.651.

[4] J. Horalek and F. Holik, "Design and Realization of the Intelligent System for Identification of the IoT Devices," *J. Telecommun. Electron. Comput. Eng.*, vol. 10, no. 1–8, 2018.
[5] A. Kolah, "Internet of Things, for Things and by Things," *EDPACS*, vol. 59, no. 1, 2019, doi: 10.1080/07366981.2019.1565338.
[6] J. Khan and M. Yuce, *Internet of Things (IoT) Systems and Applications*, Jenny Stanford Publishing, New York, United States, 2019, doi: https://doi.org/10.1201/9780429399084.
[7] M. Frustaci, P. Pace, G. Aloi, and G. Fortino, "Evaluating Critical Security Issues of the IoT World: Present and Future Challenges," *IEEE Internet Things J.*, vol. 5, no. 4, 2018, doi: 10.1109/JIOT.2017.2767291.
[8] P. P. Ray, "A Survey of IoT Cloud Platforms," *Futur. Comput. Inform. J.*, vol. 1, no. 1–2, 2016, doi: 10.1016/j.fcij.2017.02.001.
[9] V. Chang and C. Martin, "An Industrial IoT Sensor System for High-Temperature Measurement," *Comput. Electr. Eng.*, vol. 95, 2021, doi: 10.1016/j.compeleceng.2021.107439.
[10] R. Anandanatarajan, U. Mangalanathan, and U. Gandhi, "Linearization of Temperature Sensors (K-Type Thermocouple) Using Polynomial Non-Linear Regression Technique and an IoT-Based Data Logger Interface," *Exp. Tech.*, 2022, doi: 10.1007/s40799-022-00599-w.
[11] Y. Zhang, X. Zhao, G. Wang, Q. Yan, S. Li, and Y. Liu, "Researching a Simulation of Real-Time Nonlinear Dynamical Systems for Digital Power Grids in Massive IoT," *Wirel. Commun. Mob. Comput.*, vol. 2022, 2022, doi: 10.1155/2022/7153456.
[12] K. Priya Dharshini, D. Gopalakrishnan, C. K. Shankar, and R. Ramya, "A Survey on IoT Applications in Smart Cities," in *EAI/Springer Innovations in Communication and Computing*, Springer Cham, Germany, 2022, doi: 10.1007/978-3-030-66607-1_9.
[13] S. K. Goudos, P. I. Dallas, S. Chatziefthymiou, and S. Kyriazakos, "A Survey of IoT Key Enabling and Future Technologies: 5G, Mobile IoT, Sematic Web and Applications," *Wirel. Pers. Commun.*, vol. 97, no. 2, 2017, doi: 10.1007/s11277-017-4647-8.
[14] D. Tiwari, B. S. Bhati, B. Nagpal, S. Sankhwar, and F. Al-Turjman, "An Enhanced Intelligent Model: To Protect Marine IoT Sensor Environment Using Ensemble Machine Learning Approach," *Ocean Eng.*, vol. 242, 2021, doi: 10.1016/j.oceaneng.2021.110180.
[15] J. D. Stevens, D. Murray, D. Diepeveen, and D. Toohey, "Adaptalight: An Inexpensive PAR Sensor System for Daylight Harvesting in a Micro Indoor Smart Hydroponic System," *Horticulturae*, vol. 8, no. 2, 2022, doi: 10.3390/horticulturae8020105.
[16] J. Trevathan, W. Read, and A. Sattar, "Implementation and Calibration of an IoT Light Attenuation Turbidity Sensor," *Internet Things (Netherlands)*, vol. 19, 2022, doi: 10.1016/j.iot.2022.100576.
[17] N. B. Mahesa, "Rancangan Atap Otomatis Menggunakan Energi Surya Dengan Sensor LDR Berbasis IoT," *JATISI (Jurnal Tek. Inform. dan Sist. Informasi)*, vol. 8, no. 1, 2021, doi: 10.35957/jatisi.v8i1.634.
[18] Z. Deng, Y. Cao, X. Zhou, Y. Yi, Y. Jiang, and I. You, "Toward Efficient Image Recognition in Sensor-Based IoT: A Weight Initialization Optimizing Method for CNN Based on RGB Influence Proportion," *Sensors (Switzerland)*, vol. 20, no. 10, 2020, doi: 10.3390/s20102866.
[19] K. D. Choo *et al.*, "Energy-Efficient Motion-Triggered IoT CMOS Image Sensor with Capacitor Array-Assisted Charge-Injection SAR ADC," *IEEE J. Solid-State Circuits*, vol. 54, no. 11, 2019, doi: 10.1109/JSSC.2019.2939664.
[20] G. Sasi, "Motion Detection Using Passive Infrared Sensor Using IoT," *J. Phys. Conf. Ser.*, 2021, doi: 10.1088/1742-6596/1717/1/012067.
[21] Q. Zhang *et al.*, "Wearable Triboelectric Sensors Enabled Gait Analysis and Waist Motion Capture for IoT-Based Smart Healthcare Applications," *Adv. Sci.*, vol. 9, no. 4, 2022, doi: 10.1002/advs.202103694.
[22] K. Koptyra and M. R. Ogiela, "Steganography in IoT: Information Hiding with APDS-9960 Proximity and Gestures Sensor," *Sensors*, vol. 22, no. 7, 2022, doi: 10.3390/s22072612.

[23] T. D. Nguyen, T. Kim, J. Noh, H. Phung, G. Kang, and H. R. Choi, "Skin-Type Proximity Sensor by Using the Change of Electromagnetic Field," *IEEE Trans. Ind. Electron.*, vol. 68, no. 3, 2021, doi: 10.1109/TIE.2020.2975503.

[24] S. J. Moon, J. Kim, H. Yim, Y. Kim, and H. R. Choi, "Real-Time Obstacle Avoidance Using Dual-Type Proximity Sensor for Safe Human-Robot Interaction," *IEEE Robot. Autom. Lett.*, vol. 6, no. 4, 2021, doi: 10.1109/LRA.2021.3102318.

[25] M. Iwasaki *et al.*, "Capacitive-Type Pressure-Mapping Sensor for Measuring Bite Force," *Int. J. Environ. Res. Public Health*, vol. 19, no. 3, 2022, doi: 10.3390/ijerph19031273.

[26] R. Hudec, S. Matúška, P. Kamencay, and M. Benco, "A Smart IoT System for Detecting the Position of a Lying Person Using a Novel Textile Pressure Sensor," *Sensors (Switzerland)*, vol. 21, no. 1, 2021, doi: 10.3390/s21010206.

[27] T. Sangeetha, D. Kumutha, M. D. Bharathi, and R. Surendran, "Smart Mattress Integrated with Pressure Sensor and IoT Functions for Sleep Apnea Detection," *Meas. Sens.*, vol. 24, 2022, doi: 10.1016/j.measen.2022.100450.

[28] A. T. Alreshaid, J. G. Hester, W. Su, Y. Fang, and M. M. Tentzeris, "Review—Ink-Jet Printed Wireless Liquid and Gas Sensors for IoT, SmartAg and Smart City Applications," *J. Electrochem. Soc.*, vol. 165, no. 10, 2018, doi: 10.1149/2.0341810jes.

[29] S. H. Cho, J. M. Suh, T. H. Eom, T. Kim, and H. W. Jang, "Colorimetric Sensors for Toxic and Hazardous Gas Detection: A Review," *Electron. Mater. Lett.*, vol. 17, no. 1, 2021, doi: 10.1007/s13391-020-00254-9.

[30] J. B. A. Gomes, J. J. P. C. Rodrigues, R. A. L. Rabêlo, N. Kumar, and S. Kozlov, "IoT-Enabled Gas Sensors: Technologies, Applications, and Opportunities," *J. Sens. Actuator Netw.*, vol. 8, no. 4, 2019, doi: 10.3390/jsan8040057.

[31] F. Al-Turjman and I. Baali, "Machine Learning for Wearable IoT-Based Applications: A Survey," *Trans. Emerg. Telecommun. Technol.*, vol. 33, no. 8, 2022, doi: 10.1002/ett.3635.

[32] N. Bansal, "IoT Applications in Smart Homes," in *Designing Internet of Things Solutions with Microsoft Azure*, Springer International Publishing (Apress Berkeley, CA), New York, United States, 2020, doi: 10.1007/978-1-4842-6041-8_8.

[33] S. K. Datta, C. Bonnet, and N. Nikaein, "An IoT Gateway Centric Architecture to Provide Novel M2M Services," in *2014 IEEE World Forum on Internet of Things, WF-IoT 2014*, 2014, doi: 10.1109/WF-IoT.2014.6803221.

[34] K. Das and S. Moulik, "BOSS: Bargaining-Based Optimal Slot Sharing in IEEE 802.15.6-based Wireless Body Area Networks," *IEEE Internet Things J.*, 2021, doi: 10.1109/JIOT.2021.3122819.

[35] X. Zhou, "Tracking and Analysing Error in Feedback Linearized Motion Trajectory of Hydraulic Actuator Based on the Internet of Things," *Mob. Inf. Syst.*, vol. 2022, 2022, doi: 10.1155/2022/2195498.

[36] V. Zhidchenko and H. Handroos, "A Method for the Camera-Less Remote Surveillance on Hydraulically Actuated Heavy Equipment Using IoT Environment," *Int. J. Fluid Power*, vol. 23, no. 3, 2022, doi: 10.13052/ijfp1439-9776.2335.

[37] J. Kustija, D. L. Hakim, and H. Hasbullah, "Development of Internet of Things (IoT) Based Learning Media in Efforts to Improve Student Skills at the Industrial Revolution Era 4.0," in *IOP Conference Series: Materials Science and Engineering*, 2020, doi: 10.1088/1757-899X/830/4/042051.

[38] C. L. Wang and J. C. Renn, "Study on the Motion Control of Pneumatic Actuator Via Wireless Bluetooth Communication," in *Proceedings of 4th IEEE International Conference on Applied System Innovation 2018, ICASI 2018*, 2018, doi: 10.1109/ICASI.2018.8394325.

[39] M. Shirvanimoghaddam *et al.*, "Towards a Green and Self-Powered Internet of Things Using Piezoelectric Energy Harvesting," *IEEE Access*, vol. 7, 2019, doi: 10.1109/ACCESS.2019.2928523.

[40] S. Farhangdoust, G. E. Georgeson, and J.-B. Ihn, "MetaSub Piezoelectric Energy Harvesting," *Sensors*, vol. 22, no. 5, 2020, doi: 10.1117/12.2559331.

[41] J. L. Chen, M. C. Chen, C. W. Chen, and Y. C. Chang, "Architecture Design and Performance Evaluation of RFID Object Tracking Systems," *Comput. Commun.*, vol. 30, no. 9, 2007, doi: 10.1016/j.comcom.2007.04.003.

[42] T. Dahariya, A. Naik, and M. Chandra, "Study on RFID, Architecture, Service and Privacy with Limitation," *Int. J. Comput. Sci. Trends Technol.*, vol. 2, no. 6, 2014.

[43] N. Khalid, R. Mirzavand, H. Saghlatoon, M. M. Honari, and P. Mousavi, "A Three-Port Zero-Power RFID Sensor Architecture for IoT Applications," *IEEE Access*, vol. 8, 2020, doi: 10.1109/ACCESS.2020.2985711.

[44] F. Lin *et al.*, "The Design of a Lightweight RFID Middleware," *Int. J. Eng. Bus. Manag.*, vol. 1, 2009, doi: 10.5772/6776.

[45] I. Abad, C. Cerrada, J. A. Cerrada, R. Heradio, and E. Valero, "Managing RFID Sensors Networks with A General purpose RFID Middleware," *Sensors (Switzerland)*, vol. 12, no. 6, 2012, doi: 10.3390/s120607719.

[46] V. Krotov and I. Junglas, "RFID as a Disruptive Innovation," *J. Theor. Appl. Electron. Commer. Res.*, vol. 3, no. 2, 2008, doi: 10.4067/S0718-18762008000100005.

[47] G. Jezic, *Agents and Multi-Agent Systems: Technologies and Applications* Springer, Singapore, 2020. doi: https://doi.org/10.1007/978-981-13-8679-4.

[48] D. Ergenç, J. Rak, and M. Fischer, "Service-Based Resilience for Embedded IoT Networks," in *Proceedings—50th Annual IEEE/IFIP International Conference on Dependable Systems and Networks, DSN 2020*, 2020, doi: 10.1109/DSN48063.2020.00066.

[49] B. J. Praveena, N. Arivazhagan, and P. V. P. Reddy, "Blockchain Based Sensor System Design For Embedded IoT," *J. Comput. Inf. Syst.*, 2023, doi: 10.1080/08874417.2022.2155266.

[50] H. Taleb, A. Nasser, G. Andricux, N. Charara, and E. Motta Cruz, "Wireless Technologies, Medical Applications and Future Challenges in WBAN: A Survey," *Wirel. Netw.*, vol. 27, no. 8, 2021, doi: 10.1007/s11276-021-02780-2.

[51] A. V. Baidiuk, "The Use of Radio Frequency Identification Technologies for Preventing the Spread of Coronavirus," *Electron. Acoust. Eng.*, vol. 4, no. 3, 2021, doi: 10.20535/2617-0965.eae.228210.

[52] D. Pishva, "IoT: Their Conveniences, Security Challenges and Possible Solutions," *Adv. Sci. Technol. Eng. Syst.*, vol. 2, no. 3, 2017, doi: 10.25046/aj0203153.

[53] A. Ekramifard, H. Amintoosi, and A. H. Seno, "A Systematic Literature Review on Blockchain-Based Solutions for IoT Security," in *Lecture Notes on Data Engineering and Communications Technologies*, Springer Science and Business Media Deutschland GmbH, Berlin, Germany, 2020, doi: 10.1007/978-3-030-37309-2_25.

[54] M. Dave, J. Doshi, and H. Arolkar, "MQTT-CoAP Interconnector: IoT Interoperability Solution for Application Layer Protocols," in *Proceedings of the 4th International Conference on IoT in Social, Mobile, Analytics and Cloud, ISMAC 2020*, 2020, doi: 10.1109/I-SMAC49090.2020.9243377.

[55] B. Mishra and A. Kertesz, "The Use of MQTT in M2M and IoT Systems: A Survey," *IEEE Access*, vol. 8, 2020, doi: 10.1109/ACCESS.2020.3035849.

[56] Devasis Pradhan and Hla Myo Tun, "Security Challenges: M2M Communication in IoT," *J. Electr. Eng. Autom.*, vol. 4, no. 3, 2022, doi: 10.36548/jeea.2022.3.006.

[57] C. Dobrin, "Industry 4.0, M2m, Iot&S—All Equal?," *ACTA Univ. Cibiniensis*, vol. 64, no. 1, 2014, doi: 10.2478/aucts-2014-0008.

[58] S. Malik, N. Tabassum, M. Saleem, T. Alyas, M. Hamid, and U. Farooq, "Cloud-IoT Integration: Cloud Service Framework for m2m Communication," *Intell. Autom. Soft Comput.*, vol. 31, no. 1, 2022, doi: 10.32604/IASC.2022.019837.

[59] R. Djehaiche, S. Aidel, A. Sawalmeh, N. Saeed, and A. H. Alenezi, "Adaptive Control of IoT/M2M Devices in Smart Buildings Using Heterogeneous Wireless Networks," *IEEE Sens. J.*, 2023, doi: 10.1109/JSEN.2023.3247007.

[60] B. S. Chaudhari and M. Zennaro, *LPWAN Technologies for IoT and M2M Applications*, Elsevier, Amsterdam, Netherlands, pp. 1–424, 2020, doi: 10.1016/B978-0-12-818880-4.00020-X.

[61] N. Scarpato, A. Pieroni, L. Di Nunzio, and F. Fallucchi, "E-health-IoT Universe: A review," *Int. J. Adv. Sci. Eng. Inf. Technol.*, vol. 7, no. 6, 2017, doi: 10.18517/ijaseit.7.6.4467.

[62] W. E. Zhang *et al.*, "The 10 Research Topics in the Internet of Things," in *Proceedings—2020 IEEE 6th International Conference on Collaboration and Internet Computing, CIC 2020*, 2020, doi: 10.1109/CIC50333.2020.00015.

[63] B.-S. P. Lin, "Toward an AI-Enabled SDN-based 5G & IoT Network," *Netw. Commun. Technol.*, vol. 5, no. 2, 2020, doi: 10.5539/nct.v5n2p7.

[64] W. Iqbal, H. Abbas, M. Daneshmand, B. Rauf, and Y. A. Bangash, "An In-Depth Analysis of IoT Security Requirements, Challenges, and Their Countermeasures via Software-Defined Security," *IEEE Internet Things J.*, vol. 7, no. 10, 2020, doi: 10.1109/JIOT.2020.2997651.

[65] F. Tang, Z. M. Fadlullah, B. Mao, and N. Kato, "An Intelligent Traffic Load Prediction-Based Adaptive Channel Assignment Algorithm in SDN-IoT: A Deep Learning Approach," *IEEE Internet Things J.*, vol. 5, no. 6, 2018, doi: 10.1109/JIOT.2018.2838574.

[66] S. S. Jazaeri, S. Jabbehdari, P. Asghari, and H. Haj Seyyed Javadi, "Edge Computing in SDN-IoT Networks: A Systematic Review of Issues, Challenges and Solutions," *Cluster Comput.*, vol. 24, no. 4, 2021, doi: 10.1007/s10586-021-03311-6.

[67] K. H. Manguri and S. M. Omer, "SDN for IoT Environment: A Survey and Research Challenges," *ITM Web Conf.*, vol. 42, 2022, doi: 10.1051/itmconf/20224201005.

[68] S. R. Jondhale, R. Maheswar, and J. Lloret, "Fundamentals of Wireless Sensor Networks," in *EAI/Springer Innovations in Communication and Computing*, Springer, Cham, Switzerland AG, 2022, doi: 10.1007/978-3-030-74061-0_1.

[69] S. R. Jondhale, V. Mohan, B. B. Sharma, J. Lloret, and S. V. Athawale, "Support Vector Regression for Mobile Target Localization in Indoor Environments," *Sensors*, vol. 22, no. 1, 2022, doi: 10.3390/s22010358.

[70] S. J. Hsiao and W. T. Sung, "Employing Blockchain Technology to Strengthen Security of Wireless Sensor Networks," *IEEE Access*, vol. 9, 2021, doi: 10.1109/ACCESS.2021.3079708.

[71] S. R. Jondhale, M. Sharma, R. Maheswar, R. Shubair, and A. Shelke, "Comparison of Neural Network Training Functions for RSSI Based Indoor Localization Problem in WSN," in *Advances in Intelligent Systems and Computing*, Springer, Vol. 1132, pp. 112–133, 2020, doi: 10.1007/978-3-030-40305-8_7.

[72] R. Olfati-Saber and P. Jalalkamali, "Coupled Distributed Estimation and Control for Mobile Sensor Networks," *IEEE Trans. Automat. Contr.*, vol. 57, no. 10, 2012, doi: 10.1109/TAC.2012.2190184.

[73] K. H. Yeh, "A Secure IoT-Based Healthcare System with Body Sensor Networks," *IEEE Access*, vol. 4, 2016, doi: 10.1109/ACCESS.2016.2638038.

[74] J. Yang, C. Poellabauer, P. Mitra, and C. Neubecker, "Beyond Beaconing: Emerging Applications and Challenges of BLE," *Ad Hoc Netw.*, vol. 97, 2020, doi: 10.1016/j.adhoc.2019.102015.

[75] J. Yang, A. Sharma, and R. Kumar, "IoT-Based Framework for Smart Agriculture," *Int. J. Agric. Environ. Inf. Syst.*, vol. 12, no. 2, 2021, doi: 10.4018/IJAEIS.20210401.oa1.

[76] J. P. Molla *et al.*, "Energy Efficient Received Signal Strength-Based Target Localization and Tracking Using Support Vector Regression," *Energies*, vol. 16, no. 1, 2023, doi: 10.3390/en16010555.

[77] W. Osamy, A. M. Khedr, A. Salim, A. A. El-Sawy, M. Alreshoodi, and I. Alsukayti, "Recent Advances and Future Prospects of Using AI Solutions for Security, Fault Tolerance, and QoS Challenges in WSNs," *Electron.*, vol. 11, no. 24, 2022, doi: 10.3390/electronics11244122.

[78] I. F. Akyildiz, W. Su, Y. Sankarasubramaniam, and E. Cayirci, "A Survey on Sensor Networks," *IEEE Commun. Mag.*, vol. 40, no. 8, 2002, doi: 10.1109/MCOM.2002.1024422.
[79] N. Xu, "A Survey of Sensor Network Applications," *IEEE Commun. Mag.*, vol. 40, no. 8, 2002.
[80] V. Kumar, "Selecting IoT Connectivity Protocols for Rural Development Applications," *J. Mob. Multimed.*, vol. 17, no. 1–3, 2021, doi: 10.13052/jmm1550-4646.171323.
[81] L. K. Ketshabetswe, A. M. Zungeru, M. Mangwala, J. M. Chuma, and B. Sigweni, "Communication Protocols for Wireless Sensor Networks: A Survey and Comparison," *Heliyon*, vol. 5, no. 5, 2019, doi: 10.1016/j.heliyon.2019.e01591.
[82] Maitri Rashmikant Sakarvadia, "Network Topologies in Wireless Sensor Networks : A Review," *An Int. Open Access*, vol. 10, May 2022.
[83] Z. Zhang, H. Zhao, J. Zhu, and D. Li, "Research on Wireless Sensor Networks Topology Models," *J. Softw. Eng. Appl.*, vol. 03, no. 12, 2010, doi: 10.4236/jsea.2010.312137.
[84] M. López, A. Peinado, and A. Ortiz, "An Extensive Validation of a SIR Epidemic Model to Study the Propagation of Jamming Attacks Against IoT Wireless Networks," *Comput. Netw.*, vol. 165, 2019, doi: 10.1016/j.comnet.2019.106945.
[85] Devika G., A. G. Karegowda, and Ramesh D., "Survey of WSN Routing Protocols," *Int. J. Appl. Evol. Comput.*, vol. 11, no. 1, 2020, doi: 10.4018/ijaec.2020010103.
[86] J. Kaur, T. Kaur, and K. Kaushal, "Survey on WSN Routing Protocols," *Int. J. Comput. Appl.*, vol. 109, no. 10, 2015, doi: 10.5120/19226-0924.
[87] A. Čolaković and M. Hadžialić, "Internet of Things (IoT): A Review of Enabling Technologies, Challenges, and Open Research Issues," *Comput. Netw.*, vol. 144, 2018, doi: 10.1016/j.comnet.2018.07.017.
[88] P. Morillo, J. M. Orduña, M. Fernández, and I. García-Pereira, "Comparison of WSN and IoT Approaches for a Real-Time Monitoring System of Meal Distribution Trolleys: A Case Study," *Futur. Gener. Comput. Syst.*, vol. 87, 2018, doi: 10.1016/j.future.2018.01.032.
[89] C. A. Oroza, J. A. Giraldo, M. Parvania, and T. Watteyne, "Wireless-Sensor Network Topology Optimization in Complex Terrain: A Bayesian Approach," *IEEE Internet Things J.*, vol. 8, no. 24, 2021, doi: 10.1109/JIOT.2021.3082168.
[90] W. Tao, L. Zhao, G. Wang, and R. Liang, "Review of the Internet of Things Communication Technologies in Smart Agriculture and Challenges," *Comput. Electron. Agric.*, vol. 189, 2021, doi: 10.1016/j.compag.2021.106352.
[91] M. Torky and A. E. Hassanein, "Integrating blockchain and the internet of things in precision agriculture: Analysis, opportunities, and challenges," *Comput. Electron. Agric.*, vol. 178, 2020, doi: 10.1016/j.compag.2020.105476.
[92] J. Angelin Jebamalar and A. Sasi Kumar, "A Review on the Integration of Cloud Computing and Internet of Things," *Int. J. Eng. Technol.*, vol. 7, no. 2.33 Special Issue 33, 2018, doi: 10.14419/ijet.v7i2.33.15475.
[93] L. Sciullo, L. Gigli, F. Montori, A. Trotta, and M. Di Felice, "A Survey on the Web of Things," *IEEE Access*, vol. 10, 2022, doi: 10.1109/ACCESS.2022.3171575.
[94] D. Thakker, P. Patel, M. I. Ali, and T. Shah, "Semantic Web of Things for Industry 4.0," *Semant. Web.*, vol. 11, no. 6, 2020, doi: 10.3233/SW-200407.
[95] R. Sardar and T. Anees, "Web of Things: Security Challenges and Mechanisms," *IEEE Access*, vol. 9, 2021, doi: 10.1109/ACCESS.2021.3057655.
[96] F. Alhaidari, A. Rahman, and R. Zagrouba, "Cloud of Things: Architecture, Applications and Challenges," *J. Ambient. Intell. Humaniz. Comput.*, vol. 14, pp. 5957–5975, 2023, doi: 10.1007/s12652-020-02448-3.
[97] D. C. Nguyen, P. N. Pathirana, M. Ding, and A. Seneviratne, "Integration of Blockchain and Cloud of Things: Architecture, Applications and Challenges," *IEEE Commun. Surv. Tutor.*, vol. 22, no. 4, 2020, doi: 10.1109/COMST.2020.3020092.

[98] P. Bajpai, A. K. Sood, and R. J. Enbody, "The Art of Mapping IoT Devices in Networks," *Netw. Secur.*, vol. 2018, no. 4, 2018, doi: 10.1016/S1353-4858(18)30033-3.

[99] M. Noura, A. Gyrard, S. Heil, and M. Gaedke, "Automatic Knowledge Extraction to Build Semantic Web of Things Applications," *IEEE Internet Things J.*, vol. 6, no. 5, 2019, doi: 10.1109/JIOT.2019.2918327.

[100] A. Krishna, M. Le Pallec, R. Mateescu, and G. Salaün, "Design and Deployment of Expressive and Correct Web of Things Applications," *ACM Trans. Internet Things*, vol. 3, no. 1, 2022, doi: 10.1145/3475964.

[101] Q. Xiaofeng, L. Wenmao, G. Teng, H. Xinxin, W. Xutao, and C. Pengcheng, "WoT/SDN : Web of Things Architecture Using SDN," *China Commun.*, vol. 12, no. 11, 2015, doi: 10.1109/CC.2015.7366240.

[102] O. Novo and M. Di Francesco, "Semantic Interoperability in the IoT: Extending the Web of Things Architecture," *ACM Trans. Internet Things*, vol. 1, no. 1, 2020.

[103] M. Lagally and M. McCool, "IoT Interoperability with W3C Web of Things," in *Proceedings—IEEE Consumer Communications and Networking Conference, CCNC*, 2022, doi: 10.1109/CCNC49033.2022.9700546.

[104] W. Jin and D. Kim, "Resource Management Based on OCF for Device Self-Registration and Status Detection in IoT Networks," *Electron.*, vol. 8, no. 3, 2019, doi: 10.3390/electronics8030311.

[105] V. Tsiatsis, J. Höller, C. Mulligan, S. Karnouskos, and D. Boyle, *Internet of Things: Technologies and Applications for a New Age of Intelligence*, 2018, doi: 10.1016/C2017-0-00369-5.

[106] G. Kim, S. Kang, J. Park, and K. Chung, "An MQTT-Based Context-Aware Autonomous System in oneM2M Architecture," *IEEE Internet Things J.*, vol. 6, no. 5, 2019, doi: 10.1109/JIOT.2019.2919971.

[107] I. Nadim, Y. El Ghayam, and A. Sadiq, "Semantic Annotation of Web of Things Using Entity Linking," *Int. J. Bus. Anal.*, vol. 7, no. 4, 2020, doi: 10.4018/IJBAN.2020100101.

[108] A. Oliver *et al.*, "ACA Crystallographic Literacy: A Web Portal for all Things Crystallographic, by Crystallographers," *Acta Crystallogr. Sect. A Found. Adv.*, vol. 78, no. a1, 2022, doi: 10.1107/s2053273322098783.

[109] A. Nauman, Y. A. Qadri, M. Amjad, Y. Bin Zikria, M. K. Afzal, and S. W. Kim, "Multimedia Internet of Things: A Comprehensive Survey," *IEEE Access*, vol. 8, 2020, doi: 10.1109/ACCESS.2020.2964280.

[110] X. Liu, L. Wu, C. Dai, and H. C. Chao, "Compressing CNNs Using Multilevel Filter Pruning for the Edge Nodes of Multimedia Internet of Things," *IEEE Internet Things J.*, vol. 8, no. 14, 2021, doi: 10.1109/JIOT.2021.3052016.

[111] J. Yue and M. Xiao, "Coding for Distributed Fog Computing in Internet of Mobile Things," *IEEE Trans. Mob. Comput.*, vol. 20, no. 4, 2021, doi: 10.1109/TMC.2019.2963668.

[112] K. Nahrstedt, "Internet of Mobile Things: Challenges and Opportunities," in *Proceedings of the 23rd International Conference on Parallel Architectures and Compilation*, 2014, doi:10.1145/2628071.2635931.

[113] S. Aslam, M. P. Michaelides, and H. Herodotou, "Internet of Ships: A Survey on Architectures, Emerging Applications, and Challenges," *IEEE Internet Things J.*, vol. 7, no. 10, 2020, doi: 10.1109/JIOT.2020.2993411.

[114] G. Liu, R. Perez, J. A. Muñoz, and F. Regueira, "Internet of Ships: The Future Ahead," *World J. Eng. Technol.*, vol. 04, no. 03, 2016, doi: 10.4236/wjet.2016.43d027.

[115] H. H. R. Sherazi, D. Zorbas, and B. O'flynn, "A Comprehensive Survey on RF Energy Harvesting: Applications and Performance Determinants," *Sensors*, vol. 22, no. 8, 2022, doi: 10.3390/s22082990.

[116] D. Ma, G. Lan, M. Hassan, W. Hu, and S. K. Das, "Sensing, Computing, and Communications for Energy Harvesting IoTs: A Survey," *IEEE Commu. Surv. Tutor.*, vol. 22, no. 2, 2020, doi: 10.1109/COMST.2019.2962526.

[117] O. B. Akan, O. Cetinkaya, C. Koca, and M. Ozger, "Internet of Hybrid Energy Harvesting Things," *IEEE Internet Things J.*, vol. 5, no. 2, 2018, doi: 10.1109/JIOT.2017.2742663.
[118] U. S. Toro, K. Wu, and V. C. M. Leung, "Backscatter Wireless Communications and Sensing in Green Internet of Things," *IEEE Trans. Green Commun. Netw.*, vol. 6, no. 1, 2022, doi: 10.1109/TGCN.2021.3095792.
[119] H. Ali, M. Riaz, A. Bilal, and K. Ullah, "Comparison of Energy Harvesting Techniques in Wireless Body Area Network," *Int. J. Multidiscip. Sci. Eng.*, vol. 7, no. 6, 2016.
[120] P. Sharma and A. K. Singh, "A Survey on RF Energy Harvesting Techniques for Lifetime Enhancement of Wireless Sensor Networks," *Sustain. Comput. Inform. Syst.*, vol. 37, 2023, doi: 10.1016/j.suscom.2022.100836.
[121] P. Choudhary, L. Bhargava, V. Singh, M. Choudhary, and A. kumar Suhag, "A survey—Energy Harvesting Sources and Techniques for Internet of Things Devices," *Mater. Today: Proc.*, 2020, doi: 10.1016/j.matpr.2020.04.115.
[122] X. Dai *et al.*, "A Hybrid Energy Harvesting System for Self-Powered Applications in Shared Bicycles," *Sustain. Energy Technol. Assess.*, vol. 51, 2022, doi: 10.1016/j.seta.2021.101891.
[123] H. Liu, H. Fu, L. Sun, C. Lee, and E. M. Yeatman, "Hybrid Energy Harvesting Technology: From Materials, Structural Design, System Integration to Applications," *Renew. Sust. Energ. Rev.*, vol. 137, 2021, doi: 10.1016/j.rser.2020.110473.
[124] Z. Liu, Y. P. Hsu, and M. M. Hella, "A Thermal/RF Hybrid Energy Harvesting System with Rectifying-Combination and Improved Fractional-OCV MPPT Method," *IEEE Trans. Circuits Syst. I Regul. Pap.*, vol. 67, no. 10, 2020, doi: 10.1109/TCSI.2020.2982403.

3 Wireless Protocols and Technologies for the Internet of Things

3.1 WPAN TECHNOLOGIES FOR IOT

Wireless Personal Area Network (WPAN) technologies play a crucial role in connecting IoT devices within short communication ranges. These technologies enable devices to exchange data wirelessly and are designed for low-power, low-cost, and short-range communication. For instance, Bluetooth is a widely adopted WPAN technology which allows seamless wireless connections and offers low-power consumption through Bluetooth Low Energy (BLE), making it suitable for IoT devices like wearables and home automation systems. Zigbee, designed for IoT applications, provides low data rates, long battery life, and robust mesh networking capabilities. Z-Wave, commonly used in smart homes, operates in the sub-GHz (gigahertz) frequency range, supporting reliable communication through mesh networks. Thread, built on 6LoWPAN and IEEE 802.15.4 standards, offers secure and reliable connectivity in home automation. Near field communication (NFC), a short-range WPAN technology, enables contactless communication for applications like mobile payments and access control. The choice of WPAN technology depends on specific IoT requirements such as power efficiency, data rates, and interoperability needs. We will next discuss all of these technologies, one by one.

3.1.1 IEEE 802.15.4

The Institute of Electrical and Electronics Engineers (IEEE) has defined the 802 standard protocol family for physical and data link layer technologies. The IEEE 802.15.4 standard was first published in 2003 and later modified in 2006. IEEE 802.15.4 is a widely used Wireless Personal Area Network (WPAN) technology for IoT applications which is specifically designed to support low-power and low-cost wireless communication, focusing on providing reliable connectivity in environments with limited power, bandwidth, and computing resources [1, 2]. One of the main advantages of IEEE 802.15.4 for IoT is its ability to support many devices in a network. This is achieved using a star topology, whereby a single central device, such as a gateway or access point, coordinates the communication between the other devices in the network. Another key feature of IEEE 802.15.4 is its support for low-power operation. Devices that use this technology can be designed to operate on a battery for several years, making it well suited for IoT applications when power is limited and/or the devices are placed in remote or hard-to-reach locations.

DOI: 10.1201/9781003282945-3

IEEE 802.15.4 is a popular choice for WPAN technology in IoT due to its low power consumption, reliability, and ability to support many devices. It is used in a wide range of applications, including home automation, smart energy, and industrial automation, among others. It explores physical layer and media access control (MAC) protocols which are specified in the IEEE 302.15.4 standards, while Logical Link Control (LLC) layer is defined in IEEE 802.2 standards. The IEEE 802.15.4 standard defines the physical and MAC layer communication methods used to access wired (Ethernet) and wireless networks. The layered architecture of IEEE 802.15.4 standard is shown in Figure 3.1. One can see that data frames are sent via the physical layer and MAC layer to LLC for formatting [3]. Figure 3.1 shows the data flow between physical layer and MAC layer.

The Federal Communications Commission (FCC) manages the distribution of frequency bands in the United States. Table 3.1 provides the FCC-allocated frequencies for industrial, scientific, and medical applications. FCC allocates frequencies for industrial, scientific, and medical applications (ISM) for transmission power below 1 watt, which does not require licensing [4]. The MAC layer is responsible for

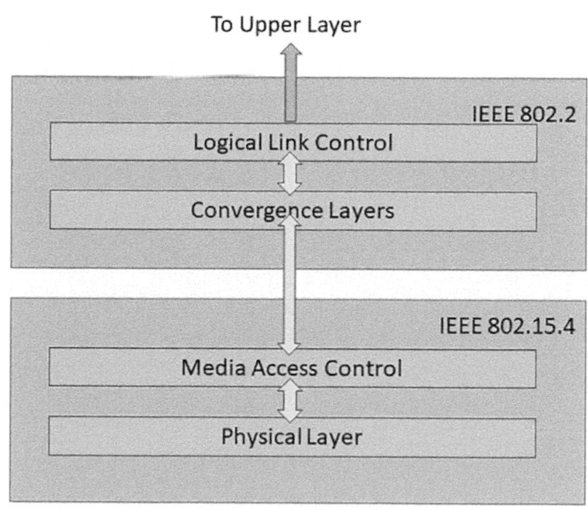

FIGURE 3.1 Data flow between physical layer and MAC layer.

TABLE 3.1
FCC-Allocated Frequencies for Industrial, Scientific, and Medical Applications

FCC Band	Frequency	Maximum Transmission Power
Industrial	902–928 MHz	< 1 W
Scientific	2.4–2.48 GHz	< 1 W
Medical	5.725–5.85 GHz	< 1 W

controlling access to the wireless medium and provides a set of functions for reliable communication between devices. Following are some of the key MAC functions defined in the standard [3, 5].

1. **Beacon Management:** The MAC layer defines a beaconing mechanism for synchronizing communication between devices. The coordinator periodically broadcasts a beacon frame, which contains information about the network such as its personal area network (PAN) identifier, super frame structure, and synchronization information. Devices can use this information to synchronize their communication with the network.
2. **Channel Access:** The MAC layer uses a contention-based channel access mechanism whereby devices compete for access to the channel. Devices can send data as soon as the channel is idle, or they can wait for a predetermined amount of time before attempting to transmit again. This helps to reduce collisions and improve the overall efficiency of the network.
3. **Frame Formatting:** The MAC layer specifies the format of the data frames used for communication between devices. The frames contain information such as the source and destination addresses, frame type, and payload. The MAC layer also defines a set of security features, such as encryption and authentication, to protect the data as it is transmitted over the network.
4. **Acknowledgments:** The MAC layer provides a mechanism for devices to acknowledge the successful receipt of data frames. When a device receives a data frame, it sends an acknowledgment frame back to the sender to confirm successful receipt. This helps to ensure reliable communication between devices.
5. **Network Topology:** The MAC layer supports two network topologies, star and peer to peer (P2P). In a star topology, all devices communicate directly with a central coordinator. In a P2P topology, devices can communicate with each other without the need for a coordinator. The MAC layer provides mechanisms for discovering neighboring devices and routing data between them.

Figure 3.2 explains the IEEE 802.15.4 frame format. While the IEEE 802.15.4 standard is well suited for low-power, low–data-rate wireless communication, it has some limitations that may make it less suitable for certain IoT applications. Thus, the developers should carefully consider the specific requirements of their application and choose the appropriate wireless communication standard accordingly.

The limitations of IEEE 802.15.4 standard are listed in what follows [6, 7].

1. **Limited Range:** The standard operates in the 2.4 GHz and 900 MHz frequency bands, which have a limited range compared to other frequency bands. This means that devices using the standard may have difficulty communicating over long distances, which can be a limitation in some IoT applications.
2. **Limited Throughput:** The standard is designed for low–data-rate applications, with a maximum data rate of 250 Kbps. This can be a limitation for

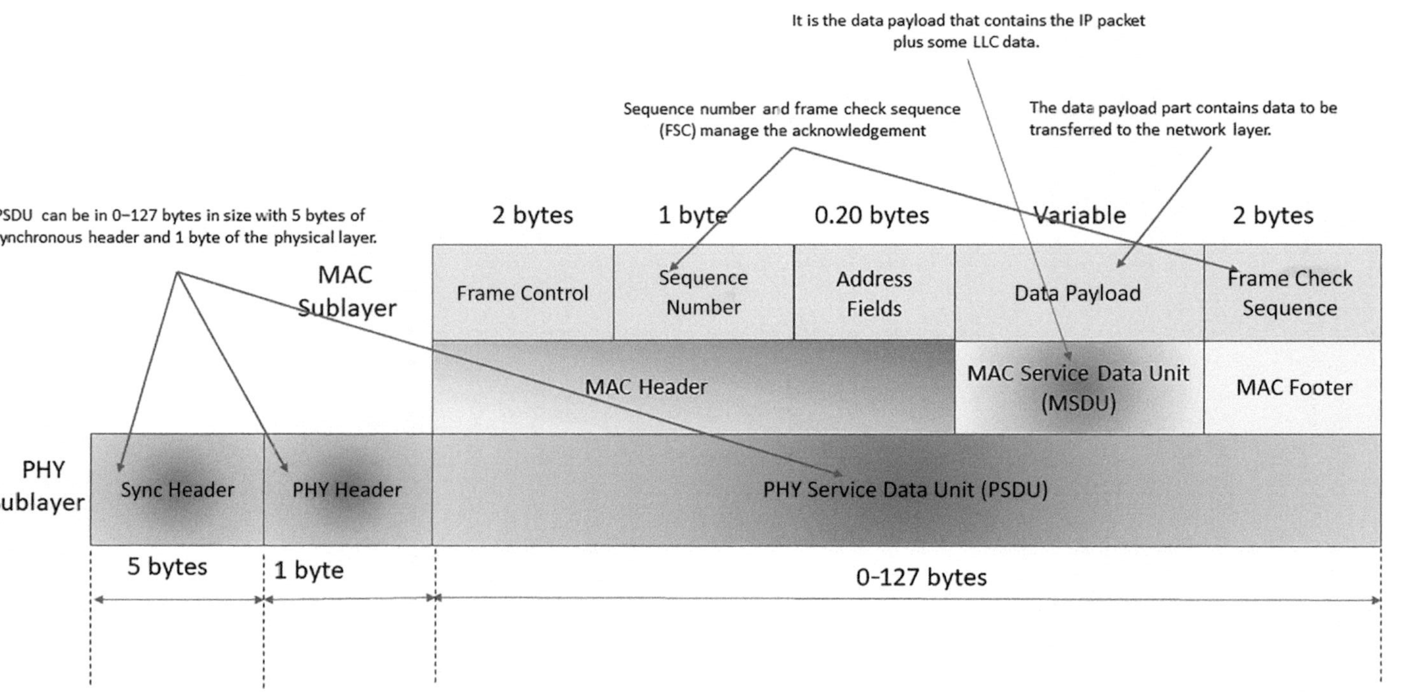

FIGURE 3.2 IEEE 802.15.4 frame format.

applications that require higher throughput, such as video streaming or real-time control systems.
3. **Limited Scalability:** The standard is designed for use in small-scale networks, such as PANs. It may be difficult to scale up to larger networks, which can be a limitation for some IoT applications that require large-scale deployments.
4. **Limited Interoperability:** The standard allows for different types of physical layer implementations, which can lead to interoperability issues between devices from different manufacturers. This can be a limitation in IoT applications that require devices from different vendors to communicate with each other.
5. **Limited Security:** While the standard provides some basic security features, such as encryption and authentication, it may not be sufficient for some IoT applications that require more robust security features.

The IEEE 802.15.4 standard is widely used in IoT applications due to its low-power, low–data-rate capabilities and its ability to support large-scale mesh networks. It is well suited for applications that require large numbers of devices to be deployed over a wide area, as well as robust security and interoperability. Some common uses of IEEE 802.15.4 in IoT include the following [1, 4, 7, 8].

1. **Smart Homes:** IEEE 802.15.4 is commonly used in smart home applications to connect various IoT devices such as sensors, thermostats, smart locks, and lighting systems. These devices can communicate with each other through a mesh network created by IEEE 802.15.4, enabling remote control and monitoring of various home systems.
2. **Industrial Automation:** IEEE 802.15.4 is widely used in industrial automation applications, enabling communication between sensors, actuators, and other devices. This can help to improve efficiency, reduce downtime, and enable predictive maintenance.
3. **Smart Cities:** IEEE 802.15.4 is used in smart city applications to connect various devices, such as traffic sensors, smart parking systems, streetlights, and environmental sensors. These devices can communicate with each other to improve traffic flow, reduce energy consumption, and monitor air quality.
4. **Healthcare:** IEEE 802.15.4 is used in healthcare applications to connect various devices, such as wearable health monitors and medical sensors, allowing for real-time monitoring of patient health data. This can help to improve patient outcomes and reduce hospital readmissions.
5. **Agriculture:** IEEE 802.15.4 is used in agriculture applications to connect various devices, such as soil moisture sensors, weather stations, and automated irrigation systems. This can help to improve crop yields and reduce water consumption.

3.1.2 Zigbee

Zigbee is a wireless communication standard that is commonly used in IoT applications due to its low-power, low–data-rate capabilities, and ability to support large-scale mesh networks. Zigbee is specifically designed for low-power applications, aiming to maximize battery life in devices. It utilizes low-duty cycles and sleep modes, allowing devices to conserve energy and operate on battery power for extended periods. In comparison, protocols like Wi-Fi and Bluetooth are more power-hungry, making them less suitable for battery-operated IoT devices. Zigbee is primarily used for two-way communication between a sensor and a control system. Like Bluetooth and Wi-Fi, it is a short-range communication and offers connectivity up to 100 meters. On the other end, Wi-Fi and Bluetooth are high–data-rate standards that support the transfer of media files, software, etc. Following are some key aspects of Zigbee that make it well suited for IoT [9, 10].

1. **Low Power Consumption:** Zigbee devices are designed to consume very little power, which makes them well suited for battery-powered IoT applications. This is achieved through features such as low-duty cycle operation, sleep modes, and low-power wake-up timers.
2. **Mesh Networking:** Zigbee supports mesh networking, which allows devices to communicate with each other through a network of intermediary nodes. This can increase the range and reliability of the network, as well as enable self-healing and self-organizing capabilities.
3. **Large-Scale Deployments:** Zigbee is designed to support large-scale deployments, with the ability to connect to tens of thousands of devices. This makes it well suited for IoT applications that require large numbers of sensors or other devices to be deployed over a wide area.
4. **Security:** Zigbee includes several security features, such as encryption, authentication, and access control. This makes it well suited for IoT applications that require secure communication and data protection.
5. **Interoperability:** Zigbee is designed to be interoperable between devices from different vendors, which can help to ensure that devices can communicate with each other and be easily integrated into larger IoT systems.

Overall, Zigbee is a popular choice for IoT applications that require low-power, low–data-rate wireless communication over large-scale mesh networks, as well as robust security and interoperability. Figure 3.3 illustrates Zigbee Architecture. Zigbee resides on top of the PHY and MAC layers defined in IEEE 802.15.4. PHY and MAC layers provide the functionality of open systems interconnection (OSI) physical and link layers [11]. This application support sublayer (APS) handles 64-bit IEEE–to–16-bit Zigbee address mapping. It routes the network layer message to a suitable application object. Each application object is identified by the endpoint ID. APS maintains a local binding table that holds the record of remote nodes and endpoints registered to receive messages from the local endpoint. APS also handles acknowledgments; retries sending messages, if not received; and data duplication. APS manages and provides support for local applications and provides mechanisms for developing and incorporating Zigbee applications. Table 3.2 shows the Zigbee network layer (NWK) frame format. The field size of Zigbee NWK format is shown in Table 3.3.

Zigbee Device Object (ZDO) is a special application running on Endpoint 0 and manages the state of Zigbee Node. ZDO initializes the APS, NWK, and security

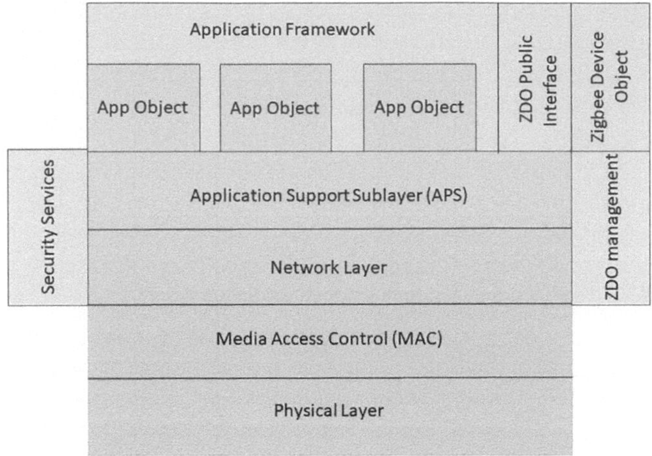

FIGURE 3.3 Zigbee architecture.

TABLE 3.2
Zigbee NWK Frame Format

Object 1	Object 2	Object 2	Object 1	Object 1	Variable
Frame control	Destination address	Source address	Radius	Sequence numbers	Frame payload
	Routing Fields				
NWK Layer					NWK payload

TABLE 3.3
Field Size of Zigbee NWK Format

Field	Field Size in Octets (8)
Frame control	1
Destination endpoint	1
Cluster identifier	1
Application profile identifier	2
Source endpoint	1
Counter	1
Payload	Variable

service provider. It provides interfacing between application objects, Zigbee device profile, and APS. It manages security policies and security configuration of a device provided by the security service provider. ZDO gathers configuration information from endpoint applications and provides device and service discovery. ZCL was added late in Zigbee architecture and defines a library of interface specifications

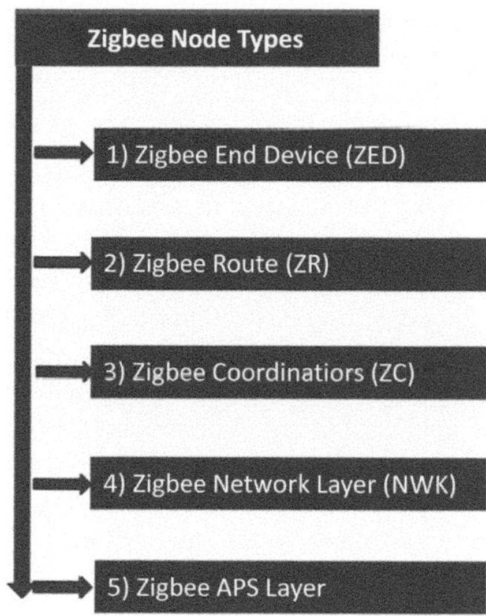

FIGURE 3.4 Zigbee node types.

like commands and attributes used for application profiles [12]. It also provides functionalities for the network interface, group formation, and management. It acts as a common mechanism for application development, even with the ongoing development of Zigbee. This provides API for Zigbee application development and Zigbee application is appointed an endpoint starting from 1.

There are various types of Zigbee nodes, as shown in Figure 3.4. Zigbee End Device (ZED) works with 802.15.4, providing reduced functionality for the device. These are battery-operated nodes that are not always ready to sense or listen. ZED must connect to a network via Zigbee Router (ZR), which acts as its parent. ZR works with 802.15.4 and provides a fully functioning device (FFD). ZR is permanently listening and can route packets once it joins the existing Zigbee network. Zigbee coordinators (ZC) work with 802.15.4 and provide an FFD. It can create a network and can also act as an 802.15.4-based PAN coordinator. It can form a network and can also connect to the existing network and can route packets—in such cases, ZC becomes ZR. Zigbee nodes are not mutually exclusive which means a ZED can also act as ZR and even as ZC. Zigbee Network Layer (NWK) provides multi-hop routing of data packets in a mesh network which is not available in 802.15.4 [13]. It uses short address allocation to nodes ranging from 0x0000 to 0XFFF7. Zigbee supports two address allocation modes: coordinator node uses short address 0x0000, while in stack profile 0x01, an address is allocated based on the position of the node in the mesh/tree topology. Each potential parent node is associated with a sub-block of network addresses (among which address is allocated to the requesting node).

Zigbee and Wi-Fi are two different wireless communication technologies that are designed for different purposes and have different strengths and weaknesses. Zigbee is a low-power, low–data-rate wireless communication technology that is primarily used for IoT devices such as smart home devices, industrial sensors, and medical devices. It is designed to be very power-efficient, which means that Zigbee devices can operate for years on a single battery charge. Zigbee also has a robust mesh networking capability, which allows Zigbee devices to relay messages to other devices, thereby extending the range of the network [9, 11]. On the other hand, Wi-Fi is a high–data-rate wireless communication technology that is designed for high-bandwidth applications such as internet access, video streaming, and online gaming. Wi-Fi has a higher power consumption than Zigbee, which means that Wi-Fi devices typically require more frequent charging or need to be plugged into a power source [11, 14]. Wi-Fi also has a limited range compared to Zigbee, and it does not have the same mesh networking capability. We can say the choice between Zigbee and Wi-Fi depends on the specific application and requirements. If you need to connect low-power IoT devices that operate on battery power and need a robust mesh networking capability, Zigbee may be a better choice. If you need to connect high-bandwidth devices that require fast data transfer rates and a broader range, Wi-Fi may be the better choice.

3.1.3 HART

The Highway Addressable Remote Transducer (HART) protocol is a digital communication protocol that is commonly used in industrial automation and control applications [15]. It is designed to provide a standard way to communicate with and control field instruments such as sensors, transmitters, and actuators. Following are some key aspects of HART that make it well suited for IoT applications [15, 16].

1. **Compatibility with Legacy Systems:** One of the main advantages of HART is that it is compatible with existing analog systems, allowing organizations to upgrade their systems gradually over time. HART devices can communicate using both analog and digital signals, which makes them compatible with both new and legacy systems.
2. **Bidirectional Communication:** HART supports bidirectional communication, which allows devices to not only receive data but also send data back to the central controller. This enables more advanced control and monitoring capabilities.
3. **Low Bandwidth Requirements:** HART is designed to operate over existing analog signal wires, which means that it has very low bandwidth requirements. This makes it well suited for IoT applications that require low-power and low-bandwidth communication.
4. **Security:** HART includes several security features, such as authentication and encryption, which help to ensure that data is transmitted securely and cannot be intercepted by unauthorized users.
5. **Standardization:** HART is an industry standard, which means that it is widely supported by many vendors and can be easily integrated into larger IoT systems. This allows organizations to choose from a wide range of compatible devices and systems, which can help to reduce costs and improve efficiency.

Overall, HART is a useful protocol for IoT applications that require low-power and low-bandwidth communication, compatibility with legacy systems, and advanced control and monitoring capabilities. The HART protocol works in two modes [15], namely: i) master-slave mode; and ii) burst mode. In HART, communication between devices typically follows a master–slave architecture. The master device, often a control system or handheld communicator, initiates communication with one or more slave devices, which are typically field devices such as sensors or actuators. Master is the main controller communication device that maintains other slave field devices and initiates communication. Slaves can be actuators, controllers, or transmitters which act based on commands from primary or secondary master mode. There can be two types of master modes: i) primary master mode (can be personal computer [PC], PLC [programmable logic controllers], or distributed control systems [DCS]); or ii) secondary master mode (can be a handheld device or PC). Burst mode is a periodic digital communication mode in which the HART device transmits bursts of digital data while maintaining the primary analog 4–20 mA signal. The bursts usually occur at predefined intervals and allow for the transmission of more extensive data packets. For some HART devices, this gives the feature of faster communication. In this mode, the slave continuously broadcasts a standard HART replay message as instructed by the master. Upon instruction from the master, the slave stops bursting until the time master receives messages at a higher rate. Figure 3.5 explains the analog and digital signals in the 4–20 mA band.

In HART, frequency shift keying (FSK) is the modulation technique used for transmitting digital data over the analog 4–20 mA current loop. FSK is a form of frequency modulation in which the carrier frequency shifts between two distinct frequencies to represent binary data. In HART, the two frequencies used for FSK modulation are the following.

1. **Mark Frequency (1.2 kHz):** This frequency represents a logical 1 or high state in the binary data. When transmitting a logical 1, the HART device modulates the carrier signal by shifting it to the mark frequency of 1.2 kHz.

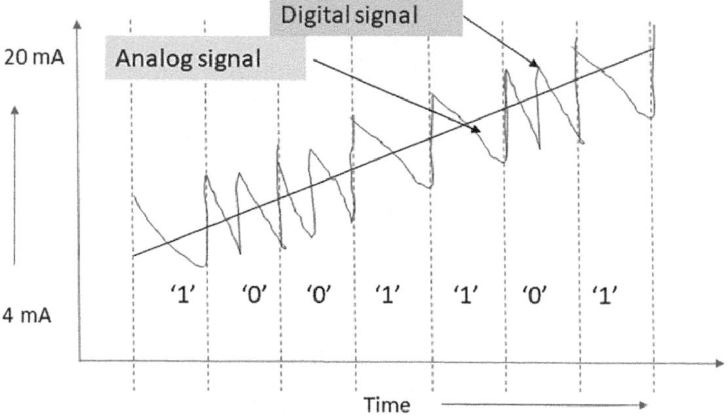

FIGURE 3.5 Analog and digital signals in 4mA–20 mA band.

2. **Space Frequency (2.2 kHz):** This frequency represents a logical 0 or low state in the binary data. When transmitting a logical 0, the HART device modulates the carrier signal by shifting it to the space frequency of 2.2 kHz.

The FSK modulation scheme allows the digital information to be superimposed on the analog 4–20 mA current loop without affecting the primary analog signal. The HART device uses FSK to transmit digital data by varying the frequency of the carrier signal according to the binary values of the data being sent. The receiving device, such as the master device or another HART device, demodulates the FSK signal to recover the transmitted binary data. By detecting the frequency shifts between the mark and space frequencies, the receiver can determine the sequence of 1s and 0s that were transmitted. FSK modulation in HART enables simultaneous transmission of both analog and digital information over the same communication channel, allowing for enhanced communication capabilities in industrial automation and control systems.

3.1.4 NFC

Near field communication (NFC) is a wireless communication protocol that is commonly used in IoT applications due to its ability to enable simple, secure, and convenient communication between devices in close proximity. Following are some key aspects of NFC that make it well suited for IoT [17, 18].

1. **Short-Range Communication:** NFC is designed for short-range communication, typically within a range of a few centimeters. This makes it well suited for IoT applications that require proximity communication, such as payment systems, access control, and inventory management.
2. **Security:** NFC includes several security features, such as encryption and authentication, which help to ensure that data is transmitted securely and cannot be intercepted by unauthorized users. This makes it suitable for applications that require secure communication and data protection.
3. **Ease of Use:** NFC is very simple to use, requiring only a simple touch or wave of a device to establish a connection. This makes it ideal for applications that require quick and convenient communication between devices, such as payment systems or smart home automation.
4. **Standardization:** NFC is an industry standard, which means that it is widely supported by many vendors and can be easily integrated into larger IoT systems. This allows organizations to choose from a wide range of compatible devices and systems, which can help to reduce costs and improve efficiency.
5. **Low Power Consumption:** NFC devices consume very little power, making them well suited for IoT applications that require low-power communication.

Overall, NFC is a useful protocol for IoT applications that require short-range, secure, and convenient communication between devices. It is particularly well suited for applications that require proximity communication, such as payment systems, access control, and inventory management. As it can be used to transfer data like (but not limited to) pictures, telephone numbers, MP3 files, digital authorization, etc. Data is transferred between two (mobile) devices that are NFC enabled or between NFC (mobile) devices and RFID cards, which are close to each other. It works on the frequency range of 13.56 MHz and provides a data transmission rate of up to 424 Kb/s which ranges from nearly 10 cm. It has the following three operating modes.

- **Passive Mode:** In this mode, NFC devices act like existing systems that are using legacy NFC standards.
- **Peer-to-Peer Mode:** In this mode, two NFC devices can exchange data/information. As the target device or destination device (listener) uses its power supply, the polling device, i.e., the device which initiates the transmission, requires less power compared to the read/write mode. This mode is standardized by ISO 18092.
- **Active Mode:** In this mode, an NFC device is active and can read/write to/from an NFC forum using authorized NFC tags, as well as passive tags.

3.1.5 Z-Wave

Z-Wave is a wireless communication protocol that is specifically designed for IoT applications, especially for smart homes and automation [19]. It is known for its ability to support many devices and provide reliable and secure communication. Z-Wave is a useful protocol for IoT applications that require reliable and secure communication between devices, especially in smart home and automation applications. Its mesh networking, low-power consumption, security, interoperability, and ease of use make it a popular choice for IoT developers and organizations. Following are some key aspects of Z-Wave that make it well suited for IoT [19, 20].

1. **Mesh Networking:** Z-Wave uses mesh networking to enable communication between devices, allowing for many devices to be connected and controlled within a single network. This makes it well suited for smart home and automation applications in which multiple devices need to be controlled from a central location.
2. **Low Power Consumption:** Z-Wave is designed to operate on low-power devices and batteries, making it energy efficient and cost effective.
3. **Security:** Z-Wave uses advanced encryption and authentication mechanisms to ensure secure communication between devices. This makes it suitable for applications that require secure communication and data protection.
4. **Interoperability:** Z-Wave is an industry standard, which means that it is widely supported by many vendors and can be easily integrated into larger IoT systems. This allows organizations to choose from a wide range of compatible devices and systems, which can help to reduce costs and improve efficiency.
5. **Ease of use:** Z-Wave is very easy to use, requiring only simple setup and configuration. This makes it ideal for applications that require quick and convenient communication between devices.

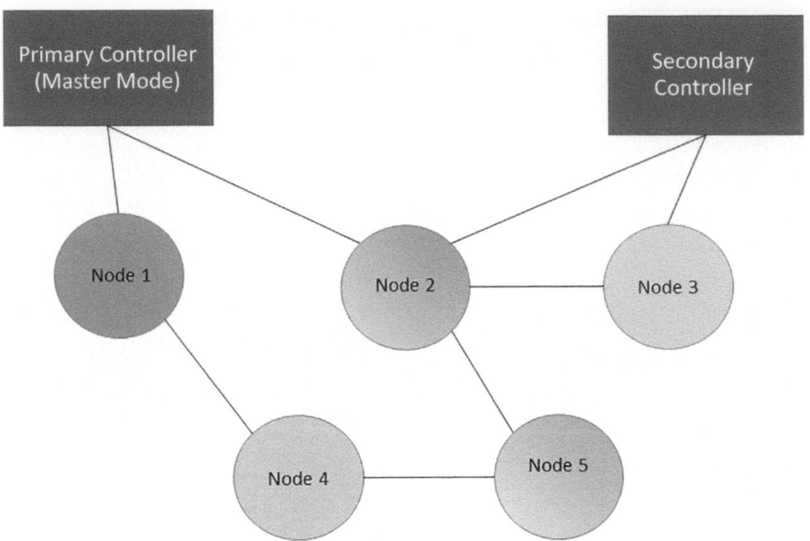

FIGURE 3.6 Simple Z-Wave Network.

Figure 3.6 illustrates a simple Z-Wave network. It must have at least one master/primary controller and can have up to 232 devices connected [19, 20]. The Z-Wave network uses a 32-bit unique identifier called "Home ID" to separate networks from one other. The primary controller contains a description of the Z-Wave network. It also controls the output and assigns the "Network or Home ID" and "Node ID" to the Z-Wave nodes during the network registration process. A secondary controller has the same "Network or Home ID" as the primary controller and remains stationary as it must maintain the routing tables. The process of assigning the "Home ID" and "Node ID" to slave devices is called "inclusion" in Z-Wave network formation. In the process of "excluding," the previously assigned "Home ID" and "Node ID" in the process of inclusion are removed. The "Home ID" and the "Node ID" are reset to zero due to exclusion. The only exception to the process is a controller—if a controller is excluded, the "Home ID" reverts to the ID programmed during manufacturing.

3.1.6 Bluetooth/BLE (Bluetooth Low Energy)

BLE is a wireless communication protocol that is widely used in IoT applications due to its low power, low cost, and short-range capabilities [21, 22]. Bluetooth/BLE is a useful protocol for IoT applications that require reliable and low-power communication between devices, especially in applications that require short-range communication. Its low power consumption, short-range communication, interoperability, security, and compatibility make it a popular choice for IoT developers and organizations. It is an eco-friendly form of Bluetooth that has been developed specifically to facilitate the IoT. Following are some key aspects of BLE that make it well suited for IoT [22, 23].

1. **Low Power Consumption:** BLE is designed to operate on low-power devices and batteries, making it energy efficient and cost effective. This makes it ideal for IoT applications in which devices may be deployed in remote or hard-to-reach areas.
2. **Short-Range Communication:** BLE has a short range, typically up to 100 meters, which makes it ideal for IoT applications in which devices need to communicate with each other in proximity.
3. **Interoperability:** BLE is an industry standard, which means that it is widely supported by many vendors and can be easily integrated into larger IoT systems. This allows organizations to choose from a wide range of compatible devices and systems, which can help to reduce costs and improve efficiency.
4. **Security:** BLE uses advanced encryption and authentication mechanisms to ensure secure communication between devices. This makes it suitable for applications that require secure communication and data protection.
5. **Compatibility:** BLE is compatible with many different types of devices, including smartphones, tablets, and computers. This allows users to easily connect and control their IoT devices using their mobile devices.

Some of the many suitable applications for BLE are fitness trackers (such as Fitbit, Misfit, etc.), smartwatches (such as the Apple Watch, Moto 360, and Pebble), beacons (Apple iBeacon, Google Eddystone), medical devices such as glucose meters and insulin pumps, and home automation devices such as door locks, light bulbs, sensors, and others as shown in Figure 3.7. Every technology has its disadvantages, and BLE is no exception. The main ones are low bandwidth, limited range (typically 30–100 meters), requirement of a gateway device to connect the end devices to the internet, and interference and noise from other protocols in the 2.4 GHz spectrum. Following are the three main software levels in the architecture of a BLE device [22].

- **Application:** The application interfacing with the stack and implementing the specific user applications.
- **Host:** The high-level layer of the protocol stack.
- **Controller:** The low-level layer of the protocol stack, including the physical layer.

3.1.7 BACnet

BACnet is a standard communication protocol for building automation and control networks developed by the American Society of Heating, Refrigerating, and Air-Conditioning Engineers (ASHRAE). It is an a widely accepted, non-proprietary object-oriented protocol which views its implementation in the form of objects. It is a communication protocol used in building automation and control systems (BACS) that provides a standard interface for exchanging data between different devices in a building automation system [24]. It is a useful protocol for IoT applications that require reliable and secure communication between devices and systems in BACS. Its interoperability, scalability, security, standardization, and flexibility make it a popular choice for IoT developers and organizations in the building automation

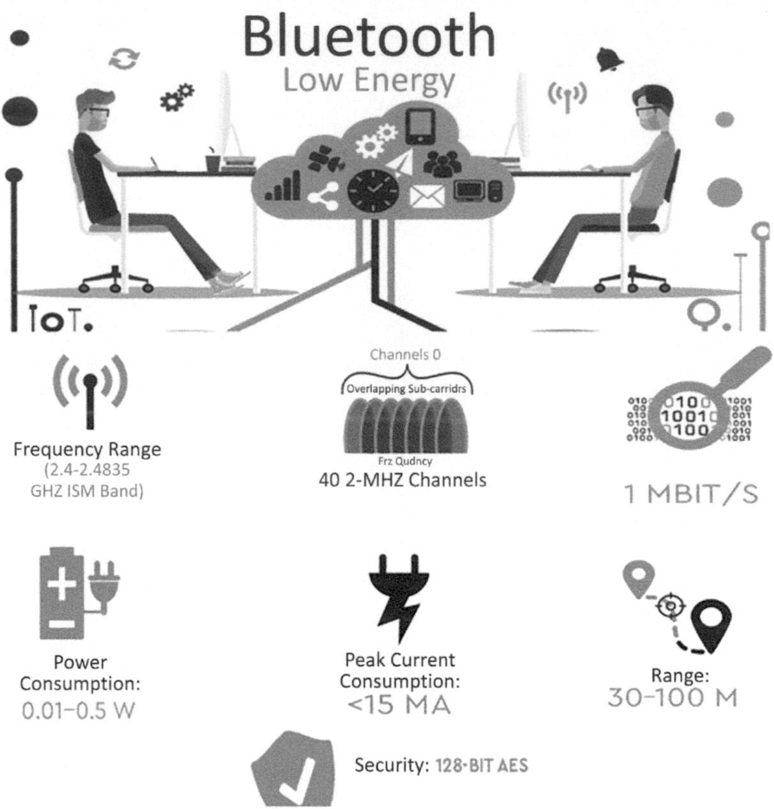

FIGURE 3.7 Overview of a BLE network.

industry. Following are some key aspects of BACnet that make it well suited for IoT [24, 25].

1. **Interoperability:** BACnet is designed to support communication between devices from different manufacturers, allowing for a more flexible and scalable building automation system. This is particularly important in IoT applications in which devices and systems may come from different vendors.
2. **Scalability:** BACnet supports a wide range of devices and systems, from simple sensors to complex HVAC systems, making it suitable for large-scale IoT applications in commercial buildings and industrial facilities.
3. **Security:** BACnet supports several security features, including authentication and encryption, to ensure secure communication between devices and systems.
4. **Standardization:** BACnet is an industry standard, which means that it is widely supported by many vendors and can be easily integrated into larger IoT systems. This allows organizations to choose from a wide range of

compatible devices and systems, which can help to reduce costs and improve efficiency.

5. **Flexibility:** BACnet supports a range of communication protocols—including Ethernet, TCP/IP, and serial communication—allowing for greater flexibility in how devices and systems are connected and controlled.

Figure 3.8 shows the three characteristics of BACnet. BACnet was designed to allow communication of BACS for applications such as HVAC control, lighting control, access control, and fire detection systems and their associated equipment. It is defined by three characteristics: objects, properties, and services [25].

BACnet provides five classes of services that are used for communication between devices in a building automation system. These five classes of services provide a comprehensive set of tools for communication and management between devices in a building automation system. They allow for efficient and effective management of building automation systems, making them an essential component of modern building automation technology. These five classes of services are the following [24].

1. **Object Access Services (BACnet Read and Write Services):** These services are used to read and write data values from and to BACnet objects. The read service is used to read the value of a property from an object, while the write service is used to set the value of a property.
2. **Alarm and Event Services:** These services are used to manage alarms and events in a building automation system. The alarm service is used to acknowledge, confirm, and reset alarms, while the event service is used to report events and changes in the system.
3. **Remote Device Management Services:** These services are used to manage remote devices in a building automation system. They include services such as device discovery, device status, and device configuration.
4. **Virtual Terminal Services:** These services provide a way to interact with devices in a building automation system using a virtual terminal. This allows users to monitor and control devices from a central location.

Objects	Properties	Services
• A logical representation of the usable entity which can be physical device, analog input, binary input, etc. • More than 30 object types.	• The information about BACnet objects are defined by its properties. • Object_identifier • Object_name • Object_type	• Services are nothing but actions that can e performed with the help of BACnet objects. • Services like read, write, input and putput.

FIGURE 3.8 Three characteristics of BACnet.

5. **File Transfer Services:** These services are used to transfer files between devices in a building automation system. They include services such as file read, file write, and file delete.

3.1.8 Modbus

Modbus is a communication protocol commonly used in industrial automation systems to establish communication between electronic devices. It was developed in 1979 by Modicon (now Schneider Electric) and has since become a standard in the industry [24]. Modbus allows for the exchange of data between devices connected over a network. Its interoperability, simplicity, scalability, security, and speed make it a popular choice for IoT developers and organizations in the industrial automation and control industry. Following are some key aspects of Modbus that make it well suited for IoT [26].

1. **Interoperability:** Modbus is a widely used and well-established protocol, which means that it is supported by many vendors and can be easily integrated into larger IoT systems. This allows organizations to choose from a wide range of compatible devices and systems, which can help to reduce costs and improve efficiency.
2. **Simplicity:** Modbus is a simple and easy-to-use protocol, requiring only basic setup and configuration. This makes it ideal for applications that require quick and convenient communication between devices.
3. **Scalability:** Modbus supports a wide range of devices and systems, from simple sensors to complex industrial control systems, making it suitable for large-scale IoT applications in industrial settings.
4. **Security:** Modbus supports several security features, including authentication and encryption, to ensure secure communication between devices and systems.
5. **Speed:** Modbus is a fast protocol, with data transmission rates of up to 115.2 Kbps, making it suitable for applications that require real-time data transmission and control.

Modbus is a messaging structure. It is used to establish client–server communication between intelligent devices. It is a de facto standard, truly open and the most widely used network protocol in the industrial manufacturing environment means of connecting industrial electronic devices. It has been implemented by hundreds of vendors on thousands of different devices to transfer discrete/analog input/output (I/O) and register data between control devices. There are several variants of the Modbus protocol, but the two most commonly used versions are Modbus RTU (remote terminal unit) and Modbus TCP/IP [26, 27].

- **Modbus RTU:** Modbus RTU is a serial communication protocol that uses binary representation for data transmission. It is typically implemented over RS-485 or RS-232 physical interfaces. In this mode, data is transmitted in a master–slave architecture, whereby one device (the master) initiates communication with one or more devices (the slaves). The communication is typically initiated by the master device sending a request to read or write data to a specific slave device. The slave device then responds with the requested data.

- **Modbus TCP/IP:** Modbus TCP/IP is a variant of Modbus that uses Ethernet as the physical layer for communication. It allows for communication over local area networks (LANs), wide area networks (WANs), or the internet. Modbus TCP/IP uses a client–server architecture, whereby one device acts as the Modbus client and initiates communication with another device acting as the Modbus server. The communication is carried out using standard TCP/IP protocols, with Modbus messages encapsulated in TCP/IP packets.

Both Modbus RTU and Modbus TCP/IP use a simple and efficient protocol structure. They define a set of function codes that specify the type of operation to be performed, such as reading or writing data, and the address of the data to be accessed. The protocol also includes error-checking mechanisms to ensure data integrity. Modbus has found widespread adoption in various industrial applications, including supervisory control and data acquisition (SCADA) systems, programmable logic controllers (PLCs), and other automation devices. It offers a straightforward and versatile means of communication between devices from different manufacturers, making it a popular choice in the industrial automation field.

3.1.9 Li-Fi

Li-Fi, short for "light fidelity," is a wireless communication technology that uses visible light, specifically the rapid flickering of light-emitting diodes (LEDs), to transmit data [28, 29]. It is a relatively new technology that aims to complement or even replace traditional Wi-Fi technology in certain applications. Li-Fi operates by modulating the intensity of LED light sources at extremely high speeds that are imperceptible to the human eye. These variations in light intensity are then detected by photodetectors, such as photodiodes, in the receiving device and converted back into data. Li-Fi is a promising technology for IoT applications that require high-speed, secure, and low-latency wireless communication. Its high-speed data transmission, security, immunity to electromagnetic interference, efficiency, and low latency make it a compelling alternative to traditional wireless communication technologies. However, its range is limited to the coverage area of the light source, which may make it unsuitable for some IoT applications that require broader coverage. Figure 3.9 explains the Li-Fi internet architecture. Following are some key aspects of Li-Fi that make it well suited for IoT [28, 30].

1. **High-Speed Data Transmission:** Li-Fi is capable of transmitting data at very high speeds, up to several gigabits per second, which makes it ideal for IoT applications that require fast data transfer rates.
2. **Security:** Unlike traditional wireless communication technologies such as Wi-Fi or Bluetooth, Li-Fi signals are confined within the physical boundaries

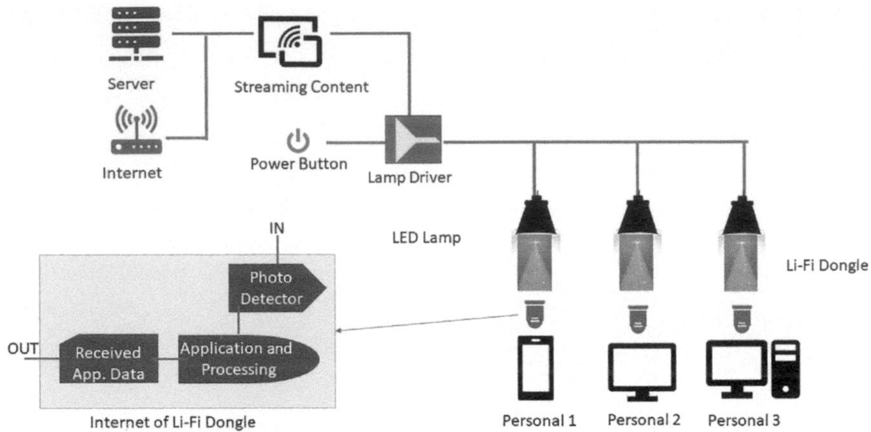

FIGURE 3.9 Li-Fi internet architecture.

of a room and cannot penetrate through walls, which makes them more secure and less prone to interception by unauthorized users.

3. **Immunity to Electromagnetic Interference:** Li-Fi is immune to electromagnetic interference, which makes it ideal for use in environments that are sensitive to electromagnetic radiation, such as hospitals or research labs.
4. **Efficiency:** Li-Fi uses LED light bulbs, which are more energy efficient than traditional Wi-Fi routers, to transmit data, making it an eco-friendly alternative for IoT applications.
5. **Low Latency:** Li-Fi has very low latency, which means that it can provide a real-time response in applications such as smart home automation or industrial control systems.

Li-Fi uses visible light communication (VLC) technology to transmit data through light waves. It operates by modulating the intensity of the light source at a very high frequency, which is then detected by a photodetector on the receiving end. The modulated light signal carries the digital data, which can be decoded by the receiver. Some potential applications of Li-Fi in IoT include the following [29, 30].

1. **Smart Homes:** Li-Fi can be used to connect various IoT devices within a home, such as smart thermostats, lighting systems, and security cameras. The fast data transfer rates and low latency of Li-Fi make it ideal for real-time communication and control.
2. **Retail:** Li-Fi can be used in retail environments to transmit information about products to customers' smartphones. For example, a store could use Li-Fi to transmit product details, pricing, and availability to customers as they browse the store.
3. **Healthcare:** Li-Fi can be used in healthcare environments to transmit patient data between devices and systems. The secure and low-latency nature of

Li-Fi makes it suitable for real-time monitoring and response in critical care environments.

4. **Industrial Automation:** Li-Fi can be used to connect IoT devices in industrial automation systems, such as sensors and robots. The high-speed data transfer rates and low latency of Li-Fi make it ideal for real-time communication and control in these environments.
5. **Smart Cities:** Li-Fi can be used to connect various IoT devices in a city, such as traffic sensors, streetlights, and public transportation systems. The high-speed data transfer rates and low latency of Li-Fi can help to improve the efficiency and safety of these systems.

Overall, Li-Fi is a promising technology for IoT applications that require high-speed, secure, and low-latency wireless communication. However, its limited range and line-of-sight requirements may make it unsuitable for some applications that require broader coverage or mobility.

3.1.10 Wi-Fi

Wi-Fi, or wireless fidelity, is a wireless communication technology that uses radio waves to transmit data between devices. Wi-Fi plays a critical role in the development and deployment of IoT systems, providing high-speed and reliable connectivity between IoT devices and systems, allowing for real-time monitoring and control, and enabling seamless interoperability between various devices and systems [2, 31]. It is widely used for IoT applications that require broad coverage, interoperability, high-speed data transfer, and low power consumption. Its long range, familiarity, interoperability, high-speed data transfer, and low power consumption make it a compelling choice for many IoT applications. However, it may not be the best choice for applications that require ultra-low power consumption or long battery life, as Wi-Fi can consume more power than other low-power wireless communication technologies such as Zigbee or LoRaWAN [32]. Following are some key aspects of Wi-Fi that make it well suited for IoT [2, 33].

1. **Range:** Wi-Fi signals can travel over a relatively long distance, which makes it ideal for IoT applications that require broad coverage, such as smart city networks or large-scale industrial automation systems.
2. **Familiarity:** Wi-Fi is a well-established and widely used technology, which means that many IoT devices and systems already support Wi-Fi connectivity. This makes it easy to integrate Wi-Fi into existing IoT networks and systems.
3. **Interoperability:** Wi-Fi is an open standard, which means that devices from different manufacturers can communicate with each other using the same protocol. This makes it easier to create an interoperable ecosystem of IoT devices and systems.
4. **High-Speed Data Transfer:** Wi-Fi can transmit data at high speeds, which makes it ideal for IoT applications that require fast data transfer rates, such as video surveillance and real-time monitoring.

5. **Low Power Consumption:** Wi-Fi can be designed to consume very little power, which makes it suitable for battery-powered IoT devices such as sensors or wearables.

The major role of Wi-Fi in IoT is to provide high-speed and reliable wireless connectivity between IoT devices and systems. Wi-Fi is well suited for IoT applications that require fast data transfer rates, such as real-time monitoring, video surveillance, and multimedia streaming. Some of the key roles of Wi-Fi in IoT include the following [34, 35].

1. **Interconnectivity:** Wi-Fi enables seamless connectivity and data exchange between various IoT devices and systems, creating an interoperable ecosystem of devices and systems.
2. **Cloud Connectivity:** Wi-Fi can be used to connect IoT devices to cloud platforms, allowing for remote monitoring, management, and control of IoT devices and systems.
3. **Real-Time Monitoring:** Wi-Fi can be used to enable real-time monitoring and control of IoT devices and systems, making it suitable for industrial automation, smart city networks, and healthcare applications.
4. **Multimedia Streaming:** Wi-Fi can support high-speed and low-latency multimedia streaming, making it ideal for smart home and entertainment applications.
5. **Scalability:** Wi-Fi is highly scalable, allowing for the connection of a large number of IoT devices and systems, and making it suitable for large-scale IoT deployments.

3.2 IP-BASED NETWORKING PROTOCOLS FOR IOT

Internet Protocol (IP)-based networking protocols are widely used in IoT applications. Some of the commonly used IP-based protocols in IoT are IPv6 (Internet Protocol version 6), 6LoWPAN (IPv6 over Low-Power Wireless Personal Area Networks), CoAP (Constrained Application Protocol), MQTT (Message Queuing Telemetry Transport), HTTP (Hypertext Transfer Protocol), and WebSocket [35, 36]. Depending on the specific IoT application and requirements, other protocols and standards may also be utilized to ensure efficient and secure communication between devices in the IoT ecosystem.

3.2.1 Overview of Networking

In the context of IoT, there are three common network topologies: star, mesh, and tree. Each of these topologies has its own advantages and disadvantages. The choice of network topology for an IoT application will depend on the specific requirements of the application, such as the number of devices, the distance between devices, the need for resilience, the cost of implementation, and the efficiency of data transmission [37]. Figure 3.10 shows the networking topologies in IoT. We will next discuss each of these topologies in detail.

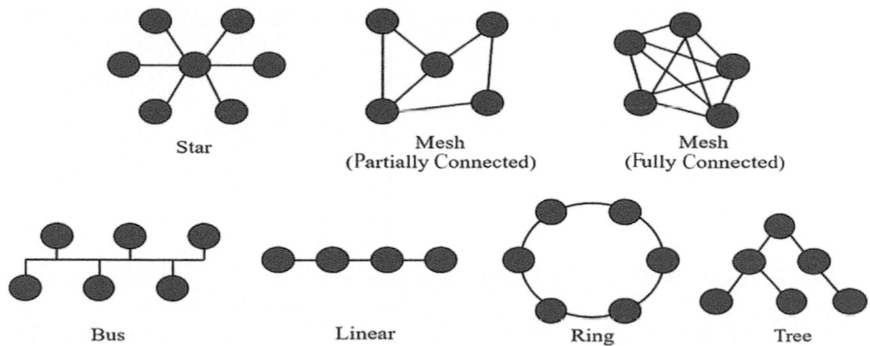

FIGURE 3.10 Networking topologies.

1. **Star Topology:** In a star topology, all IoT devices are connected to a central hub, which acts as a gateway to the internet [38]. The hub is responsible for managing the communication between the IoT devices and the internet. The advantage of a star topology is that it is simple and easy to manage, but it can be expensive to implement since it requires a central hub.
2. **Mesh Topology:** In a mesh topology, all IoT devices are connected to each other in a P2P network [38]. This means that each device can communicate directly with any other device in the network, without the need for a central hub. Mesh networks are highly resilient, since if one device fails, the network can still function. However, they can be complex to manage and can require a lot of power to operate.
3. **Tree Topology:** In a tree topology, IoT devices are connected in a hierarchical structure, with a root node at the top and branches that extend downward [37, 38]. This topology is well suited for applications in which some devices need to be located far from the central hub, but it can be less resilient than a mesh network since if a node fails, all the devices downstream of that node may also fail.

In addition to the star, mesh, and tree topologies, there are two additional network topologies that are commonly used in IoT applications: ring and linear.

1. **Ring Topology:** In a ring topology, IoT devices are connected in a circular network, whereby each device is connected to its neighbors in a ring-like structure [37, 39]. Data is transmitted in a unidirectional manner around the ring, with each device serving as a repeater for the data. Ring networks are simple to manage and can be highly resilient, since if one device fails, the data can still be transmitted around the ring in the opposite direction. However, they can be less efficient than other topologies, since data must be transmitted around the entire ring to reach its destination.
2. **Linear Topology:** In a linear topology, IoT devices are connected in a straight line, with each device connected to its neighbors in a linear fashion [37, 39].

Data is transmitted from one end of the line to the other, with each device serving as a repeater for the data. Linear networks are simple to manage and can be highly efficient since data only needs to be transmitted in one direction along the line. However, they can be less resilient than other topologies, since if one device fails, the data may not be able to reach its destination.

3.2.2 TCP/IP (IPv6)

TCP/IP (Transmission Control Protocol/Internet Protocol) is a set of networking protocols used for communication between devices on the internet. IPv6 is the latest version of the IP protocol and is designed to replace the older IPv4 protocol [40]. IPv5 (also called the Internet Stream Protocol) was an experimental protocol developed in the 1980s which was never widely deployed, and since the number 5 was already allocated, this number was not considered the successor to IPv4. Several proposals were suggested as the IPv4 successor, and each was assigned a number [41]. In the end, the one with version number 6 was selected. In the context of IoT, TCP/IP (IPv6) is used to enable communication between IoT devices and the internet. IPv6 provides a larger address space than IPv4, which is important for IoT applications in which there may be many devices that need to be connected to the internet. IPv6 also provides improved security features, which are important for ensuring the integrity and confidentiality of data transmitted between IoT devices and the internet. TCP/IP (IPv6) provides a reliable and robust communication protocol for IoT applications, allowing devices to transmit data securely and efficiently over the internet. TCP/IP (IPv6) also provides support for a range of other protocols which are commonly used in IoT applications for data transmission and management, such as HTTP and MQTT. IPv6 provides improved remote access and management for large fleets of IoT devices. Another major advantage of IPv6 is its highly efficient multicast communication feature, which all but eliminates the need for routine broadcast messaging. Thus, IPv6 includes several features that are particularly useful for IoT applications. Figure 3.11 compares IPv4 and IPv6. Some of these features include the following [40, 42].

1. **Larger Address Space:** IPv6 uses 128-bit addresses, providing a vastly larger address space compared to the 32-bit addresses used in IPv4. This makes it possible to assign unique IP addresses to a much larger number of devices, enabling the expansion of IoT networks.

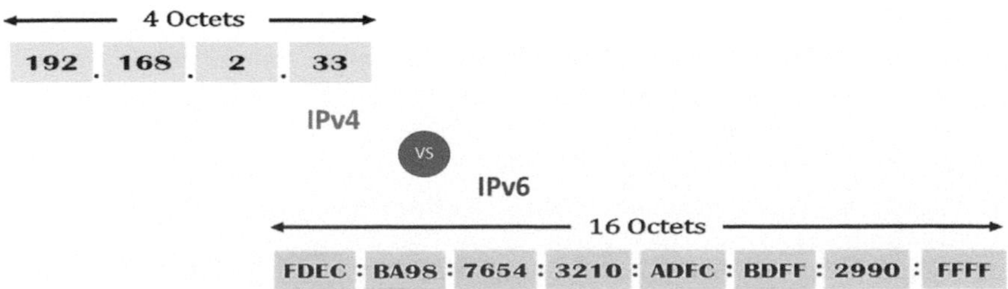

FIGURE 3.11 IPv4 vs. IPv6.

2. **Stateless Address Autoconfiguration (SLAAC):** IPv6 includes a mechanism for automatically configuring IP addresses, without the need for a central server. This can simplify the deployment and management of large IoT networks.
3. **Multicast Support:** IPv6 includes built-in support for multicasting, which is important for many IoT applications such as sensor networks and smart homes. This allows devices to receive data from multiple sources simultaneously, improving network efficiency.
4. **Quality of Service (QoS) Support:** IPv6 includes support for QoS, which allows traffic to be prioritized based on its type and importance. This is important for IoT applications in which real-time communication and low latency are critical.
5. **Extension Headers:** IPv6 includes a range of extension headers that enable additional functionality to be added to the protocol, such as authentication, encryption, and fragmentation.
6. **Mobility Support:** IPv6 includes support for mobile devices, allowing devices to seamlessly move between networks without losing their IP address. This is important for many IoT applications where devices may be moving frequently or may need to connect to multiple networks.

IPv6 uses 128-bit addresses as opposed to the 32-bit addresses used by IPv4, allowing for a substantially larger number of possible addresses. With each bit corresponding to a "0" or "1," this theoretically allows 2 ^ 128 combinations or 340 trillion, trillion, trillion addresses. By contrast, IPv4 permits 2 ^ 32 combinations for a maximum of approximately 4.7 billion addresses.

The IPv6 packet format is designed to provide a more efficient and flexible mechanism for transmitting data over the internet compared to the earlier IPv4 protocol. The IPv6 packet format is shown in Figure 3.12 [42].

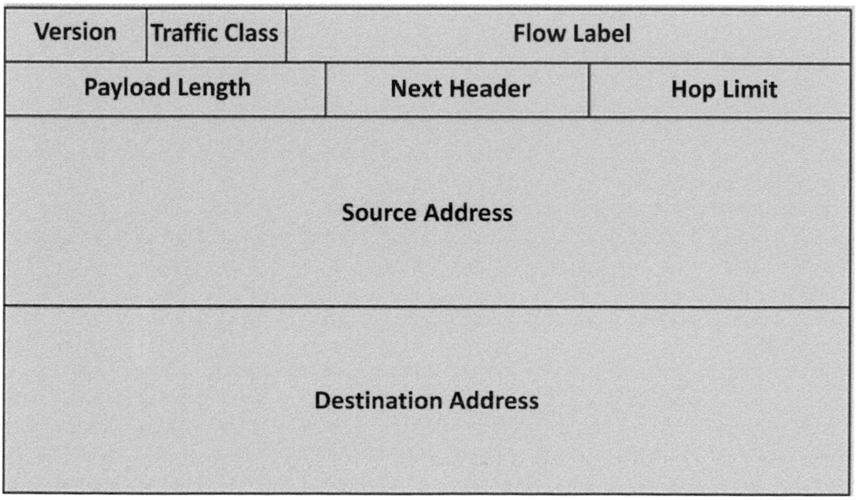

Version | Traffic Class | Flow Label
Payload Length | Next Header | Hop Limit
Source Address
Destination Address

FIGURE 3.12 IPv6 packet format.

The fields in the IPv6 packet format are:

- **Version (4 bits):** This field specifies the version of the IPv6 protocol being used, which is always set to 6.
- **Traffic Class (8 bits):** This field is used to specify the priority or type of traffic, such as voice, video, or data.
- **Flow Label (20 bits):** This field is used to identify packets belonging to the same flow, which can be used for QoS (quality of service) purposes.
- **Payload Length (16 bits):** This field specifies the length of the payload in octets.
- **Next Header (8 bits):** This field identifies the protocol used in the next header field, such as TCP or User Diagram Protocol (UDP).
- **Hop Limit (8 bits):** This field specifies the maximum number of hops that a packet can take before it is discarded.
- **Source Address (128 bits):** This field specifies the source address of the packet.
- **Destination Address (128 bits):** This field specifies the destination address of the packet.
- **Payload:** This field contains the data being transmitted in the packet.

3.2.3 6LoWPAN

6LoWPAN is a protocol designed for communication between low-power, low-bandwidth devices in IoT applications. It is a lightweight adaptation layer that allows IPv6 packets to be transmitted over low-power wireless networks, such as IEEE 802.15.4 [43]. Figure 3.13 illustrates the architecture of 6LoWPAN. 6LoWPAN Protocol is concluded by a working group in the internet area of the IETF (Internet Engineering Task Force). Rather than being an IoT application protocol technology like Bluetooth or Zigbee, 6LoWPAN is a network protocol that defines encapsulation and header compression mechanisms. It allows for the smallest devices with limited processing ability to transmit information wirelessly using an IP. It is the newest competitor to Zigbee. A powerful feature of 6LoWPAN is that while it

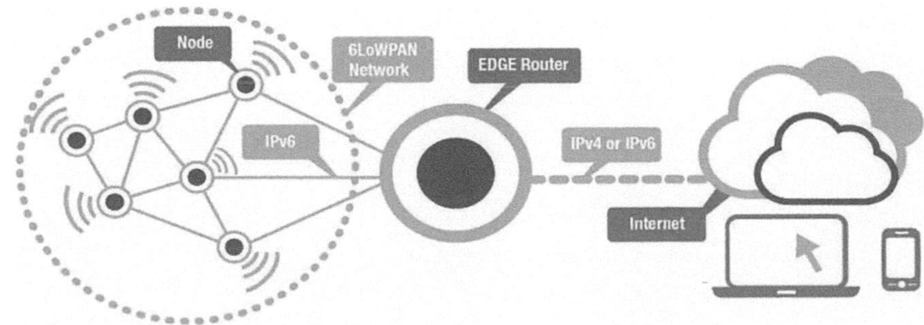

FIGURE 3.13 Architecture of 6LoWPAN.

was originally conceived to support IEEE 802.15.4 low-power wireless networks in the 2.4-GHz band, it is now being adapted and used over a variety of other networking media including Sub-1 GHz low-power RF, Bluetooth Smart, power line control (PLC, used elsewhere in this book to mean programmable logic controllers) and low-power Wi-Fi. Some of the key features of 6LoWPAN include the following [44, 45].

1. **Header Compression:** 6LoWPAN uses header compression techniques to reduce the size of IPv6 packets, making them more efficient to transmit over low-bandwidth wireless networks.
2. **Fragmentation:** 6LoWPAN can fragment large IPv6 packets into smaller packets that can be transmitted over the low-bandwidth network.
3. **Addressing:** 6LoWPAN uses 16-bit addresses instead of the 128-bit addresses used in IPv6, to reduce the size of the packet headers and to conserve battery life in low-power devices.
4. **Mesh Networking:** 6LoWPAN supports mesh networking, by which devices can forward packets for each other to extend the range of the network.
5. **Low Power Consumption:** 6LoWPAN is designed to be energy-efficient, with low overheads for packet transmission and minimal power requirements for devices.
6. **Security:** 6LoWPAN includes support for security mechanisms such as encryption and authentication to protect the privacy and integrity of data transmitted over the network.

There are several benefits of using 6LoWPAN in IoT applications, including the following [44].

1. **Efficient Use of Bandwidth:** 6LoWPAN uses header compression techniques to reduce the size of IPv6 packets, making them more efficient to transmit over low-bandwidth wireless networks. This results in a more efficient use of bandwidth, which is critical for low-power devices that have limited bandwidth.
2. **Low Power Consumption:** 6LoWPAN is designed to be energy efficient, with low overheads for packet transmission and minimal power requirements for devices. This is important for IoT devices that operate on batteries and need to conserve power to maximize their lifespan.
3. **Scalability:** 6LoWPAN supports mesh networking, whereby devices can forward packets for each other to extend the range of the network. This allows for the creation of large-scale IoT networks that can span large geographical areas.
4. **Interoperability:** 6LoWPAN is based on the standard IPv6 protocol, which is widely used and supported in the networking industry. This makes it easier to integrate 6LoWPAN devices with existing IPv6 networks and services.
5. **Security:** 6LoWPAN includes support for security mechanisms such as encryption and authentication to protect the privacy and integrity of data transmitted over the network. This is important for IoT applications that handle sensitive data, such as healthcare and financial services.

3.2.4 RPL

The Routing Protocol for Low-Power and Lossy Networks (RPL) is designed specifically for IoT devices in low-power and lossy networks (LLNs) [46, 47]. It is a key protocol for enabling communication among IoT devices and providing end-to-end communication over these networks. RPL is a proactive protocol that creates a tree-based routing topology. It uses a destination-oriented directed acyclic graph (DODAG) structure to determine the shortest path from the source to the destination node. The DODAG structure is created by selecting a root node and allowing other nodes to join the tree as leaves or branches. One of the key advantages of RPL is its ability to handle the high packet loss and low bandwidth that is common in LLNs. It achieves this by using a "rank" metric to determine the optimal route to the destination node. The rank metric considers various factors such as link quality, battery life, and latency to ensure that the most efficient path is chosen. Another advantage of RPL is its ability to support both point-to-point and multicast communication. This allows IoT devices to communicate with each other or with a group of devices, enabling a range of applications such as environmental monitoring, home automation, and industrial automation.

RPL also supports a range of security features such as authentication, confidentiality, and integrity protection. This ensures that the communication between IoT devices is secure and protected from potential threats. RPL supports the following two modes of operation: storing mode and non-storing mode [46]. Figure 3.14 shows

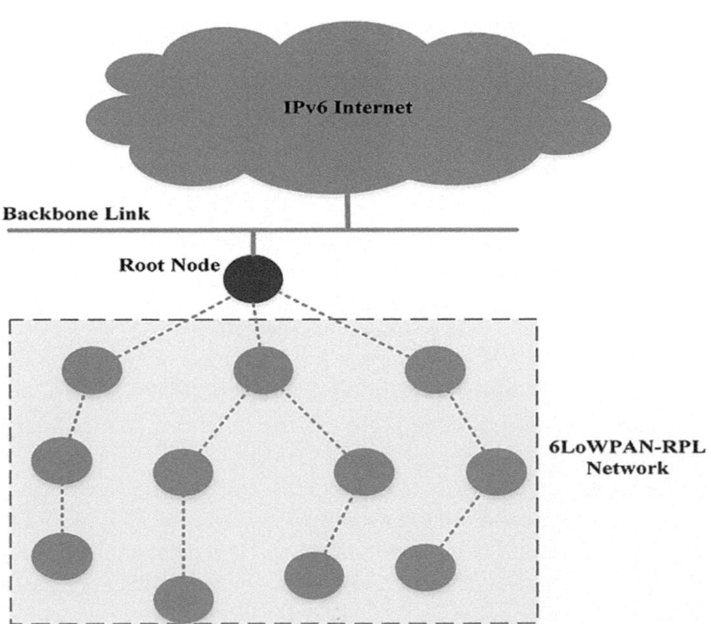

FIGURE 3.14 Architecture of Routing Protocol for Low-Power and Lossy Networks (RPL).

the architecture of RPL. These modes determine how routing information is stored and managed in the network.

- **Storing Mode:** In storing mode, all nodes in the network maintain a routing table that stores the routing information. This mode is suitable for networks with low mobility, low power consumption, and sufficient memory to store routing tables [48, 49]. In this mode, intermediate nodes along the path to the destination store routing information about the nodes and the links between them. This information is used to determine the optimal path to the destination. The nodes maintain a list of neighbors and their link qualities, allowing them to choose the best path to forward the data. Storing mode provides better routing performance as it uses an efficient and optimal routing mechanism. However, it requires more memory and processing power, which may not be suitable for all IoT devices.
- **Non-Storing Mode:** In non-storing mode, only the parent nodes along the path to the destination maintain routing information. This mode is suitable for highly dynamic and large-scale networks, where maintaining routing tables at all nodes may be impractical. In non-storing mode, the intermediate nodes forward the data to their parent node, which then routes the data to the destination node [48]. The parent nodes maintain a list of their child nodes, their link qualities, and the routes to their descendants. Non-storing mode is more scalable and suitable for networks with limited memory and processing power. However, it may not provide the same level of routing efficiency as storing mode. The RPL protocol is implemented using the Contiki operating system. This operating system primarily focuses on IoT devices, more specifically low-power wireless IoT devices. It is an open-source model and was first bought into the picture by Adam Dunkels. The RPL protocol mostly occurs in wireless sensors and networks. Other similar operating systems include T-Kernel, EyeOS, and LiteOS. The implementation of the RPL protocol for IoT devices requires the following steps [46, 48].
    1. **Select the RPL Objective Function:** The RPL objective function (OF) is used to calculate the rank of the nodes in the network, which determines their position in the DODAG structure. The OF considers various factors such as link quality, power consumption, and latency to determine the optimal path to the destination. Selecting an appropriate OF is critical to the performance of the network.
    2. **Determine the DODAG Root:** The DODAG root is the starting point of the DODAG structure and is responsible for initiating the DODAG formation. The root node is typically selected based on the network topology and the desired communication pattern.
    3. **Form the DODAG:** Once the DODAG root is selected, other nodes can join the DODAG as branches or leaves. Nodes determine their position in the DODAG based on their rank, which is calculated using the selected OF. Nodes select their preferred parent node based on their rank and the link quality to the parent node.

4. **Maintain the DODAG:** Once the DODAG is formed, it must be maintained to ensure efficient routing. This involves monitoring the link quality, updating the routing information, and handling node failures. Nodes periodically send control messages to their parent node to update the link quality and exchange routing information.
5. **Handle Data Communication:** Once the DODAG is established, data communication can occur between the nodes. Nodes use the DODAG structure to determine the optimal path to the destination node. Data packets are forwarded from node to node until they reach the destination.
6. **Handle Security:** Security is critical in IoT networks to protect against potential threats. RPL supports a range of security features such as authentication, confidentiality, and integrity protection. These features ensure that the communication between the nodes is secure and protected.

The implementation of the RPL protocol for IoT devices involves selecting the appropriate OF, determining the DODAG root, forming and maintaining the DODAG, handling data communication, and ensuring security [48]. These steps are critical to the performance and security of the IoT network. Thus, RPL is a critical protocol for enabling communication among IoT devices in low-power and lossy networks. It provides a robust and efficient routing mechanism that can handle the unique characteristics of LLNs and supports a range of security features to ensure that communication is secure and protected. In summary, the choice of mode depends on the characteristics of the IoT network, including its size, mobility, and power constraints. Both modes have their advantages and disadvantages, and selecting the appropriate mode can help optimize the performance of the network.

3.2.5 REST

REST (representational state transfer) is a protocol used in IoT to enable communication between devices and applications over the internet. It is a simple and lightweight protocol that uses HTTP to transfer data [50]. Figure 3.15 shows the REST model. The REST protocol relies on the concept of resources, which are identified by unique URIs (uniform resource identifiers). Resources represent data or functionality that can be accessed or modified using HTTP methods such as GET, PUT, POST, and DELETE.

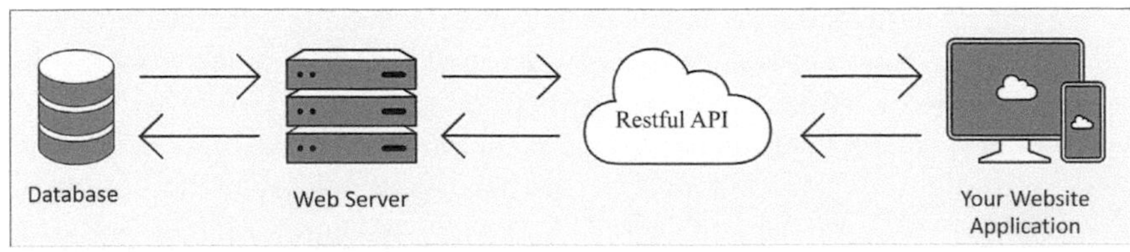

FIGURE 3.15 REST model.

Following are the key aspects of the REST protocol in IoT [35, 50].

1. **Resources:** Resources are identified by unique URIs and represent data or functionality that can be accessed or modified. In IoT, resources can include sensors, actuators, and other devices.
2. **HTTP Methods:** HTTP methods are used to interact with resources. The most commonly used HTTP methods in REST are GET, PUT, POST, and DELETE. GET is used to retrieve resource data, PUT is used to update resource data, POST is used to create a new resource, and DELETE is used to remove a resource.
3. **Representations:** Resources can be represented in various formats, such as XML (Extensible Markup Language), JSON, or binary data. The client and server can agree on a common representation format to exchange data.
4. **Stateless:** REST is a stateless protocol, which means that each request is independent and does not rely on previous requests. This simplifies communication between devices and reduces the complexity of the system.
5. **Caching:** REST supports caching, which allows frequently accessed resources to be stored locally to improve performance and reduce network traffic.
6. **Security:** REST supports various security mechanisms such as HTTPS, OAuth, and API keys to ensure secure communication between devices and applications.

In summary, the REST protocol is a lightweight and flexible protocol used in IoT to enable communication between devices and applications. It relies on the concept of resources, HTTP methods, representations, statelessness, caching, and security to provide a simple and efficient communication mechanism.

3.2.6 AMQP

AMQP (Advanced Message Queuing Protocol) is an open standard application layer protocol for message-oriented middleware [51]. It is designed to provide reliable, secure, and efficient messaging between devices and applications in IoT environments. AMQP enables the exchange of messages between devices and applications in a publish/subscribe model. It supports different messaging patterns, including point-to-point, multicast, and publish/subscribe. AMQP provides features such as message routing, queuing, and reliability to ensure that messages are delivered to their intended recipients. Overall, AMQP is an important protocol for IoT applications, providing a reliable, secure, and efficient mechanism for messaging between devices and applications. Its features for reliability, security, interoperability, scalability, and performance make it well suited to a wide range of IoT applications, from smart homes and buildings to industrial automation and healthcare monitoring. AMQP is an award-winning technology conceived by demanding users work together with technology experts to meet the need to connect systems reliably and get business done. This is an open standard for passing business messages between applications or organizations. It connects systems, feeds business processes with the information

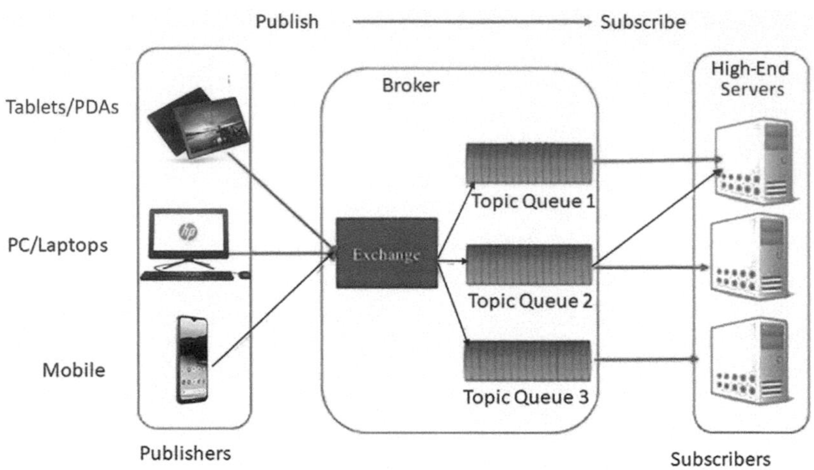

FIGURE 3.16 AMQP architecture.

they need, and reliably transmits onward the instructions that achieve their goals. Figure 3.16 shows the AMQP architecture. AMQP connects across the following.

- **Organizations:** Applications used by different organizations.
- **Technologies:** Applications running on different platforms.
- **Time:** Systems do not need to be available simultaneously.
- **Space:** Reliably operates at a distance, or over poor networks.

AMQP is designed to solve real problems completely. The capable, commoditized, multi-vendor communications ecosystem which AMQP enables creates opportunities for commerce and innovation which can transform the way business is done on the internet and in the cloud. The AMQP protocol plays a critical role in IoT by providing efficient, reliable, and standardized communication between devices and applications. It supports interoperability, scalability, and security, which are key requirements for IoT applications. Following are some key roles of the AMQP protocol in IoT [51, 52].

1. **Efficient Communication:** AMQP provides efficient and reliable communication between devices and applications. It uses a message-oriented middleware approach which allows devices to send and receive messages without the need for a dedicated connection.
2. **Standardization:** AMQP is a standardized protocol that defines a set of rules and standards for message-oriented middleware. This ensures that devices and applications can communicate with each other using a common language and protocol.
3. **Interoperability:** AMQP supports interoperability, which means that devices and applications from different vendors can communicate with each

other using the same protocol. This reduces the complexity of the system and enables devices and applications to work seamlessly together.

4. **Reliability:** AMQP provides reliable messaging, which means that messages are delivered in the order they were sent and are guaranteed to be delivered at least once. This ensures that messages are not lost or duplicated, which is critical in IoT applications.
5. **Scalability:** AMQP is scalable, which means that it can handle many devices and messages. It supports features such as message queuing and load balancing, which allows devices and applications to scale up or down as needed.
6. **Security:** AMQP supports various security mechanisms such as TLS/SSL (Transport Layer Security/Secure Socket Layer) encryption and authentication to ensure secure communication between devices and applications. This is critical in IoT applications in which security is a major concern.

3.2.7 XMPP

Extensible Messaging and Presence Protocol (XMPP) is a communication protocol that is widely used in IoT to enable real-time communication between devices and applications. Originally designed for instant messaging, XMPP has been adapted for IoT applications and is now used for a wide range of IoT use cases [53]. XMPP is an open standard communications protocol based on XML. At its root, XMPP is a chat protocol that allows for the transmission of XML fragments, i.e. data, between two network endpoints in near real time. What exactly XMPP stands for can be understood from Figure 3.17. Unlike other chat protocols, the XMPP protocol is designed for small chunks of XML data rather than large blobs or streams of binary data. To get a better understanding of what XMPP can do, we will next break down what exactly XMPP means. With these components, XMPP can handle many of the core

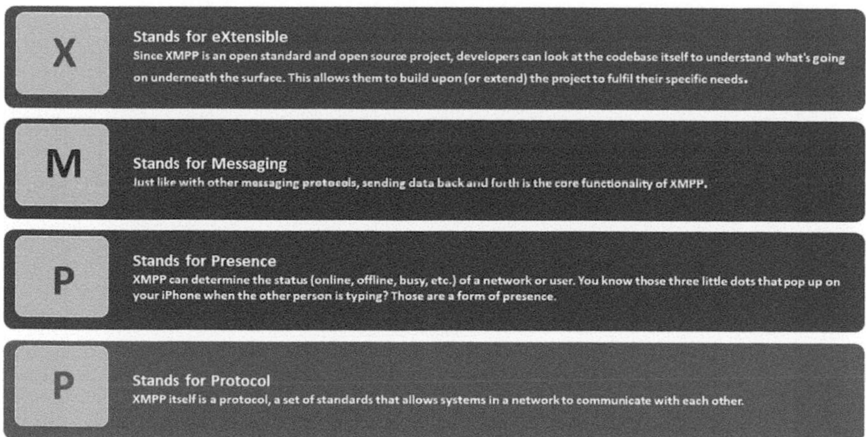

FIGURE 3.17 Definition of XMPP.

functions of a chat app including sending and receiving messages, broadcasting a user's status, managing a friends/contact list, and blocking users from sending you messages.

XMPP works on a client–server architecture [54]. This means that when you send a message via XMPP, it is first sent to a server which then routes it to the correct client (user). Each client connected to an XMPP server is assigned a unique identifier, known as a Jabber ID. The current format of the unique identifier is user@domain.com/resource.

- The user and domain parts of the unique identifier are pretty straightforward. User is the username of the person and domain.com is the domain of the client sending the message.
- Resource refers to the type of device on which the message was sent. For example, mobile or web. This part of the unique identifier is optional and is often only defined in situations when the client does not support every device.

Using this unique identifier, an XMPP server can route each message to the correct client. When a client initiates a session with an XMPP server, it opens a persistent TCP connection and starts an XML stream to the server. Once the client is identified by the server (via the unique identifier) and the connection is accepted, the server then opens an additional XML stream—with this stream going back to the client. The end result is a bidirectional stream of XML data. XMPP servers can also communicate with other XMPP servers to create a global messaging network called a "federation." A federation allows you to communicate seamlessly with a client on a different XMPP server. Figure 3.18 represents XMPP server–client architecture.

The XMPP protocol plays a critical role in IoT by providing real-time communication, messaging, presence, scalability, security, and standardization. It is widely used in IoT applications and is a popular choice for developers and organizations that require real-time communication and messaging capabilities. Following are some key roles of the XMPP protocol in IoT [53, 54].

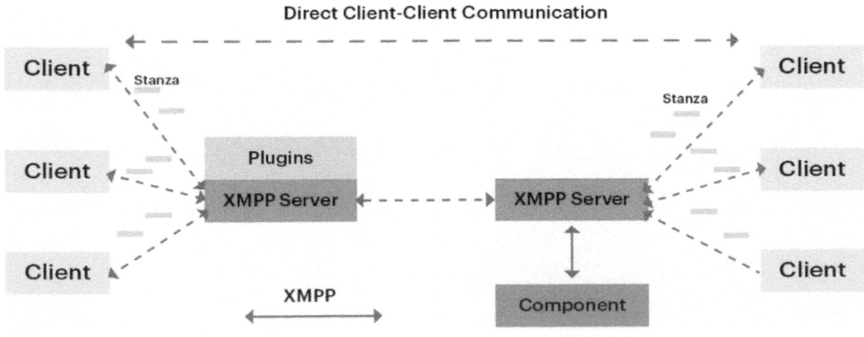

FIGURE 3.18 XMPP architecture.

1. **Real-Time Communication:** XMPP provides real-time communication between devices and applications. This is critical in IoT applications when devices need to communicate with each other in real time to exchange information and perform actions.
2. **Messaging:** XMPP supports messaging, which allows devices to send and receive messages in real time. This is useful for applications such as remote monitoring, whereby devices need to send status updates and alerts to a central server or to other devices.
3. **Presence:** XMPP supports presence, which allows devices to indicate their availability and status to other devices. This is useful for applications such as fleet management, when devices need to indicate their location and status to a central server or to other devices.
4. **Scalability:** XMPP is scalable, which means that it can handle a large number of devices and messages. It supports features such as message queuing and load balancing, which allow devices and applications to scale up or down as needed.
5. **Security:** XMPP supports various security mechanisms such as TLS/SSL encryption and authentication to ensure secure communication between devices and applications. This is critical in IoT applications in which security is a major concern.
6. **Standardization:** XMPP is a standardized protocol that is widely used in IoT. This ensures that devices and applications can communicate with each other using a common language and protocol.

3.2.8 CoAP

Constrained Application Protocol (CoAP) is a web transfer protocol that is used in constrained nodes or networks such as WSN, IoT, M2M, etc., and is targeted at IoT devices having less memory and fewer power specifications [55, 56]—hence, constrained. As it is designed for web applications, it is also known as the Web of Things Protocol. It can be used to transport data from a few bytes to thousands of bytes over web applications. It exists between the UDP and application layers. There are two modes in which CoAP messages get exchanged between CoAP client and CoAP server: with and without a separate response. With a separate response, the server notifies the client about the receipt of the request message. This will increase processing time but help in avoiding unnecessary retransmissions. CoAP IoT is an unreliable protocol due to the use of UDP. Hence, CoAP messages reach unordered or will get lost when they arrive at their destination. To make CoAP a reliable protocol, stop and wait with exponential backoff retransmission feature is incorporated in it. Duplicate detection is also introduced.

CoAP incorporates several key features that make it suitable for resource-constrained environments. First, CoAP utilizes the UDP transport protocol instead of TCP, which reduces overhead and makes it more efficient in terms of bandwidth and energy consumption [57]. This enables CoAP to be used on devices with limited processing power and memory. Second, CoAP follows a client–server model whereby devices can act as clients that request resources or servers that provide resources. It supports a request/response mechanism similar to HTTP, allowing clients to perform CRUD operations (create, read, update, delete) on resources. Another significant feature of CoAP is its support for a lightweight publish/subscribe model. It includes a resource observation feature that allows clients to subscribe to a resource and receive notifications whenever the resource changes. This feature is useful for applications that require real-time updates or event-driven interactions. CoAP also implements a flexible message format based on the REST architectural style, making it interoperable with web technologies. It uses URIs to identify resources and supports content negotiation, allowing clients and servers to exchange data in different formats such as XML or JSON. Furthermore, CoAP includes built-in support for resource discovery through a standardized protocol known as CoRE Link Format. This allows clients to discover available resources on a server dynamically, without the need for prior knowledge or manual configuration. Overall, CoAP's key features of lightweight transport, client–server model, support for resource observation, RESTful architecture, content negotiation, and resource discovery make it a suitable protocol for constrained devices and low-power networks, facilitating efficient communication and interaction within the IoT ecosystem.

Figure 3.19 depicts CoAP Architecture [55, 56]. As shown, it extends normal HTTP clients to clients having resource constraints. These clients are known as CoAP clients. Proxy device bridges the gap between a constrained environment and a typical internet environment based on HTTP protocols. The same server takes care of both HTTP and CoAP messages. the architecture of CoAP provides a lightweight, efficient, and scalable framework for communication between constrained devices and applications. Its client–server model, resource-oriented approach, RESTful message format, and support for resource observation and discovery contribute to the successful deployment of IoT solutions in resource-constrained environments. The architecture of the CoAP is designed to support communication between resource-constrained devices and applications in the context of the IoT. CoAP follows

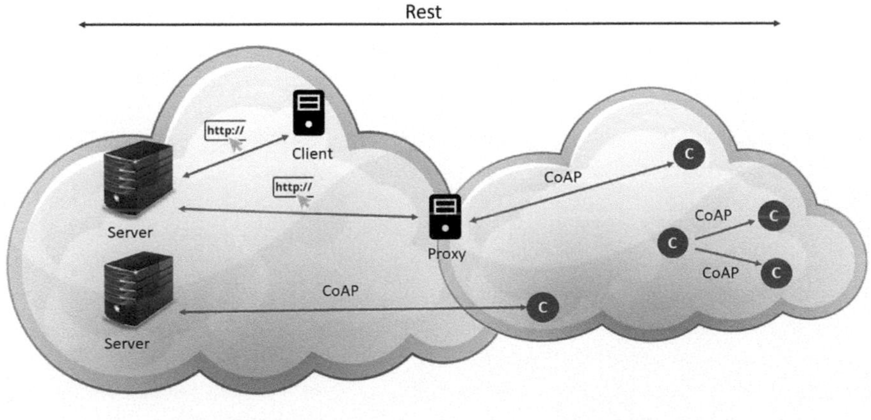

FIGURE 3.19 CoAP architecture.

a client–server model whereby devices can act as either clients or servers. At the core of CoAP is the concept of resources. A resource is a piece of information or functionality that can be accessed and manipulated by clients. Each resource is identified by a URI, which allows clients to uniquely reference and interact with the resource. CoAP uses a request/response mechanism similar to HTTP. Clients can issue requests to servers to perform operations on resources, such as retrieving resource representations, updating resource values, or deleting resources. Requests are typically made using the methods GET, POST, PUT, and DELETE, which correspond to retrieving, creating, updating, and deleting resources, respectively. CoAP employs a lightweight message format based on the REST architectural style. Messages are exchanged using the User Datagram Protocol (UDP) as the underlying transport protocol, which reduces overhead and conserves resources compared to the more heavyweight TCP. CoAP messages include headers for addressing, message type (confirmable or non-confirmable), and other control information. Additionally, CoAP incorporates a simple discovery mechanism through the CoRE Link Format. Servers can expose their available resources and associated metadata in a well-defined format, allowing clients to discover and navigate resources dynamically. Table 3.4 explains CoAP message header with description.

Figure 3.20 depicts CoAP message format consists of 4-byte header followed by a token value (from 0–8 bytes) [57]. Table 3.4 mentions the header which consists of 4 bytes, i.e., 32 bits.

TABLE 3.4
The CoAP Message Header with Description

CoAP Message Header	Description
Ver	A 2-bit unsigned integer. It mentions the CoAP version number. Set to 1.
T	A 2-bit unsigned integer. Indicates message type, viz., confirmable (0), non-confirmable (1), ACK (2), or RESET (3).
TKL	A 4-bit unsigned integer, indicating the length of the token (0–8 bytes).
Code	An 8-bit unsigned integer, it is split into two parts, viz., 3-bit class (MSBs) and 5-bit detail (LSBs).
Message ID	A 16-bit unsigned integer, it issed for matching responses and to detect message duplication.

```
 0                   1                   2                   3
 0 1 2 3 4 5 6 7 8 9 0 1 2 3 4 5 6 7 8 9 0 1 2 3 4 5 6 7 8 9 0 1
+-+-+-+-+-+-+-+-+-+-+-+-+-+-+-+-+-+-+-+-+-+-+-+-+-+-+-+-+-+-+-+-+
|Ver| T |  TKL  |      Code     |          Message ID           |
+-+-+-+-+-+-+-+-+-+-+-+-+-+-+-+-+-+-+-+-+-+-+-+-+-+-+-+-+-+-+-+-+
|   Token (if any, TKL bytes) ...
+-+-+-+-+-+-+-+-+-+-+-+-+-+-+-+-+-+-+-+-+-+-+-+-+-+-+-+-+-+-+-+-+
|   Options (if any) ...
+-+-+-+-+-+-+-+-+-+-+-+-+-+-+-+-+-+-+-+-+-+-+-+-+-+-+-+-+-+-+-+-+
|1 1 1 1 1 1 1 1|    Payload (if any) ...
+-+-+-+-+-+-+-+-+-+-+-+-+-+-+-+-+-+-+-+-+-+-+-+-+-+-+-+-+-+-+-+-+
```

FIGURE 3.20 CoAP message format.

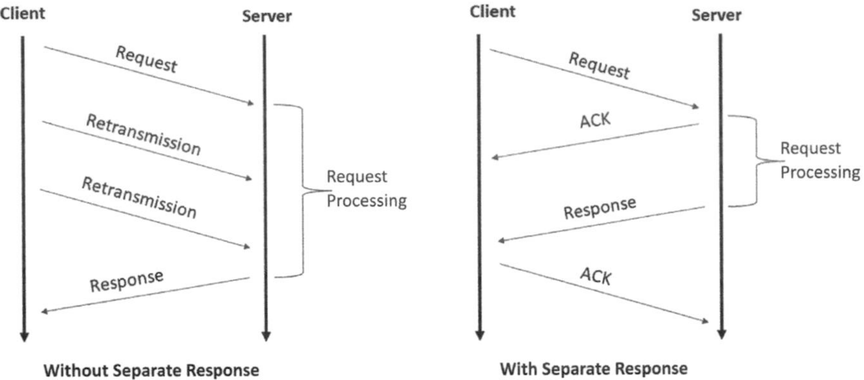

FIGURE 3.21 CoAP protocol message exchanges.

CoAP is a specialized web transfer protocol designed for resource-constrained devices and networks, such as those found in the IoT applications. CoAP follows a client–server model and utilizes a lightweight message exchange process, as shown in Figure 3.21, representing an overview of a CoAP protocol message exchange. CoAP protocol message exchanges provide a lightweight and efficient means of communication between clients and servers in constrained environments. They allow resource-constrained devices to interact with CoAP servers, retrieve information, and perform operations while minimizing resource usage.

The detailed steps during message exchange using the CoAP are as follow [55, 57, 58].

3.2.8.1 Step 1: Client Discovery

The client initiates the discovery process by sending a CoAP multicast message called a "UDP Discovery" to the CoAP multicast group address. This message allows the client to discover CoAP servers available on the network.

3.2.8.2 Step 2: Client Request

The client sends a CoAP request to a specific CoAP server. The request includes the following information.

- **Method:** Indicates the desired operation (e.g., GET, POST, PUT, DELETE).
- **URI (Uniform Resource Identifier):** Identifies the target resource on the server.
- **Message ID:** A unique identifier assigned by the client to match requests and responses.
- **Options:** Additional parameters like content type, observe, etc.
- **Payload:** Optional data to be sent along with the request.

3.2.8.3 Step 3: Server Response

The CoAP server processes the client's request and generates a corresponding response. The response includes the following information.

- **Message ID:** Matches the request message ID for identification.
- **Code:** Indicates the response status (e.g., 205 Reset Content, 404 Not Found).
- **Options:** Additional parameters like content type, observe, etc.
- **Payload:** Optional data sent back to the client as a response.

3.2.8.4 Step 4: Confirmable (CON) Message

CoAP messages can be either confirmable (CON) or non-confirmable (NON). A CON message expects an acknowledgment (ACK) from the recipient. If the client sends a CON message, it waits for an ACK before proceeding.

3.2.8.5 Step 5: Acknowledgment (ACK)

When a CoAP server receives a CON message, it sends an ACK message back to the client to confirm message delivery. The ACK message contains the message ID of the received CON message.

3.2.8.6 Step 6: Non-Confirmable (NON) Message

CoAP messages can also be sent as NON, which does not require an acknowledgment. The server may choose to respond with a NON message if it does not require reliability.

3.2.8.7 Step 7: Separate Response

In some cases, the server may decide to send the response in a separate CoAP message. This can be useful when the server needs more time to process the request or when the response is too large to fit in a single message. The client expects the separate response and waits for it.

3.2.8.8 Step 8: Message Retransmission

If the client does not receive an acknowledgment (ACK) for a CON message, it assumes the message was lost. The client retransmits the message. This ensures reliable delivery in the presence of unreliable networks.

3.2.9 MQTT

MQTT (Message Queuing Telemetry Transport) is a lightweight publish/subscribe messaging protocol and is designed to provide reliable, efficient, and secure communication between devices and applications in resource-constrained environments, especially for IoT ecosystem [52, 59]. It is a M2M connectivity protocol and is useful for connections with remote locations where a small code footprint is required and/or network bandwidth is at a premium. Figure 3.22 illustrates the schematic dataflow form sensor (machine) to device (machine). For example, MQTT has been used in sensors communicating to a broker via satellite link, over occasional dial-up connections with healthcare providers, and in a range of home automation and small device scenarios. It is also ideal for mobile applications because of its small size, low power usage, minimized data packets, and efficient distribution of

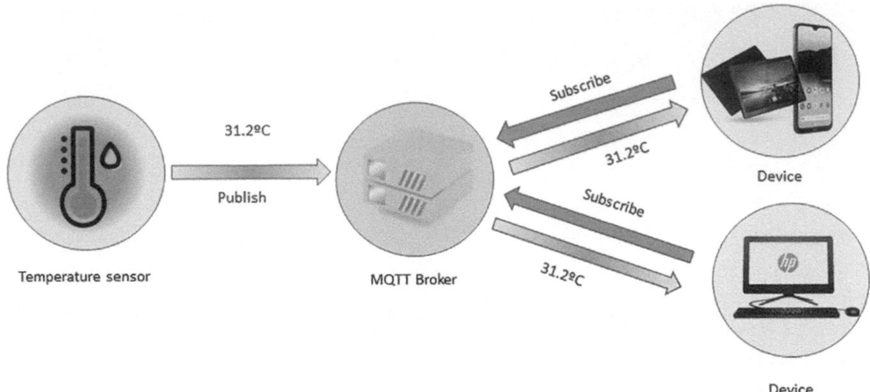

FIGURE 3.22 Schematic dataflow from sensor (machine) to device (machine).

information to one or many receivers. It is a message protocol for restricted networks (low bandwidth) and IoT devices with extremely high latency. MQTT is designed to be lightweight and low power, making it an ideal choice for IoT devices that have limited power and battery life. MQTT can be used to connect large numbers of devices, making it an ideal choice for IoT applications that require scalability. It provides a reliable messaging system that can ensure that messages are delivered even in the presence of network failures. It also provides a range of security options, including encryption, authentication, and access control, making it a secure choice for IoT applications. However, MQTT is not designed for real-time applications that require immediate response and high-speed data transfer [60]. It is not designed for transferring large amounts of data, as it is optimized for lightweight messaging. Additionally, it may not be compatible with some legacy devices or systems that use different protocols.

The MQTT broker is the center of every publish/subscribe protocol. Depending on the implementation, a broker can manage up to thousands of simultaneously connected MQTT clients [61]. The role of the MQTT broker is crucial in an IoT system, as it is responsible for managing the communication between the devices and applications. The broker receives and stores messages from publishers, and it ensures that these messages are delivered to the appropriate subscribers. The broker also handles the authentication and authorization of clients, ensuring that only authorized clients can publish or subscribe to specific topics. Some of the key functions of an MQTT broker include [59, 61]: i) accepting connections from publishers and subscribers; ii) managing MQTT topics and subscriptions; iii) filtering and routing messages between publishers and subscribers; iv) managing the QoS levels of messages; v) handling authentication and authorization of clients; and vi) providing logging and monitoring of message traffic. MQTT is used in a wide variety of industries and applications, including the following [62, 63].

1. **Industrial Automation:** MQTT is used in industrial automation applications to enable communication between sensors, actuators, and control

systems. It can be used to monitor and control machines and processes, and to collect data for analysis and optimization.

2. **Smart Home and Building Automation:** MQTT is used in smart home and building automation applications to enable communication between devices such as smart thermostats, lighting systems, and security systems. It can be used to control devices and monitor their status, and to provide real-time data to users.
3. **Healthcare:** MQTT is used in healthcare applications to enable communication between medical devices, patient monitoring systems, and healthcare applications. It can be used to collect data from medical devices and transmit it securely to healthcare applications for analysis and diagnosis.
4. **Transportation:** MQTT is used in transportation applications to enable communication between vehicles, traffic management systems, and transportation applications. It can be used to collect data on traffic conditions, vehicle performance, and driver behavior, and to optimize traffic flow and reduce congestion.
5. **Energy and Utilities:** MQTT is used in energy and utilities applications to enable communication between smart meters, energy management systems, and utility applications. It can be used to collect data on energy consumption, optimize energy usage, and improve the reliability and efficiency of energy systems.
6. **Agriculture:** MQTT is used in agriculture applications to enable communication between sensors, actuators, and agricultural management systems. It can be used to monitor soil moisture, temperature, and other environmental factors, and to optimize irrigation, fertilization, and other agricultural processes.

Getting started with MQTT in IoT is relatively easy, and there are several resources available to help you get started. Following are the steps to get started with MQTT [52, 60, 61].

1. **Choose an MQTT Broker:** An MQTT broker is a server that acts as a message broker between publishers and subscribers. You can choose from several open-source and commercial MQTT brokers, such as Mosquitto, HiveMQ, and IBM Watson IoT Platform.
2. **Choose an MQTT Client Library:** MQTT client libraries are available in several programming languages, including Python, Java, C, and C++. You can choose a client library that is compatible with your IoT device and programming language.
3. **Connect Your Device to the MQTT Broker:** Once you have chosen an MQTT broker and a client library, you can connect your device to the broker. You will need to provide the broker's address, port number, and credentials, such as username and password.
4. **Publish and Subscribe to MQTT Topics:** MQTT uses a publish/subscribe model, whereby publishers publish messages to topics and subscribers receive messages from topics. You can publish and subscribe to MQTT topics using the client library.

5. **Test Your MQTT Setup:** Once you have connected your device to the MQTT broker and published and subscribed to topics, you can test your setup by sending and receiving messages.

3.2.10 LoRa

Long Range (LoRa) is a wireless communication protocol that is widely used in IoT to enable long-range, low-power communication between devices [32, 64]. LoRa is designed to be highly scalable, efficient, and secure, making it a popular choice for IoT applications. LoRa plays a critical role in IoT by providing long-range, low-power communication that is highly scalable, efficient, secure, cost effective, and based on open standards. It is a popular choice for IoT applications that require long-range communication and low power consumption, such as smart cities, agriculture, and industrial IoT. Figure 3.23 shows a typical LoRa Network architecture. Following are some key features and roles of LoRa in IoT [32, 65].

1. **Long Range:** LoRa is designed to enable long-range communication, making it ideal for IoT applications that require devices to communicate over a large distance. LoRa can reach distances of up to 10 kilometers in rural areas and up to 2 kilometers in urban areas.
2. **Low Power:** LoRa is designed to be highly efficient in terms of power consumption, which is critical for IoT applications in which devices may need to operate on battery power for extended periods of time. LoRa devices can operate for years on a single battery charge, making them ideal for IoT applications that require long-term monitoring and sensing.
3. **Scalability:** LoRa is highly scalable, which means that it can support a large number of devices and messages. LoRa networks can be deployed in a variety of configurations, from point-to-point setups to large-scale, wide-area networks.
4. **Security:** LoRa supports various security mechanisms such as encryption and authentication to ensure secure communication between devices and applications. This is critical in IoT applications in which security is a major concern.

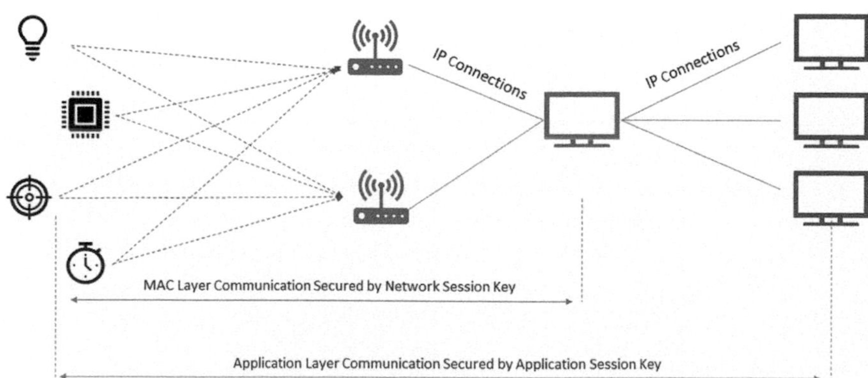

FIGURE 3.23 A typical LoRa network architecture.

5. **Cost Effectiveness:** LoRa is a cost-effective solution for IoT applications, as it requires less infrastructure and equipment than other wireless communication protocols. This makes it a popular choice for organizations that need to deploy large-scale IoT networks without incurring high costs.
6. **Standardization:** LoRa is based on open standards, which ensures that devices and applications can communicate with each other using a common language and protocol. This allows for interoperability between devices from different vendors and makes it easier for developers to create IoT applications using LoRa.

The LoRa technology in IoT consists of three main components: end devices, gateways, and network servers [44, 66].

1. **End Devices:** These are IoT devices equipped with LoRa transceivers that transmit data to gateways. End devices can be battery powered and designed for low-power consumption to enable long battery life. They can also be configured to operate in various modes, such as class A, class B, or class C, depending on their power requirements and communication needs.
2. **Gateways:** These are devices that receive data from end devices and forward it to a network server using the LoRaWAN protocol. Gateways typically use multiple channels to receive data from different end devices and transmit the data to the network server over a backhaul network such as Ethernet, Wi-Fi, or cellular.
3. **Network Server:** The LoRaWAN network server manages communication between the end devices and the gateways. It receives data from gateways and routes it to the appropriate end device using the unique device identifier (DevEUI). The network server also manages the security aspects of the communication, such as authentication and encryption.

LoRa protocol specification is developed by the LoRa Alliance. Figure 3.24 shows the LoRa Network Protocols. The end-to-end network protocol architecture is shown,

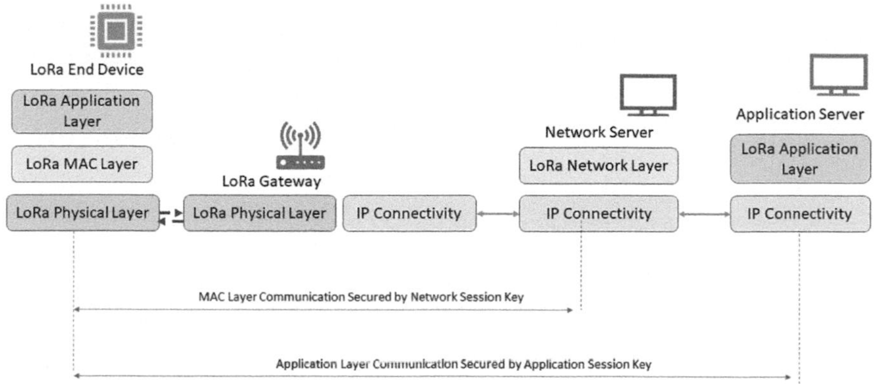

FIGURE 3.24 LoRa Network protocols.

consisting of MAC and application layers, and it operates based on the LoRa physical layer [32, 66]. The LoRaWAN protocol provides a standardized framework for communication between the end devices, gateways, and network servers, allowing for interoperability between different vendors' devices and networks. The LoRaWAN protocol uses the unlicensed ISM (industrial, scientific, and medical) band, which varies between regions, for example, 868 MHz in Europe and 915 MHz in the United States. LoRaWAN also provides different classes of operation to accommodate different power consumption and latency requirements for various IoT applications.

3.3 NETWORK AND COMMUNICATION ASPECT

Network and communication aspects play a crucial role in the IoT ecosystem. IoT devices rely on different communication protocols to send and receive data from other devices and systems. Following are some key aspects of network and communication in IoT.

1. **Protocols:** IoT devices use various communication protocols, such as Bluetooth, Wi-Fi, Zigbee, LoRaWAN, MQTT, and CoAP [67]. Each protocol has its own advantages and disadvantages in terms of range, power consumption, data rate, and security.
2. **Network Architecture:** IoT devices can be connected in different network architectures such as star, mesh, tree, and hybrid [38]. The choice of network architecture depends on the application requirements, coverage area, and the number of devices to be connected.
3. **Bandwidth and Data Rate:** IoT devices generate a large amount of data that needs to be transmitted over the network [68]. The bandwidth and data rate of the communication protocol used by the device must be able to handle the volume of data generated.
4. **Security:** IoT devices can be vulnerable to cyber-attacks, and security is a critical aspect of IoT communication. Different security mechanisms such as encryption, authentication, and authorization are used to protect IoT devices and networks [69].
5. **Power Consumption:** Many IoT devices are battery powered and designed for low power consumption to enable long battery life [68]. Communication protocols and network architectures that consume less power are preferred for IoT devices.
6. **Cloud Connectivity:** IoT devices can be connected to cloud platforms to enable remote monitoring, data analytics, and control [70]. Cloud platforms provide scalability, data storage, and data processing capabilities that are useful for IoT applications.
7. **Interoperability:** IoT devices and systems from different vendors and technologies must be able to communicate and exchange data. Standardized communication protocols and interfaces facilitate interoperability between different devices and systems.

Overall, network and communication aspects play a crucial role in the IoT ecosystem, and choosing the right communication protocol, network architecture, and security mechanism can have a significant impact on the performance and success of IoT applications.

3.3.1 Wireless Medium Access Issues

In wireless networks, medium access refers to the way in which devices share the wireless channel to transmit data. Wireless networks, such as Wi-Fi networks, face several medium access issues that can affect their performance and efficiency. These issues can be channel congestion, hidden node problem, exposed node problem, fairness issues, interference, and QoS issues [71]. Addressing these medium access issues in wireless networks often involves implementing various techniques and protocols, such as channel allocation and assignment algorithms, adaptive transmission power control, MAC layer optimizations, interference mitigation techniques, and QoS mechanisms. These approaches aim to optimize medium access, improve network performance, and provide a better user experience in wireless environments. In general, wireless medium access is prone to various issues that can affect network performance and reliability. Some of these issues include the following [66, 71, 72].

1. **Hidden Node Problem:** This occurs when two or more devices are within range of a common access point, but not within range of each other. This can result in collisions, causing two devices to transmit at the same time such that their signals interfere with each other, causing data loss.
2. **Channel Congestion:** Wireless networks operate within specific frequency bands or channels. When multiple devices compete for the same channel, channel congestion occurs. This can result in increased collisions, decreased throughput, and higher latency. The presence of neighboring Wi-Fi networks or other devices using the same frequency band can contribute to channel congestion.
3. **Exposed Node Problem:** The exposed node problem is the opposite of the hidden node problem. It occurs when a device refrains from transmitting data due to interference concerns, even though the interference would not affect the intended receiver. This results in reduced network capacity and inefficient utilization of the wireless medium. In short, it occurs when a device refrains from transmitting data to avoid interfering with another device's transmission, even though it does not actually overlap with the other device's coverage area.
4. **Fairness and Efficiency:** Fairness refers to the equitable distribution of network resources among competing devices. In wireless networks, fairness issues can arise when some devices monopolize the medium access, causing other devices to experience decreased throughput and increased latency. Unfair allocation of resources can lead to a poor user experience and hinder overall network performance. In wireless networks, it is essential to achieve a balance between fairness and efficiency. If the network is too fair, it can result in low efficiency; if it is too efficient, it can result in unfairness.
5. **Scalability:** Wireless networks must be able to scale to accommodate a large number of devices. This can be challenging due to limitations in bandwidth and the number of available channels.

6. **Interference:** Wireless networks are susceptible to interference from other wireless devices, such as Bluetooth or Wi-Fi, as well as from other sources, such as microwaves and other electronic equipment.
7. **Security:** Wireless networks are prone to security vulnerabilities, such as eavesdropping and unauthorized access. Security mechanisms must be implemented to prevent these vulnerabilities.
8. **Quality of Service (QoS):** In wireless networks, QoS is essential to ensure that traffic is prioritized appropriately and that critical data is delivered in a timely manner. However, implementing QoS in wireless networks can be challenging due to the unpredictable nature of the wireless channel.

3.3.2 MAC Protocol Survey

A MAC protocol is a set of rules and procedures that regulate the access of nodes to the communication medium in a network [71]. In the context of wireless communication, MAC protocols play a crucial role in ensuring fair and efficient access to the shared wireless medium. There are several MAC protocols used in wireless networks, including the following [5, 7].

1. **CSMA/CA (Carrier Sense Multiple Access with Collision Avoidance):** This protocol is commonly used in Wi-Fi networks and is based on the principle of listening to the medium before transmitting data. CSMA/CA allows multiple devices to share the same channel, but collisions are avoided by waiting for a random amount of time before retransmitting if the medium is busy.
2. **TDMA (Time Division Multiple Access):** TDMA is a protocol that divides the available bandwidth into time slots, allowing multiple devices to use the same channel without interference. Each device is assigned a specific time slot for transmitting data.
3. **FDMA (Frequency Division Multiple Access):** FDMA is a protocol that divides the available bandwidth into different frequency channels. Each device is assigned a specific frequency band for transmitting data.
4. **CDMA (Code Division Multiple Access):** CDMA is a protocol that uses a unique code to differentiate between different devices transmitting on the same frequency band. This allows multiple devices to transmit simultaneously without interference.
5. **ALOHA:** ALOHA is a simple MAC protocol that allows nodes to transmit data at any time, without checking if the medium is busy. If a collision occurs, the nodes retransmit their data after a random delay.
6. **Slotted ALOHA:** Slotted ALOHA divides time into fixed slots and allows nodes to transmit data only at the beginning of each slot. This reduces the likelihood of collisions and improves the efficiency of the protocol.
7. **Beacon-Enabled MAC Protocols:** These protocols use periodic beacon messages to synchronize nodes and regulate access to the wireless medium. Examples include IEEE 802.15.4, Zigbee, and Z-Wave.

The choice of MAC protocol depends on several factors, including the network topology, the number of devices in the network, the application requirements, and the available resources [71]. Each protocol has its strengths and weaknesses, and the selection of the appropriate protocol is crucial for ensuring reliable and efficient communication in wireless networks.

3.3.3 Survey of Routing Protocols

Routing protocols play a crucial role in determining the efficiency and reliability of communication in IoT networks. They play a vital role in IoT networks by establishing and maintaining device connectivity, enabling efficient data transmission, ensuring reliability, optimizing network performance, and enhancing security [73, 74]. They enable scalable and energy-efficient communication among IoT devices, prioritize traffic based on QoS requirements, and support multi-hop communication. By selecting optimal paths, avoiding congested links, and providing fault tolerance, routing protocols contribute to the seamless operation of diverse IoT applications and services. Here is a survey of some of the popular routing protocols used in IoT:

1. **RPL (IPv6 Routing Protocol for Low-Power and Lossy Networks):** RPL is a widely used routing protocol for low-power and lossy networks. It is designed for IPv6 networks and provides support for mesh topologies, multiple routing metrics, and path optimization [48]. RPL also supports the creation of multiple DODAGs to support multiple applications.
2. **AODV (Ad Hoc On-Demand Distance Vector):** AODV is a reactive routing protocol that establishes a route between nodes only when a data packet needs to be transmitted [75]. It is commonly used in wireless ad hoc networks and supports both unicast and multicast communications. AODV uses hop count as the metric to select the shortest path between source and destination.
3. **DSDV (Destination-Sequenced Distance Vector):** DSDV is a proactive routing protocol that maintains a routing table of all possible routes to a destination node. It uses sequence numbers to ensure that the latest route information is used and avoids the formation of loops [76]. DSDV is suitable for small-scale networks whereby topology is relatively stable.
4. **OLSR (Optimized Link-State Routing):** OLSR is a proactive routing protocol that uses link-state information to construct a routing table [36]. It is designed for mobile ad hoc networks and provides support for multipoint relays (MPRs) to reduce the number of broadcast messages. OLSR also supports multiple routing metrics to select the most reliable path.
5. **BATMAN (Better Approach to Mobile Ad Hoc Networking):** BATMAN is a proactive routing protocol that is optimized for mobile ad hoc networks. It uses distributed algorithms to construct and maintain a routing table and provides support for multi-path routing [36, 77]. BATMAN also supports the use of quality-of-service metrics to select the most suitable path.
6. **FSR (Fisheye State Routing):** FSR is a proactive routing protocol that uses a fisheye view to maintain a routing table. It provides support for both

unicast and multicast communications and uses a distributed algorithm to reduce the overhead of route updates [36, 77]. FSR is suitable for large-scale networks whereby the topology is relatively stable.

These are just some of the routing protocols used in IoT networks. The selection of a routing protocol depends on the specific requirements of the network, such as the size of the network, the mobility of the nodes, the reliability of the communication, and the power constraints of the devices [78].

3.3.4 Sensor Deployment and Node Discovery

Sensor deployment and node discovery are critical aspects of IoT network deployment, especially in large-scale IoT systems. These tasks involve the identification, configuration, and management of IoT devices, sensors, and nodes. Sensor deployment involves the physical installation of sensors in the environment, which can be a challenging task due to several factors such as the location, access, and power requirements of the sensors [79]. Additionally, the placement of sensors can significantly impact the accuracy and efficiency of the data collected by the sensors. Hence, careful planning and consideration are essential while deploying sensors. Node discovery is the process of identifying and adding new devices to the IoT network. The discovery process involves several steps, such as device identification, authentication, and configuration [80]. The discovery process can be challenging, especially in large-scale IoT networks to which hundreds or thousands of devices must be added.

Several protocols and technologies have been developed to simplify and automate the sensor deployment and node discovery process. For example, the Simple Network Management Protocol (SNMP) can be used to manage and monitor network devices, while the Zero Configuration Networking (Zeroconf) protocol can be used to automate device discovery and configuration [81]. Additionally, many IoT platforms and tools provide easy-to-use interfaces and APIs that simplify sensor deployment and node discovery for developers and end-users.

3.3.5 Data Aggregation and Dissemination

Data aggregation and dissemination are important aspects of IoT that involve the collection, processing, and distribution of data generated by various sensors and devices in the network [82, 83]. In IoT, data can be generated at a massive scale, and it becomes challenging to process and analyze the data in real time. Data aggregation and dissemination techniques are used to manage this data in an efficient manner. Data aggregation involves the collection and fusion of data from multiple sources to reduce the data size and improve the quality of data. Aggregated data is more concise and relevant, and it can be easily processed by applications. It also helps to reduce network traffic and save energy by reducing the number of transmissions. Data aggregation can be performed at different levels—such as node level, cluster level, and network level—depending on the application requirements.

Data dissemination involves the distribution of data to different nodes in the network, depending on the application requirements [83, 84]. Disseminated data can be used for monitoring, control, or decision-making purposes. Different techniques are used for data dissemination, such as flooding, multicast, and unicast. Flooding is a simple technique whereby data is broadcasted to all nodes in the network, which can be inefficient for large-scale networks. Multicast is a more efficient technique whereby data is transmitted only to a subset of nodes in the network. Unicast is a point-to-point communication technique whereby data is sent from one node to another node. In summary, data aggregation and dissemination techniques are crucial for efficient and effective management of data in IoT networks. These techniques can help to reduce the amount of data transmitted, save energy, and improve the scalability of IoT networks.

REFERENCES

[1] L. Alkama and L. Bouallouche-Medjkoune, "IEEE 802.15.4 Historical Revolution Versions: A Survey," *Computing*, vol. 103, no. 1, 2021, doi: 10.1007/s00607-020-00844-3.

[2] M. D. Mendy and Y. Faye, "A Comparative Study of Wireless Technologies Coexistence Mechanisms in IoT: A Survey," in *Lecture Notes in Networks and Systems*, 2021, doi: 10.1007/978-981-15-8354-4_18.

[3] S. Pollin *et al.*, "Performance Analysis of Slotted Carrier Sense IEEE 802.15.4 Medium Access Layer," *IEEE Trans. Wirel. Commun.*, vol. 7, no. 9, 2008, doi: 10.1109/TWC.2008.060057.

[4] P. Baronti, P. Pillai, V. W. C. Chook, S. Chessa, A. Gotta, and Y. F. Hu, "Wireless Sensor Networks: A Survey on the State of the Art and the 802.15.4 and ZigBee Standards," *Comput. Commun.*, vol. 30, no. 7, 2007, doi: 10.1016/j.comcom.2006.12.020.

[5] D. Striccoli, G. Boggia, and L. A. Grieco, "A Markov Model for Characterizing IEEE 802.15.4 MAC Layer in Noisy Environments," *IEEE Trans. Ind. Electron.*, vol. 62, no. 8, 2015, doi: 10.1109/TIE.2015.2403792.

[6] A. Gezer and S. Okdem, "☆Improving IEEE 802.15.4 Channel Access Performance for IoT and WSN Devices," *Comput. Electr. Eng.*, vol. 87, 2020, doi: 10.1016/j.compeleceng.2020.106745.

[7] M. Khanafer, M. Guennoun, and H. T. Mouftah, "A Survey of Beacon-Enabled IEEE 802.15.4 MAC Protocols in Wireless Sensor Networks," *IEEE Commun. Surv. Tutor.*, vol. 16, no. 2, 2014, doi: 10.1109/SURV.2013.112613.00094.

[8] C. B. Park, B. S. Park, H. J. Uhm, H. Choi, and H. S. Kim, "IEEE 802.15.4 Based Service Configuration Mechanism for Smartphone," *IEEE Trans. Consum. Electron.*, vol. 56, no. 3, 2010, doi: 10.1109/TCE.2010.5606358.

[9] Vaishali, A. M. Varsha, G. Tejaswini, and V. M. Shetty, "ZigBee Technology," *Int. J. Adv. Res. Sci. Commun. Technol.*, vol. 2, no. 1, 2022, doi: 10.48175/ijarsct-7036.

[10] T. Obaid, H. Rashed, A. Abou-Elnour, M. Rehan, M. Muhammad Saleh, and M. Tarique, "Zigbee Technology and Its Application in Wireless Home Automation Systems: A Survey," *Int. J. Comput. Netw. Commun.*, vol. 6, no. 4, 2014, doi: 10.5121/ijcnc.2014.6411.

[11] T. Agarwal, "What is ZigBee Technology, Architecture and its Applications?," *El-Pro-Cus.*, 2015. www.elprocus.com/what-is-zigbee-technology-architecture-and-its-applications/

[12] Zigbee Alliance, "ZigBee Cluster Library Specification," *Zigbee Alliance*, United States, vol. 6, January 2016.

[13] S. Farahani, "ZigBee and IEEE 802.15.4 Protocol Layers," in *ZigBee Wireless Networks and Transceivers*, Elsevier, Amsterdam, Netherlands, pp. 33–135, 2008, doi: 10.1016/b978-0-7506-8393-7.00003-0.

[14] W. Mardini, Y. Khamayseh, R. Jaradatand, and R. Hijjawi, "Interference Problem between ZigBee and WiFi," *Int. Proc. Comput. Sci. Inf. Technol.*, vol. 30, pp. 133–138, 2012.

[15] Y. Li, Y. Wang, and C. Ma, "Design of Communication System in Intelligent Instrument Based on HART Protocol," in *2015 IEEE International Conference on Mechatronics and Automation, ICMA 2015*, 2015, doi: 10.1109/ICMA.2015.7237510.

[16] F. Luo, T. Feng, and L. Zheng, "Formal Security Evaluation and Improvement of Wireless HART Protocol in Industrial Wireless Network," *Secur. Commun. Netw.*, vol. 2021, 2021, doi: 10.1155/2021/8090547.

[17] I. Turk, P. Angin, and A. Cosar, "RONFC: A Novel Enabler-Independent NFC Protocol for Mobile Transactions," *IEEE Access*, vol. 7, 2019, doi: 10.1109/ACCESS.2019.2929011.

[18] M. Al-Fayoumi and S. Nashwan, "Performance Analysis of SAP-NFC Protocol," *Int. J. Commun. Netw. Inf. Secur.*, vol. 10, no. 1, 2018, doi: 10.17762/ijcnis.v10i1.3237.

[19] I. Unwala and J. Lu, "IoT Protocols : Z-Wave and Thread," *Int. J. Futur. Revolut. Comput. Sci. Commun. Eng.*, vol. 3, no. 11, 2017.

[20] L. Babun, H. Aksu, L. Ryan, K. Akkaya, E. S. Bentley, and A. S. Uluagac, "Z-IoT: Passive Device-class Fingerprinting of ZigBee and Z-Wave IoT Devices," in *IEEE International Conference on Communications*, 2020, doi: 10.1109/ICC40277.2020.9149285.

[21] S. R. Jondhale and R. S. Deshpande, "GRNN and KF Framework Based Real Time Target Tracking Using PSOC BLE and Smartphone," *Ad Hoc Netw.*, vol. 84, 2019, doi: 10.1016/j.adhoc.2018.09.017.

[22] J. Yang, C. Poellabauer, P. Mitra, and C. Neubecker, "Beyond Beaconing: Emerging Applications and Challenges of BLE," *Ad Hoc Netw.*, vol. 97, 2020, doi: 10.1016/j.adhoc.2019.102015.

[23] A. Barua, M. A. Al Alamin, M. S. Hossain, and E. Hossain, "Security and Privacy Threats for Bluetooth Low Energy in IoT and Wearable Devices: A Comprehensive Survey," *IEEE Open J. Commun. Soc.*, vol. 3, 2022, doi: 10.1109/OJCOMS.2022.3149732.

[24] S. T. Bushby, "BACnet™: A Standard Communication Infrastructure for Intelligent Buildings," *Autom. Constr.*, vol. 6, no. 5–6, 1997, doi: 10.1016/S0926-5805(97)00029-0.

[25] S. H. Hong and S. Lee, "Design and Implementation of Fault Tolerance in the BACnet/IP Protocol," *IEEE Trans. Ind. Electron.*, vol. 57, no. 11, 2010, doi: 10.1109/TIE.2009.2038944.

[26] A. M. Kekre and A. Kothari, "MODBUS-TR: Advanced MODBUS-RTU Protocol for IoT with Auto-Discovery and Triggers," *Wirel. Pers. Commun.*, vol. 125, no. 3, 2022, doi: 10.1007/s11277-022-09684-0.

[27] I. H. Mulyadi, R. Mahdaliza, A. G. Darmoyono, S. Prayoga, and K. Kamarudin, "Modul Komunikasi Modbus RTU Over RS485 Berbasis Arduino," *J. Appl. Electr. Eng.*, vol. 5, no. 1, 2021, doi: 10.30871/jaee.v5i1.3070.

[28] M. Sasi Chandra, S. Saleem, S. L. Harish, R. Baskar, and P. C. Kishoreraja, "Li-Fi Technology and Its Applications," *Int. J. Pharm. Technol.*, vol. 8, no. 4, 2016.

[29] X. Bao, G. Yu, J. Dai, and X. Zhu, "Li-Fi: Light Fidelity-A Survey," *Wirel. Netw.*, vol. 21, no. 6, 2015, doi: 10.1007/s11276-015-0889-0.

[30] P. Goswami and M. K. Shukla, "Design of a Li-Fi Transceiver," *Wirel. Eng. Technol.*, vol. 08, no. 04, 2017, doi: 10.4236/wet.2017.84006.

[31] J. Ding, M. Nemati, C. Ranaweera, and J. Choi, "IoT Connectivity Technologies and Applications: A Survey," *IEEE Access*, vol. 8, 2020, doi: 10.1109/ACCESS.2020.2985932.

[32] A. Ikpehai *et al.*, "Low-Power Wide Area Network Technologies for Internet-of-Things: A Comparative Review," *IEEE Internet Things J.*, vol. 6, no. 2, 2019, doi: 10.1109/JIOT.2018.2883728.

[33] W. Jin, Y. G. Hong, and D. H. Kim, "Design and Implementation of a Wireless IoT Healthcare System Based on OCF IoTivity," *Int. J. Grid Distrib. Comput.*, vol. 11, no. 4, 2018, doi: 10.14257/ijgdc.2018.11.4.08.

[34] H. Pirayesh, P. K. Sangdeh, and H. Zeng, "Coexistence of Wi-Fi and IoT Communications in WLANs," *IEEE Internet Things J.*, vol. 7, no. 8, 2020, doi: 10.1109/JIOT.2020.2986110.

[35] S. Jaloudi, "Communication Protocols of an Industrial Internet of Things Environment: A Comparative Study," *Futur. Internet*, vol. 11, no. 3, 2019, doi: 10.3390/fi11030066.

[36] A. Triantafyllou, P. Sarigiannidis, and T. D. Lagkas, "Network Protocols, Schemes, and Mechanisms for Internet of Things (IoT): Features, Open Challenges, and Trends," *Wirel. Commun. Mob. Comput.*, vol. 2018, 2018, doi: 10.1155/2018/5349894.
[37] M. M. N. Sankpal, M. P. V. Chinchwade, M. R. R. Kognole, and M. K. N. Rode, "Computer Network Topologies," *Int. J. Res. Appl. Sci. Eng. Technol.*, vol. 10, no. 4, 2022, doi: 10.22214/ijraset.2022.41553.
[38] H.Andrea,"CompareandContrastNetworkTopologies(Star,Mesh,Bus,Hybridetc),"*Netw. Train.*, 2021. www.networkstraining.com/compare-and-contrast-network-topologies/
[39] A. S. Arora, S. Subramaniam, and H. A. Choi, "Logical Topology Design for Linear and Ring Optical Networks," *IEEE J. Sel. Areas Commun.*, vol. 20, no. 1, 2002, doi: 10.1109/49.974662.
[40] P. Venkata, P. Reddy, K. Mohammed, I. Ali, B. Sandeep, and T. Ravi, "Importance and Benefits of IPV6 Over IPV4: A Study," *Int. J. Sci. Res. Publ.*, vol. 2, no. 1, 2012.
[41] M. Polese, F. Chiariotti, E. Bonetto, F. Rigotto, A. Zanella, and M. Zorzi, "A Survey on Recent Advances in Transport Layer Protocols," *IEEE Commun. Surv. Tutor.*, vol. 21, no. 4, 2019, doi: 10.1109/COMST.2019.2932905.
[42] Y. Mahmood and A. Abdulqader, "A Platform for Porting IPv4 Applications to IPv6," *Int. J. Comput. Digit. Syst.*, vol. 10, no. 1, 2021, doi: 10.12785/IJCDS/100148.
[43] J. Olsson, "6LoWPAN demystified," *Texas Instrum.*, 2014. www.ti.com/lit/wp/swry013/swry013.pdf
[44] H. A. A. Al-Kashoash and A. H. Kemp, "Comparison of 6LoWPAN and LPWAN for the Internet of Things," *Aust. J. Electr. Electron. Eng.*, vol. 13, no. 4, 2016, doi: 10.1080/1448837X.2017.1409920.
[45] H. A. A. Al-Kashoash, H. Kharrufa, Y. Al-Nidawi, and A. H. Kemp, "Congestion Control in Wireless Sensor and 6LoWPAN Networks: Toward the Internet of Things," *Wirel. Netw.*, vol. 25, no. 8, 2019, doi: 10.1007/s11276-018-1743-y.
[46] M. Zaminkar, F. Sarkohaki, and R. Fotohi, "A Method Based on Encryption and Node Rating for Securing the RPL Protocol Communications in the IoT Ecosystem," *Int. J. Commun. Syst.*, vol. 34, no. 3, 2021, doi: 10.1002/dac.4693.
[47] D. Airehrour, J. A. Gutierrez, and S. K. Ray, "SecTrust-RPL: A Secure Trust-Aware RPL Routing Protocol for Internet of Things," *Futur. Gener. Comput. Syst.*, vol. 93, 2019, doi: 10.1016/j.future.2018.03.021.
[48] A. K. Mishra, O. Singh, A. Kumar, and D. Puthal, "Hybrid Mode of Operations for RPL in IoT: A Systematic Survey," *IEEE Trans. Netw. Serv. Manag.*, vol. 19, no. 3, 2022, doi: 10.1109/TNSM.2022.3159241.
[49] S. Lee, Y. Jeong, E. Moon, and D. Kim, "An Efficient MOP Decision Method Using Hop Interval for RPL-Based Underwater Sensor Networks," *Wirel. Pers. Commun.*, vol. 93, no. 4, 2017, doi: 10.1007/s11277-017-3964-2.
[50] P. N. Hardaha and S. Singh, "Structured Data REST Protocol for End to End Data Mashup," *Futur. Internet*, vol. 10, no. 10, 2018, doi: 10.3390/fi10100098.
[51] C. S. Krishna and T. Sasikala, "Healthcare Monitoring System Based on IoT Using AMQP Protocol," in *Lecture Notes on Data Engineering and Communications Technologies*, Springer Science and Business Media Deutschland GmbH, Berlin, Germany, 2019, doi: 10.1007/978-981-10-8681-6_29.
[52] N. Q. Uy and V. H. Nam, "A Comparison of AMQP and MQTT Protocols for Internet of Things," in *Proceedings—2019 6th NAFOSTED Conference on Information and Computer Science, NICS 2019*, 2019, doi: 10.1109/NICS48868.2019.9023812.
[53] R. A. Atmoko, D. Yang, M. I. Abas, A. Z. Arfianto, and R. Rahim, "Teleoperation Cloud Industrial Robot Using XMPP Protocol," *Int. J. Recent Technol. Eng.*, vol. 8, no. 3, 2019, doi: 10.35940/ijrte.C5893.098319.
[54] H. Wang, D. Xiong, P. Wang, and Y. Liu, "A Lightweight XMPP Publish/Subscribe Scheme for Resource-Constrained IoT Devices," *IEEE Access*, vol. 5, 2017, doi: 10.1109/ACCESS.2017.2742020.

[55] Z. Shelby, K. Hartke, and C. Bormann, "The Constrained Application Protocol (CoAP)," *Rfc 7252*, 2014.
[56] K. Hartke, "Observing Resources in the Constrained Application Protocol (CoAP)," *Ekp*, vol. 13, no. 3, 2015.
[57] A. G. Roselin, P. Nanda, S. Nepal, X. He, and J. Wright, "Exploiting the Remote Server Access Support of CoAP Protocol," *IEEE Internet Things J.*, vol. 6, no. 6, 2019, doi: 10.1109/JIOT.2019.2942085.
[58] M. Iglesias-Urkia, A. Orive, A. Urbieta, and D. Casado-Mansilla, "Analysis of CoAP Implementations for Industrial Internet of Things: A Survey," *J. Ambient Intell. Humaniz. Comput.*, vol. 10, no. 7, 2019, doi: 10.1007/s12652-018-0729-z.
[59] B. Mishra and A. Kertesz, "The Use of MQTT in M2M and IoT Systems: A Survey," *IEEE Access*, vol. 8, 2020, doi: 10.1109/ACCESS.2020.3035849.
[60] G. Kim, S. Kang, J. Park, and K. Chung, "An MQTT-Based Context-Aware Autonomous System in oneM2M Architecture," *IEEE Internet Things J.*, vol. 6, no. 5, 2019, doi: 10.1109/JIOT.2019.2919971.
[61] R. Banno, J. Sun, S. Takeuchi, and K. Shudo, "Interworking Layer of Distributed MQTT Brokers*," *IEICE Trans. Inf. Syst.*, vol. E102D, no. 12, 2019, doi: 10.1587/transinf.2019PAK0001.
[62] I. Sahmi, A. Abdellaoui, T. Mazri, and N. Hmina, "MQTT-PRESENT: Approach to Secure Internet of Things Applications Using MQTT Protocol," *Int. J. Electr. Comput. Eng.*, vol. 11, no. 5, 2021, doi: 10.11591/ijece.v11i5.pp4577-4586.
[63] M. Salagean and D. Zinca, "IoT Applications Based on MQTT Protocol," in *2020 14th International Symposium on Electronics and Telecommunications, ISETC 2020 — Conference Proceedings*, 2020, doi: 10.1109/ISETC50328.2020.9301055.
[64] S. Vigneshwaran, N. Karthikeyan, M. Mahalakshmi, and V. Manikandan, "A Smart Dustbin Using LoRa Technology," *Int. J. Sci. Res. Rev.*, vol. 07, no. 03, 2019.
[65] A. Rayes and S. Salam, "Industry Organizations and Standards Landscape," in *Internet of Things From Hype to Reality*, Springer Cham, Switzerland AG, 2019, doi: 10.1007/978-3-319-99516-8_11.
[66] Q. Zhou, K. Zheng, L. Hou, J. Xing, and R. Xu, "Design and Implementation of Open LORa for IoT," *IEEE Access*, vol. 7, 2019, doi: 10.1109/ACCESS.2019.2930243.
[67] H. Taleb, A. Nasser, G. Andrieux, N. Charara, and E. Motta Cruz, "Wireless Technologies, Medical Applications and Future Challenges in WBAN: A Survey," *Wirel. Netw.*, vol. 27, no. 8, 2021, doi: 10.1007/s11276-021-02780-2.
[68] K. Nahrstedt, "Internet of Mobile Things: Challenges and Opportunities," in *Proceedings of the 23rd International Conference on Parallel Architectures and Compilation*, March 2015, 2014.
[69] D. Pishva, "IoT: Their Conveniences, Security Challenges and Possible Solutions," *Adv. Sci. Technol. Eng. Syst.*, vol. 2, no. 3, 2017, doi: 10.25046/aj0203153.
[70] P. Verma and S. K. Sood, "Cloud-Centric IoT Based Disease Diagnosis Healthcare Framework," *J. Parallel Distrib. Comput.*, vol. 116, 2018, doi: 10.1016/j.jpdc.2017.11.018.
[71] T. Issariyakul, E. Hossain, and D. I. Kim, "Medium Access Control Protocols for Wireless Mobile Ad Hoc Networks: Issues and approaches," *Wirel. Commun. Mob. Comput.*, vol. 3, no. 8, 2003, doi: 10.1002/wcm.118.
[72] S. Ulukus *et al.*, "Energy Harvesting Wireless Communications: A Review of Recent Advances," *IEEE J. Sel. Areas Commun.*, vol. 33, no. 3, 2015, doi: 10.1109/JSAC.2015.2391531.
[73] Z. Shah, A. Levula, K. Khurshid, J. Ahmed, I. Ullah, and S. Singh, "Routing Protocols for Mobile Internet of Things (IoT): A Survey on Challenges and Solutions," *Electronics (Switzerland)*, vol. 10, no. 19, 2021, doi: 10.3390/electronics10192320.
[74] H. Prasad and S. Babu, "A Survey on Network Routing Protocols in Internet of Things (IOT)," *Int. J. Comput. Appl.*, vol. 160, no. 2, 2017, doi: 10.5120/ijca2017912973.

[75] M. López, A. Peinado, and A. Ortiz, "An Extensive Validation of a SIR Epidemic Model to Study the Propagation of Jamming Attacks Against IoT Wireless Networks," *Comput. Netw.*, vol. 165, 2019, doi: 10.1016/j.comnet.2019.106945.

[76] M. Gawiy, A. Al-quh, A. Al Lathaa, Z. Amran, and M. Al-Hubaishi, "Performance Analysis of Destination Sequenced Distance Vector Routing Protocol in MANET," *Int. J. Ad Hoc, Veh. Sens. Netw.*, July 2014.

[77] M. N. Bhuiyan, M. M. Rahman, M. M. Billah, and D. Saha, "Internet of Things (IoT): A Review of Its Enabling Technologies in Healthcare Applications, Standards Protocols, Security, and Market Opportunities," *IEEE Internet Things J.*, vol. 8, no. 13, 2021, doi: 10.1109/JIOT.2021.3062630.

[78] A. Nauman, Y. A. Qadri, M. Amjad, Y. Bin Zikria, M. K. Afzal, and S. W. Kim, "Multimedia Internet of Things: A Comprehensive Survey," *IEEE Access*, vol. 8, 2020, doi: 10.1109/ACCESS.2020.2964280.

[79] M. Chaudhary, N. Goyal, A. Benslimane, L. K. Awasthi, A. Alwadain, and A. Singh, "Underwater Wireless Sensor Networks: Enabling Technologies for Node Deployment and Data Collection Challenges," *IEEE Internet Things J.*, vol. 10, no. 4, 2023, doi: 10.1109/JIOT.2022.3218766.

[80] T. Yu, X. Wang, J. Jin, and K. McIsaac, "Cloud-Orchestrated Physical Topology Discovery of Large-Scale IoT Systems Using UAVs," *IEEE Trans. Ind. Inform.*, vol. 14, no. 5, 2018, doi: 10.1109/TII.2018.2796499.

[81] P. Matousek, O. Rysavy, and L. Polcak, "Unified SNMP Interface for IoT Monitoring," in *Proceedings of the IM 2021–2021 IFIP/IEEE International Symposium on Integrated Network Management*, 2021.

[82] T. Joshva Devadas, S. Thayammal, and A. Ramprakash, "IOT Data Management, Data Aggregation and Dissemination," in *Intelligent Systems Reference Library*, Springer, Berlin, Germany, Vol. 174, pp. 385–411, 2019, doi: 10.1007/978-3-030-33596-0_16.

[83] U. Bodkhe and S. Tanwar, "Taxonomy of Secure Data Dissemination Techniques for IoT Environment," *IET Softw.*, vol. 14, no. 6, 2020, doi: 10.1049/iet-sen.2020.0006.

[84] Y. Pan, S. Li, Y. Zhang, and T. Zhu, "CDA: Coordinating Data Dissemination and Aggregation in Heterogeneous IoT Networks Using CTC," *J. Netw. Comput. Appl.*, vol. 171, 2020, doi: 10.1016/j.jnca.2020.102797.

4 Data Handling and Analytics

4.1 INTRODUCTION TO BIG DATA

Before discussing the concept of Big Data, one must understand what the term data is. Data is a collection of numbers, characters, images, or other symbols that a computer uses to determine a specific action [1–3]. This data can be stored or transmitted via electrical signals. With the proliferation of sensor networks, cyber-physical systems, and the IoT in everyday life, there has been a significant increase in data collection. For instance, data is gathered every time a user logs in to an online platform, opens an app on their mobile phone, visits a website, or conducts a search on a search engine. For example, if we were to open our web browser and search for "Big Data," the process would generate a substantial amount of data. Considering the number of people who use the internet to browse various websites, upload photos, and engage in other online activities, it is evident that a considerable amount of data is generated every day. The primary sources of data include mobile devices, social media platforms, websites, digital media such as photos and videos, wireless sensors, medical records, e-commerce platforms, public surveillance systems, scientific research, and others. All this data adds up to around a quintillion bytes, with currently over 40 zettabytes of data being generated, which is equivalent to 75 times the number of grains of sand on Earth [4–6].

The origins of Big Data can be traced back to the establishment of data centers and relational databases in the 1960s and 1970s. However, it gained widespread attention in the middle of the first decade of the 2000s with the emergence of online services such as Facebook and YouTube, resulting in a significant increase in data production. Hadoop, an open-source software framework for distributed data storage and processing, was released in the same year to address the challenges of managing large datasets. NoSQL (Not only Structured Query Language) databases also became popular during this time. The IoT has further increased the production of Big Data by enabling the collection of data on consumer usage trends and product performance through connected devices [3, 6–10]. Additionally, advancements in machine learning have led to even more data being generated. Although Big Data has made significant strides, its potential is yet to be fully realized. Cloud computing has expanded its possibilities by facilitating the rapid creation of arbitrary clusters for testing small data samples. Meanwhile, graph databases are increasingly popular due to their ability to present vast amounts of data in a manner that facilitates quick and thorough analysis.

Big Data refers to datasets that are too vast for commonly used software tools to handle. The data has an enormous volume and is expanding rapidly, making it impossible for traditional data management systems to store or manage. The three

DOI: 10.1201/9781003282945-4

critical characteristics of Big Data are volume, variety, and velocity, which respectively refer to the amount of data, types of data, and processing speed [9]. It provides new insights that lead to new business opportunities. The term "Big Data" refers to techniques used for analyzing or working with datasets that are too large or complex to be processed using standard data processing applications. It is worth noting that datasets with more fields offer greater statistical power, but those with more attributes or columns may have a higher rate of false discoveries. Hence, careful analysis and management of Big Data are crucial to ensure the accuracy and reliability of results. Big Data analytics is a cutting-edge analytical approach that deals with massive, diverse datasets which comprise structured, semi-structured, and unstructured data from multiple sources. The size of these datasets ranges from terabytes to zettabytes [10]. The analysis of Big Data enables analysts, researchers, and business users to make informed decisions quickly by utilizing previously inaccessible or underutilized data. Modern analytical tools—including machine learning, text analytics, predictive analytics, statistics, data mining, and natural language processing (NLP)—help organizations uncover hidden insights from underutilized data sources. These insights can be analyzed independently or in conjunction with historical data.

4.1.1 Why Big Data?

Big Data is a popular tool used by companies to improve their operations, enhance customer service, and develop targeted marketing campaigns, all with the ultimate goal of increasing revenue. By analyzing both historical and real-time data, companies can assess market requirements, understand customer needs, and adjust their products accordingly. The combination of Big Data and machine learning enables companies to develop marketing plans and predict customer requirements, allowing them to respond quickly to demand and generate more revenue. Various industries, such as finance, education, healthcare, and securities, have already embraced Big Data [11]. In addition, medical researchers use Big Data to discover disease symptoms and risk factors, which aid doctors in diagnosing patients with illnesses and other medical conditions. The term "Big Data" encompasses not only the vast amount of data but also the technologies and techniques used to analyze and derive insights from that data. Big Data has become increasingly important as organizations seek to harness the vast amounts of data available to gain insights, make informed decisions, drive innovation, and gain a competitive edge. By leveraging Big Data analytics, organizations can uncover hidden patterns, optimize operations, enhance customer experiences, and drive growth and success in today's data-driven world. Following are several reasons why Big Data is important [12, 13].

1. **Valuable Insights:** Big Data provides organizations with the opportunity to gain valuable insights and knowledge that can drive informed decision-making. By analyzing large and diverse datasets, organizations can uncover patterns, trends, and correlations that were previously hidden. These insights can be used to identify new business opportunities, optimize processes, improve customer experiences, and make data-driven strategic decisions.

2. **Enhanced Customer Understanding:** Big Data allows organizations to better understand their customers. By analyzing customer data, including demographic information, browsing behavior, purchase history, and social media interactions, organizations can gain insights into customer preferences, needs, and behaviors. This understanding enables businesses to tailor their products, services, and marketing strategies to meet customer expectations and provide personalized experiences.
3. **Improved Operational Efficiency:** Big Data analytics can help organizations optimize their operational processes and improve efficiency. By analyzing large datasets related to production, supply chain, logistics, and maintenance, organizations can identify bottlenecks, optimize resource allocation, predict maintenance needs, and streamline operations. This can lead to cost savings, improved productivity, and better utilization of resources.
4. **Real-Time Decision-Making:** With the advancements in Big Data technologies, organizations can analyze data in real time or near real-time. This allows businesses to make timely decisions based on the most up-to-date information. For example, in industries such as finance and healthcare, real-time data analysis can enable fraud detection, risk management, and patient monitoring, leading to more proactive and effective decision-making.
5. **Innovation and Competitive Advantage:** Big Data can be a catalyst for innovation and a source of competitive advantage. By leveraging Big Data analytics, organizations can identify emerging trends, market opportunities, and customer demands. This knowledge can drive the development of innovative products, services, and business models that meet evolving customer needs and stay ahead of the competition.
6. **Data-Driven Research and Development:** Big Data plays a crucial role in research and development (R&D) efforts across various industries. By analyzing large datasets, researchers can gain insights, conduct experiments, and validate hypotheses. In fields such as healthcare, genomics, climate science, and drug discovery, Big Data analytics is transforming the R&D process, enabling breakthroughs and advancements that were not previously possible.
7. **Risk Management and Fraud Detection:** Big Data analytics can help organizations identify and mitigate risks, as well as detect fraudulent activities. By analyzing large volumes of data from multiple sources, organizations can identify patterns and anomalies that indicate potential risks or fraudulent behavior. This can be particularly valuable in industries such as finance, insurance, cyber-security, and compliance.

4.1.2 Big Data Examples

Numerous businesses employ Big Data to enhance customer experiences and increase sales. We will next look at a few of the best examples.

1. **Amazon ("Everything Under One Roof"):** Amazon is a modern consumer e-commerce business. Amazon uses vast amounts of data to make

decisions, satisfy customers, and expand sales. Amazon has access to and stores consumer data such as names, addresses, user payments, and search histories in a central database. Amazon uses this data to improve customer interactions. It optimizes the recommendation engine using Big Data collected from clients [14, 15]. It can forecast what clients want to buy more accurately the more it learns about clients. For example, when we add a specific item to our online shopping cart, Amazon displays previously added related items. Amazon highly depends on the power of pseudocode suggestions to improve user shopping experiences [16–18].

2. **Netflix:** Netflix is a streaming service that allows users to watch TV shows and movies on any internet-connected device. Netflix currently has a massive collection of TV shows, documentaries, and movies available in over 190 countries. Big Data affects Netflix content by identifying what users want to watch and their preferences [19, 20]. Thus, the user is encouraged to keep watching Netflix. Netflix pseudocode collects data by tracking users' activities and provides recommendations accordingly. Users' data that Netflix gathers includes user's location, devices that the user has used to view the content, and the moment at which the user viewed the content; the search engine saves users' past searches and repeatedly watched videos, as well as viewing dates of the content.
3. **LinkedIn:** LinkedIn is the largest professional network in the world, connecting job seekers and employers. It has 660 million users across 200 countries, making it the most popular professional social networking platform. Research released in November 2019 found that LinkedIn had over 30 million corporate profiles. More than two new people join LinkedIn every second. LinkedIn tracks every move a user makes on the site to enhance services and user experience. The recommendation engine on LinkedIn uses Big Data, which contains details on possible connections, people who have looked at users' profiles, potential jobs, and more [21]. Hadoop is a critical component of Big Data that builds the website and mobile application of LinkedIn. Services that LinkedIn provides include people you may know, skill endorsements, jobs you may be interested in, and updates in the news fee.
4. **General Electric (GE):** GE was the company that initially introduced electrically operated equipment and lighting into homes and businesses. GE announced its "Industrial Internet" vision because Big Data is now widely available. GE has placed sensors into machinery such as jet engines, gas turbines, etc. GE products include power turbines, medical scanners, and aircraft engines. These devices are constantly monitoring and recording data about their surroundings. Based on the data collected, the analytics team creates reports that help to develop new tools and other improvements to increase efficiency [22].
5. **Swiggy:** Swiggy is the ideal option for food fans. It is India's most popular online ordering and delivery platform. Swiggy already has over 20 million users in 140 cities and plans to expand further. Swiggy collects massive amounts of data every week and uses that data to improve delivery efficiency

and connect customers with the best restaurants. Customers use Swiggy to order food from nearby restaurants to deliver at their selected locations within a fixed timeframe. Rather than just using the customer's location, it uses data analytics to suggest the best restaurants on the app's home page based on the user's preferences [23]. It provides food suggestions based on previous orders and searches, allowing customers to select their preferred food easily.

4.1.3 Types of Data

Big Data consists of various data types, high velocity and extensible. Data comes in three different forms: structured, semi-structured, and unstructured [24]. We will next examine each of these three categories in more detail.

1. **Structured:** Structured data is data that has been collected and sorted systematically and can be easily retrieved. Structured data is easy to process because it has a predefined schema. Structured data refers to data that is organized and formatted in a specific way. It follows a predefined schema or data model and is typically stored in relational databases or spreadsheets. Structured data is highly organized, making it easy to search, analyze, and process. Examples of structured data include financial transactions, customer information, sensor readings with fixed attributes, and stock market data. To manage structured data, we can use SQL. An "Employee" table in a database as shown in Table 4.1 is an example of structured data.
2. **Semi-Structured:** Semi-structured data is a combination of structured and unstructured data. It contains elements of both, with some organization or metadata but without a rigid schema. Semi-structured data is often represented in formats like XML, JSON, comma-separated values (CSV), and log files. It offers more flexibility than structured data but still has some level of organization. Examples of semi-structured data include sensor data with variable attributes, web server logs, XML documents, and data from IoT devices. Semi-structured data is information that is not stored in a relational database but has particular structural characteristics that make it simpler to analyze.

TABLE 4.1
Example of Structured Data

Employee_ID	Employee_Name	Gender	Department	Salary in Lakhs
2365	Rajesh Kulkarni	Male	Finance	650000
3398	Pratibha Joshi	Female	Admin	650000
7465	Shushil Roy	Male	Admin	500000
7500	Shubhojit Das	Male	Finance	500000
7699	Priya Sane	Female	Finance	550000

Example of Semi-Structured Data

XML files or JSON documents (personal data stored in an XML file)
<rec><name>Prashant Rao</name><sex>Male</sex><age>35</age></rec>
<rec><name>Seema R.</name><sex>Female</sex><age>41</age></rec>
<rec><name>Satish Mane</name><sex>Male</sex><age>29</age></rec>
<rec><name>Subrato Roy</name><sex>Male</sex><age>26</age></rec>
<rec><name>Jeremiah J.</name><sex>Male</sex><age>35</age></rec>

3. **Unstructured:** Unstructured data refers to data that does not have a specific format or organization. It is often in the form of text, audio, video, images, social media posts, emails, and documents. Unstructured data is complex and challenging to process using traditional databases and analytics tools. However, advancements in NLP, image recognition, and machine learning techniques enable the extraction and analysis of insights from unstructured data. Examples of unstructured data include social media feeds, customer reviews, emails, and multimedia content. Unstructured data cannot be stored in a relational database since its formation or structure are unclear. Before we can analyze unstructured data, we must convert it into a structured format. Around 80% of the data collected by companies is unstructured [1]. The example of unstructured data in day-to-day life are text files and multimedia content like audio, video, images, output returned by Google searches, etc.

4.2 BIG DATA ARCHITECTURE

Big Data architecture refers to the overall framework and components that are designed to store, process, and analyze large volumes of data. It involves a combination of hardware, software, and network infrastructure that enables organizations to effectively handle Big Data and derive meaningful insights. Big Data architecture is a method for collecting, storing, and analyzing massive amounts of data for business analysis [24]. It is a Big Data solution plan based on the needs and infrastructure of commercial enterprises. The specific components and technologies used in a Big Data architecture may vary depending on the organization's requirements, data characteristics, and technological preferences. The typical Big Data architecture is as shown in Figure 4.1. The architecture should be designed to handle the challenges of Big Data—such as data volume, variety, velocity, and veracity—while providing flexibility, scalability, and security to support the organization's data-driven initiatives. A robust architecture saves money for the company by enabling trend forecasting and better decision-making. It is beneficial in the batch processing, real-time processing of Big Data, as well as predictive analytics [25].

Big Data architecture comprises the following components.

1. **Data Sources:** Data source refers to the location where the information is acquired. The process of Big Data begins with data sources. Data sources may differ depending on the application. There are two types of data sources: file data sources and machine data sources. A file data source is any entity that resembles a data repository, such as an email archive, file

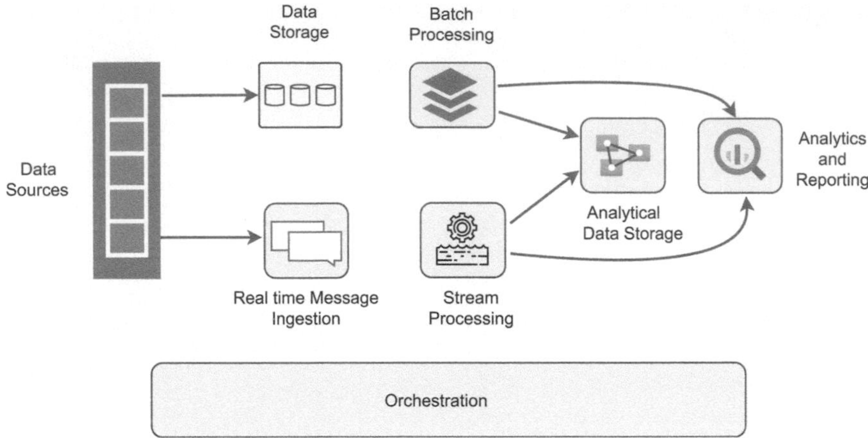

FIGURE 4.1 Big Data architecture.

sharing, or filing cabinet. The machine data source is information created by a computer process or application activity that does not require human intervention. Examples of machine data sources are computers, mobile phones, embedded systems, and other networked devices. These data can be obtained in both batch and real-time formats. The Big Data architecture is specifically designed to handle vast amounts of data from these sources [26].

2. **Real-Time Message Ingestion:** Real-time data ingestion is the process of transmitting data from a live source into an object storage system. This process involves the storage of new messages in a data store, which serves as a message buffer and supports scalable processing. In addition to various message queuing semantics, they provide stable and reliable delivery. Examples include Apache Kafka, Azure Event Hubs, and Apache Flume.
3. **Batch Processing:** A batch-processing system is required for advanced analytics because it filters, aggregates, and processes data. These are frequently long batch processes that read data from storage, process it, and then output the results to new files. The preferred batch-processing approach is Apache Hadoop [27].
4. **Stream Processing:** Real-time message intake and stream processing share many similarities. Stream processing involves the management of continuous data streams or windows and the writing of data to output sinks. Popular software used for stream processing includes Apache Spark, Apache Flink, and Storm, among others [28].
5. **Analytical Data Store:** We must collect data after processing it to analyze the entire dataset. The analytical data store is crucial because it allows for detailed analysis and centrally stores all our processed data. Analyzing transactions is not ideal. Depending on our needs, it may be a cloud-based data warehouse or a relational database.

6. **Analytics and Reporting:** After importing and processing data from various data sources, we require a data analysis tool. The data is analyzed using a variety of data analytics and visualization tools, which produce dashboards or reports after the analysis. These reports support corporate decision-making based on data.
7. **Orchestration:** Orchestration is required to move data between various systems, and automation carries this out. Data ingestion, transformation, batch and stream processing, loading into an analytical data storage system, and insight-generating analysis all require repeatable workflows. As a result, Big Data helps us continuously understand new information.

4.3 CHARACTERISTICS OF BIG DATA

Big Data can exhibit characteristics commonly referred to as the "Five Vs": volume, velocity, variety, veracity, and value [8], as shown in Figure 4.2. These characteristics define the unique aspects of Big Data and highlight the challenges and opportunities associated with it. It is important to note that there are other additional "Vs" that are sometimes associated with Big Data, such as variability (referring to the inconsistency or volatility of data), visualization (highlighting the need for effective data visualization techniques), and validity (ensuring that the data is valid and relevant to the intended analysis). These additional Vs further emphasize the complexities and considerations involved in working with Big Data.

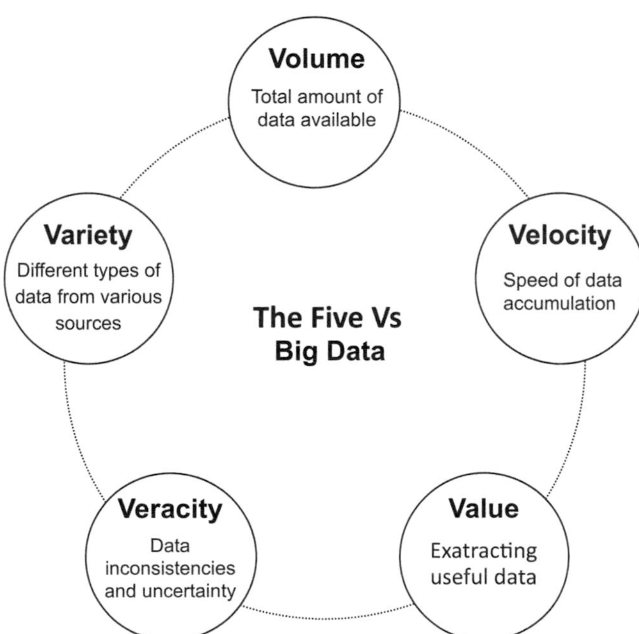

FIGURE 4.2 Characteristics of Big Data.

Understanding the characteristics of Big Data helps organizations adopt appropriate technologies, methodologies, and strategies to manage, process, and analyze large volumes of data effectively. By harnessing the power of Big Data, organizations can gain valuable insights, make data-driven decisions, and drive innovation and growth.

1. **Volume:** A consistent workflow is essential for data ingestion, transformation, and batch and stream processing, as well as loading data into an analytical data storage system and conducting analysis to generate insights. Over 350 million new posts, 4.5 billion "like" button clicks, and over 1 billion messages are produced daily on Facebook [29]. Big Data technologies are the only ones that can manage such enormous amounts of data.
2. **Velocity:** Various sources generate a vast amount of data every day. The term "velocity" refers to this unceasing, enormous flow of information [6]. It demonstrates how quickly social media usage is growing and how much Big Data is being generated every day. It is essential to control the velocity when real-time data can be generated. The crucial component of Big Data is to provide data on demand and quicker because waiting for data will be a huge waste of resources.
3. **Variety:** As was previously mentioned, there are various ways that Big Data is produced. Varieties of data produced by diverse sources are referred to as being varied. Structured, unstructured, or semi-structured are all possible. Before now, data was delivered to us in the form of tables from databases and Excel, but it is now also delivered in the form of images, audio, video, PDFs (files in Portable Document Format), and other types of files. Approximately 80% of the data is completely unstructured [14]. Structured data is just the tip of the iceberg. Thus, problems with storing, capturing, mining, and analyzing unstructured data are brought about by this variety.
4. **Veracity:** In managing Big Data, organizations need to consider the uncertainty of the data due to its inconsistency and incompleteness. The term "veracity" pertains to the degree of trustworthiness of the data [14]. It is important to note that a significant portion of the data is unstructured and irrelevant, but still essential for business development. Hence, finding alternative methods to filter or translate such data is necessary.
5. **Value:** Without knowledge, data is meaningless. There is no point in just collecting and storing Big Data unless it is analyzed and provides valuable knowledge. "Data importance" is the most important thing to be addressed in the future. Not only must the quantity of data be saved, but so must the quality of the data be stored and processed for insight. To gain insights, important, trustworthy, and reliable data must be saved, processed, and analyzed.

4.4 BIG DATA CHALLENGES

Big Data refers to the increasing volume, velocity, and variety of data generated by organizations, individuals, and machines. Handling, analyzing, and gaining insights from Big Data can be challenging due to its sheer size, complexity, and diversity.

To achieve effective decision-making and BI, it is important to address Big Data challenges such as the following [30–32].

1. **Storage and Processing:** Lack of computing power and storage space for large amounts of data.
2. **Data Quality:** Ensuring the accuracy, completeness, and relevance of data is crucial for maintaining data quality.
3. **Data Integration:** The process of data integration involves consolidating data from various sources to create a unified perspective.
4. **Privacy and Security:** Ensuring the confidentiality and protection of sensitive data.
5. **Scalability:** Being able to scale up or down as per changing demand for data analysis.

4.5 BIG DATA TECHNOLOGIES STACK

In today's data-driven world, Big Data stack has become an essential data processing infrastructure for data analytics. Big Data stack refers to the set of technologies that are used to store, process, and analyze large amounts of data effectively. The five best technologies of the Big Data stack are Apache Hadoop, Apache Spark, Apache Kafka, Apache Hive, and Apache Cassandra.

1. **Apache Hadoop:** Apache Hadoop is an open-source distributed storage and processing framework that provides a unique way of handling Big Data. It is based on the MapReduce programming model and the Hadoop Distributed File System (HDFS), which provide a scalable way to store and process large amounts of data. Hadoop is highly fault-tolerant and can handle failures of individual nodes within a cluster without any loss of data. It is widely used in various applications such as data warehousing, data processing, and data storage [28].
2. **Apache Spark:** Apache Spark is an open-source engine used for processing Big Data which provides fast processing for data analytics. It offers an in-memory data processing model that allows users to analyze data much faster than traditional disk-based systems. It can perform various tasks such as data streaming, graph processing, and machine learning. Spark is highly scalable and provides excellent performance due to its distributed processing model [28].
3. **Apache Kafka:** Apache Kafka is a messaging system that enables distributed publish-subscribe communication, facilitating real-time data streaming. It is designed to handle vast amounts of data with high throughput and low latency. Kafka provides a reliable way to store and process data streams, making it suitable for real-time analytics applications.
4. **Apache Hive:** Apache Hive is a data warehousing tool that provides an SQL-like interface to Big Data processing. It is built on top of Hadoop and provides a way to query large amounts of data stored in HDFS. Hive is designed to be highly scalable and can process petabytes of data with ease.

5. **Apache Cassandra:** Apache Cassandra is a distributed NoSQL database that provides excellent scalability, fault tolerance, and high availability. It is designed to handle large amounts of data spread across multiple nodes without any loss of data. Cassandra provides a wide range of data types and provides fast read and write operations, making it suitable for high-performance applications.

4.6 ADVANTAGES OF BIG DATA ANALYTICS

Growing Big Data is useless without data analysis. It provides organizations with a powerful toolset to harness the value of data and drive meaningful insights for better decision-making, operational efficiency, customer experiences, risk management, improved decision-making, and business growth, as illustrated in Figure 4.3. There are many advantages of Big Data analytics, including the following [19, 21].

1. **Improved Decision-Making:** Big Data analytics enables organizations to make data-driven decisions by extracting valuable insights from large volumes of structured and unstructured data. It provides a deeper understanding of customer behavior, market trends, and operational patterns, helping organizations make informed and strategic decisions.
2. **Enhanced Operational Efficiency:** Big Data analytics can identify inefficiencies and bottlenecks in business processes, allowing organizations to optimize their operations. By analyzing large datasets, organizations can uncover patterns, anomalies, and correlations, leading to process improvements, cost savings, and increased productivity.
3. **Personalized Customer Experiences:** With Big Data analytics, organizations can gain a comprehensive view of their customers by analyzing their

FIGURE 4.3 Advantages of Big Data analytics.

preferences, behaviors, and interactions. This enables personalized marketing campaigns, targeted recommendations, and tailored product offerings, enhancing the overall customer experience and driving customer satisfaction and loyalty.

4. **Improved Product Development:** Big Data analytics helps organizations gain insights into market trends, customer needs, and product performance. By analyzing customer feedback, social media data, and competitor information, organizations can make data-driven product development decisions, prioritize features, and deliver innovative solutions that meet customer demands.
5. **Enhanced Risk Management:** Big Data analytics enables organizations to identify and mitigate risks effectively. By analyzing historical and real-time data, organizations can detect patterns and anomalies that indicate potential risks, such as fraud, security breaches, or operational failures. This helps in proactive risk management and decision-making to protect the organization's assets and reputation.
6. **Better Healthcare Outcomes:** Big Data analytics plays a crucial role in the healthcare industry by analyzing large volumes of patient data, clinical records, and medical research. It helps in early disease detection, personalized treatment plans, predictive modeling, and improving patient outcomes. Additionally, it aids in population health management, resource optimization, and healthcare cost reduction.
7. **Competitive Advantage:** Organizations that effectively leverage Big Data analytics gain a competitive edge in the market. By extracting valuable insights and making data-driven decisions, organizations can identify new business opportunities, optimize operations, and deliver superior products and services. This helps in staying ahead of competitors and adapting to changing market dynamics.
8. **Real-Time Insights:** Big Data analytics enables organizations to process and analyze data in real time or near real-time, providing immediate insights and actionable intelligence. This allows organizations to respond quickly to market trends, customer demands, and operational issues, leading to faster decision-making, agility, and competitive responsiveness.
9. **Scalability and Flexibility:** Big Data analytics technologies are designed to handle large volumes of data and scale with growing data requirements. They offer flexible deployment options, such as on-premises, cloud, or hybrid environments, allowing organizations to adapt their infrastructure based on changing needs. This scalability and flexibility enable organizations to effectively manage and analyze data as it grows.
10. **Innovation and Business Growth:** Big Data analytics opens up new opportunities for innovation and business growth. By exploring and analyzing diverse datasets, organizations can uncover hidden patterns, correlations, and market trends that drive innovation and identify untapped market segments. This leads to the development of new products, services, and business models that drive growth and competitive advantage.

4.7 RELATIONSHIP BETWEEN BIG DATA AND THE INTERNET OF THINGS

The business landscape is being transformed by two technological trends: Big Data and the IoT. IoT encompasses physical devices, buildings, and vehicles that are embedded with software and sensors to facilitate data exchange and connection. On the other hand, Big Data refers to the vast amounts of information produced from various sources, including IoT devices. The two trends are interdependent, with IoT generating large amounts of data that is collected by sensors and processed by centralized systems. This data includes environmental variables like temperature, humidity, and pressure used to control and monitor the devices [33]. Big Data analytics enables companies to analyze and derive insights from IoT-generated data. IoT data is usually unstructured and requires analysis to produce meaningful insights. Big Data analytics provides the necessary tools and techniques for processing and analyzing this data. The resulting insights can be used to optimize customer behavior, operational efficiency, and other business-critical areas. Another significant benefit of the IoT and Big Data is improved decision-making. The data generated by IoT devices provides real-time insights into customer behavior, product performance, and other key areas that can affect business operations. Big Data analytics provides the tools needed to analyze this data and generate insights that can be used to make informed decisions. Furthermore, the IoT and Big Data are transforming the retail industry. Retailers are using IoT devices to track customer behavior, optimize inventory levels, and improve customer experience. Big Data analytics provides the tools needed to analyze this data and generate insights that can be used to improve business operations, increase sales, and improve the overall customer experience.

IoT systems often operate in real time or near–real time environments in which data needs to be processed and analyzed in a timely manner. Big Data analytics facilitates real-time data processing, allowing organizations to capture and analyze streaming data as it is generated. This enables proactive decision-making, instant responses to events, and timely actions based on the analyzed data. Big Data analytics provides the tools and techniques to analyze IoT data and extract actionable insights. By applying advanced analytics algorithms such as machine learning, predictive modeling, and anomaly detection, organizations can uncover hidden patterns, trends, and anomalies in the IoT data. These insights can drive operational efficiencies, predictive maintenance, optimized resource allocation, and improved decision-making. IoT systems are susceptible to security threats and anomalies due to the large attack surface and diverse devices. Big Data analytics helps in identifying security breaches, anomalies, and patterns that indicate potential threats. By analyzing IoT data in real time, organizations can detect and respond to security incidents promptly, enhancing the security posture of IoT systems. Thus, the integration of Big Data analytics with IoT systems is crucial for unlocking the full potential of IoT data and realizing its value. The relationship between Big Data and the IoT is becoming increasingly important as organizations seek to leverage the benefits of these technologies. By combining these technologies, companies can gain valuable insights into customer behavior, market trends, and operational processes that can improve business outcomes. However, it is crucial to ensure that appropriate measures are taken to safeguard data privacy and security. In countries like Africa and cities like San Francisco, wells and pumps are being equipped with smart sensors to monitor water quality and quantity. It turns out that every dollar spent on water and sanitation reduces healthcare costs by approximately $8. Smart water meters contain sensors and other advanced technological devices. The biggest challenges for the faster implementation of smart water meters are the complexity of the water supply system and financial constraints [34].

4.8 APPLICATIONS OF BIG DATA

Big Data analytics is a methodology that involves gathering, modifying, analyzing, and managing vast quantities of data to generate valuable insights. In order to gain a competitive edge and foster growth, businesses are increasingly adopting Big Data technologies for analysis. Apache Hadoop, Apache Spark, and Kafka are widely used Big Data analytics tools [23, 27]. The benefits of Big Data analytics are being leveraged across various sectors such as finance, retail, education, government, manufacturing, energy, and utilities. In the following subsections, we will explore the application of Big Data analytics in these different industries.

4.8.1 Applications of Big Data and IoT in Different Industries

There is wide variety of application areas of Big Data analytics, as illustrated in Figure 4.4.

1. **Big Data Applications in the Banking and Finance Sector:** The financial sector faces several challenges such as alerts about securities fraud, detection of card fraud, an explanation of corporate credit risk, investigating ticks, social analysis of transactions, customer data transformation, archiving of audit trails, information technology (IT) performance evaluation, and so on. The banking and finance sector has witnessed significant transformations with the advent of Big Data and IoT technologies. In the financial sector, machine learning and Big Data can be utilized to analyze stock prices in the context of social and political trends that can potentially affect the stock market [35]. Real-time monitoring of such trends empowers analysts to evaluate pertinent information and make informed decisions. The detection and prevention of fraud are largely attributable to machine

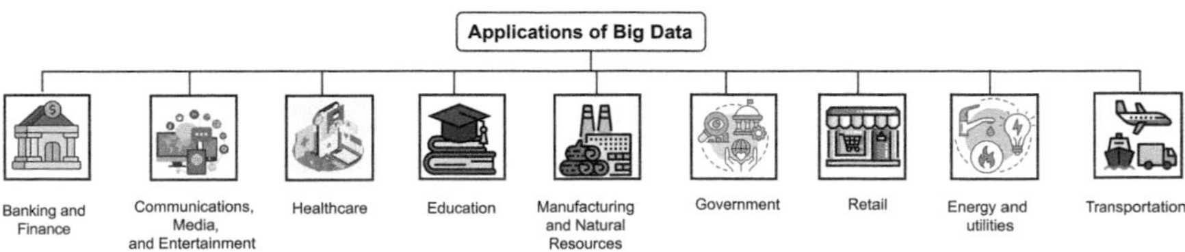

FIGURE 4.4 Applications of Big Data.

learning powered by Big Data. IoT devices can be utilized for real-time monitoring of financial transactions, detecting unusual behavior, and triggering alerts for potential fraud cases. Analytics helps to reduce the security risk that a credit card poses. When information about a valuable credit card is stolen, banks immediately freeze the card and its transactions. The customer is then made aware of the security threats. Big Data is used for trading analysis by banks, hedge funds, and other financial market participants. Trade analytics supports high-frequency trading, predictive analytics, and sentiment analysis in finance and banking. IoT devices can gather customer data from wearables, smart devices, and mobile apps, providing additional insights for personalized financial services and tailored offerings. Big Data analytics enables banks to analyze customer data and payment transactions to identify patterns and trends, improve digital banking services, and offer personalized payment solutions. IoT devices such as mobile payment terminals and contactless payment systems facilitate seamless and secure transactions, enhancing the overall payment experience. To fully understand the total cost of risk, financial institutions are using Big Data. Companies can now increase their return on investment. Companies use Big Data analytics to understand customer payment habits. Their ability to better understand their customers leads to more sales and happier customers.

2. **Big Data Uses in Communications, Media, and Entertainment:** Big Data allows companies to understand trends in customers' TV viewing preferences. It provides data on past search activity, video watch time, social media usage, reactions to trailers, and more. The media and entertainment industry uses Big Data analytics to create and market new shows based on viewer interest. In the media industry, advertisements serve as the primary source of revenue for brands. Advertisers invest considerable sums of money to feature ads during show segments. The utilization of Big Data and IoT technologies empowers companies to develop targeted ads, resulting in increased efficiency and effectiveness [36]. Big Data enables media executives, writers, and designers to produce content based on a mathematical model of popularity. Big Data platforms enable businesses to predict the success of their content rather than relying solely on intuition. Big Data assists in the prediction of actors, apps, and storylines.
3. **Big Data Uses in Healthcare Sectors:** The challenges in healthcare are to lower rising costs and improve patient outcomes. Big Data is essential for predictive analytics in healthcare. By using predictive analytics of a patient's medical history, physicians can provide superior patient care. patient protection. Clinics can make decisions that improve patient health because analytics tools can predict which patients are at risk for which diseases. Big Data is also used in electronic records in the field of medicine. Until now, the healthcare industry has struggled to keep up with the rapidly growing patient base. Each patient now has a personal set of medical records, including medication lists, medical reports, lab test results, and more. Electronic medical records in the healthcare industry enable access and maintenance of patient data. Each patient has their own record, which is done separately.

Doctors can securely share files and easily edit them when needed. By continuously monitoring the health of patients, health systems are now able to provide quality care. Many tools are available that can analyze patient data and advise physicians on appropriate actions. Patients' health is monitored by a variety of wearable sensors, including those that measure heart rate, blood pressure, and pulse. Doctors can monitor the data, reducing unnecessary hospitalization of patients. Medical researchers use Big Data analytics to predict the most successful treatments for cancer patients based on their cure rates [37, 38]. They do this by combining patient databases from different medical institutions while maintaining patient privacy. This strategy is not unique to cancer. They also use it to treat other diseases, as well.

4. **Big Data Applications in Education:** Education institutions are now able to monitor students' individual and collective performance across a range of subjects thanks to the growing use of Big Data. One can create appropriate remedies to aid in students' development. It assists institutions in creating study plans that are tailored to students' learning styles using statistical analysis of student performance across a range of subjects. They can pinpoint factors influencing student performance through data analysis and suggest workable solutions. Big Data aids students in selecting their best career paths. Based on their performance in pertinent classes and their interests, teachers can support students' career development [39, 40]. Student understanding of potential career paths is improved by Big Data. As a result, organizations can assist students in selecting a profession. Students have many opportunities to learn. Some people can only learn by reading, whereas others can only learn by writing, and some students learn things through other methods, such as watching videos. It often happens that a student is forced to fit into a certain learning structure which hinders their development. Academic performance of students suffers. Educational institutions can use Big Data analytics to design personalized courses based on student abilities. Big Data analysis identifies each student's strengths and weaknesses, and provides customized lessons and learning materials.
5. **Big Data Applications in Manufacturing and Natural Resources:** In the natural resources industries, Big Data analytics plays a crucial role in enhancing decision-making through predictive modeling. It involves gathering and integrating large sets of data that include temporal, spatial, and textual information. Similarly, the manufacturing sector can benefit from Big Data solutions to improve the quality of products, identify defects in the production process, and streamline delivery planning. Additionally, Big Data solutions can assist in enhancing energy efficiency, forecasting production, evaluating novel production techniques, and creating new manufacturing processes [41].
6. **Big Data Applications in Government Sectors:** One major challenge encountered by government agencies is effectively integrating and making data interoperable across multiple departments and agencies. This involves handling a large volume of diverse data sources within the government. Government institutions benefit greatly by the use of Big Data along with

IoT. Governments have to manage many processes and perform demanding tasks. That is why they need a platform that can handle large amounts of data. The continuously developing technology of Big Data offers an intelligent platform that facilitates the collection, cleaning, filtering, and analysis of large datasets. To improve security, legal, public sector, defense and other areas, local governments and federal agencies are using Big Data tools to streamline their operations. Big Data technology has had a major impact on defense, national security, crime prediction, cyber-security, and other industries [42, 43]. Real-time analytics is used by governments around the world to track and monitor border crossings. They monitor fleets and airspace using analytics to create multiple video streams of different objects. The performance of several military branches has improved with the introduction of Big Data and machine learning algorithms. The protection of digital assets has become a significant issue for governments in the current era of technology. To ensure the security of essential data, government agencies employ Big Data analytics and machine learning tools to monitor and investigate operations. The system keeps track of all network-connected devices and users, looks for suspicious activity or people, and sends out alerts when it does. States are now able to take more effective, dependable, and safe precautions against cyber-attacks.

7. **Big Data Applications in Retail:** The amount of data collected across retail sectors, from traditional retailers to wholesalers to online retailers, is increasing every day. This massive amount of data is produced by point-of-sale (POS) scanners, RFID scanners, loyalty cards, and more—but before Big Data analytics, this huge amounts of data was not used effectively to improve customer experience. Retailers collect customer information from credit card transactions, user logins, IP addresses, and other sources. Retailers then look at past information about consumer spending and buying habits. They can thus better anticipate customers' future purchases and provide them with tailor-made recommendations. Based on previous searches and purchases, Amazon uses Big Data to suggest products to its customers [43, 44]. Merchants can provide a better customer experience through Big Data. For example, Costco, a chain of membership warehouse stores based in Washington, uses its data collection to protect the health of its customers. Costco recently issued a warning about the possible contamination of peaches and plums. Some Costco customers who have purchased bacteria-contaminated peaches and plums received emails from the retailer. Retailers analyze social media trends using Big Data and machine learning algorithms to predict the next big thing in the industry.
8. **Big Data Applications in Energy and Utility Industries:** The energy and utility sector is continually incorporating smart technologies into its infrastructure, including cloud computing, sensors, and energy planning. These technologies produce substantial amounts of data over time. It is difficult for energy and utility companies to extract insights from this invaluable data. Smart grid dynamic energy management systems contribute significantly to

improving the flow of energy between consumers and suppliers. Big Data analytics helps analyze the massive amounts of data that Distributed Management System systems have collected for the energy and utility industries [33]. There are great tips on power management. The energy and utilities industry has considerable growth potential by implementing smart grid technology, smart meters, and increased accessibility to weather data. The utilization of Big Data and machine learning techniques can enhance the industry's operational efficiency and customer satisfaction. The real-time storage and processing of unstructured data streams are being utilized to improve the overall customer experience.

9. **Big Data Applications in the Transportation Industry:** The transportation industry faces several challenges, including an enormous influx of data from location-based social networks and applications which influence travel behavior. Additionally, the availability of high-speed data via telecommunications has added to the industry's challenges. Moreover, the transportation industry still relies on outdated social media infrastructure when predicting transportation demand. These challenges pose significant obstacles to the industry's ability to effectively predict and meet consumer demand. The government uses Big Data in the transportation sector for intelligent transportation systems, traffic management, and traffic control. Big Data and IoT technologies are also used by the private sector in the transportation industry to manage revenue, advance technology, and other things [43]. Big Data is being used by people to plan their routes to save time and fuel. Travel planning in the tourism industry also uses Big Data.
10. **Big Data Applications in the Insurance Sector:** The key challenges in the insurance industry are lack of personalized prices and services, services incorrectly routed to new segments, lack of services for specific market segments, and underutilized data collected due to hunger for better information and leak regulators. Big Data can be used by the insurance sector to provide consumer insights for more straightforward products [35, 45]. They accomplish this by analyzing data from GPS-enabled devices, social media, closed circuit television (CCTV) footage, and customer behavior predictions. The insurance industry utilizes Big Data for various purposes such as risk management, fraud detection, claims management, and real-time monitoring of claims.

4.8.2 Big Data Companies: Top Companies Using Big Data

There are several top companies across various industries that are utilizing both Big Data technology and IoT to drive innovation and gain competitive advantages. These top companies are leveraging Big Data technology and IoT to drive innovation, improve operational efficiency, enhance customer experiences, and create new business opportunities. By combining the power of IoT devices and the analytical capabilities of Big Data, these companies are unlocking valuable insights, optimizing processes, and delivering cutting-edge solutions in their respective industries. Following are some notable examples.

1. **Google:** Google's self-driving car project, Waymo, utilizes Big Data and IoT extensively. IoT sensors embedded in the vehicles collect vast amounts of real-time data, including information about road conditions, traffic patterns, and pedestrian movement. This data is then analyzed using Big Data analytics to enable autonomous driving and improve transportation efficiency [14, 46].
2. **Amazon:** Amazon uses Big Data and IoT to enhance its e-commerce operations. The Amazon Echo device, powered by the intelligent assistant Alexa, collects user data and interactions which are processed and analyzed using Big Data techniques [14]. This enables personalized recommendations, targeted advertising, and voice-controlled home automation. Additionally, Amazon Dash buttons and IoT-enabled devices facilitate seamless ordering and replenishment of products.
3. **General Electric (GE):** GE leverages Big Data analytics and IoT in its "Predix" platform. Predix collects and analyzes data from industrial machines such as turbines, generators, and medical devices [47]. The platform applies advanced analytics, machine learning, and predictive modeling to detect anomalies, optimize performance, and enable predictive maintenance. This helps reduce downtime, improve operational efficiency, and extend the lifespan of equipment.
4. **IBM:** IBM's Watson IoT platform combines IoT data with powerful AI and Big Data analytics capabilities. It enables organizations to collect, manage, and analyze data from connected devices across industries. Watson's cognitive capabilities facilitate real-time decision-making, predictive maintenance, and operational optimization. Microsoft's Big Data solutions, such as Azure Data Lake and Azure Machine Learning, further enhance data processing and analysis for IoT deployments [48, 49].
5. **Microsoft:** Microsoft's Azure IoT platform offers a comprehensive suite of services for managing, analyzing, and deriving insights from IoT data. Azure IoT Hub securely connects and collects data from devices, while Azure IoT Suite provides pre-configured solutions for specific industries. Microsoft's Big Data analytics services, such as Azure Data Lake and Azure Machine Learning, enable organizations to process and analyze vast amounts of IoT data, uncover patterns, and derive actionable insights [50, 51].
6. **Cisco:** Cisco provides networking infrastructure and solutions for IoT deployments. Its IoT offerings include connectivity solutions, security solutions, and data management platforms. Cisco's Big Data analytics capabilities enable organizations to process, analyze, and gain insights from the massive amounts of data generated by IoT devices [50]. This helps optimize IoT deployments, improve operational efficiency, and enhance security.
7. **Siemens:** Siemens utilizes Big Data and IoT technologies in various domains, including energy management, industrial automation, and smart cities. Siemens' MindSphere platform serves as an IoT operating system, collecting and analyzing data from connected devices. The platform enables real-time monitoring, predictive maintenance, and performance optimization [50]. Siemens combines IoT data with Big Data analytics to drive operational efficiencies, improve energy utilization, and create sustainable smart city solutions.

8. **Intel:** Intel provides hardware solutions for IoT devices and platforms. Its processors and chips power a wide range of IoT devices, enabling data collection and processing at the edge. Intel also offers Big Data analytics platforms, such as Intel IoT Analytics, which facilitate the processing and analysis of IoT data at scale [50]. These solutions help organizations extract valuable insights from IoT data, enabling real-time decision-making and driving innovation.
9. **Tesla:** Tesla utilizes Big Data and IoT technologies in its electric vehicles. Tesla vehicles are equipped with a multitude of sensors and systems that collect data related to vehicle performance, battery usage, and driving behavior. This data is continuously analyzed using Big Data techniques to optimize vehicle performance, improve energy efficiency, and enhance the overall driving experience. Tesla also utilizes over-the-air software updates to continuously improve its vehicles based on real-time data analysis [52].
10. **Philips:** Philips applies Big Data and IoT in its healthcare solutions. Connected medical devices collect patient data, which is then analyzed using Big Data analytics. This enables remote patient monitoring, early detection of health issues, and personalized treatment plans. Philips' HealthSuite platform integrates IoT data with electronic health records (EHRs) and other data sources, facilitating comprehensive health data analysis, clinical decision support, and population health management [53].

4.9 IOT AND BIG DATA USE CASES

There are many use cases of IoT and Big Data such as smart home automation, Industrial IoT (IIoT), smart cities, healthcare monitoring, supply chain optimization, precision agriculture, energy management, transportation and fleet management, retail analytics, environmental monitoring, and so on. These use cases highlight the diverse applications of IoT and Big Data technologies across industries, ranging from optimizing energy consumption and improving healthcare outcomes to enhancing transportation systems and enabling sustainable practices. For instance, IoT devices such as smart thermostats, smart lighting systems, and connected appliances collect data on energy usage, occupancy patterns, and user preferences. This data, when combined with Big Data analytics, enables homeowners to optimize energy consumption, automate routine tasks, and enhance home security. In manufacturing environments, IoT sensors embedded in machines, equipment, and production lines capture real-time data on performance, maintenance needs, and environmental conditions. Big Data analytics applied to this data can enable predictive maintenance, optimize production processes, and improve overall operational efficiency. We will next discuss how IoT and Big Data technologies are deployed in smart home automation, IIoT, and smart cities.

Smart Home Automation [50, 54]

1. **Deployment:** IoT devices such as smart thermostats, smart lighting systems, and connected appliances are installed in homes. These devices are connected to a central hub or a cloud-based platform that collects data from the devices.

2. **Data Collection:** The IoT devices collect data on energy consumption, occupancy patterns, and user preferences. This data is transmitted to the central hub or cloud platform for analysis.
3. **Data Analytics:** Big Data analytics algorithms analyze the collected data to identify patterns, trends, and anomalies. This analysis helps in optimizing energy usage, automating routine tasks, and providing personalized experiences.
4. **Control and Automation:** Based on the analysis results, commands are sent back to the IoT devices to control actions such as adjusting the temperature, turning lights on or off, and activating appliances.
5. **Benefits:** These include increased energy efficiency, cost savings on utilities, enhanced home security, and personalized home experiences.

Industrial Internet of Things (IIoT) [55, 56]

1. **Deployment:** IoT sensors are embedded in machines, equipment, and production lines within manufacturing environments. These sensors are connected to a network or a central data aggregation system.
2. **Data Collection:** IoT sensors continuously collect real-time data on various parameters such as temperature, pressure, vibration, and machine performance. The data is transmitted to the central system for further processing.
3. **Data Analytics:** Big Data analytics algorithms process the collected data to identify patterns, deviations, and potential issues. This analysis helps in predicting maintenance needs, optimizing production processes, and improving overall operational efficiency.
4. **Decision Support:** Based on the analysis results, actionable insights and alerts are generated to inform operators and maintenance teams about potential failures, required maintenance actions, and process optimizations.
5. **Benefits:** These include reduced downtime, improved equipment reliability, optimized production processes, and cost savings through efficient resource allocation.

Smart Cities [57, 58]

1. **Deployment:** IoT sensors and devices are deployed across urban areas and integrated into infrastructure, buildings, and public spaces. These devices are connected to a network or a central data platform.
2. **Data Collection:** IoT sensors capture data on various aspects such as traffic flow, air quality, waste management, energy consumption, and public services. The collected data is transmitted to the central platform.
3. **Data Analytics:** Big Data analytics algorithms process the data in real time or in batches to extract insights and patterns. This analysis helps in optimizing traffic management, resource allocation, environmental sustainability, and urban planning.
4. **Decision-Making and Automation:** The analyzed data is used to inform decision-making processes for traffic control, resource management, emergency response, and infrastructure planning. Automation systems can be triggered based on the analysis results to optimize services and operations.

5. **Benefits:** These include reduced traffic congestion, improved air quality, optimized waste management, enhanced citizen safety, and efficient use of resources.

4.10 DATA HANDLING TECHNOLOGIES

Data handling technologies encompass a wide range of tools, techniques, and practices used to manage data throughout their lifecycles. These technologies facilitate data collection, storage, processing, analysis, and presentation. The data collection is possible with the help of IoT sensors, wearable devices, RFID, and data acquisition systems. Sensors capture data from the physical environment or devices. They can measure various parameters such as temperature, humidity, pressure, motion, and more. Wearable devices, like fitness trackers or smartwatches, collect personal health and activity data. RFID tags and readers are used for automatic identification and tracking of objects or assets [59]. The data acquisition systems collect data from various sources, perform analog-to-digital conversion, and transmit it to the back-end systems. There are various kinds of databases that can be used for data storage purposes. Traditional databases—such as MySQL, PostgreSQL, or Oracle—store structured data using tables, rows, and columns. The NoSQL databases—like MongoDB, Cassandra, and Redis—handle unstructured or semi-structured data, providing scalability and flexibility. Data warehouses integrate and store data from various sources for business intelligence and reporting purposes. Services like Amazon S3, Google Cloud Storage, and Microsoft Azure Blob Storage offer scalable and secure storage for large volumes of data. Technologies like Hadoop Distributed File System (HDFS) enable distributed storage of Big Data across multiple nodes [28].

Technologies like Apache Hadoop, Apache Spark, and Apache Flink provide distributed processing capabilities for large-scale data analysis. Platforms like Apache Kafka and AWS Kinesis process and analyze real-time streaming data. Techniques like data mining, predictive analytics, and machine learning algorithms extract insights and patterns from data. Tools such as Tableau, Power BI, and D3.js can then help in visualizing and presenting data in a meaningful way. Tools like Apache NiFi, Informatica, or Talend facilitate the extraction, transformation, and loading of data from various sources into a target system. These data handling technologies collectively enable organizations to effectively manage and leverage data for decision-making, insights, and innovation. The choice of specific technologies depends on the nature of data, scale, requirements, and organizational goals [60].

4.10.1 Flow of Data

The flow of data refers to the movement and transfer of data within an IoT system. It involves capturing, transmitting, processing, storing, and analyzing data generated by IoT devices. Some key technologies involved in managing the flow of data include the following [26, 30].

1. **IoT Gateways:** IoT gateways act as intermediaries between IoT devices and the cloud or data center. They aggregate data from multiple devices,

perform initial data processing, and transmit it to the cloud or data center for further analysis.
2. **Communication Protocols:** Various communication protocols—such as MQTT, CoAP, and HTTP—facilitate data transmission between IoT devices, gateways, and back-end systems.
3. **Data Streaming Platforms:** Streaming platforms like Apache Kafka and AWS Kinesis enable real-time ingestion and processing of data streams. They handle the high volume and velocity of data generated by IoT devices and ensure efficient and reliable data flow.
4. **Data Pipelines:** Data pipelines orchestrate the movement of data through various stages, including data ingestion, transformation, enrichment, and storage. Technologies like Apache NiFi and Apache Airflow help in designing and managing data pipelines.

4.10.2 Data Acquisition

Data acquisition refers to the process of collecting data from different sources, including IoT devices, sensors, and other data-generating entities. Key technologies involved in data acquisition include the following [25, 26, 61].

1. **IoT Sensors:** Sensors play a crucial role in capturing data from the physical environment. They can measure various parameters such as temperature, humidity, pressure, motion, and more. Examples include temperature sensors, accelerometers, and GPS sensors.
2. **IoT Protocols:** Protocols like Bluetooth Low Energy (BLE), Zigbee, Wi-Fi, and cellular networks enable communication between IoT devices and data acquisition systems. They ensure seamless data transfer from sensors to the back-end infrastructure.
3. **Edge Computing:** Edge computing brings computational capabilities closer to the data source, reducing latency and bandwidth requirements. It enables data pre-processing and filtering at the edge devices themselves, minimizing data transmission and storage costs.
4. **Data Acquisition Systems:** Data acquisition systems collect data from sensors, perform analog-to-digital conversion, and transmit it to the back-end systems. These systems can include microcontrollers, data loggers, and specialized hardware modules.

4.10.3 Data Storage

Data storage involves securely storing and managing the vast amounts of data generated by IoT devices. Some key technologies for data storage in IoT systems are the following [8, 25].

1. **Relational Databases:** Traditional relational databases—such as MySQL, PostgreSQL, and Oracle—are commonly used for structured data storage in IoT applications. They provide ACID (atomicity, consistency, isolation, and durability) compliance, and support complex queries.

2. **NoSQL Databases:** NoSQL databases—including MongoDB, Cassandra, and DynamoDB—are designed to handle large volumes of unstructured or semi-structured data generated by IoT devices. They offer scalability, flexibility, and high availability.
3. **Data Lakes:** Data lakes, built on technologies like Apache Hadoop and Amazon S3, store vast amounts of raw and unprocessed data. They provide a centralized repository for storing diverse data types, enabling future analysis and exploration.
4. **Cloud Storage:** Cloud storage services—such as Amazon S3, Google Cloud Storage, and Microsoft Azure Blob Storage—offer scalable and cost-effective options for storing IoT data. They provide durability, accessibility, and easy integration with other cloud services.

4.10.4 Introduction to Hadoop

Hadoop is designed to address the challenges posed by Big Data, which refers to extremely large and complex datasets that cannot be easily managed, processed, or analyzed using traditional computing approaches [62, 63]. Hadoop provides a scalable, fault-tolerant, and cost-effective framework for storing, processing, and analyzing Big Data, enabling organizations to derive valuable insights and make data-driven decisions. Hadoop enables the storage and processing of massive amounts of data, ranging from terabytes to petabytes and beyond. It allows organizations to store and analyze data that exceeds the capacity of a single machine or traditional storage systems. Its distributed nature allows it to scale horizontally by adding more machines to a cluster. This scalability ensures that as data volume increases, processing capacity can be easily expanded by adding more nodes to the cluster. Hadoop's distributed file system (HDFS) stores data across multiple machines in a cluster. This enables data locality, which means that processing tasks can be performed on the same nodes where the data resides. By minimizing data movement across the network, Hadoop reduces network congestion and improves overall performance. Hadoop's MapReduce model allows for parallel processing of data [64]. It breaks down tasks into smaller sub-tasks and distributes them across the cluster, allowing multiple machines to work on different parts of the dataset simultaneously. This parallelism leads to faster processing times for Big Data analytics. Additionally, Hadoop's ecosystem offers a wide range of tools and frameworks that integrate with Hadoop, such as Hive for data warehousing, Pig for data analysis, Spark for in-memory processing, and HBase for real-time data storage. This flexibility allows organizations to build custom solutions tailored to their specific needs. The key components of Hadoop include the following [63, 65].

1. **Hadoop Distributed File System (HDFS):** This is the primary storage system of Hadoop. HDFS divides files into blocks and distributes them across multiple machines in a cluster, enabling high fault tolerance and data locality.
2. **MapReduce:** MapReduce is a programming model used for processing and analyzing data stored in Hadoop [64]. It allows developers to write distributed data processing tasks by defining map and reduce functions. The map

function processes input data and produces intermediate key-value pairs, while the reduce function performs aggregation on the intermediate data to generate the final results.

3. **YARN (Yet Another Resource Negotiator):** YARN is a resource management system in Hadoop that handles resource allocation and scheduling tasks across the cluster. It allows different data processing frameworks—like MapReduce, Apache Spark, and Apache Flink—to run on the same Hadoop infrastructure.

4.11 INTRODUCTION TO DATA ANALYTICS

The term "Big Data Analytics" describes the process of analyzing large amounts of different datasets using the latest analytical methods. Big Data analytics enables analysts, researchers, and business users to harness Big Data that was previously inaccessible and unusable for faster and more effective decision-making [4, 8, 38]. Companies use this analytics tool to glean valuable insights from a mountain of unstructured and raw data, e.g., hidden patterns, undiscovered correlations, market trends and customer preferences. Using statistical methods (such as measures of central tendencies, graphs, etc.), information systems software (such as data mining and sorting routines), and operations research methods (such as linear programming), analysis aims to explore, visualize, identify, and find patterns or trends in communicating data [66, 67]. For example, weather data collected by meteorology agencies can be analyzed and used to predict weather conditions. Furthermore, the creation of successful new products depends on business data analytics. How to use data analytics as a powerful tool to gain competitive advantage and uncover new business opportunities is revealed by the analytics process in the age of Big Data. Its many uses include marketing, fraud detection and credit risk assessment. The different methods of analysis fall into the following categories.

4.11.1 Types of Data Analytics

Different strategies are required for the various types of data. There are four major types of Big Data analytics: namely descriptive analytics, diagnostic analytics, predictive analytics, and prescriptive analytics, as shown in Figure 4.5 [61, 68].

1. **Descriptive Analytics:** Descriptive analytics is regarded as a tool for identifying patterns within a particular customer segment. It simplifies and condenses historical data into a form that can be read. Descriptive analytics involves examining past events and trends to gain insights and understand patterns [12]. It enables the generation of reports on a company's financial metrics, such as earnings and sales, in a more efficient manner. By delving deeper into the data, further information can be obtained. Examples of descriptive analytics include market basket analysis's use of summary statistics, clustering, and association rules. Descriptive analytics is employed by various businesses, including Dow Chemical Company. Using its historical data, the company made better use of its lab and office space.

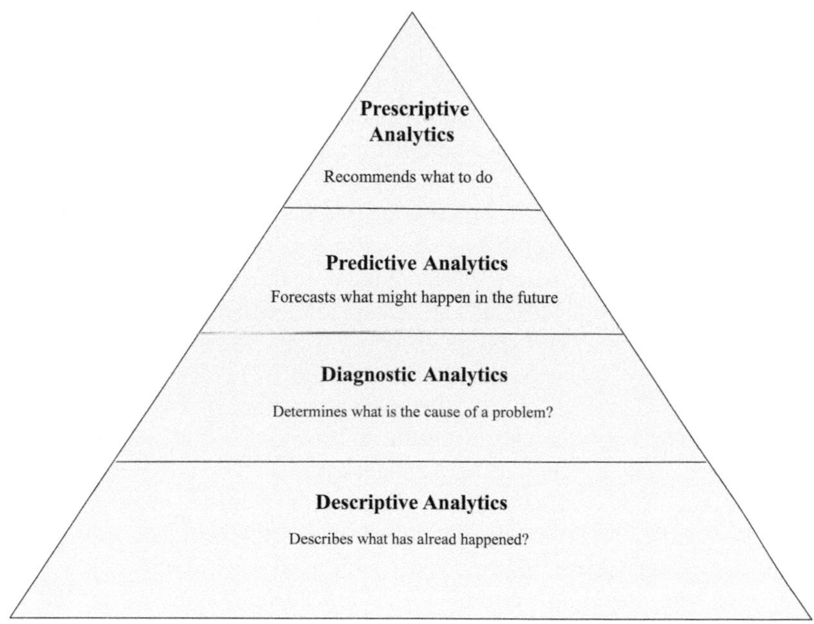

FIGURE 4.5 Types of data analytics.

2. **Diagnostic Analytics:** As the name suggests, diagnostic analysis provides a diagnosis of the problem. It provides a complete understanding of the cause of the problem. When looking for the cause of an incident, data scientists turn to analytics. Diagnostic analysis techniques include drilling, data mining, data recovery, outage analysis, and customer health analysis, among others [12, 69]. In business, diagnostic analytics help you explore the usage patterns of your most loyal customers and what drives the leading churn rates. An e-commerce business could be a use case for diagnostic analytics. Note that even though customers are adding items to their carts, the company's sales are down. Possible causes of this problem include expensive shipping, insufficient payment options, or incorrect form loading. Companies use diagnostic analytics to determine the exact cause of a problem and then work to fix it.
3. **Predictive Analytics:** Predictive analytics is a methodology that utilizes statistical algorithms and machine learning techniques to examine past data and discern patterns, connections, and interdependencies, using this knowledge to anticipate forthcoming events or tendencies [12, 68]. The approach involves analyzing data to predict potential outcomes or behaviors, allowing businesses to make informed decisions. The process of predictive analytics typically requires large amounts of historical data, which is used to build and train predictive models. These models can then be applied to new data to generate predictions about potential future events or behaviors. Predictive analytics is used extensively in a wide range of industries, including finance,

healthcare, marketing, and manufacturing. It has proven to be an effective tool for risk identification and mitigation, decision-making improvement, and business process optimization. Overall, predictive analytics has grown in importance in recent years as organizations seek to leverage the power of data and analytics to gain a competitive advantage and achieve business success.

4. **Prescriptive Analytics:** Prescriptive analytics refers to a type of data analysis that is focused on identifying the best course of action that can be taken to achieve a particular desired outcome or goal. This type of analytics is based on advanced algorithms and statistical models that analyze historical data, current trends, and predicted future events to provide recommendations on the best course of action to take [12, 68]. Prescriptive analytics can be used in a wide range of industries such as healthcare, finance, marketing, and logistics. For example, in healthcare, it can be used to prescribe the most effective treatment plan for a patient based on their medical history and current condition. In finance, it can be used to optimize investment strategies by taking into account market trends and risk levels. The main goal of prescriptive analytics is to provide decision-makers with actionable insights that can help them make informed decisions that can lead to improved outcomes. These insights can be presented in various forms such as dashboards, reports, and visualizations that can be easily interpreted by non-technical stakeholders. In conclusion, prescriptive analytics is an important data analysis technique that can help organizations make data-driven decisions that can lead to better outcomes. By leveraging advanced statistical models and algorithms, prescriptive analytics can provide valuable insights that can inform decision-making across a wide range of industries [27]. In business literature, the terms analytics, business analytics (BA), and business intelligence (BI) are often used interchangeably to refer to processes that turn data into useful information. However, descriptive, predictive, diagnostic, and prescriptive analytics all have different goals and methods. Any of four different analysis processes can be used. These terms are defined for your convenience in what follows.
   a) **Business Analytics (BA):** A recent article claims that business analytics transcends the scope of pure analytics. It utilizes a blend of various techniques such as descriptive (depicting what is happening), predictive (discerning the reason behind it, discovering new trends, and forecasting what will occur next), diagnostic (analyzing why it happened), and prescriptive (suggesting the best way forward) methods to generate distinctive and valuable insights that lead to measurable improvement in business performance [29, 70]. The data used for analysis can come from company reports, databases, and data that is housed in the cloud. Reporting results on BI is a part of business analysis processes, and further attempts are made to explain why the results occur based on the analysis.
   b) **Business Intelligence (BI):** BI is an approach that focuses on the analysis of data through the creation of reports and queries. It involves the integration of data obtained from various sources, including a reported

BA approach. BI aims to provide insights and answers to critical business questions such as the current state of affairs, where it is happening, and what steps need to be taken based on past experiences [29, 70].

The use of BA and BI has been prevalent in the reporting and comprehension of historical events based on structured data obtained from database management systems [71]. However, with the continuous growth of Big Data, these techniques can be integrated with Big Data analytics methods to extract useful insights from data by using analytical techniques and tools. These techniques are applied in various areas including structured data analytics, text analytics, web analytics, network analytics, and mobile analytics. The large amount and fast pace of Big Data create a chance to use analytical tools to predict future trends and uncover novel insights.

4.11.2 Statistical Models

Statistical models are a key component of data analytics and are used to analyze and interpret data. Statistical models provide a framework for interpreting and understanding data. They help uncover patterns, relationships, and trends in the data, allowing analysts to gain insights and make informed decisions. Statistical models enable prediction and forecasting. By analyzing historical data, models can be trained to make predictions about future outcomes or behaviors. This is particularly useful in areas such as sales forecasting, demand planning, and risk assessment [72]. Statistical models provide a rigorous framework for hypothesis testing. They help determine whether observed differences or relationships in data are statistically significant or occurred by chance. This is crucial for drawing valid conclusions and making data-driven decisions. These models assist in identifying the most relevant features or variables that contribute to the outcome of interest. They help reduce the dimensionality of data by selecting the most informative features, improving model performance and interpretability. These models allow for model validation and evaluation to assess their performance. Techniques such as cross-validation and metrics like accuracy, precision, recall, and receiver operating characteristic (ROC) curves help evaluate the effectiveness of the models and compare different approaches. Following are some commonly used statistical models in data analytics [73, 74].

- **Linear Regression:** Linear regression is used to model the relationship between a dependent variable and one or more independent variables. It helps understand how the independent variables influence the dependent variable and make predictions based on the observed data.
- **Logistic Regression:** Logistic regression is used when the dependent variable is categorical or binary. It estimates the probability of an event occurring based on the values of the independent variables.
- **Decision Trees:** Decision trees are used for classification and regression analysis. They create a tree-like model of decisions and their possible consequences. Each node represents a feature or attribute, and branches represent possible outcomes based on that feature.

- **Random Forest:** Random forest is an ensemble learning method that combines multiple decision trees to improve accuracy and reduce overfitting. It is commonly used for classification and regression tasks.
- **Support Vector Machines (SVM):** SVM is a supervised learning algorithm used for classification and regression analysis. It separates data into different classes by finding an optimal hyperplane that maximizes the margin between classes.
- **Naïve Bayes:** Naïve Bayes is a probabilistic classification algorithm based on Bayes' theorem. It assumes that the presence of a particular feature in a class is unrelated to the presence of other features; hence, the term "naïve."
- **Clustering Algorithms:** Clustering algorithms—such as K-means, hierarchical clustering, and density-based spatial clustering of applications with noise (DBSCAN)—group similar data points together based on their similarities or distances. They are used for unsupervised learning tasks to discover patterns and groupings in data.
- **Time Series Analysis:** Time series analysis models time-dependent data to understand patterns and make predictions. It involves techniques like autoregressive integrated moving average (ARIMA), exponential smoothing, and seasonal decomposition.
- **Principal Component Analysis (PCA):** PCA is a dimensionality reduction technique used to reduce the complexity of high-dimensional data. It transforms the data into a lower-dimensional space while preserving the most important information.
- **Neural Networks:** Neural networks, including deep learning models, are used for complex pattern recognition, image and speech recognition, NLP, and other tasks [75]. They mimic the functioning of the human brain by using interconnected nodes (neurons) organized in layers.

4.11.3 Analysis of Variance

Analysis of variance (ANOVA) is a statistical technique used in data analytics to analyze the variance between different groups or factors in a dataset [76]. It is particularly useful for comparing means and determining whether there are significant differences among multiple groups. It provides a systematic and rigorous approach to analyzing differences between groups. It helps to identify significant factors that contribute to variations in the outcome variable. In the context of data analytics, ANOVA can provide valuable insights by answering questions such as the following [77].

1. Are there significant differences between groups?
2. Which group(s) differ significantly from others?
3. How much of the variability is explained by different factors?
4. Is there evidence to support specific hypotheses?
5. How should resources be allocated or decisions be made based on group differences?
6. What is the appropriate experimental design?

ANOVA enables researchers to draw conclusions about the significance of differences based on statistical evidence. It facilitates the comparison of multiple groups simultaneously, saving time and resources. In the context of data analytics, ANOVA can bc applied in several ways, including the following [78, 79].

1. **Comparing Group Means:** ANOVA is used to compare means across multiple groups. For example, in a clinical trial, researchers may want to compare the effectiveness of different treatments on patient outcomes. ANOVA can help determine if there are significant differences in outcomes within the treatment group.
2. **Testing Hypotheses:** ANOVA allows analysts to test specific hypotheses about group means. They can formulate null and alternative hypotheses to determine if there are significant differences in means. By calculating the F-statistic and comparing it to the critical value, analysts can make conclusions about the significance of the differences.
3. **Variance Decomposition:** ANOVA helps decompose the total variance in the data into different components, such as the variance between groups and the variance within groups. This decomposition provides insights into the proportion of variance explained by the factors under investigation.
4. **Post Hoc Analysis:** After conducting ANOVA and identifying significant differences between groups, post-hoc analysis can be performed to determine which specific group means differ significantly. Multiple comparison tests, such as Tukey's HSD (honestly significant difference) test or Bonferroni correction, can be used for pairwise comparisons.
5. **Experimental Design:** ANOVA is an essential tool in experimental design. It helps determine the appropriate sample size, statistical power, and the number of treatment groups required to detect significant differences. It aids in designing experiments that maximize the chances of detecting true effects while minimizing the influence of confounding factors.

4.11.4 Data Dispersion

Data dispersion, also known as data variability or spread, refers to the extent to which data points in a dataset are spread out or distributed. It provides information about the spread or range of values within the dataset and is a measure of the degree of variability or diversity in the data [80]. In the context of statistical analysis and data analytics, understanding data dispersion is important, as it helps to assess the variability of the data points and provides insights into the distribution of values. Key measures of data dispersion include the following [80, 81].

1. **Range:** The range is the simplest measure of data dispersion and represents the difference between the maximum and minimum values in the dataset. It provides a basic understanding of the spread of values but is sensitive to outliers.
2. **Variance:** Variance measures the average squared deviation of each data point from the mean. It quantifics the spread of values around the mean and

provides an indication of how much individual data points deviate from the average. Higher variance indicates greater dispersion.

3. **Standard Deviation:** Standard deviation is the square root of the variance and provides a measure of the average deviation of data points from the mean. It is widely used in data analysis as it provides a more interpretable measure of dispersion, and its value is in the same unit as the data.
4. **Interquartile Range (IQR):** The interquartile range represents the range between the 25th and 75th percentiles of the data. It is less sensitive to outliers compared to the range and provides a measure of the spread of the central 50% of the data. It is often used in robust statistical analysis.
5. **Coefficient of Variation (CV):** The coefficient of variation is the ratio of the standard deviation to the mean, expressed as a percentage. It is used to compare the relative dispersion of datasets with different scales. A higher CV indicates a higher relative dispersion.

Data dispersion is a crucial aspect of data analysis, as it provides information about the spread and variability of data points. Measures of dispersion help in assessing data quality, understanding data distribution, detecting outliers, and making comparisons between datasets. They contribute to a comprehensive analysis and interpretation of data. Understanding data dispersion is valuable in several ways, including the following [82, 83].

1. **Identifying Outliers:** Data dispersion helps identify outliers, which are data points that significantly deviate from the rest of the data. Outliers can impact the analysis and interpretation of data, and detecting them is important for data quality and anomaly detection.
2. **Assessing Data Quality:** Data dispersion can provide insights into the quality of data. Highly dispersed data may indicate measurement errors, data inconsistencies, or the presence of influential factors that affect the variability of the data.
3. **Understanding Data Distribution:** Data dispersion helps in understanding the distribution of values within the dataset. It provides information about the spread and variability of the data, which can be used to assess the shape of the distribution, detect skewness or asymmetry, and choose appropriate statistical models.
4. **Comparing and Contrasting Data:** Data dispersion allows for comparisons between datasets. It helps in comparing the spread of values across different groups, populations, or time periods. Comparisons of data dispersion can provide insights into differences or similarities in variability.

4.11.5 Contingence and Correlation

In the context of data analysis and statistics, contingency and correlation are two important concepts that help to understand the relationships and associations between variables in a dataset. Contingency analysis focuses on the relationship between categorical variables and helps identify associations or dependencies, whereas correlation analysis examines the linear relationship between continuous variables and measures the strength and direction of the association [84, 85].

Contingency refers to the dependence or relationship between two categorical variables in a dataset. It is often analyzed using a contingency table, also known as a cross-tabulation or a contingency matrix. A contingency table displays the frequency counts or proportions of each combination of categories for the two variables. Contingency analysis helps to determine if there is a statistically significant association between the variables. It involves calculating various statistical measures such as chi-square test, Fisher's exact test, or G-test. These tests assess whether the observed frequencies in the contingency table deviate significantly from the expected frequencies, assuming independence between the variables. Contingency analysis is particularly useful in analyzing categorical data, such as survey responses, demographic characteristics, or outcomes in medical studies. It helps to identify relationships, dependencies, or associations between variables and can provide insights into the patterns or trends within the data.

Correlation, on the other hand, measures the strength and direction of the linear relationship between two continuous variables in a dataset [86]. It quantifies how the variables move together or relate to each other. Correlation analysis helps to determine whether a change in one variable is associated with a change in the other variable. The correlation coefficient is a common measure used in correlation analysis. It ranges between −1 and 1, where −1 indicates a perfect negative correlation, 1 indicates a perfect positive correlation, and 0 indicates no correlation. The correlation coefficient is calculated using statistical methods such as Pearson correlation, Spearman correlation, or Kendall's tau. Correlation analysis is valuable for understanding the relationship between variables, and it can provide insights into the direction and strength of the association. It helps in identifying dependencies, trends, or patterns in the data. Correlation analysis is widely used in fields such as finance, economics, social sciences, and market research to explore the relationships between variables and make informed decisions. It is important to note that correlation does not imply causation. While a correlation between two variables indicates an association, it does not necessarily imply that one variable causes the other. Causation requires additional analysis and considerations beyond correlation.

4.11.6 Regression Analysis

Regression analysis is a statistical technique used to model and analyze the relationship between a dependent variable and one or more independent variables. It helps to understand how changes in the independent variables are associated with changes in the dependent variable. In the context of data analysis, regression analysis is widely used for prediction, forecasting, and understanding the impact of variables on an outcome of interest. The key components of regression analysis are as follows.

1. **Dependent Variable:** The dependent variable, also known as the response variable or outcome variable, is the variable that we want to predict or explain. It represents the variable of interest in the analysis, and its values are influenced by the independent variables.

2. **Independent Variables:** The independent variables, also known as predictor variables or explanatory variables, are the variables that are believed to influence or explain the variation in the dependent variable. They are used to make predictions or estimate the effect of the independent variables on the dependent variable.
3. **Regression Model:** A regression model is constructed to represent the relationship between the dependent variable and independent variables. The model specifies the functional form and the parameters that quantify the relationship. The most common form is the linear regression model, with the relationship assumed to be a linear combination of the independent variables.
4. **Estimation:** The regression model is estimated using statistical techniques to estimate the parameters. The most common method is ordinary least squares (OLS), which minimizes the sum of the squared differences between the observed values of the dependent variable and the predicted values from the regression model.
5. **Model Evaluation:** Once the regression model is estimated, it is evaluated to assess its accuracy of fit and statistical significance. Evaluation includes analyzing the coefficients, conducting hypothesis tests, assessing model assumptions, and examining accuracy-of-fit measures such as R-squared or adjusted R-squared.
6. **Inference and Interpretation:** Regression analysis allows for making inferences about the relationship between the variables. The estimated coefficients indicate the direction and magnitude of the effect of the independent variables on the dependent variable. The significance of the coefficients and their confidence intervals provide insights into the statistical significance of the relationships.

4.11.7 Precision and Error Limits

In the context of statistical analysis and measurement, precision and error limits are important concepts that help to assess the accuracy and reliability of measurements. Precision reflects the consistency and reproducibility of measurements, with higher precision indicating less variability. Error limits provide a measure of uncertainty and represent the range within which the true value is expected to lie with a certain level of confidence. Understanding precision and error limits helps in assessing the accuracy and reliability of measurements and making informed decisions based on statistical analysis. Precision refers to the degree of consistency and reproducibility in the measurements or results obtained from a statistical analysis. It reflects the level of agreement among repeated measurements or observations of the same quantity. A precise measurement or result has a small amount of random variability and provides consistent values. In statistical terms, precision is often quantified using measures such as standard deviation, variance, or CV. A smaller standard deviation or variance indicates higher precision and less variability among the measurements. Conversely, a larger standard deviation or variance indicates lower precision and more variability among the measurements. Precision is crucial in ensuring the reliability and consistency of measurements. It helps to determine the level of confidence we can have in the obtained results. Highly precise measurements are desirable as they minimize random errors and provide more reliable information for decision-making.

Error limits, also known as margin of error or confidence intervals, represent the range within which the true value of a parameter is expected to lie with a certain level of confidence. When making statistical inferences or estimating unknown values, error limits provide a measure of uncertainty associated with the estimated value. The error limits are calculated based on the precision of the measurements and the selected level of confidence. The confidence level indicates the probability that the true value falls within the calculated error limits. Commonly used confidence levels are 95% and 99%. For example, if a measurement is reported as 10 ± 0.5 with a 95% confidence level, it means that the true value is expected to be within the range of 9.5–10.5 with 95% confidence. The error limits provide a sense of the potential variability or uncertainty associated with the measurement. Error limits are useful in interpreting and communicating the results of statistical analyses. They help to convey the range of possible values for a parameter and provide a sense of the reliability of the estimation. Error limits also assist in comparing measurements or results from different sources and assessing the significance of observed differences.

4.12 CHALLENGES IN IOT WITH BIG DATA ANALYTICS

The rapid growth of various applications in IoT also leads to various challenges that need to be addressed [43, 87]. While the combination of IoT systems and Big Data analytics offers significant benefits, there are also several challenges that need to be addressed for successful implementation. The main challenges of IoT using Big Data analytics are as follows.

1. **Data Storage and Management:** The data generated by internet-enabled devices is constantly increasing, and the storage capacity of Big Data systems is limited, so storing and managing such a large amount of data becomes one of the biggest challenges. There is a need to design mechanisms and frameworks to collect, store, and process this data [2, 6].
2. **Data Visualization:** We are already aware that data generated is heterogeneous, i.e., it becomes challenging to directly visualize this data because it is structured, unstructured, and semi-structured in a variety of formats. Data preparation is necessary for better understanding and visualization, which will lead to more timely and accurate industrial decision-making and increased industry productivity [8].
3. **Confidentiality and Privacy:** Every intelligent object integrated into a network with a global reach constitutes an IoT system, whether it is used by people or machines. This raises concerns about information leakage and privacy. Since the produced data contains the personal information of users, it is important that privacy and confidentiality are maintained.
4. **Integrity:** Connected devices can collect information, communicate, share information, and perform analytics for a variety of applications. These tools ensure that users will not share their data indefinitely. In order to successfully

meet scalability and integrity requirements, data collection methods must follow a set of procedures and rules.

5. **Power Captivity:** For the smooth and continuous operation of IoT operations, internet-enabled devices should be connected to an endless power supply. These devices must be deployed with lightweight mechanisms because they have memory, processing, and energy limitations.
6. **Analytics Complexity:** Extracting valuable insights from IoT data requires advanced analytics techniques, including machine learning, predictive modeling, and real-time analytics. Developing and deploying complex analytics models, algorithms, and infrastructure require specialized skills and expertise.

REFERENCES

[1] M. Bansal, I. Chana, and S. Clarke, "A Survey on IoT Big Data," *ACM Comput. Surv.*, vol. 53, no. 6, 2021, doi: 10.1145/3419634.

[2] M. S. Hadi, A. Q. Lawey, T. E. H. El-Gorashi, and J. M. H. Elmirghani, "Big Data Analytics for Wireless and Wired Network Design: A Survey," *Comput. Netw.*, vol. 132, 2018, doi: 10.1016/j.comnet.2018.01.016.

[3] Y. Hajjaji, W. Boulila, I. R. Farah, I. Romdhani, and A. Hussain, "Big Data and IoT-Based Applications in Smart Environments: A Systematic Review," *Compu. Sci. Rev.*, vol. 39, 2021, doi: 10.1016/j.cosrev.2020.100318.

[4] M. R. Anawar, S. Wang, M. Azam Zia, A. K. Jadoon, U. Akram, and S. Raza, "Fog Computing: An Overview of Big IoT Data Analytics," *Wirel. Commun. Mob. Comput.*, vol. 2018, 2018, doi: 10.1155/2018/7157192.

[5] M. Mohammadi, A. Al-Fuqaha, S. Sorour, and M. Guizani, "Deep Learning for IoT Big Data and Streaming Analytics: A Survey," *IEEE Commun. Surv. Tutor.*, vol. 20, no. 4, 2018, doi: 10.1109/COMST.2018.2844341.

[6] M. Bansal, I. Chana, and S. Clarke, "A Survey on IoT Big Data: Current Status, 13 V's Challenges, and Future Directions," *ACM Comput. Surv.*, vol. 53, no. 6, 2021, doi: 10.1145/3419634.

[7] M. A. Amanullah *et al.*, "Deep Learning and Big Data Technologies for IoT Security," *Comput. Commun.*, vol. 151, 2020, doi: 10.1016/j.comcom.2020.01.016.

[8] M. Marjani *et al.*, "Big IoT Data Analytics: Architecture, Opportunities, and Open Research Challenges," *IEEE Access*, vol. 5, 2017, doi: 10.1109/ACCESS.2017.2689040.

[9] R. Khamisy-Farah *et al.*, "Big Data for Biomedical Education with a Focus on the Covid-19 Era: An Integrative Review of the Literature," *Int. J. Environ. Res. Public Health*, vol. 18, no. 17, 2021, doi: 10.3390/ijerph18178989.

[10] N. AlNuaimi, M. M. Masud, M. A. Serhani, and N. Zaki, "Streaming Feature Selection Algorithms for Big Data: A Survey," *Appl. Comput. Inform.*, vol. 18, no. 1–2, 2022, doi: 10.1016/j.aci.2019.01.001.

[11] G. Koffikalipe and R. K. Behera, "Big Data Architectures: A Detailed and Application Oriented Analysis," *Int. J. Innov. Technol. Explor. Eng.*, vol. 8, no. 9, 2019, doi: 10.35940/ijitee.h7179.078919.

[12] S. Sasikala, D. D. Renuka, and R. Kumar, "Introduction to Big Data Analytics," in *Research Practitioner's Handbook on Big Data Analytics*, Apple Academic Press, Florida, USA, 2023, doi: 10.1201/9781003284543-1.

[13] A. Singla, N. Bali, and D. Chaudhary, "Big Data and Its Applications," *J. Technol. Manag. Grow. Econ.*, vol. 11, no. 2, 2020, doi: 10.15415/jtmge.2020.112008.

[14] T. N. Hewage, M. N. Halgamuge, A. Syed, and G. Ekici, "Review: Big Data Techniques of Google, Amazon, Facebook and Twitter," *J. Commun.*, vol. 13, no. 2, 2018, doi: 10.12720/jcm.13.2.94-100.

[15] J. Woo and M. Mishra, "Predicting the Ratings of Amazon Products Using Big Data," *Wiley Interdiscip. Rev.: Data Min. Knowl. Discov.*, vol. 11, no. 3, 2021, doi: 10.1002/widm.1400.

[16] M. N. Halgamuge, G. Ekici, T. N. Hewage, and A. Syed, "Review: Big Data Techniques of Google, Amazon, Facebook and Twitter Article in Journal of Communications February," *J. Commun.*, vol. 13, no. 2, 2018.

[17] Amazon, "Amazon EMR—Big Data Platform—Amazon Web Services," *Amazon*, 2020.

[18] B. Marr, "Amazon: Using Big Data to Understand Customers," *Bernard Marr Co.*, 2019.

[19] V. Heredia-Ruiz, A. C. Quirós-Ramírez, and B. E. Quiceno-Castañeda, "Netflix: Content Catalog and Television Flow in Times of Big Data," *Rev. Comun.*, vol. 20, no. 1, 2021, doi: 10.26441/RC20.1-2021-A7.

[20] M. Dixon, "How Netflix Used Big Data and Analytics to Generate Billions," *Selerity*, vol. 4, 2019.

[21] J. M. Norvaisas and J. "Yoni" Karpfen, "Little Data, Big Data and Design at LinkedIn," *Ethnogr. Prax. Ind. Conf. Proc.*, vol. 2014, no. 1, 2014, doi: 10.1111/1559-8918.01029.

[22] R. Sumbaly, J. Kreps, and S. Shah, "The 'Big Data' Ecosystem at LinkedIn," in *Proceedings of the ACM SIGMOD International Conference on Management of Data*, 2013, doi: 10.1145/2463676.2463707.

[23] M. Sharmila Begum, G. Jayashree, Z. Mahaboob Asfia, R. Subhasri, and L. Vishnu Priya, "Predicting the Prices of Bitcoin Using Data Analytics," *Turk. J. Comput. Math.*, vol. 12, no. 10, pp. 1487–1501, 2021.

[24] P. Ghavami, "Chapter 1 Introduction to Big Data," in *Big Data Management*, De Gruyter, Berlin, Germany, 2020, doi: 10.1515/9783110664065-001.

[25] D. Solodovnikova and L. Niedrite, "Handling Evolution in Big Data Architectures," *Balt. J. Mod. Comput.*, vol. 8, no. 1, 2020, doi: 10.22364/BJMC.2020.8.1.02.

[26] M. MacAk, M. Ge, and B. Buhnova, "A Cross-Domain Comparative Study of Big Data Architectures," *Int. J. Coop. Inf. Syst.*, vol. 29, no. 4, 2020, doi: 10.1142/S0218843020300016.

[27] J. Lee, B. Kim, and J. M. Chung, "Time Estimation and Resource Minimization Scheme for Apache Spark and Hadoop Big Data Systems with Failures," *IEEE Access*, vol. 7, 2019, doi: 10.1109/ACCESS.2019.2891001.

[28] K. Sharmila, S. Kamalakkannan, R. Devi, and C. Shanthi, "Big Data Analysis Using Apache Hadoop and Spark," *Int. J. Recent Technol. Eng.*, vol. 8, no. 2, 2019, doi: 10.35940/ijrte.A2128.078219.

[29] C. Giebe, L. Hammerström, and D. Zwerenz, "Big Data & Analytics as a Sustainable Customer Loyalty Instrument in Banking and Finance," *Financ. Mark. Inst. Risks*, vol. 3, no. 4, 2019, doi: 10.21272/fmir.3(4).74-88.2019.

[30] U. Sivarajah, M. M. Kamal, Z. Irani, and V. Weerakkody, "Critical Analysis of Big Data Challenges and Analytical Methods," *J. Bus. Res.*, vol. 70, 2017, doi: 10.1016/j.jbusres.2016.08.001.

[31] M. J. Anwar, A. Q. Gill, F. K. Hussain, and M. Imran, "Secure Big Data Ecosystem Architecture: Challenges and Solutions," *Eurasip J. Wirel. Commun. Netw.*, vol. 2021, no. 1, 2021, doi: 10.1186/s13638-021-01996-2.

[32] A. L'Heureux, K. Grolinger, H. F. Elyamany, and M. A. M. Capretz, "Machine Learning with Big Data: Challenges and Approaches," *IEEE Access*, vol. 5, 2017, doi: 10.1109/ACCESS.2017.2696365.

[33] J. Lloret, J. Tomas, A. Canovas, and L. Parra, "An Integrated IoT Architecture for Smart Metering," *IEEE Commun. Mag.*, vol. 54, no. 12, 2016, doi: 10.1109/MCOM.2016.1600647CM.

[34] D. Garcia Valverde, D. González Vidal, J. Quevedo Casin, V. Puig Cayuela, and J. Saludes Closa, "Water Demand Estimation and Outlier Detection From smart Meter Data Using Classification and Big Data Methods," *New Dev. IT Water Conf.*, 2015.

[35] C. A. Moturi, V. O. Okemwa, and D. O. Orwa, "Big Data Analytics Capability for Digital Transformation in the Insurance Sector," *Int. J. Big Data Manag.*, vol. 2, no. 1, 2022, doi: 10.1504/ijbdm.2022.119435.

[36] A. Nurhayati, "A Survey on Big Data in the Media and Entertainment Industry," *ITEJ (Information Technol. Eng. Journals)*, vol. 4, no. 2, 2019, doi: 10.24235/itej.v4i2.50.

[37] V. Jagadeeswari, V. Subramaniyaswamy, R. Logesh, and V. Vijayakumar, "A study on Medical Internet of Things and Big Data in Personalized Healthcare System," *Heal. Inf. Sci. Syst.*, vol. 6, no. 1, 2018, doi: 10.1007/s13755-018-0049-x.

[38] K. Batko and A. Ślęzak, "The Use of Big Data Analytics in Healthcare," *J. Big Data*, vol. 9, no. 1, 2022, doi: 10.1186/s40537-021-00553-4.

[39] S. Khan and S. Alqahtani, "Big Data Application and Its Impact on Education," *Int. J. Emerg. Technol. Learn.*, vol. 15, no. 17, 2020, doi: 10.3991/ijet.v15i17.14459.

[40] X. Li *et al.*, "Curriculum Reform in Big Data Education at Applied Technical Colleges and Universities in China," *IEEE Access*, vol. 7, 2019, doi: 10.1109/ACCESS.2019.2939196.

[41] H. N. Dai, H. Wang, G. Xu, J. Wan, and M. Imran, "Big Data Analytics for Manufacturing Internet of Things: Opportunities, Challenges and Enabling Technologies," *Enterp. Inf. Syst.*, vol. 14, no. 9–10, 2020, doi: 10.1080/17517575.2019.1633689.

[42] S. Dash, S. K. Shakyawar, M. Sharma, and S. Kaushik, "Big Data in Healthcare: Management, Analysis and Future Prospects," *J. Big Data*, vol. 6, no. 1, 2019, doi: 10.1186/s40537-019-0217-0.

[43] A. I. Torre-Bastida, J. Del Ser, I. Laña, M. Ilardia, M. N. Bilbao, and S. Campos-Cordobés, "Big Data for Transportation and Mobility: Recent Advances, Trends and Challenges," *IET Intell. Transp. Syst.*, vol. 12, no. 8, 2018, doi: 10.1049/iet-its.2018.5188.

[44] E. S. Silva, H. Hassani, and D. Ø. Madsen, "Big Data in Fashion: Transforming the Retail Sector," *J. Bus. Strategy*, vol. 41, no. 4, 2020, doi: 10.1108/JBS-04-2019-0062.

[45] S. Venkatesh, "Big Data—Can it Make a Big Impact in the Insurance Sector?," *J. Insur. Inst. India*, vol. 6, no. 4, 2019.

[46] D. Gupta, S. Bhatt, M. Gupta, O. Kayode, and A. S. Tosun, "Access Control Model for Google Cloud IoT," in *Proceedings—2020 IEEE 6th Intl Conference on Big Data Security on Cloud, BigDataSecurity 2020, 2020 IEEE Intl Conference on High Performance and Smart Computing, HPSC 2020 and 2020 IEEE Intl Conference on Intelligent Data and Security, IDS 2020*, 2020, doi: 10.1109/BigDataSecurity-HPSC-IDS49724.2020.00044.

[47] H. A. A. Al-Kashoash and A. H. Kemp, "Comparison of 6LoWPAN and LPWAN for the Internet of Things," *Aust. J. Electr. Electron. Eng.*, vol. 13, no. 4, 2016, doi: 10.1080/1448837X.2017.1409920.

[48] IBM, "IBM Watson IoT Platform," *Console.Bluemix.Net*, 2020.

[49] C. Newswire, "IBM Announces Major Blockchain Collaboration with Dole, Driscoll's, Golden State Foods, Kroger, McCormick and Company, McLane Company, Nestlé, Tyson Foods, Unilever and Walmart to Address Food Safety Worldwide," *IBM-Food-Safety*, 2017.

[50] N. Bansal, "Designing Internet of Things Solutions with Microsoft Azure: A Survey of Secure and Smart Industrial Applications," Springer International Publishing (Apress Berkeley, CA), New York, United States, 2020, doi: 10.1007/978-1-4842-6041-8.

[51] M. van Rijmenam, "The Organisation of Tomorrow: How AI, Blockchain and Analytics Turn Your Business into a Data Organisation," Taylor and Francis, Oxfordshire, England, pp. 1–192, 2019, doi: 10.4324/9780429279973.

[52] M. I. Baig, L. Shuib, and E. Yadegaridehkordi, "Big Data in Education: A State of the Art, Limitations, and Future Research Directions," *Int. J. Educ. Technol. High. Educ.*, vol. 17, no. 1, 2020, doi: 10.1186/s41239-020-00223-0.

[53] R. Pastorino *et al.*, "Benefits and Challenges of Big Data in Healthcare: An Overview of the European Initiatives," *Eur. J. Public Health*, vol. 29, 2019, doi: 10.1093/eurpub/ckz168.

[54] K. C. Chu, E. Turatsinze, K. C. Chang, Y. W. Zhou, F. H. Chang, and M. T. Wang, "A Survey of Common IOT Communication Protocols and IOT Smart-X Applications

of 5G Cellular," in *Smart Innovation, Systems and Technologies*, Springer Science and Business Media Deutschland GmbH, Berlin, Germany, Vol. 211, pp. 114–122, 2021, doi: 10.1007/978-981-33-6420-2_15.

[55] J. Sengupta, S. Ruj, and S. Das Bit, "A Comprehensive Survey on Attacks, Security Issues and Blockchain Solutions for IoT and IIoT," *J. Netw. Comput. Appl.*, vol. 149, 2020, doi: 10.1016/j.jnca.2019.102481.

[56] S. Jaloudi, "Communication Protocols of an Industrial Internet of Things Environment: A Comparative Study," *Futur. Internet*, vol. 11, no. 3, 2019, doi: 10.3390/fi11030066.

[57] K. L. M. Ang, J. K. P. Seng, E. Ngharamike, and G. K. Ijemaru, "Emerging Technologies for Smart Cities' Transportation: Geo-Information, Data Analytics and Machine Learning Approaches," *ISPRS Int. J. Geo-Inf.*, vol. 11, no. 2, 2022, doi: 10.3390/ijgi11020085.

[58] P. Datta and B. Sharma, "A Survey on IoT Architectures, Protocols, Security and Smart City Based Applications," in *8th International Conference on Computing, Communications and Networking Technologies, ICCCNT 2017*, 2017, doi: 10.1109/ICCCNT.2017.8203943.

[59] J. L. Chen, M. C. Chen, C. W. Chen, and Y. C. Chang, "Architecture Design and Performance Evaluation of RFID Object Tracking Systems," *Comput. Commun.*, vol. 30, no. 9, 2007, doi: 10.1016/j.comcom.2007.04.003.

[60] ThingSpeak, "IoT Analytics—ThingSpeak Internet of Things," *ThingSpeak*, 2020.

[61] S. Misra and S. Bera, "Introduction to Big Data Analytics," in *Smart Grid Technology*, Cambridge University Press, England, pp. 38–48, 2018, doi: 10.1017/9781108566506.005.

[62] A. H. Ali and M. Z. Abdullah, "A Novel Approach for Big Data Classification Based on Hybrid Parallel Dimensionality Reduction Using Spark Cluster," *Comput. Sci.*, vol. 20, no. 4, 2019, doi: 10.7494/csci.2019.20.4.3373.

[63] Z. Wu, Y. Li, A. Plaza, J. Li, F. Xiao, and Z. Wei, "Parallel and Distributed Dimensionality Reduction of Hyperspectral Data on Cloud Computing Architectures," *IEEE J. Sel. Top. Appl. Earth Obs. Remote Sens.*, vol. 9, no. 6, 2016, doi: 10.1109/JSTARS.2016.2542193.

[64] S. M. Marzuni, A. Savadi, A. N. Toosi, and M. Naghibzadeh, "Cross-MapReduce: Data Transfer Reduction in Geo-Distributed MapReduce," *Futur. Gener. Comput. Syst.*, vol. 115, 2021, doi: 10.1016/j.future.2020.09.009.

[65] T. White, "Hadoop: The Definitive Guide," O'Reilly Media, Inc., California, United States, vol. 54, 2015.

[66] B. Davazdahemami, "Using Big Data Analytics and Statistical Methods for Improving Drug Safety," PhD Thesis report submitted to the Faculty of Graduate College of the Oklahoma State University, 2019.

[67] A. Gandomi and M. Haider, "International Journal of Information Management Beyond the Hype : Big Data Concepts, Methods, and Analytics," *Int. J. Inf. Manage.*, vol. 35, no. 2, 2015, doi: 10.1016/j.ijinfomgt.2014.10.007.

[68] P. Maroufkhani, R. Wagner, W. K. Wan Ismail, M. B. Baroto, and M. Nourani, "Big Data Analytics and Firm Performance: A Systematic Review," *Information (Switzerland)*, vol. 10, no. 7, 2019, doi: 10.3390/INFO10070226.

[69] I. Lee and G. Mangalaraj, "Big Data Analytics in Supply Chain Management: A Systematic Literature Review and Research Directions," *Big Data Cogn. Comput.*, vol. 6, no. 1, 2022, doi: 10.3390/bdcc6010017.

[70] J. Ausmus, R. S. De Carvalho, A. K. Chen, Y. N. Velaga, and Y. Zhang, "Big Data Analytics and the Electric Utility Industry," in *2019 International Conference on Smart Grid Synchronized Measurements and Analytics, SGSMA 2019*, 2019, doi: 10.1109/SGSMA.2019.8784657.

[71] J. Yin and V. Fernandez, "A Systematic Review on Business Analytics," *J. Ind. Eng. Manag.*, vol. 13, no. 2, 2020, doi: 10.3926/jiem.3030.

[72] C. Schaefer and A. Makatsaria, "Framework of Data Analytics and Integrating Knowledge Management," *Int. J. Intell. Netw.*, vol. 2, 2021, doi: 10.1016/j.ijin.2021.09.004.

[73] B. Chakraborty, R. Sen, and A. K. Mandal, "A Survey on Machine Learning Techniques for THz Image Analysis," in *Terahertz Biomedical and Healthcare*

Technologies, Elsevier, Amsterdam, Netherlands, pp. 167–176, 2020, doi: 10.1016/b978-0-12-818556-8.00009-4.

[74] H. Kour and N. Gondhi, "Machine Learning Techniques: A Survey," Innovative Data Communication Technologies and Application Lecture Notes on Data Engineering and Communications Technologies, Springer International Publishing, United States, pp. 266–275, 2020, doi: 10.1007/978-3-030-38040-3_31.

[75] N. Milosevic, *Introduction to Convolutional Neural Networks*, Apress, New York, United States, 2020, doi: 10.1007/978-1-4842-5648-0.

[76] K. Molugaram and G. S. Rao, "ANOVA (Analysis of Variance)," in *Statistical Techniques for Transportation Engineering*, Elsevier, Amsterdam, Netherlands, pp. 451–462, 2017, doi: 10.1016/b978-0-12-811555-8.00011-8.

[77] P. Stoker, G. Tian, and J. Y. Kim, "Analysis of Variance (Anova)," in *Basic Quantitative Research Methods for Urban Planners*, Taylor and Francis, England, pp. 197–219, 2020, doi: 10.4324/9780429325021-11.

[78] E. G. M. Hui, *Learn R for Applied Statistics: With Data Visualizations, Regressions, and Statistics*, Apress Media LLC., New York, United States, pp. 1–243, 2018, doi: 10.1007/978-1-4842-4200-1.

[79] P. Dangeti, *Statistics for Machine Learning: Techniques for Exploring Supervised, Unsupervised, and Reinforcement Learning Models with Python and R*, Packt Publishing, Birmingham, UK, 2017.

[80] K. F. Sellers, "Introduction: Count Data Containing Dispersion," in *The Conway–Maxwell–Poisson Distribution*, Cambridge University Press, England, pp. 1–21, 2023, doi: 10.1017/9781108646437.002.

[81] S. Lee, "Scholarly Research in Music: Shared and Disciplinary-Specific Practices", Taylor and Francis, England, Second Edition, pp. 1–246, 2022, doi: 10.4324/9781003153924.

[82] M. D. Robinson and G. K. Smyth, "Small-Sample Estimation of Negative Binomial Dispersion, with Applications to SAGE data," *Biostatistics*, vol. 9, no. 2, 2008, doi: 10.1093/biostatistics/kxm030.

[83] R. Petrich and A. Delan, "Considerations for the Application of Precipitation Data for Dispersion Modeling," *Gefahrstoffe Reinhaltung der Luft*, vol. 82, no. 7–8, 2022.

[84] J. Y. Liang, C. J. Feng, and P. Song, "A Survey on Correlation Analysis of Big Data," *Jisuanji Xuebao/Chinese J. Comput.*, vol. 39, no. 1, 2016, doi: 10.11897/SP.J.1016.2016.00001.

[85] L. Husamaldin and N. Saeed, "Big Data Analytics Correlation Taxonomy," *Inf.*, vol. 11, no. 1, 2020, doi: 10.3390/info11010017.

[86] P. Dahlgren, "Social Media and Counter-Democracy: The Contingences of Participation," in *Lecture Notes in Computer Science (Including Subseries Lecture Notes in Artificial Intelligence and Lecture Notes in Bioinformatics)*, Vol. 7444, pp. 1–12, 2012, doi: 10.1007/978-3-642-33250-0_1.

[87] O. Elijah, T. A. Rahman, I. Orikumhi, C. Y. Leow, and M. N. Hindia, "An Overview of Internet of Things (IoT) and Data Analytics in Agriculture: Benefits and Challenges," *IEEE Internet Things J.*, vol. 5, no. 5, 2018, doi: 10.1109/JIOT.2018.2844296.

5 Roles of Cloud Computing, Fog Computing, and Edge Computing

5.1 CLOUD ANALYTICS FOR IOT APPLICATIONS

Cloud analytics for IoT applications refers to the use of cloud computing platforms and data analytics techniques to process, analyze, and gain insights from the vast amount of data generated by Internet of Things (IoT) devices. IoT devices generate a tremendous amount of data from various sources such as sensors, actuators, and connected devices. This data, often referred to as IoT data or sensor data, can be structured or unstructured and is typically generated in real time or near real time. Cloud analytics provides the infrastructure and tools to effectively manage and analyze this data, extracting valuable information and enabling intelligent decision-making. The evolution of computing technology can be traced back to the 1940s and 1950s, with the advent of the first commercial computer. The evolution of cloud computing since then has been illustrated in Figure 5.1. This marked the beginning of a new era in the computing industry, whereby organizations could store and process data electronically. Mainframe computers emerged during the 1960s, capable of supporting multiple users at once and processing large amounts of data. The 1990s saw the widespread adoption of desktop and portable computers, enabling individuals to perform complex computing tasks from their homes and offices. The turn of the millennium brought the mass adoption of the internet, revolutionizing the way people communicate and access information. Furthermore, the emergence of cloud computing since 2007 has dramatically altered the way businesses store and process data, leveraging distributed systems and associated peripherals, virtualization, Web 2.0, service-oriented architecture (SOA), and utility computing to provide efficient and cost-effective computing services [1–4].

5.1.1 Introduction to Cloud Computing

Cloud computing is a technological advancement that enables the distribution of computing services via the internet, encompassing servers, storage, databases, networking, software, analytics, and intelligence, among other resources [5, 6]. It essentially provides computing resources as a service, whereby third-party providers possess and operate the resources for the benefit of the end-users. This eliminates the need for end-users to worry about the hardware and software infrastructure and

DOI: 10.1201/9781003282945-5

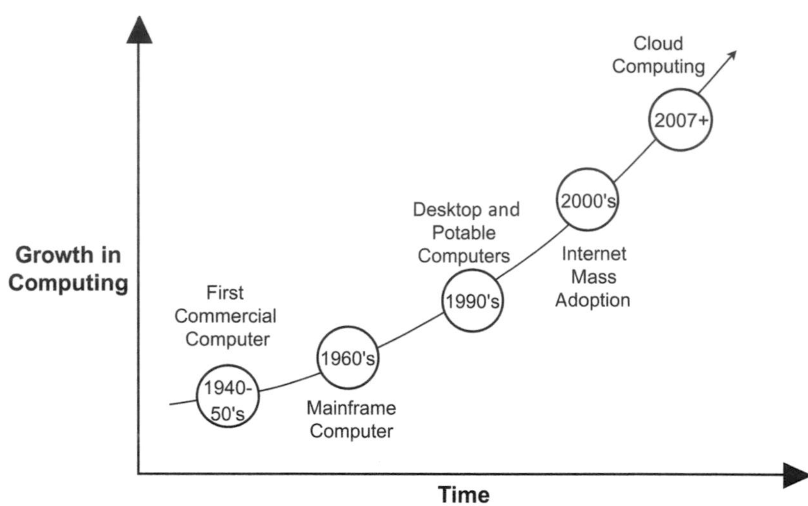

FIGURE 5.1 Evolution of cloud computing.

their locations, as the resources are accessible through the internet via a metaphorical "cloud." The flexibility and scalability of cloud computing have made it an attractive option for individuals and organizations alike, allowing them to focus on their core activities while leaving the complexities of IT infrastructure to cloud providers.

The advent of cloud computing has resulted in a shift from on-premises software and hardware to a networked, remote resource, freeing companies from the need to invest in labor, expertise, or capital for the maintenance of such resources. The emergence of cloud computing has led to the rise of various cloud providers, including major players like AWS and Microsoft Azure [5, 6]. Cloud computing offers an alternative to on-premises data centers, which require users to manage everything, from hardware and virtualization to installing operating systems, applications, and configuring network and storage (See Figure 5.2) [4]. In contrast, cloud vendors are responsible for purchasing and maintaining hardware, and they offer a range of software and platform services that can be rented based on usage. The cloud infrastructure provides an internet-based platform that makes it easy for users to manage computing, storage, networking, and application resources.

Cloud computing technology can be broadly categorized into three types: public cloud, private cloud, and hybrid cloud, as illustrated in Figure 5.3 [2, 5, 6]. The distinguishing characteristics of each type are as follows.

- **Public Cloud:** Public clouds refer to cloud resources that are owned and operated by a third-party cloud service provider. Users access computing resources, such as servers, software, and storage, through the internet. Public clouds are open to multiple users and are usually priced according to usage.
- **Private Cloud:** Private clouds are exclusive to a single business or organization. These resources may be located on-site or hosted by a third-party.

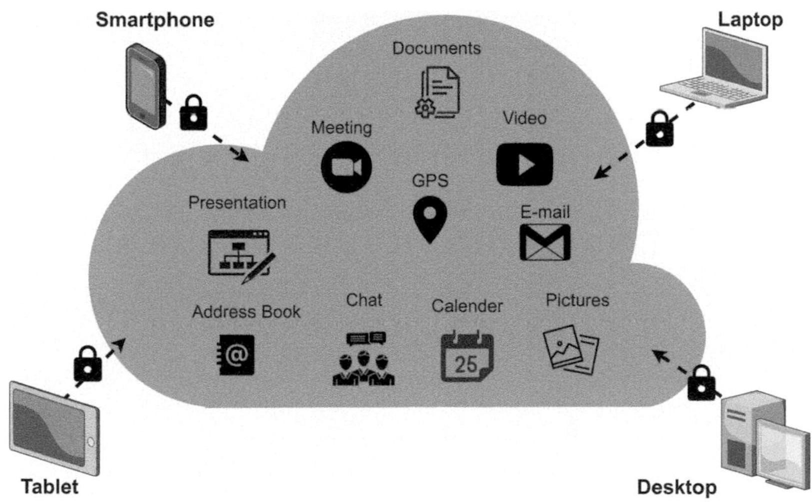

FIGURE 5.2 Application of the cloud.

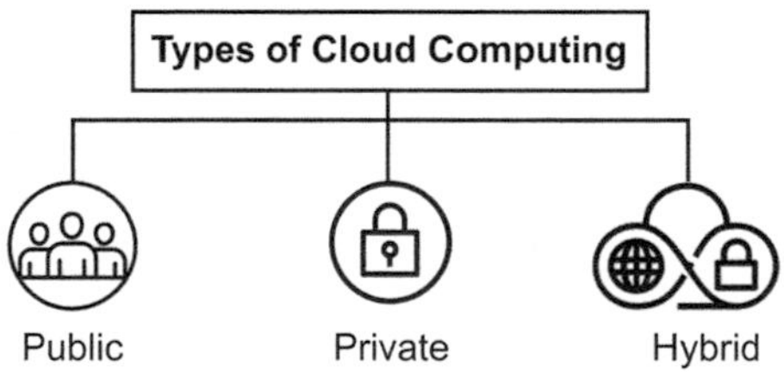

FIGURE 5.3 Types of cloud computing.

Private clouds are typically more secure than public clouds, as access is restricted to authorized personnel only.

- **Hybrid Cloud:** Hybrid clouds are a combination of public and private clouds. Data and applications are shared between the two, allowing for greater flexibility and deployment options. Hybrid clouds allow businesses to take advantage of the scalability and cost effectiveness of public clouds, while also ensuring the security and compliance of private clouds.

5.1.2 Differences between Cloud Computing and Fog Computing

Cloud computing and fog computing are two computing platforms that help companies manage their communication effectively and efficiently. Fog computing, also known as fogging, is an extension of cloud computing that allows for instant connections in data centers with multiple edge nodes over physical devices [7–9]. Fog computing creates a link between cloud computing and the internet of things, making it possible to process data locally across various nodes. The key contrasts between cloud computing and fog computing are explained in the following [3, 8, 10].

1. **Architecture:** Cloud computing architecture is centralized, with data processed in large data centers, while fog computing architecture is decentralized, with data processed at the edge of the network.
2. **Processing:** In cloud computing, data is processed in a remote data center, while in fog computing, data is processed locally on multiple edge nodes.
3. **Latency:** Cloud computing has higher latency as it involves transferring data to remote data centers, while fog computing has lower latency due to the local processing of data.
4. **Bandwidth:** In cloud computing, large amounts of bandwidth are required to transmit data to remote data centers, while in fog computing, less bandwidth is required as data is processed locally.
5. **Security:** Cloud computing offers a high level of security through data encryption and other security measures, while fog computing offers additional security measures due to its decentralized architecture.
6. **Use cases:** Cloud computing is ideal for applications that require significant computational power, storage, and data processing, while fog computing is better suited for applications that require real-time processing, low latency, and data proximity.

5.1.3 The Next Evolution of Cloud Computing

Cloud computing has progressed from its fundamental notion of supplying computing resources on-demand through the internet, to more advanced services that address diverse business requirements. The next evolution of cloud computing centers around delivering software, platforms, and infrastructure as services—commonly known as SaaS, PaaS, and IaaS, as illustrated in Figure 5.4.

1. **Software-as-a-Service (SaaS):** SaaS is a model in which a cloud provider hosts a software application and offers it to customers over the internet.

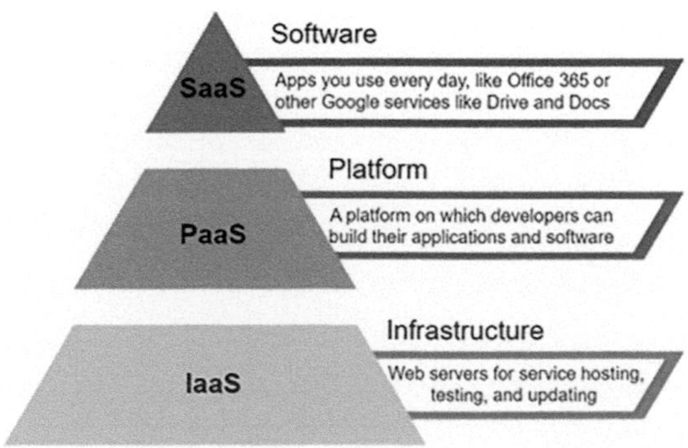

FIGURE 5.4 Development of cloud computing.

This enables customers to access the software without having to install or maintain it themselves. They can use a web browser or thin client to access the software. SaaS examples include email services, office applications, and customer relationship management (CRM) software.

2. **Platform-as-a-Service (PaaS):** PaaS is a type of cloud service that enables customers to develop, operate, and manage applications without being concerned about the underlying infrastructure [11–13]. The cloud provider manages the infrastructure, operating system, and middleware, allowing the customers to concentrate on the development and deployment of their applications. Google App Engine and Microsoft Azure are examples of PaaS.
3. **Infrastructure-as-a-Service (IaaS):** IaaS is a cloud computing model that enables users to access and manage computing resources such as servers, storage, and networking over the internet [11–13]. It allows businesses to build their own IT infrastructure without the need to invest in or maintain physical hardware. Popular examples of IaaS providers include Amazon Web Services (AWS) and Microsoft Azure.

The next evolution of cloud computing involves the integration of these services into a seamless platform, offering customers the flexibility to choose the services that best suit their needs. This integration will provide a more comprehensive and efficient solution for businesses, enabling them to focus on their core operations and drive innovation.

5.1.3.1 Advantages of Cloud Computing

Cloud computing offers various benefits to organizations, including the following.

1. **Cost Effectiveness:** Cloud computing services offer a cost-effective solution for businesses to avoid upfront capital investments required for purchasing hardware and software. This is because cloud services are charged based on the pay-as-you-go model, whereby businesses only pay for the resources they utilize.
2. **Speed:** Cloud resources can be accessed quickly and easily within a few clicks, without any delays associated with the setup of hardware and software.
3. **Scalability:** Cloud computing provides businesses with the ability to adjust their resources in accordance with their evolving needs, resulting in improved flexibility and efficiency. This scalability enables companies to efficiently allocate resources based on demand fluctuations, ultimately leading to better utilization of resources.
4. **Productivity:** Cloud computing simplifies hardware and software maintenance, allowing IT teams to focus on achieving business goals instead.
5. **Reliability:** Cloud computing offers dependable data backup and recovery options that are both cost effective and efficient, guaranteeing uninterrupted business operations.
6. **Security:** Many cloud vendors offer robust security policies, technologies, and controls that enhance the security of the data stored in the cloud.

5.1.4 The Role of Cloud Computing in IoT

The term "cloud" denotes a centralized framework that enables the transmission and distribution of data and files to distant data centers via the internet. It provides a centralized location for accessing various data and programs, which facilitates easy accessibility. On the other hand, IoT refers to the interconnectivity of devices through the internet. IoT devices can store real-time and historical data, analyze and control devices for effective decision-making, and monitor activity performance. The IoT has revolutionized data collection, processing, and transmission, offering numerous benefits across various industries, including healthcare, agriculture, transportation, and energy management. By integrating IoT with cloud computing, innovative solutions have been developed that provide valuable insights into intricate systems and improve operational efficiency [14].

The integration of cloud computing is essential for the success of the IoT [1, 8, 14]. This technology allows users to perform computing tasks using services provided over the internet. The convergence of IoT and cloud technologies has resulted in futuristic technologies that will bring numerous benefits. The rapid technological advancements have led to a surge in the amount of data being stored, processed, and accessed. The biggest innovations are related to the interplay between IoT and cloud technologies, which enables the use of powerful sensor data flow processing and new monitoring services. For example, cloud computing can be utilized to store and upload sensor data for future smart monitoring and activation with other devices. The primary aim is to transform data into insights that can enhance profitable and productive operations.

Cloud computing, like IoT, is aimed at increasing the efficiency of daily tasks. In the context of IoT, cloud computing plays a crucial role in storing and managing IoT data, making it easily accessible. Additionally, it is worth noting that cloud computing is an effective method for transmitting significant volumes of data generated by IoT devices across the internet. While IoT generates massive amounts of data, cloud computing provides the path for this data to reach its destination. According to AWS, cloud computing has the following four main benefits [15, 16].

- It eliminates the need to guess infrastructure capacity needs in advance.
- It allows for cost savings by only paying for the resources that are used, resulting in greater savings as volume increases.
- The platform can be deployed worldwide within minutes.
- It offers developers the advantage of fast and flexible resource allocation.

5.1.4.1 Benefits and Functions of IoT Cloud

The combination of IoT and cloud computing offers numerous benefits and functions [5, 8, 9, 14]. Following are some of them.

1. IoT cloud computing provides multiple connectivity options, allowing for large network access. Cloud computing resources are available to users via different devices, including laptops, tablets, and mobile devices. This convenience, however, requires network access points.

2. IoT cloud computing is accessible on-demand as a web service, requiring only an internet connection. Developers can access it without special permission or assistance.
3. Users can scale IoT cloud computing services to meet their needs. It allows for quick and flexible expansion of storage space, software settings, and user capacity, enabling deep computing power and storage.
4. Resource pooling in cloud computing fosters collaboration and strengthens connections among users.
5. With the increasing number of IoT devices and automation, security has become a major concern. Cloud solutions provide dependable authentication and encryption protocols to address these concerns.
6. IoT cloud computing is cost effective, as users pay only for service they use. Service providers measure usage statistics.

Thus, the combination of cloud computing and IoT will bring about significant changes in the management of information [2]. The cloud is the most suitable technology to handle the analysis, storage, and access to IoT data, depending on its deployment model. The cloud can be accessed from any device, anywhere, due to its on-demand nature and internet connectivity. As hybrid cloud usage increases, businesses are experiencing its advantages and adopting it. Cloud computing will continue to create new opportunities for IoT with computing power, reliability, and connectivity as the three main components that will transform the IoT landscape.

5.1.5 Connecting IoT to the Cloud

The IoT produces a large volume of data known as Big Data. This data can be difficult for businesses to manage and store. However, cloud computing provides models and platforms that can help companies efficiently handle and analyze the data generated by IoT. AWS and Microsoft Azure are two cloud platforms that offer solutions like digital lifecycle management (DLM), application enablement platforms (AEPs), and digital twins, which are virtual replicas of a physical asset or system that enables real-time monitoring, modeling, and simulation [17, 18]. The IoT ecosystem is supported by various cloud services and platforms, each with its own role. Some platforms offer advanced features, like machine learning and business intelligence tools, which allow for complex data analysis using SQL queries. The cloud's scalability and agility principles make it a revolutionary technology on a global scale. Its ability to support IoT initiatives has made it an essential tool for achieving success in the IoT.

There are several key reasons why the cloud is essential for the success of the IoT. First, cloud solutions can facilitate the widespread adoption of IoT initiatives. Additionally, the cloud's ability to scale allows for the easy addition of new devices and applications to the IoT ecosystem. Finally, the cloud's agility enables quick adaptation to changing circumstances and requirements, making it an invaluable tool for companies looking to stay competitive in the rapidly evolving world of IoT.

Cloud computing and the IoT can improve daily tasks by working together [8, 9]. The IoT produces a lot of data, which can be transferred using cloud computing. Cloud providers use a pay-per-use model, so customers only pay for what they use. Using cloud hosting saves money by using economies of scale. Cloud computing allows for remote data storage and access, which lets developers work on projects without delays.

- **Remote Computing Capability:** The capability of remote computing is made possible by cloud technology, which allows IoT devices to exceed traditional appliances such as refrigerators and air conditioners. The cloud provides vast storage space, removing the need for on-premises infrastructure. The advent of 5G and improved internet speeds has made cloud services more widely available, enabling businesses to conveniently access remote computing resources. The combination of IoT and cloud technology has transformed the way we interact with devices, making remote access and control easier and more efficient [7, 13].
- **Security and Privacy:** The growth of IoT devices has led to significant security concerns. However, cloud technology has emerged as a possible solution to enhance the security of IoT devices. Through preventive, detective, and corrective control measures, the cloud offers a wide range of security features, including authentication and encryption protocols [1, 8, 9]. These protocols provide users with secure and robust security measures. Furthermore, biometric technology can also be used to manage and safeguard user identities in IoT products. Cloud technology provides an increased level of security that can help mitigate the risks associated with IoT devices.
- **Data Integration:** The evolution of the IoT has enabled businesses to utilize connected devices to gain valuable insights into their critical business processes. Although these devices have increased operational efficiency and reduced costs, they also generate an immense amount of data that may overwhelm analytics platforms. Cloud-based solutions have become a crucial tool in managing this data overload, providing robust data integration capabilities that can effectively handle the vast amount of data generated from multiple sources [1, 8, 9]. By storing, processing, and analyzing data from enterprise systems and connected devices in a centralized location, companies can better understand their operations and make informed decisions to drive growth and success.
- **Low Threshold:** In the current era of technology, plug-and-play hosting services are becoming increasingly popular for IoT innovations. This trend makes cloud hosting an attractive option for IoT devices, as it eliminates the requirement for bulky equipment or hardware that may not meet the agility demands of IoT devices. The emergence of innovative cloud hosting solutions has significantly reduced entry barriers for IoT-based companies, enabling them to implement large-scale IoT plans with ease. Overall, the use of cloud hosting for IoT is proving to be a game-changer for the industry, making it easier for companies to implement IoT-based solutions at scale [8, 9, 13].
- **Business Continuity:** Cloud computing solutions are highly regarded for their flexibility and dependability in maintaining business continuity. The cloud-based services rely on a network of servers spread across various

locations, allowing them to store replicated copies of data in multiple data centers. This redundancy feature ensures that IoT-based operations remain operational even if one of the servers becomes unavailable due to a technical issue or other reasons, while also reducing the risk of data loss. This quality of the cloud services is well-documented in research [8, 13].

- **Communication between Devices:** IoT devices and services require interconnectivity to function effectively. Cloud-based solutions provide a convenient and efficient way to connect and communicate with IoT devices. They provide various APIs—including Cloudflare, CloudCache, and Dropstr—that allow seamless interaction between connected devices and smartphones. This interconnectivity creates opportunities for the development of connected technology [11–13].

5.1.6 Challenges in the Integration of IoT with Cloud

The integration of cloud computing and IoT has the potential to accelerate the growth of the internet. However, implementing this integration poses several challenges, ranging from handling large amounts of data to managing network communication protocols and sensor networks, as described in the following.

- **Handling Large Amounts of Data:** Handling large amounts of data generated by millions of devices can be overwhelming and may compromise the overall application performance. While following the NoSQL movement may offer benefits, it is still an untested solution for managing Big Data in the cloud [8, 9].
- **Network and Communication Protocol:** M2M communication is essential in the Cloud and IoT, as different devices with varying protocols must be able to communicate with each other. Managing the transition can be challenging, particularly in non-mobile applications. To promote mobility, Wi-Fi and Bluetooth have been utilized as temporary measures in some cases [2, 8, 9].
- **Sensor Networks:** Sensor networks are essential for measuring and interpreting precise environmental indicators. However, efficiently managing vast quantities of sensor data has always been a significant obstacle. The cloud presents opportunities for consolidating sensor data, but it also raises concerns regarding privacy and security [2, 8, 10].

5.2 CLOUD OF THINGS

The Cloud of Things (CoT) is an advanced technology that combines cloud computing (CC) with IoT to create an efficient cloud-based system for managing and monitoring IoT devices from a remote location [19–21]. This new paradigm offers a novel business model that increases efficiency by allowing users to connect their devices and machines to the cloud and monitor them from anywhere. The CoT enables organizations to access and analyze vast amounts of data generated by IoT devices, thus enabling them to make informed decisions in real time. It provides a cost-effective solution to store and process data from IoT devices, resulting in significant savings for organizations. Overall, the CoT has the potential to revolutionize industries by providing a seamless and scalable platform for managing and controlling IoT devices.

The widespread use of IoT devices has resulted in a substantial increase in the amount of data generated. This data cannot be stored locally and temporarily due to its vast quantity. Additionally, the storage capacity and virtual resource utilization required for IoT data are significant. To address this issue, cloud computing is being integrated with IoT, creating what is now known as the CoT. This integration has greatly improved the processing and analysis of IoT-generated data, facilitating the development of advanced smart applications [21, 22].

The IoT has emerged as a crucial component for several application areas, such as healthcare, smart homes, smart cities, smart energy, smart mobility, smart surveillance, smart logistics, and environmental monitoring [19, 23, 24]. Several CoT platforms are available in the market, including ThingSpeak, OpenIoT, CloudPlugs, AWS IoT, and Nimbits. Despite its advantages, the concept of CoT also faces several challenges that need to be addressed. These challenges include issues related to security and privacy, excessive data communication, energy efficiency, protocol support, service discovery, scalability, deployment of IPv6, resource allocation, identity management, data storage location, and QoS provision. To address these issues, researchers and practitioners in the field of IoT must focus on developing secure and efficient CoT platforms that can provide quality services while addressing the concerns of end-users.

5.2.1 Grid/SOA and Cloud Computing

Grid/SOA (service-oriented architecture) and cloud computing are two related but distinct concepts in the field of distributed computing. Grid computing involves the coordinated use of a large number of interconnected computers or resources to solve complex computational problems. It focuses on sharing and coordinating distributed computing resources, such as processing power, storage, and data, across multiple organizations or entities. Grid computing aims to create a virtual supercomputer by aggregating resources from various sources and making them available for computational tasks. It typically relies on middleware software to manage resource discovery, job scheduling, data management, and security. Grid computing is often used for scientific research, large-scale data processing, and high-performance computing, whereas SOA is an architectural approach that emphasizes the design and development of modular, loosely coupled services. It involves breaking down software applications into smaller, independent services that can be easily combined and reused. These services are designed to be self-contained, well-defined, and communicate with each other using standard protocols and interfaces. SOA enables the creation of flexible, interoperable systems by promoting service composition and orchestration. It provides a modular and scalable architecture for building distributed applications and integrating various software components and systems.

Cloud computing refers to the delivery of on-demand computing resources over the internet. It provides access to a shared pool of configurable computing resources—such as servers, storage, databases, and software applications—that can be rapidly provisioned and released with minimal management effort. Grid computing and SOA are architectural concepts and approaches that can be utilized within a cloud computing environment. Cloud computing provides the infrastructure and service delivery models to enable the deployment and utilization of grid computing and SOA principles. The cloud can serve as the underlying platform for hosting and managing the distributed resources, services, and applications built using grid computing and SOA. The important cloud computing technologies are virtualization, SOA, grid computing, and utility computing [22–24]. We will next discuss each of these in detail.

5.2.1.1 Virtualization

Virtualization involves creating a virtual environment on a server that can support multiple operating systems, applications, and storage devices. It is commonly used in cloud computing to optimize the use of virtual machines, which function like physical computers and can execute various tasks on demand [24]. By using virtualization, cloud computing enhances resource utilization, reduces costs, and increases the scalability and flexibility of IT infrastructure. The use of virtualization in cloud computing has increased the efficiency of computing systems by maximizing resource utilization, reducing costs, and improving the scalability and flexibility of IT infrastructure. Therefore, virtualization has become a crucial aspect of modern computing systems, enabling users to optimize their computing resources and enhance their IT capabilities.

5.2.1.2 Service-Oriented Architecture (SOA)

SOA is a system that enables organizations to access cloud-based computing solutions based on their changing business needs [22], with or without cloud computing. One of the primary advantages of SOA is its easy maintenance, platform independence, and high scalability. SOA comprises two major roles: service providers and service consumers. SOA is a flexible and adaptable architecture that enables organizations to access cloud-based solutions as needed, making it an essential tool in modern business environments. It is basically a software design principle that involves the use of loosely coupled, reusable software components or services to facilitate the development of distributed systems. There are three key components of SOA: service provider, service consumer, and service registry, as shown in Figure 5.5.

1. **Service Provider:** The service provider is responsible for creating and publishing web services that can be consumed by other applications. It is responsible for implementing the logic and functionality of the service and making it available for use over a network.
2. **Service Consumer:** The service consumer is an application that consumes the web services published by the service provider. It uses the functionality provided by the web service to perform its own tasks.
3. **Service Registry:** The service registry acts as a directory of available web services. It allows service consumers to discover and locate the appropriate web service for their needs. It also helps to manage and maintain information about the available services.

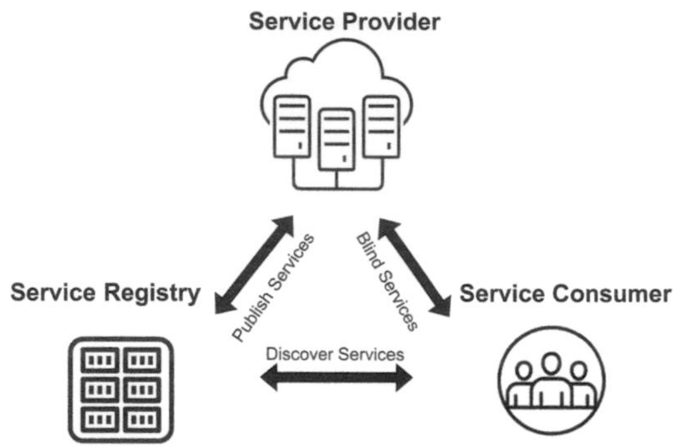

FIGURE 5.5 Service-oriented architecture.

In the context of SOA, the service provider creates and publishes web services that are consumed by service consumers. The service registry acts as an intermediary, allowing service consumers to locate and use the appropriate web service. The service provider and service consumer are often developed independently, and can be written in different programming languages, making SOA a highly flexible and scalable approach to building distributed systems. The three components work together to create a loosely coupled architecture, where changes to one component have minimal impact on the others, improving system flexibility and maintainability. The SOA is shown in Figure 5.5.

5.2.1.3 Grid Computing

Grid computing, also referred to as distributed computing, is an architecture that utilizes computing resources from various locations to achieve a shared goal It involves connecting parallel nodes to form a computer cluster that can operate on any operating system. The grid is comprised of three types of machines, as illustrated in Figure 5.6.

- **Control Node:** A group of servers that manage and administer the entire network.
- **Provider:** A computing device that contributes its computational resources to the network's resource pool.
- **User:** A computer that utilizes the network resources offered by the providers. Users can access the grid computing network to perform computationally intensive tasks that require significant computational resources.

Grid computing finds applications in various fields, including automated teller machines (ATMs), back-end infrastructures, and marketing research. In ATM networks, grid computing can be used to ensure the seamless operation of the network, especially during peak periods of activity. In back-end infrastructures, grid computing can be used to improve the efficiency of data processing and storage operations. Marketing research can leverage grid computing to analyze large amounts of data

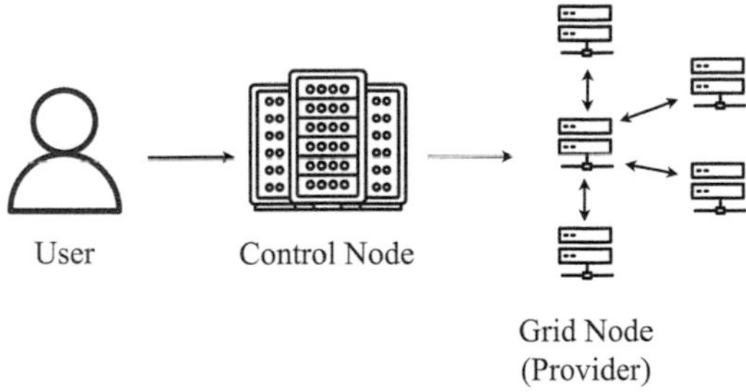

FIGURE 5.6 Grid computing.

quickly and accurately, enabling researchers to draw meaningful conclusions in a timely manner. In summary, grid computing is a powerful tool that allows organizations to harness the collective power of multiple computing resources to achieve their computational goals. The control node, provider, and user machines work together seamlessly to ensure the efficient operation of the network, enabling users to access vast amounts of computational resources quickly and easily.

5.2.1.4 Utility Computing

Utility computing is a service model that has become increasingly popular. It provides on-demand computing resources, including computation, storage, and programming services through an API, and charges based on usage. Its detailed architecture is shown in Figure 5.7. It allows for efficient utilization of resources while minimizing associated costs. Large corporations like Amazon and Google have created their own utility services for computing, storage, and applications. These services offer more flexibility and easier management [21, 25, 26]. The utility computing process involves several steps. First, a client sends a data request to the service provider. The provider then applies the request to their available computing resources and processes it accordingly. If necessary, the data may be modified by the service provider before being returned to the client as a storage data reply. In some cases, the storage data may need to be relayed to another location or system. The service provider may also receive a modified data request, which it would process and return to the client as a data response. Throughout this process, the service provider ensures that the computing resources are utilized efficiently, reducing costs and providing value to the client.

Overall, utility computing provides an effective means of accessing computing resources on demand while minimizing associated costs. As more organizations adopt this service model, we can expect to see continued innovation and evolution in the field, further improving its efficiency and effectiveness. Cloud computing and grid computing have different ownership models, scalability approaches, resource access methods, and cost structures. Cloud computing focuses on providing scalable, on-demand services through a centralized provider, while grid computing emphasizes resource sharing and collaboration among distributed entities. In cloud computing, the computing resources (servers, storage, networks) are owned and managed by

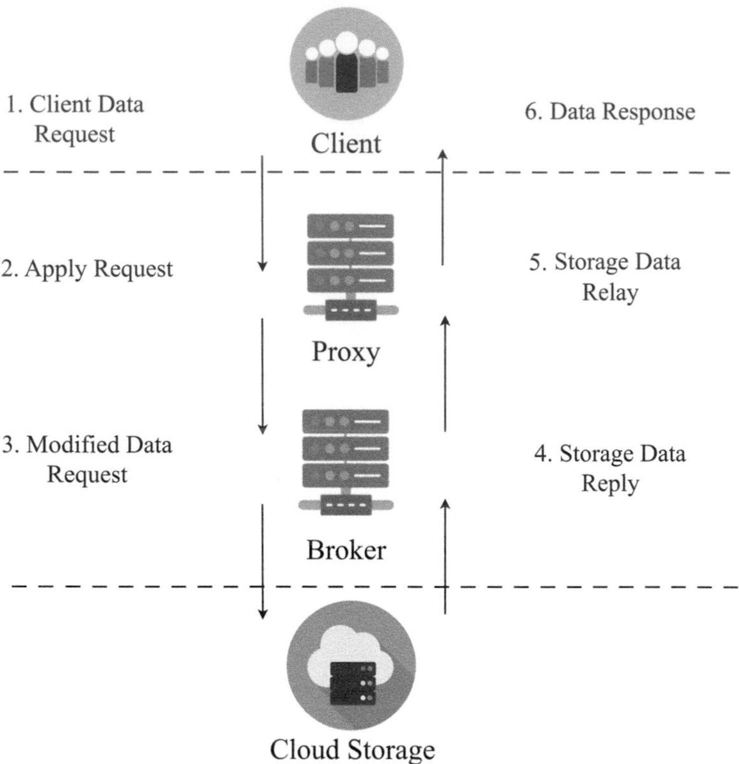

FIGURE 5.7 Utility computing.

a cloud service provider, who offers them as services to users on a pay-per-use basis. Users do not have direct control over the underlying infrastructure but can provision and manage resources within the provider's infrastructure. In grid computing, the resources are typically owned and controlled by different organizations or entities that collaborate to pool their resources. Each organization retains control over its resources and determines how they are utilized. Table 5.1 describes the differences between cloud computing and grid computing in detail [25, 26].

5.2.2 Cloud Middleware

Cloud middleware refers to the software that provides a bridge between different cloud applications, services, and systems. It enables communication and integration between these different components by providing a common platform and set of services that facilitate the sharing of data and resources. Middleware is essential for building scalable and resilient cloud-based architectures and can help organizations to reduce the complexity of their IT infrastructure. Cloud middleware includes a range of technologies such as messaging systems, application servers, databases, and APIs that are designed to work together to provide a seamless and efficient cloud

TABLE 5.1
Difference between Cloud Computing and Grid Computing

Cloud Computing	Grid Computing
Cloud computing is a technology that delivers on-demand computing resources and services over the internet, including storage, processing power, and software applications. The primary purpose of cloud computing is to provide users with scalable and flexible computing resources as per their requirements.	Grid computing is a distributed computing model that connects multiple computers and resources to solve complex computing problems. The primary purpose of grid computing is to provide a shared pool of computing resources to solve large-scale computing problems that a single computer cannot solve.
Cloud computing architecture is centralized, such that resources are located at a single data center, and users access these resources through the internet. The resources are virtualized, and users can easily scale up or down, as per their requirements.	Grid computing architecture is decentralized, such that resources are distributed across multiple locations and the system coordinates the resources to work together to solve a computing problem.
Cloud computing resources are allocated dynamically based on user demand. The system automatically allocates resources to the user as per their requirements, and users pay only for the resources they use.	Grid computing resources are allocated statically based on the system's predefined rules. The system administrator manually assigns the resources to a specific task, and users do not have the flexibility to scale the resources up or down.
Cloud computing providers ensure data security by implementing robust security measures such as firewalls, encryption, and access control. The users have limited control over the security measures implemented by the cloud provider.	Grid computing systems have a distributed security model whereby each resource owner is responsible for implementing security measures for their resources. The system administrator has limited control over the security of the resources.

computing environment. It acts as a layer between the cloud applications and services and their underlying infrastructure, providing a set of services that are independent of the specific applications or systems being used.

Middleware can also provide a range of other benefits for organizations using cloud computing. For example, it can help to improve security by providing a layer of protection between applications and the underlying infrastructure. It can also help to reduce the costs associated with managing and maintaining complex IT environments by providing a common platform for managing and monitoring different components. Overall, cloud middleware is a critical component of modern cloud computing architectures, providing a range of services and technologies that enable organizations to build and manage complex cloud-based systems with ease.

5.2.3 Cloud Standards: Cloud Providers and Systems

Cloud standards refer to a set of guidelines, specifications, and protocols that define the technical and operational requirements for cloud computing. These standards provide a common language and framework that cloud providers and users can use to ensure interoperability, security, reliability, and portability of cloud services and applications. Cloud providers are companies that offer cloud computing services. Examples of such providers are AWS, Microsoft Azure, Google Cloud, and IBM Cloud. These providers provide a variety of cloud services, including IaaS, PaaS, and SaaS. Each cloud provider has its own set of standards and protocols that define how its services are implemented and used. Cloud systems refer to the software and hardware components that make up a cloud computing environment. These systems include virtual machines, storage devices, networking equipment, and software applications. Cloud systems are designed to be highly scalable, flexible, and reliable, and they are managed and maintained by cloud providers. The importance of cloud standards lies in the fact that they ensure that cloud services and applications are compatible across different cloud providers and systems. This enables users to migrate their applications and data from one cloud provider to another without significant downtime or data loss. Standards also ensure that cloud services are secure, reliable, and performant, which is critical for mission-critical applications and services.

Some of the key cloud standards organizations include the International Organization for Standardization (ISO), the National Institute of Standards and Technology (NIST), the Cloud Security Alliance (CSA), and the Open Cloud Consortium (OCC). These organizations work together to develop and promote cloud standards that are widely adopted by cloud providers and users. In conclusion, cloud standards are essential for ensuring interoperability, security, reliability, and portability of cloud services and applications. Cloud providers and systems must adhere to these standards to ensure that their services are compatible with other cloud providers and systems and that they meet the needs of their users.

5.2.4 Mobile Cloud Computing (MCC)

Mobile computing allows individuals to access data and information from any location through their mobile devices. This technology transfers data, voice, and video through a network, enabling individuals to access information on-the-go. Mobile computing initially focused on serving consumers; however, organizations have now incorporated mobile systems to integrate their business applications and processes. This integration allows employees to work remotely, saving both time and money. The integration of mobile computing, cloud computing, and wireless networks has given rise to a technology called MCC. This technology offers rich computational resources to mobile users, network operators, and cloud computing providers [27, 28]. MCC enables the execution of rich mobile applications on a variety of mobile devices. Data processing and storage occur externally to the mobile devices, providing benefits such as extended battery life, improved data storage and processing capacity, enhanced synchronization, improved reliability and scalability, and easy integration. MCC comprises five types of cloud resources: distant mobile cloud, distant immobile cloud, proximate mobile computing entities, proximate immobile computing entities, and hybrid. The MCC architecture consists of a front-end layer, middle layer, and cloud layer, as illustrated in Figure 5.8.

MCC applications refer to software programs that are accessible via the internet through portable devices. These applications are designed to be used on-the-go and

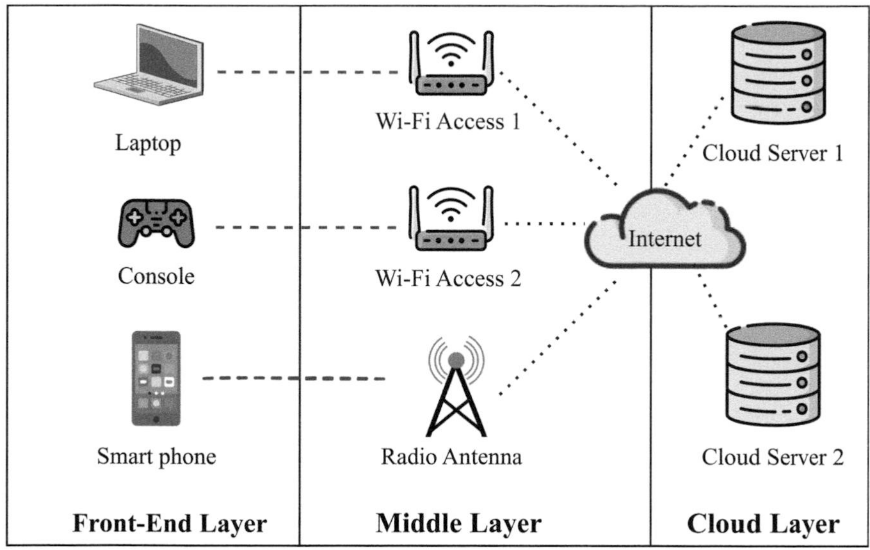

FIGURE 5.8 Typical framework of mobile cloud computing architecture.

can be accessed from anywhere using mobile devices. There are numerous examples of mobile cloud solutions that are widely used in the real world. Some of these examples include the following [27, 28].

- **Email:** This is a commonly used example of mobile cloud technology. Gmail, Outlook, and Yahoo Mail are some of the popular mobile email apps that can be accessed through portable devices.
- **Social Media:** Mobile social networking apps such as Twitter, Instagram, and Facebook allow real-time data sharing. These apps enable users to store data and share videos with others.
- **Commerce:** Mobile commerce apps, such as banking and e-commerce apps, use MCC to provide scalable processing power to users. This allows users to access and use these apps on-the-go.
- **Healthcare:** With mobile healthcare apps, MCC enables massive amounts of instantaneous data storage in the cloud that can be accessed through a mobile device. This makes it easy to access patient records and other medical information on-the-go.

There are several challenges associated with MCC [27, 28]. MCC faces a major challenge due to its dependence on radio waves. This results in slower accessing speeds, approximately three times slower than a wired network due to the limited wavelength available to mobile devices. Threat management on mobile devices is challenging, as wireless networks are more susceptible to information loss than wired networks. Therefore, ensuring security and privacy is of utmost importance. Users often experience network breakdowns, transportation crowding, out-of-coverage signals, etc., which affect the accessibility and storage of data. Low-frequency signals may also contribute to poor access speeds. MCC is required to support various operating system platforms, such as iOS, Android, and Windows Phone, to ensure efficient performance. Therefore, it is crucial to maintain compatibility with each platform. The Intelligent Radio Network Access (IRNA) technique manages the performance of different mobile platforms. Mobile devices have limitations in terms of battery life and energy consumption due to their reduced power. The use of MCC exacerbates the battery usage of these devices, leading to significant concern. To access applications and perform other operations, it is crucial to have long-lasting batteries. However, when the code being modified is small, offloading can result in increased energy consumption compared to local processing.

5.2.5 The Cloud of Things Architecture

Cloud computing provides three distinct models: IaaS, PaaS, and SaaS. These models enable users to create, store, and use applications and data via the cloud. The CoT concept involves connecting IoT devices to cloud-based services and platforms, enabling seamless communication, data storage, processing, and analysis. It leverages the capabilities of cloud computing—such as scalability, flexibility, and data management—to enhance the functionality and value of IoT deployments. By integrating IoT devices with the cloud, the CoT enables centralized management, remote monitoring, and control of IoT devices and their data. It provides a scalable infrastructure for storing and analyzing the vast amounts of data generated by IoT devices, facilitating real-time insights and decision-making. The CoT also has various forms, such as Identity-and-Policy-Management-as-a-Service, Big-Data-Analytics-as-a-Service, Database-as-a-Service, Sensor-as-a-Service, Data-as-a-Service, Sensing-as-a-Service, and Video-Monitoring-as-a-Service [22–25]. These objects are connected through multiple networked environments.

5.3 FOG COMPUTING

In January 2014, Cisco proposed the concept of "fog computing" as an expansion of cloud computing that operates at the enterprise network's edge. This approach, named after ground-level fog, refers to nodes located between the host and the cloud. The primary goal of fog computing is to enable computing, storage, and networking services to be delivered between end devices and data centers by bringing computational capabilities closer to the host machine. The concept gained popularity, leading IBM to introduce a similar term—"edge computing"—in 2015. Fog computing is an intermediate layer that bridges the gap between cloud data centers and IoT devices or sensors [29, 30]. It offers storage, computational services, and networking capabilities in close proximity to IoT devices or sensors. Fog computing expands on the concept of edge computing, which seeks to bring data processing closer to the data source. However, the limited resources of edge devices make it difficult to support multiple IoT applications, resulting in resource conflicts and increased latency. By integrating edge devices with cloud resources, fog computing addresses these limitations. It places processing nodes between end devices and cloud data centers, reducing latency and enhancing efficiency [31]. The use of fog computing has the potential to overcome the current challenges faced by IoT data stored in remote data centers.

5.3.1 When to Use Fog Computing

Fog computing can be employed in various situations, such as the following [29–31].

1. Selective data transmission to the cloud, whereby only specific data is transmitted for long-term storage and accessed less frequently by the host.
2. The need for multiple services across different geographic locations, especially in a wide area.
3. Devices that require extensive computations and processing can benefit from fog computing.
4. Fog computing is used in real-world examples such as IoT devices, the IIoT that includes devices with sensors and cameras, and the CAR 2 CAR Communication Consortium (C2C-CC) in Europe.

In summary, fog computing is a promising technology that provides efficient and reliable data processing and storage for a variety of scenarios. Its flexibility and ability to handle data at the network edge make it a popular choice for many industries and applications.

5.3.2 Advantages and Limitations of Fog Computing

Fog computing is an effective approach for reducing the amount of data that needs to be transmitted to the cloud. It achieves this by shortening the distance that data needs to travel, saving network bandwidth and reducing response time while improving security by keeping data close to the host. Following are some of the key advantages of fog computing [9, 29, 32].

- **Low Latency:** Fog computing offers resources for data processing that are located close to the devices. This results in reduced latency, which is crucial for real-time data processing applications. By processing data locally, fog computing significantly reduces the time taken to process data and improves the overall performance of the system.
- **Better Security:** Fog computing provides localized data processing, enhancing security. By processing data locally, security policies can be implemented on a local basis, allowing for better protection of sensitive data. Furthermore, fog computing can reduce the risk of data breaches as it limits the amount of data that needs to be transmitted over a network.
- **Reduced Operation Cost:** By processing data locally, fog computing saves network bandwidth and infrastructure costs. This approach reduces the need for a large central cloud infrastructure, resulting in significant cost savings.
- **Scalability:** Fog computing is a highly scalable solution that enables rapid addition of devices to the network. Devices can be easily scaled up on an on-demand basis, ensuring that the network is always able to handle increased demand.

- **Flexibility:** Fog computing allows multiple devices from different platforms to connect and share data without any hindrance. This flexibility enables organizations to develop new applications and services easily, as they can easily connect to the network and start processing data. Additionally, fog computing can be used in a variety of applications, including healthcare, manufacturing, transportation, and more.

Fog computing has some drawbacks, as outlined in sources [7, 31]. One issue is congestion that can arise between the host and fog node due to increased traffic or heavy data flow. Additionally, adding an extra layer between the host and cloud can lead to increased power consumption. Scheduling tasks can also become challenging, as it requires coordination between the host, fog nodes, and the cloud. Moreover, managing data can be a tedious task as it involves encryption-decryption for data transmission, which can further expose the data.

Fog computing has certain drawbacks, such as:

- **Authentication:** Fog computing involves a large number of interconnected devices, which makes it challenging to authenticate each device due to its distributed nature.
- **Scheduling:** Moving tasks between fog devices, fog nodes, and cloud servers creates scheduling issues.
- **Power Consumption:** Fog nodes consume more power than centralized cloud architecture, which can be a concern.
- **Fog Servers:** Proper placement of fog servers is necessary to ensure optimal service delivery.

5.3.3 Need for Fog Computing

Fog computing was introduced by Cisco in 2012 to address the challenges faced by IoT applications in transferring large amounts of data to the cloud. IoT applications generate vast amounts of data that require analysis for decision-making and action-taking. However, transferring this data to the cloud can lead to problems such as latency, excessive bandwidth usage, delayed real-time responses, and centralized data location [4, 29, 32]. Fog computing aims to minimize these challenges by bringing computation closer to end devices, resulting in reduced latency and more efficient bandwidth usage. With the increase in sensor-based devices, storing and processing data on the cloud becomes costly and time-consuming. Therefore, placing resources near the end devices decreases processing time and reduces costs. Overall, fog computing is a promising solution to overcome the challenges of IoT applications in cloud environments.

5.3.4 Fog Computing Architecture

Fog computing is an architectural approach to computing whereby the storage, computation power, data, and applications are located between the cloud and the physical device. This allows for efficient processing of data and applications closer to the source, reducing latency and enhancing overall performance [7, 29, 32]. Fog nodes, which are the devices comprising the fog infrastructure, are responsible for these functionalities, and they are placed closer to the host. This proximity to the host allows for faster processing as data is processed almost immediately where it is generated. This faster processing improves the efficiency of the system and enhances security, which is why fog computing has been instrumental in the growth of the IoT. Fog computing is particularly useful in IoT devices that require quick and large amounts of processing.

5.3.5 Working of Fog Computing

Fog computing is an architectural approach that utilizes the services of end devices like routers, switches, and multiplexers for storage, computation, and processing. It is composed of physical and logical network elements, software, and hardware, which connect a large number of devices [8, 30]. The distribution of fog nodes, both physically and geographically, along with the topology and protocols used, are key features of this architecture. The architecture of fog computing consists of three layers: the cloud computing layer, the fog computing layer, and the edge layer, as shown in Figure 5.9 [4, 29, 32]. The cloud computing layer is responsible for storing and processing data in a centralized data center. The fog computing layer serves as an intermediate layer that enables distribution of computation and storage functions between the cloud and the edge. The edge layer refers to end devices where data is generated and collected.

Fog architecture involves the distribution of functions at different layers, the use of various protocols, and the constraints imposed at different layers. The distribution of fog nodes plays a significant role in this architecture, as it determines the physical

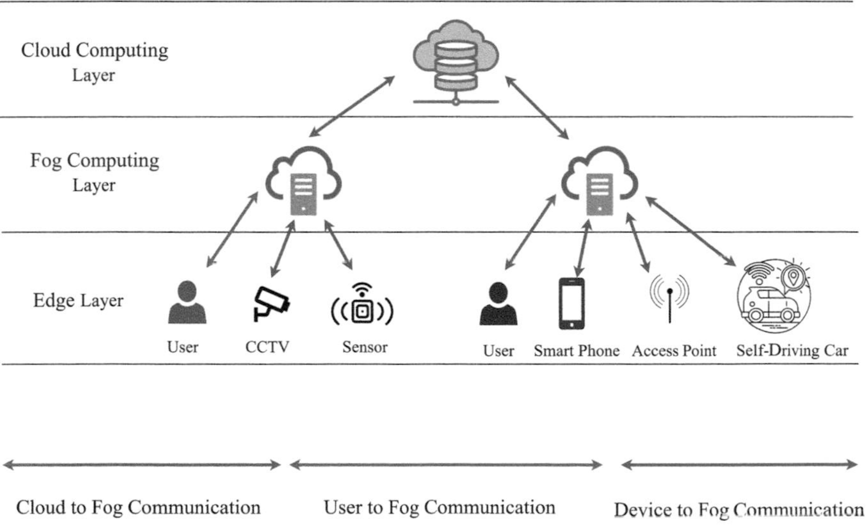

FIGURE 5.9 Layers in fog computing architecture.

and geographical distribution of computing resources. The choice of protocols and the number of protocols used are also important, as they affect the efficiency and reliability of the network. Constraints are imposed at different layers to ensure data security, privacy, and QoS.

5.3.6 Layered Fog Computing Architecture

Fog computing is a technology that operates with a layered architecture consisting of six layers. Following is a simplified breakdown of each layer [30, 33, 34].

- **Physical and Virtualization Layer:** This layer comprises physical and virtual nodes that collect data using sensors. The data is sent to upper layers through gateways for processing and filtering.
- **Monitoring Layer:** This layer monitors nodes and their tasks, application performance, and energy usage of fog nodes.
- **Pre-Processing Layer:** This layer analyzes collected data and filters out irrelevant information, ensuring that only useful information is collected.
- **Temporary Storage Layer:** This layer temporarily stores and distributes data using storage virtualization devices such as NAS (network-attached storage), fiber channel (FC), and iSCSI (Microsoft's Internet Small Computer Systems Interface).
- **Security Layer:** Security measures such as privacy, integrity, encryption, and decryption of data are implemented in this layer. Privacy includes usage, data, and location privacy.
- **Transport Layer:** The pre-processed data is uploaded to the cloud for permanent storage through smart gateways.

5.4 EDGE COMPUTING

Edge computing refers to the practice of bringing computing resources closer to the data source or "edge" of a network. It involves processing, storing, and analyzing data locally on devices or edge servers, rather than transmitting it to a centralized cloud or data center for processing. In simpler terms, edge computing shifts some of the computing tasks and data processing from a centralized location (like the cloud) to the edge of the network, closer to where the data is generated. This approach helps address the limitations and challenges posed by latency, bandwidth, reliability, and privacy concerns in certain applications. By processing data at the edge, edge computing enables real-time or near–real-time analysis, faster response times, and reduced network congestion. It can be particularly useful in scenarios in which immediate action is required, such as industrial automation, autonomous vehicles, remote monitoring, and smart city applications. Edge computing can take various forms, including edge devices (e.g., IoT devices with processing capabilities), edge servers, gateways, or dedicated edge computing platforms. These edge components perform computational tasks, data filtering, analytics, and decision-making locally, often in conjunction with cloud-based services for centralized management and coordination.

5.4.1 What Is Edge Computing?

Edge computing refers to a decentralized computing paradigm that brings computation and data storage closer to the edge of the network—closer to the data source or end-user devices. It involves processing, analyzing, and storing data at or near the point of generation, rather than transmitting it to a centralized cloud or data center for processing. Edge computing aims to bring computing resources closer to the data source to overcome the limitations of traditional centralized processing, optimize network utilization, enhance real-time capabilities, and improve the overall performance and efficiency of applications that rely on timely data processing and analysis. Edge computing is a relatively new paradigm that has emerged due to the massive growth of information generated by IoT devices. While centralized cloud computing has been a standard platform for data processing and storage, it has become costly as the amount of data generated increases. The cloud's architecture is data-centric and efficient, but it creates transmission latency and increases response time when the distance between the user and the cloud is large. Edge computing offers a solution to this problem by providing real-time computing capabilities that are closer to the user, reducing transmission latency and improving response times. Edge computing is a promising technology for meeting the growing demand for real-time computing in the IoT era [31, 34]. Edge computing finds applications in various domains, including industrial IoT, smart cities, autonomous vehicles, healthcare monitoring, retail, and more. It complements cloud computing by providing a distributed and localized computing infrastructure that complements the centralized capabilities of the cloud.

As demand for cloud services grows, there are limitations on access and bandwidth for latency-sensitive applications. Edge computing platforms offer a solution by relocating cloud computing and data storage closer to the user. These platforms use small edge servers between the cloud and the user to process applications, reducing data transport time and increasing availability. The technology aims to compute logics and data on the edge network, reducing the need for data to return to the central server for every function executed by an IoT device [7, 31]. This approach offloads workloads from the cloud server, processing them closer to the user's device, which improves application response times and maintains low latency.

5.4.2 What Is the Need for Edge Computing?

Edge computing is a relatively novel concept that has gained popularity due to the demand for faster and more effective data processing. The key idea of edge computing is to process data closer to its origin, rather than sending it to a central data center for processing. This has several advantages, including reducing latency, improving bandwidth utilization, and enhancing security. Edge computing is particularly useful in scenarios where real-time data processing is required, such as in IoT, autonomous vehicles, and industrial automation. By bringing processing power closer to the data source, edge computing can enable faster, more efficient, and more reliable data processing. This can provide various benefits to both businesses and consumers.

5.4.3 Challenges in Edge Computing

Edge computing faces several challenges and issues, including the following [35–37].

- **Privacy and Security of Data:** Edge computing requires advanced security schemes to ensure the privacy and security of data. Different encryption mechanisms should be introduced to encrypt data during transit between different distributed nodes connected via the internet. Decentralized infrastructure is also necessary to replace the centralized, top-down model.
- **Scalability:** The distributed network structure of edge computing makes scalability challenging. The heterogeneity of devices and their varying energy and performance constraints, as well as dynamic conditions and reliability of connections, create several issues [37]. The need for increased security requirements can also lead to latency between communicating nodes, slowing down the scaling factor of edge computing.
- **Reliability:** Ensuring the dependability of service delivery is critical in edge computing. It is important for each device to maintain the network topology of the entire distributed system to identify errors and offer recovery measures. The reliability levels of the connection technology employed may vary, and the precision of data generated at the edge could be affected by environmental factors. Therefore, it is crucial to manage failovers effectively to maintain service reliability.
- **Speed:** Edge computing is expected to deliver speedy services to end-users by utilizing analytical and computational resources in close proximity to the source [36]. This approach facilitates rapid communication and surpasses the performance of conventional cloud computing systems.
- **Efficiency:** Edge computing becomes more efficient when advanced analytical tools are located closer to end-users. This enables the execution of sophisticated AI and analytical tools on the edge of the system, resulting in enhanced operational efficiency and numerous benefits for the overall system [35, 36, 38].

5.4.4 Why Edge Computing?

Edge computing is a cutting-edge technology that has the potential to improve efficiency, reduce costs, and increase security [28, 37]. Edge computing enables efficient and timely processing of data at the edge of the network, bringing computation closer to the data source, and providing benefits such as reduced latency, improved scalability, enhanced privacy, and better utilization of network resources. Following are some reasons why this technology is beneficial.

- **Real-Time Response:** Edge computing enables quick responses to data as it is generated, eliminating any delay in processing. This feature is particularly useful in smart applications and devices.
- **Data Stream Acceleration:** This technology facilitates real-time processing of data without any lag. This is important in self-driving car technology and offers critical benefits to businesses.

- **Efficient Data Processing:** Edge computing allows for large-scale data processing in close proximity to its source. This reduces the use of internet bandwidth, resulting in cost savings and improved accessibility to applications in remote locations.
- **Security:** Edge computing offers an added layer of security by providing the ability to process sensitive data at the furthest distance from public clouds, keeping it secure.

5.4.5 Applications of Edge Computing

As more devices become connected to the internet, the demand for edge computing is increasing. Following are five potential applications of edge computing.

1. **Transportation:** Edge computing can play a crucial role in autonomous vehicles by utilizing sensors to process data close to the vehicle, saving time. The Automotive Edge Computing Consortium plans to focus on connected car solutions [39]. Edge computing can also benefit trains, airplanes, and other forms of transportation.
2. **Healthcare:** Wearable health devices can analyze data in real time to help doctors evaluate patients. Edge computing can make data collection and processing faster and more secure, allowing doctors to access cloud applications more quickly [36–38].
3. **Manufacturing:** Edge computing can move operational technology to the edge computing platforms for running processes like predictive maintenance, reducing the data that goes to the cloud [40].
4. **Grid Edge Control and Analytics:** Edge computing can provide advanced real-time monitoring and analytics for distributed energy resources like renewables, reducing overall cost and avoiding outages and overcompensation [41].
5. **Remote Monitoring of Oil and Gas:** Edge computing allows for real-time safety monitoring of oil and gas systems, preventing malfunctions and disasters [41].
6. **Traffic Management:** Smart transportation systems like self-driving cars use edge computing to analyze and optimize real-time traffic data, reducing network expenses and operating processing and storage costs [37, 39, 42].
7. **Edge Video Orchestration:** Edge computing resources can optimize the delivery of heavy bandwidth videos by orchestrating, caching, and distributing video files closely to devices, reducing service costs and avoiding quality issues associated with mobile networks [36, 37, 43].

5.4.6 Benefits and Limitations of Edge Computing

Following are some of the benefits of edge computing.

- **Speed:** It is an indispensable factor in various fields, especially in computer science. Companies and industries require high-speed technology to avoid financial losses and save lives. For instance, financial organizations need fast data processing to prevent significant financial losses. In the healthcare industry, timely processing of data can mean the difference between saving or losing a patient's life. In service-providing industries, slow computing can irritate customers and have negative impacts on the industry. Edge computing offers a viable solution to these issues by providing exceptionally fast computing speeds [35, 37]. Edge computing reduces network latency, and IoT devices can process data at edge data centers, eliminating the need to send data back to centralized servers.

- **Security of Data:** Edge computing provides a significant advantage in terms of data security as it allows for data to be stored near its source, distributing data processing tasks across multiple data centers and devices. This decentralization of data makes it more difficult for cyber-attackers to access confidential information and launch DDoS attacks [1, 42]. Furthermore, by storing data locally, it is easier to monitor and secure it, ensuring that industries can maintain the privacy and confidentiality of their data.
- **Scalability of Data:** Scaling data becomes a simpler task with the utilization of edge computing. This method involves the acquisition of edge devices that possess a high level of computational power to enhance the capacity of the edge network. Companies do not have to construct their own centralized data centers to meet their data requirements. By combining edge computing with colocation services, it becomes possible to extend the edge network. This eliminates the need for companies to purchase new equipment for expanding their IT infrastructure. Instead, they can simply invest in a few IoT devices to broaden their network. Ultimately, this approach enables companies to save money on equipment purchases [36, 38].
- **Faster Data Processing:** Collaborative IoT applications may cause server slowdowns when generating a large volume of data. Centralizing these applications could lead to increased complexities for both the server and the connected IoT devices. Moreover, if the server malfunctions, the connected devices would also malfunction. Edge computing offers a solution by allowing local or nearby access to data, thereby reducing costs associated with data movement to a central server and decreasing data processing time. This results in more efficient data processing, and when the network is not constantly exchanging data, it saves network clustering and promotes data sharing between nodes only when necessary [35–37].
- **Cost Effectiveness:** Edge computing has gained popularity as a cost-effective alternative to traditional technologies. This is because it reduces expenses associated with data storage, network usage, data processing, and data transmission. Additionally, it facilitates compatibility among modern, legacy, and smart IoT devices by translating communication protocols used by older devices into a language that modern devices and the cloud can comprehend [35–37]. This eliminates the need to purchase new IoT devices as existing or older ones can be easily connected through edge computing. Additionally, edge computing allows devices to operate even without high-speed internet connectivity, which is crucial for cloud functionalities.

- **High Speed and Low Latency:** Edge computing is a technology that aims to reduce latency and improve data processing performance by bringing data closer to the user, instead of sending it to a centralized cloud server network. This approach allows for faster, more secure data sharing without latency issues. When combined with 5G technology, edge computing can reduce latency to just 1 millisecond, further enhancing its benefits [44].
- **Reduced Internet Bandwidth Usage and Associated Costs:** The use of edge computing can lead to a significant reduction in both internet bandwidth usage and costs. This is since data processing takes place at the edge network, which frees up server resources for other cloud-specific operations. As a result, server resource utilization and associated costs can be reduced [37, 44].
- **Responsive and Robust Application Performance:** Deploying the processing logic to a local edge environment can enhance application performance, making it more responsive and robust. This approach can improve business efficiency and reliability by enabling critical operations to be performed in a local environment without the risk of network disconnects causing response timeouts [40, 41, 45].
- **Distributed Security:** Distributed security is a major benefit of edge computing due to its ability to process data locally, reducing direct interaction with the cloud. This approach minimizes the risk of DDoS attacks, which can potentially cripple networks and compromise security [1, 46].
- **Increased Reliability:** Edge computing is known for its ability to improve reliability by operating micro data centers in a variety of environments. This eliminates interruptions that may arise from internet and cloud-based services. By bringing computing resources closer to the user, edge computing enables the deployment of robust, secure, and intelligent on-premises infrastructure [20, 47].

The disadvantages associated with edge computing include the following [35–38].

- **Increased Storage Requirement:** Since data is stored and processed at various locations, edge computing requires additional storage, which can be costly.
- **Security Risks:** The distributed nature of edge computing creates security risks as it becomes more difficult to detect cyber-threats and identify thefts. Adding new IoT devices also poses a potential risk for data breaches.
- **High Cost:** Edge computing can be expensive despite the savings it can bring in terms of purchasing new devices.
- **Advanced Infrastructure Requirement:** Edge computing requires advanced infrastructure to process data effectively.
- **Limited Resource Pooling:** Edge computing has limited capabilities for resource pooling, which can hinder its ability to utilize resources effectively.
- **Peripheral Limitations:** Edge computing is limited in terms of the number of peripherals it can support.

5.4.7 Edge Computing vs. Cloud Computing

Edge computing and cloud computing are two distinct technologies that serve different purposes, and while edge computing will not replace cloud computing, it will have an impact on it. Edge computing will enhance cloud computing by providing less complex solutions for handling complex data [35, 37, 44, 48]. Table 5.2 presents some key differences that set edge computing apart from cloud computing.

5.4.8 Potential Industries Using Edge Computing

Edge computing is a technology that enables processing data and analytics closer to the source of data, rather than sending it to a central location. It can be implemented in various industries, including the following.

1. **Healthcare:** Edge computing can be used to analyze patient data and provide real-time feedback to healthcare professionals [49–51]. It can also help in remote monitoring of patients and assist in detecting critical health issues.
2. **Manufacturing:** Edge computing can enhance manufacturing processes by providing real-time monitoring of equipment performance and detecting defects, which can help in preventing downtime.

TABLE 5.2
Difference between Edge Computing and Cloud Computing

Edge Computing	Cloud Computing
Edge computing is ideal for organizations with limited financial resources, such as mid-level organizations.	Cloud computing is recommended for managing and processing a high volume of complex and massive data. Therefore, organizations dealing with massive data storage use cloud computing.
Edge computing enables the utilization of various programming languages on diverse platforms, each having a unique runtime.	Cloud computing operates on a particular platform and employs a specific programming language.
Edge computing is responsible for handling time-critical information by performing data processing tasks at the edge of the network.	Cloud computing is a type of data processing that is not constrained by time. This means that the data processing is not dependent on specific timeframes.
Edge computing employs a distributed model and performs data processing at remote locations. It follows a decentralized approach, enabling it to operate closer to the source of the data it is processing.	Cloud computing adopts a centralized approach to manage and process data at centralized locations.
Edge computing enables organizations to utilize their current IoT devices and enhance their capabilities without having to buy new devices.	Cloud computing requires the use of new IoT devices to replace existing ones, which is a costly and time-consuming process.
Edge computing is the future of computing.	Cloud computing is the currently existing technology.

3. **Transportation:** The implementation of edge computing can assist in monitoring traffic patterns and providing real-time information to drivers, which can improve safety and reduce traffic congestion.
4. **Energy:** Edge computing can be used to optimize the performance of energy grids and reduce energy waste, which can lower costs for both consumers and energy providers.
5. **Retail:** Retail stores can utilize edge computing to track customer behavior, analyze shopping patterns, and provide personalized recommendations to customers.
6. **Agriculture:** Edge computing can help farmers to monitor crop growth, optimize water usage, and detect soil quality, which can improve crop yield and reduce waste.

In conclusion, edge computing has a wide range of applications and can be implemented in various industries to improve efficiency, productivity, and cost effectiveness.

5.4.9 Challenges of Edge Computing

Edge computing is a technology that brings data processing and storage closer to the source or device that generates it. Although it has many advantages, it also presents some challenges, such as the following.

- **Security:** Edge devices are often located in remote and unsecured locations, making them vulnerable to cyber-attacks. To overcome this challenge, edge computing systems need to incorporate strong security measures such as encryption and access control [8, 35].
- **Device Management:** Managing and maintaining edge devices can be difficult, as they are often located in hard-to-reach areas. This can lead to issues such as device downtime or reduced performance [44]. To address this challenge, edge computing systems should include tools for remote management and maintenance.
- **Data Integration:** Edge devices often use different protocols or data formats, making it difficult to integrate them with existing systems [1, 46]. This can result in data silos and reduced efficiency. To address this challenge, edge computing systems should include tools for data integration and management.
- **Network Latency:** Edge computing relies on processing data closer to the source, but this can lead to increased network latency if the devices are too far from the central system. This can impact real-time data processing and application performance [25, 52].
- **Power and Resource Constraints:** Edge devices often have limited power and resources, such as battery life or processing capacity. This can affect the performance and scalability of edge computing systems, especially for large-scale deployments.

In conclusion, while edge computing offers many benefits, it also presents several challenges that need to be addressed. These challenges include security, device management, and data integration. By overcoming these challenges, organizations can fully realize the potential of edge computing and take advantage of its many benefits.

5.5 DATA ANALYSIS OPTIONS: EDGE, CLOUD, OR COMBINATION?

There are three main options for data analysis: edge, cloud, or a combination of both. In edge computing, data analysis is performed directly on the edge devices or edge servers near the data source. This approach offers real-time or near–real-time analytics and immediate insights at the edge. It is beneficial when low latency and immediate decision-making are critical, as it eliminates the need to transmit data to the cloud for analysis. Edge data analysis is suitable for applications for which quick response times and localized decision-making are essential, such as real-time monitoring, predictive maintenance, and autonomous systems. In cloud computing, data analysis is performed on centralized cloud servers. Data is transmitted from edge devices to the cloud for processing, storage, and analysis. Cloud data analysis allows for extensive computational resources, scalability, and advanced analytics capabilities. It is suitable for applications that require complex data processing, large-scale analytics, historical data analysis, and machine learning models. Cloud data analysis also provides a centralized view and facilitates cross-device or cross-location analysis.

A combination of edge and cloud data analysis can be employed to leverage the benefits of both paradigms. In this approach, initial data filtering and lightweight analysis are performed at the edge for quick insights and immediate actions, then selected data or aggregated results are transmitted to the cloud for further processing, in-depth analysis, long-term storage, and complex modeling. The hybrid approach allows for a balance between real-time analysis at the edge and the extensive computational power and resources of the cloud. It is suitable for applications for which a combination of low latency and centralized processing is required, such as smart cities, remote monitoring, and distributed systems. We will next briefly summarize each of these options.

Edge Computing

- Data is analyzed locally on the device where it was collected, such as a smartphone or sensor device.
- Provides faster response times since the data does not need to be sent to the cloud for analysis.
- Suitable for applications that require real-time analysis or are in locations where internet connectivity is limited or unreliable.
- Edge devices may have limited processing power and storage capacity, which can limit the complexity of analysis that can be performed.

Cloud Computing

- Data is analyzed on remote servers in the cloud, typically using powerful computing resources.

- Offers virtually unlimited processing power and storage capacity for data analysis.
- Suitable for applications that require complex analysis or require large amounts of data to be processed.
- May have slower response times due to data transfer and processing times.
- Requires a reliable and high-speed internet connection.

Combination of Edge and Cloud Computing

- Combines both edge and cloud analysis to leverage the benefits of both options.
- Enables real-time analysis of data on the edge, while also allowing for more complex analysis to be performed in the cloud.
- Suitable for applications that require both real-time analysis and complex analysis.
- Requires a reliable and high-speed internet connection, as well as edge devices with sufficient processing power and storage capacity.

When it comes to data analysis in the context of edge computing and cloud computing, there are multiple options available, and the choice depends on various factors such as the nature of the data, application requirements, and resource availability. Ultimately, the choice between edge, cloud, or a combination of both will depend on the specific requirements of the application, including factors such as response time, processing power, and internet connectivity.

REFERENCES

[1] D. Liu, Z. Yan, W. Ding, and M. Atiquzzaman, "A Survey on Secure Data Analytics in Edge Computing," *IEEE Internet Things J.*, vol. 6, no. 3, 2019, doi: 10.1109/JIOT.2019.2897619.

[2] M. Díaz, C. Martín, and B. Rubio, "State-of-the-Art, Challenges, and Open Issues in the Integration of Internet of Things and Cloud Computing," *J. Netw. Comput. Appl.*, vol. 67, 2016, doi: 10.1016/j.jnca.2016.01.010.

[3] A. Alam, I. Ullah, and Y. K. Lee, "Video Big Data Analytics in the Cloud: A Reference Architecture, Survey, Opportunities, and Open Research Issues," *IEEE Access*, vol. 8, 2020, doi: 10.1109/ACCESS.2020.3017135.

[4] A. Yassine, S. Singh, M. S. Hossain, and G. Muhammad, "IoT Big Data Analytics for Smart Homes with Fog and Cloud Computing," *Futur. Gener. Comput. Syst.*, vol. 91, 2019, doi: 10.1016/j.future.2018.08.040.

[5] F. Pop, J. Kolodziej, and B. D. Martino, *Resource Management for Big Data Platforms: Algorithms, Modelling, and High-Performance Computing Techniques (Computer Communications and Networks)*, Springer, Switzerland, 2016, doi: 10.1007/978-3-319-44881-7.

[6] H. Rahman *et al.*, "Advances in Intelligent Systems and Computing 1199 Progress in Advanced Computing and Intelligent Engineering," *Inf. Syst.*, vol. 34, pp. 1–34, 2021.

[7] P. Maciel *et al.*, "A Survey on Reliability and Availability Modeling of Edge, Fog, and Cloud Computing," *J. Reliab. Intell. Environ.*, vol. 8, no. 3, 2022, doi: 10.1007/s40860-021-00154-1.

[8] F. Firouzi, B. Farahani, and A. Marinšek, "The Convergence and Interplay of Edge, Fog, and Cloud in the AI-Driven Internet of Things (IoT)," *Inf. Syst.*, vol. 107, 2022, doi: 10.1016/j.is.2021.101840.

[9] S. Sharma and M. Sajid, "Integrated Fog and Cloud Computing Issues and Challenges," *Int. J. Cloud Appl. Comput.*, vol. 11, no. 4, 2021, doi: 10.4018/IJCAC.2021100110.

[10] R. Muñoz *et al.*, "Integration of IoT, Transport SDN, and Edge/Cloud Computing for Dynamic Distribution of IoT Analytics and Efficient Use of Network Resources," *J. Light. Technol.*, vol. 36, no. 7, 2018, doi: 10.1109/JLT.2018.2800660.

[11] C. M. Mohammed and S. R. Zeebaree, "Sufficient Comparison Among Cloud Computing Services: IaaS, PaaS, and SaaS: A Review," *Int. J. Sci. Bus.*, vol. 5, no. 2, 2021.

[12] IBM, "Defining IaaS, PaaS and SaaS," *IaaS, PaaS and SaaS—IBM Cloud Service Models*, 2019.

[13] B. Kepes, "Understanding the Cloud Computing Stack SaaS, PaaS, IaaS," *Rackspace Support Network*, pp. 1–20, 2013.

[14] M. Alam, K. A. Shakil, and S. Khan, *Internet of Things (IoT): Concepts and Applications*, Springer International Publishing, Switzerland, 2020, doi: 10.1007/978-3-030-37468-6.

[15] Amazon, "Amazon EMR—Big Data Platform—Amazon Web Services," *Amazon*, 2020.

[16] J. Woo and M. Mishra, "Predicting the Ratings of Amazon Products Using Big Data," *Wiley Interdiscip. Rev.: Data Min. Knowl. Discov.*, vol. 11, no. 3, 2021, doi: 10.1002/widm.1400.

[17] J. Shi, L. Jin, and J. Li, "The Integration of Azure Sphere and Azure Cloud Services for Internet of Things," *Appl. Sci.*, vol. 9, no. 13, 2019, doi: 10.3390/app9132746.

[18] R. M. H. Al-Sayyed, W. A. Hijawi, A. M. Bashiti, I. AlJarah, N. Obeid, and O. Y. Adwan, "An Investigation of Microsoft Azure and Amazon Web Services From Users' Perspectives," *Int. J. Emerg. Technol. Learn.*, vol. 14, no. 10, 2019, doi: 10.3991/ijet.v14i10.9902.

[19] D. C. Nguyen, P. N. Pathirana, M. Ding, and A. Seneviratne, "Integration of Blockchain and Cloud of Things: Architecture, Applications and Challenges," *IEEE Commun. Surv. Tutor.*, vol. 22, no. 4, 2020, doi: 10.1109/COMST.2020.3020092.

[20] A. A. A. Ari *et al.*, "Enabling Privacy and Security in Cloud of Things: Architecture, Applications, Security & Privacy Challenges," *Appl. Comput. Inform.*, 2019, doi: 10.1016/j.aci.2019.11.005.

[21] H. Abualese, T. Al-Rousan, and B. Al-Shargabi, "A New Trust Framework for E-Government in Cloud of Things," *Int. J. Electron. Telecommun.*, vol. 65, no. 3, 2019, doi: 10.24425/ijet.2019.129791.

[22] M. M. E. Mahmoud *et al.*, "Enabling Technologies on Cloud of Things for Smart Healthcare," *IEEE Access*, vol. 6, 2018, doi: 10.1109/ACCESS.2018.2845399.

[23] F. Callegati, S. Giallorenzo, A. Melis, and M. Prandini, "Cloud-of-Things Meets Mobility-as-a-Service: An Insider Threat Perspective," *Comput. Secur.*, vol. 74, 2018, doi: 10.1016/j.cose.2017.10.006.

[24] A. Farahzadi, P. Shams, J. Rezazadeh, and R. Farahbakhsh, "Middleware Technologies for Cloud of Things: A Survey," *Digit. Commun. Netw.*, vol. 4, no. 3, 2018, doi: 10.1016/j.dcan.2017.04.005.

[25] J. M. Myerson, "Cloud Computing Versus Grid Computing," *IBM*, pp. 1–9, 2009.

[26] S. M. Hashemi and A. K. Bardsiri, "Cloud Computing Vs. Grid Computing," *ARPN J. Syst. Softw.*, vol. 2, no. 5, 2012.

[27] T. H. Noor, S. Zeadally, A. Alfazi, and Q. Z. Sheng, "Mobile Cloud Computing: Challenges and Future Research Directions," *J. Netw. Comput. Appl.*, vol. 115, 2018, doi: 10.1016/j.jnca.2018.04.018.

[28] N. Fernando, S. W. Loke, and W. Rahayu, "Mobile Cloud Computing: A Survey," *Futur. Gener. Comput. Syst.*, vol. 29, no. 1, 2013, doi: 10.1016/j.future.2012.05.023.

[29] P. Bellavista, J. Berrocal, A. Corradi, S. K. Das, L. Foschini, and A. Zanni, "A Survey on Fog Computing for the Internet of Things," *Pervasive Mob. Comput.*, vol. 52, 2019, doi: 10.1016/j.pmcj.2018.12.007.

[30] C. Mouradian, D. Naboulsi, S. Yangui, R. H. Glitho, M. J. Morrow, and P. A. Polakos, "A Comprehensive Survey on Fog Computing: State-of-the-Art and Research Challenges," *IEEE Commun. Surv. Tutor.*, vol. 20, no. 1, 2018, doi: 10.1109/COMST.2017.2771153.

[31] G. M. Mujthaba, A. Alameen, and M. Kolhar, "Cloud Servers and Fog or Edge Computing with Their Limitations & Challenges," *Int. J. Sci. Technol. Res.*, vol. 9, no. 3, 2020.

[32] M. R. Anawar, S. Wang, M. Azam Zia, A. K. Jadoon, U. Akram, and S. Raza, "Fog Computing: An Overview of Big IoT Data Analytics," *Wirel. Commun. Mob. Comput.*, vol. 2018, 2018, doi: 10.1155/2018/7157192.

[33] G. Mokhtari, A. Anvari-Moghaddam, and Q. Zhang, "A New Layered Architecture for Future Big Data-Driven Smart Homes," *IEEE Access*, vol. 7, 2019, doi: 10.1109/ACCESS.2019.2896403.

[34] S. Kunal, A. Saha, and R. Amin, "An Overview of Cloud-Fog Computing: Architectures, Applications with Security Challenges," *Secur. Priv.*, vol. 2, no. 4, 2019, doi: 10.1002/spy2.72.

[35] W. Shi, J. Cao, Q. Zhang, Y. Li, and L. Xu, "Edge Computing: Vision and Challenges," *IEEE Internet Things J.*, vol. 3, no. 5, 2016, doi: 10.1109/JIOT.2016.2579198.

[36] T. Qiu, J. Chi, X. Zhou, Z. Ning, M. Atiquzzaman, and D. O. Wu, "Edge Computing in Industrial Internet of Things: Architecture, Advances and Challenges," *IEEE Commun. Surv. Tutor.*, vol. 22, no. 4, 2020, doi: 10.1109/COMST.2020.3009103.

[37] R. Buyya and S. N. Srirama, *Fog and Edge Computing: Principles and Paradigms*, pp. 1–471, Wiley, Hoboken, New Jersey, United States, 2019, doi: 10.1002/9781119525080.

[38] J. Cao, Q. Zhang, and W. Shi, "Challenges and Opportunities in Edge Computing," in *SpringerBriefs in Computer Science*, Springer, Switzerland, 2018, doi: 10.1007/978-3-030-02083-5_5.

[39] G. Yan and Q. Qin, "The Application of Edge Computing Technology in the Collaborative Optimization of Intelligent Transportation System Based on Information Physical Fusion," *IEEE Access*, vol. 8, 2020, doi: 10.1109/ACCESS.2020.3008780.

[40] K. Kubiak, G. Dec, and D. Stadnicka, "Possible Applications of Edge Computing in the Manufacturing Industry—Systematic Literature Review," *Sensors*, vol. 22, no. 7, 2022, doi: 10.3390/s22072445.

[41] J. Wang, L. Wu, K. K. R. Choo, and D. He, "Blockchain-Based Anonymous Authentication with Key Management for Smart Grid Edge Computing Infrastructure," *IEEE Trans. Ind. Inform.*, vol. 16, no. 3, 2020, doi: 10.1109/TII.2019.2936278.

[42] X. Li, T. Chen, Q. Cheng, S. Ma, and J. Ma, "Smart Applications in Edge Computing: Overview on Authentication and Data Security," *IEEE Internet Things J.*, vol. 8, no. 6, 2021, doi: 10.1109/JIOT.2020.3019297.

[43] A. Ullah, H. Dagdeviren, R. C. Ariyattu, J. DesLauriers, T. Kiss, and J. Bowden, "MiCADO-Edge: Towards an Application-level Orchestrator for the Cloud-to-Edge Computing Continuum," *J. Grid Comput.*, vol. 19, no. 4, 2021, doi: 10.1007/s10723-021-09589-5.

[44] N. Hassan, K. L. A. Yau, and C. Wu, "Edge Computing in 5G: A Review," *IEEE Access*, vol. 7, 2019, doi: 10.1109/ACCESS.2019.2938534.

[45] R. F. Hussain, M. A. Salehi, and O. Semiari, "Serverless Edge Computing for Green Oil and Gas Industry," in *IEEE Green Technologies Conference*, vol. 2019, April 2019, doi: 10.1109/GreenTech.2019.8767119.

[46] M. J. Anwar, A. Q. Gill, F. K. Hussain, and M. Imran, "Secure Big Data Ecosystem Architecture: Challenges and Solutions," *Eurasip J. Wirel. Commun. Netw.*, vol. 2021, no. 1, 2021, doi: 10.1186/s13638-021-01996-2.

[47] J. Granjal, E. Monteiro, and J. Sa Silva, "Security for the Internet of Things: A Survey of Existing Protocols and Open Research Issues," *IEEE Commun. Surv. Tutor.*, vol. 17, no. 3, 2015, doi: 10.1109/COMST.2015.2388550.

[48] B. Bajic, I. Cosic, B. Katalinic, S. Moraca, M. Lazarevic, and A. Rikalovic, "Edge Computing vs. Cloud Computing: Challenges and Opportunities in Industry 4.0," in *Annals of DAAAM and Proceedings of the International DAAAM Symposium*, vol. 30, no. 1, 2019, doi: 10.2507/30th.daaam.proceedings.120.

[49] S. Dash, S. K. Shakyawar, M. Sharma, and S. Kaushik, "Big Data in Healthcare: Management, Analysis and Future Prospects," *J. Big Data*, vol. 6, no. 1, 2019, doi: 10.1186/s40537-019-0217-0.

[50] R. Pastorino *et al.*, "Benefits and Challenges of Big Data in Healthcare: An Overview of the European Initiatives," *Eur. J. Public Health*, vol. 29, 2019, doi: 10.1093/eurpub/ckz168.

[51] A. Singla, N. Bali, and D. Chaudhary, "Big Data and Its Applications," *J. Technol. Manag. Grow. Econ.*, vol. 11, no. 2, 2020, doi: 10.15415/jtmge.2020.112008.

[52] B. P. Bhattarai *et al.*, "Big Data Analytics in Smart Grids: State-of-Theart, Challenges, Opportunities, and Future Directions," *IET Smart Grid.*, vol. 2, no. 2, 2019, doi: 10.1049/iet-stg.2018.0261.

6 Internet of Things in the Era of 5G

6.1 5G

5G is the latest advancement in mobile network technology, succeeding the current 4G LTE (long-term evolution) networks. It has been developed to address the increasing demand for data and connectivity in modern society, including the massive expansion of the Internet of Things (IoT), which involves billions of connected devices, as well as emerging innovations [1, 2]. 5G refers to the fifth generation of wireless technology for cellular networks. It is the latest advancement in mobile communications and offers significant improvements over its predecessors, 3G and 4G. It is important to note that the deployment of 5G networks is an ongoing process, and the full potential of 5G will be realized over time as more infrastructure is built and as new applications and services are developed to leverage its capabilities.

One of the significant advantages of 5G technology is its low latency, which refers to the time taken for devices to communicate with each other over a wireless network. 5G's response time is anticipated to be as low as 1 ms (millisecond), compared to 100 ms for 3G and 30 ms for 4G networks [3]. This faster response time creates new possibilities for connected applications that require real-time communication. 5G provides significantly faster data speeds compared to 4G and 3G. While 4G networks typically offer download speeds of up to several hundred megabits per second (Mbps), 5G can achieve multi-gigabit per second (Gbps) speeds. This ultra-fast speed enables quicker downloads, seamless streaming of high-definition content, and improved real-time communication. 5G offers significantly lower latency compared to 4G and 3G. While 4G networks typically have a latency of around 30–50 ms, 5G aims to reduce it to less than 10 ms. This reduced latency is crucial for applications that require near–real-time responsiveness, such as online gaming, remote surgery, and autonomous vehicles. 5G networks have a much higher capacity to handle a massive number of connected devices simultaneously. This improved capacity is achieved by utilizing higher radio frequencies, advanced antenna technologies, and network virtualization techniques. 5G can support up to 1 million devices per square kilometer, while 4G can handle around 4,000 devices per square kilometer. This increased connectivity is essential for the growing IoT ecosystem and enables the seamless connection of numerous smart devices in smart homes, cities, and industries. 5G introduces a concept called "network slicing," which allows the creation of multiple virtual networks on a shared physical infrastructure. This enables network operators to tailor the network's characteristics, such as speed, capacity, and latency, to meet specific requirements of different applications and industries. Network slicing enhances efficiency, flexibility, and customization possibilities for diverse use cases, ranging from autonomous vehicles to industrial automation. 5G utilizes

DOI: 10.1201/9781003282945-6

several technological advancements to deliver its enhanced performance. These include higher-frequency millimeter waves, Massive MIMO (multiple input/multiple output) antenna systems, beamforming, and advanced modulation techniques. These technologies enable the efficient use of available spectrum, increase network capacity, and improve signal quality.

6.1.1 What Is 5G?

5G technology enables a wide range of applications across various sectors. 5G provides faster download and upload speeds, allowing for seamless streaming of high-definition videos, virtual reality (VR), augmented reality (AR), and immersive gaming experiences on mobile devices. 5G enables the massive deployment of IoT devices, as it can handle a significantly higher number of connected devices compared to previous generations. 5G enables telemedicine and remote healthcare services by providing reliable and high-bandwidth connections. It facilitates real-time video consultations, remote patient monitoring, and the transmission of large medical imaging files, improving access to healthcare in remote areas and enabling more efficient healthcare delivery.

The terms massive machine-type communications (mMTC), ultra-reliable and low-latency communications (URLLC), and enhanced mobile broadband (eMBB) are directly related to the development and implementation of 5G technology. They represent different service categories or use cases that 5G networks are designed to support, as illustrated in Figure 6.1. These categories were defined by the International Telecommunication Union (ITU) to provide a framework for understanding the

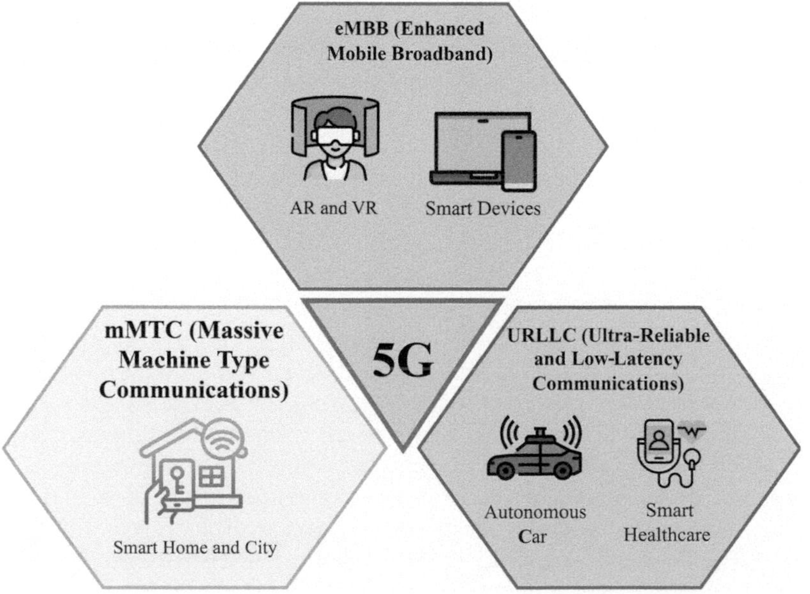

FIGURE 6.1 Range of application areas that 5G supports.

diverse requirements and applications of 5G. 5G networks are designed to be highly versatile and capable of supporting a wide range of use cases, from massive machine-type communications to URLLC, and enhanced mobile broadband services. Each of these service categories has specific characteristics and requirements, and 5G networks are designed to address these requirements. Overall, these three service categories—mMTC, URLLC, and eMBB—represent different use cases and requirements in the 5G ecosystem. 5G networks are designed to accommodate the diverse needs of IoT devices, critical applications, and high-bandwidth services, offering enhanced connectivity, reliability, low latency, and high data rates to support a wide range of applications and industries.

The mMTC refers to the capability of 5G networks to handle massive numbers of devices or sensors that require low-power, low-cost, and low-complexity connectivity. It focuses on supporting applications involving a large-scale deployment of IoT devices. These devices typically transmit small amounts of data infrequently, but in extremely high quantities. Examples of mMTC applications include smart cities, industrial automation, agricultural monitoring, and environmental monitoring. The goal of mMTC is to enable efficient and scalable communication for a massive number of IoT devices, allowing them to send and receive data reliably without overwhelming the network infrastructure. mMTC emphasizes energy efficiency, extended coverage, and optimized resource utilization to accommodate the vast number of connected devices. URLLC focuses on providing ultra-reliable, low-latency, and high-reliability communication services for critical applications that demand stringent requirements in terms of latency, reliability, and availability. URLLC is designed to support time-critical and mission-critical applications that cannot tolerate any delay or disruption in communication. Examples of URLLC applications include autonomous vehicles, industrial automation, remote surgery, and public safety systems. The key characteristics of URLLC are extremely low latency, high reliability, and determinism in communication. These applications require near-instantaneous response times, high availability, and very low error rates. The network infrastructure is optimized to provide low-latency transmission, ultra-reliable connectivity, and prioritization of critical traffic to meet the stringent requirements of URLLC applications. On the other hand, eMBB focuses on delivering enhanced mobile broadband services that provide significantly higher data rates, capacity, and improved user experience compared to previous generations of mobile networks. eMBB targets applications that require high-speed data transmission, multimedia streaming, VR, and AR experiences. Examples of eMBB applications include 4K/8K video streaming, online gaming, virtual meetings, and immersive media. eMBB aims to provide faster download and upload speeds, improved network capacity, and reduced latency compared to previous network technologies. It enables high-bandwidth applications and services that demand large data transfer, high-quality video streaming, and real-time interactive experiences.

6.1.2 What Will 5G Enable?

The advent of 5G technology promises to revolutionize the way we interact with the internet, as it provides faster download speeds, lower latency, and better connectivity.

This will enable new applications, services, and business opportunities that were previously unimaginable. With advancements in AI, data processing, and cellular communication, the wireless data exchange has become faster, and 5G is expected to take mobile performance from the current LTE Cat 20's top speed of 2.4 Gbps to nearly 20 Gbps [1, 2]. Thus, 5G can serve as a viable alternative to wired fiber optic networks in providing high-speed data networking. Moreover, IoT solutions are expected to connect over 50 billion devices by 2030, further driving the demand for 5G technology. Although the rollout of 5G is ongoing, its evolution in communications promises to bring about a faster and smarter future for the world. Following are three major categories of use case for 5G.

1. **Massive Machine-to-Machine Communications:** Massive M2M refers to the exchange of information and data between multiple devices without human intervention. This involves a network of connected sensors, devices, and machines communicating with each other to collect and share data in real time. M2M has significant potential to improve efficiency, reduce costs and improve decision-making in industries such as healthcare, manufacturing, transportation, and smart cities [3].
2. **Ultra-Reliable Low Latency Communications:** URLLC refers to a type of communication that provides high-quality and fast connectivity with high reliability. This technology is essential for complex industries such as healthcare, autonomous vehicles, and industrial automation. It ensures that data is transmitted quickly and with minimal delay to allow efficient and real-time decision-making. Additionally, the system is designed to prevent any loss or interruption of data, making it highly reliable [4].
3. **Enhanced Mobile Broadband:** Enhanced mobile broadband (eMBB) refers to the advancement of mobile network technology that provides higher data rates, increased capacity and improved reliability for faster and more seamless connectivity. With eMBB, users can experience faster downloads, smoother streaming, and more efficient transmission of data, enabling a wide range of new applications and services. eMBB is a key component of 5G networks and enables a more connected and automated future [5].
4. **The Game-Changer for Community Development:** 5G technology is set to be a game-changer for community development. With its lightning-fast speed and low latency, 5G networks will bring new possibilities to everything from education and healthcare to transportation and entertainment. This means that communities can expect faster, more reliable communication and access to cutting-edge technologies that will help them grow and thrive. Ultimately, 5G has the potential to revolutionize the way we live, work, and play, making it an essential tool for community development in the 21st century.
5. **Benefits of 5G for Business and Industry:** 5G technology offers numerous benefits for businesses and industries, including faster data transfer rates, lower latency, higher connectivity density, and improved network reliability. This allows for more efficient and effective communication, real-time data analysis, and faster decision-making. Additionally, 5G can support emerging

technologies like the IoT, AR, and VR, enabling new business models and revenue streams. Overall, 5G can help businesses stay competitive and drive innovation [6].

6.1.3 What Is 5G IoT?

5G is a recent wireless communication technology that seeks to enhance global connectivity. It involves a new framework, known as 5G NR, and an entirely new core network. This system standardizes the concept of multiple access, which includes various connectivity technologies like satellites, Wi-Fi, fixed lines, and cellular networks. 5G is capable of connecting more devices at higher speeds and minimizing lag, resulting in an exceptional user experience regardless of the device, application, or service. Additionally, it supports massive cellular IoT technologies, which are cost effective and low power, with comprehensive indoor and outdoor coverage, secure connectivity and authentication, easy deployment, and scalable capacity upgrades. Businesses, city developers, and other industrial organizations can take advantage of 5G's adaptability to connect more devices with better capabilities at lower costs [7, 8].

As discussed in Section 6.1.1, 5G is a broad term encompassing advancements in wireless technology, whereas 5G IoT focuses specifically on leveraging 5G to enhance connectivity and enable the seamless integration of a massive number of IoT devices. 5G refers to the overall fifth-generation wireless technology for cellular networks. It encompasses a range of advancements in mobile communications, including faster speeds, lower latency, higher capacity, and network slicing. 5G aims to provide an enhanced mobile broadband experience and support a wide array of applications beyond IoT. On the other hands, 5G IoT specifically focuses on leveraging 5G technology to enable and optimize the IoT ecosystem. It involves connecting and managing a massive number of IoT devices, enabling seamless communication between them and harnessing the benefits of 5G for IoT use cases. 5G encompasses a broader range of applications and services, including enhanced mobile broadband, IoT, autonomous vehicles, and more. 5G IoT specifically focuses on IoT use cases and how 5G can improve connectivity and efficiency for IoT devices. 5G provides improved connectivity and capacity overall, but 5G IoT focuses on optimizing connectivity specifically for IoT devices. It aims to address the unique requirements of IoT applications such as low power consumption, wide coverage, and support for a massive number of devices. 5G enables various use cases beyond IoT, such as high-definition video streaming, AR, VR, and mission-critical applications. 5G IoT, on the other hand, emphasizes IoT-specific applications like smart cities, industrial automation, agriculture, healthcare monitoring, and asset tracking.

6.1.4 Mobile IoT Systems are Paving the Way for 5G

Mobile IoT (MIoT) systems are playing an increasingly crucial role in paving the way for 5G wireless network technology. This technology has revolutionized the way our communication and networking systems function, leading to increased connectivity and collaboration across different platforms. This chapter examines the definition of MIoT systems and highlights their advantages in the present-day environment. It also delves into the opportunities and future scope of this technology in the coming years [9, 10]. MIoT refers to a set of low-power wireless technologies that enables interconnectivity between various devices, such as sensors, machines, and other internet-enabled devices, using cellular networks. This technology allows these devices to communicate directly with each other without requiring human intervention. MIoT technologies include Narrowband IoT (NB-IoT) and Long-Term Evolution for Machines (LTE-M), both of which are specially engineered for low-power, low–data-rate applications. These technologies have significant advantages in terms of their power efficiency, reliability, and range [11].

In today's world, the increasing use of connected smart devices has created a large demand for stable and efficient communication networks. MIoT systems are designed to address this need and offer several advantages over traditional connectivity methods, including the following [12].

1. **Power Efficiency:** MIoT networks utilize low-power connectivity that enables devices to function for extended periods, even with limited battery life.
2. **Cost Effectiveness:** The deployment and maintenance of MIoT networks are highly cost effective, making them ideal for IoT devices that require minimal data transfer.
3. **Global Coverage:** MIoT networks are based on cellular technology, providing an extensive coverage area that enables devices to communicate over long distances.
4. **High Security:** MIoT networks feature advanced security protocols that ensure the safety and integrity of data exchange between devices.

6.1.5 Current Applications of 5G IoT

The introduction of 5G technology has revolutionized the field of the IoT. It has enabled high-speed, low-latency communication with vast numbers of IoT devices, opening up a range of new possibilities for IoT applications including the following [10, 11].

1. **Smart Cities:** 5G IoT facilitates the deployment of smart city solutions that enhance city management, optimize transportation systems, and improve the quality of life for residents. It enables real-time communication between various city systems and devices, such as traffic lights, parking meters, and environmental sensors. 5G IoT enables real-time monitoring of traffic flow, congestion, and accidents. This data can be used to optimize traffic signals, reroute vehicles, and improve overall transportation efficiency. With 5G IoT, utility companies can deploy smart meters and sensors to monitor energy consumption, optimize distribution, and integrate renewable energy sources. This leads to better energy management and reduced environmental impact. 5G IoT can allow for enhanced public safety through real-time video surveillance, smart cameras, and facial recognition systems. It enables

quicker emergency response, crime prevention, and overall improvement in public safety measures. 5G IoT sensors and connectivity facilitate real-time parking space availability information, guiding drivers to vacant spots and reducing traffic congestion caused by searching for parking. These use cases demonstrate the diverse applications of 5G IoT in smart cities, aiming to improve efficiency, sustainability, safety, and citizen satisfaction. They showcase the potential for transformative changes in urban environments by harnessing the power of connectivity, data analytics, and automation.

2. **Industrial IoT:** 5G IoT offers a significant boost to industrial IoT, enabling real-time monitoring and control of complex industrial processes. It can help optimize manufacturing processes, improve inventory management, and enhance worker safety. 5G IoT enables real-time communication and control of industrial robots and automated systems. This allows for efficient production processes, increased productivity, and improved worker safety. With 5G IoT, businesses can track and manage their assets in real time, including inventory, equipment, and vehicles. This leads to optimized asset utilization, reduced downtime, and enhanced supply chain efficiency. 5G IoT devices and sensors can monitor equipment and machinery in real time, collecting data on performance, temperature, vibration, and other parameters. This data is then used to predict maintenance needs, schedule repairs, and minimize unplanned downtime. 5G IoT enables real-time monitoring and analysis of production processes, ensuring product quality and reducing defects. It allows for remote inspections, automated quality control, and faster response to deviations. 5G IoT devices in the supply chain enable real-time tracking of goods, monitoring conditions such as temperature, humidity, and location. This improves inventory management, reduces losses, and enhances overall supply chain visibility.
3. **Telemedicine:** 5G IoT facilitates the deployment of telemedicine solutions, enabling doctors to remotely monitor the health of patients in real time. It can help improve the quality of care and reduce healthcare costs. 5G IoT enables the real-time monitoring of patients' vital signs and health parameters through wearable devices and sensors. This allows healthcare providers to remotely monitor patients' conditions, detect abnormalities, and provide timely interventions. With 5G connectivity, healthcare professionals can conduct virtual consultations and telemedicine visits with patients, regardless of their geographic location. This enables access to medical expertise and care without the need for in-person visits. 5G IoT allows for the seamless integration of mobile health applications with healthcare systems. This enables remote access to EHRs, medication reminders, health tracking, and personalized health management. 5G IoT supports wearable devices, such as smartwatches and fitness trackers, that can monitor and transmit health-related data to healthcare providers. This data can be used for preventive care, health monitoring, and early detection of health issues.
4. **Autonomous Vehicles:** 5G IoT is essential for enabling the deployment of autonomous vehicles. It enables real-time communication between vehicles and other devices, such as road infrastructure, to enhance safety and

efficiency. 5G IoT enables real-time communication between autonomous vehicles, allowing them to exchange information about their position, speed, and direction. This enhances safety by enabling collision avoidance and cooperative driving. 5G IoT enables communication between autonomous vehicles and infrastructure, such as traffic signals, road signs, and parking systems. This allows vehicles to receive real-time information about road conditions, traffic congestion, and available parking spaces. 5G IoT allows for remote monitoring and control of autonomous vehicles. This enables real-time tracking of vehicle location, status, and performance. It also allows for over-the-air software updates and diagnostics. 5G IoT facilitates fleet management for autonomous vehicles, allowing operators to monitor vehicle performance, fuel consumption, and maintenance needs in real time. This improves operational efficiency and reduces downtime. These use cases demonstrate the potential of 5G IoT in revolutionizing the autonomous vehicle industry by enabling advanced communication, data exchange, and intelligent decision-making for safer, efficient, and connected transportation systems.

5. **Energy Management:** 5G IoT enables more efficient management of energy grids and can help reduce energy consumption. It enables real-time monitoring of energy consumption and optimizes the distribution of energy. It enables real-time communication and processing, facilitating the deployment of smart solutions that enhance efficiency, safety, and sustainability. 5G IoT enables real-time monitoring and control of power generation, distribution, and consumption in smart grids. This allows for efficient load balancing, demand response management, and integration of renewable energy sources. 5G IoT facilitates the collection and analysis of energy data from smart meters, sensors, and devices. This data can be used to identify energy consumption patterns, detect anomalies, and optimize energy usage in homes, buildings, and industrial facilities. 5G IoT enables intelligent lighting and HVAC systems that can adjust their operation based on occupancy, ambient conditions, and energy demand. This helps optimize energy usage and create comfortable and energy-efficient environments. 5G IoT supports the management and optimization of electric vehicle (EV) charging infrastructure. It enables real-time monitoring of charging stations, load balancing, and integration with renewable energy sources, promoting the adoption of electric vehicles. These use cases highlight how 5G IoT can transform energy management by enabling real-time monitoring, control, and optimization of energy resources, promoting energy efficiency, grid stability, and sustainability.

6.1.6 Future 5G Use Cases

In recent years, MIoT devices have become increasingly prevalent, with smart homes, synced watch and phone devices, and fitness apps being common examples. As the speed and performance capabilities of 5G technology continue to develop, these devices will become even more ubiquitous, and the future of 5G is expected to look radically different over the next 20 years [12]. Large-scale automation is anticipated to extend to vehicles and utility services such as waste management and energy production, facilitated by smart grids and environmental monitoring technology that can reduce greenhouse gases and pollution. The potential benefits of this technology include the ability to wirelessly charge a smart car in a parking garage and then remotely instruct the vehicle to drive to the user's office, as well as enabling farmers in rural areas to monitor and track crops, livestock, and machinery more effectively using drones and super-dense sensor networks.

The COVID-19 pandemic brought about a paradigm shift in remote work which is expected to endure as a new corporate norm, and 5G technology will facilitate the integration of remote work with smart homes. Users will be able to optimize power usage and stream their preferred entertainment from any location. These technological advancements will lead to increased efficiency, smarter cities, and personalized information streams for users. The future of 5G technology holds numerous exciting use cases across various industries. Following are some potential future 5G use cases.

1. **Autonomous Vehicles:** 5G can play a crucial role in enabling connected and autonomous vehicles. With its low latency and high reliability, 5G networks can facilitate real-time communication between vehicles, infrastructure, and pedestrians, enhancing safety and enabling advanced features like cooperative collision avoidance, traffic optimization, and remote vehicle control.
2. **Smart Cities:** 5G will greatly contribute to the development of smart cities by enabling efficient infrastructure management and improved quality of life. It can support connected systems for smart traffic management, intelligent energy grids, waste management, environmental monitoring, public safety, and enhanced public services like smart lighting, parking, and transportation.
3. **Industry 4.0:** 5G can revolutionize industrial automation and manufacturing processes. It enables real-time monitoring and control of machinery, robotics, and supply chains, leading to increased productivity, efficiency, and cost savings. With features like network slicing, 5G can provide dedicated and secure connectivity for different industrial applications within a factory or industrial environment.
4. **Remote Healthcare:** 5G has the potential to transform healthcare delivery by enabling remote diagnostics, telemedicine, and remote surgery. High-speed and low-latency connections allow doctors to remotely examine patients, conduct surgeries with robotic assistance, and provide medical services in underserved areas through connected devices and virtual consultations.
5. **Extended Reality (XR):** 5G can enhance AR and VR experiences by providing high-speed, low-latency connections. This opens up possibilities for immersive gaming, interactive training simulations, remote collaboration in various industries, and virtual tourism.
6. **Energy and Utilities:** 5G can optimize energy distribution, monitor utility infrastructure, and enable smart grid management. It facilitates real-time

data collection from smart meters, sensors, and devices, allowing utilities to better manage energy consumption, reduce waste, and enhance sustainability.

These are just a few examples of the potential future use cases for 5G. As the technology continues to evolve and more industries embrace its capabilities, we can expect to see even more innovative applications and transformative changes in various sectors.

6.2 INDUSTRIAL INTERNET OF THINGS

The IoT is an expanding network of physical objects with internet connectivity via IP addresses. These objects communicate with other internet-enabled devices and systems, and examples of everyday IoT devices include Wi-Fi doorbells and smart refrigerators. Industrial Internet of Things (IIoT) is a subcategory of IoT aimed at industrial applications [13]. Its focus is on connecting machines to other machines or data management systems to create "smart factories," and it is interchangeable with Industry 4.0, a term coined in Europe that refers to the Fourth Industrial Revolution.

IIoT refers to the application of intelligent sensors and actuators to enhance industrial and manufacturing processes. It is also known as Industry 4.0 and harnesses the potential of smart machines and real-time analytics to extract valuable insights from data generated by traditional machinery [14, 15]. The underlying principle of IIoT is that machines equipped with smart sensors are better at collecting and analyzing data in real time than humans, thereby facilitating faster and more accurate decision-making. Through connected sensors and actuators, companies can detect inefficiencies and problems at an earlier stage, saving time and money, and supporting business intelligence efforts. In the manufacturing sector, IIoT has immense potential to improve quality control, promote sustainable practices, ensure supply chain traceability, and enhance overall efficiency. It plays a crucial role in industrial processes such as predictive maintenance, field service, energy management, and asset tracking [16–18].

The IIoT enables real-time monitoring and analysis of industrial processes, machinery, and equipment. By collecting and analyzing data from various sensors and devices, organizations can gain valuable insights into their operations, identify inefficiencies, optimize workflows, and reduce downtime. This leads to improved operational efficiency, cost savings, and better resource utilization. IIoT solutions enable predictive maintenance, which involves monitoring equipment and systems in real time to detect signs of potential failures or maintenance needs. By utilizing sensor data and advanced analytics, organizations can predict when equipment is likely to malfunction and proactively schedule maintenance activities. This approach reduces unplanned downtime, extends equipment lifespan, and minimizes maintenance costs. IIoT solutions enhance workplace safety by continuously monitoring and analyzing environmental conditions, equipment performance, and worker behavior. Connected sensors and devices can detect hazardous situations, send real-time alerts, and trigger automated safety measures to mitigate risks. This helps prevent accidents, improve worker safety, and improve compliance with safety regulations.

IIoT applications can improve supply chain visibility and efficiency. By tracking assets, inventory, and shipments in real time, organizations can optimize logistics, reduce delays, and enhance inventory management. The IIoT also enables end-to-end traceability, ensuring product quality and facilitating compliance with regulatory requirements. IIoT solutions help organizations optimize energy consumption by monitoring and controlling energy-intensive processes and systems. Real-time data on energy usage, coupled with advanced analytics, enables organizations to identify energy-saving opportunities, implement energy management strategies, and reduce their environmental footprint.

6.2.1 What Is the Industrial Internet of Things?

Industry 4.0 represents a new era in the evolution of manufacturing and supply chain management (SCM). The IIoT offers significant opportunities for industries to optimize their operations, improve productivity, enhance safety, and drive innovation. By leveraging IoT technologies and data analytics, organizations can gain a competitive edge in the increasingly interconnected industrial landscape. It is characterized by a strong focus on interconnectivity, automation, machine learning, and real-time data analysis [17]. This concept, also referred to as IIoT or smart manufacturing, involves the integration of physical production and operations with digital technology, Big Data, and machine learning. Industry 4.0 provides a more comprehensive and interconnected ecosystem for businesses, enabling them to access real-time insights across processes, partners, products, and people. It is not just about investing in new technology to enhance manufacturing efficiency, but rather a complete transformation of how businesses operate and grow. Industry 1.0 to Industry 4.0 refers to the four major industrial revolutions that have shaped the evolution of manufacturing and industrial processes (Figure 6.2). Basically, the transition from Industry 1.0 to Industry 4.0 represents a significant shift in manufacturing paradigms, leveraging technological advancements to drive efficiency, productivity, and competitiveness in the industrial sector.

- **The First Industrial Revolution:** Also known as Industry 1.0, the First Industrial Revolution took place between the late 1700s and early 1800s,

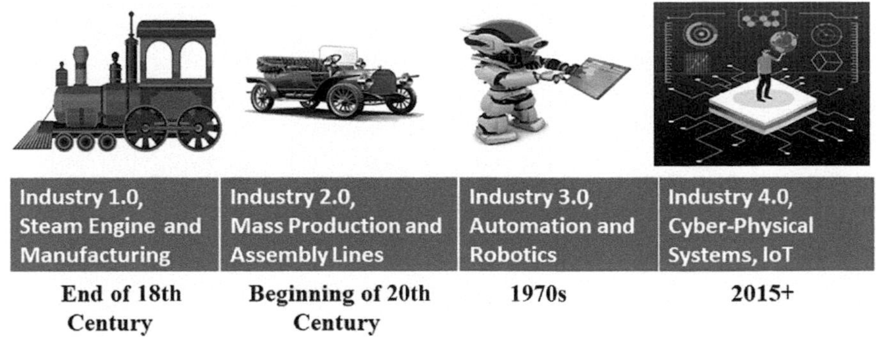

FIGURE 6.2 Historical evolution of the Industrial Internet of Things.

when manufacturing evolved from manual labor aided by work animals to steam and water-powered engines and machine tools [18]. Industry 1.0 was characterized by the mechanization of production through the introduction of water and steam power. This led to the development of factories and the transition from manual labor to machine-based production.

- **The Second Industrial Revolution:** Also known as Industry 2.0, the second phase emerged in the early 20th century with the introduction of electricity in factories, which increased efficiency and made factory machinery more mobile. The assembly line was introduced to boost productivity during this phase [19, 20]. Industry 2.0 was driven by advancements in electricity and the introduction of mass production techniques. The assembly line and interchangeable parts revolutionized manufacturing, enabling increased efficiency and productivity.
- **The Third Industrial Revolution:** Also known as Industry 3.0, the Third Industrial Revolution, which began in the late 1950s, was characterized by the integration of electronic and eventually computer technology into factories, emphasizing digital technology and automation. Industry 3.0 marked the era of automation and computerization. It involved the adoption of computers, electronics, and IT in manufacturing processes. This led to the emergence of programmable logic controllers (PLCs) and computer-controlled systems, enabling more sophisticated automation and control.
- **The Fourth Industrial Revolution:** Also known as Industry 4.0, the Fourth Industrial Revolution has emerged in recent decades. It builds on the digital technology emphasized in previous phases and takes it to a whole new level by incorporating interconnectivity through the IoT, real-time data, and cyber-physical systems. Industry 4.0 offers a comprehensive, interlinked, and holistic approach to manufacturing by digitally connecting partners, vendors, products, and people [21]. This enables business owners to better control and understand every aspect of their operations, leveraging instant data to boost productivity, improve processes, and drive growth. Industry 4.0 represents the integration of digital technologies, the IoT, and data-driven decision-making in manufacturing and industrial processes. It involves the use of advanced analytics, artificial intelligence (AI), robotics, and cyber-physical systems to create "smart factories" that are highly connected and intelligent. Industry 4.0 aims to enable real-time data exchange, automation, and optimization of production processes, leading to increased efficiency, flexibility, and customization. Industry 4.0 is characterized by the convergence of physical and digital systems, the use of Big Data analytics, cloud computing, and the IoT to create a connected ecosystem. It encompasses technologies such as AI, machine learning, additive manufacturing (3D printing), and autonomous systems. The goal is to create highly adaptable and responsive manufacturing systems that can meet changing demands, enable personalized production, and drive innovation.

6.2.2 Basic IIoT Concepts and Glossary of Terms

The IIoT pertains to the integration of advanced technologies with industrial infrastructures to enable intelligent processes, automated decision-making, information sharing, and optimized operations. The IIoT ecosystem includes a broad range of hardware devices, software applications, sensors, and connectivity technologies that enable real-time data acquisition, analysis, and processing. The following glossary of terms provides a basic overview of the most commonly used IIoT concepts and terminology [22].

1. **IoT:** The IoT is an overarching concept that refers to the interconnectivity of all kinds of devices, appliances, and machines, enabling them to exchange data and perform tasks.
2. **IIoT:** IIoT is a specific type of IoT that focuses on the integration of industrial equipment and infrastructures to enable data-driven decision-making and operational optimization.
3. **Edge Computing:** Edge computing refers to the decentralized processing of data on devices close to their source, reducing the load on central servers and enabling faster processing.
4. **Cloud Computing:** Cloud computing refers to the delivery of computer resources and services over the internet, including storage, processing power, and databases.
5. **Machine Learning:** Machine learning is a type of AI that enables computer programs to learn from data and improve their performance without being explicitly programmed.
6. **Big Data:** Big Data refers to extremely large datasets that require advanced technologies and methods to analyze and extract insights.
7. **Predictive Maintenance:** Predictive maintenance uses data analysis and machine learning to predict when maintenance is needed on industrial equipment, reducing downtime and maintenance costs.
8. **Digital Twin:** A digital twin is a virtual replica of a physical asset or system that enables real-time monitoring, modeling, and simulation.
9. **Cyber-security:** Cyber-security refers to the protection of computer systems and networks from cyber-threats such as hacking, malware, and data breaches.

6.2.3 Industry 4.0: Sub-Components

Industry 4.0 is an advanced manufacturing approach that combines modern technologies to enhance productivity and efficiency in the manufacturing process. The following sub-components of Industry 4.0 are important to understand.

6.2.3.1 The Cloud

Cloud computing is a fundamental technology that underpins the connected and intelligent systems of Industry 4.0. In this context, the cloud refers to a distributed network of servers, storage devices, and software applications that can be accessed remotely over the internet in a scalable and on-demand manner. In Industry 4.0, the cloud plays a crucial role in enabling the real-time collection, analysis, and sharing of data from smart sensors, machines, and devices. This data can then be used to optimize processes, improve quality, and drive innovation. Cloud computing also provides a flexible and affordable platform for hosting virtualized applications, digital services, and AI algorithms. This allows companies to rapidly scale their operations, experiment with new business models, and offer personalized products and services to their customers [23].

Moreover, the cloud enables secure and reliable communication between different stakeholders in the Industry 4.0 ecosystem, including suppliers, manufacturers, service providers, and customers. This can help to increase transparency, efficiency, and collaboration across the value chain. Overall, the cloud has emerged as an essential technology for realizing the full potential of Industry 4.0, enabling companies to stay competitive and agile in an increasingly complex and dynamic market environment.

6.2.3.2 Sensors and Connected Devices

Industry 4.0 is a new phase in the ongoing Industrial Revolution, characterized by the integration of digital and physical systems to create a highly automated and interconnected production environment. One of the major components of Industry 4.0 is the use of sensors and connected devices. Sensors are devices that detect and measure physical phenomena such as temperature, pressure, and vibration. They are used in various stages of the production process to monitor the performance of machines and equipment, detect faults, and optimize production. Connected devices refer to the multitude of devices that are connected to a network, such as cameras, smartphones, and computers. In Industry 4.0, connected devices are used to gather and transmit data from sensors and other sources, creating a vast network of information.

By using sensors and connected devices, the production environment becomes more flexible, efficient, and cost effective. Production processes can be monitored in real time, allowing for quicker response times and preventive maintenance. Connected devices also allow for the integration of data from different sources, enabling predictive analytics to optimize production. Overall, the use of sensors and connected devices is a crucial part of Industry 4.0 and has the potential to transform the way industries operate [24, 25].

6.2.3.3 Augmented Reality

Augmented Reality (AR) refers to a technology that superimposes digital information on top of the physical world through a device such as a smartphone or wearable headset. In the context of Industry 4.0, AR has the potential to revolutionize manufacturing and supply chain operations by providing real-time and context-sensitive information to workers [26]. AR can be used in several ways in Industry 4.0. For example, it can be used to overlay digital instructions and graphics onto physical objects, enabling workers to assemble and operate machinery with greater efficiency and accuracy. AR can also be used to provide workers with immersive training experiences, allowing them to practice complex processes in a virtual environment before attempting them in the real world.

In addition, AR can help companies optimize their supply chain operations by providing real-time data on inventory and logistics. For example, AR can be used to track shipments and provide workers with information on the contents of a package or the location of a product in a warehouse. Overall, AR has the potential to significantly increase productivity, efficiency, and safety in the manufacturing and logistics industries. As Industry 4.0 continues to evolve, we can expect to see even more innovative applications of AR in these fields.

6.2.3.4 Artificial Intelligence

Artificial intelligence (AI) refers to the development of computer systems that can perform tasks that normally require human cognition, such as learning, decision-making, and problem-solving. In the context of Industry 4.0, AI plays a key role in transforming the manufacturing industry to smart manufacturing by providing advanced data analytics, automation, and predictive maintenance [27]. Industry 4.0 integrates digital technologies such as AI, machine learning, Big Data, and IoT to create a smart manufacturing ecosystem. AI is at the forefront of this revolution and has the potential to create significant efficiencies in the production processes of industries. For instance, AI-powered predictive maintenance can help minimize downtime by predicting maintenance needs before a failure occurs, reducing costs and improving productivity. AI-powered automation can also reduce the need for manual intervention, freeing up labor resources for other tasks.

6.2.3.5 Big Data

Big Data in relation to Industry 4.0 refers to the massive amount of complex data produced and collected from various sources and devices. Industry 4.0 is a term used to describe the integration of advanced technologies such as IoT, AI, and robotics into industrial processes to increase efficiency, productivity, and sustainability. In Industry 4.0, Big Data is essential because it provides insights and actionable information that can be used to improve decision-making and optimize processes. Data is collected from sensors, machines, and other connected devices, and analyzed using AI algorithms to identify patterns, predict outcomes, and recommend actions. By harnessing the power of Big Data, Industry 4.0 companies can achieve greater levels of automation, customization, and quality control, while also reducing waste, energy consumption, and production costs. This, in turn, leads to increased competitiveness and customer satisfaction, as companies can deliver products faster, cheaper, and with higher accuracy. Overall, Big Data plays a crucial role in Industry 4.0 by enabling companies to leverage the vast amounts of data generated by industrial processes to drive innovation, improve efficiency, and achieve sustainable growth [28].

6.2.3.6 Digital Twin

Digital twin is a concept that has emerged as a key component of Industry 4.0. It refers to a virtual replica of a physical system, product, or process that is highly accurate and detailed. The digital twin can be used for a range of purposes, from simulating the behavior of the physical system to monitoring its performance in real time. The use of digital twin technology is expected to revolutionize manufacturing and other industries by improving product design, increasing efficiency, reducing downtime, and minimizing the need for physical testing. Digital twin technology involves the use of sensors, data analytics and machine learning algorithms to create a virtual replica of the physical system. This digital replica is then linked to the physical system using IoT technology. This allows for the real-time monitoring of the physical system, as well as the ability to simulate different scenarios using the virtual replica.

One of the key benefits of digital twin technology is its ability to improve product design. By creating a virtual replica of a product, manufacturers can test and optimize the design before it is physically produced. This can help to reduce costs and improve quality. Additionally, digital twin technology can improve efficiency by allowing for predictive maintenance. By monitoring the performance of a physical system in real time, manufacturers can identify potential issues before they occur, and schedule maintenance before downtime occurs. In conclusion, digital twin technology is a key component of Industry 4.0, and has the potential to revolutionize manufacturing and other industries. By creating a virtual replica of physical systems, products and processes, manufacturers can improve product design, increase efficiency, reduce downtime, and minimize the need for physical testing [29].

6.2.3.7 Cyber-Security

Cyber-security in relation to Industry 4.0 refers to the measures taken to protect digital assets—such as information, devices, and networks—against unauthorized access, theft, damage, or modification. Industry 4.0 is the integration of cutting-edge technologies such as AI, IoT, Big Data analytics, and cloud computing. This integration aims to develop intelligent and interconnected factories, machinery, and systems [30]. As Industry 4.0 continues to evolve and transform industries, cyber-threats are also becoming increasingly sophisticated and complex. Cyber-attackers can exploit vulnerabilities in connected devices and networks to gain access to sensitive data, disrupt operations, or cause physical harm. Therefore, organizations need to implement effective cyber-security strategies to safeguard their digital assets.

One key aspect of cyber-security in Industry 4.0 is the design and implementation of secure-by-design technology solutions. This involves building security features into IoT devices, networks, and software applications from the outset, rather than adding them on later. This approach helps to minimize the risk of cyber-attacks and provides a more reliable and resilient system. Another essential aspect of cyber-security is threat intelligence and detection. This involves using advanced analytics technologies such as machine learning and AI to monitor networks and identify suspicious activities or patterns. This enables organizations to respond quickly and efficiently to cyber-threats before they can cause significant damage. Furthermore, cyber-security requires a solid understanding of regulations and compliance standards such as the European Union's General Data Protection Regulation (GDPR) and the U.S. National Institute of Standards and Technology (NIST) Cybersecurity Framework. Organizations need to ensure that they are complying with these standards and that their cyber-security policies and procedures are up to date. In conclusion, cyber-security is a critical aspect of Industry 4.0, given the significant risks that come with innovative and connected digital technologies. By adopting a secure-by-design approach, leveraging advanced analytics, and complying with industry regulations and standards, organizations can effectively protect themselves against cyber-attacks and achieve a secure and successful digital transformation.

6.2.3.8 Additive Manufacturing and Digital Scanning

Additive manufacturing is a technological process that enables the creation of three-dimensional objects by layering materials on top of each other, using a digital model. The process involves the use of specialized machines, known as 3D printers, which deposit thin layers of material—such as plastic, metal, or ceramic—one layer at a time to build the final product. Additive manufacturing, also known as 3D printing or rapid prototyping, has revolutionized the manufacturing industry, facilitating the production of more complex parts and reducing costs, time, and waste [31]. On the other hand, digital scanning is the process of taking a physical object and converting it into a digital model. This is done using specialized software and hardware such as lasers and cameras that capture the object's shape and size. The resulting digital model can be used for a variety of purposes, including design and analysis, quality inspection, and reverse engineering. Together, additive manufacturing and digital scanning have transformed the manufacturing industry, enabling faster prototyping, rapid customization, and on-demand production. In addition, these technologies have reduced waste and material costs, and have led to new business models, such as distributed manufacturing.

6.2.4 Who Is Industry 4.0 Right for?

Industry 4.0 technology and solution providers can help organizations achieve improved efficiency and profitability, among other benefits. However, it is essential to assess whether an organization is suited to adopt this technology. Industry 4.0 is useful to a wide range of stakeholders in various industries. Industry 4.0 offers significant benefits to manufacturing companies. It enables them to enhance operational efficiency, optimize production processes, reduce costs, improve product quality, and increase productivity. By leveraging technologies like automation, IoT, AI, and Big Data analytics, manufacturing companies can achieve greater agility, flexibility, and responsiveness in their operations. Industry 4.0 has the potential to transform the work environment and empower workers. It can lead to the development of new job roles that focus on managing and maintaining advanced technologies. Additionally, by automating repetitive and mundane tasks, workers can be freed up to focus on more creative and complex tasks, leading to increased job satisfaction and skill development. Industry 4.0 enables companies to deliver products and services that are better customized to meet individual customer needs. Through real-time data analytics and IoT connectivity, companies can gather customer insights, personalize products, improve customer service, and enhance the overall customer experience.

Industry 4.0 technologies allow for better visibility and collaboration across the supply chain. Supply chain partners can leverage real-time data and analytics to improve demand forecasting, optimize inventory management, enhance logistics and transportation efficiency, and enable seamless information sharing among stakeholders. Industry 4.0 opens up new opportunities for equipment and machinery manufacturers. By incorporating IoT sensors and connectivity in their products, they can provide advanced monitoring, predictive maintenance, and remote management capabilities. This helps in reducing downtime, enhancing equipment performance, and providing value-added services to customers. Industry 4.0 creates a demand for specialized services and technologies to support the implementation and integration of advanced systems. Service providers and technology vendors offering IoT platforms, cloud computing, cyber-security solutions, data analytics tools, and consulting services play a crucial role in enabling companies to adopt and leverage Industry 4.0 technologies.

The following factors can help determine an organization's suitability for Industry 4.0 technology [26–29].

1. The organization operates in a highly competitive industry with a significant number of tech-savvy players.
2. The organization faces difficulties in recruiting employees to fill vacant positions.
3. The organization desires better visibility throughout its supply chain.
4. The organization aims to identify and address problems before they escalate.
5. The organization seeks to provide its team members with informed, up-to-date, and relevant views of production and business processes.
6. The organization wants access to richer and more timely analytics.
7. The organization requires assistance in digitizing and making sense of information.
8. The organization aims to improve customer satisfaction and experience.
9. The organization wants to improve or maintain product quality.
10. The organization seeks to implement an integrated enterprise resource planning system that encompasses various functional areas such as inventory management, financials, CRM, SCM, planning, and manufacturing execution.
11. The organization requires a consistent and flexible view of production and business operations tailored to specific areas or users within the organization.
12. The organization wants real-time insights to facilitate better decision-making.

The deployment of sensors and IoT devices in the manufacturing shop floor introduces additional vulnerabilities that require convergence between IT security and OT (operational technology) security. Industrial systems such as robots and digital automation platforms also require strong cyber-security to ensure their safety [23]. The integration of machine learning and AI in industrial systems has introduced new security risks such as attacks that target deep neural networks like poisoning and evasion attacks. These security challenges necessitate a comprehensive approach to secure industrial systems starting from the device level, and extending to the edge and cloud levels. Additionally, the exchange of digital models for 3D printing necessitates the encryption of sensitive data to protect intellectual property rights [26–28]. In conclusion, organizations that satisfy most of these criteria mentioned can consider evaluating Industry 4.0 technology and solution providers while allocating the necessary resources for deployment. Overall, Industry 4.0 benefits various stakeholders involved in manufacturing and related industries, enabling them to achieve higher efficiency, productivity, innovation, and customer satisfaction. It has the potential to drive economic growth, competitiveness, and sustainable development in a digitized and interconnected world.

6.2.5 Benefits of Adopting an Industry 4.0 Model

Industry 4.0 covers the entire product life cycle and supply chain, comprising various aspects such as design, sales, inventory, scheduling, quality, engineering, customer service, and field service. It provides all stakeholders with accurate real-time insights into production and business processes, facilitating more comprehensive and timely analytics. Following is a non-exhaustive list of some benefits that adopting an Industry 4.0 model can offer to businesses [32, 33].

1. **Increased Competitiveness:** In today's business landscape, Amazon's success in optimizing logistics and SCM highlights the need for other businesses to invest in technology and solutions to improve their own operations. Implementing Industry 4.0 systems and processes can enable businesses to provide the same level of service (or better) as Amazon, thereby maintaining their competitiveness.
2. **Attraction of a Younger Workforce:** Organizations that embrace advanced and contemporary Industry 4.0 technologies are in a more favorable position to appeal to and retain younger employees.
3. **Enhanced Collaboration:** Industry 4.0 solutions can boost collaboration between departments, increase efficiency, allow predictive and prescriptive analytics, and enable people at all levels to leverage real-time data and intelligence to make better decisions.
4. **Proactive Issue Resolution:** The integration of predictive analytics, real-time data, internet-connected machinery, and automation can enhance the ability of businesses to identify and address potential maintenance and SCM issues proactively.
5. **Cost Reduction and Profitability:** Industry 4.0 technologies allow for the management and optimization of all aspects of manufacturing processes and supply chain and provide access to real-time data and insights. This can lead to smarter and faster decision-making, increased efficiency, and—ultimately—profitability.

The use of IT systems and enterprise applications such as enterprise resource planning (ERP) and manufacturing execution systems (MES) has been prevalent in the manufacturing industry for several decades. However, the true transformative aspect of Industry 4.0 lies in the expanded use of embedded sensors throughout the value chain [24, 25]. These sensors convert manufacturing assets into cyber-physical systems and allow for numerous optimizations that were previously impossible. For instance, embedded sensors can monitor machines' conditions and optimize maintenance schedules, thereby reducing unplanned downtimes and maximizing their utilization. They also enable continuous quality monitoring of products and parts as part of quality management. The collection and analysis of data from embedded sensors and other IIoT technologies facilitate product innovation and the creation of new business opportunities. Overall, embedded sensors play a crucial role in increasing efficiencies by converting raw digital data into actionable insights and automation actions on the factory floor [24].

6.2.6 IIoT Stack and 5G

IIoT refers to the use of internet-connected devices in industrial settings to collect and analyze data to improve efficiency and productivity. The IIoT stack comprises four main elements—intelligent assets, data communications, applications and analytics, and people—as shown in Figure 6.3. These four elements form the IIoT stack, creating an interconnected ecosystem that enables the seamless flow of data, intelligent asset management, data analysis, and human interaction. The integration and collaboration of these elements empower organizations to leverage the full potential of IIoT in industrial settings by driving digital transformation, operational efficiency, and innovation.

1. **Intelligent Assets:** Intelligent assets are an essential component of the IIoT stack. These assets may include industrial robots, IoT-enabled machinery, and other IoT devices that contain connected sensors, embedded sensors, and RFID (radio frequency identification) readers [34]. These sensors collect data and transmit it to the applications and analytics layer for processing and analysis. These intelligent assets form the foundation of the IIoT ecosystem by capturing and transmitting data from the industrial environment. Examples include sensors on machines, smart meters, connected vehicles, and wearable devices.
2. **Data Communications:** The data communications layer enables the transmission of data from intelligent assets to IT applications or other internet-connected objects. Data communications encompass the networks, protocols, and connectivity technologies that enable the transfer of data between intelligent assets and other components of the IIoT ecosystem. This includes wired and wireless networks, such as Ethernet, Wi-Fi, cellular networks, and industrial communication protocols like MQTT, OPC-UA, and Modbus. Data communications ensure seamless and reliable data exchange

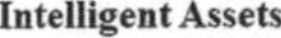

FIGURE 6.3 IIoT stack elements.

within the IIoT system. This layer includes various communication protocols, such as Wi-Fi, Ethernet, Bluetooth, and cellular connectivity [35]. It ensures that data is transmitted efficiently and securely.

3. **Applications and Analytics:** Applications and analytics are the third layer of the IIoT stack. These components collect and analyze data from intelligent assets and IoT devices, and they are typically integrated into a cloud infrastructure [36]. The applications and analytics layer enables organizations to gain insights from the data collected, optimize operations, and make data-driven decisions [37]. This element involves the software applications, platforms, and analytics tools used to process, analyze, and derive insights from the collected data. IIoT applications can range from real-time monitoring and control systems to advanced analytics platforms that enable predictive maintenance, asset optimization, and operational efficiency. These applications enable data visualization, predictive modeling, anomaly detection, and other analytical capabilities to make informed decisions and drive business value.
4. **People:** The people element of the IIoT stack represents the human users who interact with the IIoT system and utilize the insights and information generated by the intelligent assets and analytics. This includes various stakeholders such as operators, technicians, engineers, managers, and decision-makers who leverage IIoT data and applications to optimize processes, improve productivity, and make informed business decisions. People play a crucial role in interpreting and acting upon the insights provided by the IIoT system [38].

The newly developed standard for mobile networks called 5G has been designed to provide fast data throughput rates and low latency. With 5G, download speeds of up to 20 Gbps and sub-millisecond latency can be supported. The introduction of 5G technology is expected to affect the adoption of IIoT devices in the following two main ways [38].

- The fast data transfer speeds and minimal delay offered by 5G technology have the potential to enable real-time sharing of information between devices. This capability will be beneficial in various applications, such as autonomous vehicles and intelligent urban environments.
- 5G's high speed and low latency will likely result in device proliferation, enabling IIoT devices to be used in remote sites where lack of high-speed connectivity previously made IIoT use impractical.

Edge computing is also becoming increasingly important for IIoT applications. Edge computing involves data collection and processing close to the field, within infrastructures like edge clusters, IoT gateways, and edge devices. This is particularly useful for real-time, low-latency applications that cannot tolerate delays in transferring and processing data in the cloud. Edge computing offers improved data security compared to cloud computing by keeping data within the local edge devices instead of transmitting it to external cloud data centers of the manufacturing enterprise [39]. Moreover, performing edge analytics, which includes utilizing AI algorithms on edge devices, proves to be significantly more energy-efficient than cloud-based analytics [40]. As a result, industrial enterprises typically utilize both cloud computing and edge computing for their IIoT use cases, depending on the application's specific demands [41].

6.3 WHAT IS NB-IOT?

In today's world, connectivity and communication have become an essential aspect of our daily lives. IoT has revolutionized the way we communicate and interact with our electronic devices. The IoT infrastructure and the devices connected to it require a stable and reliable network connection that can transmit and receive data. This is where the Narrowband Internet of Things (NB-IoT) comes in. NB-IoT is a low-power wide-area network (LPWAN) technology specifically designed for IoT devices [42]. The history of NB-IoT dates to 2012, when a group of companies—including Nokia, Qualcomm, and Huawei—started working on the creation of a specialized IoT network called LTE-M (Long-Term Evolution for Machines). This network was designed to provide stable and reliable connectivity for IoT devices. However, LTE-M had some limitations, such as high-power consumption and relatively high cost per device. To overcome these limitations, the 3rd Generation Partnership Project (3GPP) in late 2014 proposed the development of a new network for low-power devices. This led to the introduction of NB-IoT as a new standard for IoT networks. NB-IoT became an official 3GPP standard in June 2016 [43].

The concept of NB-IoT is based on the use of cellular networks to provide connectivity to IoT devices. NB-IoT is a wireless communication technology that is designed to provide stable and reliable connectivity to IoT devices. NB-IoT networks operate in the licensed spectrum, which ensures a high-quality service and data security. NB-IoT uses narrowband radio-frequency channels to transmit data with low power consumption, making it ideal for IoT devices [44]. NB-IoT networks have three deployment options: in-band, standalone, and guard-band. In-band deployment involves using a portion of an existing LTE cellular network to provide NB-IoT coverage, which allows seamless integration of NB-IoT devices into the existing LTE infrastructure. Standalone deployment, on the other hand, is a separate dedicated network built specifically for IoT devices, with no integration with the existing cellular network. Guard-band deployment involves using the space between existing cellular networks to deploy NB-IoT, which is an efficient way to utilize scarce resources. NB-IoT operates in the 800 MHz band and lower, which is a licensed spectrum that is exclusively dedicated to IoT devices. The technology is designed to operate in areas with poor coverage, such as underground parking lots, basements, and remote areas. NB-IoT also has a coverage range of up to 100 kilometers, which is significantly higher than other LPWAN technologies currently available [45]. NB-IoT technology is designed to offer several benefits over other IoT connectivity options, such as Wi-Fi and Bluetooth. NB-IoT offers improved coverage, low power consumption, and secure communication, making it an ideal choice for several IoT use cases [46].

1. **Improved Coverage:** NB-IoT offers improved coverage compared to other LPWAN technologies. The technology is designed to operate in areas with

poor coverage, such as underground parking lots, basements, and remote areas. NB-IoT networks have a penetration rate of up to 20 dB, which means the signal can penetrate through walls and other obstacles, ensuring connectivity even in hard-to-reach areas.

2. **Low Power Consumption:** One of the essential features of NB-IoT is low power consumption. The technology is specifically designed to minimize the power consumption of IoT devices, which means the devices can operate for several years without requiring a battery change. The technology uses narrowband radio-frequency channels to transmit data, which reduces the power consumption of the device significantly.
3. **Secure Communication:** NB-IoT uses licensed spectrum frequencies, which ensures a high-quality service and data security. The technology also uses advanced encryption methods to secure communication between devices, ensuring data privacy and security.

6.3.1 Features of NB-IoT

NB-IoT is a wireless communication technology designed specifically for the IoT. Following are some important features of NB-IoT [47].

1. **Low Power Consumption:** NB-IoT is designed to consume minimal power, making it an ideal solution for devices that need to operate with low power for extended periods.
2. **Wide Area Coverage:** NB-IoT is designed to work in challenging environments with low signal strength, which allows it to provide better coverage over a wider area.
3. **Low Device Cost:** NB-IoT technology is relatively inexpensive to implement, which makes it an affordable option for IoT device manufacturers.
4. **Secure Communication:** NB-IoT uses secure encryption protocols to ensure that communication between devices and the network is secure.
5. **Improved Data Transmission:** With a higher data transmission rate, NB-IoT enables fast and reliable data transmission over long distances, even in low signal environments.
6. **Compatibility with Existing Cellular Networks:** NB-IoT is designed to work with existing 4G LTE networks, which makes it easier to deploy and reduces the need for building new infrastructure.
7. **Scalable and Future-Proof:** NB-IoT is highly scalable and can handle many devices, making it future-proof as IoT networks continue to grow.

6.3.2 NB-IoT Frequency Spectrum

NB-IoT is a wireless communication technology that enables devices to transmit data over long distances with low power consumption. This technology makes use of a specific frequency spectrum for communication. NB-IoT operates in the licensed spectrum, specifically within the cellular spectrum bands allocated for the deployment of IoT devices. The frequency spectrum used by NB-IoT varies across different

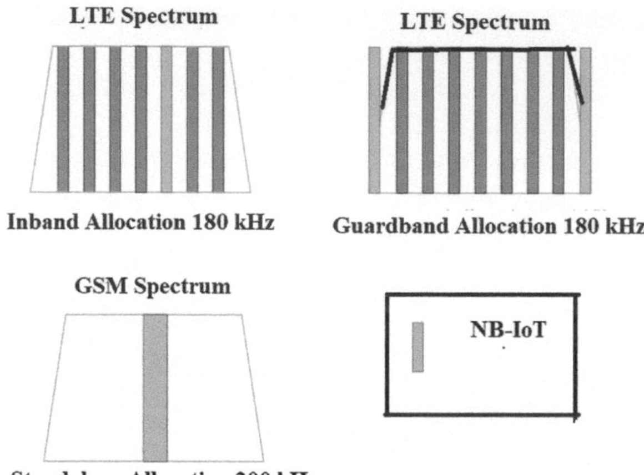

FIGURE 6.4 NB-IoT frequency spectrum.

regions and countries, depending on the regulatory framework and spectrum allocation policies. However, there are certain frequency bands that are commonly used for NB-IoT deployment worldwide [46, 47]. The frequency spectrum for NB-IoT typically falls within the following frequency bands such as Band 5, Band 8, Band 20, and so on, as shown in Figure 6.4.

Band 5 operates in the frequency range of 824–849 MHz for uplink and 869–894 MHz for downlink. This frequency band is commonly used for NB-IoT deployments in North America, Latin America, and some parts of Asia. It provides good coverage and propagation characteristics, making it suitable for outdoor and indoor IoT applications. Band 8 operates in the frequency range of 880–915 MHz for uplink and 925–960 MHz for downlink. Band 8 NB-IoT deployments in Europe, Africa, and some parts of Asia and the Pacific often utilize the 900 MHz band. It offers good coverage and penetration capabilities, making it suitable for wide-area IoT application. Band 20 operates in the frequency range of 832–862 MHz for uplink and 791–821 MHz for downlink. NB-IoT deployments in Europe, Russia, and some parts of Asia utilize the 800 MHz band. It provides good coverage and can penetrate obstacles effectively, making it suitable for applications requiring long-range connectivity. The spectrum is suitable for low-power, low–data-rate applications, such as smart metering, asset tracking, and remote monitoring. The NB-IoT frequency spectrum has a higher resistance to interference and can support many devices in a single cell.

6.3.3 What Are the Advantages and Applications of Using NB-IoT?

NB-IoT is a standard for wireless communication that is specifically designed for IoT devices. It offers a range of benefits over other wireless technologies like Bluetooth, Wi-Fi or Zigbee, which makes it an ideal choice for IoT applications. Its wide coverage, low power consumption, cost effectiveness, scalability, security, reliability, and compatibility with existing networks contribute to its appeal as an efficient and reliable connectivity solution for IoT deployments. Following are some of the advantages of using NB-IoT [46, 47].

1. **Wide Coverage:** NB-IoT provides excellent coverage, even in hard-to-reach areas such as basements, underground spaces, and remote locations. Its superior signal penetration capabilities allow for connectivity in challenging environments, enabling IoT devices to communicate effectively over long distances.
2. **Low Power Consumption:** NB-IoT is designed to operate with low power consumption, enabling battery-powered IoT devices to operate for extended periods without frequent recharging or battery replacement. This makes NB-IoT ideal for applications in which long battery life is crucial, such as remote monitoring, asset tracking, and environmental sensing.
3. **Scalability:** NB-IoT supports massive device connectivity, enabling the deployment of large-scale IoT solutions. It can handle a high density of connected devices in a given area, making it well suited for applications requiring a large number of IoT devices, such as smart cities, industrial automation, and asset tracking.
4. **Secure Communication:** NB-IoT incorporates robust security mechanisms to protect IoT data and ensure secure communication. It utilizes encryption protocols, secure authentication, and data integrity measures, safeguarding sensitive information transmitted between IoT devices and the network. This helps address the security concerns associated with IoT deployments.
5. **High Reliability:** NB-IoT networks provide reliable connectivity, minimizing the risk of data loss or disruption. The technology is designed to operate in licensed spectrum bands, ensuring interference-free communication. This reliability is particularly important for critical applications such as healthcare monitoring, industrial automation, and public safety systems.
6. **Cost Effective:** NB-IoT offers cost advantages in terms of both infrastructure deployment and device connectivity. It utilizes existing cellular infrastructure, allowing for cost-efficient deployment and leveraging economies of scale. Additionally, NB-IoT chipsets and modules are designed to be cost effective, making them suitable for low-cost IoT device deployments.
7. **Coexistence with Cellular Networks:** NB-IoT can coexist with existing cellular networks—including 2G, 3G, and 4G networks—which allows seamless integration and backward compatibility. This compatibility enables a smooth transition and integration of NB-IoT with existing network infrastructure, reducing deployment complexities and facilitating adoption.

NB-IoT is basically a LPWAN technology specifically designed for connecting low-cost IoT devices over long distances. It offers several key advantages, such as long battery life, deep indoor penetration, and excellent coverage in challenging environments. NB-IoT can be used in smart city applications like smart streetlights, waste management, and traffic monitoring. NB-IoT can be used in agricultural applications like soil moisture monitoring, weather forecasting, and irrigation control.

NB-IoT can be used in healthcare applications like patient monitoring, health tracking, and medication reminders. NB-IoT can be used in industrial automation applications like smart factories, SCM, and asset tracking. NB-IoT can also be used in smart home applications like home automation, energy management, and security systems. We will next discuss few dominant applications in detail.

1. **Smart Metering:** NB-IoT enables remote monitoring and management of utility meters, such as electricity, gas, and water meters. It facilitates automated meter reading, accurate data collection, and real-time tracking of consumption. This enhances efficiency in utility management, enables better resource planning, and allows for timely billing and demand response initiatives.
2. **Asset Tracking:** NB-IoT enables cost-effective and energy-efficient tracking of assets across different industries. It allows organizations to monitor and manage the location, condition, and movement of assets in real time. This is particularly beneficial for tracking high-value goods, logistics management, supply chain optimization, and theft prevention.
3. **Environmental Monitoring:** NB-IoT can be used to monitor various environmental parameters, such as air quality, pollution levels, humidity, and temperature. This data can be collected from remote locations and used to analyze and improve environmental conditions, support urban planning, and enhance public health and safety.
4. **Agriculture:** NB-IoT enables smart agriculture applications, including soil monitoring, irrigation management, and livestock tracking. It helps farmers optimize water usage, monitor crop health, and improve overall agricultural productivity. NB-IoT can also facilitate precision farming techniques, enabling targeted application of fertilizers and pesticides based on real-time data.
5. **Smart Cities:** NB-IoT contributes to the development of smart cities by enabling a wide range of applications. It can be used for smart parking systems, waste management, street lighting control, public safety monitoring, and intelligent transportation systems. NB-IoT enables efficient resource utilization, enhances citizen services, and improves overall quality of life.
6. **Healthcare Monitoring:** NB-IoT can be utilized for remote patient monitoring, telemedicine, and healthcare tracking applications. It enables the collection of vital health data from patients in real time, allowing healthcare providers to monitor their conditions remotely and provide timely interventions. NB-IoT facilitates improved healthcare access, reduces hospital visits, and enhances patient care.
7. **Industrial Automation:** NB-IoT can be integrated into industrial automation systems for remote monitoring and control of equipment and processes. It enables predictive maintenance, enhances equipment uptime, and reduces operational costs. By connecting sensors and devices, NB-IoT enables the collection of data from industrial environments, supporting data-driven decision-making and process optimization.

6.3.4 How Does NB-IoT Differ from Sigfox and LoRa?

NB-IoT is a technology used for LPWANs aimed at facilitating the communication of low data rates from connected objects. NB-IoT is generally used for devices that only require sending and receiving small amounts of data, such as tracking or monitoring devices [48, 49]. NB-IoT, Sigfox, and LoRa are all LPWAN technologies designed for IoT applications. It is important to note that the selection of NB-IoT, Sigfox, or LoRa depends on various factors such as specific use cases, desired coverage, data requirements, power consumption constraints, and available infrastructure. Each technology has its strengths and limitations, and is suitable for different IoT applications based on the specific requirements and priorities of the deployment. Although they serve a similar purpose of providing long-range, low-power connectivity for IoT devices, the following are some key differences between them [50, 51].

1. **Network Architecture:** NB-IoT and LoRa operate on licensed radio spectrum, whereas Sigfox operates on unlicensed radio spectrum. NB-IoT uses a traditional cellular network infrastructure with base stations, while LoRa uses a gateway architecture for data routing. Sigfox, on the other hand, uses a star network topology. NB-IoT operates within the existing cellular network infrastructure. It utilizes licensed spectrum and operates alongside traditional cellular technologies like 2G, 3G, and 4G. In contrast, Sigfox and LoRa operate on unlicensed spectrum and require the deployment of dedicated gateways or base stations to create a network infrastructure.
2. **Spectrum Availability:** NB-IoT operates in spectrum bands which are licensed, regulated, and allocated by authorities such as telecommunications regulatory bodies. Sigfox and LoRa, on the other hand, operate in unlicensed spectrum bands which are available for public use without the need for specific licenses.
3. **Data Rates:** NB-IoT generally has higher data rates than both LoRa and Sigfox. NB-IoT provides peak data rates of up to 250 Kbps, while LoRa's data rates range from 0.3–50 Kbps depending on the configuration. Sigfox only offers data rates of up to 100 bps.
4. **Power Consumption:** NB-IoT is designed to be highly power-efficient, and it can operate on batteries for up to 10 years. LoRa also has low power consumption but consumes more power than NB-IoT. Sigfox is the most power-efficient of the three technologies. In other words, NB-IoT is optimized for low power consumption, allowing devices to operate on battery power for extended periods. Sigfox and LoRa also offer low-power capabilities but may consume slightly more power compared to NB-IoT devices.
5. **Coverage:** NB-IoT provides better coverage than both LoRa and Sigfox, with better penetration into buildings and underground. LoRa's coverage depends on the location and terrain, while Sigfox provides minimal coverage and is mostly used in urban areas. In general, Sigfox and LoRa are designed to provide long-range coverage, often spanning several kilometers. They are suitable for applications that require wide-area coverage. NB-IoT also offers good coverage but may have slightly shorter-range capabilities.

6. **Scalability:** NB-IoT leverages existing cellular infrastructure, which enables it to benefit from the extensive coverage and scalability of cellular networks. Sigfox and LoRa networks require the deployment of dedicated gateways or base stations, making their scalability dependent on the expansion of the network infrastructure.
7. **Cost:** The cost of deploying and operating NB-IoT, Sigfox, and LoRa networks can vary. NB-IoT leverages existing cellular infrastructure, which may result in higher infrastructure costs. Sigfox and LoRa networks require the deployment of dedicated gateways or base stations, which may have associated costs. The cost of devices and network services also varies between the different technologies.

REFERENCES

[1] V. Mohanan, R. Budiarto, and I. Aldmour, *Powering the Internet of Things with 5G Networks*, IGI Global, Pennsylvania, United States, pp. 1–304, 2017, doi: 10.4018/978-1-5225-2799-2.

[2] S. Sicari, A. Rizzardi, and A. Coen-Porisini, "5G In the Internet of Things Era: An Overview on Security and Privacy Challenges," *Comput. Netw.*, vol. 179, 2020, doi: 10.1016/j.comnet.2020.107345.

[3] M. R. Palattella, "Internet of Things in the 5G Era : Enabling Technologies and Business Models," *IEEE J. Sel. Areas Commun.*, vol. 34, no. 3, pp. 510–527, December 2015, doi: 10.1109/JSAC.2016.2525418.

[4] N. Varsier, L. A. Dufrene, M. Dumay, Q. Lampin, and J. Schwoerer, "A 5G New Radio for Balanced and Mixed IoT Use Cases: Challenges and Key Enablers in FR1 Band," *IEEE Commun. Mag.*, vol. 59, no. 4, 2021, doi: 10.1109/MCOM.001.2000660.

[5] K. Shafique, B. A. Khawaja, F. Sabir, S. Qazi, and M. Mustaqim, "Internet of Things (IoT) for Next-Generation Smart Systems: A Review of Current Challenges, Future Trends and Prospects for Emerging 5G-IoT Scenarios," *IEEE Access*, vol. 8, 2020, doi: 10.1109/ACCESS.2020.2970118.

[6] M. Torres Vega *et al.*, "Immersive Interconnected Virtual and Augmented Reality: A 5G and IoT Perspective," *J. Netw. Syst. Manag.*, vol. 28, no. 4, 2020, doi: 10.1007/s10922-020-09545-w.

[7] M. R. Palattella *et al.*, "Internet of Things in the 5G Era: Enablers, Architecture, and Business Models," *IEEE J. Sel. Areas Commun.*, vol. 34, no. 3, 2016, doi: 10.1109/JSAC.2016.2525418.

[8] R. S. Alonso, I. Sittón-Candanedo, Ó. García, J. Prieto, and S. Rodríguez-González, "An Intelligent Edge-IoT Platform for Monitoring Livestock and Crops in a Dairy Farming Scenario," *Ad Hoc Netw.*, vol. 98, 2020, doi: 10.1016/j.adhoc.2019.102047.

[9] S. K. Goudos, P. I. Dallas, S. Chatziefthymiou, and S. Kyriazakos, "A Survey of IoT Key Enabling and Future Technologies: 5G, Mobile IoT, Sematic Web and Applications," *Wirel. Pers. Commun.*, vol. 97, no. 2, 2017, doi: 10.1007/s11277-017-4647-8.

[10] A. El Mahjoubi, T. Mazri, and N. Hmina, "NB-IoT and eMTC: Engineering Results Towards 5G/IoT Mobile Technologies," *Int. J. Interact. Mob. Technol.*, vol. 13, no. 1, 2019, doi: 10.3991/ijim.v13i01.9728.

[11] F. Ghavimi and H. H. Chen, "M2M Communications in 3GPP LTE/LTE-A Networks: Architectures, Service Requirements, Challenges, and Applications," *IEEE Commun. Surv. Tutor.*, vol. 17, no. 2, 2015, doi: 10.1109/COMST.2014.2361626.

[12] M. Beale, H. Uchiyama, and J. C. Clifton, "IoT Evolution: What's Next?," *IEEE Wirel. Commun.*, vol. 28, no. 5, 2021, doi: 10.1109/MWC.2021.9615126.

[13] CtiGroup, "IoT vs IIoT," *PT. Computrade Technology International*, 2016.
[14] X. Wang, L. T. Yang, Y. Wang, L. Ren, and M. J. Deen, "ADTT: A Highly Efficient Distributed Tensor-Train Decomposition Method for IIoT Big Data," *IEEE Trans. Ind. Inform.*, vol. 17, no. 3, 2021, doi: 10.1109/TII.2020.2967768.
[15] A. Esfahani *et al.*, "A Lightweight Authentication Mechanism for M2M Communications in Industrial IoT Environment," *IEEE Internet Things J.*, vol. 6, no. 1, 2019, doi: 10.1109/JIOT.2017.2737630.
[16] Y. K. Teoh, S. S. Gill, and A. K. Parlikad, "IoT and Fog Computing based Predictive Maintenance Model for Effective Asset Management in Industry 4.0 Using Machine Learning," *IEEE Internet Things J.*, vol. 10, no. 3, pp. 2087–2094, 2021, doi: 10.1109/JIOT.2021.3050441.
[17] A. Dridi, H. Afifi, H. Moungla, and J. Badosa, "A Novel Deep Reinforcement Approach for IIoT Microgrid Energy Management Systems," *IEEE Trans. Green Commun. Netw.*, vol. 6, no. 1, 2022, doi: 10.1109/TGCN.2021.3112043.
[18] T. Hafeez, L. Xu, and G. McArdle, "Edge Intelligence for Data Handling and Predictive Maintenance in IIoT," *IEEE Access*, vol. 9, 2021, doi: 10.1109/ACCESS.2021.3069137.
[19] S. K. Tan and S. Rajah, "Evoking Work Motivation in Industry 4.0," *SAGE Open*, vol. 9, no. 4, 2019, doi: 10.1177/2158244019885132.
[20] M. Xu, J. M. David, and S. H. Kim, "The Fourth Industrial Revolution: Opportunities and Challenges," *Int. J. Financ. Res.*, vol. 9, no. 2, 2018, doi: 10.5430/ijfr.v9n2p90.
[21] N. Matkovčíková, "Methods Used in Personnel Audit in Companies Operating in the Slovak Republic in the Stage of Industrial Revolution 4.0," *SHS Web Conf.*, vol. 83, 2020, doi: 10.1051/shsconf/20208301043.
[22] S. D. Milic and B. M. Babic, "Toward the Future—Upgrading Existing Remote Monitoring Concepts to IIoT Concepts," *IEEE Internet Things J.*, vol. 7, no. 12, 2020, doi: 10.1109/JIOT.2020.2999196.
[23] Y. Lu, J. Li, and Y. Zhang, "Privacy-Preserving and Pairing-Free Multirecipient Certificateless Encryption With Keyword Search for Cloud-Assisted IIoT," *IEEE Internet Things J.*, vol. 7, no. 4, 2020, doi: 10.1109/JIOT.2019.2943379.
[24] V. P. Gupta, "Smart Sensors and Industrial IoT (IIoT): A Driver of the Growth of Industry 4.0," in *Smart Sensors for Industrial Internet of Things*, Springer Science and Business Media Deutschland GmbH, Berlin, Germany, pp. 37–49, 2021, doi: 10.1007/978-3-030-52624-5_3.
[25] J. Arm *et al.*, "Automated Design and Integration of Asset Administration Shells in Components of Industry 4.0," *Sensors*, vol. 21, no. 6, 2021, doi: 10.3390/s21062004.
[26] J. Rosales, S. Deshpande, and S. Anand, "IIoT Based Augmented Reality for Factory Data Collection and Visualization," *Procedia Manuf.*, vol. 53, 2021, doi: 10.1016/j.promfg.2021.06.062.
[27] S. Zhu, K. Ota, and M. Dong, "Green AI for IIoT: Energy Efficient Intelligent Edge Computing for Industrial Internet of Things," *IEEE Trans. Green Commun. Netw.*, vol. 6, no. 1, 2022, doi: 10.1109/TGCN.2021.3100622.
[28] P. Qvist-Sørensen, "Applying IIoT and AI—Opportunities, Requirements and Challenges for Industrial Machine and Equipment Manufacturers to Expand Their Services," *Cent. Eur. Bus. Rev.*, vol. 9, no. 2, 2020, doi: 10.18267/j.cebr.234.
[29] D. Guo, R. Y. Zhong, Y. Rong, and G. G. Q. Huang, "Synchronization of Shop-Floor Logistics and Manufacturing Under IIoT and Digital Twin-Enabled Graduation Intelligent Manufacturing System," *IEEE Trans. Cybern.*, vol. 53, no. 3, pp. 2005–2016, 2023, doi: 10.1109/TCYB.2021.3108546.
[30] K. Tange, M. De Donno, X. Fafoutis, and N. Dragoni, "A Systematic Survey of Industrial Internet of Things Security: Requirements and Fog Computing Opportunities," *IEEE Commun. Surv. Tutor.*, vol. 22, no. 4, 2020, doi: 10.1109/COMST.2020.3011208.

[31] M. Ammar, A. Haleem, M. Javaid, S. Bahl, and A. S. Verma, "Implementing Industry 4.0 Technologies in Self-Healing Materials and Digitally Managing the Quality of Manufacturing," *Mater. Today: Proc.*, vol. 52, 2021, doi: 10.1016/j.matpr.2021.09.248.
[32] I. S. Khan, M. O. Ahmad, and J. Majava, "Industry 4.0 and Sustainable Development: A Systematic Mapping of Triple Bottom Line, Circular Economy and Sustainable Business Models Perspectives," *J. Clean Prod.*, vol. 297, 2021, doi: 10.1016/j.jclepro.2021.126655.
[33] D. Alami and W. ElMaraghy, "A Cost Benefit Analysis for Industry 4.0 in a Job Shop Environment Using a Mixed Integer Linear Programming Model," *J. Manuf. Syst.*, vol. 59, 2021, doi: 10.1016/j.jmsy.2021.01.014.
[34] J. Navarro-Ortiz, S. Sendra, P. Ameigeiras, and J. M. Lopez-Soler, "Integration of LoRaWAN and 4G/5G for the Industrial Internet of Things," *IEEE Commun. Mag.*, vol. 56, no. 2, 2018, doi: 10.1109/MCOM.2018.1700625.
[35] I. Gehrke, M. Schauss, D. Küsters, and T. Gries, "Experiencing the Potential of Closed-Loop PLM Systems Enabled by Industrial Internet of Things," *Procedia Manuf.*, vol. 45, 2020, doi: 10.1016/j.promfg.2020.04.091.
[36] Q. Zhao, "Presents the Technology, Protocols, and New Innovations in Industrial Internet of Things (IIoT)," in *EAI/Springer Innovations in Communication and Computing*, Springer Science and Business Media Deutschland GmbH, Berlin, Germany, pp. 39–56, 2020, doi: 10.1007/978-3-030-32530-5_3.
[37] D. Enireddy, D. Bharathy, D. Anselin Nisha, and D. Babu, "Open Source Cloud Application Solution with PaaS, SaaS and IaaS," *Turkish J. Physiother. Rehabil.*, vol. 32, no. 3, 2021.
[38] C. M. Mohammed and S. R. Zeebaree, "Sufficient Comparison Among Cloud Computing Services: IaaS, PaaS, and SaaS: A Review," *Int. J. Sci. Bus.*, vol. 5, no. 2, 2021.
[39] N. Hassan, K. L. A. Yau, and C. Wu, "Edge Computing in 5G: A Review," *IEEE Access*, vol. 7, 2019, doi: 10.1109/ACCESS.2019.2938534.
[40] K. Takishi, S. Fabre, F. Marsala, and P. Liu, "Gartner—Magic Quadrant for 5G Network Infrastructure for Communications Service Providers," *Gartner*, February, 2021.
[41] H. Ren, D. Anicic, and T. A. Runkler, "Towards Semantic Management of On-Device Applications in Industrial IoT," *ACM Trans. Internet Technol.*, vol. 22, no. 4, 2022, doi: 10.1145/3510820.
[42] K. Mikhaylov *et al.*, "Multi-Radio Perspectives for Massive MTC Localization: Energy Consumption and Utility," in *International Congress on Ultra Modern Telecommunications and Control Systems and Workshops*, vol. 2019, October 2019, doi: 10.1109/ICUMT48472.2019.8970969.
[43] R. Fujdiak *et al.*, "Security in Low-Power Wide-Area Networks: State-of-the-Art and Development Toward the 5G," in *LPWAN Technologies for IoT and M2M Applications*, Elsevier, Amsterdam, Netherlands, pp. 373–396, 2020, doi: 10.1016/B978-0-12-818880-4.00018-1.
[44] C. Drubin, "Tech Vendor Marketing of Blockchain, 5G, Indoor Location and Autonomous Vehicle Solutions Not Resonating with US Enterprises," *Microw. J.*, vol. 60, no. 7, 2017.
[45] S. Bartoletti, A. Conti, D. Dardari, and A. Giorgetti, "5G Localization and Context-Awareness," *Whitepaper*, pp. 167–188, 2019.
[46] M. B. Hassan, E. S. Ali, R. A. Mokhtar, R. A. Saeed, and B. S. Chaudhari, "NB-IoT: Concepts, Applications, and Deployment Challenges," in *LPWAN Technologies for IoT and M2M Applications*, Elsevier, Amsterdam, Netherlands, pp. 119–144, 2020, doi: 10.1016/B978-0-12-818880-4.00006-5.
[47] Y. B. Lin, H. C. Tseng, Y. W. Lin, and L. J. Chen, "NB-IoTtalk: A Service Platform for Fast Development of NB-IoT Applications," *IEEE Internet Things J.*, vol. 6, no. 1, 2019, doi: 10.1109/JIOT.2018.2865583.

[48] S. Y. Wang, J. E. Chang, H. Fan, and Y. H. Sun, "Comparing the Performance of NB-IoT, LTE Cat-M1, Sigfox, and LoRa for IoT End Devices Moving at High Speeds in the Air," *J. Signal Process. Syst.*, vol. 94, no. 1, 2022, doi: 10.1007/s11265-021-01660-4.
[49] N. L. Ismail, M. Kassim, M. Ismail, and R. Mohamad, "A Review of Low Power Wide Area Technology in Licensed and Unlicensed Spectrum for IoT Use Cases," *Bull. Electr. Eng. Inform.*, vol. 7, no. 2, 2018, doi: 10.11591/eei.v7i2.1174.
[50] B. Vejlgaard, M. Lauridsen, H. Nguyen, I. Z. Kovacs, P. Mogensen, and M. Sorensen, "Coverage and Capacity Analysis of Sigfox, LoRa, GPRS, and NB-IoT," in *IEEE Vehicular Technology Conference*, vol. 2017, June 2017, doi: 10.1109/VTCSpring.2017.8108666.
[51] K. Mekki, E. Bajic, F. Chaxel, and F. Meyer, "A Comparative Study of LPWAN Technologies for Large-Scale IoT Deployment," *ICT Express*, vol. 5, no. 1, 2019, doi: 10.1016/j.ictc.2017.12.005.

7 The Role of Blockchain Technology in the Internet of Things

7.1 BLOCKCHAIN TECHNOLOGY IN IOT

IoT is reshaping incumbent industries into smart industries featuring data-driven decision-making. However, intrinsic features of IoT result in a number of challenges such as decentralization, poor interoperability, and privacy and security vulnerabilities. Blockchain technology brings the opportunities in addressing the challenges of IoT. Blockchain is essentially a perfect complement to IoT with its improved interoperability, privacy, security, reliability and scalability [1, 2]. A blockchain is a chain of blocks which contain information. Each block records all of the recent transactions, and once completed, that block goes into the blockchain as a permanent database. Each time a block gets completed, a new block is generated. Blockchain can be used for the secure transfer of money, property, contracts, etc., without requiring a third-party intermediary like bank or government [3, 4]. Blockchain is a software protocol, but it could not be run without the internet (like Simple Mail Transfer Protocol [SMTP] used in email).

7.1.1 Introduction to Blockchain

Blockchain technology was described in 1991 by the research scientist Stuart Haber and W. Scott Stornetta [5]. They wanted to introduce a computationally practical solution for time-stamping digital documents so that they could not be backdated or tampered with. They developed a system using the concept of a cryptographically secured chain of blocks to store the time-stamped documents. However, the invention of blockchain technology is credited to a person or group of people using the pseudonym Satoshi Nakamoto. The concept of blockchain was first described in a white paper titled "Bitcoin: A Peer-to-Peer Electronic Cash System" in 2008, which was published under the name Satoshi Nakamoto [6]. The paper proposed a decentralized digital currency system that used a public ledger called a blockchain to record transactions. However, despite many attempts to uncover the true identity of Satoshi Nakamoto, the inventor(s) of blockchain technology remains unknown to this day. The blockchain would be maintained by a network of nodes that verify and record transactions in a secure and tamper-proof way. In 2009, the first Bitcoin software was released by Nakamoto, which implemented the blockchain system described in the white paper. The first Bitcoin transaction took place shortly after, where Nakamoto sent ten Bitcoins to a developer named Hal Finney. Since

DOI: 10.1201/9781003282945-7

then, blockchain technology has evolved and expanded beyond its original use case of digital currency. It has found applications in industries such as finance, healthcare, supply chain management (SCM), and more, due to its secure and transparent nature. Blockchain can be defined as a chain of blocks that contain information. The technique is intended to timestamp digital documents so that it is not possible to backdate them or tamper with them. The purpose of blockchain is to solve the double records problem without the need for a central server. The blockchain is used for the secure transfer of items like money, property, contracts, etc., without requiring a third-party intermediary like bank or government [1, 2]. The blockchain is a software protocol (like SMTP is for email). However, blockchain could not be run without the internet. It is also called a meta-technology as it affects other technologies. It is comprised of several pieces: a database, software application, some connected computers, etc. A blockchain is a constantly growing ledger which keeps a permanent record of all the transactions that have taken place in a secure, chronological, and immutable way.

The use of blockchain technology in IoT has the potential to revolutionize the way we interact with connected devices by addressing the security and privacy challenges that come with increased connectivity. Blockchain technology provides a decentralized and secure way to store and share data, which is particularly important in IoT systems whereby data is generated and shared across multiple devices and networks. One of the main benefits of using blockchain technology in IoT is the increased security it provides. By using a distributed ledger system, data can be stored in a tamper-proof and immutable manner, which makes it much more difficult for hackers to tamper with or steal data [7, 8]. This can be particularly important in sectors such as healthcare, in which patient data needs to be protected and secured at all times. In addition to security, blockchain technology can also improve the efficiency and transparency of IoT systems. By using smart contracts, for example, devices can automate certain processes, reducing the need for intermediaries and increasing the speed and efficiency of transactions. Furthermore, the transparency of blockchain technology can provide greater visibility into SCM, enabling businesses to track the movement of goods and verify their authenticity. Despite the potential benefits, there are also challenges to using blockchain technology in IoT. For example, the high computational power required for blockchain transactions can be a challenge in IoT systems, which are often constrained by limited processing power and battery life [9, 10]. Additionally, the interoperability of different blockchain platforms and devices can also be a challenge, requiring standardization and collaboration across different stakeholders. The key characteristics of blockchain technology are the following [3].

- **Decentralized Nature:** No controlling power or point of failure.
- **Immutable:** Ledgers can't be altered without the network agreeing to it.
- **Facilitates Trustless Transactions:** Unalterable ledger means transactions can be made to unknown parties with a minimum of risk.
- **Distributed Processing Power:** Decentralized nature means the network shares the load.

Important terms related with blockchain technology include the following [9, 11].

- **Ledger:** It is a file that is constantly growing.
- **Permanent:** Once the transaction goes inside a blockchain, you can put up it permanently in the ledger.
- **Secure:** Blockchain places information in a secure way. It uses very advanced cryptography to make sure that the information is locked inside the blockchain.
- **Chronological:** Every transaction happens following the previous one.
- **Immutable:** As transactions are built into the blockchain, this ledger can never be changed.

Overall, the use of blockchain technology in IoT has the potential to enhance the security, privacy, and efficiency of connected devices. However, careful consideration needs to be given to the specific use case and implementation, taking into account the unique challenges and limitations of both blockchain technology and IoT system.

7.1.2 Who Uses Blockchain?

Blockchain technology is used by a wide range of stakeholders, including individuals, businesses, governments, and non-profit organizations. The most well-known use case of blockchain technology is its use as the underlying technology for cryptocurrencies such as Bitcoin and Ethereum, which allows individuals to send and receive digital currencies without the need for intermediaries like banks. Beyond cryptocurrencies, businesses across various industries have also started to adopt blockchain technology for a range of applications, such as SCM, digital identity verification, and smart contracts [10–13]. For instance, in the supply chain industry, companies like Walmart and Maersk have started to use blockchain technology to track the movement of goods and improve the efficiency and transparency of their supply chains. Governments are also exploring the potential of blockchain technology to improve transparency, security, and efficiency in various areas, such as voting systems, land registry, and taxation. For example, the Republic of Estonia has implemented a blockchain-based digital identity system that allows citizens to securely access government services and sign documents online.

Blockchain technology can be integrated into multiple areas. The primary use of blockchain is as a distributed ledger for crypto currencies. It shows great promise across a wide range of business applications like banking, finance, government, healthcare, insurance, media and entertainment, retail, etc. Blockchain technology is used by a wide range of individuals and organizations, including individuals who use it for secure online transactions, businesses that use it to track supply chain information, and governments that use it to maintain secure records [14, 15]. Finally, non-profit organizations are also using blockchain technology to support various social and environmental initiatives. For instance, the World Food Program has implemented a blockchain-based system to track food distribution in refugee camps, while organizations like Plastic Bank and Charity Water are using blockchain technology to facilitate donations and track the impact of their programs [16]. Overall, blockchain-based transactions offer a secure and transparent way to transfer assets and data, and have potential applications in various industries such as finance, SCM, and healthcare.

We will next discuss how blockchain can be used in day-to-day life. Imagine a group of friends who want to keep track of their expenses while traveling together. They decide to use a blockchain-based app to record all the transactions. Each time a transaction occurs, it is added to a block, which contains information about the transaction, such as the sender, recipient, and amount. The block is then verified by the network of computers in the blockchain network, ensuring that the transaction is valid and that the sender has enough funds to make the payment. Once the block is verified, it is added to the existing chain of blocks, forming a permanent record of all the transactions. Because each block contains a reference to the previous block in the chain, it is virtually impossible to alter any previous transaction without being detected by the network. This decentralized and transparent system ensures that all transactions are secure, immutable, and tamper-proof, eliminating the need for a central authority to verify and validate transaction [2, 17]. Some specific examples of industries using blockchain include the following.

- **Financial Services:** Banks and other financial institutions are experimenting with blockchain technology to improve the speed and security of financial transactions [18, 19]. One example of using blockchain technology in the financial services domain is for cross-border payments. Traditionally, cross-border payments involve multiple intermediaries and can take several days to settle. This process is also associated with high transaction fees and exchange rate risks. Blockchain technology can streamline this process by creating a decentralized, immutable ledger that can facilitate peer-to-peer (P2P) transactions without the need for intermediaries. This can significantly reduce transaction costs and settlement times. For instance, the blockchain-based payment solution provider Ripple offers a cross-border payment solution that leverages its XRP cryptocurrency to enable near-instant settlement of transactions [20]. The platform allows financial institutions to transfer funds in any currency, and the payment is processed within seconds using the XRP cryptocurrency as a bridge currency. Blockchain-based cross-border payment solutions can also enhance transparency, security, and compliance. All transactions are recorded on the blockchain, providing a transparent record of all activities. The decentralized nature of the blockchain also makes it difficult for bad actors to tamper with the data or commit fraud.
- **Supply Chain Management:** Companies are using blockchain to track products as they move through the supply chain, from manufacturers to retailers to consumers [21]. One example of using blockchain technology in the SCM domain is to enhance traceability and transparency. Supply chains involve multiple stakeholders, such as suppliers, manufacturers, distributors, retailers, and customers. The lack of transparency and visibility into the supply chain can create inefficiencies and delays, increasing the

risk of fraud and counterfeiting. Blockchain technology can address these challenges by creating a decentralized, immutable ledger that can securely record and track every transaction in the supply chain [22, 23]. This creates a transparent, tamper-proof record of all activities, making it easier to identify and resolve any issues that arise in the supply chain. For instance, Walmart is using blockchain technology to track the provenance of food products in its supply chain. The company has partnered with IBM to develop a blockchain-based platform that allows it to track the origin, processing, and shipping of food products from farm to store. This provides Walmart and its customers with more information about the source and quality of the food products they buy, enhancing transparency and trust. Another example is Maersk, the global shipping company, which is using blockchain technology to track and manage the movement of cargo in its supply chain. The company has partnered with IBM to develop a blockchain-based platform that enables it to securely track the movement of goods from port to port. This improves visibility and transparency, reduces paperwork, and enhances security and efficiency.

- **Healthcare:** Blockchain technology is being used to securely store and share medical records, as well as to track the supply of prescription drugs [13]. One example of using blockchain technology in the healthcare domain is to improve patient data management and privacy. Healthcare organizations store large volumes of sensitive patient data, such as medical records, test results, and personal information. This data is often siloed and fragmented, making it difficult for healthcare providers to access and share patient data securely and efficiently. Blockchain technology can address these challenges by creating a secure, decentralized, and immutable ledger that allows patients to control and share their medical data with healthcare providers securely. Patients can grant access to their data to specific healthcare providers, which can enhance patient care and reduce medical errors. For instance, MedRec is a blockchain-based platform that allows patients to store and share their medical records securely [14, 18]. The platform uses smart contracts to manage access to patient data and allows patients to control who can access their data. This provides patients with more control over their data and enhances privacy and security. Another example is Medicalchain, a blockchain-based platform that allows patients to manage their medical data and connect with healthcare providers securely. The platform uses blockchain technology to create a tamper-proof record of all medical transactions and uses encryption to ensure data privacy and security. This allows patients to access their medical data from anywhere and share it with healthcare providers securely.
- **Real Estate:** Blockchain technology is being used to digitize property records and make the buying and selling processes more efficient [24]. One example of using blockchain technology in the real estate domain is to streamline property transactions and enhance transparency. Real estate transactions involve multiple parties, such as buyers, sellers, real estate agents, lawyers, and financial institutions. These transactions can be complex and

time-consuming, involving multiple steps, paperwork, and intermediaries. Blockchain technology can address these challenges by creating a decentralized, tamper-proof ledger that can securely record and track all the steps in a real estate transaction. This can reduce transaction times, streamline the process, and reduce the need for intermediaries, reducing costs and increasing transparency. For instance, Propy is a blockchain-based platform that allows real estate transactions to be completed entirely online, using smart contracts to automate the process [25]. The platform allows buyers to browse properties, complete transactions, and handle the transfer of ownership securely and efficiently. Another example is the use of blockchain to digitize property titles and deeds. This can eliminate the need for physical paperwork and make it easier to transfer ownership securely. In countries where property rights are unclear or disputed, blockchain technology can provide a transparent and tamper-proof record of ownership, enhancing security and trust in the real estate market. For example, the government of Dubai has launched a blockchain-based platform called "The Dubai Blockchain Strategy" which aims to digitize all property transactions by 2020 [26]. The platform will use blockchain technology to create a secure and tamper-proof record of all property transactions, enhancing transparency and reducing fraud in the real estate market.

- **Gaming:** Blockchain technology is being used to create in-game digital assets that can be bought, sold, and traded on the open market [27]. One example of using blockchain technology in the gaming industry is to create a more transparent and secure marketplace for in-game assets. In-game assets—such as virtual currencies, items, and skins (items of clothing, armor, etc., for customizing the appearance of a player's avatar)—have become increasingly valuable, and players are willing to spend real money to acquire them. Blockchain technology can address some of the challenges associated with in-game assets by creating a decentralized, tamper-proof ledger that tracks the ownership and transactions of these assets. This can provide more transparency, security, and liquidity in the in-game asset marketplace, allowing players to buy and sell assets more efficiently and with greater confidence. For instance, games such as CryptoKitties and Decentraland use blockchain technology to create unique and tradable virtual assets [28]. These assets are stored on the blockchain, allowing players to prove ownership and transfer them securely and efficiently. Another example is the use of blockchain technology to create decentralized gaming platforms. These platforms enable developers to create games that operate entirely on the blockchain, providing more transparency and fairness in gameplay. Players can earn cryptocurrencies by playing these games, and they can use these currencies to buy in-game assets or trade them on cryptocurrency exchanges. For example, *Gods Unchained* is a blockchain-based trading card game that allows players to earn and trade unique virtual assets. The game operates on the Ethereum blockchain, allowing players to prove ownership and trade assets securely and efficiently.

- **Cryptocurrency:** Blockchain technology is used by many digital currencies like Bitcoin and Ethereum, which are decentralized and operate without a central authority [29, 30]. One example of using blockchain in the crypto industry is for the creation and transfer of cryptocurrencies. Cryptocurrencies such as Bitcoin, Ethereum, and Litecoin are all created, transferred, and stored using blockchain technology. In the case of Bitcoin, for example, each transaction is verified by a network of nodes on the blockchain, which ensures the security and integrity of the transaction. The blockchain maintains a ledger of all transactions on the network, which is decentralized and publicly accessible. This means that no one person or organization has control over the Bitcoin network, making it a trustless and transparent system. Furthermore, blockchain technology allows for the creation of smart contracts, which are self-executing contracts with the terms of the agreement written into lines of code. Smart contracts can be used for a variety of purposes, including the creation and distribution of tokens, the establishment of governance structures for decentralized organizations, and the automation of financial transactions.

7.1.3 The Need for Blockchain

Blockchain is a decentralized, distributed digital ledger that records transactions in a secure, immutable, and transparent manner. The need for blockchain arose from the shortcomings of traditional centralized systems, which are prone to fraud, cyberattacks, and single points of failure. Smart contracts can be used to automate processes, reduce the need for intermediaries and ensure that the terms of the contract are carried out efficiently and securely using blockchain technology. Blockchain technology can bring transparency, security, and efficiency to various industries, making it a valuable tool for many businesses and organizations. Following are some of the key reasons why blockchain technology is necessary.

- **Time Reduction:** In the financial industry, blockchain can allow the quicker settlement of trades. It does not take a lengthy process for verification, settlement, and clearance [18, 31]. It is because of a single version of agreed-upon data available between all stakeholders.
- **Unchangeable Transactions:** Blockchain registers transactions in a chronological order which certifies the inalterability of all operations, meaning that when a new block is added to the chain of ledgers, it cannot be removed or modified [18, 30]. One of the key features of blockchain technology is the immutability or inalterability of transactions recorded on the blockchain. Once a transaction is added to the blockchain, it becomes part of a permanent and unchangeable record that is stored on multiple nodes across the network. The inalterability of blockchain-based transactions is achieved through the use of cryptographic hash functions, which create a unique digital fingerprint for each transaction. Each block on the blockchain contains a hash of the previous block, which creates a chain of blocks that cannot be modified without altering the entire blockchain. In order to

alter a transaction on the blockchain, an attacker would need to alter the entire blockchain, which would require a massive amount of computational power and resources. This makes it virtually impossible to tamper with the blockchain without being detected. Moreover, most blockchain networks use consensus mechanisms such as proof-of-work (PoW) or proof-of-stake (PoS) which ensure that all nodes on the network agree on the validity of each transaction before it is added to the blockchain [6, 32]. This makes it very difficult for an attacker to introduce fraudulent transactions onto the blockchain.

- **Reliability:** Blockchain certifies and verifies the identities of all interested parties. This removes double records, reducing rates and accelerating transactions [7, 31]. Blockchain-based transactions are considered reliable because they rely on a decentralized network of computers called nodes that work together to validate and confirm each transaction. These nodes use complex mathematical algorithms to ensure the integrity of the data stored on the blockchain, making it very difficult to tamper with or alter. Furthermore, because blockchain transactions are processed by a network of nodes rather than a central authority, they are resistant to attacks or attempts at manipulation. In order to hack the network, an attacker would need to compromise a majority of the nodes, which is extremely difficult given the size and decentralization of most blockchain networks. In summary, the reliability of blockchain-based transactions comes from the use of a decentralized network of nodes, cryptographic hashing to ensure data integrity, and resistance to attacks due to the difficulty of compromising a large and diverse network.
- **Security:** Blockchain uses very advanced cryptography to make sure that the information is locked inside the blockchain. It uses distributed ledger technology (DLT) whereby each party holds a copy of the original chain, so the system remains operative, even if a large number of other nodes fail [33, 34]. Blockchain technology provides a high level of security through the use of cryptography, consensus mechanisms, and DLT. This makes it virtually impossible for any individual or organization to tamper with the data on the blockchain. For example, the blockchain-based platform Ethereum provides secure smart contract execution, which allows for the development of decentralized applications.
- **Collaboration:** This allows each party to transact directly with each other without requiring a third-party intermediary [7, 33]. Blockchain technology enables trust in transactions without the need for intermediaries like banks, lawyers, or other third parties. This is achieved through the use of cryptographic algorithms that ensure the authenticity and integrity of the data being recorded on the blockchain. For example, Bitcoin uses blockchain technology to facilitate P2P transactions without the need for a central authority.
- **Decentralized:** It is decentralized because there is no central authority supervising anything. There are standards which govern how every node exchanges the blockchain information. This method ensures that all

transactions are validated, and all valid transactions are added one by one [7, 33]. Blockchain technology enables decentralization, which means that there is no central authority or single point of failure. This makes it more resilient to cyber-attacks and provides greater freedom and control for users. For example, the blockchain-based social media platform Steemit allows users to create and share content without the need for a central authority.
- **Traceability:** Blockchain technology allows for the tracking and tracing of goods and assets throughout the supply chain, making it easy to identify any issues or problems that may arise [33]. Blockchain technology provides transparency in transactions by allowing all participants to view the transactions and their history. This helps to reduce fraud and increase accountability. For example, in SCM, blockchain technology can be used to track the movement of goods from the source to the end consumer, enabling consumers to verify the authenticity of the products.
- **Cost Savings:** By removing intermediaries and automating processes, blockchain technology can greatly reduce the cost of transactions and operations [21]. Blockchain technology provides a more efficient and cost-effective way to manage transactions and data. This is achieved through the elimination of intermediaries and the use of automation. For example, Ripple facilitates cross-border payments in a more efficient and cost-effective manner compared to traditional methods.

7.1.4 Challenges of Integrating Blockchain Technology with IoT

There are several challenges when it comes to integrating blockchain technology with IoT [10, 21, 35–37]. These challenges include scalability, interoperability, security, complexity, and cost, which will require collaboration and innovation among stakeholders in the blockchain and IoT ecosystems. Some of the main challenges include the following.

1. **Scalability:** The number of devices connected to the IoT is expected to reach into the billions, and blockchain technology needs to be able to handle the large number of transactions and data generated by these devices. One of the biggest challenges of integrating blockchain with IoT is scalability. IoT generates a vast amount of data, and blockchain is inherently slow in processing large volumes of data. The consensus algorithms used by most blockchain networks require a high degree of computational power, which makes it challenging to process IoT data in real time [2, 15]. Therefore, scaling blockchain to support IoT applications is a significant challenge. One example of scalability issues when integrating blockchain with IoT is in the energy sector. IoT devices can be used to monitor energy usage and enable more efficient energy distribution. However, the sheer amount of data generated by these devices can be difficult to process with traditional blockchain networks. The IOTA network is an example of a blockchain-based platform designed specifically for IoT applications, which uses a different consensus mechanism called Tangle to achieve scalability.

2. **Security:** IoT devices are vulnerable to hacking and other security breaches, and blockchain technology needs to provide a secure way to store and transmit data. Security is another major concern when integrating blockchain with IoT. Blockchain provides a secure way to store and transfer data, but it does not necessarily guarantee the security of IoT devices. IoT devices can be vulnerable to cyber-attacks, and if these devices are connected to a blockchain network, they can potentially compromise the entire network. Ensuring the security of IoT devices is critical to the successful integration of blockchain with IoT [29, 38]. For example, in the automotive industry, connected cars can be vulnerable to hacking, which could result in serious safety risks. To address this challenge, projects like the Mobility Open Blockchain Initiative (MOBI) consortium have been established, aiming to develop secure blockchain-based solutions for the automotive industry.
3. **Interoperability:** Different blockchain platforms and IoT devices may not be compatible with each other, which can make it difficult to integrate the two technologies. Another challenge is interoperability between different blockchain networks and IoT devices. IoT devices operate on different platforms and protocols, which can make it difficult to integrate them with blockchain networks [39, 40]. For example, some IoT devices may use Wi-Fi or Bluetooth, while others may use Zigbee or Z-Wave. These different protocols can make it challenging to establish a common language that can be used to communicate with blockchain networks. For example, in the healthcare sector, there are many different types of medical devices that use different protocols, making it difficult to integrate them with a blockchain network. To address this challenge, projects have been developed such as the health Nexus blockchain platform, which aims to provide a common language for communication between different healthcare devices.
4. **Latency:** Some blockchain platforms have high latency, which can make it difficult for real-time applications such as IoT to function efficiently. Latency refers to the time delay between the transmission of data and its receipt at the receiving end. When integrating IoT with blockchain, latency can be a significant challenge [1, 11]. This is because the consensus algorithms used by most blockchain networks are designed to ensure that all nodes in the network agree on the current state of the ledger. This process can be time-consuming, and it can result in delays in processing IoT data. In IoT applications, real-time data processing is often critical. For example, in a smart city application, IoT devices can be used to monitor traffic patterns and adjust traffic signals in real time to optimize traffic flow. In this case, even small delays in data processing can result in significant impacts on traffic flow. Latency can be particularly challenging in public blockchain networks like Bitcoin and Ethereum, which can have high transaction processing times. These networks can also become congested during periods of high demand, resulting in even longer processing times.
5. **Energy Consumption:** Some blockchain protocols, such as PoW, are very energy-intensive, making it difficult to use them in IoT devices with limited power resources. Energy consumption is a significant issue when integrating

IoT with blockchain. This is because the consensus algorithms used by most blockchain networks require a significant amount of computational power to process transactions and maintain the integrity of the ledger. This high computational demand can lead to increased energy consumption, which can be a significant concern in IoT applications in which devices are often battery powered and have limited energy resources [11, 37]. The energy consumption issue is particularly pronounced in public blockchain networks like Bitcoin and Ethereum, which rely on PoW consensus algorithms. In PoW, miners compete to solve a mathematical problem, and the first to solve the problem receives a reward in the form of newly minted cryptocurrency. However, this requires significant computational power and results in a significant energy consumption. The energy consumption of the Bitcoin network alone is estimated to be around 128 TWh per year, which is equivalent to the annual energy consumption of a small country like Argentina.

6. **Standardization and Regulation:** As the technology is new and still evolving, there is a lack of clear regulation and standardization, which could impede the widespread adoption of blockchain in IoT. Standardization and regulation are important issues when integrating IoT with blockchain. Standardization refers to the development of common protocols and interfaces that allow IoT devices and blockchain networks to communicate and interact with each other seamlessly. Regulation refers to the development of legal frameworks that govern the use of IoT and blockchain technologies and ensure compliance with relevant laws and regulation. Standardization is important because it ensures that IoT devices and blockchain networks can communicate with each other effectively, without the need for custom interfaces or special programming [37, 41]. This can help to reduce costs and increase interoperability, making it easier for developers to create new IoT blockchain application. Regulation is important because it ensures that IoT blockchain applications are developed and used in a way that is safe and secure, and that protects the privacy and security of users. This is particularly important given the sensitive nature of IoT data and the potential for blockchain networks to store and process large amounts of personal information. Some of the challenges associated with standardization and regulation when integrating IoT with blockchain include: lack of standards, regulatory uncertainty, data privacy and security, and interoperability. Thus, it is important to develop common standards and protocols for IoT blockchain applications, as well as legal frameworks that promote innovation while protecting the privacy and security of users. This will require collaboration between industry stakeholders, regulators, and policymakers, as well as ongoing efforts to address emerging technological and regulatory issues.
7. **Complexity:** The integration of blockchain technology into IoT systems can be complex and requires a high level of technical expertise [9, 37]. Blockchain technology is complex and requires a high degree of technical expertise to implement and maintain. Integrating blockchain with IoT can add another layer of complexity to an already complex system. This can make it challenging for organizations to implement and manage these systems,

which can slow down adoption. For example, in the supply chain industry, there are many different stakeholders involved in the movement of goods, each with their own systems and processes. Integrating blockchain with IoT can require significant coordination and technical expertise to ensure that the systems work together seamlessly. To address this challenge, projects have been developed like the VeChain blockchain platform, which aims to simplify the integration of blockchain with supply chain systems.

8. **Cost:** Integrating blockchain with IoT can be expensive [37]. The hardware and software required to support blockchain networks can be costly, and organizations may need to invest in new infrastructure to support these systems. Additionally, the cost of maintaining these systems can be high, as they require a high degree of technical expertise. For example, in the agriculture industry, IoT devices can be used to monitor crop health and enable more efficient irrigation. However, the cost of implementing these devices, along with the cost of supporting a blockchain network to process the data, can be a significant barrier to adoption. To address this challenge, projects have been developed like the AgriLedger blockchain platform, which aims to provide affordable blockchain-based solutions for small-scale farmers.

7.2 KEY CHARACTERISTICS OF BLOCKCHAIN

Blockchain technology has the potential to enhance the security, scalability, and interoperability of the IoT by providing a secure and decentralized way to store and transmit data. Some of the potential uses of blockchain technology in IoT include SCM, device identity and access management, sensor data management, smart contracts, and micro-payments [18, 19, 21]. Overall, the integration of blockchain technology with IoT has the potential to create more secure, efficient, and transparent systems for managing and utilizing data from IoT devices. Basically, the blockchain is a decentralized digital ledger that records transactions across a network of computers. The key characteristics of blockchain technology important while integrating it with IoT are the following [10, 35, 36].

1. **Decentralization:** Blockchain technology is a decentralized system that allows multiple parties to access and validate the same data without the need for a central authority [37]. The decentralized nature of blockchain means that there is no central authority controlling it. Instead, the network is made up of a distributed network of nodes or computers that work together to verify and record transactions. This means that there is no single point of failure and that the network is thus resistant to censorship, manipulation, and attacks. The devices in the network communicate directly with each other, making the system more resilient and less susceptible to attacks.
2. **Immutable:** Once data is recorded on a blockchain, it cannot be altered or deleted. This ensures the integrity and authenticity of the data. The information stored on the blockchain is considered to be tamper-proof and immutable because once data is added to the blockchain, it cannot be

altered or deleted [1, 37]. This is because each block in the blockchain is linked to the previous block, forming a chain that is secured by advanced cryptographic algorithms. Any attempt to change the data in a block would require changing all subsequent blocks in the chain, which is practically impossible due to the large number of nodes on the network. This ensures the integrity and authenticity of data generated by IoT devices, which is crucial for applications such as SCM and smart cities.

3. **Transparency:** All transactions on a blockchain are visible to everyone on the network, creating transparency and accountability. All participants in the blockchain network have access to the same information, and all transactions are visible to anyone on the network. This transparency promotes trust and accountability among participants because everyone can see what is happening on the network, and any attempt to manipulate the data would be immediately apparent [3, 37].
4. **Security:** Blockchain uses advanced cryptographic techniques to secure the data generated by IoT devices or financial transactions, making it difficult for hackers to tamper with the data. Blockchain uses advanced cryptographic techniques, such as public-key cryptography, to secure transactions and protect against hacking and fraud [1, 12]. Each transaction is verified by multiple nodes on the network, and a consensus mechanism is used to ensure that all nodes agree on the validity of transactions. This makes it extremely difficult for hackers to manipulate the data on the blockchain.
5. **Smart contract:** A smart contract is a self-executing contract with the terms of the agreement written into code. It allows for the automation of processes and the execution of transactions without the need for intermediaries. This reduces transaction costs and increases efficiency because there is no need for intermediaries or manual processing of contracts. Blockchain-based IoT systems can use smart contracts to automate the execution of agreements between IoT devices [1, 12]. Smart contracts can be used to define the terms of a transaction, such as the price of goods, delivery time, and payment term.
6. **Interoperability:** Blockchain technology can be integrated with other technologies and systems, making it possible to share data across different platforms and networks. This interoperability enables devices from different manufacturers and with different protocols to communicate with each other seamlessly [1, 11]. For example, blockchain can be used to track the supply chain of goods from the manufacturer to the retailer, integrating with other technologies such as RFID tags and IoT devices.
7. **Consensus:** Blockchain uses a consensus mechanism, such as PoW or PoS, to ensure that all nodes on the network agree on the validity of transactions [2, 42]. This helps to prevent double-spending and other types of fraud. For example, in the PoW consensus mechanism used by Bitcoin, miners compete to solve complex mathematical problems, and the first miner to solve the problem gets to add a new block to the blockchain. This creates a trustless and decentralized system whereby all participants can agree on the validity of transactions without the need for a central authority.

Overall, a blockchain-based IoT system can provide a high level of trust, transparency, and security, making it an ideal solution for a wide range of applications, from smart cities to industrial automation to healthcare.

7.3 BENEFITS OF COMBINING BLOCKCHAIN AND IOT

The IoT and blockchain are two revolutionary technologies that have the potential to transform various industries. While IoT refers to the interconnectedness of physical devices, blockchain is a decentralized, immutable ledger technology that provides a secure and transparent way of recording transactions. Combining IoT and blockchain technology can bring numerous benefits, including increased security, improved transparency, and enhanced efficiency. The integration of IoT and blockchain opens the door for new possibilities that inherently reduce inefficiencies, enhance security, and improve transparency for all involved parties while enabling secured M2M transactions [33, 37]. The coupling of these technologies allows a physical asset to be tracked from the moment raw materials are mined, for example, and among every step of the supply chain until it is with the end consumer. IoT can extend trust to a blockchain network as it builds trust between devices [36, 37]. Participants of the blockchain network reduce chances of data tampering before being added to a blockchain because human intervention is not involved in the flow of the data. It also reduces or eliminates additional costs involved with intermediaries and can substantially decrease the time it takes to settle a lawsuit because all the case information is easily audited. Adding each of your partners to a network as a "node" is much less costly than building a full-on integration (and then maintaining it).

For instance, healthcare is important application domain for blockchain and IoT. IoT devices can be used to monitor patient health, providing real-time data on vital signs, medication adherence, and other health indicators. By combining blockchain and IoT, it is possible to create a more secure and transparent healthcare ecosystem [14, 43]. Blockchain can be used to securely store and manage patient health data, enabling healthcare providers to access patient data in real time and make data-driven decisions. Smart contracts can be used to automate healthcare processes, such as insurance claims processing and medical record management, reducing the risk of errors or fraud. Manufacturing is yet another important application domain for blockchain and IoT. IoT devices can be used to monitor the production process, providing real-time data on machine performance, inventory levels, and production output. By combining blockchain and IoT, it is possible to create a more efficient and transparent manufacturing ecosystem. Blockchain can be used to securely store and manage production data, enabling stakeholders to optimize the manufacturing process and reduce waste. Smart contracts can be used to automate manufacturing processes, such as inventory management and quality control, reducing the risk of errors or delays. In conclusion, the combination of blockchain and IoT can bring numerous benefits in various important IoT application domains, including smart cities, SCM, energy management, healthcare, and manufacturing. By leveraging the strengths of these two technologies, it is possible to create more secure, efficient, and transparent ecosystems that can drive innovation and growth in these industries.

Blockchain technology can provide several benefits when applied to the IoT, including the following [10, 35, 36].

- **Enhanced Security:** One of the most significant benefits of combining IoT and blockchain is enhanced security. IoT devices are connected to the internet, which makes them vulnerable to cyber-attacks. Hackers can exploit vulnerabilities in IoT devices to gain access to sensitive data, such as personal information or financial records. However, by combining IoT and blockchain technology, it is possible to create a secure and decentralized system that is much harder to hack. Blockchain technology incorporates security with the ability to verify and allow transactions originated by a trusted party, as well as encryption while data is being transmitted and stored [19, 31]. Blockchain technology provides transparency about who has access and who is making transactions, as well as a record of all of the interactions. Plus, blockchain adds a security layer in terms of encryption: the removal of single point of failure and the ability to quickly identify the weak link in the entire network. Blockchain's decentralized and distributed architecture can help secure IoT devices and networks by making it difficult for hackers to access or manipulate data. Blockchain's decentralized architecture makes it more secure than traditional centralized systems. In a blockchain network, each node holds a copy of the ledger, and all nodes must agree on the validity of transactions before they are added to the blockchain. This makes it extremely difficult for hackers to manipulate the blockchain, as they would need to compromise a majority of the nodes simultaneously—which is practically impossible [44, 45]. Moreover, blockchain technology can be used to authenticate IoT devices, ensuring that only authorized devices are connected to the network. Each device can have a unique identifier that is stored on the blockchain, making it virtually impossible to impersonate or hack the device. This enhanced security can be particularly useful in industries such as healthcare, in which data privacy is of utmost importance.
- **Reduced Costs:** By automating the transaction validation and processing steps on blockchain, the entire IoT ecosystem can be made proactive at a reduced cost [21]. Blockchain can eliminate the need for intermediaries, such as centralized servers or third-party providers, thereby reducing costs associated with maintaining and managing IoT networks. For instance, blockchain and IoT can be used to create a transparent and secure SCM system. IoT devices can track the movement of goods throughout the supply chain, while blockchain can provide an immutable and transparent record of all transactions. This can help reduce the cost of managing the supply chain by improving efficiency and reducing the risk of fraud and errors. IoT devices can be used to monitor and manage assets such as machinery, equipment, and vehicles. Blockchain can provide a secure and transparent record of asset ownership and maintenance history. This can help reduce the cost of asset management by improving efficiency and reducing the risk of theft and maintenance errors [2]. Smart contracts can be used to automate various processes and reduce the need for intermediaries. This can help reduce

the cost of executing contracts and transactions by eliminating the need for manual processes and intermediaries. Blockchain and IoT can be used to create a secure and transparent record of product origin and authenticity. This can help reduce the cost of counterfeiting by making it easier to identify and track counterfeit products.

- **Speed of Transactions:** One of the main benefits of combining blockchain and IoT is that it can significantly increase the speed of transactions. Blockchain provides a decentralized and secure way of managing data and transactions, which can help reduce transaction times and increase efficiency. IoT devices can be used to gather real-time data, which can then be stored on the blockchain in a secure and transparent manner. This is especially true for supply chain transactions with multiple suppliers, producers, distributors, and consumers. With the blockchain serving as a shared ledger to a degree, untrusted parties can exchange data directly with one another, eliminating the manual processes and increasing the speed of transactions [30, 33, 34]. When IoT is combined with blockchain, transactions can be processed more quickly and without the need for intermediaries or centralized authorities. For instance, in the case of SCM, real-time data from IoT sensors can be used to trigger smart contracts, which can then execute transactions automatically without any human intervention. This can significantly reduce transaction times and increase efficiency.
- **Increased Transparency and Traceability:** Blockchain's immutable and tamper-proof ledger can provide a clear and auditable record of all transactions and interactions between IoT devices. The combination of blockchain and IoT can also improve traceability, which is essential in various industries, such as healthcare and agriculture [16, 46, 47]. By assigning a unique identifier to each IoT device and storing this identifier on the blockchain, it is possible to track the device's movements and transactions throughout its lifecycle. For example, in the healthcare industry, IoT devices can be used to monitor patient health and the data generated by these devices can be stored on the blockchain. This can enable healthcare providers to track patient health over time and identify potential health issues before they become more severe. In the agriculture industry, IoT devices can be used to monitor crop growth and the data generated by these devices can be stored on the blockchain. This can enable farmers to track the growth and location of their crops, which can help them optimize their farming practices and reduce waste.
- **Scalability:** Another benefit of combining blockchain and IoT is scalability. Blockchain has traditionally faced scalability issues due to its limited processing power and storage capacity. However, with the use of IoT devices, the scalability of blockchain can be greatly increased. Blockchain can handle a large number of transactions simultaneously, making it suitable for IoT networks that include billions of devices [8]. IoT devices can be used to gather and process data, which can then be stored on the blockchain. This can help reduce the processing load on the blockchain network, making it more scalable. Additionally, with the use of off-chain solutions such as state

channels or sidechains, IoT devices can process transactions and interactions off the main blockchain, further increasing scalability.

- **Better Data Management:** Combining blockchain and IoT can also bring significant benefits in terms of data management. IoT devices generate vast amounts of data which can be difficult to manage and process. Blockchain provides a secure and transparent way of storing and managing this data, which can be accessed and used by multiple parties without the risk of tampering or manipulation [48, 49]. Blockchain can enable secure and efficient data sharing between IoT devices, which can improve data analytics and decision-making capabilities. With the use of blockchain, data generated by IoT devices can be securely stored and managed, ensuring the integrity and authenticity of the data. Additionally, with the use of smart contracts, data can be automatically processed and validated, reducing the risk of errors or fraud.
- **Improved Data Privacy:** The combination of blockchain and IoT can also improve data privacy. IoT devices generate a vast amount of data, much of which can be sensitive or confidential. By storing this data on the blockchain, it is possible to ensure that only authorized parties have access to the data [9, 49]. Moreover, blockchain technology can be used to enable data sharing without compromising data privacy. By creating a permissioned blockchain network, it is possible to control access to the data stored on the blockchain. This can be particularly useful in industries such as healthcare, in which patient data privacy is of utmost importance.

Thus, as more industries adopt IoT devices, we can expect to see increasing interest in combining blockchain and IoT technology in the coming years. The blockchain can affect most of the application areas of IoT. For instance, smart cities are built on the foundation of IoT devices and sensors, which collect data on various aspects of city life, such as traffic flow, air quality, and waste management [26, 50]. By combining blockchain and IoT, it is possible to create a more secure, efficient, and transparent smart city ecosystem. The blockchain can be used to securely store and manage the data generated by IoT devices in a smart city. This can enable city administrators to make data-driven decisions and optimize city services. Additionally, blockchain can be used to create a secure and transparent system for managing the exchange of value in a smart city ecosystem, such as the payment for transportation or energy service. SCM is another important application domain for blockchain and IoT. IoT devices can be used to monitor the movement of goods and products throughout the supply chain, providing real-time information on their location, condition, and status. By combining blockchain and IoT, it is possible to create a more secure and transparent supply chain ecosystem. Blockchain can be used to store and manage the data generated by IoT devices, enabling stakeholders to track the movement of goods and products from production to delivery. Smart contracts can be used to automate supply chain processes and reduce the risk of fraud or error. Energy management is an important application domain for both IoT and blockchain. IoT devices can be used to monitor energy consumption and production, providing real-time data on energy usage and availability [10, 51]. By combining blockchain and IoT, it is possible to create a more efficient and decentralized energy management system. Blockchain can be used to securely store and manage the data generated by IoT devices, enabling stakeholders to optimize energy production and distribution. Smart contracts can be used to automate energy transactions and enable P2P energy trading, reducing the reliance on centralized energy providers.

7.4 HOW BLOCKCHAIN TRANSACTIONS WORK

A key component of IoT is data. In order to operate, an IoT network must send and receive large amounts of sensitive data. One such example is the security access data that is required for the August Smart Lock, a household IoT device that lets users replace their house key with their smartphone by allowing the user to lock and unlock the door with their smartphone, a keycard, or a traditional key [52]. This smart lock allows homeowners to unlock their home just by using their phone, without the need for a key. Naturally, homeowners need to be assured that no unauthorized person is going to be able to steal entry code data and gain access to their home. This means that the IoT network must be secure at all times. Not only that, data is often transferred between devices that have different administrators and data usage policies, thereby creating a challenging management environment that also requires close attention to data security. Blockchain has the potential to dramatically increase both the security and level of automation of certain data transactions [18, 29, 35]. The technology allows for the creation of individual blocks of data in the form of a chain. As each new block is added to the last, it forms what is, in essence, a digital ledger containing all the information ever added to the blockchain. Since the data on each new block is partly calculated from information held on the previous block in the blockchain, in order to alter a block, an unauthorized individual would have to change the information on all the blocks linked to it to prevent the change from being immediately noticed. In the case of a cryptocurrency blockchain, for example, this may well mean having to change every single block on the chain. The really exciting thing about blockchain technology is that it operates as a P2P decentralized network. As such a network, blockchain does not require any controlling party to function [30]. This has enormous implications for many of the business processes we all rely on today.

A blockchain transaction is a digital exchange of value that is recorded on a decentralized digital ledger. In the process of a blockchain-based transaction, a user typically initiates a transaction by creating a digital signature using their private key [53]. This signature serves as proof of their identity and authorization to transfer the funds. This transaction is then broadcasted to the network of computers (the nodes which make up the blockchain). The nodes on the network validate the transaction by verifying the digital signature and checking that the user has sufficient funds to complete the transaction. Once the transaction is validated, it is grouped with other transactions into a block. Each block contains a unique code, called a "hash" that links it to the previous block. The block is added to the blockchain through a process called mining, which involves solving a complex mathematical problem [53, 54]. This process ensures the integrity of the blockchain by making it difficult for any one user to tamper with the transaction history. Once the block is added to the blockchain, the transaction is considered complete, and the funds are transferred from the sender's account to the recipient's account. The transaction information is visible to all the participants in the network, providing transparency and immutability.

A blockchain transaction is a transfer of cryptocurrency from one digital wallet to another. It involves a series of steps that occur within a decentralized network of nodes. Blockchain transactions are secure and transparent due to the decentralized nature of the network and the use of cryptographic algorithms to verify and validate transactions. The transactions are recorded in a public ledger, which is visible to all participants in the network, providing transparency and accountability. The steps detailed in the example of the following steps are based on a typical blockchain protocol called PoW, but there are other types of consensus mechanisms (PoS, delegated PoS, etc.) that can be used to validate the transactions and add them to the blockchain [18, 38, 53].

1. **Initiation of Transaction:** The sender creates a digital wallet and requests to send a certain amount of cryptocurrency to the recipient's wallet. The sender signs the transaction with their private key, which is a unique code to which only they have access.
2. **Verification and Validation:** The transaction is broadcasted to the network of nodes. Each node in the network verifies and validates the transaction to ensure that the sender has sufficient funds in their wallet and that the transaction is legitimate.
3. **Recording the Transaction in a Block:** Once the transaction is verified and validated, it is recorded in a block, along with other transactions. The block is then added to the blockchain through a process called mining. Mining is the process of solving a complex mathematical problem, which requires a significant amount of computing power. The first miner to solve the problem is rewarded with a certain amount of cryptocurrency for their work.
4. **Confirmation:** Once the block of transactions is added to the blockchain, it becomes a permanent part of the public ledger, and the transaction is considered confirmed. This means that it cannot be altered or reversed. The recipient's wallet now has the cryptocurrency that was sent, and the transaction is complete.

7.5 HOW TO SECURE IOT WITH BLOCKCHAIN

The application of blockchain into IoT networks is one of the most exciting long-term uses of this great new technology. Individuals as well as businesses all around the globe stand to benefit from more secure IoT networks, which will help secure all aspects of IoT use and allow everyone to feel more trust that their data is safe. The enhanced security environment that blockchain facilitates will massively help to overcome people's apprehensions when it comes to using an increasing number of smart devices in their daily lives [48, 55]. Knowing that using a smart lock for your home is safer than using a physical key, for example, will greatly speed up the transition we all make to use such smart technology [52, 53]. In the same way that self-driving cars promise to make driving part of what we now call "leisure time," smart devices using blockchain technology will help automate many more aspects of our daily chores, leaving us all with more time to sit back and enjoy life. IoT operates a distributed client/server model that requires an administrator to manage the network. This centralized authority is the weak point when it comes to IoT cyber-security.

To operate normally, IoT devices rely on this authority to determine how they behave. If there is a breach of security at the central authority, the information being sent by the smart devices is then largely at the mercy of the hackers. This makes attacking the central authority very appealing to cyber-hackers, as large amounts of data can be collected in one go. A series of cyber-attacks occurred in 2017, many of which exploited this weakness and allowed hackers to make off with sensitive data relating to hundreds of millions of U.S. citizens. Since the decentralized nature of blockchain technology would negate any central attack, hackers would have to target individual nodes on the network in order to try to obtain the data they want. In a blockchain network, smart devices are able to actively participate in validating transactions. This means that the network would be able to guard against any hack by validating predetermined "acceptable" behavior for any irregularities [35, 37, 53]. Once a device on the network was identified as not behaving correctly, it could be isolated to prevent it from being used to access further sensitive data or being used to unlock a person's home, etc. However, keep in mind that IoT security is a complex issue and the blockchain alone is not a silver bullet—integration with other technologies such as encryption, access control, and intrusion detection will play a crucial role in the IoT security. Blockchain-based IoT systems can be vulnerable to various types of attacks, including the following [1, 44].

1. **Sybil Attacks:** This involves an attacker creating multiple fake identities in the network to gain control and manipulate the system.
2. **Eclipse Attacks:** An attacker takes control of a victim's network node, isolating it from the rest of the network, and controlling the information flow to and from the victim's node.
3. **DDoS Attacks:** Distributed Denial of Service (DDoS) attacks involve flooding the network with traffic, rendering it unavailable to legitimate users.
4. **51% Attacks:** In a blockchain network, an attacker with control over more than half of the network's computing power can manipulate transactions, reverse transactions, or even double-spend coins.
5. **Smart Contract Attacks:** Smart contracts on the blockchain can be vulnerable to coding errors, which can lead to loss of funds or unauthorized access to sensitive information.
6. **Blockchain Network Disruption:** An attacker can disrupt the network by manipulating the consensus protocol, preventing nodes from agreeing on the state of the network.
7. **Malware Attacks:** Malware can be injected into IoT devices, compromising the security of the blockchain network.

To protect against these types of attacks, blockchain-based IoT systems should be designed with security in mind. This includes implementing robust security measures such as encryption, multi-factor authentication, and regular updates to software and firmware. In addition, organizations should conduct regular security audits and testing to identify vulnerabilities and address them proactively. One potential solution to the security challenges of IoT is blockchain technology. Following are some ways in which blockchain can be used to secure IoT.

1. **Immutable Records:** To ensure the security of data on IoT devices, a blockchain-based immutable record system can be implemented. The data generated by IoT devices can be stored in blocks and added to the blockchain in a decentralized manner, ensuring that the data is tamper-proof and secure. For instance, VeChain, a blockchain-based SCM platform, uses a combination of RFID tags and blockchain technology to track and verify the authenticity of luxury products [56]. The data generated by the RFID tags is stored on the VeChain blockchain, creating a tamper-proof record of the product's journey through the supply chain.
2. **Decentralized Architecture:** A decentralized architecture can be implemented by creating a network of IoT devices that communicate with each other without the need for a central point of control. Each device can have its own copy of the blockchain, making it difficult for attackers to take down the entire network. For instance, IOTA, a DLT platform designed specifically for IoT, uses a unique architecture called the Tangle [57]. The Tangle is a directed acyclic graph (DAG) that allows IoT devices to communicate with each other in a decentralized manner. By eliminating the need for miners, IOTA achieves a high level of scalability and energy efficiency.
3. **Identity Management:** Another way to use blockchain is to secure the identity of IoT devices; for example, by using blockchain-based digital identity certificates [9, 24]. It is also possible to use blockchain-based data marketplaces to monetize the data generated by IoT devices, allowing for secure and transparent sharing of data among devices and organizations. Identity management for IoT devices can be achieved by creating a unique identity for each device and storing it on the blockchain. This ensures that only authorized devices can access the network and that each device's actions can be tracked and audited. For instance, the blockchain-based IoT platform Filament uses a proprietary hardware device called a Blocklet to enable secure communication between IoT devices. Each Blocklet has its own unique identity, which is stored on the blockchain. This ensures that only authorized devices can access the network and that all transactions are secure.
4. **Smart Contracts:** One way to secure the IoT with blockchain is to use blockchain-based smart contracts to secure communication between IoT devices [9, 11]. Smart contracts can be used to ensure that only authorized devices can access and transmit data on the network. Smart contracts can be used to automate the verification process for transactions between IoT devices. These contracts can be programmed to execute automatically when certain conditions are met, reducing the risk of human error and ensuring that all transactions are secure. For instance, the blockchain-based IoT security

platform Atonomi uses smart contracts to automate the process of device authentication and authorization. The smart contracts are used to verify that each device is authorized to access the network and that all transactions are secure.

5. **Data Encryption:** Data encryption for IoT devices can be achieved by using a combination of symmetric and asymmetric encryption. The data can be encrypted with a symmetric key, which is then encrypted with an asymmetric key and stored on the blockchain. For instance, Ambrosus, a blockchain-based IoT platform for SCM, uses a combination of encryption and blockchain technology to ensure the security of data generated by IoT devices [58]. The data is encrypted using a combination of symmetric and asymmetric encryption, and the encrypted data is stored on the Ambrosus blockchain, ensuring that the data is secure and tamper-proof.

7.6 HOW TO SECURE IOT WITH BLOCKCHAIN: THE PROBLEM OF CENTRALIZATION

The IoT is a rapidly growing network of interconnected devices that communicate with each other to automate and optimize various processes. While IoT brings numerous benefits, it also raises security concerns, as it involves the exchange of sensitive data between devices. Blockchain technology can provide a solution to the security challenges of IoT by ensuring the confidentiality, integrity, and availability of data. However, the problem of centralization can undermine the security benefits of blockchain technology. In the context of a blockchain IoT system, the problem of centralization refers to the concentration of power and control in the hands of a few entities, or nodes [59]. This can occur when a single entity or group of entities control the majority of the nodes or computing power in the network. We will next discuss few examples of the problems associated with centralization:

1. **Facebook's Data Privacy Issues:** Facebook is a centralized platform that stores a vast amount of personal data of its users. In 2018, it was revealed that the political consulting firm Cambridge Analytica had gained unauthorized access to millions of Facebook users' data without their consent [60]. This data was then used to influence the 2016 U.S. presidential election. This case highlighted the problem of centralization and the potential for abuse of power.
2. **Bitcoin's Scalability Problem:** Bitcoin is a decentralized cryptocurrency that relies on a network of computers to process transactions. However, the blockchain technology that underlies Bitcoin can only handle a limited number of transactions per second, leading to slow transaction times and high transaction fees during peak usage. This scalability problem is partly due to the decentralized nature of Bitcoin, which makes it difficult to coordinate upgrades to the network [61].
3. **U.S. Healthcare System:** The healthcare system in the United States is highly centralized, with a few large insurance companies controlling a significant portion of the market. This centralization has led to high healthcare

costs and limited access to care for some individuals [59, 62]. Additionally, the centralized system has been criticized for its lack of transparency and accountability.
4. **Amazon's Market Dominance:** Amazon is a centralized platform that has become the dominant player in the online retail space. This dominance has allowed Amazon to exert significant control over the market, which has led to concerns about antitrust violations and unfair competition. Additionally, Amazon's centralization has raised concerns about the company's power to influence consumer behavior and shape the broader economy [59].

In each case, centralization has led to concentration of power, lack of accountability, and potential for abuse. Centralization can undermine the security and efficiency of the blockchain IoT system in several ways, including the following [59, 62, 63].

1. **Single Point of Failure:** When one node or entity has control over the majority of the nodes in the network, it becomes a single point of failure. This means that if the central node fails or is compromised, the entire network could become vulnerable to attacks.
2. **Reduced Privacy:** A centralized blockchain IoT system may be more vulnerable to privacy breaches, as a single entity can potentially access and control all the data transmitted within the network.
3. **Slower Transaction Processing:** A centralized system can also lead to slower transaction processing, as all transactions must go through the central entity, which can create a bottleneck.

To address the problem of centralization in blockchain IoT systems, decentralized architectures can be used. These architectures distribute power and control across the network, allowing all nodes to participate in decision-making and eliminating the need for a central authority. In a decentralized system, each node has equal rights, and decisions are made through consensus among the nodes. This can improve the security and efficiency of the blockchain IoT system, making it more resilient to attacks and faster in processing transactions. By implementing a decentralized blockchain architecture, IoT devices can communicate securely without relying on a central authority. This can prevent unauthorized access to data and ensure that the network remains resilient to attacks.

7.7 HOW IT LOOKS FOR ARCHITECTURE-MINDED PEOPLE

From an architectural perspective, blockchain is a DLT that uses a decentralized network of nodes to maintain a constantly growing list of records, called blocks. Each block contains a timestamp and a link to the previous block, forming a chain of blocks (hence the name "blockchain"). One key feature of blockchain is its consensus mechanism, which allows the network to reach agreement on the state of the ledger without relying on a central authority [62]. This is achieved through the use of cryptographic techniques, such as digital signatures and hashing, to ensure the integrity of the ledger and prevent tampering. The architecture of a blockchain network can vary depending on the specific implementation, but generally, it consists of three main components: the nodes, the consensus mechanism, and the storage layer [9, 42].

- **Nodes:** The nodes are the individual devices or computers that participate in the network and maintain copies of the ledger.
- **Consensus Mechanism:** The consensus mechanism is the process by which the nodes agree on the state of the ledger. Different blockchain implementations use different consensus mechanisms, such as PoW and PoS.
- **Storage Layer:** The storage layer is responsible for maintaining the ledger and providing access to the data stored on it. This can include a database or a distributed file system.

From an architectural point of view, the decentralized nature of blockchain offers several benefits, such as increased security and resilience against single points of failure. However, it also poses certain challenges, such as scalability and interoperability, which need to be addressed when designing a blockchain-based system [11, 37]. In an IoT blockchain architecture, the various layers play specific roles in ensuring the secure and efficient operation of the system, as illustrated in Figure 7.1. The application layer provides the interface for users and devices to interact with the blockchain, enabling the implementation of various IoT use cases. The distributed computing layer ensures the decentralized and secure nature of the IoT blockchain system, maintaining the consensus protocol and executing smart contracts. The platform layer provides the necessary tools and resources for developing, deploying, and managing IoT Blockchain applications, enabling developers to create secure and interoperable solutions. The infrastructure layer supports the physical and networking components of the IoT blockchain system, facilitating the seamless integration and reliable operation of IoT devices with the blockchain network. The integration of blockchain into the IoT is still in its early stages and there are still

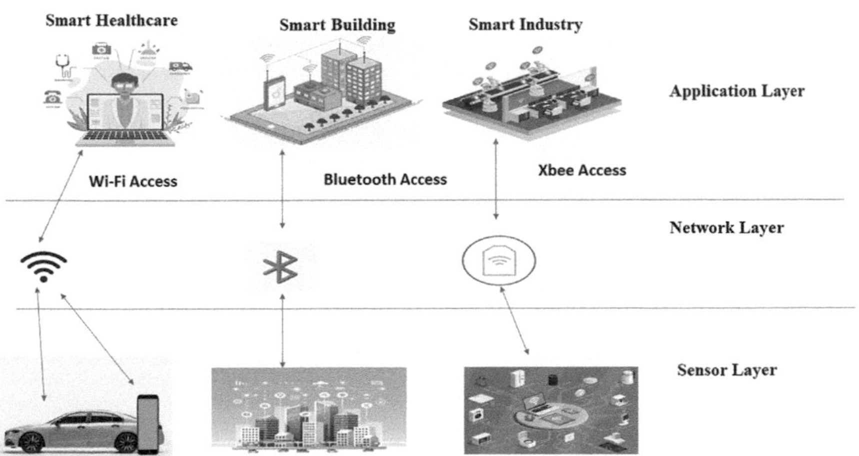

FIGURE 7.1 IoT blockchain architecture.

many challenges that need to be addressed, such as scalability, interoperability, and energy efficiency [33, 37].

1. **Application Layer:** The application layer is responsible for handling the user interfaces and application-specific functionalities in the IoT blockchain system. It includes the applications and services that interact with users or other systems. This layer enables the implementation of various IoT use cases, such as smart contracts, asset tracking, SCM, and energy management. The application layer provides the interface for users and devices to interact with the blockchain and access the stored data and functionalities.
2. **Distributed Computing Layer:** The distributed computing layer is the core layer that manages the blockchain network and the consensus mechanism. It handles the DLT and ensures the decentralized and secure nature of the system. This layer includes nodes or peers that participate in the blockchain network, validate transactions, and maintain the consensus protocol. It is responsible for executing smart contracts, validating transactions, and securing the blockchain against malicious activities. The distributed computing layer ensures transparency, immutability, and trust in the IoT blockchain system.
3. **Platform Layer:** The platform layer provides the infrastructure and tools for developing, deploying, and managing IoT blockchain applications. It includes the software frameworks, development kits, and APIs that facilitate the creation and integration of IoT devices and applications with the blockchain network. The platform layer offers features like identity management, data encryption, data integration, and access control. It provides developers with the necessary tools and resources to build scalable, interoperable, and secure IoT blockchain applications.
4. **Infrastructure Layer:** The infrastructure layer comprises the underlying hardware and networking components that support the IoT blockchain system. It includes the physical devices, sensors, gateways, communication protocols, cloud infrastructure, and data storage systems. This layer ensures the connectivity, scalability, and reliability of the IoT devices and their integration with the blockchain network. The infrastructure layer handles data acquisition, transmission, storage, and processing. It plays a critical role in enabling the seamless integration of IoT devices with the blockchain, allowing for real-time data exchange and secure transactions.

In the context of the IoT, blockchain architecture can be used to secure communication and data sharing among IoT devices [2]. One way to do this is by using blockchain-based smart contracts to control access to the network and ensure that only authorized devices (nodes) can transmit data. When a user initiates a transaction, it is broadcasted to all the nodes in the network. Each node then verifies the transaction to ensure that it is valid and that the user has the necessary funds to complete the transaction. Once the transaction is validated, it is added to a block, along with other transactions. When a block is full, it is broadcasted to all the nodes in the network for validation. Each node verifies the block to ensure that it follows the rules of the blockchain protocol and that all the transactions in the block are valid. Once a block is validated, it is added to the blockchain, and the process starts again. The beauty of the blockchain architecture is that it is decentralized, meaning that no single entity controls the network. Instead, it is maintained by a network of nodes that work together to ensure the integrity of the data. This makes it difficult for anyone to manipulate the blockchain, ensuring the security and immutability of the data stored within it. An IoT blockchain architecture typically includes the following components [10, 38, 48, 54].

- **IoT Devices:** These are the physical devices that collect and transmit data, such as sensors and actuators. They typically have limited computing power and connectivity capabilities.
- **Blockchain Nodes:** These are the devices or computers that participate in the blockchain network and maintain copies of the ledger. They can range from powerful servers to small, low-power devices. Nodes are the individual computers that make up the blockchain network. Each node contains a copy of the blockchain ledger and works together with other nodes to validate transactions and add them to the ledger. Nodes can be operated by anyone, making the network decentralized.
- **Transactions:** Transactions are the records of value transfer between two parties on the blockchain. Each transaction is validated by the nodes on the network to ensure its authenticity, accuracy, and compliance with the rules of the blockchain protocol.
- **Blocks:** Blocks are the groups of validated transactions that are added to the blockchain in a sequential manner. Each block contains a unique identifier, a list of validated transactions, a timestamp, and a reference to the previous block in the chain, forming an unbreakable chain of blocks.
- **Smart Contracts:** These are self-executing contracts with the terms of the agreement between buyer and seller being directly written into lines of code. They can be used to automate the process of access control and data sharing among IoT devices. Smart contracts are self-executing contracts that are stored on the blockchain. They are used to automate complex transactions and enforce the rules of the blockchain network.
- **Data Storage:** This component is responsible for storing the data generated by the IoT devices. It can be a centralized database or a decentralized distributed file system.
- **Consensus Mechanism:** This component is responsible for maintaining the integrity of the ledger and ensuring that all nodes agree on the state of the network. This can be achieved through different mechanisms such as PoW or PoS. The consensus mechanism is the algorithm that governs how nodes on the network agree on the current state of the blockchain ledger. It ensures that all nodes agree on the same version of the blockchain and that no single node can manipulate the ledger. The consensus layer is responsible for ensuring that all nodes in the network agree on the state of the ledger. It includes the consensus algorithm, which determines how nodes reach consensus on which transactions to add to the ledger.

- **Application Layer:** This is the layer where the actual IoT application runs, the layer that connects the IoT devices to the blockchain network, and the layer which allows the devices to interact with the smart contracts and the data storage. This layer is where the user interacts with the blockchain network. It includes the user interface and the application logic that enables users to create and execute transactions.
- **Cryptography:** Cryptography is used to secure the blockchain network by providing encryption and digital signatures for transactions and blocks. It ensures that only authorized parties can access and modify the data on the blockchain.

7.8 IS BLOCKCHAIN THE SOLUTION TO IOT SECURITY?

Security of IoT devices is an ongoing problem. The largely unregulated IoT market leaves plenty of room for device hacking. When considering applications such as smart homes and smart cars, this lack of security can be a real concern. A hacker, for example, could take over a self-driving car with someone in it, or make purchases based on access levels given to an IoT system. With all of the data that is collected and passed between IoT devices, strong security is a must. There is no single best way to secure IoT devices, as the appropriate security measures will depend on the specific device and its intended use case [33, 37]. However, some common solutions for securing IoT systems include the following [8, 41, 44].

1. **Blockchain:** As mentioned earlier, blockchain technology can provide a decentralized, tamper-proof, and transparent ledger for recording and verifying transactions and data exchanges between IoT devices. It can enhance the security of IoT devices by providing a secure and transparent communication platform.
2. **Encryption:** Encryption is the process of converting plaintext into ciphertext, which makes it difficult for unauthorized parties to access the data. It is a commonly used security measure for protecting IoT devices and data. However, encryption alone may not be sufficient to protect IoT devices from sophisticated cyber-attacks.
3. **Digital Signatures:** The use of digital signatures is a cryptographic technique that is used to authenticate the identity of the sender and ensure the integrity of the data being transmitted. Digital signatures can be used to verify the authenticity of data and ensure that it has not been tampered with during transmission.
4. **Secure Boot:** Secure boot is a security feature that ensures that the software running on IoT devices is authentic and has not been tampered with. It verifies the authenticity of the firmware before it is loaded, preventing unauthorized access to the device.
5. **Trusted Platform Modules (TPMs):** TPMs are hardware security modules that are used to store and manage cryptographic keys and other sensitive data. They can be used to ensure the authenticity of data and protect against cyber-attacks.

All these solutions have their own advantages and limitations, and their effectiveness depends on the specific requirements of the IoT system and the level of security required. A combination of these solutions can be used to enhance the security of IoT devices and protect them from cyber-attacks. It is important to note that blockchain is not necessarily better than other security options like encryption, digital signatures, secure boot, or trusted platform modules (TPMs) [25, 64]. Each of these security measures has its own strengths and limitations, and their effectiveness will depend on the specific requirements of the IoT system and the level of security required. However, blockchain can provide several unique advantages for IoT security that other security options may not be able to offer. Blockchain technology can help to secure IoT devices by providing a decentralized, tamper-proof, and transparent ledger that can record and verify all transactions and data exchanges between devices. The advantages of blockchain for securing IoT system include the following [7, 31, 33].

1. **Decentralized Trust:** Blockchain technology allows for a decentralized trust model, whereby trust is established through a network of nodes rather than relying on a centralized authority. This can be especially valuable for IoT devices that may not have a centralized entity responsible for their security.
2. **Tamper-Proof Ledger:** Blockchain technology uses cryptographic hashing to create a tamper-proof and transparent ledger that records all transactions and data exchanges between IoT devices. This can provide an immutable record of all activities on the network, making it easier to detect and prevent malicious activity.
3. **Transparency:** Blockchain technology can provide transparency into the activities of IoT devices and their interactions with other devices on the network. This can help to identify potential security risks and enable faster response to security incidents.
4. **Resilience to Attacks:** The distributed nature of blockchain technology makes it more resilient to attacks and less susceptible to a single point of failure. Even if some nodes in the network are compromised, the remaining nodes can continue to operate and maintain the security of the network.

Thus, blockchain technology has the potential to enhance security for IoT devices by providing secure, decentralized, and tamper-proof storage of data and transactions. However, it is important to note that blockchain alone is not a complete solution for IoT security and it should be used in conjunction with other security measures such as secure communication protocols, device authentication, and regular software updates. One need to keep the software on IoT devices up to date with the latest security patches (firmware updates). However, these updates can be risky as they can be intercepted by hackers. Blockchain can be used to create a secure and transparent system for firmware updates, whereby updates are validated by multiple nodes on the network before being applied. Additionally, the scalability and energy consumption issues of blockchain-based systems need to be addressed before they can be widely adopted in IoT. For instance, possible secure communication protocols for blockchain-based IoT include the following [65–67].

1. **MQTT-SN (MQTT for Sensor Networks):** This protocol is designed to work on top of the MQTT protocol, which is widely used in IoT applications. MQTT-SN provides a lightweight messaging protocol that supports data transfer between IoT devices and the blockchain network.
2. **Zigbee:** Zigbee is a low-power, wireless communication protocol that is specifically designed for IoT devices. It provides secure communication using Advanced Encryption Standard (AES) encryption and can be used in conjunction with blockchain technology.
3. **Ethereum Whisper:** Ethereum Whisper is a messaging protocol that is designed for communication between decentralized applications. It uses a P2P network and provides secure communication between IoT devices and the blockchain network.
4. **IOTA:** IOTA is a distributed ledger technology that is specifically designed for IoT devices. It uses a unique consensus mechanism called the Tangle, which provides secure communication between IoT devices and the blockchain network.
5. **Hyperledger Fabric:** Hyperledger Fabric is a blockchain framework that is specifically designed for enterprise applications. It provides secure communication using various encryption techniques and can be used in conjunction with IoT devices.

7.9 BLOCKCHAIN IOT USE CASES

Blockchain empowers the IoT devices to enhance security and bring transparency in IoT ecosystems. Blockchain offers a scalable and decentralized environment to IoT devices, platforms, and applications. Apart from various financial institutes, a wide range of companies have planned to experience the blockchain's potential. On the other hand, the IoT opens up countless opportunities for businesses to run smart operations. Every device around us is now equipped with sensors, sending data to the cloud [7, 31]. Therefore, combining these two technologies can make the systems efficient. Following are a few blockchain enterprise use cases on how combining IoT with blockchain can have a significant impact across multiple industries [14, 15, 18, 19].

1. **Supply Chain and Logistics:** A global supply chain network involves many stakeholders, such as brokers, raw material providers, etc. It complicates the end-to-end visibility. The supply chain can also extend over months of time and consist of many payments and invoices. Due to the involvement of multiple stakeholders, delivery delays have become the biggest challenge. Therefore, companies are working on making their vehicles IoT-enabled to track their movement throughout the shipment process. Due to the lack of transparency and complications in the current supply chain and logistics, blockchain and IoT combined can enhance the network's reliability and

traceability [21]. The combination of blockchain and IoT technology can provide significant benefits in the supply chain and logistics domain, such as increasing efficiency, transparency, and security. One of the most significant use cases is in supply chain traceability. By integrating IoT sensors into products and shipments, data can be collected throughout the supply chain, including information about temperature, location, and other relevant parameters. This data can then be recorded on a blockchain ledger, creating an immutable record of the product's journey from origin to destination. This enables supply chain participants to track the product's movement in real time, identify any potential delays or problems, and ensure compliance with regulations and quality standards. In case of any issues, the supply chain participants can quickly identify the root cause, as the data is transparent and tamper-proof. Another use case is in logistics optimization. IoT sensors can be used to monitor the status of vehicles, including fuel levels, maintenance needs, and driver behavior. This data can be combined with blockchain-based smart contracts that automatically trigger payments and optimize routes, reducing costs and improving delivery times. Finally, blockchain and IoT can help mitigate counterfeiting and fraud in the supply chain [21, 22]. By creating an immutable record of a product's journey, it becomes easier to identify fake products and prevent them from entering the supply chain. Additionally, smart contracts can automate the verification of product authenticity, ensuring that only legitimate products are allowed to continue through the supply chain. Following are a few examples of companies using blockchain and IoT in the supply chain and logistics domain.

a) **Walmart:** Walmart has been exploring the use of blockchain and IoT to improve supply chain traceability and food safety. In a pilot project, the company used blockchain to track the journey of mangoes from farms in Mexico to Walmart's shelves in the United States. IoT sensors were used to monitor the temperature and humidity of the mangoes throughout their journey, and the data was recorded on a blockchain ledger [68]. This enabled Walmart to quickly identify any issues, such as a break in the cold chain, and take corrective action.
b) **Maersk and IBM:** Maersk and IBM partnered to create a blockchain-based platform for global trade called TradeLens [69]. The platform uses IoT sensors to track shipments and record data such as temperature, location, and customs documentation on a blockchain ledger. This enables all parties involved in the supply chain to access a transparent and tamper-proof record of the shipment's journey. By using TradeLens, Maersk and IBM aim to reduce the time and cost of global trade, while increasing transparency and security.
c) **Nestlé:** Nestlé has been using blockchain and IoT to improve the traceability and sustainability of its supply chain. In a pilot project, the company used blockchain to track the journey of milk from farms in New Zealand to factories in the Middle East [70]. IoT sensors were used to monitor the temperature and humidity of the milk throughout its journey, and the data was recorded on a blockchain ledger. This enabled Nestlé to

ensure that the milk was transported under appropriate conditions and to verify its sustainability credentials.

2. **Automotive Industry:** Blockchain technology can help in creating secure, transparent, and tamper-proof records of transactions between multiple parties in the automotive industry, such as suppliers, manufacturers, dealers, and consumers. This can help in reducing fraud, improving efficiency, and ultimately lowering costs. In addition, blockchain technology can help in managing and sharing data in a secure and transparent way. For example, blockchain-based platforms can be used to securely store and share vehicle data, such as maintenance history, accident history, and ownership records, with various stakeholders in the automotive industry. This can help improve the transparency and accuracy of vehicle data, which can be useful for buyers and sellers of used cars. Connecting IIoT solutions in the automotive sector with the decentralized network enables multiple users to exchange crucial information easily and quickly [71, 72]. For example, NetObjex is an IoT platform and solutions provider that specializes in blockchain, AI, and machine learning technologies. The company offers a variety of IoT solutions for different industries, including SCM, smart cities, healthcare, and energy. NetObjex provides a platform for businesses to create and manage their own IoT networks and applications, with a focus on secure data sharing and analysis [73]. The platform includes features such as device management, data analytics, and real-time monitoring, and it can be customized to fit specific industry needs. The automotive industry is an exciting blockchain IoT use case, as the combined technology can disrupt automated fuel payment, autonomous cars, smart parking, and automated traffic control. Smart contracts are being used in the automotive industry to automate and streamline processes such as vehicle leasing, financing, and insurance. For example, a smart contract could automatically trigger a payment to a lender when a car lease payment is due. We will next discuss few examples of how blockchain technology is being used in the automotive industry.
   a) **Supply Chain Management:** BMW Group, Ford, Renault and General Motors are among the automakers that have started using blockchain technology to improve their SCM systems [21, 22]. Blockchain technology can help in creating an immutable record of every transaction between suppliers, manufacturers, and dealers, providing a clear, transparent, and secure view of the entire supply chain. This can help in reducing fraud, minimizing errors, improving efficiency, and ultimately reducing costs.
   b) **Digital Identity and Vehicle History:** CarVertical is a blockchain-based platform that enables car owners to create a digital identity for their vehicles [72]. The platform uses blockchain technology to create an immutable record of the vehicle's history, including its ownership, accident history, and maintenance records. This can help potential buyers to make informed decisions about purchasing a used car.
   c) **Car Sharing:** The German automaker Daimler has launched a blockchain-based car-sharing service called Car2Go [74]. The platform enables users to rent cars on an hourly basis and pay using a digital

wallet. The platform uses blockchain technology to ensure that the rental agreements are secure, transparent, and immutable.

d) **Autonomous Vehicle Data Management:** In 2019, MOBI announced the launch of a blockchain-based data sharing platform for autonomous vehicles [75]. The platform is designed to enable autonomous vehicles to securely and anonymously share data with each other, such as location, speed, and road conditions. This can help in improving the safety and efficiency of autonomous vehicles.

e) **EV Charging:** The Energy Web Foundation (EWF) has developed a blockchain-based platform called the EW Origin that tracks the source of renewable energy used to charge electric vehicles [76]. The platform enables users to verify the source of the energy and ensure that it is coming from a renewable source. This can help in promoting the use of renewable energy and reducing carbon emissions from electric vehicles.

f) **Vehicle Maintenance:** In 2017, Toyota Research Institute (TRI) announced a partnership with blockchain startup Oaken Innovations to develop a blockchain-based platform for managing vehicle maintenance and payments [77]. The platform enables car owners to securely store and share vehicle data, such as maintenance history and warranty information, with repair shops and dealerships. It also enables secure and transparent payments for vehicle repairs and maintenance services.

g) **Car Insurance:** Insurwave is a blockchain-based platform that enables insurers, brokers, and customers to manage and track marine insurance policies [19]. The platform uses blockchain technology to create a secure and transparent record of policy transactions, claims, and payments. Insurwave has also partnered with BMW Group to develop a blockchain-based platform for automotive insurance.

h) **Vehicle Security:** VeChain is a blockchain-based platform that enables car owners to track the location and condition of their vehicles in real time [56]. The platform uses blockchain technology to create a secure and tamper-proof record of the vehicle's data, including its location, speed, and condition. This can help in reducing the risk of vehicle theft and fraud.

i) **Autonomous Vehicle Payments:** The blockchain-based startup Cognitiv+ is developing a platform for autonomous vehicles to securely and automatically make payments for services such as parking, tolls, and charging [72]. The platform uses blockchain technology to create a secure and transparent record of the transactions, enabling autonomous vehicles to pay for services without human intervention.

3. **Smart Homes:** Smart IoT-enabled devices play a crucial role in our day-to-day lives. IoT blockchain enables the home security system to be managed remotely from the smartphone [12, 50], but the traditional centralized approach to exchange information generated by IoT devices lacks security standards and ownership of data. Blockchain could elevate the smart home to the next level by solving security issues and removing centralized infrastructure. As the technology continues to develop, we can expect to see

more innovative applications in this space. Following are some examples of how blockchain and IoT have been applied in the smart home domain.

a) **Power Ledger:** Power Ledger is an Australian company that is using blockchain technology to allow homeowners to sell excess energy generated by their solar panels to others on the same network [78]. The company's platform uses IoT sensors to track energy production and consumption, ensuring that transactions are secure and transparent.
b) **Ambrosus:** Ambrosus is a Swiss company that is using blockchain and IoT to create a smart home ecosystem that focuses on food safety [58]. The company's system tracks the entire supply chain of food products, from farm to table, using IoT sensors to monitor temperature, humidity, and other conditions. This information is stored on the blockchain, making it tamper-proof and transparent.
c) **Slock.it:** Slock.it is a German company that has developed a smart lock that can be controlled using blockchain technology [79]. The lock is connected to the IoT, allowing homeowners to monitor access to their property and control who has permission to enter. The blockchain ensures that all transactions are recorded and secure.
d) **Provenance:** Provenance is a UK-based company that is using blockchain and IoT to create a more transparent supply chain for consumer goods [80]. The company's system tracks products from the factory to the store using IoT sensors and records all transactions on the blockchain. This allows consumers to see exactly where their products come from and how they were produced.
e) **Filament:** Filament is a U.S. company that has developed a blockchain-enabled IoT platform for the smart home [81]. The company's system uses blockchain to ensure that all devices on the network are secure and tamper-proof. It also uses IoT sensors to monitor the environment, allowing homeowners to control temperature, humidity, and other conditions remotely.
f) **Telstra:** Telstra, a telecommunications company based in Australia, is working to improve the security of smart homes. In 2020, the company launched a new platform called Telstra Smart Home Protect, which is designed to protect customers from cyber-threats such as hacking, malware, and phishing attacks [82]. Telstra is taking steps to address the growing security concerns associated with smart homes, and Telstra Smart Home Protect is one example of how the company is working to protect its customers from cyber-threats. Telstra uses its network to identify and block malicious traffic before it reaches a customer's smart home devices. The platform monitors connected devices for unusual activity and alerts customers if it detects any suspicious behavior. Telstra offers web filtering to block known malicious websites and protect customers from phishing attacks.

4. **Sharing Economy:** The sharing economy has become a widely adopted concept around the world. Blockchain could help create decentralized, shared economy applications to earn considerable revenue by sharing the

goods seamlessly [17]. Following are two case studies of blockchain and IoT applications in the sharing economy domain.

a) **Share&Charge:** Share&Charge is a blockchain-based platform for electric vehicle (EV) charging which uses IoT devices to enable secure and automated payments between EV drivers and charging station owners. The platform uses blockchain technology to create a secure and transparent ledger of charging transactions, which can be accessed and audited by all parties involved. IoT sensors and smart contracts are used to automate the charging and payment process, ensuring that drivers are only charged for the exact amount of energy they use, and that charging station owners are paid promptly for their services [83]. Share&Charge is an example of how blockchain and IoT can be used to create a more efficient and secure sharing economy, by enabling P2P transactions and eliminating the need for intermediaries. By using blockchain to create a trusted and transparent ledger of transactions, and IoT devices to automate the charging and payment process, Share&Charge is able to create a seamless and frictionless user experience for EV drivers and charging station owners.

b) **WePower:** WePower is a blockchain-based platform for renewable energy sharing which uses IoT devices to enable transparent and automated tracking of energy production and consumption. The platform allows individuals and businesses to buy and sell renewable energy directly, using blockchain technology to create a transparent and secure ledger of energy transactions. IoT sensors and smart contracts are used to automatically track energy production and consumption, ensuring that all transactions are accurately recorded and verified. WePower is an example of how blockchain and IoT can be used to create a more sustainable and decentralized sharing economy by enabling the sharing and trading of renewable energy directly between individuals and businesses [84]. By using blockchain to create a transparent and secure ledger of energy transactions, and IoT devices to automate the tracking and verification of energy production and consumption, WePower is able to create a more efficient and equitable energy market.

5. **Pharmaceutical Industry:** The pharmaceutical industry is responsible for developing, manufacturing, and distributing pharmaceutical drugs. Tracking the complete journey of the process is difficult. Blockchain and IoT can be used in the pharmaceutical industry to improve SCM, enhance drug safety and authenticity, and increase efficiency in clinical trials. One of the main challenges in the pharmaceutical industry is ensuring the safety and efficacy of drugs, as well as the accuracy and integrity of data in clinical trials. Blockchain technology can provide a secure and transparent platform for tracking drug provenance, monitoring drug quality, and recording clinical trial data [85]. By using blockchain to create a tamper-proof and auditable record of drug transactions, pharmaceutical companies can improve drug safety and efficacy, and ensure the accuracy and integrity of clinical trial data. IoT devices can also be used to monitor drug quality, track drug shipments, and provide real-time data on drug efficacy and safety. By using IoT

sensors to monitor temperature, humidity, and other environmental factors that can affect drug quality, pharmaceutical companies can ensure that drugs are stored and transported under the appropriate conditions. IoT devices can also be used to track the movement of drugs through the supply chain, from production to distribution to consumption, providing real-time data on drug availability, inventory levels, and other key metrics. Following are two case studies of blockchain and IoT applications in the pharmaceutical domain.

a) **MediLedger:** MediLedger is a blockchain-based platform for tracking and verifying pharmaceuticals which uses IoT devices to enable real-time monitoring of the supply chain [86]. The platform allows pharmaceutical manufacturers, distributors, and pharmacies to track the movement of drugs through the supply chain, from production to distribution to consumption. IoT sensors are used to track the location, temperature, and other key metrics of each drug shipment, ensuring that drugs are stored and transported under the appropriate conditions. MediLedger is an example of how blockchain and IoT can be used to create a more secure and transparent pharmaceutical supply chain by enabling real-time tracking and verification of drug shipments. By using blockchain to create a tamper-proof and auditable record of drug transactions and IoT devices to monitor the movement and conditions of drug shipments, MediLedger is able to improve the safety and efficiency of the pharmaceutical supply chain.

b) **Chronicled:** Chronicled is a blockchain-based platform for tracking and verifying the authenticity of pharmaceutical products, which uses IoT devices to enable real-time monitoring of drug quality and provenance [87]. The platform allows pharmaceutical companies to track the movement of drugs through the supply chain, from production to distribution to consumption, using blockchain technology to create a secure and transparent record of each transaction. IoT sensors are used to monitor the quality and authenticity of each drug shipment, ensuring that drugs are not counterfeit or adulterated. Chronicled is an example of how blockchain and IoT can be used to combat the problem of counterfeit and substandard drugs, which is a major issue in many parts of the world. By using blockchain to create a tamper-proof and auditable record of drug transactions, and IoT devices to monitor the quality and provenance of drug shipments, Chronicled is able to improve the safety and efficacy of the pharmaceutical supply chain, and protect patients from the harm caused by counterfeit and substandard drugs.

6. **Agriculture:** For maximum customer satisfaction, it is essential to grow more food for the increased population while minimizing environmental footprints, and ensuring transparency across the supply chain. Blockchain, coupled with IoT, has the potential to reshape the food production industry from farm to grocery to home [46, 88]. Installing IoT sensors in the farms and sending data directly to the blockchain can help enhance the food supply chain to a greater extent. The combination of blockchain and IoT can bring significant benefits to the agriculture industry by increasing transparency,

reducing fraud, and ensuring the safety and quality of food products. We will next explore a few case studies of application of IoT and blockchain to improve the agricultural supply chain.

a) **AgriDigital:** AgriDigital is an Australian company that uses blockchain technology to streamline agricultural supply chains [89], using IoT sensors to track the movement of crops from the field to the warehouse, and then blockchain to record the transactions between farmers, buyers, and distributors. This allows for greater transparency in the supply chain and helps to reduce the risk of fraud.

b) **TE-FOOD:** TE-FOOD is a blockchain-based food traceability platform that uses IoT sensors to track the movement of livestock and crops [90]. The company has implemented its technology in several countries, including Vietnam, where TE-FOOD is working with the government to track the movement of pork to prevent the spread of African swine fever.

c) **Ambrosus:** Ambrosus is a blockchain-based food traceability platform that uses IoT sensors to track the temperature, humidity, and other environmental factors that can affect the quality of food [58]. The company has worked with several food producers and distributors to ensure that their products are of the highest quality and are delivered safely to consumers.

d) **Provenance:** Provenance is a blockchain-based platform that allows consumers to trace the origin of their food products [80], using IoT sensors to track the movements of crops and livestock, and then record the information on the blockchain. This allows consumers to see where their food came from and how it was produced.

7. **Water Management:** Leaking water fixtures can result in 1 trillion gallons of waste water per year in the United States. IoT and blockchain technologies can be used for water management to improve efficiency, transparency, and sustainability. IoT devices can be used to monitor water usage, quality, and environmental conditions in real time. This data can be collected and analyzed to identify patterns and potential inefficiencies, which can help to optimize water usage and reduce waste. Blockchain technology can be used to securely store and share data between stakeholders such as water utilities, regulators, and consumers [91]. Blockchain can provide a transparent and tamper-proof ledger of water usage and quality data, which can help to build trust between stakeholders and improve regulatory compliance. Moreover, blockchain technology can also enable the P2P trading of water rights between stakeholders. By using blockchain technology, water rights can be securely and transparently traded, which can help to ensure that water is allocated efficiently and sustainably. In addition, the combination of IoT and blockchain technologies can also help to improve disaster management related to water resources. By using IoT devices and blockchain technology, real-time data on water usage and quality can be collected and shared during natural disasters, such as floods or droughts, to help emergency responders

manage water resources more effectively. We will next explore a few case studies of application of IoT and blockchain to improve water management.

a) **Veolia Water Technologies:** Veolia Water Technologies, a water treatment and management company, collaborated with BlockApps, a blockchain solutions provider, to develop a blockchain-enabled IoT platform for water treatment plants [92]. The platform uses sensors and IoT devices to monitor water quality, usage, and other parameters in real time. The data is stored on a private blockchain network, which enables secure data sharing and improves data integrity. The platform also allows for automatic billing and payments, which streamlines the billing process and reduces the risk of errors.
b) **Aquai:** Aquai is a water management platform that uses blockchain and IoT technologies to optimize water usage and reduce waste in industrial and agricultural settings. The platform uses sensors and IoT devices to collect real-time data on water usage, quality, and environmental conditions. The data is then stored on a blockchain network, which enables secure and transparent data sharing between stakeholders, such as farmers, suppliers, and regulators. Aquai also uses machine learning algorithms to analyze the data and provide insights into water usage patterns and potential inefficiencies. The platform can provide recommendations to users on how to optimize their water usage and reduce waste. In addition to improving water management, Aquai also has the potential to enable the trading of water rights between stakeholders. By using blockchain technology, Aquai can provide a secure and transparent platform for the P2P trading of water rights, which can help to ensure that water is allocated efficiently and sustainably.
c) **"Drone on the Volga":** The "Drone on the Volga" project is an example of how IoT and blockchain technologies can be used for water management. The project was initiated by the Russian government to monitor and regulate water use in the Volga River basin. The project used drones equipped with IoT sensors to collect data on water quality, usage, and environmental conditions. The data was then transmitted to a blockchain-based platform, which enabled secure and transparent data sharing between stakeholders, such as water utilities, regulators, and consumers [93]. The blockchain platform used smart contracts to automate the water usage monitoring process and to ensure compliance with regulations. The smart contracts could automatically notify regulators and water utilities if there was a violation of regulations, such as exceeding water usage limits. The platform also enabled the P2P trading of water rights, which helped to ensure that water was allocated efficiently and sustainably. The use of drones and IoT sensors allowed for real-time monitoring of water resources, which enabled prompt response to potential problems, such as water pollution or excessive water usage. The use of blockchain technology ensured that the data was tamper-proof and transparent, which helped to build trust between stakeholders and improve regulatory compliance.

7.10 THE FUTURE OF BOTNETS IN THE INTERNET OF THINGS

A botnet is a network of internet-connected devices—such as computers, smartphones, and IoT devices—that are infected with malicious software, also known as malware [94, 95]. The infected devices, also called bots or zombies, are controlled remotely by a single attacker, who can use them to carry out various activities without the knowledge or consent of their owners. Botnets can be used for a wide range of malicious activities, such as sending spam emails, launching DDoS attacks, stealing sensitive data, installing additional malware on the compromised devices, and performing click fraud. Botnets can also be used to generate revenue through various illegal means, such as mining cryptocurrency using the computing power of the infected devices. The size and complexity of botnets can vary greatly, ranging from a few hundred bots to millions of bots. The most sophisticated botnets use advanced techniques to evade detection and maintain their control over the infected devices. Preventing and mitigating the damage caused by botnets is a major challenge for cyber-security experts and law enforcement agencies. The IoT is a rapidly growing field that involves connecting everyday objects to the internet, enabling them to send and receive data and be controlled remotely. However, as more and more IoT devices are being deployed, they are becoming an attractive target for cybercriminals looking to build botnets. One of the main challenges with IoT devices is that they often have weak security protections and are not regularly updated with security patches, making them vulnerable to attacks. Additionally, many IoT devices have default usernames and passwords that are easy to guess or are hard-coded into the device firmware, making it easier for attackers to gain control of them.

As a result, botnets that target IoT devices are expected to become more prevalent in the future. These botnets can be used for a variety of malicious activities, such as launching DDoS attacks, mining cryptocurrency, and stealing sensitive data [96, 97]. Furthermore, as IoT devices become more integrated into our daily lives and critical infrastructure, the potential impact of botnet attacks on them could be much more severe than attacks on traditional computing devices. Botnets have already been used to launch large-scale attacks that have caused significant disruptions to internet services. For example, in 2016, the Mirai botnet was used to launch a massive DDoS attack against domain name service (DNS) provider Dyn which resulted in widespread outages for popular websites such as Twitter, Spotify, and Netflix. One of the main drivers behind the rise of IoT botnets is the sheer number of connected devices that are being deployed. These devices often have weak security protections and are easy to compromise, which makes them an attractive target for attackers. Once an attacker gains control of an IoT device, they can use it to communicate with other compromised devices and build a botnet. For example, the Reaper botnet is an IoT botnet that was first discovered in 2017. It targets vulnerable IoT devices such as routers, IP cameras, and network-attached storage (NAS) devices. Once it infects a device, it attempts to spread to other vulnerable devices on the same network, using a variety of exploits and default credentials. The Reaper botnet is particularly concerning because it is modular and can be updated with new capabilities, making it difficult to detect and stop. Another example of an IoT botnet is the Satori botnet, which was first discovered in 2018 [98, 99]. This botnet targets IoT devices that have open Telnet ports, which are used for remote management. Once it infects a device, it installs a cryptocurrency miner and uses the device's computing resources to mine for cryptocurrency. The Satori botnet is particularly sophisticated because it uses a decentralized P2P architecture, which makes it more difficult to take down. As IoT devices become more prevalent in our daily lives and critical infrastructure, the impact of botnet attacks targeting them could be severe. For example, a botnet could be used to launch a large-scale attack on a power grid or a water treatment plant, causing widespread disruption and potentially even loss of life. Therefore, it is crucial for manufacturers to prioritize security in their IoT devices and for consumers to take steps to secure their devices. Additionally, cyber-security professionals and law enforcement agencies will need to continue to develop new strategies to detect and mitigate botnet attacks targeting IoT devices.

Typically, the bot herder will hijack a network of computer systems to create a botnet and then use it to execute various types of cyber-attacks like scams, brute force attacks, malware invasions, etc. A bot-master then directs a group of hacked computers using remote commands. After compiling the bots, the herder utilizes command programming to control their other behaviors and aid the bot-master in fulfilling the ultimate ulterior motive [96]. The operator in command of the botnet may have set up the swarm or could be renting it from a third party with access to the devices. Each malware-infected endpoint device that is taken over is referred to as a zombie computer or bot. These devices function blindly in response to commands programmed by the bot herder but often without the user's notice. The majority of botnets are designed to be simple to manage and control. They allow a single computer to take over many infected systems through a command-and-control (C&C) server operated by the herder. These botnets accomplish a variety of malicious tasks, including gaining control of the victim's computer, stealing data, spying on user activity by recording keystrokes or collecting photos, sending spam messages, and executing DDoS attacks.

The purpose of all botnets is the same—i.e., to use one or more computers remotely to launch a large-scale and difficult-to-trace attack—but different types of botnets approach this object in different ways [95, 96, 100]. Some of the most commonly used types of botnets include the following.

1. **Botnets Using Internet Relay Chat:** Botnets using Internet Relay Chat (IRC) is one of the oldest and most traditional types of botnets. In this type of botnet, the infected computers connect to an IRC server and wait for commands from the botnet operator. The operator can then send commands to the infected computers using IRC channels, which can be used for various purposes, including DDoS attacks, spam campaigns, data theft, and more. IRC botnets can be very powerful because they allow the operator to control a large number of infected computers from a single point of control. However, they can also be relatively easy to detect because IRC traffic is less commonly used for legitimate web browsing activity. As a result, many botnet operators have moved away from IRC botnets in favor of other types of botnets, such as HTTP or P2P botnets. It is important to be aware of the different types of botnets and take appropriate measures to protect your

devices from infection. This can include installing antivirus software, keeping software up to date, and avoiding suspicious links and downloads.

2. **Automated Botnets:** The term "automated botnets" does not describe a specific type of botnet, but rather a description of how some botnets are managed and operated. These botnets operate autonomously, with no human intervention or control. They infect victims and consume their resources, such as the local central processing unit (CPU) and network bandwidth, to launch DDoS assaults at the hacker's command [97, 101]. This specific type or category of botnets is designed in a manner that is difficult to detect, even if one uses antivirus protection. Most botnets are automated in some way, meaning that they are designed to operate without direct human intervention. They may be programmed to perform specific actions—such as sending spam emails, launching DDoS attacks, or mining cryptocurrencies—based on instructions received from the C&C server. However, some botnets are also managed by human operators who can monitor the botnet's activity, issue commands, and adjust its behavior as needed. In these cases, the botnet may still be automated in terms of its operation, but it may also have a higher degree of flexibility and adaptability based on the operator's decisions. Regardless of whether a botnet is fully automated or managed by a human operator, it can still pose a serious threat to online security. It is important to take steps to protect your devices from infection and to stay vigilant against suspicious online activity. This can include installing antivirus software, keeping software up to date, and avoiding suspicious links and downloads.
3. **Hypertext Transfer Protocol (HTTP) Botnets:** HTTP botnets are botnets that use HTTP to communicate between the infected computers and the C&C server [97]. This type of botnet can be difficult to detect because HTTP traffic is commonly used for legitimate web browsing activity. The bot herder delivers instructions via the HTTP protocol, and the bots access the server for new updates and actions. Thanks to the HTTP protocol, the herder can camouflage the activities as regular internet traffic and evade detection by existing detection methods like desktop firewalls.
4. **P2P Botnets:** A P2P network is a computer network in which two or more computers are linked and share resources (such as content, storage, and CPU cycles) through direct exchange rather than going through a server or authority that administers centralized resources [102]. P2P botnets are botnets that use a decentralized, P2P network to communicate between the infected computers and the C&C server. In this type of botnet, each infected computer can act as both a client and a server, allowing the botnet to operate even if some of the computers are taken offline or removed from the network. P2P botnets can be difficult to shut down because there is no central point of control. P2P botnets are more difficult to set up than IRC or HTTP botnets, but they are more resilient since they are not dependent on a centralized server. Instead, each bot functions as both client and server, generating and sharing information with other botnet devices [102]. The attacker does not have to configure a specific server for this sort of system architecture.

However, they retain total control over the nefarious actions performed by compromised devices. Both HTTP botnets and P2P botnets can be used for various purposes, including DDoS attacks, spam campaigns, data theft, and cryptocurrency mining [101, 102]. It is important to be aware of these types of botnets and take appropriate measures to protect your devices from infection, such as installing antivirus software, keeping software up to date, and avoiding suspicious links and downloads.

5. **Manual Botnets:** The "manual" botnet, also known as Zerp, which is a type of botnet that has been active since at least 2018. The manual botnet is a Linux-based botnet that is primarily used for mining cryptocurrency, specifically Monero [101, 103]. The manual botnet targets vulnerable servers running unsecured software or outdated versions of software with known vulnerabilities. Once a server is infected, it can be used to mine Monero and perform other malicious activities, such as spreading malware to other computers on the network. Like all types of botnets, the manual botnet is a threat to online security and can cause significant harm to infected computers and networks. It is important to take steps to protect your devices from infection and to stay vigilant against suspicious online activity. This can include installing antivirus software, keeping software up to date, and avoiding suspicious links and downloads.
6. **Backdoor Botnets:** A backdoor botnet is not a specific type of botnet, but rather a common feature of many botnets. A backdoor is a secret entrance or method of bypassing normal authentication or security controls which can be used by a botnet operator to maintain control over an infected computer or network. On a computer, network, or software program, a backdoor is any technique by which both authorized and unauthorized users may defeat standard security measures to get high-level user access (also known as root access). Once inside, hackers may pilfer personal and financial information, run other software, and control linked devices. Backdoor botnets use compromised machines to corrupt other devices and add these to a collection of bots that the perpetrator may command [97, 101]. In the context of a botnet, a backdoor is typically created when a computer is infected with malware that opens a "backdoor" port or service. This port or service can then be used by the botnet operator to communicate with the infected computer, issue commands, and receive data. Backdoors can be difficult to detect because they are designed to be hidden and operate covertly. However, they can also be used by other malicious actors to gain unauthorized access to a computer or network.
7. **Spam-Sending Botnets:** a spam-sending botnet is a specific type of botnet that is designed to send large volumes of unsolicited or unwanted emails, also known as spam. These botnets are often used to spread phishing scams, malware, and other types of online threats. Spam-sending botnets are typically composed of large numbers of infected computers known as "zombies" or "bots" that are controlled by a central C&C server. The C&C server sends instructions to the bots, which then send out spam emails to targeted recipients. These types of botnets are programmed to send millions, if not

billions, of unwanted spam messages to their intended recipients from infected devices all over the globe. Spambots gather email addresses from online forums, websites, guestbooks, and other locations where the target may have provided their email address [95, 96, 101]. These types of botnets are controlled and commanded by a bot-master for remote process execution. To avoid detection and improve their success rate, spam-sending botnets often use a variety of tactics, such as spoofing the sender's email address, using multiple IP addresses to hide their location, and using social engineering techniques to trick recipients into opening or clicking on malicious links. Spam-sending botnets can cause significant harm to online security and can be difficult to detect and mitigate. It is important to take steps to protect your devices from infection and to stay vigilant against suspicious emails and online activity. This can include using spam filters, avoiding suspicious links and downloads, and keeping software up to date.

7.10.1 Thingbots: Concept

An IoT botnet is a group of hacked computers, smart appliances and internet-connected devices that have been co-opted for illicit purposes [104, 105]. A conventional botnet is made up of computers that have been remotely accessed without the owners' knowledge and set up to forward transmissions to other computers on the internet. If you replaced botnet computers with IoT devices such as smartwatches, medical devices, smart alarms, and other similar devices, you end up being a part of the botnet that only contains IoT devices, which is known as a thingbot. Thingbots are a type of botnet that target IoT devices, such as routers, webcams, and other smart devices, in order to compromise and control them for malicious purposes. Thingbots can be used for a variety of purposes, such as launching DDoS attacks, spreading malware, and stealing sensitive information. They are often controlled by remote attackers who use them to carry out coordinated attacks, making it difficult to track down the source of the attacks. One of the main reasons why thingbots are so effective is because many IoT devices have weak security features or default passwords that are easy to guess. This makes it relatively easy for attackers to gain control of them and use them as part of a botnet. As the number of IoT devices continues to grow, the threat posed by thingbots is likely to increase, as well. These devices can be controlled by an owner to launch attacks, steal sensitive data, or facilitate other malicious activities. We have already seen a few of these in the last couple of years. Due to their ubiquity and the fact that they are usually connected directly to the internet, wireless routers and modems are the primary targets for thingbots [99, 104, 105].

Thingbots are created by cybercriminals who seek to exploit and compromise IoT devices for malicious purposes. The motivations behind creating thingbots can vary, but they are generally created to carry out cyber-attacks or other illegal activities, such as stealing sensitive data, launching DDoS attacks, or spreading malware. Some of the most common motivations for creating thingbots include financial gain, political or ideological objectives, and personal vendettas. For example, cybercriminals may create thingbots to steal personal information or financial data which they can then use for financial gain. In other cases, thingbots may be created to disrupt the operations of a political adversary or to spread a particular message or ideology. Thingbots can also be used as a tool for revenge or personal attacks, such as targeting an individual or organization that the creator has a grudge against. In addition to cybercriminals, there have been cases when nation-state actors have been accused of creating thingbots for espionage or cyber-warfare purposes. These attacks can be highly sophisticated and may involve the use of advanced malware and hacking techniques. Regardless of the motivations behind their creation, thingbots pose a significant threat to individuals, businesses, and organizations that use IoT devices. It is important to take steps to secure IoT devices and prevent them from becoming part of a botnet, and to have measures in place to detect and respond to thingbot attacks if they do occur.

Dealing with thingbots can be a challenging task, as they are designed to be difficult to detect and control. However, following are several steps that can be taken to reduce the risk of thingbot attacks and mitigate their impact [94, 97, 99, 103].

1. **Secure IoT Devices:** The first step in preventing thingbot attacks is to secure IoT devices by changing default passwords, updating firmware, and disabling unnecessary services or features. IoT devices are often targeted by thingbots because they have weak security features or default passwords that are easy to guess. By changing the default passwords and keeping firmware up to date, organizations can prevent thingbots from gaining control of these devices. Disabling unnecessary services or features can also reduce the attack surface and make it more difficult for thingbots to exploit vulnerabilities.
2. **Use Network Security Tools:** Implementing network security tools such as firewalls, intrusion detection and prevention systems, and antivirus software can help detect and block thingbot activity. Firewalls can be used to block unauthorized traffic and prevent thingbots from communicating with C&C servers. Intrusion detection and prevention systems can be used to detect and block suspicious activity on the network, such as scanning for vulnerable devices or attempting to exploit known vulnerabilities. Antivirus software can be used to detect and remove malware that may be used by thingbots.
3. **Regularly Update Software:** Regularly updating software and security patches for IoT devices can help prevent vulnerabilities that thingbots can exploit. Many thingbots exploit known vulnerabilities in software to gain control of devices, so keeping software up to date is critical in preventing these attacks.
4. **Monitor Network Traffic:** Monitoring network traffic for unusual or suspicious activity can help detect and respond to thingbot attacks. Organizations should monitor network traffic for unusual spikes in traffic, attempts to access known vulnerable services, or attempts to connect to suspicious IP addresses. By monitoring network traffic, organizations can detect thingbot activity early and take steps to prevent further damage.
5. **Educate Users:** Educating users about the risks of thingbots and the importance of maintaining good security practices can help prevent devices from

becoming part of a botnet. Users should be encouraged to change default passwords, keep software up to date, and report any suspicious activity on their devices. By educating users, organizations can reduce the risk of thingbot attacks and create a culture of security awareness.

6. **Implement Network Segmentation:** Implementing network segmentation can help contain the impact of a thingbot attack and prevent it from spreading to other parts of the network. By separating IoT devices from other parts of the network, organizations can limit the impact of a thingbot attack and prevent it from spreading to other devices.
7. **Work with Security Experts:** Organizations can work with security experts to assess their security posture and develop a comprehensive security strategy that includes thingbot prevention and response measures. Security experts can help identify vulnerabilities in IoT devices and recommend strategies for securing them. They can also provide guidance on responding to thingbot attacks and minimizing the impact of these attacks.

7.10.2 Elements of Typical IRC Bot Attack

Internet Relay Chat (IRC) is a network of internet servers that use a specific protocol through which individuals can hold real-time online conversations via personal computers (PCs) and other devices [94, 103]. Many of today's botnets utilize IRC to communicate with bot-infected machines, which is typically referred to as a "ping flood." This attack overloads the victim's internet connection with an amount of ICMP data exceeding the connection's capacity, potentially causing a disconnection from the IRC network. For the duration of the attack, the user's internet connection remains hindered. A typical IRC bot attack typically involves the use of malware or malicious software to gain control of a victim's computer, and then use that control to connect the victim's computer to an IRC channel [103, 104]. The attacker then uses the victim's computer to carry out various actions, such as sending spam messages, launching DDoS attacks, or stealing personal information [96, 99]. The goal of the attacker is typically to use the network of infected computers (botnet) to carry out these actions on a large scale. Additionally, the attacker may also use the botnet to control the infected computers remotely, often using the IRC protocol to communicate with the bots.

Basically, the IRC bot attacks are a type of cyber-attack that involves the use of an automated software program, known as a bot, to gain unauthorized access to an IRC server or channel. These attacks can be carried out for a variety of malicious purposes, such as stealing sensitive data, spreading malware, or conducting DDoS attacks. Following are some of the common elements of a typical IRC bot attack [103, 106].

1. **Botnet Recruitment:** The attacker creates or finds a pre-existing botnet, a collection of bots that are programmed to carry out specific tasks. Often these botnets are controlled by a C&C server operated by the attacker.
2. **Reconnaissance:** The botnet then probes potential targets such as IRC servers and channels seeking to find ones which can be exploited.

3. **Exploitation:** The botnet attacks IRC servers or channels using a variety of exploits to gain control of the server or channel. One common method is by exploiting vulnerabilities in the server software, such as buffer overflow attacks. Another method is to use social engineering tactics to trick users into giving up their login credentials.
4. **Bot Deployment:** Once the attacker gains control of the server or channel, the botnet deploys the bot on the server. The bot then waits for commands from the C&C server.
5. **Malicious Activities:** The attacker can use the bot for various malicious activities such as spamming, DDoS attacks, and spreading malware.
6. **Concealment:** To avoid detection, the bot may use various techniques to conceal its presence and activity, such as encrypting communications with the C&C server, using random nicknames, and hiding in system processes.
7. **Persistence:** To ensure continued access and control, the bot may install backdoors or other methods of persistence on the compromised system.

7.10.3 Malicious Use of Bots and Botnet

While botnets may be deemed an attack unto itself, they are an ideal instrument for conducting large-scale frauds and cybercrimes [94, 97]. The following are examples of popular botnet attacks:

1. **Distributed Denial of Service (DDoS):** DDoS is a type of cyber-attack in which a large number of compromised computers (known as a botnet) are used to flood a target server or network with traffic, overwhelming its capacity and causing it to become unavailable to legitimate users [96]. The goal of a DDoS attack is to disrupt normal operations or to bring down a website or online service entirely. The attack typically works by exploiting vulnerabilities in devices or servers that allow the attacker to gain control over them, and then using these compromised devices to flood the target with traffic. This traffic may be generated in a variety of ways, including by sending large amounts of data to the target, or by repeatedly requesting connections to the target in order to exhaust its resources. DDoS attacks can be difficult to mitigate because they often come from a large number of sources, making it difficult to distinguish legitimate traffic from the attack traffic. There is, however, a variety of techniques that can be used to detect and mitigate DDoS attacks, such as filtering out malicious traffic, diverting traffic to alternative servers, or limiting the rate of incoming traffic to the target.
2. **Sniffing and Keylogging Botnet Attacks:** Sniffing and keylogging are two types of botnet attacks that are commonly used by cybercriminals to steal sensitive information from victims [96, 103]. Sniffing botnet attacks involve the use of malware to intercept and capture data that is transmitted over a network, such as usernames, passwords, and other confidential information. This is done by capturing and analyzing network packets, which contain data transmitted between devices on the network. The attacker can

then use this information to gain unauthorized access to systems or to steal sensitive data. Keylogging botnet attacks involve the use of malware to capture and record every keystroke entered by a user on a compromised device. This allows the attacker to capture sensitive information such as login credentials, credit card numbers, and other confidential data. Both of these types of botnet attacks can be used to steal sensitive information on a large scale, as the attacker can control a large number of compromised devices and capture data from all of them simultaneously. It is important for users to take steps to protect themselves from these types of attacks, such as keeping their software up to date, using strong passwords, and being cautious when opening email attachments or clicking on links from unknown sources.

3. **Botnet-Driven Phishing:** Botnet-driven phishing is a type of cyber-attack in which a botnet is used to distribute phishing emails to a large number of potential victims [103]. Phishing is a technique used by cybercriminals to trick users into providing sensitive information, such as login credentials or credit card numbers, by disguising themselves as a trustworthy entity. In a botnet-driven phishing attack, the botnet is used to send out large volumes of emails that are designed to look like they are from a legitimate source, such as a bank or online retailer. The emails may contain links to fake websites that are designed to look like the real thing but are actually designed to capture the user's information. The use of a botnet in these attacks allows the attacker to send out a large number of emails quickly and efficiently, increasing the chances that some users will fall for the phishing scam. The botnet can also be used to evade detection by sending out the emails from a large number of different IP addresses, making it difficult for security systems to block the attack. To protect themselves from botnet-driven phishing attacks, users should be cautious when opening emails from unknown senders or clicking on links contained within these emails. They should also be aware of the warning signs of phishing, such as emails that request sensitive information or emails that contain spelling and/or grammatical errors, or unusual formatting. It is also important for users to keep their software up to date and to use security software to help detect and prevent these types of attacks.
4. **Large-Scale Spam Attacks:** A large-scale spam attack is a type of cyber-attack in which a large number of unsolicited emails are sent to a large number of recipients, often with the intention of delivering malware, phishing scams, or other types of malicious content [103]. Spam emails are typically sent using a botnet. The botnet can be used to send out millions of spam emails in a short amount of time, allowing the attacker to reach a large number of potential victims. To protect themselves from large-scale spam attacks, users should be cautious when opening emails from unknown senders or clicking on links contained within these emails. They should also be aware of the warning signs of spam, such as emails that contain grammatical errors or unusual formatting. It is also important for users to keep their software up to date and to use security software to help detect and prevent

these types of attacks. Spam emails can be used for a variety of purposes, including the following.

a) **Phishing Scams:** The spam email may contain a link to a fake website that is designed to look like a legitimate site, such as a bank or online retailer. The user is then tricked into entering their login credentials or other sensitive information, which is then captured by the attacker.
b) **Malware Distribution:** The spam email may contain a file attachment or a link to a website that is designed to deliver malware, such as a virus or a Trojan horse. Once the user downloads or clicks on the link, the malware is installed on their computer.
c) **Scams:** The spam email may contain a message that is designed to trick the user into sending money or providing personal information to the attacker.

5. **Data Breach Perpetrated via Botnet:** A data breach perpetrated via botnet is a type of cyber-attack in which a botnet is used to gain unauthorized access to sensitive information stored on a computer or network [94, 97]. Botnets are created by infecting computers and other internet-connected devices with malware, allowing them to be controlled remotely by a hacker. Once a botnet is established, the hacker can use it to launch a variety of attacks, including data breaches. In this type of attack, the botnet is used to scan for vulnerabilities in a target system and then exploit those vulnerabilities to gain access to sensitive data. The botnet may be programmed to collect certain types of information, such as credit card numbers, passwords, or personal identifying information, and then transmit that data back to the hacker. Data breaches perpetrated via botnets can be particularly damaging because they can allow a hacker to gain access to large amounts of sensitive information quickly and easily. In addition, because the attack is being carried out by a network of compromised devices, it can be difficult to detect and trace back to its source. Organizations can protect themselves against botnet-based attacks by implementing strong security measures, such as firewalls, antivirus software, and intrusion detection systems, and by regularly updating their software and systems to ensure that they are protected against known vulnerabilities.
6. **Cryptocurrency Mining and Clipping:** Cryptocurrency mining is the process of validating transactions and adding them to the blockchain ledger of a cryptocurrency, such as Bitcoin. A cryptocurrency clipping attack, also known as cryptojacking, is a type of cyber-attack that involves stealing cryptocurrency by gaining unauthorized access to someone else's computer or mobile device and using it to mine cryptocurrency [94, 97]. The attacker will typically install mining software on the victim's device without their knowledge or consent, and then use their computing power and energy to mine cryptocurrency for their own benefit. The impact of a cryptocurrency clipping attack can be significant. It can slow down the victim's computer or mobile device, increase energy usage, and reduce battery life. In addition, it can also cause financial loss for the victim, as

the attacker may be able to earn significant amounts of cryptocurrency without their knowledge. To protect against cryptocurrency clipping attacks, users should take steps to secure their devices, such as keeping their software up to date, using strong passwords, and avoiding downloading suspicious files or clicking on suspicious links. In addition, organizations should implement security measures such as firewalls, antivirus software, and intrusion detection systems to detect and prevent these types of attacks.

7. **Brute Force Attacks:** A brute force attack is a type of cyber-attack that involves trying every possible combination of characters or passwords until the correct one is found. In other words, the attacker will systematically try every possible password until they gain access to a system or account. Brute force attacks can be used to crack encrypted passwords, gain access to secure systems, or steal sensitive information [107]. The attack can be carried out using software tools that automate the process, allowing the attacker to try thousands or even millions of combinations per second. Brute force attacks can be very effective if the attacker has enough time and computing power to try all possible combinations. However, they can also be time consuming and resource intensive, especially if the password is long or complex. To protect against brute force attacks, users should use strong passwords that are difficult to guess. This includes using a combination of upper- and lower-case letters, numbers, and special characters. In addition, organizations should implement security measures such as limiting login attempts, using multi-factor authentication, and monitoring their systems for signs of suspicious activity.

REFERENCES

[1] M. A. Ferrag, M. Derdour, M. Mukherjee, A. Derhab, L. Maglaras, and H. Janicke, "Blockchain Technologies for the Internet of Things: Research Issues and Challenges," *IEEE Internet Things J.*, vol. 6, no. 2, 2019, doi: 10.1109/JIOT.2018.2882794.

[2] L. Zhu, K. Gai, and M. Li, *Blockchain Technology in Internet of Things*, Springer International Publishing, Berlin, Germany, 2019, doi: 10.1007/978-3-030-21766-2.

[3] A. Aoun, A. Ilinca, M. Ghandour, and H. Ibrahim, "A Review of Industry 4.0 Characteristics and Challenges, with Potential Improvements Using Blockchain Technology," *Comput. Ind. Eng.*, vol. 162, 2021, doi: 10.1016/j.cie.2021.107746.

[4] M. Parmar and H. J. Kaur, "Comparative Analysis of Secured Hash Algorithms for Blockchain Technology and Internet of Things," *Int. J. Adv. Comput. Sci. Appl.*, vol. 12, no. 3, 2021, doi: 10.14569/IJACSA.2021.0120335.

[5] J. Klein, "'Money Was the Sizzle': Blockchain Pioneer W. Scott Stornetta Assesses Satoshi's Work," *breakermag.com*, 2019.

[6] S. Squarepants, "Bitcoin: A Peer-to-Peer Electronic Cash System," *SSRN Electron. J.*, 2022, doi: 10.2139/ssrn.3977007.

[7] A. M. Al-asmari, R. I. Aloufi, and Y. Alotaibi, "A Review of Concepts, Advantages and Pitfalls of Healthcare Applicationsin Blockchain Technology," *Int. J. Comput. Sci. Netw. Secur.*, vol. 21, no. 5, 2021.

[8] A. Ekramifard, H. Amintoosi, and A. H. Seno, "A Systematic Literature Review on Blockchain-Based Solutions for IoT Security," in *Lecture Notes on Data Engineering*

and Communications Technologies, Springer Science and Business Media Deutschland GmbH, Berlin, Germany, 2020, doi: 10.1007/978-3-030-37309-2_25.

[9] M. N. M. Bhutta *et al.*, "A Survey on Blockchain Technology: Evolution, Architecture and Security," *IEEE Access*, vol. 9, 2021, doi: 10.1109/ACCESS.2021.3072849.

[10] P. K. Sharma, N. Kumar, and J. H. Park, "Blockchain Technology Toward Green IoT: Opportunities and Challenges," *IEEE Netw.*, vol. 34, no. 4, 2020, doi: 10.1109/MNET.001.1900526.

[11] B. K. Mohanta, D. Jena, S. S. Panda, and S. Sobhanayak, "Blockchain Technology: A Survey on Applications and Security Privacy Challenges," *Internet Things (Netherlands)*, vol. 8, 2019, doi: 10.1016/j.iot.2019.100107.

[12] J. Xie *et al.*, "A Survey of Blockchain Technology Applied to Smart Cities: Research Issues and Challenges," *IEEE Commun. Surv. Tutor.*, vol. 21, no. 3, 2019, doi: 10.1109/COMST.2019.2899617.

[13] C. C. Agbo, Q. H. Mahmoud, and J. M. Eklund, "Blockchain Technology in Healthcare: A Systematic Review," *Healthcare (Switzerland)*, vol. 7, no. 2, 2019, doi: 10.3390/healthcare7020056.

[14] P. Zhang, D. C. Schmidt, J. White, and G. Lenz, "Blockchain Technology Use Cases in Healthcare," in *Advances in Computers*, Academic Press Inc., Cambridge, England, Vol. 111, pp. 1–41, 2018, doi: 10.1016/bs.adcom.2018.03.006.

[15] K. Zīle and R. Strazdiņa, "Blockchain Use Cases and Their Feasibility," *Appl. Comput. Syst.*, vol. 23, no. 1, 2018, doi: 10.2478/acss-2018-0002.

[16] H. Kim and M. Laskowski, "Agriculture on the Blockchain: Sustainable Solutions for Food, Farmers, and Financing," *SSRN Electron. J.*, 2018, doi: 10.2139/ssrn.3028164.

[17] S. Huckle, R. Bhattacharya, M. White, and N. Beloff, "Internet of Things, Blockchain and Shared Economy Applications," *Procedia Comput. Sci.*, vol. 58, pp. 461–466, 2016, doi: 10.1016/j.procs.2016.09.074.

[18] S. Van Hijfte, "Blockchain and Industry Use Cases," in *Decoding Blockchain for Business*, Berkeley, CA, Apress, 2020, doi: 10.1007/978-1-4842-6137-8_3.

[19] D. Popovic *et al.*, "Understanding Blockchain for Insurance Use Cases," *Br. Actuar. J.*, 2020, doi: 10.1017/S1357321720000148.

[20] M. Benji and M. Sindhu, "A Study on the Corda and Ripple Blockchain Platforms," in *Advances in Intelligent Systems and Computing*, 2019, doi: 10.1007/978-981-13-1882-5_16.

[21] M. M. Queiroz, R. Telles, and S. H. Bonilla, "Blockchain and Supply Chain Management Integration: A Systematic Review of the Literature," *Supply Chain Manag.*, vol. 25, no. 2, 2020, doi: 10.1108/SCM-03-2018-0143.

[22] P. C. Sauer, G. Orzes, and G. Culot, "Blockchain in Supply Chain Management: A Multiple Case Study Analysis on Setups, Contingent Factors, and Evolutionary Patterns," *Prod. Plan. Control.*, 2022, doi: 10.1080/09537287.2022.2153078.

[23] H. Treiblmaier, "The Impact of the Blockchain on the Supply Chain: A Theory-Based Research Framework and a Call for Action," *Supply Chain Manag.*, vol. 23, no. 6, 2018, doi: 10.1108/SCM-01-2018-0029.

[24] J. H. Huh and S. K. Kim, "Verification Plan Using Neural Algorithm Blockchain Smart Contract for Secure p2p Real Estate Transactions," *Electron.*, vol. 9, no. 6, 2020, doi: 10.3390/ELECTRONICS9061052.

[25] D. P. Shelke, P. Sangle, S. Saswadkar, P. Gundawar, and K. Kadale, "Blockchain in Real Estate," *Int. J. Res. Appl. Sci. Eng. Technol.*, vol. 11, no. 1, 2023, doi: 10.22214/ijraset.2023.48159.

[26] S. Dubai, "Dubai Blockchain Strategy," *Smart Dubai*, 2016.

[27] J. Zhao, Y. Chi, Z. Wang, V. C. M. Leung, and W. Cai, "CloudArcade: A Blockchain Empowered Cloud Gaming System," in *BSCI 2020 — Proceedings of the 2nd ACM International Symposium on Blockchain and Secure Critical Infrastructure, Co-located with AsiaCCS 2020*, 2020, doi: 10.1145/3384943.3409420.

[28] A. Serada, T. Sihvonen, and J. T. Harviainen, "CryptoKitties and the New Ludic Economy: How Blockchain Introduces Value, Ownership, and Scarcity in Digital Gaming," *Games Cult.*, vol. 16, no. 4, 2021, doi: 10.1177/1555412019898305.
[29] M. Crosby, Nachiappan, P. Pattanayak, S. Verma, and V. Kalyanaraman, "Blockchain Technology—Beyond Bitcoin," *Berkley Eng.*, no. 2, pp. 6–19, 2016.
[30] A. Sharma and P. Gupta, "Blockchain Revolution," in *Research Anthology on Convergence of Blockchain, Internet of Things, and Security*, IGI Global, Pennsylvania, United States, pp. 1128–1152, 2021, doi: 10.4018/978-1-6684-7132-6.ch060.
[31] B. Wu and T. Duan, "The Advantages of Blockchain Technology in Commercial Bank Operation and Management," in *ACM International Conference Proceeding Series*, 2019, doi: 10.1145/3340997.3341009.
[32] S. Khan, W. K. Lee, and S. O. Hwang, "Aechain: A Lightweight Blockchain for IoT Applications," *IEEE Consum. Electron. Mag.*, vol. 11, no. 2, 2022, doi: 10.1109/MCE.2021.3060373.
[33] J. Golosova and A. Romanovs, "The Advantages and Disadvantages of the Blockchain Technology," in *2018 IEEE 6th Workshop on Advances in Information, Electronic and Electrical Engineering, AIEEE 2018 — Proceedings*, 2018, doi: 10.1109/AIEEE.2018.8592253.
[34] K. Y. Kang, "Cryptocurrency and Double Spending History: Transactions with Zero Confirmation," *Econ. Theory*, pp. 453–491, 2022, doi: 10.1007/s00199-021-01411-3.
[35] B. K. Mohanta, D. Jena, U. Satapathy, and S. Patnaik, "Survey on IoT Security: Challenges and Solution Using Machine Learning, Artificial Intelligence and Blockchain Technology," *Internet Things (Netherlands)*, vol. 11, 2020, doi: 10.1016/j.iot.2020.100227.
[36] M. Torky and A. E. Hassanein, "Integrating Blockchain and the Internet of Things in Precision Agriculture: Analysis, Opportunities, and Challenges," *Comput. Electron. Agric.*, vol. 178, 2020, doi: 10.1016/j.compag.2020.105476.
[37] Y. Lu, "The Blockchain: State-of-the-Art and Research Challenges," *J. Ind. Inf. Integr.*, vol. 15, 2019, doi: 10.1016/j.jii.2019.04.002.
[38] B. Cao *et al.*, "Performance Analysis and Comparison of PoW, PoS and DAG Based Blockchains," *Digit. Commun. Netw.*, vol. 6, no. 4, 2020, doi: 10.1016/j.dcan.2019.12.001.
[39] S. Schmid *et al.*, "An Architecture for Interoperable IoT Ecosystems," in *Lecture Notes in Computer Science (Including Subseries Lecture Notes in Artificial Intelligence and Lecture Notes in Bioinformatics)*, 2017, doi: 10.1007/978-3-319-56877-5_3.
[40] R. Banno, J. Sun, S. Takeuchi, and K. Shudo, "Interworking Layer of Distributed MQTT Brokers*," *IEICE Trans. Inf. Syst.*, vol. E102D, no. 12, 2019, doi: 10.1587/transinf.2019PAK0001.
[41] E. A. Shammar, A. T. Zahary, and A. A. Al-Shargabi, "A Survey of IoT and Blockchain Integration: Security Perspective," *IEEE Access*, vol. 9, 2021, doi: 10.1109/ACCESS.2021.3129697.
[42] T. Ali Syed, A. Alzahrani, S. Jan, M. S. Siddiqui, A. Nadeem, and T. Alghamdi, "A Comparative Analysis of Blockchain Architecture and Its Applications: Problems and Recommendations," *IEEE Access*, vol. 7, 2019, doi: 10.1109/ACCESS.2019.2957660.
[43] K. N. Griggs, O. Ossipova, C. P. Kohlios, A. N. Baccarini, E. A. Howson, and T. Hayajneh, "Healthcare Blockchain System Using Smart Contracts for Secure Automated Remote Patient Monitoring," *J. Med. Syst.*, vol. 42, no. 7, 2018, doi: 10.1007/s10916-018-0982-x.
[44] J. Sengupta, S. Ruj, and S. Das Bit, "A Comprehensive Survey on Attacks, Security Issues and Blockchain Solutions for IoT and IIoT," *J. Netw. Comput. Appl.*, vol. 149, 2020, doi: 10.1016/j.jnca.2019.102481.
[45] S. J. Hsiao and W. T. Sung, "Employing Blockchain Technology to Strengthen Security of Wireless Sensor Networks," *IEEE Access*, vol. 9, 2021, doi: 10.1109/ACCESS.2021.3079708.

[46] S. Neethirajan and B. Kemp, "Digital Livestock Farming," *Sens. Bio-Sens. Res.*, vol. 32, 2021, doi: 10.1016/j.sbsr.2021.100408.
[47] M. Imran, U. Zaman, Imran, J. Imtiaz, M. Fayaz, and J. Gwak, "Comprehensive Survey of IoT, Machine Learning, and Blockchain for Health Care Applications: A Topical Assessment for Pandemic Preparedness, Challenges, and Solutions," *Electronics (Switzerland)*, vol. 10, no. 20, 2021, doi: 10.3390/electronics10202501.
[48] M. S. Ali, M. Vecchio, M. Pincheira, K. Dolui, F. Antonelli, and M. H. Rehmani, "Applications of Blockchains in the Internet of Things: A Comprehensive Survey," *IEEE Commun. Surv. Tutor.*, vol. 21, no. 2, 2019, doi: 10.1109/COMST.2018.2886932.
[49] I. Al_Barazanchi *et al.*, "Blockchain Technology—Based Solutions for IOT Security," *Iraqi J. Comput. Sci. Math.*, vol. 3, no. 1, pp. 53–63, 2022, doi: 10.52866/ijcsm.2022.01.01.006.
[50] S. Hakak, W. Z. Khan, G. A. Gilkar, M. Imran, and N. Guizani, "Securing Smart Cities through Blockchain Technology: Architecture, Requirements, and Challenges," *IEEE Netw.*, vol. 34, no. 1, 2020, doi: 10.1109/MNET.001.1900178.
[51] S. K. Singh, Y. Pan, and J. H. Park, "Blockchain-Enabled Secure Framework for Energy-Efficient Smart Parking in Sustainable City Environment," *Sustain. Cities Soc.*, vol. 76, 2022, doi: 10.1016/j.scs.2021.103364.
[52] M. Fuller, M. Jenkins, and K. Tjølsen, "Security Analysis of the August Smart Lock," *Minor*, 2017.
[53] B. Singhal, G. Dhameja, and P. S. Panda, "How Blockchain Works," in *Beginning Blockchain*, Apress, New York, United States, pp. 31–148, 2018, doi: 10.1007/978-1-4842-3444-0_2.
[54] R. Hobeck, C. Klinkmüller, H. M. N. D. Bandara, I. Weber, and W. M. P. van der Aalst, "Process Mining on Blockchain Data: A Case Study of Augur," in *Lecture Notes in Computer Science (Including Subseries Lecture Notes in Artificial Intelligence and Lecture Notes in Bioinformatics)*, 2021, doi: 10.1007/978-3-030-85469-0_20.
[55] A. Banafa, "How to Secure the Internet of Things (IoT) with Blockchain," *DataFloq*, 2016.
[56] M. Hussey, "What Is VeChain (VET) ? | The Beginner's Guide—Decrypt," *Decrypt*, 2019.
[57] M. Ben Hassine, M. Kmimech, H. Hellani, and L. Sliman, "Toward a Mixed Tangle-Blockchain Architecture," in *Frontiers in Artificial Intelligence and Applications*, 2020, doi: 10.3233/FAIA200568.
[58] N. Varatharaj and S. T. Ramalingam, "Enabling Continuous Connectivity Services for Ambrosus Blockchain Application by Incorporating 5G-Multilevel Machine Learning Orchestrations," *J. Intell. Fuzzy Syst.*, vol. 42, no. 4, 2022, doi: 10.3233/JIFS-211745.
[59] Y. Kano and T. Nakajima, "A Novel Approach to Solve a Mining Work Centralization Problem in Blockchain Technologies," *Int. J. Pervasive Comput. Commun.*, vol. 14, no. 1, 2018, doi: 10.1108/IJPCC-D-18-00005.
[60] J. Sanders and D. Patterson, "Facebook Data Privacy Scandal: A Cheat Sheet," *TechRepublic*, 2019.
[61] Q. Zhou, H. Huang, Z. Zheng, and J. Bian, "Solutions to Scalability of Blockchain: a Survey," *IEEE Access*, vol. 8, 2020, doi: 10.1109/aCCESS.2020.2967218.
[62] P. P. Ray, Di. Dash, K. Salah, and N. Kumar, "Blockchain for IoT-Based Healthcare: Background, Consensus, Platforms, and Use Cases," *IEEE Syst. J.*, vol. 15, no. 1, 2021, doi: 10.1109/JSYST.2020.2963840.
[63] T. Salman, M. Zolanvari, A. Erbad, R. Jain, and M. Samaka, "Security Services Using Blockchains: A State of the Art Survey," *IEEE Commun. Surv. Tutor.*, vol. 21, no. 1, 2019, doi: 10.1109/COMST.2018.2863956.
[64] M. Huang, S. Cao, X. Li, K. Huang, and X. Zhang, "Defending Data Poisoning Attack via Trusted Platform Module and Blockchain Oracle," in *IEEE International Conference on Communications*, 2022, doi: 10.1109/ICC45855.2022.9838252.

[65] N. Islam, M. S. Rahman, I. Mahmud, M. N. A. Sifat, and Y. Z. Cho, "A Blockchain-Enabled Distributed Advanced Metering Infrastructure Secure Communication (BC-AMI)," *Appl. Sci.*, vol. 12, no. 14, 2022, doi: 10.3390/app12147274.

[66] M. Kim, S. Yu, J. Lee, Y. Park, and Y. Park, "Design of Secure Protocol for Cloud-Assisted Electronic Health Record System Using Blockchain," *Sensors (Switzerland)*, vol. 20, no. 10, 2020, doi: 10.3390/s20102913.

[67] M. Wazid, A. K. Das, S. Shetty, and M. Jo, "A Tutorial and Future Research for Building a Blockchain-Based Secure Communication Scheme for Internet of Intelligent Things," *IEEE Access*, vol. 8, 2020, doi: 10.1109/ACCESS.2020.2992467.

[68] D. Galvin, "IBM and Walmart: Blockchain for Food Safety," *IBMBlockchain*, 2017.

[69] IBM Corporation, "Maersk and IBM Introduce TradeLens Blockchain Shipping Solution," *IBM Newsroom*, 2018.

[70] R. Aitken, "IBM Forges Blockchain Collaboration with Nestlé & Walmart in Global Food Safety," *Forbes*, 2017.

[71] T. Lawson, "Accelerating Technology Disruption in the Automotive Market—Blockchain in the Automotive Industry," *Deloitte*, 2018.

[72] F. Gîrbacia, D. Voinea, R. Boboc, M. Duguleană, and C. C. Postelnicu, "Toward Blockchain Adoption for the Automotive Industry," *IOP Conf. Ser. Mater. Sci. Eng.*, vol. 1220, no. 1, 2022, doi: 10.1088/1757-899x/1220/1/012026.

[73] C. Koban, M. Falaleyeva, M. Spravtseva, R. Moiseev, and S. Khan, "Modeling User-Centric Threats in Smart City: A Hybrid Threat Modeling Method," in *Proceedings of IEEE/ACS International Conference on Computer Systems and Applications, AICCSA*, 2022, doi: 10.1109/AICCSA56895.2022.10017885.

[74] D. Linke and S. Strahringer, "Blockchain Integration Within an ERP System for the Procure-to-Pay Process: Implementation of a Prototype with SAP S/4HANA and Hyperledger Fabric in the Daimler AG," *HMD Prax. der Wirtschaftsinformatik*, vol. 55, no. 6, 2018.

[75] N. Prakash, D. G. Michelson, and C. Feng, "CVIN: Connected Vehicle Information Network," in *IEEE Vehicular Technology Conference*, 2020, doi: 10.1109/VTC2020-Spring48590.2020.9128642.

[76] J. Morris, "The Energy Web Foundation: Bringing Blockchain Technology to the Grid," *RMI Outlet*, February 2017.

[77] J. Shieber, "Toyota Turns to Blockchain to Drive Autonomous Vehicle Adoption," *Tech Crunch*, 2017.

[78] S. J. Alsunaidi and F. A. Khan, "Blockchain-Based Distributed Renewable Energy Management Framework," *IEEE Access*, vol. 10, 2022, doi: 10.1109/ACCESS.2022.3196457.

[79] I. Allison, "RWE and Slock.it—Electric Cars Using Ethereum Wallets Can Recharge by Induction at Traffic Lights," *International Business Times*, 2016.

[80] H. M. Kim and M. Laskowski, "Toward an Ontology-Driven Blockchain Design for Supply-Chain Provenance," *Intell. Syst. Accounting, Financ. Manag.*, vol. 25, no. 1, 2018, doi: 10.1002/isaf.1424.

[81] N. Bansal, "IoT Applications in Smart Homes," in *Designing Internet of Things Solutions with Microsoft Azure*, Apress, New York, United States, pp. 135–156, 2020, doi: 10.1007/978-1-4842-6041-8_8.

[82] M. van Rijmenam, *The Organisation of Tomorrow: How AI, Blockchain and Analytics Turn Your Business into a Data Organisation*, Taylor and Francis, New York, United States, pp. 1–192, 2019, doi: 10.4324/9780429279973.

[83] Y. Li and B. Hu, "A Consortium Blockchain-Enabled Secure and Privacy-Preserving Optimized Charging and Discharging Trading Scheme for Electric Vehicles," *IEEE Trans. Ind. Inform.*, vol. 17, no. 3, 2021, doi: 10.1109/TII.2020.2990732.

[84] Y. Tian, R. E. Minchin, K. Chung, J. Woo, and P. Adriaens, "Towards Inclusive and Sustainable Infrastructure Development Through Blockchain-Enabled Asset Tokenization: An Exploratory Case Study," *IOP Conf. Ser. Mater. Sci. Eng.*, vol. 1218, no. 1, 2022, doi: 10.1088/1757-899x/1218/1/012040.

[85] A. Ghadge, M. Bourlakis, S. kamble, and S. Seuring, "Blockchain Implementation in Pharmaceutical Supply Chains: A Review and Conceptual Framework," *Int. J. Prod. Res.*, vol. 61, no. 13, pp. 6633–6651, 2022, doi: 10.1080/00207543.2022.2125595.

[86] MediLedger, "MediLedger—Blockchain solutions for Pharma companies," *www.mediledger.com/*, 2019.

[87] P. H. Diamandis and S. Kotler, "The Future Is Faster Than You Think: How Converging Technologies Are Transforming Business," *Inquiry*, vol. 26, no. 1, 2020.

[88] S. Narasimmasubramanian and S. Arumuga Perumal, "A Study on Intelligence Agriculture Using Blockchain with IoT," *Int. J. Eng. Res. Technol.*, vol. 9, no. 5, 2021.

[89] X. Xu, I. Weber, and M. Staples, "Case Study: AgriDigital: Blockchain Technology in the Trade and Finance of Agriculture Supply Chains," *Archit. Blockchain Appl.*, pp. 239–255, 2019.

[90] A. Botelho, I. R. Silva, L. Ribeiro, M. S. Lopes, and M. Au-Yong-Oliveira, "Improving Food Transparency Through Innovation and Blockchain Technology," in *Proceedings of the European Conference on Innovation and Entrepreneurship, ECIE*, 2020, doi: 10.34190/EIE.20.034.

[91] U. W. Chohan, "Blockchain and Environmental Sustainability: Case of IBM's Blockchain Water Management," *SSRN Electron. J.*, 2019, doi: 10.2139/ssrn.3334154.

[92] Enterprise Ethereum Alliance, "White Paper der Enterprise Ethereum Alliance," *www.entethalliance.org*, 2017.

[93] I. Berman *et al.*, "Trustable Environmental Monitoring by Means of Sensors Networks on Swarming Autonomous Marine Vessels and Distributed Ledger Technology," *Front. Robot. AI*, vol. 7, 2020, doi: 10.3389/frobt.2020.00070.

[94] N. L. Cleveland, "Bots & Botnet: An Overview," *Inf. Secur.*, vol. 401, 2001.

[95] H. Singh and A. Bijalwan, "A survey on Malware, Botnets and their detection," *Int. J. Adv. Eng. Res. Sci.*, vol. 3, no. 3, 2016.

[96] N. Hoque, D. K. Bhattacharyya, and J. K. Kalita, "Botnet in DDoS Attacks: Trends and Challenges," *IEEE Commun. Surv. Tutor.*, vol. 17, no. 4, 2015, doi: 10.1109/COMST.2015.2457491.

[97] G. Vormayr, T. Zseby, and J. Fabini, "Botnet Communication Patterns," *IEEE Commun. Surv. Tutor.*, vol. 19, no. 4, 2017, doi: 10.1109/COMST.2017.2749442.

[98] D. K. Bhattacharyya and J. K. Kalita, *DDoS Attacks: Evolution, Detection, Prevention, Reaction, and Tolerance*, CRC Press, Florida, United States, pp. 1–283, 2016.

[99] F. Hussain *et al.*, "A Two-Fold Machine Learning Approach to Prevent and Detect IoT Botnet Attacks," *IEEE Access*, vol. 9, 2021, doi: 10.1109/ACCESS.2021.3131014.

[100] D. Pishva, "IoT: Their Conveniences, Security Challenges and Possible Solutions," *Adv. Sci. Technol. Eng. Syst.*, vol. 2, no. 3, 2017, doi: 10.25046/aj0203153.

[101] M. Mahmoud, M. Nir, and A. Matrawy, "A Survey on Botnet Architectures, Detection and Defences," *Int. J. Netw. Secur.*, vol. 17, no. 3, 2015.

[102] R. A. Rodríguez-Gómez, G. Maciá-Fernández, P. García-Teodoro, M. Steiner, and D. Balzarotti, "Resource Monitoring for the Detection of Parasite P2P Botnets," *Comput. Netw.*, vol. 70, 2014, doi: 10.1016/j.comnet.2014.05.016.

[103] R. Sharma and A. Thakral, "Identifying Botnets: Classification and Detection," *Int. J. Innov. Technol. Explor. Eng.*, vol. 8, no. 9 Special Issue, 2019, doi: 10.35940/ijitee.I1021.0789S19.

[104] G. L. Nguyen, B. Dumba, Q. D. Ngo, H. V. Le, and T. N. Nguyen, "A Collaborative Approach to Early Detection of IoT Botnet," *Comput. Electr. Eng.*, vol. 97, 2022, doi: 10.1016/j.compeleceng.2021.107525.

[105] T. Trajanovski and N. Zhang, "An Automated and Comprehensive Framework for IoT Botnet Detection and Analysis (IoT-BDA)," *IEEE Access*, vol. 9, 2021, doi: 10.1109/ACCESS.2021.3110188.
[106] S. Aanjankumar and S. Poonkuntran, "An Efficient Soft Computing Approach for Securing Information Over GAMEOVER Zeus Botnets with Modified CPA Algorithm," *Soft Comput.*, vol. 24, no. 21, 2020, doi: 10.1007/s00500-020-04956-y.
[107] S. K. Wanjau, G. M. Wambugu, and G. N. Kamau, "SSH-Brute Force Attack Detection Model Based on Deep Learning," *Int. J. Comput. Appl. Technol. Res.*, vol. 10, no. 01, 2021, doi: 10.7753/ijcatr1001.1008.

8 A Practical Approach to Development of the Internet of Things

8.1 PYTHON

Python is a high-level, interpreted programming language known for its simplicity, readability, and versatility. Python was created by Guido van Rossum, a Dutch programmer who started developing Python in the late 1980s and released the first version, Python 0.9.0, in February 1991. Guido van Rossum is often referred to as the "benevolent dictator for life" (BDFL) of the Python programming language due to his continued involvement in its development and guidance over the years. Python has been a widely used programming language in various domains, including web development, data analysis, scientific computing, AI, and of course, IoT [1, 2]. Python offers several advantages compared to other programming languages in the IoT domain, making it a popular choice among developers. For instance, Python is known for its simplicity and readability, making it easy for developers to write and understand code. Its clean syntax and straightforward structure allow programmers to quickly prototype and develop IoT applications. This simplicity reduces the learning curve for beginners and enables faster development cycles. Python's simplicity, community support, platform independence, data analytics capabilities, rapid prototyping, connectivity, and extensive documentation make it an excellent choice for IoT development. Its ease of use, versatility, and robust ecosystem contribute to faster development cycles, efficient data processing, and seamless integration within the IoT ecosystem.

Python is an interpreted programming language. Speaking in more clear words, Python programs are executed directly by an interpreter without the need for prior compilation into machine code. When you run a Python program, the interpreter reads the source code line by line, translates it into bytecode, and executes it immediately [3]. This interpretive nature allows for interactive development, rapid prototyping, and easier debugging. Python's dynamic nature and interpreted execution make it an ideal choice for rapid prototyping and iterative development. Developers can quickly test ideas, experiment with different approaches, and make changes on the fly. This agility is particularly valuable in the IoT domain, in which requirements and specifications may evolve rapidly. Python's quick feedback loop accelerates the development process, allowing for faster time to market.

8.1.1 Introduction to Python

As discussed earlier, Python has several applications including web development, data analysis, scientific computing, mathematics, AI, and, IoT [4, 5]. Python focuses

DOI: 10.1201/9781003282945-8

on code readability. It is a dynamic and interpreted programming language. It supports multiple programming paradigms. Generally, Python has fewer steps than Java and C. Python is also called a general-purpose programming language. However, Python supports object-oriented programming (OOP) paradigms, enabling developers to structure code using classes and objects. OOP principles like encapsulation, inheritance, and polymorphism help organize complex codebases and promote code reusability. Python empowers beginners and experienced programmers alike to embark on exciting coding adventures and can be used for software development, mathematics, web development, and system scripting. Developers use Python on the server side to develop web applications. Python can handle big and complex data easily. It can work on Windows, Mac, Linux, and Raspberry Pi platforms. Python can be treated as procedural, functional, object-oriented, etc. With the scripting language, you can develop desktop applications and web applications. It also translates into binary languages like Java. Python has a large and active community of developers who contribute to its extensive ecosystem [6]. This community-driven nature means that there are numerous libraries, frameworks, and tools available specifically for IoT development in Python. This wealth of resources simplifies IoT application development by providing pre-built modules for common tasks such as handling sensor data, communication protocols, and data visualization.

Python has powerful web frameworks, such as Django and Flask, which can be utilized for building IoT web applications and interfaces [7]. These frameworks provide a structured and scalable approach to developing IoT dashboards, control panels, and data visualization tools. Python's integration with web frameworks facilitates the creation of user-friendly interfaces to monitor and control IoT devices remotely. It can be used alongside software to create workflows, it can connect to database systems, and it can read and modify files. Python is a versatile programming language that offers a wide range of applications. It is particularly well suited for handling Big Data and performing complex mathematical operations. Whether for rapid prototyping or developing production-ready software, Python provides a powerful toolset. It is platform-independent, capable of running on various operating systems such as Windows, Mac, and Linux, and even on devices like Raspberry Pi. One of the key advantages of Python is its simple syntax, which resembles the English language and makes it easy to read and write code. Additionally, Python's concise syntax allows developers to accomplish tasks with fewer lines of code compared to some other programming languages. Being an interpreted language, Python enables immediate execution of code, facilitating quick prototyping and development cycles. Moreover, Python supports multiple programming paradigms, including procedural, object-oriented, and functional programming, offering flexibility in coding approaches. Python also has robust libraries and frameworks for data analytics and machine learning, such as NumPy, Pandas, and TensorFlow. These tools enable IoT developers to process and analyze the vast amounts of data generated by IoT devices. Python's integration with machine learning and AI allows for advanced data processing, predictive modeling, and decision-making capabilities in IoT applications.

The latest major version of Python is Python 3, which introduced several enhancements and improvements over its predecessor, Python 2. While Python 2 is no longer actively developed, it still maintains a significant user base due to existing codebases and compatibility requirements [8]. Python's design philosophy focuses on readability, making it easy for developers to understand and write code. The language incorporates elements from the English language, as well as mathematical conventions. Unlike some programming languages that use semicolons or parentheses to complete a command, Python uses new lines. Additionally, Python utilizes whitespace and indentation to define the scope of loops, functions, and classes, in contrast to the use of curly brackets in many other programming languages.

8.1.2 Why Use Python in IoT?

For many developers, Python is considered as the language of preference in the market. It is simple to learn, has clean syntax, and has a large online community supporting it. Python becomes a great choice when it comes to IoT. It can be either used for the back-end side of development or the software development of devices. Moreover, Python is available to work on Linux devices, and we can make use of MicroPython for microcontrollers [9]. Python is the coding language that we can use to reduce the volume of data that we need to deal with, accessible in the cloud. Python recognizes the needs regardless of whether we create the IoT project from scratch or interact with actuators, sensors, and accessories. Two of the many benefits of working with Python for IoT devices are the large number of libraries for all types of platforms and the speed it offers at which code can be developed. In addition to its versatility, Python is commonly used for developing device prototypes [10]. It provides a convenient platform for quickly building and testing proof-of-concept models. While Python is an interpreted language and may not offer the same level of performance as languages like C, C++, or Java, it still performs well in many cases. In scenarios in which performance optimization is required, portions of the Python code can be rewritten in languages like C, C++, or Java while retaining the overall functionality of the system. This flexibility allows developers to strike a balance between rapid prototyping in Python and achieving optimal performance through code optimization in other languages. With the rise of edge computing in IoT, Python's integration with AI and machine learning libraries becomes even more significant. Python's extensive support for frameworks like TensorFlow, Keras, and PyTorch enables developers to deploy machine learning models directly on edge devices [11]. This capability empowers IoT devices to perform real-time data analysis, decision-making, and predictive analytics without relying on cloud services, reducing latency and enhancing privacy.

The rapidly changing automotive industry has been revolutionized by IoT, making driving safe and efficient. IoT has unleashed a range of benefits in agriculture from improving productivity to diminishing crop failure risks. The capability of IoT to diagnose a problem and avoid failure of the system is helping in preventing the breakdown scenario. The usage of IoT devices has increased year over year. More than 8 billion IoT devices were registered from 2016–2018. As per the analysis of IoT experts, the count of IoT devices by the end of 2025 will reach more than 80 billion [12], and the market value of IoT will reach $7 trillion. As the IoT is evolving continuously, it can be difficult to analyze which tools are more useful in IoT development. Many programming languages are used to develop IoT devices—but which programming languages are most efficient in IoT development? Python is one of the most popular programming languages for IoT. The coding flexibility and dynamic nature of Python helps developers in creating intelligent IoT devices. Python provides robust support for various communication protocols used in IoT, such as MQTT, CoAP, and HTTP. Its versatility in networking and integration enables seamless connectivity between IoT devices, gateways, and cloud services. Python's ability to interface with external devices, sensors, and APIs simplifies data exchange and enables interoperability within an IoT ecosystem. Python benefits from extensive documentation and a wealth of learning resources. Its popularity in diverse domains, including IoT, has led to the availability of comprehensive tutorials, guides, and community-driven support forums. Developers can quickly find solutions to common problems and get assistance from the vibrant Python community.

A database is a no-brainer when it comes to most IoT applications. All IoT devices send data to the internet. A database is required to can store generated data. MySQL is the go-to relational database for most developers [13]. In this regard, MySQLdb is a very convenient little tool that circumvents the need to execute shell commands within a Python script to read and write to a database, and Python comes into the picture. You can also use other programming languages along with Python such as Assembly, C, C++, Java, JavaScript, PHP, and many more. As compared with a Java programming language, the Python is quite a favorite language for IoT developers. The reasons behind using Python in IoT development are its specific features [3, 5, 6], as explained in what follows.

- **Easy to Code:** One of the distinguishing features of Python is its use of whitespace and indentation for code identification and block structure. Unlike many other programming languages that rely on curly braces ({}) or other explicit symbols to define code blocks, Python utilizes indentation to denote the beginning and end of blocks [1, 3]. This design choice eliminates the need for excessive punctuation and forces developers to write clean and well-organized code. By enforcing consistent indentation, Python encourages a standardized coding style that enhances code readability and maintainability. The absence of curly braces reduces visual clutter and allows developers to focus on the logic and flow of the code rather than the syntax itself. Python's clear and consistent syntax eliminates common errors related to mismatched braces or incorrect block structure. Overall, Python's reliance on whitespace and indentation for code identification contributes to its simplicity, readability, and reduced cognitive load, making it an attractive choice for beginners and experienced developers alike.
- **Simple Syntax:** Python is renowned for its simple and intuitive syntax, which bears a resemblance to the English language [5]. This characteristic sets it apart from many other programming languages and contributes to its readability and ease of use. Python's syntax is designed to be clear and expressive, allowing developers to write code that is easy to understand and maintain. Its syntax emphasizes the use of whitespace and indentation to delineate blocks of code, such as loops, functions, and conditionals. This clean and visually appealing syntax reduces the need for excessive

punctuation or complex syntax structures, making Python code more natural and human-readable. The English-like syntax of Python helps beginners grasp programming concepts more easily and allows experienced developers to write code more quickly and efficiently.

- **Interpreted Language:** Python operates on an interpreter system, which means that code can be executed directly without the need for compilation. This immediate execution capability offers several advantages, particularly in terms of quick prototyping and development. With Python, developers can write code and see the results instantaneously. They can quickly test ideas, experiment with different approaches, and iterate their code in real time. This rapid prototyping ability is highly beneficial in scenarios in which fast development cycles and iterative design processes are crucial [14, 15]. The interpreted nature of Python eliminates the overhead of compiling code before execution. Developers can write code and execute it immediately, saving valuable time during the development phase. This immediate feedback loop enables developers to identify and fix errors or make modifications on the spot, enhancing productivity and reducing development time.
- **Embeddable:** Python offers the capability to integrate code written in other programming languages such as C++, Java, or C. This feature allows developers to leverage the strengths and performance benefits of other languages while still enjoying the flexibility and simplicity of Python. Python provides several mechanisms for integrating with other languages. Additionally, Python supports the use of extensions, which are modules or libraries written in other languages and loaded into Python [16]. These extensions can be used to optimize performance-critical sections of code by implementing them in languages like C or C++.
- **Extensible:** Python is known for its simplicity and conciseness, allowing developers to write programs with fewer lines of code compared to some other programming languages. Python provides built-in data structures—such as lists, dictionaries, and sets—which are expressive and efficient for handling various types of data. These data structures often simplify complex operations and reduce the number of lines required to manipulate and process data. Python is a dynamically typed language, which means that variable types are determined at runtime. This flexibility eliminates the need for explicit type declarations, reducing code verbosity [17]. Additionally, Python's type inference capabilities automatically deduce variable types based on context, further reducing the need for explicit type annotations. Python encourages code reusability through functions, classes, and modules. By writing reusable functions and organizing code into modular components, developers can achieve code reuse, leading to shorter overall code length.
- **Portable:** Python code is highly portable, meaning that you can write code once and run it on different machines and operating systems without the need for significant modifications. This portability is one of the advantages of using Python and contributes to its widespread adoption. The Python

programming language is designed to be cross-platform compatible [17]. The Python interpreter is available for different operating systems, ensuring that Python code can be executed on multiple platforms without modification. This allows developers to write code that works seamlessly across various machines and operating systems.

- **Free and Open Source:** Python is an open-source programming language, which means that its source code is freely available to the public. The source code of Python is publicly accessible and can be downloaded from the official Python website or from various repositories. This allows developers to view and study the implementation details of the language, understand how different features work, and contribute to its development [3, 18]. As an open-source language, Python grants users the freedom to modify the source code according to their needs. This flexibility enables developers to customize Python's behavior, add new features, or fix issues to suit their specific requirements. This ability to modify the language's source code is one of the key advantages of open-source software. With open-source licensing, Python allows users to distribute and redistribute the language and its modifications freely. This means that developers can share their customized versions of Python, distribute applications built with Python, or include Python as part of their software packages without any licensing restrictions.
- **Community Supports:** Python has indeed gained significant popularity and has a large and active community of users and developers supporting its advancements. The Python community consists of experienced developers, educators, and enthusiasts who actively share their knowledge and expertise through various channels. Online forums, mailing lists, social media groups, and dedicated community websites provide platforms for users to seek help, ask questions, and share insights [8]. This culture of knowledge sharing fosters learning and supports newcomers in understanding and utilizing Python effectively. The Python community organizes numerous events and conferences worldwide, bringing together users, developers, and experts. These events provide opportunities to network, learn from industry leaders, and stay up to date with the latest developments in the Python ecosystem. Prominent examples include PyCon, EuroPython, and regional Python conferences which feature presentations, workshops, and discussions on a wide range of topics related to Python.
- **Easy to Learn:** Python is designed with a clear and concise syntax that emphasizes readability. Its code structure resembles the English language, making it easier to understand and follow. Python avoids complex symbols and syntax, such as semicolons or curly braces, which are common in languages like C++ and Java. This simplicity reduces the learning curve and allows beginners to focus on problem-solving rather than worrying about intricate language details [8]. Python's popularity has led to the availability of numerous learning resources, including tutorials, documentation, online courses, and community forums. These resources cater to beginners and

provide step-by-step guidance, interactive examples, and practical exercises to help learners grasp the language concepts effectively.

- **Easy to Debug:** Python is often considered easier to debug than are languages like C++ and C. One of the reasons for this is that Python is an interpreted language, which means that the code is executed line by line during runtime, allowing for easier identification and resolution of errors. Python's syntax and error messages are designed to be user-friendly and informative. When an error occurs, Python provides detailed error messages that typically point to the exact line of code where the issue occurred, making it easier to identify and fix the problem. The error messages often include specific information about the nature of the error, helping developers understand and resolve it more effectively. Python offers several powerful debugging tools that facilitate the identification and resolution of issues [8]. The most commonly used tool is the Python debugger, pdb, which allows developers to pause the execution of the code at specific breakpoints, inspect variables and their values, step through the code line by line, and analyze the program's state. This interactive debugging capability enables developers to examine the code's behavior and identify any logical or runtime errors.

8.1.3 Python: Getting Started

The software for Python is available on the official Python website python.org created by the Python community or it can be downloaded from Google free of cost [17, 19]. Once Python is installed, you can start writing your first lines of code. Python uses a simple and intuitive syntax, making it easy to understand and read. You can write Python code in any text editor or use specialized IDEs such as PyCharm, Visual Studio Code, or Jupyter Notebook [20]. These IDEs provide a range of features that facilitate code writing, debugging, and project management. Python's interactive shell, called the Python REPL (Read-Eval-Print Loop), is an excellent tool for experimenting and learning. You can access the Python REPL by opening a terminal or command prompt and typing "python" to start an interactive Python session. In the REPL, you can enter commands or write code line by line, instantly seeing the output as you go. This interactive nature of Python enables rapid prototyping and quick feedback during development.

To deepen your Python skills, there are numerous online resources available. Python documentation provides comprehensive guides and references, explaining the language's features and usage [19, 20]. Online tutorials, video courses, and interactive coding platforms like Codecademy and DataCamp offer structured learning paths for beginners. Furthermore, the Python community is known for its friendliness and willingness to help. Participating in forums, attending local meetups, or joining online communities like Stack Overflow and Reddit can provide valuable insights and support. In summary, getting started with Python is an accessible and rewarding experience. With its simplicity, extensive resources, and supportive community, Python empowers beginners and experienced programmers alike to embark on exciting coding adventures.

8.1.4 Downloading and Installing Python

There are various Python versions for use and new Python releases come from time to time. For instance, Python 3.9.6 version for Windows 10 was released in Summer 2021 [20, 21]. The latest version of Python can be downloaded from the official Python website www.python.org/downloads/ and installed on a machine. Python is available for various operating systems, including Windows, macOS, and Linux. The download size of the Python installation package is relatively small, around 25 MB. After downloading the installer, you can run it and follow the installation wizard to install Python on your machine. During the installation process, you may have the option to customize the installation and select additional features or components. Once Python is installed, it typically requires an additional 90 MB of disk space. This includes the core Python interpreter, standard library modules, and other necessary files. The disk space required may vary slightly depending on the specific Python version and configuration. It is worth noting that Python can be installed as either a 32-bit or 64-bit application, depending on your system architecture. It is recommended to install the appropriate version (64-bit) for better performance and compatibility, especially if you are working with large datasets or computationally intensive tasks.

In addition to installing Python, Eclipse is an IDE widely used for programming in various languages, including Python. Eclipse provides a rich set of features for coding, debugging, and managing projects. To work with Python in Eclipse, you will need to install the appropriate Python plugin or extension for Eclipse, such as PyDev [5, 17]. It is important to note that Eclipse itself is not required to use Python. Python can be run and developed using any text editor or dedicated Python IDE. However, if you prefer using Eclipse for Python development, make sure to install the compatible Python plugin or extension to enable Python-specific features and functionality within the Eclipse IDE. We will next discuss Python installation step by step.

8.1.4.1 Downloading

1. Consider that we want to install Python version 3.9.6. Once you open the www.python.org/downloads/ website, following webpage appears as shown in Figure 8.1 [17].
2. On the Downloads page, scroll down to the section titled "Python 3.9.6" (or search for it using the search box on the page). Under the Python 3.9.6 section, you will find various installation files for different operating systems. Select the appropriate installer for your system. For example, if you are using a Windows 64-bit operating system, you would choose "Windows installer (64-bit)." Once you click on "Python 3.9.6," the following window will appear as shown in Figure 8.2 [17].

   Then just click on the "Save File" button. Once the download is complete, locate the downloaded file on your computer. By default, it is usually found in your "Downloads" folder, as shown in the Figure 8.3 [17].
3. Double-click on the downloaded file to run the installer. Follow the installation wizard's instructions to complete the installation process. Make sure to select the options you prefer during the installation, such as adding Python

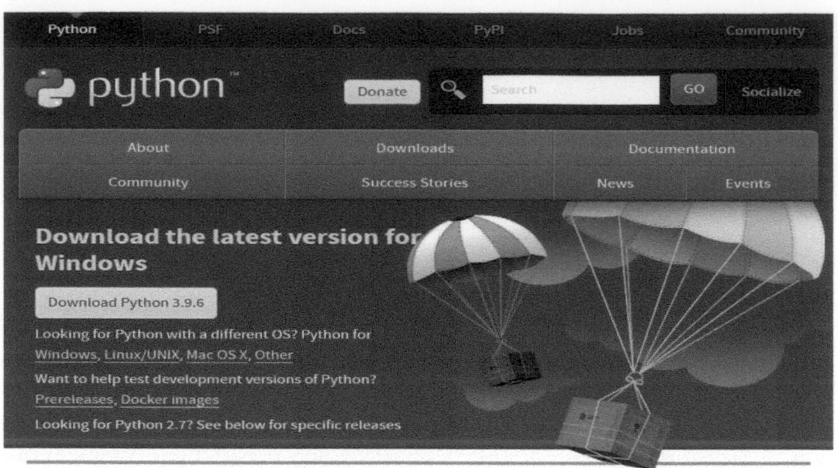

FIGURE 8.1 Python website home page.

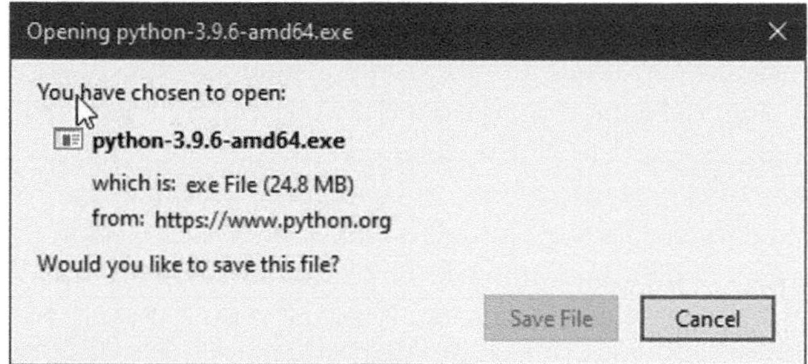

FIGURE 8.2 Opening python-3.96-amd64.exe.

python-3.9.6-amd64.exe	7/8/2021 12:02 PM	Application	25,428 KB

FIGURE 8.3 File name: python-3.96-amd64.exe.

to the system PATH or installing pip (Python package manager). After the installation is finished, you should have Python 3.9.6 installed on your system.

8.1.4.2 Installing

1. Once we run the file entitled python-3.9.6-amd64.exe, a "Python 3.9.6 Setup" screen will appear, as shown in Figure 8.4 [17].
2. If you are confident that the installer is legitimate and from a trusted source, click the "Yes" button in the user account control (UAC) pop-up window

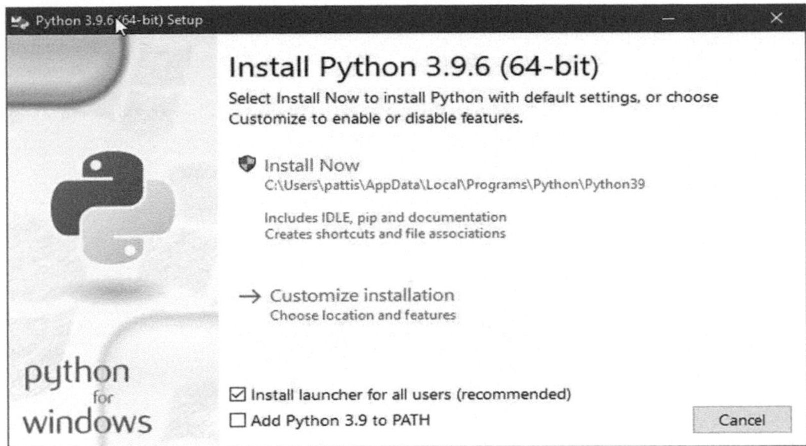

FIGURE 8.4 Pop-up window showing start of installation Python 3.9.6.

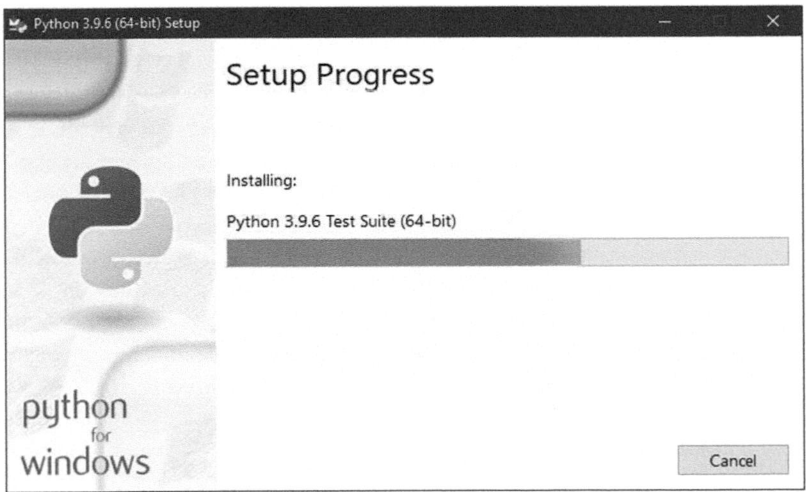

FIGURE 8.5 Progress bar of installation for Python 3.9.6.

to allow the installation process to continue. The installer will then proceed with the installation or upgrade of Python on your system.

3. The progress of the installation of "Python 3.9.6 (64-bit) Setup" looks like on the system as shown in Figure 8.5 [17].

   Once the installation is finished, following pop-up window showing "Setup was successful" appears, as shown in Figure 8.6 [17].

8.1.5 File Handling

Python provides support for file handling, which allows users to perform operations such as reading and writing files. The file handling capabilities in Python are

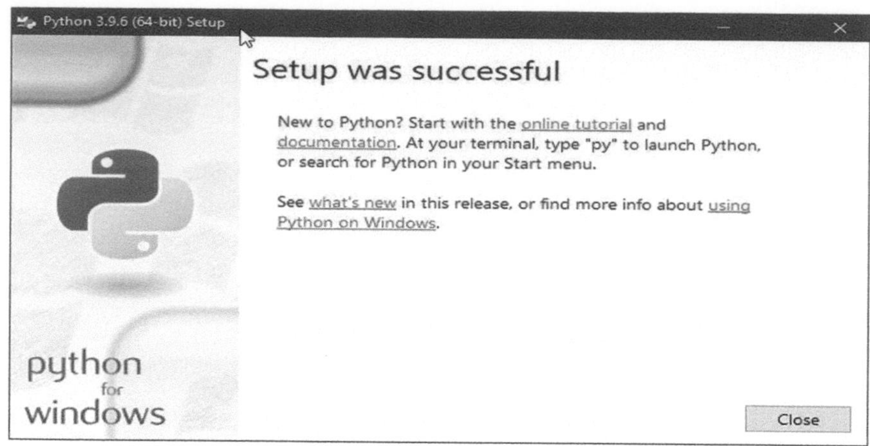

FIGURE 8.6 Pop-up window showing successful installation of Python 3.9.6.

designed to be straightforward and concise. In Python, files can be handled in two modes: text mode and binary mode [3, 5]. Text mode is used for handling text files, whereby the content is composed of characters and each line is terminated by an end of line (EOL) character like a comma (,) or a new line character. Binary mode is used for handling binary files, which contain non-textual data. File handling in Python is a powerful and versatile tool that can be used to perform a wide range of operations. However, it is important to carefully consider the advantages and disadvantages of file handling when writing Python programs to ensure that the code is secure and reliable, and that it performs well. Python also provides other methods and techniques for file handling, such as reading files line by line, appending content to an existing file, handling errors during file operations, and more. These concepts make file handling in Python relatively easy and concise compared to some other programming languages. The pros and cons associated with file handling using Python include the following [1, 8, 18].

8.1.5.1 Pros

- **Versatility:** File handling in Python allows you to perform a wide range of operations, such as creating, reading, writing, appending, renaming, and deleting files.
- **Flexibility:** File handling in Python is highly flexible, as it allows you to work with different file types (e.g., text, binary, CSV, etc.), and to perform different operations on files (e.g. read, write, append, etc.).
- **User-Friendly:** Python provides a user-friendly interface for file handling, making it easy to create, read, and manipulate files.
- **Cross-Platform:** Python file handling functions work across different platforms (e.g. Windows, Mac, Linux), allowing for seamless integration and compatibility.

8.1.5.2 Cons

- **Error-Prone:** File handling operations in Python can be prone to errors, especially if the code is not carefully written or if there are issues with the file system (e.g. file permissions, file locks, etc.).
- **Security Risks:** File handling in Python can also pose security risks, especially if the program accepts user input that can be used to access or modify sensitive files on the system.
- **Complexity:** File handling in Python can be complex, especially when working with more advanced file formats or operations. Careful attention must be paid to the code to ensure that files are handled properly and securely.
- **Performance:** File handling operations in Python can be slower than in other programming languages, especially when dealing with large files or performing complex operations.

8.1.5.3 Working of open() Function

In Python, before performing any operations on a file, you need to open it using the **open**() function. The **open**() function takes two parameters: the file name and the mode. The **filename** parameter represents the name or path of the file you want to open. The **mode** parameter specifies the purpose for which you are opening the file. It is a string that can take various values, depending on the operation you want to perform.

```
f = open (filename, mode)
```

Some common modes include:

- **r:** Read mode (default). Opens the file for reading.
- **w:** Write mode. Opens the file for writing. If the file does not exist, it creates a new file. If the file exists, it truncates (clears) the file before writing.
- **a:** Append mode. Opens the file for writing. If the file exists, it appends the new content at the end of the file without truncating the existing content. If the file does not exist, it creates a new file.
- **x:** Exclusive creation mode. Opens a file for exclusive creation. If the file already exists, the operation fails.

There are additional modes and options available for handling binary files, reading files in text mode, and more. You can refer to the Python documentation for a comprehensive list of file modes and their descriptions. Remember to close the file after you have finished working with it by calling the **close**() method on the file object. This ensures that any changes are saved and resources are properly released.

8.1.5.4 Working of read() Mode

In Python, one way to read the contents of a file is by using the **read**() method on a file object. The **read**() method reads the entire content of the file and returns it as a string. In the following example, we open the file named "example.txt" in read mode using the **open**() function. Then, we call the **read**() method on the file object (**file.read**()) to read the entire content of the file [18].

```
# Python code to illustrate read() mode
file = open("example.txt", "r")
print (file.read())
file.close()
```

Finally, we print the content and close the file using the **close**() method. It is important to close the file after you have finished reading or performing any operations on it to free up system resources and ensure that any changes are saved properly.

8.1.5.5 Creating a File Using write() Mode

In Python, you can create a new file using the write mode ("w") when opening the file. If the file does not exist, it will be created, and if it already exists, its content will be truncated (cleared) before writing new content. Following is an example that demonstrates how to create a file and write content to it using the write mode [18].

```
# Python code to create a file
file = open('example.txt','w')
file.write("This is the content of the file")
file.close()
```

In the preceding example, we open a file named "example.txt" in write mode by passing "w" as the second argument to the **open**() function. If the file already exists, its content will be erased. Then, we use the **write**() method on the file object **file.write**() to write the desired content to the file. In this case, we write the string "This is the content of the file." Finally, we close the file using the **close**() method. Closing the file ensures that any changes are saved properly and resources are released. After running this code, a new file named "example.txt" will be created in the current working directory, and it will contain the specified content. Make sure to provide the correct file path if you want to create the file in a specific location other than the current working directory.

8.1.5.6 Using Write Along with the with() Function

We can also use the write function along with the with() function [8, 18].

```
# Python code to illustrate with () along with write ()
with open("file.txt", "w") as f:
        f.write("Hello World!!!")
```

8.1.5.7 split() Using File Handling

We can also split lines using file handling in Python. This splits the variable when space is encountered. You can also split using any characters as we wish. Following is the code.

```
with open ("file.text", "r") as file:
        data = file.readlines()
        for line in data:
                word = line.split()
                print (word)
```

There are also various other functions that help to manipulate the files and their contents. You can explore various other functions in Python Docs.

8.1.5.8 Example: Implementing all the Functions in File Handling

```
import os
def create_file(filename):
        try:
                with open(filename, 'w') as f:
                        f.write('Hello, world!\n')
                print("File "+ filename + "created successfully.")
        except IOError:
                print("Error: could not create file "+ filename)

def read_file(filename):
        try:
                with open(filename, 'r') as f:
                        contents = f.read()
                        print(contents)
        except IOError:
                print("Error: could not read file "+ filename)

def append_file(filename, text):
        try:
                with open(filename, 'a') as f:
                        f.write(text)
```

```
            print("Text appended to file "+ filename + "successfully.")
        except IOError:
            print("Error: could not append to file "+ filename)

def rename_file(filename, new_filename):
        try:
            os.rename(filename, new_filename)
            print("File "+ filename + "renamed to "+ new_filename + "suc-
            cessfully.")
        except IOError:
            print("Error: could not rename file "+ filename)

def delete_file(filename):
        try:
            os.remove(filename)
            print("File "+ filename + "deleted successfully.")
        except IOError:
            print("Error: could not delete file "+ filename)

if __name__ == '__main__':
        filename = "example.txt"
        new_filename = "new_example.txt"

        create_file(filename)
        read_file(filename)
        append_file(filename, "This is some additional text.\n")
        read_file(filename)
        rename_file(filename, new_filename)
        read_file(new_filename)
        delete_file(new_filename)
```

Output

```
File example.txt created successfully.
Hello, world!

Text appended to file example.txt successfully.
Hello, world!
This is some additional text.

File example.txt renamed to new_example.txt successfully.
Hello, world!
This is some additional text.

File new_example.txt deleted successfully.
```

8.1.5.9 With Statement

with statement in Python is used in exception handling to make the code cleaner and much more readable. It simplifies the management of common resources like file streams. Unlike the previously discussed implementations, there is no need to call file.close() when using with statement. The with statement itself ensures proper acquisition and release of resources.

8.1.5.10 Syntax

```
with open filename as file:
```

```
# Program to show various ways to read data from a file.
L = ["This is Delhi \n", "This is Paris \n", "This is London \n"]
# Creating a file
with open("myfile.txt", "w") as file1:
        # Writing data to a file
        file1.write("Hello \n")
        file1.writelines(L)
        file1.close() # to change file access modes

with open("myfile.txt", "r+") as file1:
        # Reading from a file
        print(file1.read())
```

Output

```
Hello
This is Delhi
This is Paris
This is London
```

8.1.5.11 Writing to File in Python

There are two ways to write in a file.

write(): Inserts the string str1 in a single line in the text file.

```
File_object.write(str1)
```

writelines(): For a list of string elements, each string is inserted in the text file. Used to insert multiple strings at a single time.

```
File_object.writelines(L) for L = [str1, str2, str3]
```

8.1.5.12 Example

```
# Python program to demonstrate writing to file
# Opening a file
file1 = open('myfile.txt', 'w')
L = ["This is Delhi \n", "This is Paris \n", "This is London \n"]
s = "Hello\n"

# Writing a string to file
file1.write(s)

# Writing multiple strings at a time
file1.writelines(L)
file1.close()

# Checking if the data is written to file or not
file1 = open('myfile.txt', 'r')
print(file1.read())
file1.close()
```

Output

```
Hello
This is Delhi
This is Paris
This is London
```

8.2 EMBEDDED SUITES FOR IOT

An embedded suite for IoT refers to a collection of software tools, frameworks, and components specifically designed to support the development and deployment of IoT solutions on embedded systems [22, 23]. It provides a comprehensive set of resources that enable developers to build, manage, and maintain IoT applications efficiently. An embedded suite may include a lightweight and optimized operating system designed for resource-constrained devices commonly used in IoT applications. Examples of such operating systems include FreeRTOS, Contiki, TinyOS, and RIOT. The suite may provide development tools such as IDEs, compilers, debuggers, and simulators tailored for IoT application development. These tools help developers write, test, and debug code specifically for embedded systems. Some embedded suites offer built-in capabilities for data analytics and machine learning. This enables the processing and analysis of IoT data at the edge, allowing real-time insights, anomaly detection, predictive maintenance, and other intelligent capabilities.

The embedded suite may include a board support package (BSP) that provides the necessary drivers, libraries, and tools to interface with the specific hardware components on the development board [24]. This enables developers to utilize the board's features and functionalities efficiently. The goal of an embedded suite for IoT is to simplify and streamline the development process, enhance device functionality, and accelerate time to market for IoT solutions. By providing a comprehensive set of tools and frameworks tailored for embedded systems, developers can focus on building innovative applications and services while leveraging the capabilities of IoT devices.

8.2.1 Development Boards

Python is a versatile programming language that offers several useful libraries and frameworks for IoT development. The popular development boards for IoT in Python include: Raspberry Pi, PyBoard, ESP8266, and ESP32 with Micropython.

8.2.1.1 Python on Raspberry Pi

Python is one of the most popular programming languages used on the Raspberry Pi platform. The Raspberry Pi offers a low-cost, versatile solution for various projects, including IoT applications, home automation, robotics, and more. Python's simplicity, readability, and extensive libraries make it an ideal choice for programming on the Raspberry Pi. One of the primary advantages of using Python on Raspberry Pi is its ability to interact with the general-purpose input/output (GPIO) pins. Python libraries like RPi.GPIO provide a simple interface for controlling and reading the GPIO pins, allowing you to connect and control external devices such as sensors, light-emitting diodes (LEDs), motors, and more [9, 16]. Raspberry Pi supports both Python 2 and Python 3. However, it is recommended to use Python 3, as it is the latest version and offers better support and future-proofing. Python on Raspberry Pi allows you to utilize the extensive collection of Python packages and libraries available. These packages cover a wide range of domains, including web development, data analysis, machine learning, IoT protocols, and more. You can use tools pip command (Python package installer) to easily install and manage these packages. Thus, running Python on Raspberry Pi provides a user-friendly and powerful platform for developing a wide range of projects. Its simplicity, extensive libraries, and GPIO integration make it an ideal choice for beginners and experienced developers alike. Whether you are building a simple IoT application or a complex robotics project, Python on Raspberry Pi can help you bring your ideas to life.

8.2.1.2 Python on PyBoard

The Pyboard with an STM32F405RG microcontroller is yet another a popular choice for Python-based IoT development. The Pyboard is a development board specifically designed for running MicroPython, which is a lightweight implementation of Python optimized for microcontrollers [25]. The Pyboard is a small microcontroller board designed specifically for MicroPython, a lean and efficient implementation of Python that is optimized for microcontrollers and embedded systems. MicroPython on the Pyboard supports a significant portion of the Python language syntax, including control structures (if-else, loops), functions, classes, and modules. However, not all Python features and modules are available in MicroPython due to the resource constraints of microcontrollers. PyBoard executes MicroPython, which is a lightweight implementation of the standard CPython interpreter [14]. It allows you to quickly prototype and develop projects that involve hardware interfacing, automation, robotics, and more. Whether you are a beginner or an experienced developer, Python on the Pyboard offers an accessible platform for exploring the world of embedded systems and microcontroller programming. The MicroPython is basically an efficient implementation of the Python 3 programming language that includes a small subset of the Python standard library and is optimized to run on microcontrollers and in constrained environments. The MicroPython pyboard is a compact electronic circuit board that runs MicroPython on the bare metal, giving you a low-level Python operating system that can be used to control all kinds of electronic projects. MicroPython is packed full of advanced features such as an interactive prompt, arbitrary precision integers, closures, list comprehension, generators, exception handling, and more—yet, it is compact enough to fit and run within just 256K of code space and 16K of random access memory (RAM). The Pyboard connects to a personal computer (PC) via universal serial bus (USB), providing the following two main functionalities for programming and file storage [25].

- **USB Flash Drive Mode:** When you connect the Pyboard to a PC using the USB cable, it appears as a USB flash drive. You can access the Pyboard's file system from your computer and easily transfer Python scripts or other files to and from the Pyboard. This allows you to conveniently store and manage your Python scripts directly on the Pyboard.
- **Serial Python Prompt (REPL):** In addition to the USB flash drive functionality, the Pyboard also provides a serial Python prompt called the REPL (Read-Eval-Print Loop). The REPL allows you to interactively write and execute Python code directly on the Pyboard. This is a useful feature for instant programming and testing on the Pyboard without the need for an external development environment. The REPL provides real-time feedback and can be accessed through a terminal or serial console program on your PC.

MicroPython is an entire rewrite of the Python (version 3.4) programming language to fit and execute on a microcontroller. It involves various optimization for efficiency and consumes quite less RAM. MicroPython executes bare metal on the PyBoard, necessarily providing us with an operating system based on Python. The in-built pyb module consists of functions and classes in order to control the peripherals available on the board, like I2C, UART, ADC, DAC, and SPI. The board's dimensions are impressive with dimensions of 33 mm × 43 mm, and weighing only 6 grams.

8.2.1.3 ESP8266, ESP32 with MicoPython

Python can also be used on popular microcontroller boards like ESP8266 and ESP32. These boards are based on the Espressif Systems' Wi-Fi–enabled microcontrollers, which provide a powerful and cost-effective platform for IoT applications. ESP8266 and ESP32 boards come with a variety of built-in features and peripherals, such as GPIO pins, UART, I2C, SPI, and Wi-Fi connectivity [26, 27]. MicroPython allows you to interact with these hardware interfaces using Python code, enabling you to control sensors, actuators, and communicate with other devices. Both ESP8266 and ESP32 have dedicated firmware versions of MicroPython that are specifically optimized for these boards. These firmware versions include the necessary drivers and libraries to access the board's features and peripherals. Python scripts can be developed on a computer using a preferred code editor or integrated development environment (IDE). Once the code is written, it can be transferred to the ESP8266 or ESP32 board for execution. Various tools and utilities are available to facilitate the code transfer process, including ampy, rshell, and esptool.

In summary, Raspberry Pi offers computational power and versatility, making it suitable for projects that require running complex software and multimedia applications. Pyboard is optimized for MicroPython, providing precise timing and low-level control for embedded systems. ESP8266 and ESP32 boards are cost-effective options with built-in Wi-Fi connectivity, making them ideal for wireless IoT projects that require low power consumption. The choice of board depends on the specific requirements of your project, including the computational needs, power constraints, and connectivity options [28].

8.2.2 Introduction to Arduino, Raspberry Pi, and Their Components

Arduino is an open-source electronics platform that has gained popularity for its simplicity and versatility in creating interactive projects. It consists of both hardware and software components, enabling users to develop and control various electronic devices and system. The Arduino hardware typically comprises a microcontroller board with digital and analog input/output (I/O) pins and various other components such as resistors, capacitors, and LEDs [29]. The Arduino IDE is a software tool specifically designed for Arduino development. It offers a user-friendly interface that simplifies the process of writing, compiling, and uploading code to the Arduino board. The IDE is based on the Processing programming language and simplifies the programming process for beginners and experienced users alike. One of the key advantages of Arduino is its extensive library support. The Arduino community has developed numerous libraries that provide pre-written code for various functions, making it easier to interface with sensors, motors, displays, and other electronic components. This significantly reduces the complexity of coding and allows users to focus on the specific functionalities of their projects. Arduino supports a wide range of input and output devices, including buttons, switches, sensors (e.g., temperature, humidity, light), motors, displays (e.g., LCD [liquid crystal display], OLED [organic light-emitting diodes]), and communication modules (e.g., Bluetooth, Wi-Fi, Ethernet). By combining these components and utilizing the Arduino platform, users can create projects such as home automation systems, robots, wearable devices, interactive art installations, and much more. Arduino has several key features that contribute to its popularity and versatility. Following are some of its notable features [29, 30].

1. **Open Source:** Arduino is an open-source platform, which means that its hardware design, software, and documentation are freely available for anyone to

access, modify, and distribute. This fosters collaboration, community-driven development, and the sharing of knowledge and resources.

2. **Simple and Beginner-Friendly:** Arduino is designed with simplicity in mind, making it accessible even to those with limited programming or electronics experience. The Arduino IDE provides an easy-to-use interface for writing and uploading code, and the programming language is based on C/C++ but with simplified functions and syntax.
3. **Cross-Platform Compatibility:** The Arduino IDE is compatible with multiple operating systems—including Windows, macOS, and Linux—allowing users to work with their preferred system. It ensures that Arduino is accessible to a wide range of users regardless of their operating system.
4. **Extensive Library Support:** Arduino benefits from a vast library ecosystem that offers pre-written code for various functions and devices. These libraries simplify the integration of sensors, actuators, communication modules, and other components into projects, reducing the complexity of coding and accelerating development.
5. **Versatile Input/Output (I/O) Capabilities:** Arduino boards have a range of digital and analog I/O pins, which can be used to interface with a wide variety of electronic components and peripherals. These pins allow users to read data from sensors, control actuators like motors and LEDs, and communicate with other devices using protocols such as I2C, SPI, and UART.
6. **Expandability:** Arduino boards often have additional pins and connectors—such as power pins, communication interfaces, and specialty pins—that provide expandability and compatibility with various shields and modules. Shields are add-on boards that offer specific functionalities like wireless communication, motor control, and display integration, expanding the capabilities of Arduino projects.
7. **Cost Effectiveness:** Arduino boards are relatively affordable compared to other microcontroller platforms, making them accessible to hobbyists, students, and enthusiasts on a budget. Additionally, the open-source nature of Arduino enables users to create their own versions of the board, further reducing costs.
8. **Strong Community Support:** Arduino has a large and active community of users worldwide. Online forums, websites, and social media platforms provide platforms for sharing projects, troubleshooting, and seeking guidance. The community's collaborative nature ensures that newcomers can find assistance and inspiration while working on their projects.

There are several types of Arduino boards available, each with its own features and specifications. Although there are several types of boards, the most popular Arduino boards are Arduino Uno, Arduino Nano, and Arduino Mega [31]. The Arduino Uno is one of the most widely used boards. Figure 8.7 shows the ATmega328P microcontroller, which offers 14 digital I/O pins (of which six can be used as PWM [pulse width modulation] outputs), six analog input pins, a USB connection for programming and power, and other essential components. It is a great choice for beginners and small to medium-sized projects. The Arduino Nano is a compact version of the

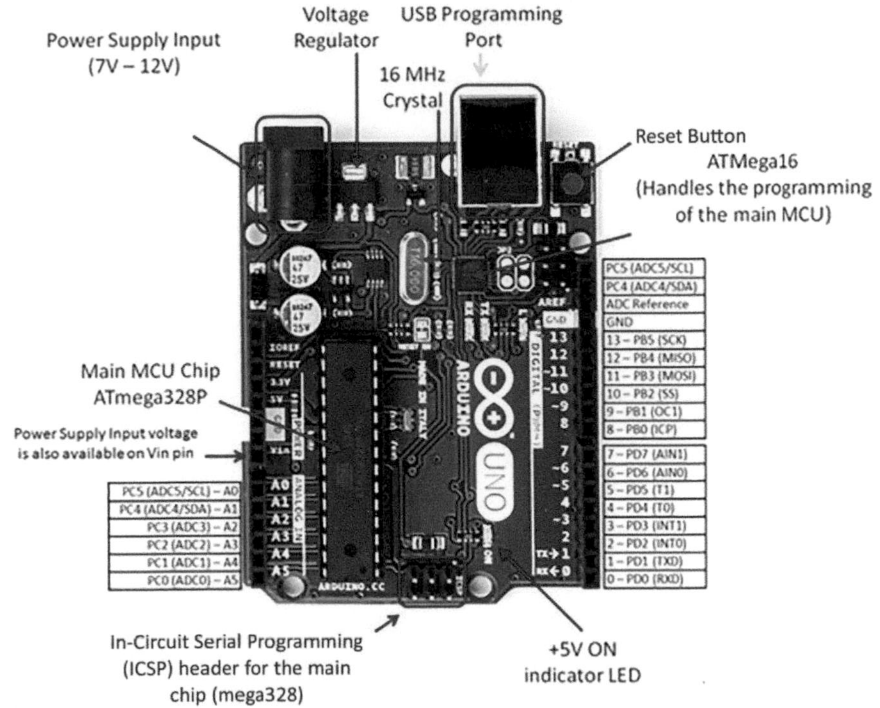

FIGURE 8.7 ATmega328P microcontroller.

Arduino Uno. It is similar in functionality to the Uno but comes in a smaller form. The Nano is often used in projects in which space is limited or when a more discreet design is desired. The Arduino Mega is a board that provides a significant increase in memory, I/O pins, and overall capabilities compared to the Uno. It is based on the ATmega2560 microcontroller and offers 54 digital I/O pins (of which 15 can be used as PWM outputs), 16 analog inputs, and multiple communication interfaces. The Mega is suitable for complex projects that require a large number of inputs and output. The Arduino Uno pin diagram is shown in Figure 8.7 [32].

Raspberry Pi boards are credit card–sized computers that consist of a system-on-a-chip (SoC) processor, memory, storage, I/O ports, and various other components [10, 14]. They typically include high-definition multimedia interface (HDMI) or composite video output, USB ports, Ethernet, Wi-Fi, Bluetooth, and a microSD card slot for storage. Raspberry Pi can run various operating systems, with the most popular being the Linux-based Raspberry Pi OS (formerly known as Raspbian). It provides a familiar desktop environment and a wide range of software packages compatible with Linux. Raspberry Pi models vary in terms of processing power. The earlier models had ARM-based processors with single-core CPUs, while the newer ones, such as the Raspberry Pi 4, feature quad-core or even octo-core CPUs. This increased processing power allows for more demanding tasks and applications. One of the distinguishing features of Raspberry Pi is its general-purpose input/output

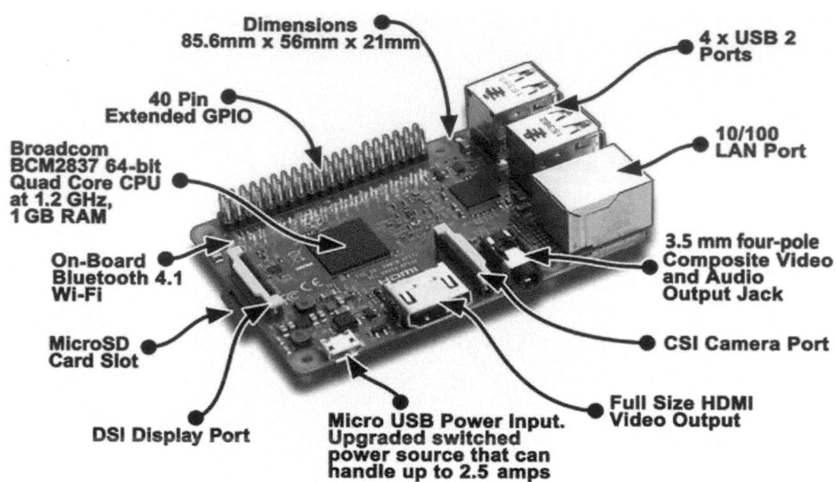

FIGURE 8.8 Raspberry Pi 3 Model B board.

(GPIO) pins. These pins allow you to connect and control external devices and components, such as sensors, actuators, LEDs, and motors. They provide a way to interact with the physical world and enable the creation of diverse projects. Raspberry Pi supports a wide range of programming languages, including Python, C/C++, Java, and more, and thereby allows users to choose the language with which they are most comfortable for programming their projects. Raspberry Pi also has a large community of developers who share tutorials, projects, and support. Raspberry Pi has the ability to handle multimedia tasks, including playing high-definition videos, serving as a media center, and running retro gaming emulators. Its HDMI output allows for connecting to monitors or TVs, providing a complete multimedia experience.

There are several types of Raspberry Pi boards available such as Raspberry Pi Model A and Model B, Raspberry Pi Zero and Raspberry Pi Zero W, Raspberry Pi 2 Model, Raspberry Pi 3 Model B, and so on, each offering different features and specifications. Figure 8.8 shows the Raspberry Pi 3 model B board [33]. For instance, Model A and Model B were the initial releases of Raspberry Pi. They featured a single-core ARM CPU, SD card slot, HDMI output, USB ports, and GPIO pins. The Model B had additional features like more USB ports and an Ethernet port. The Raspberry Pi 3 Model B and its updated version, the Raspberry Pi 3 Model B+, offer additional enhancements: a quad-core CPU, 1 GB of RAM, Wi-Fi, Bluetooth, four USB ports, an Ethernet port, an HDMI output, and GPIO pins.

Raspberry Pi and Arduino are both popular platforms for electronics and computing projects, but they have distinct features and use cases. Following is a comparison of some key features [10, 29, 34].

1. **Processing Power:** Raspberry Pi boards have more processing power compared to Arduino boards. Raspberry Pi incorporates a complete computer system—including a processor, memory, and storage—allowing it to handle

complex tasks and run a full operating system. Arduino, on the other hand, uses microcontrollers with comparatively lower processing capabilities, suitable for simpler tasks and real-time control.

2. **Operating System:** Raspberry Pi can run a variety of operating systems, including Linux-based Raspberry Pi OS, providing a desktop-like environment with access to a wide range of software. Arduino typically uses a simplified programming environment specific to its platform, without a full operating system.
3. **Input/Output (I/O) Capabilities:** Arduino is known for its extensive I/O capabilities, especially the availability of numerous digital and analog pins. These pins allow direct interfacing with various electronic components, making Arduino ideal for physical computing and sensor-based projects. Raspberry Pi also offers GPIO pins, but they are relatively limited in number compared to Arduino. Raspberry Pi's GPIO pins are often used for simple I/O tasks or interfacing with external devices.
4. **Connectivity:** Raspberry Pi boards come with built-in connectivity options—such as Ethernet, Wi-Fi, and Bluetooth—which make them easier to connect to networks and communicate with other devices. While Arduino boards may require additional modules or shields to achieve similar connectivity, they can be more power-efficient and suitable for low-power and battery-powered projects.
5. **Software Development:** Raspberry Pi supports a wide range of programming languages, including Python, C/C++, Java, and more. It offers a full software development environment with access to extensive libraries and tools. Arduino has its own simplified programming language based on C/C++ and a dedicated IDE that simplifies the coding process, and is well suited for beginners.
6. **Community and Ecosystem:** Both Raspberry Pi and Arduino have large and active communities. However, Arduino has a longer history and a more extensive ecosystem of libraries, shields, and projects specifically designed for Arduino boards. The Arduino community is known for its beginner-friendly resources and a vast range of project examples and tutorials. Raspberry Pi's community is also vibrant, with a focus on software development, IoT projects, and multimedia application.
7. **Cost:** Arduino boards are generally more affordable than Raspberry Pi boards, making them suitable for cost-sensitive projects or when simplicity and real-time control are the primary requirements. Raspberry Pi boards provide more computing power and functionality, but they are generally higher in price due to their additional features and capabilities.

Ultimately, the choice between Raspberry Pi and Arduino depends on the specific requirements of the project. Raspberry Pi is well suited for applications that require a full-fledged computer system, multimedia capabilities, and network connectivity. With its extensive I/O and real-time control capabilities, Arduino is often preferred for physical computing, robotics, and sensor-based projects in which simplicity, low-power operation, and real-time responsiveness are key.

8.2.3 Recognizing the Input/Output

Both Arduino and Raspberry Pi offer various I/O capabilities for interacting with the physical world. Arduino boards excel in their extensive digital and analog I/O, making them well suited for physical computing and sensor-based projects, whereas Raspberry Pi provides GPIO pins, along with additional communication interfaces like I2C (inter-integrated circuit), SPI (serial peripheral interface), and UART (universal asynchronous receiver-transmitter), making it a more versatile platform for projects that require networking, multimedia, and the ability to run a full operating system [10, 14]. Arduino boards typically have multiple digital pins that can be configured as either input or output. These pins operate with binary logic, meaning they can be set to either high (5 V) or low (0 V) states. Digital input pins can read the state of external devices, such as buttons or switches, by detecting whether the input is high or low. Digital output pins can send signals to control LEDs, relays, or other digital components by setting them to either high or low states. Arduino boards generally include several analog input pins. These pins use analog-to-digital converters (ADCs) to convert continuous voltage values into digital values that the Arduino can read. Analog input pins are used to measure the voltage from analog sensors, such as temperature sensors or light sensors. The ADC resolution determines the precision of the analog-to-digital conversion. Some digital pins on Arduino boards support PWM output, which allows for the simulation of analog output by rapidly toggling the digital pin between high and low states. The duty cycle—or the ratio of the high time to the total period—determines the average voltage applied to a component. PWM is commonly used to control the brightness of an LED or the speed of a motor.

Compared with Arduino, the Raspberry Pi boards include a set of GPIO pins that can be configured as either input or output [33]. These pins operate at 3.3 V logic levels. Raspberry Pi GPIO pins are capable of digital input and output, similar to Arduino. You can set the pins to high or low states for output, and read their states as input. However, it is important to note that Raspberry Pi's GPIO pins have a lower current handling capacity compared with Arduino's digital pins. Raspberry Pi has dedicated pins for I2C communication. I2C is a serial communication protocol that allows multiple devices to be connected on the same bus, using only two wires for communication: SDA (serial data line) and SCL (serial clock line). The I2C protocol enables communication with various devices, such as sensors, LCD monitors, and EEPROM memory chips. Raspberry Pi also has dedicated pins for SPI communication. SPI is a synchronous serial communication protocol commonly used to communicate with devices such as sensors, displays, and memory modules. It utilizes four wires for communication: SCLK (serial clock), MOSI (master out slave in), MISO (master in slave out), and SS/CE (slave select/chip enable). Raspberry Pi boards include a UART interface for serial communication. UART allows asynchronous serial communication between the Raspberry Pi and other devices. It uses two pins: TX (transmit) and RX (receive) for sending and receiving data. UART is often used to communicate with devices like GPS modules, Bluetooth modules, and other serial devices.

8.3 OPEN SERVICE PLATFORMS FOR IOT CLOUD COMPUTING

Open-service platforms for IoT cloud computing are platforms which provide a framework and infrastructure for developing and deploying IoT applications in the cloud [35, 36]. These platforms offer a set of services and tools that enable developers to build, integrate, and manage IoT applications and devices more easily. These platforms provide a foundation for developing IoT applications by handling the complexity of device management, data processing, and communication. They often support various communication protocols, security features, and integration with other cloud services, making it easier for developers to focus on building innovative IoT solutions. Following are some notable open service platforms for IoT cloud computing.

1. **AWS IoT Core:** AWS IoT Core is a managed cloud service offered by Amazon Web Services (AWS) [37]. It allows connected devices to securely interact with cloud applications and other devices. The platform provides a set of services and features to facilitate IoT application development. Key features of AWS IoT Core include the following [38, 39].
   a) **Device Registry and Management:** AWS IoT Core offers a device registry to manage information about IoT devices, including device metadata, authentication, and permissions. It allows you to securely register, track, and manage devices at scale.
   b) **MQTT and RESTful APIs:** The platform supports both the MQTT (Message Queuing Telemetry Transport) and RESTful APIs, enabling devices to send and receive messages to and from the cloud. This ensures efficient and reliable communication between devices and cloud applications.
   c) **Message Broker:** AWS IoT Core includes a message broker that allows devices and applications to publish and subscribe to topics. It enables the decoupling of producers and consumers, allowing multiple devices and applications to exchange data seamlessly.
   d) **Rules Engine:** The Rules Engine enables the processing of IoT data in real time. It allows you to define rules and actions to filter, transform, and route messages based on specific conditions. This enables data enrichment and automation of tasks based on IoT data.
   e) **Integration with AWS Services:** AWS IoT Core integrates with other AWS services such as AWS Lambda, Amazon Kinesis, Amazon S3, and Amazon DynamoDB [37, 40]. This integration allows you to easily process, analyze, store, and visualize IoT data using familiar AWS services.
2. **Azure IoT Hub:** Azure IoT Hub is a fully managed cloud service provided by Microsoft Azure [40]. It enables bidirectional communication between IoT devices and the Azure cloud, offering a range of features to build scalable and secure IoT applications. Key features of Azure IoT Hub include the following [41–43].
   a) **Device Identity and Management:** Azure IoT Hub allows you to securely register, provision, and manage IoT devices. It provides unique

identities and keys for devices, ensuring secure authentication and access control.

b) **Messaging and Communication:** The platform supports various protocols such as MQTT, AMQP, and HTTPS, enabling efficient and reliable communication between devices and cloud applications. It also supports device-to-cloud and cloud-to-device messaging.

c) **Device Twins:** Azure IoT Hub provides device twins, which are JSON documents that represent the state and metadata of each device. Device twins allow synchronized communication between devices and applications, enabling remote configuration and monitoring.

d) **Direct Methods:** Azure IoT Hub supports direct methods, which enable cloud applications to invoke methods on devices and receive responses. This facilitates remote control and management of devices.

e) **Integration with Azure Services:** Azure IoT Hub seamlessly integrates with other Azure services such as Azure Functions, Azure Stream Analytics, Azure Logic Apps, and Azure Machine Learning. This integration allows you to process, analyze, and act upon IoT data using a wide range of Azure services.

3. **Google Cloud IoT Core:** Google Cloud IoT Core is a cloud-based service provided by Google Cloud Platform (GCP) that offers a scalable infrastructure for connecting, managing, and ingesting data from IoT devices [44]. It provides a robust set of features for building IoT solutions. Key features of Google Cloud IoT Core include the following [44, 45].

a) **Device Registration and Management:** Google Cloud IoT Core offers device registration and management capabilities. It allows you to register devices, assign unique identities, and manage device configurations at scale.

b) **MQTT and HTTP Protocols:** The platform supports both MQTT and HTTP protocols for device communication. This enables devices to securely publish and subscribe to messages using standard protocols.

c) **Pub/Sub-Messaging:** Google Cloud IoT Core integrates with Google Cloud Pub/Sub, a messaging service for publication and subscribing (pub/sub) that provides real-time, asynchronous communication between devices and applications. It enables high-throughput, scalable messaging and data ingestion.

d) **Device Configuration and Control:** You can remotely configure device properties, update firmware, and send commands to devices using the device management capabilities of Google Cloud IoT Core. This enables efficient device management at scale.

8.4 RESOURCE MANAGEMENT TECHNIQUES FOR CLOUD-BASED IOT ENVIRONMENTS

Resource management techniques play a crucial role in optimizing the performance, scalability, and efficiency of cloud-based IoT environments [46]. Following are some key resource management techniques used in cloud-based IoT environments [46, 47].

1. **Resource Provisioning:** Resource provisioning involves allocating and provisioning computational resources (such as virtual machines, containers, or serverless functions) based on the requirements of IoT applications and devices. Dynamic resource provisioning techniques adjust the resource allocation dynamically based on changing workloads and demand. This ensures that IoT applications have sufficient resources to handle varying data volumes and computational needs.
2. **Load Balancing:** Load balancing techniques distribute the incoming workload across multiple servers or resources to ensure optimal resource utilization and prevent overloading. In the context of cloud-based IoT environments, load balancing is essential to distribute the processing and communication load across available resources to avoid bottlenecks and improve performance.
3. **Scalability and Elasticity:** Scalability and elasticity are critical for handling the dynamic nature of IoT workloads. Scalability refers to the ability to add or remove resources to meet the changing demands of IoT applications. Elasticity takes scalability a step further by automatically scaling resources based on workload fluctuations. Techniques like horizontal scaling, auto-scaling, and dynamic resource allocation enable cloud-based IoT environments to adapt to varying workloads efficiently.
4. **Quality of Service (QoS) Management:** QoS management ensures that IoT applications and services meet the defined performance requirements and service level agreements (SLAs). QoS management techniques monitor and control factors such as response time, throughput, reliability, and availability. This includes mechanisms for prioritizing critical IoT data, managing network bandwidth, and enforcing resource allocation policies to guarantee desired levels of performance and reliability.
5. **Energy Efficiency:** Energy efficiency is crucial for IoT devices, which are often resource constrained and battery powered. Resource management techniques in cloud-based IoT environments aim to minimize energy consumption by optimizing resource utilization, minimizing data transmission, and employing energy-saving mechanisms such as sleep modes or adaptive power management.
6. **Data Management and Processing:** Efficient data management and processing techniques are essential for handling the massive amounts of data generated by IoT devices. This includes techniques like data filtering, aggregation, compression, and stream processing. Cloud-based IoT environments leverage distributed data storage systems, database technologies, and Big Data processing frameworks to handle IoT data effectively.
7. **Predictive Analytics and Machine Learning:** Predictive analytics and machine learning techniques can be applied to analyze historical data, predict future IoT workloads, and make proactive resource management decisions. By leveraging machine learning models, resource management systems can

dynamically allocate resources, predict failures, optimize energy consumption, and enhance overall system performance.
8. **Security and Privacy:** Resource management techniques should incorporate robust security and privacy measures to protect IoT devices, data, and communications. This includes techniques like access control, encryption, authentication, and intrusion detection systems to ensure the integrity, confidentiality, and privacy of IoT resources and data.

Effective resource management techniques in cloud-based IoT environments enhance performance, scalability, energy efficiency, and security, enabling seamless operation and optimal utilization of resources in complex IoT ecosystems. We will next discuss a case study of smart grid energy management that highlight the implementation of resource management techniques in cloud-based IoT environments. Smart grids leverage IoT technologies to monitor and manage energy consumption in real time. A cloud-based IoT environment can effectively manage the resources in such a scenario. In this case study, a utility company implemented resource management techniques to optimize energy distribution and consumption.

1. **Resource Provisioning:** The cloud-based IoT environment dynamically provisions computational resources based on the demand for energy monitoring and control. It allocates additional resources during peak periods to handle high data volumes and computational requirements.
2. **Load Balancing:** Load balancing techniques distribute the incoming energy data across multiple servers to avoid overloading and ensure efficient processing. It allows for effective utilization of resources and maintains the responsiveness of the system.
3. **Scalability and Elasticity:** The cloud-based IoT environment automatically scales resources based on the fluctuating energy demand. It can dynamically add or remove resources to handle varying workloads, ensuring efficient energy management.
4. **Quality of Service Management:** QoS techniques are employed to ensure reliable and timely energy data processing. Response time and availability of the system are carefully monitored to meet the defined performance requirements and SLAs.

8.5 DATA MANAGEMENT FOR IOT

Data management for the IoT involves handling and processing the vast amounts of data generated by IoT devices. Effective data management in IoT is crucial because IoT devices generate enormous volumes of data in real time. Efficient data management is necessary to handle and process this data effectively, ensuring that valuable insights are not lost in the overwhelming volume [40, 48]. IoT applications often require real-time or near-real-time data processing. Data management systems must be capable of ingesting, analyzing, and responding to IoT data in a timely manner to enable real-time decision-making and automation. IoT data comes in various formats and from diverse sources. Data management techniques are needed to handle different data types, integrate data from multiple devices and platforms, and ensure interoperability for effective analysis. Ensuring data quality is crucial for accurate analysis and decision-making. Data management practices help validate and cleanse IoT data, reducing errors, inconsistencies, and biases that could affect the reliability of insights derived from the data. Following are some key aspects of data management for the IoT [48, 49].

1. **Data Collection:** IoT devices gather data from various sources, such as sensors, actuators, and embedded systems. This data can include environmental readings, user interactions, machine-generated data, and more.
2. **Data Storage:** Due to the massive scale of IoT data, efficient storage mechanisms are required. Cloud-based storage solutions, distributed file systems, and databases are commonly used to store and manage IoT data. Depending on the use case, data may be stored locally on edge devices or centralized in the cloud.
3. **Data Processing:** IoT data often requires pre-processing and filtering to extract relevant information and reduce the overall volume. Real-time analytics and stream processing techniques are employed to analyze and extract valuable insights from the continuous stream of IoT data.
4. **Data Integration:** IoT devices generate data in various formats and protocols. Data integration involves aggregating data from different devices, platforms, and sources, ensuring compatibility and uniformity for analysis and decision-making.
5. **Data Security and Privacy:** IoT devices generate sensitive data requiring robust security measures to protect against unauthorized access, data breaches, and privacy violations. Encryption, access controls, secure communication protocols, and data anonymization techniques are used to safeguard IoT data.
6. **Data Governance and Compliance:** Organizations must establish data governance policies and compliance frameworks to ensure proper data handling, consent management, and adherence to regulations such as GDPR (the European Union's General Data Protection Regulation).
7. **Data Lifecycle Management:** Managing the entire lifecycle of IoT data involves capturing, storing, analyzing, archiving, and eventually disposing of the data when it is no longer needed. Data retention policies and data lifecycle management strategies are necessary to optimize storage costs and ensure compliance.
8. **Data Analytics and Machine Learning:** IoT data holds valuable insights that can be extracted using various analytics techniques. Machine learning algorithms and predictive analytics enable organizations to derive actionable intelligence, detect anomalies, and make data-driven decisions based on IoT data.
9. **Data Visualization and Reporting:** Presenting IoT data in a visual and understandable format is crucial for decision-makers. Data visualization tools and dashboards help stakeholders gain insights, monitor key metrics, and track IoT system performance.

Proper data management enables organizations to extract meaningful insights from IoT data, leading to data-driven decision-making, process optimization, and improved operational efficiency [38, 50, 51]. IoT data analysis can identify patterns and anomalies that indicate potential equipment failures. Proactive maintenance based on these insights can help prevent costly breakdowns, minimize downtime, and optimize maintenance schedules. IoT data management enables organizations to understand customer behavior, preferences, and usage patterns. This knowledge can be leveraged to personalize products, services, and experiences, leading to improved customer satisfaction and loyalty. IoT data management opens up opportunities for innovative business models, such as Product-as-a-Service and subscription-based offerings. It also enables organizations to monetize data by providing data-driven services and insights to customers and partners.

8.6 THINGSPEAK FOR IOT

ThingSpeak is an IoT platform and analytics service provided by MathWorks, the company behind the programming language MATLAB [52]. It is designed to enable developers and IoT enthusiasts to collect, analyze, and visualize sensor data from connected devices. There are sensors all around—in our homes, smartphones, automobiles, city infrastructure, and industrial equipment. Sensors detect and measure information about all sorts of things like temperature, humidity, and pressure, and they communicate that data in some form, such as a numerical value or electrical signal. ThingSpeak is an IoT platform provided by MathWorks that enables you to collect, analyze, and visualize data from IoT devices. It offers a range of features for data storage, visualization, analysis, and integration with other services [53]. With ThingSpeak, you can easily send data from your devices to the cloud, where it is stored in private or public channels. Storing data in the cloud provides convenient access to your data from anywhere. Once the data is in a ThingSpeak channel, you can analyze and visualize it using a wide range of customizable options such as line plots, bar graphs, and maps. Additionally, ThingSpeak allows you to perform calculations on the data, integrate with social media and web services, and interact with other devices. Overall, ThingSpeak provides a powerful solution for managing IoT data, enabling you to gain insights and make informed decisions based on the data collected from your devices. Using online analytical tools, you can explore and visualize data. You can discover relationships, patterns, and trends in data; you can calculate new data; and you can visualize it in plots, charts, and gauges. ThingSpeak can provide access to MATLAB to help you make sense of data. Developers can create rules and triggers based on IoT data to automate actions or generate alerts using MATLAB. This allows them to respond to events or conditions in real time and take appropriate actions in their IoT ecosystem.

ThingSpeak provides several key features for IoT developers. It allows IoT developers to easily collect data from sensors and connected devices. It supports various communication protocols such as RESTful APIs and MQTT, making it compatible with a wide range of IoT devices. Developers can send data to ThingSpeak in real time or batch mode, depending on their application requirements. It offers built-in visualization tools to create customizable dashboards and plots for visualizing IoT data. Developers can easily create charts, graphs, gauges, and maps to display their data in a visually appealing manner. These visualizations help monitor trends, identify patterns, and gain insights from the collected IoT data. It allows integration with popular cloud platforms such as AWS IoT, Google Cloud IoT Core, and Microsoft Azure IoT Hub [40, 42, 43]. This integration capability enables developers to leverage the power of multiple platforms and services, expanding the functionality of their IoT applications. ThingSpeak offers an open API, allowing developers to extend its functionality and integrate it with their own applications or third-party services. Developers can develop custom applications, scripts, and plugins to interact with ThingSpeak's data and functionality, tailoring it to their specific IoT requirements. Additionally, the ThingSpeak community provides support, resources, and examples, making it easier for developers to get started and overcome challenges in their IoT projects.

We will next discuss a case study of environmental monitoring in smart agriculture. We know that agricultural productivity depends heavily on environmental factors such as temperature, humidity, and soil moisture. Monitoring these parameters in real time is crucial for optimizing crop growth, irrigation management, and overall farm efficiency. A farmer wants to implement an IoT solution to monitor and analyze environmental conditions on their farm. In order to address this issue, the farmer can use ThingSpeak as the IoT platform for collecting and analyzing environmental data [52]. The steps to be followed in this solution will be are as follows [52, 54, 55].

1. **Sensor Deployment:** The farmer deploys various sensors across the farm to capture environmental data. Temperature and humidity sensors are installed to measure atmospheric conditions, while soil moisture sensors are placed in different locations to monitor soil moisture levels.
2. **Data Collection and Transmission:** Each sensor is connected to a microcontroller or IoT device that collects data from the sensors and transmits it to ThingSpeak. The microcontroller is programmed to periodically read sensor values and send the data to ThingSpeak using the ThingSpeak API or MQTT protocol. The data transmission can be done using wired or wireless connectivity options, depending on the farm's infrastructure.
3. **ThingSpeak Configuration:** The farmer sets up a ThingSpeak channel for each type of sensor data. For example, there will be separate channels for temperature, humidity, and soil moisture. The channels are configured to receive and store the incoming data from the sensors. The data can be sent to ThingSpeak using JSON or CSV format, depending on the chosen data format.
4. **Data Visualization:** Using ThingSpeak's built-in visualization tools, the farmer creates customized dashboards to monitor the environmental data. Line charts are created to display the temperature and humidity trends over time, while bar graphs or gauges are used to visualize soil moisture levels. The visualizations help the farmer quickly identify any anomalies or trends that require attention.
5. **Alerts and Notifications:** ThingSpeak's MATLAB Analysis app is utilized to set up rules and triggers based on predefined thresholds. For example, if the

soil moisture level drops below a certain threshold, an alert can be generated and sent to the farmer's email or mobile device. This allows the farmer to take prompt action, such as initiating irrigation or adjusting watering schedules.

6. **Historical Data Analysis:** ThingSpeak's MATLAB Analytics app is leveraged to perform advanced analysis on the collected data. The farmer can apply statistical analysis, identify correlations between different environmental factors, and gain insights into the impact of specific conditions on crop health and productivity. This analysis aids in making informed decisions for optimizing farming practices.

This case study demonstrates how ThingSpeak can be utilized in an IoT application for environmental monitoring in smart agriculture. By leveraging ThingSpeak's features, the farmer can make data-driven decisions, optimize resource allocation, and enhance overall farm productivity. Speaking in more specific words, the farmer can gain the following benefits by implementing a ThingSpeak-based solution.

- **Real-time Monitoring:** The farmer can monitor environmental conditions on the farm in real time, enabling timely interventions and adjustments to optimize crop growth and resource management.
- **Data-Driven Decision-Making:** By analyzing historical data, the farmer can identify patterns and trends, allowing for data-driven decision-making. This includes adjusting irrigation schedules, optimizing fertilization, and improving overall farm efficiency.
- **Proactive Alerts:** With ThingSpeak's alerts and notifications, the farmer receives timely alerts when critical thresholds are breached, allowing for immediate action to prevent crop damage or losses.
- **Visualization and Insights:** ThingSpeak's visualization tools and analytics capabilities provide a clear understanding of the environmental factors affecting crop health. The farmer can easily visualize and interpret the data, gaining valuable insights for improved farming practices.

REFERENCES

[1] K. A. Lambert, *Fundamentals of Python Data Structures*, USA, Cengage Learning PTR, Boston, Massachusetts, United States, 2019.

[2] P. Virtanen *et al.*, "SciPy 1.0: Fundamental Algorithms for Scientific Computing in Python," *Nat. Methods*, vol. 17, no. 3, 2020, doi: 10.1038/s41592-019-0686-2.

[3] M. Lutz, *Learning Python*, Icarus, Sussex, England, vol. 78, no. 1, 2007, doi: 10.1016/0019-1035(89)90077-8.

[4] E. Gottlieb, "The Design and Implementation of a Modern Systems Programming Language," *Spring*, 2011.

[5] M. L. Scott, *Programming Language Pragmatics, Second Edition*, Morgan Kaufmann, Massachusetts, United States, 2005.

[6] G. Hackeling, *Mastering Machine Learning with Scikit-Learn*, Packt Publishing Ltd, Birmingham, UK, 2014.

[7] S. Campbell, "Flask vs Django: What's the Difference Between Flask & Django?," *Guru99*, 2021.

[8] E. Matthes, *Python Crash Course; A Hands-On, Project-Based Introduction to Programming, Third Edition*, No Starch Press, San Francisco, CA, 2019.

[9] S. Yamanoor and S. Yamanoor, *Python Programming with Raspberry Pi*, Packt Publishing, Birmingham, UK, 2017.

[10] J. Cicolani, *Beginning Robotics with Raspberry Pi and Arduino*, Apress, New York, United States, 2021, doi: https://doi.org/10.1007/978-1-4842-6891-9.

[11] IDC Study, "AIoT: How IoT Leaders Are Breaking Away," *SAS Inst. Inc*, 2019.

[12] S. K. Goudos, P. I. Dallas, S. Chatziefthymiou, and S. Kyriazakos, "A Survey of IoT Key Enabling and Future Technologies: 5G, Mobile IoT, Sematic Web and Applications," *Wirel. Pers. Commun.*, vol. 97, no. 2, 2017, doi: 10.1007/s11277-017-4647-8.

[13] D. I. Bayem, H. O. Osuagwu, and C. F. Ugwu, "A Web-Based Aggregate Information Portal," *Eur. J. Electr. Eng. Comput. Sci.*, vol. 5, no. 3, 2021, doi: 10.24018/ejece.2021.5.3.323.

[14] C. Bell, *Beginning Sensor Networks with XBee, Raspberry Pi, and Arduino: Sensing the World with Python and MicroPython*, Apress Media LLC, New York, United States, 2020, doi: 10.1007/978-1-4842-5796-8.

[15] B. Kim and G. Henke, "Easy-to-Use Cloud Computing for Teaching Data Science," *J. Stat. Data Sci. Educ.*, vol. 29, no. S1, 2021, doi: 10.1080/10691898.2020.1860726.

[16] W. Donat, *Learn Raspberry Pi Programming with Python*, Apress, New York, United States, 2018, doi: 10.1007/978-1-4842-3769-4.

[17] www.python.org/downloads/release/python-396/accessed on: 17/07/2023.

[18] R. Nayak and N. Gupta, "File Handling," in *Python for Engineers and Scientists*, CRC Press, Florida, United States, pp. 271–288, 2022, doi: 10.1201/9781003219125-10.

[19] R. G. McClarren, "Getting Started in Python," in *Computational Nuclear Engineering and Radiological Science Using Python*, Elsevier, Amsterdam, Netherlands, 2018, doi: 10.1016/b978-0-12-812253-2.00002-9.

[20] S. Jessen, "Getting Started with Data Science Using Python," *IBM Press Pearson plc*, 2021.

[21] Plotly, "Getting Started with Plotly in Python," *Plotly*, 2022.

[22] S. Committee, *IEEE Standard for Software Verification and Validation IEEE Standard for Software Verification and Validation*, Institute of Electrical and Electronics Engineers, New Jersey, United States, vol. 1998, pp. 1–110, July 1998.

[23] R. Rehim, *Python Penetration Testing Cookbook*, Packt Publishing, Birmingham, UK, 2017.

[24] F. Hüning, *Embedded Systems für IoT*, Springer Berlin Heidelberg, Heidelberg, Germany, 2019, doi: 10.1007/978-3-662-57901-5.

[25] A. Ju, D. Chen, and J. Tang, "Design of Educational Robot Platform Based on Graphic Programming," in *Advances in Intelligent Systems and Computing*, 2020, doi: 10.1007/978-981-15-2568-1_53.

[26] Y. R. S. Kumar, T. Nivethetha, P. Priyadharshini, and U. Jayachandiran, "Smart Glasses for Visually Impaired People with Facial Recognition," in *2022 International Conference on Communication, Computing and Internet of Things, IC3IoT 2022 — Proceedings*, 2022, doi: 10.1109/IC3IOT53935.2022.9768012.

[27] R. K. Kodali and K. S. Mahesh, "Low Cost Ambient Monitoring Using ESP8266," in *Proceedings of the 2016 2nd International Conference on Contemporary Computing and Informatics, IC3I 2016*, 2016, doi: 10.1109/IC3I.2016.7918788.

[28] S. A. Strom and M. Strom, "Embedded Measurement and Control Applications Utilizing Python on the Pocket Beaglebone," in *ASEE Annual Conference and Exposition, Conference Proceedings*, 2020, doi: 10.18260/1-2-34517.

[29] A. S. Ismailov and Z. B. Jo'rayev, "Study of Arduino Microcontroller Board," *Sci. Educ. Sci. J.*, vol. 3, no. 3, 2022.

[30] V. M. Cvjetkovic and M. Matijevic, "Overview of Architectures with Arduino Boards as Building Blocks for Data Acquisition and Control Systems," *Int. J. Online Eng.*, vol. 12, no. 7, 2016, doi: 10.3991/ijoe.v12i07.5818.

[31] Yogesh, "Introduction to Arduino UNO Board," in *Programming and Interfacing with Arduino*, CRC Press, Florida, United States, 2021, doi: 10.1201/9781003201700-1.
[32] https://osoyoo.com/2017/06/26/introduction-of-raspberry-pi-gpio/ Accessed On: 17/07/2023.
[33] Raspberry Pi, "Raspberry Pi 4 Model B Specifications—Raspberry Pi," *Raspberry Pi Foundation*, 2020.
[34] D. Albright, "Arduino Vs Raspberry Pi: A Detailed Comparison," *Digital Trends*, 2015.
[35] IBM, "IBM Watson IoT Platform," *Console.Bluemix.Net*, 2020.
[36] F. Alhaidari, A. Rahman, and R. Zagrouba, "Cloud of Things: Architecture, Applications and Challenges," *J. Ambient Intell. Humaniz. Comput.*, vol. 14, no. 5, pp. 5957–5975, 2020, doi: 10.1007/s12652-020-02448-3.
[37] N. Kewate, "A Review on AWS—Cloud Computing Technology," *Int. J. Res. Appl. Sci. Eng. Technol.*, vol. 10, no. 1, 2022, doi: 10.22214/ijraset.2022.39802.
[38] H. Yoo, R. C. Park, and K. Chung, "IoT-Based Health Big-Data Process Technologies: A Survey," *KSII Trans. Internet Inf. Syst.*, vol. 15, no. 3, 2021, doi: 10.3837/tiis.2021.03.009.
[39] S. Dhanasekar, E. Ilankhatir, S. Divakar, and D. Vennila, "A Survey on IoT Architecture," *Int. J. Adv. Sci. Res. Dev.*, vol. 6, no. 4, 2019, doi: 10.26836/ijasrd/2019/v6/i4/60402.
[40] K. S. Mohamed, "IoT Cloud Computing, Storage, and Data Analytics," in *The Era of Internet of Things*, Springer International Publishing, Berlin, Germany, 2019, doi: 10.1007/978-3-030-18133-8_4.
[41] R. Stackowiak, "Azure IoT Hub," in *Azure Internet of Things Revealed*, 2019, doi: 10.1007/978-1-4842-5470-7_4.
[42] C. Pham, D. T. Nguyen, Y. Njah, N. H. Tran, K. K. Nguyen, and M. Cheriet, "Share-to-Run IoT Services in Edge Cloud Computing," *IEEE Internet Things J.*, vol. 9, no. 1, 2022, doi: 10.1109/JIOT.2021.3085777.
[43] Y. Zhang, Y. Sun, R. Jin, K. Lin, and W. Liu, "High-Performance Isolation Computing Technology for Smart IoT Healthcare in Cloud Environments," *IEEE Internet Things J.*, vol. 8, no. 23, 2021, doi: 10.1109/JIOT.2021.3051742.
[44] Google, "Google Cloud IoT Core documentation," *Google Cloud Documentation*, 2020.
[45] D. Gupta, S. Bhatt, M. Gupta, O. Kayode, and A. S. Tosun, "Access Control Model for Google Cloud IoT," in *Proceedings—2020 IEEE 6th Intl Conference on Big Data Security on Cloud, BigDataSecurity 2020, 2020 IEEE Intl Conference on High Performance and Smart Computing, HPSC 2020 and 2020 IEEE Intl Conference on Intelligent Data and Security, IDS 2020*, 2020, doi: 10.1109/BigDataSecurity-HPSC-IDS49724.2020.00044.
[46] A. Javadpour, G. Wang, and S. Rezaei, "Resource Management in a Peer to Peer Cloud Network for IoT," *Wirel. Pers. Commun.*, vol. 115, no. 3, 2020, doi: 10.1007/s11277-020-07691-7.
[47] T. M. Pham and T. T. L. Nguyen, "Optimization of Resource Management for NFV-Enabled IoT Systems in Edge Cloud Computing," *IEEE Access*, vol. 8, 2020, doi: 10.1109/ACCESS.2020.3026711.
[48] Y. Wang, K. Yang, W. Wan, Y. Zhang, and Q. Liu, "Energy-Efficient Data and Energy Integrated Management Strategy for IoT Devices Based on RF Energy Harvesting," *IEEE Internet Things J.*, vol. 8, no. 17, 2021, doi: 10.1109/JIOT.2021.3068040.
[49] H. Zhang, X. Zhang, Z. Guo, H. Wang, D. Cui, and Q. Wen, "Secure and Efficiently Searchable IoT Communication Data Management Model: Using Blockchain as a New Tool," *IEEE Internet Things J.*, vol. 10, no. 14, pp. 11985–11999, 2021, doi: 10.1109/JIOT.2021.3121482.
[50] Gazali, S. Kaur, and I. Singh, "Artificial Intelligence Based Clinical Data Management Systems: A Review," *Inform. Med. Unlocked*, vol. 9, 2017, doi: 10.1016/j.imu.2017.09.003.

[51] T. Joshva Devadas, S. Thayammal, and A. Ramprakash, "IOT Data Management, Data Aggregation and Dissemination," in *Intelligent Systems Reference Library*, 2019, doi: 10.1007/978-3-030-33596-0_16.

[52] ThingSpeak, "IoT Analytics—ThingSpeak Internet of Things," *ThingSpeak*, 2020.

[53] V. Viegas, J. M. D. Pereira, P. Girão, and O. Postolache, "Study of Latencies in ThingSpeak," *Adv. Sci. Technol. Eng. Syst.*, vol. 6, no. 1, 2021, doi: 10.25046/aj060139.

[54] M. Jagatheesan and G. Janaki, "Weather Monitoring System Using IoT for Smart Farming," *ECS Trans.*, vol. 107, no. 1, 2022, doi: 10.1149/10701.17439ecst.

[55] A. A. Mohammed, M. A. N. Al-hayanni, and H. M. Azzawi, "Detection and Segmentation the Affected Brain Using ThingSpeak Platform Based on IoT Cloud Analysis," *Period. Eng. Nat. Sci.*, vol. 9, no. 2, 2021, doi: 10.21533/pen.v9i2.1918.

9 The Internet of Things for Healthcare

9.1 IOT AS A KEY IN THE DIGITAL HEALTHCARE SYSTEM

The IoT is revolutionary technology that has brought significant advancements in the healthcare industry. This technology has transformed the traditional healthcare delivery system into a more efficient, cost-effective, and patient-centered approach. With IoT, healthcare providers now have the ability to collect, exchange, and analyze real-time data from connected medical devices and wearables. This data has the potential to improve patient outcomes, optimize care delivery, and reduce healthcare costs [1, 2]. The concept of IoT in healthcare is not a new one. The concept of telemedicine can be traced back to the early 20th century with the advent of radio and telephone technology. In the 1920s, radio waves were used to transmit medical information and consultations between medical professionals in remote locations. In the 1950s and 1960s, the telephone was used for remote consultations and medical advice. However, it was not until the 1970s and 1980s that telemedicine as we know it today began to take shape with the development of videoconferencing technology. In 1973, the first telemedicine demonstration took place between the University of Nebraska and the Norfolk State Hospital, and in 1974 the first telemedicine program was established at Massachusetts General Hospital [3, 4]. Since then, with the advancements in technology, telemedicine has expanded to include a variety of remote healthcare services, including remote monitoring, teleconsultation, teletriage, and tele-education, all of which are now part of the larger concept of the IoMT and the IoT in healthcare. The combination of Wi-Fi connectivity, sensors, and cloud infrastructure can enable continuous data collection, analysis, and remote monitoring of patients' health conditions, facilitating timely interventions and improved patient care. Wi-Fi provides the wireless network infrastructure that enables the seamless communication between IoT devices, sensors, and the central monitoring system. Wi-Fi connectivity allows for real-time transmission of data from sensors and devices to the cloud for analysis and monitoring. The cloud can serve as a central repository for storing and processing the vast amount of data generated by remote patient monitoring (RPM) devices and sensors. Cloud platforms provide scalable and secure storage, ensuring that patient data is protected and accessible to authorized healthcare professionals. A detailed explanation of cloud computing can be found in Section 5.1.1. Figure 9.1 demonstrates how a doctor can check patients physically, and how the real-time patient health-related measurements can be transmitted with other medical remote expert in a wireless fashion.

IoT has played a crucial role in the evolution of the digital healthcare system. The use of IoT in healthcare is centered on three key areas: RPM [5], clinical data management (CDM) [6], and healthcare asset management (HAM) [7, 8]. RPM is one

DOI: 10.1201/9781003282945-9

FIGURE 9.1 Combination of Wi-Fi, IoT sensors, and the cloud in disease diagnosis.

of the most significant applications of IoT in healthcare. RPM is a technology-based healthcare delivery method that uses digital tools to monitor patients' health status outside of the traditional healthcare setting. RPM allows healthcare providers to remotely monitor a patient's vital signs, symptoms, and other health data in real time or at regular intervals. It involves the use of connected medical devices and wearables to monitor the health status of patients in real time. The data collected from these devices is transmitted to healthcare providers, who can use it to make informed decisions about the patient's care. RPM typically involves the use of various medical devices—such as blood pressure monitors, pulse oximeters, glucose meters, and wearables like smartwatches or fitness trackers—to collect and transmit patient data to healthcare providers. This data is then analyzed by healthcare providers to identify any changes or patterns that may indicate a deterioration in the patient's health status, allowing for early intervention or adjustment of the treatment plan. A typical RPM scenario is illustrated in Figure 9.2, with various medical devices and sensors interfaced with the IoT network such that healthcare providers can remotely monitor the health status of patients and collect real-time data for analysis. RPM can be particularly beneficial for patients with chronic conditions—such as diabetes, hypertension, or heart disease—who require ongoing monitoring and management. By allowing patients to receive care in their own homes, RPM can improve access to care, reduce hospital readmissions, and lower healthcare costs. Patients are no longer required to visit a healthcare facility for routine check-ups, reducing the cost of care and increasing the overall efficiency of the healthcare delivery system.

CDM is another area where IoT has made a significant impact in the healthcare industry. CDM in the context of IoT refers to the process of managing and analyzing clinical data generated from various IoT devices used in healthcare. IoT devices—such as wearables, implantable devices, and medical sensors—generate vast amounts

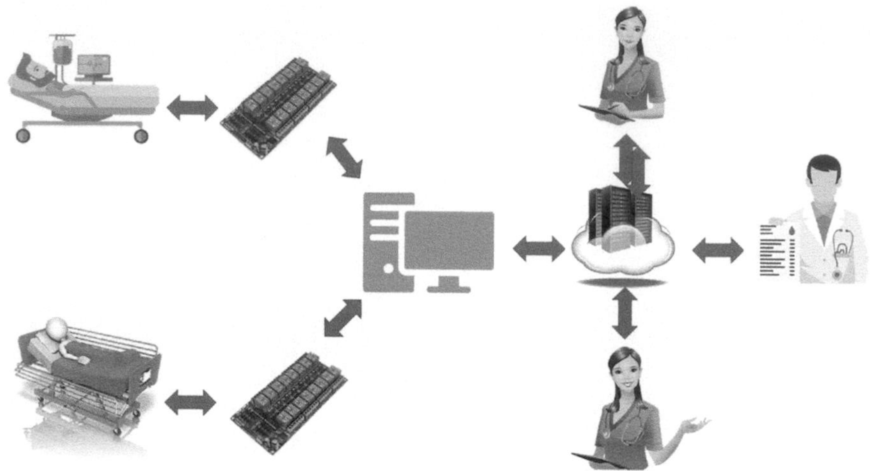

FIGURE 9.2 A typical remote patient monitoring scenario.

of data that needs to be collected, processed, and stored securely for analysis and use in clinical research. With the implementation of electronic health records (EHRs) and other digital health tools, healthcare providers can now access patient data from anywhere, at any time [9]. This data can help providers make better-informed decisions about patient care, leading to better health outcomes. The process of CDM in the context of IoT involves the collection of data from various IoT devices, integration of data from multiple sources, data cleaning, data transformation, and data analysis. The data collected from IoT devices can be used for various purposes, including real-time monitoring of patients, identifying disease patterns and trends, and predicting disease progression. In addition to managing the data generated from IoT devices, CDM in the context of IoT also involves ensuring data quality, confidentiality, and security. This includes the use of secure data transmission protocols, data encryption, and access control mechanisms to prevent unauthorized access to sensitive patient data. Overall, effective CDM in the context of IoT can help improve the quality of care delivered to patients, advance clinical research, and enhance healthcare outcomes [6, 10].

HAM has also benefited from the implementation of IoT in healthcare. Using connected devices and sensors, healthcare providers can efficiently manage their medical equipment and other assets. This has led to reduced downtime, increased efficiency, and cost savings. HAM in the context of IoT refers to the process of tracking and managing medical equipment, supplies, and other assets using IoT devices and technologies. The goal of HAM is to improve the efficiency and accuracy of inventory management, reduce costs, and improve patient care. IoT devices, such as RFID tags and sensors, can be attached to medical equipment, supplies, and other assets to track their location, usage, and maintenance needs in real time [7, 10]. This data can be collected and transmitted to a central database or cloud-based platform for analysis and decision-making. HAM using IoT can help hospitals and healthcare organizations to optimize their inventory management processes, reduce waste, and improve the allocation of resources. It can also help to improve patient safety by ensuring that medical equipment is properly maintained and available when needed. Additionally, IoT-enabled asset management systems can provide real-time data on the status of equipment and supplies, allowing hospitals to identify potential issues before they become critical. This can help to prevent equipment downtime, reduce maintenance costs, and improve the overall efficiency of healthcare operations. Overall, HAM using IoT can help to improve the quality of care delivered to patients, increase operational efficiency, and reduce costs for healthcare organizations.

Overall, IoT is a key enabler of digital healthcare systems and has the potential to transform healthcare delivery. By leveraging the power of IoT devices and data analytics, healthcare professionals can improve patient outcomes, reduce costs, and enhance the overall patient experience. Thus, the IoT is a key component in digital healthcare systems for several reasons including the following.

1. **Remote Patient Monitoring:** IoT devices such as wearables and sensors can monitor vital signs, track medication adherence, and detect changes in a patient's condition [5]. This can be especially useful for patients with chronic conditions who require ongoing monitoring. RPM enables healthcare professionals to track patients' health in real time, even when they are not physically present in the clinic or hospital. This can reduce hospitalizations and emergency room visits, and it can improve patient outcomes.
2. **Improved Efficiency and Accuracy:** IoT devices can automate many tasks and reduce the need for manual data entry, which can save time and reduce errors [10, 11]. For example, a smart pill bottle can automatically log medication usage and send alerts to patients when it is time to take their medication. This can reduce the risk of medication errors and improve patient adherence to treatment plans.
3. **Personalized Medicine:** IoT devices can collect and analyze large amounts of data on individual patients, such as their activity levels, sleep patterns, and dietary habits [12]. This can enable healthcare professionals to provide personalized treatment plans that are tailored to the specific needs of each patient. For example, a diabetes patient's glucose levels can be monitored in real time, enabling the healthcare professional to adjust treatment plans based on the patient's current condition.
4. **Cost Savings:** IoT devices can reduce healthcare costs by enabling remote monitoring and reducing hospitalizations [12]. For example, a remote monitoring system for patients with chronic conditions can reduce hospital readmissions and emergency room visits. Additionally, IoT devices can help healthcare professionals identify potential health issues before they become more serious, reducing the need for costly interventions.
5. **Improved Patient Experience:** IoT devices can provide patients with more control over their healthcare and enable them to be more engaged in their treatment. For example, a mobile app that tracks a patient's medication usage and provides reminders can help patients feel more empowered and in control of their health [12, 13]. Additionally, IoT devices can provide patients

with access to their health data, enabling them to make more informed decisions about their healthcare.

The use of IoT in healthcare is not without its challenges. The collection and management of vast amounts of data comes with the risk of data breaches and privacy concerns. Healthcare providers must ensure that patient data is protected at all times through the implementation of robust security protocols [14, 15]. Another challenge of IoT implementation in healthcare is the issue of interoperability. The data collected from various sources must be integrated into a single platform to be useful. Therefore, healthcare providers and device manufacturers must work together to establish industry-wide standards for data exchange and interoperability [16, 17]. In conclusion, IoT has revolutionized the healthcare industry, enabling a more patient-centered, cost-effective, and efficient healthcare delivery system. Healthcare providers must continue to leverage IoT and other digital health tools to improve patient outcomes, optimize care delivery, and reduce healthcare costs. However, healthcare providers must address the challenges of data security, interoperability, and regulatory compliance to successfully implement IoT in healthcare [18, 19].

9.2 HOW IOT HELPS IN HEALTHCARE PROCESSES

Wearable technology has revolutionized the healthcare industry by providing real-time data to both patients and healthcare providers. Wearable technology devices such as smartwatches, fitness trackers, and other medical devices are used to monitor and track vital signs such as heart rate, blood pressure, blood glucose levels, and other health metrics. These devices enable RPM, which reduces the need for hospital visits and allows for timely interventions. Wearable technology can also help patients manage their health conditions, promote healthy lifestyle choices, and prevent illnesses [20, 21]. Recently, the COVID-19 pandemic has accelerated the adoption of IoT in healthcare as RPM became essential to prevent the spread of the virus. Wearable technology, such as pulse oximeters and temperature sensors, enabled patients to monitor their health at home, reducing the risk of exposure to the virus. Healthcare providers also relied on remote monitoring to monitor patients with COVID-19, reducing the need for hospital admissions. The pandemic highlighted the importance of IoT in healthcare, and its adoption is expected to continue to grow [22, 23].

To set up an end-to-end healthcare IoT system, several key elements are required. First, the system needs to have a reliable and secure network infrastructure that can support the transfer of data from wearable devices to the cloud. The system also needs to have a data storage and analytics platform to store and process the data generated by the devices. The platform should be able to integrate with other healthcare systems to enable seamless data exchange. The system also needs to have an intuitive user interface that allows patients and healthcare providers to access the data generated by the devices. Machine learning can be implemented in healthcare IoT products to improve the accuracy of data analysis and predictions [24, 25]. Machine learning algorithms can be used to identify patterns and anomalies in the data generated by the devices, enabling early detection of health conditions and timely interventions. Machine learning can also be used to personalize healthcare interventions based on the patient's health metrics, history, and preferences. Data analytics can be used in healthcare IoT to extract meaningful insights from the vast amount of data generated by wearable devices [26, 27]. Analytics can help healthcare providers identify trends, patterns, and correlations in the data, enabling them to make informed decisions about patient care. Analytics can also help patients understand their health metrics, identify areas for improvement, and track progress toward their health goals. The introduction of 5G networks has opened up new possibilities for healthcare IoT [2, 28]. 5G networks offer faster data transfer speeds, lower latency, and higher bandwidth, enabling real-time RPM, telemedicine, and other healthcare applications. 5G networks can also support the use of AR and VR technologies in healthcare, enabling immersive training and simulation for healthcare professionals and patients.

IoT-based healthcare systems generally follow several steps. First, the wearable device is connected to the network infrastructure and begins transmitting data to the cloud. The data is then stored and processed by the data storage and analytics platform. The platform generates insights and alerts based on the data analysis, which are then presented to healthcare providers and patients through an intuitive user interface. Healthcare providers can use the insights to make informed decisions about patient care, while patients can use the interface to monitor their health metrics and receive personalized recommendations for improving their health [26, 27]. As the system continues to collect data, the insights and recommendations become more accurate and personalized over time. The process of using IoT in healthcare can be broken down into the following steps [14, 29].

1. **Data Collection:** IoT devices are used to collect and transmit real-time patient health data. These devices can include wearable sensors, medical monitoring devices, and implantable medical devices. The data collected can include vital signs such as heart rate, blood pressure, and respiratory rate, as well as activity level, sleep patterns, and medication adherence.
2. **Data Analysis:** The data collected from IoT devices is then analyzed using machine learning algorithms and other advanced analytics techniques. This analysis helps to identify patterns and trends in the data that can be used to develop personalized treatment plans for individual patients. For example, the data can be used to identify patients who are at risk of developing complications, such as diabetic foot ulcers, and intervene early to prevent these complications from developing.
3. **Remote Monitoring:** IoT devices can also be used for RPM, allowing healthcare providers to monitor patients outside of traditional clinical settings. This can be especially useful for patients who are recovering from surgery or who have chronic conditions that require ongoing monitoring. Remote monitoring can also help to reduce hospital readmissions and improve patient outcomes.
4. **Telemedicine:** IoT devices can also be used to facilitate telemedicine, allowing patients to connect with healthcare providers remotely. This can include virtual consultations, remote diagnostics, and even remote surgery. Telemedicine can help to improve access to healthcare services, particularly for patients who live in rural or underserved area.

5. **Operational Efficiency:** IoT devices can also be used to improve operational efficiency in healthcare settings. For example, IoT devices can be used to track the location and availability of medical equipment, reducing the time and effort required to locate and prepare equipment for use. IoT devices can also be used to automate administrative tasks such as patient scheduling and billing.

Overall, IoT has the potential to revolutionize healthcare by improving patient outcomes, increasing access to healthcare services, and improving operational efficiency. However, the implementation of IoT in healthcare must be carefully managed to ensure patient privacy and security, as well as to address regulatory and ethical concerns.

9.3 APPLICATIONS OF IOT TECHNOLOGY IN HEALTHCARE

IoT technology has been revolutionizing the healthcare industry by introducing a plethora of applications [30, 31]. IoT technology can be used to track the number of steps taken by patients, encouraging them to exercise and maintain a healthy lifestyle. Smart saline drips can automatically notify medical staff when they need to be refilled. Real-time location tracking systems are becoming popular in healthcare facilities for inventory management and equipment tracing. This technology allows hospitals to track equipment movement and use, improving visibility of potential equipment shortages and preventing the spread of infections. Another application of IoT in healthcare is ingestible sensors. Patients can swallow a pill containing sensors, which can detect whether they have taken their medication at the right time and alert them through a mobile app. Smart IoT-based dustbins have been developed to minimize contact between medical staff and clinical waste, such as sharp objects, preventing accidental injuries. IoT-enabled asthma inhalers can monitor patients and automatically alert physicians if any abnormalities are detected. Device monitoring can also help healthcare professionals keep track of equipment and clinical materials, reducing the risk of misplaced items. Some of the key applications of IoT technology in healthcare are described in the following subsections.

9.3.1 Remote Patient Monitoring

RPM is a system of healthcare delivery that enables the collection of patient data outside of traditional healthcare settings, usually at a patient's home or workplace. Its goal is to improve the quality and efficiency of healthcare delivery by delivering to healthcare providers real-time, continuous data about a patient's health [5]. IoT technology is increasingly being used in RPM, enabling the collection of data from a variety of sources such as wearables, sensors, and mobile devices. The use of IoT technology in RPM provides several benefits such as the following.

- **Improved Patient Outcomes:** Remote monitoring enables healthcare providers to detect and respond to changes in a patient's condition in real time, leading to early intervention and improved outcomes.

- **Enhanced Patient Engagement:** Patients can actively participate in their care by using wearable devices and mobile apps to track their health and receive feedback on their progress.
- **Increased Efficiency:** By monitoring patients remotely, healthcare providers can reduce the need for in-person visits, leading to cost savings and increased efficiency.

The process of RPM using IoT technology typically involves the following steps [21, 32].

1. **Data Collection:** Wearable devices, sensors, and other IoT devices collect data such as vital signs, activity levels, and medication adherence.
2. **Data Transmission:** The data collected by IoT devices is transmitted wirelessly to a cloud-based platform, where it is stored and analyzed.
3. **Data Analysis:** The data is analyzed by algorithms and machine learning models to identify trends, patterns, and potential health risks.
4. **Alert Generation:** If the data indicates a potential health risk, an alert is generated and healthcare providers are notified.
5. **Intervention:** Healthcare providers can intervene as necessary, providing guidance, support, and care to patients.

9.3.2 Smart Healthcare Systems

IoT can be used to develop smart healthcare systems that can provide various benefits to patients, healthcare providers, and medical facilities. It can be a game-changer in the healthcare industry by enabling smart healthcare systems that can improve patient care, reduce costs, and enhance the efficiency of medical facilities [2, 33]. IoT can be used to track medical assets such as equipment, devices, and medicines in hospitals and clinics. This can help prevent theft, loss, and misplacement of critical medical assets, resulting in better patient care and cost savings. IoT can be used to predict when medical equipment needs maintenance or repair. This can help prevent downtime and improve the reliability and availability of medical equipment, which is critical in healthcare settings. IoT can be used to enable telemedicine services, which allow doctors to provide medical consultations to patients remotely [3]. This can be especially useful in rural or underserved areas where there is a shortage of healthcare providers. IoT can be used to manage hospital resources such as energy consumption, lighting, and waste management. This can help hospitals reduce costs and improve their sustainability efforts. IoT can be used to improve patient safety by monitoring patients' movements and activities. This can help prevent falls and other accidents, especially in elderly or vulnerable patients. MIoT can help hospitals optimize their operations and improve patient outcomes by integrating medical devices and systems, such as EHRs, medical imaging equipment, and patient monitoring systems. This allows healthcare professionals to access real-time patient data and make informed decisions quickly.

9.3.3 Telemedicine

Telemedicine refers to the use of telecommunication and information technologies to provide healthcare services remotely. It allows healthcare professionals to diagnose, treat, and monitor patients from a distance, using video conferencing, remote monitoring devices, and other communication technologies. IoT technology can be used to develop telemedicine platforms that enable patients to connect with healthcare providers remotely [34]. These platforms can incorporate video conferencing, remote monitoring, and other communication technologies to facilitate virtual consultations. Following are some of the needs and advantages of telemedicine [7].

1. **Improved Access to Care:** Telemedicine allows patients to access healthcare services from the comfort of their homes, eliminating the need for in-person visits to clinics and hospitals. This is particularly beneficial for patients who live in remote or underserved areas, where access to healthcare services may be limited.
2. **Convenience and Flexibility:** Telemedicine enables patients to schedule appointments at a time that is convenient for them, without having to take time off work or travel long distances to see a healthcare provider. This can lead to higher patient satisfaction and adherence to treatment plans.
3. **Reduced Healthcare Costs:** Telemedicine can reduce healthcare costs by eliminating the need for in-person visits, reducing hospital readmissions, and decreasing the use of emergency room services. This is particularly beneficial for patients with chronic conditions who require frequent monitoring and follow-up care.
4. **Improved Patient Outcomes:** Telemedicine can improve patient outcomes by providing timely interventions and preventing the progression of chronic conditions. Remote monitoring devices can track vital signs and alert healthcare providers to potential health issues before they become more serious.
5. **Increased Efficiency:** Telemedicine can increase the efficiency of healthcare delivery by reducing wait times, decreasing paperwork, and allowing healthcare providers to see more patients in less time.
6. **Better Provider Collaboration:** Telemedicine can facilitate collaboration between healthcare providers, allowing them to share patient data and consult with specialists in real time. This can lead to more coordinated care and better outcomes for patients.

Overall, telemedicine is a valuable tool for improving access to care, reducing healthcare costs, and improving patient outcomes. It has the potential to transform the way healthcare is delivered, making it more convenient, efficient, and accessible for patients and healthcare providers alike.

9.3.4 Drug Development

IoT technology can be used in several ways to improve the drug development process, drug safety, and medication adherence. Following are some examples.

1. **Smart Pill Bottles:** IoT-enabled smart pill bottles can track when a patient takes their medication and provide reminders if the patient misses a dose [35]. This information can be transmitted to healthcare providers, enabling them to monitor patient adherence and adjust treatment plans as needed. Smart pill bottles can also be used to monitor medication levels and provide alerts when it is time to refill a prescription.
2. **Temperature Monitoring:** IoT sensors can be used to monitor the temperature of medications during storage and transportation [11]. This is important because some medications are sensitive to temperature and can degrade if they are not stored at the correct temperature. By monitoring the temperature of medications in real time, healthcare providers can ensure that medications are stored and transported correctly, maintaining their effectiveness and safety.
3. **Clinical Trials:** IoT devices can be used in clinical trials to collect data from participants in real time. For example, wearables can be used to track physical activity levels and sleep patterns, providing researchers with information on how the drug is affecting participants' daily lives [36]. IoT devices can also be used to collect data on adverse events and side effects, enabling researchers to monitor the safety of the drug in real time.
4. **Supply Chain Management:** IoT technology can be used to track and manage the supply chain of medications. For example, sensors can be used to monitor the temperature and humidity of medications during transportation and storage, ensuring that they are stored under the correct conditions [37]. IoT technology can also be used to track medication shipments in real time, enabling healthcare providers to monitor the location of medications and prevent drug shortage.

Overall, IoT technology has the potential to transform the drug development process, improving drug safety and efficacy, and enhancing patient outcomes through better medication adherence.

9.3.5 Medical Robots

In the context of the IoT, medical robots can be connected to other healthcare devices and systems, allowing for a more streamlined and efficient healthcare process. IoT-enabled medical robots can collect and transmit data in real time, allowing healthcare providers to monitor patient health and adjust treatments as needed [38]. Medical robots are increasingly being used in various healthcare settings to improve patient outcomes and enhance the overall quality of care. Following are some of the most common applications of medical robots [30, 38, 39].

1. **Surgery:** Medical robots are used to assist surgeons in performing minimally invasive procedures that require precision and accuracy, such as laparoscopic surgery. The robots are controlled by the surgeon, who uses a console to guide the robotic arms to perform the procedure.

2. **Rehabilitation:** Medical robots are used in physical therapy to help patients recover from injuries or surgeries. The robots can provide repetitive and controlled movements that help patients regain strength and mobility.
3. **Diagnosis:** Medical robots can be used for imaging and diagnosis. For example, robotic systems can be used for computed tomography (CT), magnetic resonance imaging (MRI), and ultrasound scans, which can help doctors detect and diagnose various medical conditions.
4. **Drug Delivery:** Medical robots can be used to deliver drugs to specific areas of the body. This targeted drug delivery can reduce the risk of side effects and improve the effectiveness of treatments.
5. **Telemedicine:** Medical robots can be used for telemedicine consultations. Patients can interact with healthcare providers remotely through a robot, allowing them to receive medical advice and treatment without leaving their homes.
6. **Elderly Care:** Medical robots can be used to assist elderly patients with daily tasks such as getting out of bed, walking, and taking medication.
7. **Emergency Response:** Medical robots can be used to respond to emergencies such as natural disasters or terrorist attacks. Robots can be used to search for survivors, deliver medical supplies, and perform other tasks in hazardous environments.

IoT-enabled medical robots can also be used to automate routine tasks and reduce human error. For example, a robot in a pharmacy can receive prescription orders from healthcare providers, prepare medications, and deliver them to patients [7, 39]. This can improve the accuracy of medication dispensing and reduce wait times for patients. Overall, IoT-enabled medical robots have the potential to transform healthcare by improving patient outcomes, increasing efficiency, and reducing healthcare costs. However, it is important to ensure that proper security and privacy measures are in place to protect sensitive patient information and prevent unauthorized access to medical devices and systems.

9.4 HEALTHCARE IOT CHALLENGES, SECURITY ISSUES, AND RISKS

The IoT has revolutionized the healthcare industry by providing innovative solutions that enhance the quality of patient care. Healthcare IoT has made it possible to remotely monitor patients, automate medical devices, and enhance medication management. However, the implementation of IoT in healthcare also presents several challenges and security risks that need to be addressed to ensure safe and effective healthcare delivery. Secure healthcare IoT devices have become increasingly important in the healthcare industry. The dominant challenges associated with Healthcare IoT include the following.

1. **Interoperability:** One of the biggest challenges of healthcare IoT is the lack of interoperability among different devices and systems. Interoperability is the ability of different systems and devices to

communicate and exchange information with each other seamlessly. The lack of interoperability can lead to data silos, duplication of efforts, and increased operational costs [40].

2. **Security and Data Privacy:** IoT devices can be vulnerable to security breaches, leaving patient data and sensitive information at risk. Healthcare IoT systems must be designed with strong security measures in place to prevent unauthorized access and protect patient privacy. Healthcare IoT involves collecting sensitive patient data, including personal health information, medical history, and biometric data. This data needs to be protected from unauthorized access, theft, and misuse. Data breaches can result in significant financial losses, reputational damage, and legal liabilities. Healthcare IoT devices and systems are vulnerable to cyber-attacks, such as malware, ransomware, and phishing attacks [40]. These attacks can compromise the confidentiality, integrity, and availability of patient data, disrupt healthcare operations, and pose a significant risk to patient safety. Healthcare IoT devices, such as medical implants and wearables, are often connected to the internet, making them susceptible to hacking and malware. A compromised device can potentially harm the patient or result in inaccurate data, leading to incorrect diagnoses and treatment plans.
3. **Integration:** Healthcare IoT involves integrating various devices and systems into a cohesive network. This can be a complex and time-consuming process that requires significant investment in infrastructure and expertise [41].
4. **Data Management:** Healthcare IoT generates a large amount of data that needs to be managed efficiently. This includes collecting, storing, analyzing, and sharing data in a secure and timely manner. Effective data management is crucial for ensuring accurate diagnoses, personalized treatment plans, and better patient outcomes [20, 26].
5. **Regulatory Compliance:** Healthcare IoT devices must comply with strict regulatory standards, such as the U.S. Health Insurance Portability and Accountability Act (HIPAA), to protect patient privacy and ensure the safety and efficacy of medical devices [42]. Compliance with these standards can be challenging, particularly for smaller healthcare providers and startups.
6. **Cost:** Healthcare IoT devices and systems can be expensive to develop, implement, and maintain. Healthcare providers must carefully consider the costs and benefits of implementing IoT technology to ensure that they are investing in technologies that will deliver long-term value [41].

Overall, while there are many potential benefits to Healthcare IoT, addressing these challenges will be essential to ensuring that the technology is used effectively and safely in healthcare settings. IoT devices have been adopted in the healthcare industry because they provide the ability to monitor patient vitals in real time, improve patient outcomes, and streamline healthcare operations. However, these devices are susceptible to cyber-attacks that can result in data breaches, which can compromise patient safety and privacy. Securing healthcare IoT devices is crucial to protect patients' privacy, ensure the integrity of medical data, and prevent unauthorized access to critical medical equipment. Following are some actions that can be taken to secure healthcare IoT devices.

1. **Encryption:** Encryption is the process of converting data into a coded language that can only be accessed by authorized individuals. It is a critical tool to protect patient data and prevent unauthorized access. All data transmitted over IoT devices should be encrypted to protect against cyber-threats. Sensitive data such as patient health information should be encrypted to prevent unauthorized access or interception [41, 43]. Encryption can be applied at various levels, including data transmission, data storage, and authentication mechanisms.
2. **Access Control:** Access control is a security measure that allows only authorized individuals to access sensitive data. Access control should be implemented in all healthcare IoT devices to prevent unauthorized access to patient data [41]. Access controls should be implemented to ensure that only authorized personnel can access IoT devices and their data. This can include role-based access control, which restricts access based on a user's job function, or attribute-based access control, which restricts access based on a user's attributes such as location or time of day.
3. **Regular Updates:** IoT devices are often targeted by cybercriminals because they are often not updated with the latest security patches. Regular updates are critical to ensure that the device is protected against known security threats. IoT devices should be updated regularly with the latest security patches and software updates to fix any known security vulnerabilities. Healthcare organizations should have a process in place for identifying vulnerabilities and applying the necessary updates in a timely manner [24, 43].
4. **Authentication:** Authentication is the process of verifying the identity of an individual or device. Multi-factor authentication should be implemented on all healthcare IoT devices to prevent unauthorized access. Healthcare IoT devices should have strong authentication mechanisms to prevent unauthorized access. This can be achieved by using methods such as two-factor authentication, which requires users to provide two forms of identification to access the device, or biometric authentication, which uses unique biological characteristics such as fingerprints or facial recognition to identify users [41, 44].
5. **Network Segmentation:** Network segmentation is the process of dividing a network into smaller sub-networks to improve security. Healthcare IoT devices should be isolated from other network devices to prevent unauthorized access. Network segmentation involves dividing a network into smaller sub-networks to isolate IoT devices from other network components [45]. This reduces the attack surface and limits the spread of any potential security breaches.
6. **Risk Assessment:** A risk assessment should be performed on all healthcare IoT devices to identify potential vulnerabilities and implement necessary security measures [45]. Healthcare organizations should conduct regular security assessments of their IoT devices to identify any vulnerabilities and

address them in a timely manner. This can include penetration testing, vulnerability scans, and risk assessments. Intrusion detection and prevention systems can be used to monitor network traffic and identify any suspicious activity. These systems can detect and block potential security breaches before they can cause harm.

7. **Data Protection:** Data protection measures such as data backups and disaster recovery plans should be implemented to ensure that patient data is protected in the event of a cyber-attack.
8. **Train Staff on Security Best Practices:** Healthcare staff should be trained on how to identify and respond to security incidents and promote best security practices [41]. This can include training on how to identify phishing emails, how to use strong passwords, and how to securely store and transmit data.
9. **Use Secure Protocols:** IoT devices should use secure communication protocols such as HTTPS (Hypertext Transfer Protocol Secure) and TLS/SSL (Transport Layer Security/Secure Socket Layer) encryption to ensure that data is transmitted securely over the network [46]. These protocols encrypt data in transit and protect against eavesdropping and data interception.
10. **Implement a Robust Incident Response Plan:** Healthcare organizations should develop a comprehensive incident response plan that outlines the steps to be taken in case of a security breach or incident. This plan should include procedures for detecting, containing, and mitigating the impact of any security incidents, as well as communication protocols for notifying relevant stakeholders [41, 43].

9.5 WIRELESS BODY AREA NETWORK (WBAN)

In today's world, technology has advanced to the point where we can now measure our physical activities and health status with a small device that can be worn on the body. These devices are part of a Wireless Body Area Network, also known as a WBAN. A WBAN is a network of wireless devices that are worn on or implanted into the human body to collect and transmit data to other devices or systems. Basically, a WBAN is a type of wireless network that enables communication between small, low-power sensors or devices placed on or inside the human body [29, 47]. These sensors can monitor various physiological and environmental parameters, such as heart rate, blood pressure, body temperature, respiration rate, and oxygen saturation levels. The data collected by these sensors can be transmitted wirelessly to an external device or server for processing and analysis. The main advantage of WBANs is their ability to provide continuous, real-time monitoring of an individual's health and well-being. For example, a patient with a chronic health condition can use a WBAN to monitor their vital signs and receive alerts if their condition worsens. Athletes and fitness enthusiasts can use WBANs to track their physical activity levels and optimize their training routines. Military and industrial applications can use WBANs to monitor workers' safety and well-being in hazardous environments. WBANs are highly sensitive to power consumption, size, and weight constraints. The sensors must be small and unobtrusive, and the battery life must be long enough to support continuous operation for an extended period. To achieve this, WBANs use low-power wireless communication protocols, such as Bluetooth Low Energy (BLE), Zigbee, or Wi-Fi Direct [48, 49].

The concept of WBANs has been around for a few decades, but it was not until the early 2000s that the technology began to take off. The initial idea was to use WBANs to monitor the vital signs of patients in hospitals and clinics, allowing healthcare providers to track their condition in real time without the need for intrusive wires and cables [50]. As the technology improved, researchers began to see the potential for WBANs in other areas, such as sports and fitness tracking. Today, there are a variety of wearable devices that can monitor everything from heart rate and blood pressure to steps taken and calories burned. These devices can be used by individuals to track their own health and fitness goals, or by researchers to collect data on large groups of people. One of the key benefits of WBANs is their ability to transmit data wirelessly. This means that devices can be worn discreetly and comfortably without the need for wires or cables. Additionally, the data collected by these devices can be transmitted in real time, allowing for immediate analysis and action if necessary. The communication protocols used in WBANs must be efficient and reliable, as the sensors are typically located in or around the human body, which can cause interference and signal attenuation. To address this, WBANs use specialized communication protocols that are optimized for low power consumption and can handle interference and signal loss [31, 51]. These protocols typically use frequency hopping, which enables the sensors to switch between different channels to avoid interference and maintain a stable connection. In conclusion, WBANs offer a promising solution for real-time monitoring of human health and well-being. With the increasing demand for personalized healthcare and remote monitoring, WBANs are expected to play a significant role in the future of healthcare and wellness.

However, there are also some challenges associated with WBANs. For example, ensuring the security and privacy of the data collected by these devices is a major concern [52, 53]. Additionally, the devices themselves must be small, lightweight, and energy-efficient to be worn comfortably for extended periods of time. Simply put, WBANs face several challenges, including security and privacy concerns. The data transmitted by WBANs contains sensitive personal and medical information, and it must therefore must be protected against unauthorized access and use. To address this, WBANs use encryption and authentication mechanisms to secure the communication between the sensors and the external device or server. Despite these challenges, the potential benefits of WBANs are enormous. They have the potential to revolutionize healthcare, sports and fitness, and many other areas of our lives. As the technology continues to improve, we can expect to see even more innovative applications of WBANs in the years to come.

9.6 WBAN ARCHITECTURE

A WBAN architecture is the structure or organization of the system components that make up a WBAN. It defines the roles and responsibilities of each component, the communication protocols and interfaces between components, and the overall system behavior [50, 54]. A WBAN architecture typically includes the following components.

1. **Sensors:** These are the devices that collect data from the human body, such as heart rate, temperature, and movement. Sensors may be attached to the body or implanted under the skin.
2. **Body Area Network (BAN):** This is the wireless network that connects the sensors to the gateway or external device. The BAN may use various wireless communication technologies such as Bluetooth, Zigbee, or Wi-Fi.
3. **Gateway:** This is the device that receives the data from the sensors and forwards it to an external network, such as the internet or a local area network (LAN). The gateway may be a smartphone, tablet, or computer.
4. **Cloud or Server:** This is where the data is stored and processed. Cloud-based services can provide scalable and secure storage, as well as access to sophisticated data analysis tools.

The WBAN architecture can be designed in various ways, depending on the specific requirements of the application. Some common types of WBAN architectures include centralized, decentralized, clustered, and hybrid architectures [55]. The choice of architecture will depend on factors such as the number of sensors, the data rate, the power consumption, and the reliability and robustness of the network. there are several types of WBAN architectures proposed in the literature. These architectures have different advantages and disadvantages, depending on the application requirements. The choice of architecture depends on factors such as the number of sensors, the data rate, the power consumption, and the reliability and robustness of the network [55, 56]. Following are a few examples.

- **Centralized Architecture:** In this architecture, all the data from the sensors on the body are collected by a central node or hub. The central node is responsible for processing the data and communicating with external devices.
- **Clustered Architecture:** In this architecture, the sensors are organized into clusters, with each cluster having a cluster head. The cluster heads communicate with a central node, which is responsible for collecting and processing the data.
- **Decentralized Architecture:** In this architecture, the sensors communicate with each other in a P2P fashion, without the need for a central node. The sensors can collaborate to process the data and make decisions.
- **Hybrid Architecture:** This architecture combines two or more of the previously outlined architectures to create a customized solution that meets the specific requirements of the application.

The preferred architecture for a WBAN depends on the specific requirements of the application. Each architecture has its own advantages and disadvantages, and the choice of architecture should be based on factors such as its number of sensors, data rate, and power consumption, and the reliability and robustness of the network. For example, a centralized architecture may be preferred when there are a large number of sensors that generate a high volume of data and when real-time processing is required [55]. On the other hand, a decentralized architecture may be preferred when the network needs to be more resilient to individual sensor failures or when there is a need for low power consumption. Ultimately, the choice of architecture will depend on the specific requirements of the application, and a careful analysis of the trade-offs between different architectures will be necessary to make an informed decision [12].

A layered architecture is a common approach to designing WBAN systems. The layered architecture separates the system into a set of hierarchical layers, each of which performs a specific function in the communication process. This approach simplifies the design and implementation of the system, making it easier to develop, maintain, and modify. A layered WBAN architecture typically consists of the following layers [29, 47, 49].

1. **Physical Layer:** This is the lowest layer of the architecture, and it is responsible for transmitting and receiving data over the wireless channel. The physical layer handles issues such as signal modulation, channel coding, and channel access.
2. **Data Link Layer:** This layer is responsible for ensuring reliable communication between the sensors and the gateway. It handles issues such as packet framing, error detection and correction, and flow control.
3. **Network Layer:** This layer is responsible for managing communication between the sensors and the gateway. It handles issues such as addressing, routing, and network topology.
4. **Transport Layer:** This layer is responsible for ensuring reliable end-to-end communication between the sensors and the gateway. It handles issues such as packet segmentation, retransmission, and congestion control.
5. **Application Layer:** This layer is responsible for the interaction between the WBAN system and the external devices or services. It handles issues such as data formatting, data compression, and security.

Each layer of the architecture communicates with the adjacent layers using well-defined interfaces and protocols. This modular design makes it easier to modify and update individual layers without affecting the entire system. Additionally, the layered architecture enables interoperability between different WBAN systems, as long as they conform to the same set of protocols and interfaces. The layered architecture is not a type of WBAN architecture in the same sense as centralized, decentralized, clustered, or hybrid architectures. Rather, it is a design approach that can be applied to any of these architectures to simplify the development and maintenance of the system [55, 56]. In other words, the layered architecture is orthogonal to the other types of WBAN architectures, meaning it can be used in combination with any of them. For example, a centralized WBAN architecture can be designed using a layered approach, with the physical, data link, network, transport, and application layers clearly defined and separated. Similarly, a decentralized or clustered architecture can be designed using a layered approach to simplify the communication between sensors and the gateway. In fact, the layered architecture is often used in conjunction with other types of WBAN architectures to improve the reliability, scalability, and maintainability of the system. For example, a hybrid architecture that combines centralized and decentralized elements can be designed using a layered approach to create a modular and flexible system.

9.7 WHAT MAKES WEARABLES SO SEXY?

Wearable technology has come a long way since its inception, and it has become a crucial part of our lives. Wearables are electronic devices that can be worn on the body and are designed to track various metrics related to health, fitness, and well-being. These devices can also be used to receive and respond to notifications, make phone calls, and control smart home devices. Wearable sensors are small electronic devices that can be worn on the body, often integrated into clothing or accessories, to measure various aspects of a person's health and activity [22, 50]. The convenience, personalization, connectivity, data collection, and style of wearable sensors have contributed to their increasing popularity and appeal in recent years. Wearable sensors are easy to use and can provide continuous monitoring of health and fitness metrics without requiring any effort from the user. Wearable sensors can be customized to track specific metrics, such as heart rate, sleep quality, or step count, depending on the user's needs and goals. Many wearable sensors can connect to smartphones or other devices, allowing users to easily access and track their data and receive alerts or notifications. Wearable sensors can provide a wealth of data about a person's health and activity which can be used to track progress, identify trends, and make informed decisions about lifestyle choices [57, 58]. Wearable sensors have evolved beyond the clunky, unattractive devices of the past and are now available in a wide range of styles and designs, from discreet fitness trackers to fashionable smartwatches. Wearables can track various health metrics, such as heart rate, blood pressure, and sleep patterns. This information can be used to identify potential health issues and make lifestyle changes to improve overall health. Wearables can help individuals set fitness goals and track their progress toward them. This can motivate individuals to stay active and make healthy choices. Wearables allow individuals to stay connected to their digital lives without being tied to a phone or computer. They can receive notifications, make phone calls, and control smart home devices from their wrist. Wearables can be used to track the location of individuals, which can be useful in emergency situations and is particularly important for children and elderly individuals. Wearables can be customized to meet the specific needs and preferences of individuals. This makes them a valuable tool for individuals with unique health or fitness requirements.

Wearable sensors are designed to be worn on the body, typically on the wrist, chest, or ankle. These sensors are designed to measure various health and activity metrics such as heart rate, physical activity, sleep quality, and blood glucose levels, among others [59, 60]. Overall, wearable sensors are becoming increasingly popular in healthcare and fitness settings, as they provide valuable insights into a person's health and activity levels, which can help them make informed decisions about their lifestyle and improve their overall well-being. Following are some examples of common types of wearable sensors.

1. **Accelerometers:** These are one of the most common types of wearable sensors. These sensors measure movement and acceleration, which can be used to track steps taken, distance traveled, and physical activity. Accelerometers can be found in many fitness trackers, smartwatches, and other wearable devices, and they are often used to monitor exercise intensity, set goals, and track progress [41, 61].
2. **Heart Rate Sensors:** These are another common type of wearable sensor. These sensors measure the user's heart rate, which can be used to monitor exercise intensity, track recovery after workouts, and detect irregular heartbeats. Heart rate sensors can be found in many fitness trackers and smartwatches, and they are often used in conjunction with other sensors, such as accelerometers, to provide a more comprehensive view of the user's health and fitness [62].
3. **Temperature Sensors:** These are used to measure the user's body temperature, which can be used to monitor fever and detect early signs of illness. These sensors can be found in some wearable devices, such as smart thermometers, and are often used in healthcare settings to monitor patients' temperature remotely.
4. **Electrocardiogram (ECG) Sensors:** These are used to measure the electrical activity of the heart, which can be used to detect arrhythmias, heart disease, and other cardiac issues. ECG sensors can be found in some smartwatches and other wearable devices, and are often used in clinical settings to monitor patients with cardiovascular conditions [1, 63].
5. **Blood Pressure Sensors:** These are used to measure the user's blood pressure, which can be used to monitor hypertension and other cardiovascular conditions. These sensors can be found in some smartwatches and other wearable devices, and they are often used in clinical settings to monitor patients' blood pressure remotely [1].
6. **Sleep Sensors:** These are used to measure the user's sleep quality and patterns, which can be used to monitor sleep disorders and recommend lifestyle changes for better sleep. These sensors can be found in some wearable devices, such as sleep trackers, and are often used to provide personalized recommendations for improving sleep quality [7].
7. **Blood Glucose Sensors:** These are used to measure the user's blood glucose levels, which can be used to monitor diabetes and adjust insulin doses accordingly. These sensors can be found in some wearable devices, such as continuous glucose monitoring (CGM) systems, and are often used to provide real-time data on blood glucose levels to help patients manage their diabetes more effectively [33, 64].
8. **Sweat Sensors:** These are used to measure the user's sweat levels, which can be used to monitor hydration and electrolyte balance during physical activity [7, 1]. These sensors can be found in some wearable devices, such as smart fabrics and patches, and are often used to provide real-time data on hydration levels during exercise.

9.8 WHAT ARE THE WEAKNESSES OF WBAN AND WEARABLES?

Wearable technology and WBAN have become increasingly popular in recent years, providing a range of benefits in healthcare, fitness, and everyday life. However, as with any technology, there are also potential weaknesses that need to be considered. WBANs can have several problems when used in real-time applications. Real-time applications require data to be transmitted in near-real time to provide immediate feedback or enable timely decisions. However, WBANs may face several challenges that can affect their real-time performance. For instance, in RPM, whereby healthcare providers remotely monitor patients' vital signs, activity levels, and other health-related data using wearable devices and WBANs, several challenges can arise [5, 65]. First, limited battery life can be a major issue in RPM, as continuous monitoring is required. If the battery runs out of charge, the device may stop functioning, leading to gaps in monitoring data. Second, limited range can be a problem if the patient moves away from the monitoring device or the healthcare provider's range of monitoring equipment. Third, security is crucial in RPM, as the data transmitted from the wearable devices to the healthcare provider's systems must be secure to protect the sensitive health information of patients. Data breaches can lead to severe consequences for both patients and healthcare providers. Finally, accuracy can be affected by factors such as patient movements, sweating, and skin conditions. This can lead to inaccurate data and a lack of confidence in the monitoring results, making it challenging for healthcare providers to make informed decisions about patient care [14, 29].

We will next explore few more cases showing limitations of wearables and WBAN. Wearable fitness trackers are popular among fitness enthusiasts, but they have limitations. For example, the accuracy of the sensors can be affected by sweat or movement, leading to incorrect measurements [14, 29]. Additionally, some users may find the device uncomfortable to wear during workouts, which can limit their usage. WBANs are used in industrial settings for monitoring worker safety, but they also have limitations. For example, the range of the devices may be limited by obstacles or interference from other equipment, leading to missed monitoring data. Additionally, the devices may not be suitable for use in harsh environments such as extreme temperatures or exposure to chemicals. Wearables are used in elderly care to monitor the health and safety of seniors, but they also have limitations. For example, some elderly individuals may have difficulty using the devices or may experience discomfort or skin irritation from wearing them. Additionally, the accuracy of the sensors can be affected by factors such as tremors or other physical conditions, leading to inaccurate monitoring data [21]. Wearables are used in sports to monitor athletes' performance and prevent injuries, but they also have limitations. For example, the devices may be uncomfortable to wear during activity or may not be suitable for use in water-based sports. Additionally, the accuracy of the sensors can be affected by factors such as body position or the athlete's movements, leading to inaccurate data.

Overall, WBANs can face several challenges in real-time applications that can affect their performance. These challenges must be carefully considered when deploying WBANs in real-time applications to ensure that they provide the desired level of performance. We will next summarize key areas where wearable technology and WBANs may fail. Following are 12 points that explore some of the limitations of WBANs and wearables.

1. **Limited Battery Life:** Most wearables and WBAN devices rely on batteries for power, and their battery life can be limited. This can be particularly problematic for devices that need to be worn continuously or for extended periods, such as those used for tracking patients with chronic conditions [66]. WBANs rely on batteries to function, and the small size of these devices means that the battery capacity is often limited. This can be a significant issue in real-time applications when continuous monitoring is required, and the battery may not last long enough to provide the desired level of real-time performance.
2. **Interference:** WBANs operate in the same frequency band as many other wireless devices, which can cause interference and degrade the quality of the signal. This interference can lead to packet loss, signal distortion, or delays in data transmission, affecting real-time performance [49].
3. **Data Accuracy:** The accuracy of data collected by wearables and WBAN devices can be affected by a range of factors, including the quality of the sensors used, the positioning of the device on the body, and the user's movements. The accuracy of sensors used in wearables can be limited by factors such as motion, sweat, and body hair [54, 67]. This can affect the reliability of the data collected and limit the usefulness of the devices.
4. **Security Risks:** Security is a significant concern in WBANs and wearables, particularly in healthcare applications via which sensitive data is being transmitted. These devices can be vulnerable to hacking, and encryption protocols must be implemented to protect against data breaches. Wearable devices and WBANs can be vulnerable to hacking and other security threats, potentially compromising sensitive data such as medical records [34, 55].
5. **Limited Interoperability:** There are a variety of different wearable devices and WBAN systems available, and they may not always be compatible with one another, making it difficult to integrate data from multiple sources [55].
6. **Limited Bandwidth:** WBANs have limited bandwidth due to the low power of the devices and the frequency bands in which they operate. This can limit the amount of data that can be transmitted at any given time, leading to delays in real-time applications [55].
7. **Network Congestion:** This can occur in crowded environments with many devices operating in close proximity, leading to delays in data transmission and affecting real-time performance [55].
8. **Cost:** WBANs and wearables can be expensive, particularly when used in healthcare applications for which high-quality sensors and materials are required. The cost of these devices can limit their adoption in certain settings.
9. **Privacy Concerns:** Wearable devices and WBANs can collect a significant amount of personal data, raising concerns about privacy and data protection.
10. **Comfort:** Wearables must be comfortable to be worn for extended periods in order to encourage people to use them. The design of the device can affect

its comfort level, and some individuals may experience skin irritation or discomfort from the materials used in the device [54, 55].

11. **Technical Complexity:** Wearable devices and WBANs can be technically complex, requiring specialized knowledge to set up and operate effectively.
12. **Limited Range:** The range of a WBAN is limited due to the low power of the devices and the frequency bands they operate in. This can restrict the use of WBANs in large environments and outdoor areas [51, 55].

9.9 WBAN APPLICATIONS

Once upon a time, WBANs were a futuristic concept that existed only in the minds of scientists and engineers. However, with the advent of new technologies and advancements in wireless communication, WBANs have become a reality, revolutionizing the healthcare industry. WBANs have several applications in healthcare, sports, and other fields. Following are some of the most common applications of WBANs.

1. **Healthcare Monitoring:** One of the primary applications of WBANs is in healthcare monitoring. These networks can be used to monitor the vital signs of patients in real time, providing doctors and nurses with up-to-date information that can be used to diagnose and treat diseases. WBANs are extensively used in healthcare to monitor patients' vital signs and health conditions [29, 34]. For example, a patient with heart disease can wear a sensor on their chest to monitor their heart rate and detect potential arrhythmias. Similarly, patients with diabetes can wear a sensor on their skin to monitor their blood glucose levels. WBANs enable doctors and nurses to remotely monitor patients' health conditions and detect potential health problems before they become critical. This can lead to more proactive and personalized healthcare, reducing hospitalizations, and improving patients' outcomes. WBANs are also used in rehabilitation and physical therapy to monitor patients' movements and muscle activity, allowing healthcare providers to customize rehabilitation programs for each patient's needs [48].
2. **Disease Management:** WBAN have great potential for disease management as they enable real-time monitoring of vital signs and other physiological parameters of patients. This information can be used to diagnose and manage various diseases. WBANs can also be used to manage chronic diseases, such as diabetes and heart disease [11]. By collecting and analyzing data from patients' WBANs, doctors can identify patterns and trends that can be used to adjust treatment plans and improve outcomes. WBANs consist of a set of wearable and implantable sensors that communicate with each other and with a central monitoring system. These sensors can be placed on the body or implanted under the skin to measure parameters such as heart rate, blood pressure, glucose levels, oxygen saturation, and body temperature. The data collected from these sensors can be transmitted wirelessly to a central monitoring system, which can be located in a hospital or at the patient's home. This system can analyze the data in real time and provide alerts if any abnormality is detected. This can help physicians to

provide early intervention and prevent complications. WBANs can be used to monitor glucose levels continuously and transmit the data to a central monitoring system. This can help patients and physicians to adjust medication and diet accordingly. WBANs can monitor heart rate, blood pressure, and oxygen saturation in real time. This can help physicians to diagnose and manage conditions such as arrhythmias and heart failure. WBANs can monitor breathing rate and oxygen saturation levels in patients with respiratory diseases such as asthma and chronic obstructive pulmonary disease (COPD) [68]. This can help physicians to adjust medication and provide early intervention if necessary.

3. **Elderly Care:** WBANs can also be used to monitor the health and well-being of elderly individuals who live alone or in assisted living facilities. These networks can alert caregivers if there are any changes in a patient's vital signs or if they experience a fall or other emergency [62].
4. **Sports Performance:** WBANs are also being used in sports to monitor athletes' performance and prevent injuries. These networks can be used to track a player's heart rate, body temperature, and other vital signs, providing coaches with real-time feedback that can be used to improve performance and prevent injuries [50, 69]. WBANs are increasingly used in sports to monitor athletes' performance and prevent injuries. For example, a soccer player can wear a sensor on their leg to track their movements, such as running speed, distance covered, and changes in direction. Coaches and trainers can use this data to adjust training programs and prevent injuries. WBANs can also monitor an athlete's heart rate, respiratory rate, and other physiological parameters, which can help coaches tailor training regimens to maximize performance.
5. **Military Applications:** In military applications, WBANs can be used to monitor soldiers' vital signs and detect signs of fatigue or stress. These networks can also be used to track soldiers' location and movement, providing commanders with valuable information in real time. WBANs are used in the military to monitor soldiers' health conditions, detect potential health problems, and prevent injuries. Soldiers in combat can wear sensors to monitor their vital signs, such as heart rate and blood pressure, and to detect potential health hazards, such as dehydration or heatstroke [31, 70]. WBANs also enable soldiers to communicate with each other and their commanders in real time, enhancing their situational awareness and improving their response to emergencies. WBANs can also monitor soldiers' movements, enabling commanders to track their positions and plan operations accordingly.
6. **Disaster Management:** WBANs can be utilized in disaster management for various purposes such as real-time monitoring of vital signs of disaster victims, tracking and locating first responders, and facilitating communication between rescue workers. These networks can provide real-time information on the condition of emergency personnel and help identify areas where resources are needed. WBANs can play a crucial role in improving the effectiveness of disaster management operations by providing real-time

data and situational awareness to the first responders and healthcare workers. In the event of a disaster, medical personnel need to quickly triage and prioritize the treatment of victims. WBANs can be used to monitor the vital signs of disaster victims in real time, including heart rate, blood pressure, oxygen saturation, and respiratory rate [31, 70]. This can help healthcare workers to quickly identify the most critical patients and provide appropriate treatment. WBANs can be used to track and locate the first responders in real time. This can help disaster management personnel to coordinate rescue efforts and allocate resources more effectively. WBANs can be used to facilitate communication between rescue workers in the field. This can help to coordinate rescue efforts and ensure that everyone is working toward the same goals. WBANs can be used to monitor the environmental conditions in disaster zones, including temperature, humidity, and air quality. This can help to identify potential hazards and ensure that rescue workers are working in safe conditions. Thus, WBANs can be a valuable tool for disaster management, providing real-time data and situational awareness to first responders and healthcare workers. By improving the effectiveness of rescue efforts, WBANs can help to save lives and reduce the impact of disasters on communities.

7. **Workplace Safety:** In industries such as construction and mining, WBANs can be used to monitor the health and safety of workers. These networks can detect signs of fatigue or stress and alert managers if workers are in danger [71]. WBANs can be used in workplace safety to monitor workers' exposure to hazardous materials, to prevent ergonomic injuries, to detect heat stress, to improve emergency response, and to monitor workers' health. The collected data can be used to create safer and healthier workplaces, reducing accidents and injuries and improving workers' well-being. WBANs can be used to monitor workers' exposure to hazardous materials such as chemicals, fumes, and dust in real time. Sensors can be attached to a worker's clothing or protective equipment to measure the concentration of these materials. The collected data can be used to alert workers and supervisors to potential hazards, helping them to take appropriate action to avoid exposure. WBANs can also be used to monitor workers' movements and postures to prevent ergonomic injuries. Sensors can be attached to a worker's clothing or equipment to measure their movements, such as bending and twisting, and to detect potential ergonomic hazards such as repetitive motion injuries. The collected data can be used to design workstations and equipment that minimize ergonomic risks and to develop training programs that help workers to adopt safe work practices. WBANs can be used to monitor workers' exposure to heat in real time. Sensors can be attached to a worker's clothing or protective equipment to measure their body temperature and heart rate [31, 56]. The collected data can be used to detect heat stress and to alert workers and supervisors to potential health hazards, helping them to take appropriate action to avoid heat-related illnesses. WBANs can be used to improve emergency response in the workplace. For example, workers can wear sensors that can detect if they fall or become incapacitated. The

collected data can be used to alert supervisors and emergency responders to potential emergencies, allowing them to respond quickly and effectively. WBANs can be used to monitor workers' health in real time. Sensors can be attached to a worker's clothing or equipment to measure their vital signs, such as heart rate and blood pressure, and to detect potential health problems such as respiratory issues or fatigue. The collected data can be used to develop personalized health plans for workers and to monitor their health over time.

8. **Entertainment:** WBANs can also be used in gaming to provide a more immersive experience. These networks can be used to track a player's movements and vital signs, providing feedback that can be used to adjust the game's difficulty level and create a more engaging experience. WBANs are used in the entertainment industry to create immersive experiences for viewers. For example, sensors attached to a person's body can enable them to control a virtual character in a video game or simulate the experience of being inside a movie [31, 56]. WBANs can also be used to track audience members' movements and reactions to a performance, enabling performers to tailor their act to the audience's preferences.
9. **Environmental Monitoring:** WBANs can be used in environmental monitoring to track pollution levels and other environmental factors. These networks can provide real-time data on air and water quality, helping researchers identify areas where pollution is most severe and track the effectiveness of remediation efforts [49, 56]. WBANs can be used to monitor air quality in real time. For example, sensors can be attached to a person's clothing to measure the concentration of pollutants such as carbon monoxide, sulfur dioxide, and nitrogen oxide in the air. The collected data can be used to create a real-time air quality map that provides information about pollution hotspots, helping authorities to take appropriate action to reduce pollution. WBANs can also be used to monitor water quality in real time. For example, sensors can be attached to a person's wrist or ankle to measure water temperature, pH levels, and the concentration of pollutants such as heavy metals and pesticides. The collected data can be used to detect water contamination and to identify the sources of pollutants, helping authorities to take appropriate action to protect water resources. WBANs can be used to monitor weather conditions in real time. For example, sensors can be attached to a person's clothing to measure temperature, humidity, and atmospheric pressure. The collected data can be used to create a real-time weather map that provides information about weather patterns and helps authorities to predict and respond to severe weather events such as storms and hurricanes. WBANs can also be used to monitor wildlife in real time. For example, sensors can be attached to animals such as birds and bats to measure their movements, activity levels, and other physiological parameters [29, 49]. The collected data can be used to track the migration patterns of animals and to monitor their health and behavior, helping authorities to protect endangered species and to better understand the ecology of wildlife populations.

10. **Industrial:** WBANs are used in the industrial sector to monitor workers' health conditions and prevent accidents. For example, workers in hazardous environments, such as factories or mines, can wear sensors to monitor their exposure to toxic gases or other hazardous substances. WBANs can also monitor workers' movements, such as their posture and gait, to detect potential ergonomic hazards and prevent musculoskeletal injuries [49, 69]. By monitoring workers' health and safety in real time, WBANs can help employers create safer and healthier workplaces, reducing accidents and injuries.

REFERENCES

[1] N. Gupta and S. Paiva, "IoT and ICT for Healthcare Applications," in *EAI/Springer Innovations and Communication and Computing Series,* Springer Cham, New York, United States, 2020, doi: 10.1007/978-3-030-42934-8.

[2] M. Gupta, G. Chaudhary, and V. H. C. de Albuquerque, *Smart Healthcare Monitoring Using IoT with 5G*, CRC Press, Florida, United States, 2021, doi: 10.1201/9781003171829.

[3] Z. Yang, B. Liang, and W. Ji, "An Intelligent End-Edge-Cloud Architecture for Visual IoT-Assisted Healthcare Systems," *IEEE Internet Things J.*, vol. 8, no. 23, 2021, doi: 10.1109/JIOT.2021.3052778.

[4] M. N. Bhuiyan, M. M. Rahman, M. M. Billah, and D. Saha, "Internet of Things (IoT): A Review of Its Enabling Technologies in Healthcare Applications, Standards Protocols, Security, and Market Opportunities," *IEEE Internet Things J.*, vol. 8, no. 13, 2021, doi: 10.1109/JIOT.2021.3062630.

[5] J. C. Pritchett *et al.*, "Association of a Remote Patient Monitoring (RPM) Program With Reduced Hospitalizations in Cancer Patients With COVID-19," *JCO Oncol. Pract.*, vol. 17, no. 9, 2021, doi: 10.1200/op.21.00307.

[6] Gazali, S. Kaur, and I. Singh, "Artificial Intelligence Based Clinical Data Management Systems: A Review," *Inform. Med. Unlocked*, vol. 9, 2017, doi: 10.1016/j.imu.2017.09.003.

[7] T. A. Rashid, C. Chakraborty, and K. Fraser, "Advances in Telemedicine for Health Monitoring: Technologies, Design and Applications," in *The Institution of Engineering and Technology*, pp. 1–297, London, England, 2020, doi: 10.1049/PBHE023E.

[8] J. B. Rousek, K. Pasupathy, D. Gannon, and S. Hallbeck, "Asset Management in Healthcare: Evaluation of RFID," *IIE Trans. Healthc. Syst. Eng.*, vol. 4, no. 3, 2014, doi: 10.1080/19488300.2014.938207.

[9] P. Yadav, M. Steinbach, V. Kumar, and G. Simon, "Mining Electronic Health Records (EHRs): A Survey," *ACM Comput. Surv.*, vol. 50, no. 6, 2018, doi: 10.1145/3127881.

[10] S. Razdan and S. Sharma, "Internet of Medical Things (IoMT): Overview, Emerging Technologies, and Case Studies," *IETE Tech. Rev. (IETE, India)*, vol. 39, no. 4, 2022, doi: 10.1080/02564602.2021.1927863.

[11] A. Ghubaish, T. Salman, M. Zolanvari, D. Unal, A. Al-Ali, and R. Jain, "Recent Advances in the Internet-of-Medical-Things (IoMT) Systems Security," *IEEE Internet Things J.*, vol. 8, no. 11, 2021, doi: 10.1109/JIOT.2020.3045653.

[12] N. Scarpato, A. Pieroni, L. Di Nunzio, and F. Fallucchi, "E-Health-IoT Universe: A Review," *Int. J. Adv. Sci. Eng. Inf. Technol.*, vol. 7, no. 6, 2017, doi: 10.18517/ijaseit.7.6.4467.

[13] F. Sadoughi, A. Behmanesh, and N. Sayfouri, "Internet of Things in Medicine: A Systematic Mapping Study," *J. Biomed. Inform.*, vol. 103, 2020, doi: 10.1016/j.jbi.2020.103383.

[14] S. Abbas, "An Innovative IoT Service for Medical Diagnosis," *Int. J. Electr. Comput. Eng.*, vol. 10, no. 5, 2020, doi: 10.11591/ijece.v10i5.pp4918-4927.

[15] P. Verma and S. K. Sood, "Cloud-Centric IoT Based Disease Diagnosis Healthcare Framework," *J. Parallel Distrib. Comput.*, vol. 116, 2018, doi: 10.1016/j.jpdc.2017.11.018.
[16] A. Aborujilah, A. E. F. M. Elsebaie, and S. A. Mokhtar, "IoT MEMS: IoT-Based Paradigm for Medical Equipment Management Systems of ICUs in Light of COVID-19 Outbreak," *IEEE Access*, vol. 9, 2021, doi: 10.1109/ACCESS.2021.3069255.
[17] K. H. Yeh, "A Secure IoT-Based Healthcare System with Body Sensor Networks," *IEEE Access*, vol. 4, 2016, doi: 10.1109/ACCESS.2016.2638038.
[18] R. Senthilkumar, R. S. Ponmagal, and K. Sujatha, "Efficient Health Care Monitoring and Emergency Management System Using IoT," *Int. J. Control Theory Appl.*, vol. 9, no. 4, 2016.
[19] K. Intawong, W. Boonchieng, P. Lerttrakarnnon, E. Boonchieng, and K. Puritat, "A-SA SOS: A Mobileand IoT-based Pre-hospital Emergency Service for the Elderly and Village Health Volunteers," *Int. J. Adv. Comput. Sci. Appl.*, vol. 12, no. 4, 2021, doi: 10.14569/IJACSA.2021.0120465.
[20] T. Saheb and L. Izadi, "Paradigm of IoT Big Data Analytics in the Healthcare Industry: A Review of Scientific Literature and Mapping of Research Trends," *Telemat. Inform.*, vol. 41, 2019, doi: 10.1016/j.tele.2019.03.005.
[21] V. Jagadeeswari, V. Subramaniyaswamy, R. Logesh, and V. Vijayakumar, "A Study on Medical Internet of Things and Big Data in Personalized Healthcare System," *Heal. Inf. Sci. Syst.*, vol. 6, no. 1, 2018, doi: 10.1007/s13755-018-0049-x.
[22] J. Hayward, "Wearable Technology 2018–2028: Markets Players Forecast," *IDTechEx,* Cambridge, UK, 2018.
[23] M. J. Hayward, D. G. Chansin, and D. H. Zervos, "Wearable Technology 2017–2027: Markets, Players, Forecasts," *IDTechEx*, Cambridge, UK, 2017.
[24] A. Aldahiri, B. Alrashed, and W. Hussain, "Trends in Using IoT with Machine Learning in Health Prediction System," *Forecasting*, vol. 3, no. 1, 2021, doi: 10.3390/forecast3010012.
[25] H. Bolhasani, M. Mohseni, and A. M. Rahmani, "Deep Learning Applications for IoT in Health Care: A Systematic Review," *Inform. Med. Unlocked*, vol. 23, 2021, doi: 10.1016/j.imu.2021.100550.
[26] M. D. Lytras, K. T. Chui, and A. Visvizi, "Data Analytics in Smart Healthcare: The Recent Developments and Beyond," *Appl. Sci. (Switzerland)*, vol. 9, no. 14, 2019, doi: 10.3390/app9142812.
[27] L. Wang and C. A. Alexander, "Big Data Analytics in Medical Engineering and Healthcare: Methods, Advances and Challenges," *J. Med. Eng. Technol.*, vol. 44, no. 6, 2020, doi: 10.1080/03091902.2020.1769758.
[28] J. M. C. Brito, "Technological Trends for 5G Networks Influence of E-Health and IoT Applications," *Int. J. E-Health Med. Commun.*, vol. 9, no. 1, 2018, doi: 10.4018/IJEHMC.2018010101.
[29] H. Taleb, A. Nasser, G. Andrieux, N. Charara, and E. Motta Cruz, "Wireless Technologies, Medical Applications and Future Challenges in WBAN: A Survey," *Wirel. Netw.*, vol. 27, no. 8, 2021, doi: 10.1007/s11276-021-02780-2.
[30] A. Singh Rajput, S. Singh, D. Mehta, and S. Patil, "IoT in Medical Analytics: Technological Advancement for Health Management," *Shashikant Patil Int. J. Innov. Adv. Comput. Sci. IJIACS ISSN*, vol. 6, 2017.
[31] S. Ullah *et al.*, "A Comprehensive Survey of Wireless Body Area Networks," *J. Med. Syst.*, vol. 36, no. 3, 2012, doi: 10.1007/s10916-010-9571-3.
[32] D. C. Klonoff, "Fog Computing and Edge Computing Architectures for Processing Data from Diabetes Devices Connected to the Medical Internet of Things," *J. Diabetes Sci. Technol.*, vol. 11, no. 4, 2017, doi: 10.1177/1932296817717007.
[33] M. Alshamrani, "IoT and Artificial Intelligence Implementations for Remote Healthcare Monitoring Systems: A Survey," *J. King Saud Univ.—Comput. Inf. Sci.*, vol. 34, no. 8, 2022, doi: 10.1016/j.jksuci.2021.06.005.

[34] P. K. D. Pramanik, A. Nayyar, and G. Pareek, "WBAN: Driving e-Healthcare Beyond Telemedicine to Remote Health Monitoring: Architecture and Protocols," in *Telemedicine Technologies: Big Data, Deep Learning, Robotics, Mobile and Remote Applications for Global Healthcare*, Elsevier, Amsterdam, Netherlands, pp. 89–119, 2019, doi: 10.1016/B978-0-12-816948-3.00007-6.

[35] M. Aldeer, R. E. Howard, R. P. Martin, and J. Ortiz, "Unobtrusive Patient Identification Using Smart Pill-Bottle Systems," *Internet Things (Netherlands)*, vol. 14, 2021, doi: 10.1016/j.iot.2021.100389.

[36] W. Iqbal, H. Abbas, M. Daneshmand, B. Rauf, and Y. A. Bangash, "An In-Depth Analysis of IoT Security Requirements, Challenges, and Their Countermeasures via Software-Defined Security," *IEEE Internet Things J.*, vol. 7, no. 10, 2020, doi: 10.1109/JIOT.2020.2997651.

[37] M. Hua, I. K. W. Lai, and H. Tang, "Analysis of Advertising and a Points-Exchange Incentive in a Reverse Supply Chain for Unwanted Medications in Households Based on Game Theory," *Int. J. Prod. Econ.*, vol. 217, 2019, doi: 10.1016/j.ijpe.2019.02.004.

[38] T. K. Morimoto, E. W. Hawkes, and A. M. Okamura, "Design of a Compact Actuation and Control System for Flexible Medical Robots," *IEEE Robot. Autom. Lett.*, vol. 2, no. 3, 2017, doi: 10.1109/LRA.2017.2676240.

[39] R. A. Beasley, "Medical Robots: Current Systems and Research Directions," *J. Robot.*, vol. 2012, 2012, doi: 10.1155/2012/401613.

[40] A. Mavrogiorgou, A. Kiourtis, K. Perakis, S. Pitsios, and D. Kyriazis, "IoT in Healthcare: Achieving Interoperability of High-Quality Data Acquired by IoT Medical Devices," *Sensors (Basel).*, vol. 19, no. 9, 2019, doi: 10.3390/s19091978.

[41] L. Minh Dang, M. J. Piran, D. Han, K. Min, and H. Moon, "A Survey on Internet of Things and Cloud Computing for Healthcare," *Electron.*, vol. 8, no. 7, 2019, doi: 10.3390/electronics8070768.

[42] K. N. Griggs, O. Ossipova, C. P. Kohlios, A. N. Baccarini, E. A. Howson, and T. Hayajneh, "Healthcare Blockchain System Using Smart Contracts for Secure Automated Remote Patient Monitoring," *J. Med. Syst.*, vol. 42, no. 7, 2018, doi: 10.1007/s10916-018-0982-x.

[43] F. Alshehri and G. Muhammad, "A Comprehensive Survey of the Internet of Things (IoT) and AI-Based Smart Healthcare," *IEEE Access*, vol. 9, 2021, doi: 10.1109/ACCESS.2020.3047960.

[44] P. K. Dhillon and S. Kalra, "Multi-Factor User Authentication Scheme for IoT-Based healthcare Services," *J. Reliab. Intell. Environ.*, vol. 4, no. 3, 2018, doi: 10.1007/s40860-018-0062-5.

[45] P. T. Le, C. C. Chang, Y. H. Li, Y. C. Hsu, and J. C. Wang, "Antialiasing Attention Spatial Convolution Model for Skin Lesion Segmentation with Applications in the Medical IoT," *Wirel. Commun. Mob. Comput.*, vol. 2022, 2022, doi: 10.1155/2022/1278515.

[46] A. Abayomi-Alli, A. J. Ikuomola, O. A. Aliyu, and O. Abayomi-Alli, "Development of a Mobile Remote Health Monitoring System—MRHMS," *African J. Comput. ICT.*, vol. 7, no. 4, 2014.

[47] F. Al-Turjman, *Internet of Nano-Things and Wireless Body Area Networks (WBAN)*, CRC Press, Florida, United States, pp. 1–241, 2019, doi: 10.1201/9780429243707.

[48] S. Ayed, L. Chaari, and A. Fares, "A Survey on Trust Management for WBAN: Investigations and Future Directions," *Sensors (Switzerland)*, vol. 20, no. 21, 2020, doi: 10.3390/s20216041.

[49] I. Al_Barazanchi, Y. Niu, S. Nazeri, W. Hashim, A. A. Alkahtani, and H. R. A. Shaheed, "A Survey on Short-Range WBAN Communication; Technical Overview of Several Standard Wireless Technologies," *Period. Eng. Nat. Sci.*, vol. 9, no. 4, 2021, doi: 10.21533/pen.v9i4.2444.

[50] F. Al-Turjman and I. Baali, "Machine Learning for Wearable IoT-Based Applications: A Survey," *Trans. Emerg. Telecommun. Technol.*, vol. 33, no. 8, 2022, doi: 10.1002/ett.3635.

[51] K. Das and S. Moulik, "BOSS: Bargaining-Based Optimal Slot Sharing in IEEE 802.15.6-Based Wireless Body Area Networks," *IEEE Internet Things J.*, vol. 10, no. 4, pp. 2945–2953, 2021, doi: 10.1109/JIOT.2021.3122819.

[52] M. Asam *et al.*, "Challenges in Wireless Body Area Network," *Int. J. Adv. Comput. Sci. Appl.*, vol. 10, no. 11, 2019, doi: 10.14569/IJACSA.2019.0101147.

[53] J. V. Ananthi and P. S. H. Jose, "A Perspective Review of Security Challenges in Body Area Networks for Healthcare Applications," *Int. J. Wirel. Inf. Netw.*, vol. 28, no. 4, 2021, doi: 10.1007/s10776-021-00538-3.

[54] A. S. Shibghatullah and I. Al Barazanchi, "An Analysis of the Requirements for Efficient Protocols in WBAN," *J. Telecommun. Electron. Comput. Eng.*, vol. 6, no. 2, 2014.

[55] D. Rathee, S. Rangi, S. K. Chakarvarti, and V. R. Singh, "Recent Trends in Wireless Body Area Network (WBAN) Research and Cognition Based Adaptive WBAN Architecture for Healthcare," *Health Technol.*, vol. 4, no. 3, 2014, doi: 10.1007/s12553-014-0083-x.

[56] R. Singh, S. Sinha, S. Anand, and M. Sen, "Wireless Body Area Network: An Application of IoT and Its Issuses—A Survey," in *Advances in Intelligent Systems and Computing*, Springer, Vol. 1120, pp. 285–293, 2020, doi: 10.1007/978-981-15-2449-3_24.

[57] M. Saravanan, J. Ajayan, S. R. Jondhale, and P. Mohankumar, "An Overview of Energy Harvesting Techniques for Future Internet of Things Applications," in EAI/Springer Innovations in Communication and Computing, Springer Cham, Switzerland AG, 2020, doi: 10.1007/978-3-030-34328-6_7.

[58] S. R. Jondhale, V. Mohan, B. B. Sharma, J. Lloret, and S. V. Athawale, "Support Vector Regression for Mobile Target Localization in Indoor Environments," *Sensors*, vol. 22, no. 1, 2022, doi: 10.3390/s22010358.

[59] T. W. Tseng, C. T. Wu, and F. Lai, "Threat Analysis for Wearable Health Devices and Environment Monitoring Internet of Things Integration System," *IEEE Access*, vol. 7, 2019, doi: 10.1109/ACCESS.2019.2946081.

[60] A. Barua, M. A. Al Alamin, M. S. Hossain, and E. Hossain, "Security and Privacy Threats for Bluetooth Low Energy in IoT and Wearable Devices: A Comprehensive Survey," *IEEE Open J. Commun. Soc.*, vol. 3, 2022, doi: 10.1109/OJCOMS.2022.3149732.

[61] A. Shamayleh, M. Awad, and J. Farhat, "IoT Based Predictive Maintenance Management of Medical Equipment," *J. Med. Syst.*, vol. 44, no. 4, 2020, doi: 10.1007/s10916-020-1534-8.

[62] Imran, N. Iqbal, S. Ahmad, and D. H. Kim, "Health Monitoring System for Elderly Patients Using Intelligent Task Mapping Mechanism in Closed Loop Healthcare Environment," *Symmetry (Basel).*, vol. 13, no. 2, 2021, doi: 10.3390/sym13020357.

[63] A. M. Koya and P. P. Deepthi, "Plug and Play Self-Configurable IoT Gateway Node for Telemonitoring of ECG," *Comput. Biol. Med.*, vol. 112, 2019, doi: 10.1016/j.compbiomed.2019.103359.

[64] T. M. Fernández-Caramés, I. Froiz-Míguez, O. Blanco-Novoa, and P. Fraga-Lamas, "Enabling the Internet of Mobile Crowdsourcing Health Things: A Mobile Fog Computing, Blockchain and IoT Based Continuous Glucose Monitoring System for Diabetes Mellitus Research and Care," *Sensors (Switzerland)*, vol. 19, no. 15, 2019, doi: 10.3390/s19153319.

[65] A. Ikpehai *et al.*, "Low-Power Wide Area Network Technologies for Internet-of-Things: A Comparative Review," *IEEE Internet Things J.*, vol. 6, no. 2, 2019, doi: 10.1109/JIOT.2018.2883728.

[66] J. Yang, C. Poellabauer, P. Mitra, and C. Neubecker, "Beyond Beaconing: Emerging Applications and Challenges of BLE," *Ad Hoc Netw.*, vol. 97, 2020, doi: 10.1016/j.adhoc.2019.102015.

[67] P. Sambandam, M. Kanagasabai, R. Natarajan, M. G. N. Alsath, and S. Palaniswamy, "Miniaturized Button-Like WBAN Antenna for Off-Body Communication," *IEEE Trans. Antennas Propag.*, vol. 68, no. 7, 2020, doi: 10.1109/TAP.2020.2980367.

[68] H. Chung, C. Jeong, A. K. Luhach, Y. Nam, and J. Lee, "Remote Pulmonary Function Test Monitoring in Cloud Platform via Smartphone Built-in Microphone," *Evol. Bioinforma.*, vol. 15, 2019, doi: 10.1177/1176934319888904.

[69] R. Li, D. T. H. Lai, and W. S. Lee, "A Survey on Biofeedback and Actuation in Wireless Body Area Networks (WBANs)," *IEEE Revi. Biomed. Eng.*, vol. 10, 2017, doi: 10.1109/RBME.2017.2738009.

[70] E. E. Egbogah and A. O. Fapojuwo, "Achieving Energy Efficient Transmission in Wireless Body Area Networks for the Physiological Monitoring of Military Soldiers," in *Proceedings—IEEE Military Communications Conference MILCOM*, 2013, doi: 10.1109/MILCOM.2013.233.

[71] F. Wu, T. Wu, and M. R. Yuce, "An Internet-of-Things (IoT) Network System for Connected Safety and Health Monitoring Applications," *Sensors (Switzerland)*, vol. 19, no. 1, 2019, doi: 10.3390/s19010021.

Index

T

U

V

W

Z